AF708535

# Dissolution of Marriage

Family Law Series

**Judge Joyce Hens Green**

**John V. Long**

**Roberta L. Murawski**

**SHEPARD'S/McGRAW-HILL**
P.O. Box 1235
Colorado Springs, Colorado 80901

McGRAW-HILL BOOK COMPANY
New York • St. Louis • San Francisco • Colorado Springs
Auckland • Bogotá • Hamburg • Johannesburg • London
Madrid • Mexico • Milan • Montreal • New Delhi • Panama
Paris • São Paulo • Singapore • Tokyo • Toronto

Copyright © 1986 by McGraw-Hill, Inc. All rights reserved. Printed in the United States of America. Except as permitted under the United States Copyright Act of 1976, no part of this publication may be reproduced or distributed in any form or by any means, or stored in a data base or retrieval system, without the prior written permission of the publisher.

12345678910 SHHA 895432109876

**Library of Congress Cataloging-in-Publication Data**

Green, Joyce.
Dissolution of marriage.

(Family law series)
Includes index.
1. Divorce—Law and legislation—United States.
2. Custody of children—United States. 3. Equitable distribution of marital property—United States.
I. Long, John V. II. Murawski, Roberta. III. Title.
IV. Series.
KF535.G74 1986 346.7301'66 86-13822
347.306166

ISBN 0-07-172056-1

**ISBN 0-07-172056-1**

The authors fondly dedicate this book to the memory of the late Samuel Green. His wisdom and compassion as a family law practitioner for more than 30 years have continued to guide us in our work. Without his inspiration, this book would have not been possible.

# Acknowledgments

The authors wish to acknowledge those who provided valuable assistance at various stages of this book, to whom we remain indebted: Deana Frances Dudley, Esquire, Cynthia B. Mynhier, Joan Peterson, and the library staff of the National Law Center at George Washington University in Washington, D.C.

# Preface

Family law is a dynamic, rapidly expanding area of the law. In the past three decades, this once-stable legal field has virtually exploded with changes and trends as it has adapted to the fact that the United States divorce rate is the highest in the world. The statisticians now tell us that half of all marriages will end in divorce and that half of America's minors will live in single-parent families. Contemporary family law touches virtually every sphere of life.

The family law practitioner has not only kept pace with this phenomenal growth but, more importantly, has been instrumental in developing new ideas on behalf of clients' rights in the interest of society. The family lawyer's position in the Bar has gained greater respect, prominence, and responsibility. The Family Law Section is the fastest growing section of the American Bar Association, reflecting the increased impact of this area of the law.

It is no longer enough for the family lawyer to know about local divorce grounds and other state statutes relating to custody and property in order to successfully serve clients and society. An increasingly sophisticated family law practitioner must have a substantial understanding of economics, taxes, financial planning, accounting, contracts, torts, real property, mediation, family counseling and human behavior, among others, and must also be familiar with federal law in many cases.

Therefore, the attorney in this field needs tools to assist him or her in developing a basis for understanding the rapidly changing areas. *Dissolution of Marriage*, like its companion volume, *Marriage and Family Law Agreements*, is designed to educate and assist the family law practitioner in providing the best possible representation in this complex changing field. National in scope, this book concentrates on three areas, providing historical analysis of the societal influences which have culminated in trends comprising the most pressing family law issues of our times. Without this historical analysis, it is impossible to understand current trends and dissolution issues.

The first part of this book addresses the most widereaching change in American family law in this century: the shift from fault to no-fault divorce. An analysis of historic fault grounds and defenses which still exist in some jurisdictions is followed by a description of the forces which contributed to the emergence and accelerated acceptance of no-fault divorce. This discussion is especially useful for young lawyers in this field who may lack the personal experience of the transition from fault-dominated divorce law to no-fault divorce, yet who have clients who desire justice in a fault-precipitated breakup. The various forms of no-fault divorce grounds are described, and an historical overview of jurisdictional issues is provided.

No-fault divorce was spurred in part by the desire to allow spouses to leave a marriage with dignity. This desire for dignity has also formed the basis for the trend of nonadversarial divorce, which particularly in the 1980s has led to greater recourse to arbitration and mediation. These trends are discussed, with emphasis on ethical issues for the family law practitioner.

The no-fault divorce trend has created a dramatically different kind of divorce proceeding by shifting the focus away from the cause of the breakup to the resolution of custody and property issues. In Part Two of *Dissolution of Marriage*, the authors explore the historic evolution in custody law. The emergence of a stronger emphasis on the best interests of the child has diminished the historical preferences—first, for the father, and later, for the mother—for custodial parent. The idea that children, as human beings, possess rights and that their welfare is the primary concern of the courts has fostered growth of a controversial trend favoring *joint custody* in both parents. Highlighting the nonadversarial resolution of custody disputes, joint custody diminishes the separation and polarization of the parents in the child's eyes and provides the child with the nurturing influence of both parents. A trend with an uncertain future, joint custody is often an ideal rather than a viable reality. It is imperative for the protection of the children that the practitioner be well-versed in the various definitions or forms of joint custody as well as its advantages and risks.

Part Three emphasizes, following more general discussion of property division, a critical trend arising from the contemporary treatment of marriage as an economic partnership. In a society where many couples devote time and financial resources toward one spouse's career and income potential rather than real property, it follows that, upon divorce, economic factors as evinced by degrees, licenses, pensions, and other employment benefits can be valued and divided.

A social inequity has been suggested by recent research on the economic consequences to wives who have worked to put their husbands through school, for example. Upon divorce, these women generally are not eligible for alimony because they are self-supporting even if they have limited income and career potential. A parent who retains custody of the children but receives inadequate support payments may be expected to drop to a lower standard of living than existed during the marriage. The noncustodial parent, who is usually the husband, on the other hand, may be left with an increased earning capacity and a bright career future, according to economic studies.

The idea of including so-called career assets in the classification of marital or community property to be divided upon divorce is a product of lawyer creativity arising out of recent sociological and economic research. *Dissolution of Marriage* provides a thorough analysis of this trend, with a particular focus on pensions.

This book is designed to assist the practitioner involved in these exciting and challenging areas of family law. The family lawyer, in addition to being an advocate, must also be responsive to the human needs of clients. This means being sensitive, understanding, pragmatic, and artful in negotiation. The family lawyer also must be financially adept and able to anticipate the future. Because he or she is dealing with the basic unit of human life when representing clients in divorce situations, lawyers with compassion and understanding must have extensive knowledge to protect their clients' legal interests.

Perhaps the most extraordinary aspect of this area of the law is that evolution is continuing rapidly, necessitating understanding the trends and the underpinnings of unanswered questions. Because the future is unknown, it challenges the lawyer to keep abreast of new trends in family law in order to more effectively serve individuals and society at large. All lawyers choosing to enter this field have a responsibility to be alert to new developments and constantly sensitive to their clients' human needs. *Dissolution of Marriage* emphasizes this unique, exciting, and professional responsibility.

# Authors

### Joyce Hens Green

Joyce Hens Green specialized in domestic relations, estate and personal injury litigation in the District of Columbia and Virginia, following graduation from George Washington University's National Law Center. Those years included law partnership with her husband, the late Samuel Green, co-author of *Marriage and Family Law Agreements* (Shepard's/McGraw-Hill 1984) and parent partnership rearing their children, Jimmy, June, and Michael. Appointed to the Superior Court of the District of Columbia as an Associate Judge, she was the first presiding judge of its family law division immediately prior to her appointment in 1979 to the federal bench. She continues to serve as Judge, United States District Court for the District of Columbia. She has been President, Women's Bar Association of the District of Columbia, Chairman, Executive Women in Government, recipient of the Women's Legal Defense Fund award, lecturer in trial advocacy at Harvard Law School, Fellow of the American Bar Foundation and Fellow, American Academy of Matrimonial Lawyers.

### John V. Long

John V. Long was graduated from the University of Chicago Law School and has served as adjunct professor of law at the College of Law, Ohio State University, and the School of Law, Catholic University of America. He also served as a legal advisor to the Chairman, National Labor Relations Board.

He was chairperson of the Domestic Relations Committee of the District of Columbia Bar Association for five years, member, Steering Committee, Family Law Section of the D.C. Bar, 1976-1982; 1985-1987, vice chairman, Committee on International Support Procedures, Family Law Section of the American Bar Association, 1983-1986 and chairman, 1986- . He is a member of the Maryland Bar Association and has been a lawyer in private practice of family law in the District of Columbia and Maryland for 20 years. Elected, Fellow, American Academy of Matrimonial Lawyers, 1984- , Reporter on United States law,

Conference on International Jurisdiction in Family Law of the International Association of Lawyers, the Hague, September 1985.

He is co-author of *The Real and Illusory Changes of the 1977 Marriage and Divorce Act (District of Columbia)*, 27 Cath UL Rev 469 (1978) and *Marriage and Family Law Agreements* (Shepard's/McGraw-Hill 1984).

**Roberta L. Murawski**

Roberta L. Murawski was graduated Magna Cum Laude in 1979 from the State University of New York at Buffalo, where she was Phi Beta Kappa and received English Department honors. She was graduated from the National Law Center at the George Washington University in Washington, D.C. in 1982. She is a member of the District of Columbia Bar, the Women's Bar Association of the District of Columbia, the Maryland Bar Association, the Virginia State Bar, and the American Bar Association. She worked closely with the late Samuel Green, Esquire and John V. Long, Esquire in the production of *Marriage and Family Law Agreements* (Shepard's/McGraw-Hill 1984), researching and supervising researchers, writing, and editing. Ms. Murawski is now in the private practice of law with Herbert Rubenstein and Associates, P.C. in Washington, D.C., Maryland, and Virginia.

# Contents

## Summary

## Detailed

# Part One

## Divorce and Dissolution

# 1 Introduction to Divorce

## §1.01 Divorce Generally

Marriage, which, apart from religious significance, is a form of social regulation and organization and a mechanism for human survival, has never been a stable institution.[1] From very early times, various societies have regulated divorce or dissolution of marriage through laws and customs and have determined the status of spouses, the division of property, and the custody of children. Customs and procedures range from a unilateral repudiation by the husband for no reason, to a divorce by mutual agreement, to the doctrine of the absolute indissolubility of marriage.[2]

In the United States, the law of divorce was established on the belief that divorce was a remedy for an innocent spouse and a punishment for a guilty spouse who had breached the marriage contract.[3] Each state promulgated laws stating fault-based grounds which, if proven by an innocent party, provided a court with a justification for terminating the marriage.[4] Divorce, as viewed within this system, "is the culmination of a tragedy in human experience often worse than death itself. . . . "[5]

The problems created by fault divorce were the product of a conflict between the system's goals, values, and morals, and the actions of the people who wanted divorce. The integrity of the judicial system was so severely threatened by the subterfuge of the letter and the spirit of divorce law that a great movement toward no-fault divorce developed on various levels of society all over the world.[6] Every state in the United States has a no-fault ground for divorce.

No-fault divorce has, in turn, shifted the emphasis away from breaches of the marriage contract or reasons for the breakdown of marriage to the financial aspects of the marriage. Despite some criticism of no-fault divorce, it may be said that the no-fault movement truly has been one of monumental proportion and importance which has reflected the change in the make-up of our society.

The change in divorce may be clearly viewed if compared with the change in marriage, and with the societal developments which reflect those changes. Called *companionship marriage* or *urban marriage* or *modern marriage,* marriage has become a transformed institution, influenced by the urbanization of our society and the increased independence of women, among other factors. The new functions of marriage and family have shifted towards comfort, companionship, love, and support. As one authority has noted:

---

[1] *See* W. Goodsell, A History of Marriage and the Family 30-33 (1934); 1 G. Howard, A History of Matrimonial Institutions 224-49 (reprinted 1964); 3E. Westermarck, The History of Human Marriage 267-78 (5th ed rewritten 1925); J. Udry, The Social Context of Marriage 511 (1966).

[2] *See* **§§1.02-1.09.**

[3] *See* **§§1.09-1.26.**

[4] *See* **§§1.10-1.18.**

[5] Lichtenberger, *Divorce Legislation,* in Selected Essays on Family Law 862, 867 (1950).

[6] *See* **§§2.01-2.06.** *See also* M. Rheinstein, Marriage Stability, Divorce and the Law (1972).

> [This] has increased the difficulty of finding the mate by whom the new needs will be satisfied. It is comparatively easier to find a wife who is a good housekeeper, an efficient helper on the farm, and a good mother to a flock of children, or a husband who is a good provider, than a mate who is an ever ready congenial companion, who shares not only our sorrows and troubles, but also our tastes, interests, and our circle of acquaintances, and who remains congenial in all these respects and many more not only in the youthful years of early love and bliss but through all the vicissitudes and transformation of a lifetime with its growth in body, mind and soul. In all these more subtle aspects of marriage we need more, expect more, and we are more easily disappointed.[7]

As the functions, roles, and expectations of marriage and the family have changed, so have the roles, functions and expectations of the institution of divorce. The law, in its never-ending attempt to maintain pace with social conduct, has developed a system of no-fault divorce which, in many jurisdictions, has been renamed *dissolution* in order to remove all negative connotation. However, even where fault has been eliminated as a cause of action for divorce, it continues to be a factor in custody, support, and property determinations.[8]

The system of dissolution has created both problems and innovations. A serious drawback may be the loss of the bargaining power by a fault-free wife. At the same time that no-fault grounds were adopted, most common law jurisdictions revised their statutory concepts of marital property to include all property acquired during the marriage except by gift or inheritance.[9] It was believed that the enlargement of the property subject to division by the divorce court would provide women with the protection necessary so that they would not need the bargaining power of the fault grounds. Whether this has worked out in practice is not clear.[10]

The fact that divorces are easier to obtain has taken its toll on the legal system. Except for small claims cases, divorce cases occupy the largest share of the country's civil law docket, and some cases last for many years.[11] The litigated issues concentrate on property division and child custody. Alternative methods of dispute resolution such as mediation have appeared in the divorce system.[12]

In the wake of no-fault divorce, annulments have become infrequent.

---

[7] Rheinstein, *The Law of Divorce and the Problem of Marriage Stability*, 9 Vand L Rev 633, 655-56 (1956).

[8] *See* **chs 6, 7, 8, 9, & 10.**

[9] *See* **ch 10.**

[10] *See* Weitzman, *The Economics of Divorce: Social and Economic Consequences of Property, Alimony, and Child Support Awards*, 28 UCLA L Rev 1181 (1981).

[11] Press, with Clauses, Burger, Abramson, McCormick & Cavazos, *Divorce American Style*, Newsweek, Jan 10, 1983, at 42.

[12] *See* **ch 5.**

However, annulment remains a viable exit from marriage, especially for those whose religious teachings condemn divorce.

## §1.02 —Historical Background

It is interesting and helpful to view the history of divorce to better understand its contemporary form. An examination of the types, forms, and procedures of divorce in specific cultures and societies which have influenced our system in a historical perspective demonstrates the development of the role of the law in divorce.

Customs in some societies involving the right to divorce, fault in divorce, property distribution, support and child custody in divorce, the right to remarry, and the redefinition of status after divorce may be traced directly back to early cultures. It is especially important to see how the canon law, the ecclesiastical courts, and the early American colonists influenced divorce law in America.

## §1.03 —Hebrew and Greek Divorce

From the time of the Patriarchs to the Roman occupation of Palestine in 65 B.C., two primary characteristics of Hebrew divorce were that a husband had a unilateral right to divorce his wife for any reason, and that divorce was a private action, unsupervised by the public or by law.[13]

To divorce his wife, a husband had to give his wife a bill of divorcement, or *get* which usually included the words *Be thou divorced (or separated) from me.* The ease of divorce may be explained by the fact that the early Hebrews practiced wife purchase, whereby a wife was considered chattel.

Before the birth of Christ, however, the rabbinical schools expressed disapproval of divorce and attempted to impose a fault system upon Hebrew divorce customs.[14] The rabbis increased the details and formalities of the bill

---

[13] Falk, Jewish Matrimonial Law in the Middle Ages 113 (1966). The Bible restricted divorce in two instances: where the husband falsely accused his wife of antenuptial unchastity, and where the husband was forced to marry the wife after he had raped her. *See Deut* 21:14,22:28-29 (King James).

[14] *See especially Mal* 2:14-16:

> Yet ye say, Why? Because the Lord hath been witness between thee and the wife of thy youth, against whom thou hast dealt treacherously; yet is she thy companion, and the wife of thy covenant.
>
> And did not he make one? Yet had he the residue of the spirit. And why one? That he might seek a godly seed. Therefore, take heed to your spirit, and let none deal treacherously against the wife of his youth.
>
> For the Lord, the God of Israel, saith that he hateth putting away. . . .

Two rabbinical schools, Hillel and Shammai, offered different interpretations of *Deut* 24:1, which stated that a husband may divorce a wife if "it came to pass that she found no favor in his eyes, because he hath found some uncleanness in her." The Hillel's interpretation, which was followed for centuries, provided that anything displeasing to the husband was a proper ground for divorce.

of divorcement. Fault grounds were enunciated, including adultery, flagrant disregard of moral decency, refusal to cohabit for a year or more, change of religion, and physical "disease" such as barrenness or leprosy.[15] Rabbinical law, influenced by Roman law, recognized divorce grounds for the Hebrew wife, although adultery was not included among them.[16]

Eventually the rabbis enforced divorces against couples with or without their consent if the marriage was in conflict with rabbinical law. The rabbis also invalidated marriages which could not fulfill the marital purpose of procreation.

Greek divorce paralleled Hebrew divorce. The rights and privileges of divorce belonged to the husband, who could repudiate his wife before witnesses for no reason.[17] A Greek husband had the duty to divorce his wife if she was barren or committed adultery, because both conditions frustrated the purpose of Greek marriage, which was to perpetuate the *gens,* or clan. However, in Sparta, where the city-state placed more importance on a strong army than on pure citizenry, adultery was not considered a justifiable ground for divorce.[18]

A Greek wife had very few rights and privileges with divorce. She was entitled to return of her dowry, whether she was guilty or innocent, but she lost custody of the children and was required to return to her father's family and legal authority. It was also very difficult for her to obtain a divorce. Legally she was considered an *incapable.*[19] There also was more public disapproval for a divorce obtained by the wife than for a divorce obtained either by a husband or by mutual consent of the spouses.

## §1.04 —Roman Divorce

Family historians have divided the Roman Empire into two periods for

---

15 W. Goodsell, A History of Marriage and the Family 72 (1934).

16 *See* **§1.04.** The wife's grounds included physical impotence if admitted by the husband, change of religion, extreme dissoluteness, refusal to support, continued mistreatment, commission of crime followed by escape from the country, postmarital affliction with a loathsome disease, or pursuit of a disgusting trade.

17 3 E. Westermarck, The History of Human Marriage 318 (5th ed rewritten (1925).

18 See W. Goodsell, A History of Marriage and the Family 99 (1934), which notes that "sex relations were much freer among the Spartans than the Athenians. If a Spartan had no children or had become old, he might and frequently did encourage his wife to have intercourse with some younger and more vigorous man in order to raise up children to continue his name."

19 R. Flacelieure, Daily Life in Greece at the Time of Pericles 65-66 (1959), which states that the only way a Greek woman could get a divorce was to submit a written claim for a divorce before the archon, the traditional protector of all such incapables. This was extremely difficult in light of the fact that Athenian women especially were customarily confined to their homes, and were rarely allowed to be on the streets.

convenient study of the Roman family.[20] The first period is from the dawn of the Roman legend to the Punic Wars in 202 B.C. The second period ranged from the end of the Punic Wars to the fourth century and the influence of Christianity.

In the early period the patriarchal Roman family was stable, simple, and rigid. Divorce was rare, and the wife's father, who controlled a married couple's legal rights, could terminate the marriage if he so desired.[21]

The Laws of the Twelve Tables, compiled in approximately 450 B.C. and considered the commencement of the written legal history of the Empire,[22] expressly recognized the right of a husband to divorce his wife. Although generally a private custom, divorce in early Rome was checked by public opinion and the watchful eye of the censor who would, in his official capacity, rebuke a husband who unjustifiably repudiated his wife.

The three Punic Wars brought many changes to Roman society which in turn upset the stability of the family in Rome. Divorce was popular, and marriage was not. The men were absent for long periods of time, and women emerged as a wealthy, independent class.[23]

Increased wealth, slaves, leisure time, and upper class conspicuous consumption produced an increase of individualism in Rome which included an unwillingness to remain in an unsatisfactory marriage.[24] Both the husband and wife could divorce at will.[25] Marriages for limited purposes were common, many for only money, social position, or political gain.[26] The epidemic of

---

[20] *See* W. Goodsell, A History of Marriage and the Family 115 (1934); S. Queen & J. Adams, The Family In Various Cultures 129 (1952).

[21] See 3 E. Westermark, The History of Human Marriage 320-21 (5th ed rewritten 1925), where the author notes that legend indicated that Romulus, a founder of Rome, had forbidden the repudiation of wives, except for adultery or wine drinking, on the threat of forfeiture of all property.

[22] J. Sandys, A Companion to Latin Studies 303 (3d ed 1929).

[23] W. Goodsell, *supra* note 20, at 129-30, noted that both the father's power over his daughters and the husband's power over his wife declined during this period. She even linked the increased celibacy in Rome during this time to the resentment the Roman man held for the rich, learned, ambitious, dominating, and independent woman.

[24] S. Queen & J. Adams, *supra* note 20, at 141.

[25] W. Goodsell, *supra* note 20, at 144, conveyed the attitude of men toward divorce through a story in Plutarch's *Lives:*

> Aemilius was asked why he had divorced his wife Papira and he replied, stretching out his shoe: "Is it not beautiful? Is it not new? But none of you can tell where it pinches me. In fact some men divorce their wives for great and manifest faults, yet the little but constant irritation which proceeds from incompatible tempers and habits, though unnoticed by the world at large, does gradually produce between married people breaches which cannot be healed."

[26] The stories of the scandalous marriages and divorces of Rome after the Punic Wars could match any soap opera on television today! *See generally* J. Balsdon, Roman Women, Their History and Their Habits 219-21 (1963); J. Carcopino, Daily Life in Ancient Rome 96-97 (1940); W. Goodsell, *supra* note 23, at 146; P. Grimal, The Civilization of Rome 124-25 (1963); S. Queen & J. Adams, *supra* note 20, at 144; 3 E. Westermarck, *supra* note 21, at 323.

divorce reached scandalous proportions.[27]

Emperor Augustus attempted to restrict divorce by enacting the Lex Julia de Adulteris in 18 B.C. This law required a party who desired a divorce to execute a *repudium,* a written statement renouncing the marriage, in the presence of seven witnesses, all full Roman citizens. It also made adultery a crime and required that a husband divorce his adulterous wife.[28]

Another characteristic of the Roman divorce after the Punic Wars was the mandatory property settlement. If a husband divorced his wife for minor grounds, or was at fault himself, he was required to return his wife's dowry, or *dos.* Needless to say, this had a chilling effect on husbands of rich wives.[29] If the wife divorced the husband, or was at fault, the husband might retain one-sixth of the dowry for each child of the marriage, up to a maximum of one-half the dowry.[30] The husband retained custody of the children. Eventually the practice developed whereby a husband set aside some antenuptial property, called gift for the sake of marriage or *donatio propter nuptias,* for the express purpose of satisfying his wife's claims against him if he occasioned a divorce through his fault or initiative.[31]

Eventually, the Christian reaction against these "pagan" Romans influenced the practices of divorce. But until then, Roman society was in a turmoil which sounds astonishingly like contemporary Western society:

> The unassailable rock had cracked and crumbled away on every side. Then, the woman was strictly subjected to the authority of her lord and master; now, she is his equal, his rival, if not his *imperatrix.* Then, husband and wife had all things in common; now, their property is almost entirely separate. Then, she took pride in her own fertility; now, she fears it. Then, she was faithful; now, she is capricious and depraved. Divorces then were

---

[27] 3 E. Westermarck, *supra* note 21, at 323, cites some statistics:

> Almost all the well-known ladies of the Ciceronian age were divorced at least once, and Seneca said that some women counted their years, not by consuls, but by their husbands. Ovid and Pliny the Younger married three times, Caesar and Antony four, Sulla and Pompey five; and such cases must have been frequent. On the stone erected to a certain Turia by her husband in the early days of the Empire it is said, "seldom do marriages last until death undivorced."

[28] J. Carcopino, *supra* note 26, states that the divorce epidemic continued despite Augustus's law, or perhaps because of it.

[29] J. Balsdon, *supra* note 26, at 219, states:

> For divorce has always had its crude financial aspect; and when a husband had no better ground of divorcing his wife than the fact he found her company tedious, he was frequently restrained, no doubt, by the chill realization that he could not divorce her without replacing her dowry. Cicero was at his wits' end to find the necessary money when he divorced Terentia in late 47 or early 46 B.C., and it is probable that when he died four years later, the dowry was still not repaid.

[30] *Id,* 220.

[31] S. Queen & J. Adams, *supra* note 20, at 144-45.

rare; now they follow so close on each other's heels that, as Martial says, marriage has become merely a form of legalised adultery.[32]

## §1.05 —Early Christian Divorce

The development of the Christian doctrine of divorce was influenced by the teachings of Jesus and Saint Paul, the writings of the early church fathers, and the fusion of the Roman society with the Christian society.

Jesus's words on divorce generated great confusion among church fathers because in Matthew's gospel, Jesus stated that adultery was a ground for divorce, while in Mark's and Luke's gospels, no such ground is mentioned.[33]

Saint Paul's writings provided the foundation for the early church's doctrine of divorce. In his letter to the Romans, Paul declared that a woman is bound by law to her husband for as long as he lives, and may remarry only if he dies.[34] In his first letter to the Corinthians, Paul stated: "[a]nd unto the married I command, yet not I, but the Lord, Let not the wife depart from the husband: but and if she does depart, let her remain unmarried, or be reconciled to her husband: and let not the husband put away his wife."[35] However, Paul did provide an exception for faithful Christians whose unbelieving spouses left them, maintaining that these spouses were "not under bondage in these cases. . . ."[36]

Because the foundation for the early church's divorce doctrine was controversial and ambiguous, the church fathers adopted no well-defined position on divorce for four centuries. The development of a specific Christian divorce doctrine was also hindered because the early Christians were a diverse people

---

[32] J. Carcopino, *supra* note 26, at 100.

[33] Matthew's treatment of the subject is as follows, at *Matt* 19:3-9:

> The Pharisees also came unto him, tempting him, and saying unto him, Is it lawful to put away his wife for any cause? And he answered and said unto them, Have ye not read that he which made them at the beginning made them male and female, And said For this cause shall a man leave father and mother, and shall cleave to his wife: and they twain shall be one flesh? Wherefore they are no more twain, but one flesh? What therefore God hath joined together, let not man put asunder. They say unto him, Why did Moses then command to give a writing of divorcement and to put her away? He saith unto them, Moses because of the hardness of your hearts suffered you to put away your wives: but from the beginning it was not so. And I say unto you, Whosoever shall put away his wife, except it be for fornication, and shall marry another, committeth adultery: and whoso marrieth her which it put away committeth adultery.

See also *Luke* 16:18 which states that "[w]hosoever putteth away his wife and marrieth another, committeth adultery: and whosoever marrieth her that is put away from her husband committeth adultery."

[34] *Rom* 7:2-3.

[35] 1 *Cor* 7:10-11.

[36] 1 *Cor* 7:12.

of many cultures, languages, and countries, many of which did recognize a right to divorce.[37]

Christianity spread, and the belief that marriage was a sacred union also spread. In the fifth century, the church fathers finally concluded that marriage could be terminated only upon specific grounds, including adultery. In 407 A.D., at the Council of Carthage, the church laid down the strict doctrine of the indissolubility of marriage.

The church's teachings still conflicted with societal actions, however, until the Roman emperors recognized Christianity as the official religion and promulgated strict laws on the subject of divorce. The pronouncement of marriage as a sacrament in the eleventh century fortified its position as an indissoluble union. Yet, as one marriage historian noted:

> [T]here yet remained a twofold task which it would still require centuries to accomplish. On the one hand, the discordant utterances of the Fathers, the popes, and the councils had to be harmonized or explained away; while, at the same time, the results thus gained had to be exactly formulated and wrought into the intricate system of matrimonial jurisprudence.[38]

## §1.06 —Anglo-Saxon Divorce

Anglo-Saxon divorce customs were a product of Germanic, Roman, and early Christian influences. The Germanic tribes of Angles, Saxons, and Jutes which eventually unified England and gave it its first king originally practiced purchase marriage.[39] Therefore, the husband most likely had the sole right of repudiation, although this is uncertain because historical information in this area is scarce.[40]

The Code of Aethelberht, enacted around 602 A.D., and considered the earliest laws written in the English language, has been interpreted as allowing divorce at will, but as punishing arbitrary repudiation.[41] Teutonic folk-laws, local records of Germanic tribes' customs and traditions, provided for divorce by mutual agreement for many of the tribes.[42]

The Christians' inevitable influence resulted in the establishment of fault grounds for divorce for the Anglo-Saxons. The Christians' doctrine of

---

[37] *See* **§§1.03-1.04.**

[38] 2 G. Howard, A History of Matrimonial Institutions 47 (reprint 1964).

[39] *See generally* G. Keeton, English Law, The Judicial Constitution 10 (1974); 1 World Book Encyclopedia 440-41 (1983).

[40] W. Goodsell, A History of Marriage and the Family 210 (1934); 2 G. Howard, A History of Matrimonial Institutions 34 (reprint 1964); 2 F. Pollock & F. Maitland, History of English Law 392 (1895, reprinted 1978); S. Queen & J. Adams, The Family in Various Cultures 183 (1952).

[41] 2 G. Howard, *supra* note 40, at 35.

[42] W. Goodsell, *supra* note 40, at 210.

indissolubility clashed with the tribes' divorce upon mutual consent, producing the fault ground compromise which persisted until Christianity's influence became the law of England.[43]

## §1.07 —Divorce and the Canon Law

The practitioner should be aware of the strong influence of the Catholic Church and the Church of England over the law of divorce. Church doctrine has been a dominant force in the establishment of American divorce law, as will be seen repeatedly in future sections.

In the fifth century, the Council of Carthage declared that marriage was an indissoluble bond. The fifth and sixth centuries also brought the decline of the Roman emperors' power of legislation in Western Europe. Control of marriage and divorce fell into the hands of the Christian church through its canonists and ecclesiastical courts. In England these courts would retain control until 1857.

The doctrine of indissolubility was extremely difficult for the church to enforce in societies which had historically provided a right of repudiation for one or both spouses. It became clear to church officials and canonists that the only way to enforce their doctrine of the indissolubility of marriage was to obtain control over the divorce procedures.

In 505 A.D., the Council of Agde declared that a divorce was not valid until the ecclesiastical authority approved of a divorce ground which was being used in the temporal court. Until this time, the temporal courts merely dictated penal sentences for a guilty party in a divorce action, and did not nullify or enforce what was essentially a self-divorce.

The temporal courts began enforcing the decisions of the ecclesiastical authority, and the ecclesiastical courts' power began to build. In the middle of the tenth century, the great canonists Gratian and Peter Lombard revised, recorded, and attempted to harmonize the declarations of the church fathers, the councils, the Popes, and the bishops' manuals, to form a complete system of divorce jurisprudence. The ecclesiastical courts' participation also contributed to the reconciliation of the various authorities into a comprehensive canon law.[44]

The jurisdiction of the church courts included all questions of marriage, such as nullity and separation, and an elaboration of the rules governing legiti-

---

[43] W. Goodsell, *supra* note 40, at 211-12; S. Queen & J. Adams, *supra* note 40, at 183.

[44] 2 G. Howard, A History of Matrimonial Institutions 51 (reprint 1964), states that "[t]hrough special pleading and violent assumption, unscrupulous twisting and suppressing of texts, earnest argument and childish allegory, the law of divorce was gradually brought into some degree of harmony with the sacramental theory of marriage."

macy.[45] From the twelfth century onward, the ecclesiastical courts and rules had undoubted control over marriage and divorce all over Christian Europe.[46]

Despite the doctrine of the indissolubility of marriage, the church courts recognized two legal processes which were popularly and misleadingly called divorces.[47] One was the divorce *a vinculo matrimonii,* which was a decree of nullity for some lack of marital capacity which rendered the marriage void from its inception, void ab initio.[48] This process was abused by people in unhappy marriages with the necessary wealth and influence to secure a decision from an ecclesiastical court that no true marriage existed.[49]

The other process was the divorce *a mensa et thoro,* the divorce from bed and board, which was a judicial separation useful for situations of marital discord unaccompanied by any forbidden impediments. The divorce a mensa et thoro was granted for gross misconduct, usually adultery or cruelty, which made it impossible for the parties to live together. The ecclesiastical court ordered the couple to live apart, while forbidding remarriage.

It should also be noted that the canon law provided for an absolute divorce in three extremely narrow cases.[50] Papal dispensations were also available to those well-to-do people who wanted either to remarry after a divorce or to marry *within* the forbidden degrees.

Thus, it appears that the strict doctrine of the indissolubility of marriage of the canon law had many exceptions.

## §1.08 —The Reformation and Beyond

The Reformation brought to light many of the abuses and inconsistencies of the canon law's divorce doctrine. The early Protestants rebelled against the canon law and struggled to produce a satisfying doctrine of their own.

---

[45] G. Keeton, English Law, The Judicial Constitution 57 (1974).

[46] 2 J. Bryce, Studies in History and Jurisprudence 825 (1901).

[47] *Id.* See also 2 G. Howard, *supra* note 44, at 52-53, where he states that "the name 'divorce' is retained as a rubric in the collection of canons; and it is used in two senses, neither of which corresponds with its ancient and proper meaning as a complete dissolution of the bond of true wedlock."

[48] J. Madden, Handbook of the Law of Persons and Domestic Relations 257 (1931); 2 F. Pollock & F. Maitland, History of English Law 393 (reprint 1978).

[49] See 2 F. Pollock & F. Maitland, *supra* note 48, at 393 n 1, where the authors declare that "in medieval practice the decree of nullity often served the purpose of true divorce; spouses who had quarrelled began to investigate their pedigrees and were unlucky if they could discover no impedimentum didimens."

[50] See Kelly, *Marriage, Divorce, and Annulment,* 4 Jurist 246, 273 (1944), which describes the three exceptions. The first is called the Pauline Privilege, because it was first enunciated by the Apostle Paul. An absolute divorce could be granted if a newly converted person's spouse refused to be converted or cohabit peacefully with the new convert. The convert could only remarry a believer, however.

The canon law also provided that an unconsummated marriage bond could be validly dissolved by one party's entering a religious order or by direct intervention from the Pope. The third case is called the Petrine Privilege, and it is a combination of the first two cases.

Two important influences over divorce during this time were Luther's reclassification of marriage as a worldly thing and his rejection of the jurisdiction of the existing ecclesiastical courts.[51] This gave rise to a question of whether self-divorce was sufficient, or whether the intervention of some authority was necessary to dissolve the marriage.

The Protestants tended to look to the Roman law for guidance, but still were bound by the Scriptures. Instead of adding more grounds for divorce, the reformers leaned toward broader definitions of adultery and malicious prosecution, and favored ad hoc decisions by the courts.[52]

The Christian church established a stricter divorce doctrine as a result of the Reformation. The grounds for divorce a mensa et thoro (permanent judicial separation) were reduced to adultery. The wealthy citizens of England turned to the Parliament for decrees of absolute divorce.

In 1857 Parliament established the Court of Divorce and Matrimonial Causes. It had the jurisdiction and powers of the ecclesiastical courts, the legislature's ability to grant absolute divorces, and the power to award damages for criminal conversation which formerly belonged to the common law courts.[53]

Thus, the power of the ecclesiastical courts over divorce was ended.

## §1.09 —Early American Divorce

There is nothing surprising about the rule of English jurisprudence which dictates that colonists settling in an uninhabited land will take with them those laws of their mother country which are suited to their new circumstances.[54] Generally, the American colonists, rebellious in nature and struggling for survival, did not follow the laws and procedures of their home countries regarding divorce.[55] Unique circumstances such as the harsh pioneer conditions, the abandonment of spouses in the old country, the desire to populate the new land, and a rejection of certain beliefs of the old country contributed to a new treatment of divorce in America.[56]

---

[51] 2 G. Howard, A History of Matrimonial Institutions 68 (reprint 1964).

[52] *See* W. Goodsell, A History of Marriage and the Family 266-68 (1934); 2 G. Howard, *supra* note 51, at 60-85.

[53] 1 W. Holdsworth, History of English Law 623 (7th ed 1956).

[54] *See* J. Bishop, Marriage, Divorce and Separation §116 (1891); 2 G. Howard, A History of Matrimonial Institutions 366 (reprint 1964).

[55] *See* S. Green & J. Long, Marriage and Family Law Agreements §1.08 (1984).

[56] *See* N. Blake, The Road to Reno 48 (1962); *An Essay on Marriage: Or the Lawfulness of Divorce,* in the Colonial American Family 3 (D. Rothman & S. Rothman eds 1972).

The attitude of the colonists eventually resulted in their independence and the establishment of the United States of America. This same attitude influenced the treatment of divorce. In 1788, an anonymous Philadelphia author, disturbed by the news of an unhappy wife's suicide, published *An Essay on Marriage* which extolled the advantages of a liberal divorce policy:

America has been famous for her love of liberty, and hatred of tyranny of every

In New England, where marriage was viewed as a civil contract, a liberal divorce policy was established as a reaction "against the forms and abuses of the ancient canonical and ecclesiastical systems."[57] Legislative divorces were common in the New England colonies. The assemblies frequently granted divorces, exercising concurrent jurisdiction with the law tribunals.

In the southern colonies, the Church of England was established, and English divorce law and customs were generally followed. However, the southern and middle colonies did not establish any tribunal equivalent to England's ecclesiastical courts. Equity courts were granting petitions for alimony despite the fact that no statute awarded such jurisdiction.[58]

In the southern and middle colonies, divorce either did not exist or was a rarely exercised legislative or executive power. After the Revolution, the states reluctantly entrusted divorce jurisdiction to the courts. Each new state enacted laws specifying grounds for divorce; New England and the states of the Old Northwest were liberal, while South Carolina and New York were the most conservative.[59]

## §1.10 Historical Grounds for Divorce

As seen in previous sections, in many early societies parties were required to prove that their spouses were at fault in the marriage in order to be able to divorce.[60] The establishment of fault grounds as a basis for divorce became a tool by which society attempted to discourage divorce. Nowhere was this practice more effective than in case of the Christian church.[61]

In attempting to establish the doctrine of the indissolubility of marriage, the church forbade absolute divorces. Upon proof of a spouse's adultery, cruelty, or unnatural practices which fit the *crime* of a violation of the sacred marital vow, the church allowed the divorce a mensa et thoro, to suspend the cohabitation

---

> kind. . . . Therefore, it is hoped, the same spirit of indulgence will extend still further - to those unhappy individuals, mixed among every class of mankind, who are frequently united together in the worst of bondage to each other; occasioned by circumstances not in their power to foresee, or prevent, at the time of their union; which should entitle them to relief from humane legislators and the rest of mankind. We believe it will be readily admitted, that there is no circumstance in life, on which our happiness so much depends as being suitably united together in marriage; and that no foresight that people are capable of, at that time, is sufficient to foresee, or prevent, the many causes that are likely to destroy the felicity of that union; and that it is equally certain, that various causes do destroy it, and render them completely miserable; from hence arises the necessity of divorce in such situations, under such restrictions as may be deemed necessary.

*Id* 3-4.

[57] 2 G. Howard, *supra* note 54, at 330.

[58] 2 G. Howard, *supra* note 54, at 367.

[59] N. Blake, *supra* note 56, at 48-79.

[60] *See* **§§1.02-1.09.**

[61] *See* **§1.07.**

obligation of marriage while continuing other duties and obligations. Divorce from bed and board was granted as a relief to an innocent spouse and as a punishment of a guilty spouse.

When the English Parliament transferred divorce jurisdiction from the eccelesiastical courts to the state courts by enacting the Matrimonial Causes Act of 1857, the fault-oriented system remained intact.[62] In fact, the notion of fault was taken to the American colonies where, as one commentator has noted, "when post-revolution America drafted its divorce legislation, the fault concept was compulsively carried over into our own legal system where it remained to this day."[63] Each state developed its own body of law which, among other things, enumerated grounds for divorce.

The traditional fault divorce grounds stemmed from the Biblical ground of adultery. These grounds included cruelty, desertion, impotence, imprisonment, intoxication, nonsupport, and insanity.[64] At one time, adultery was a ground for absolute divorce in all states.[65]

In the United States, for many years, public policy supported the statutory fault divorce system. The state had an interest in protecting and preserving the integrity and stability of marriage. Therefore, the state not only prohibited divorce by mutual agreement of the parties, but required that divorces be granted for *just causes*, or on fault grounds.[66] The party who desired a divorce was required to go to court and prove that the other spouse was guilty of specific marital misconduct which was a statutorily enunciated ground.

Although used much less frequently, the fault system still exists in most states. That existence, however, warrants discussion.[67]

## §1.11 —Adultery

Historically, adultery has been an important divorce ground, used frequently during the era of the ecclesiastical courts, established as the sole divorce ground in 1857 in England when Parliament transferred divorce jurisdiction to state

---

[62] Walker, *Beyond Fault: An Examination of Patterns of Behavior in Response to Present Divorce Laws*, 10 J Fam L 267, 273 (1971).

[63] *Id* 273-74.

[64] 2 C. Vernier, American Family Laws 5 (1931). *See* **§§1.11-1.18.**

[65] 2 C. Vernier, *supra* note 64, at 18. *See* **§1.11.**

[66] See Lichtenberger, *Divorce Legislation*, in Selected Essays on Family Law 862 (1950), where the author summarized divorce practice at that time:

> A divorce cannot be secured in any state in the Union unless and until it can be established by positive proof in a court of record that at some specific time in the past the marriage *de facto* has been destroyed through the operation of causes designated as "legal grounds" in the state of residence. In the absence of such proof the petition is denied.

[67] *See* **§§1.11-1.18.**

courts, and carried over by the colonists into the law of early America.[68] Public policy has long condemned adultery as the cardinal sin of marital misconduct. It has been believed that no violation of the marital vow is more serious or destructive to a marriage than adultery.[69]

The law in the United States has reflected this public policy in two ways. In many states, adultery was statutorily defined as a crime. Some of these statutes still exist today, although they are rarely enforced.[70]

For many years, however, adultery was a divorce ground in every United States jurisdiction which allowed absolute divorce.[71] Adultery was the only divorce ground in New York from 1787 to 1966.[72] In 1985, 30 states and the District of Columbia still included adultery as a ground in their divorce statutes.[73]

The adultery ground has a history of sexual prejudice. At common law the

---

[68] *See* H. Clark, The Law of Domestic Relations in the United States 281 (1968); Mueller, *Inquiry Into the State of a Divorceless Society*, 18 U Pitt L Rev 545, 550 (1957); Ohlson, *Adultery: A Review*, 17 BUL Rev 328 (1937); **§§1.02-1.09.**

[69] Ohlson, *supra* note 68, at 329-30. In fact, the seventh commandment brought down by Moses from Mount Sinai was: "Thou shalt not commit adultery." *Exod* 20:14.

[70] *See, e.g.,* DC Code Ann §22-1002 (1981) (fornication); Fla Stat Ann §§798.01-.03 (West 1976); Md Ann Code art 27, §4 (1982); Mass Ann Laws ch 272, §12 (Michie/Law Co-op 1980); NY Penal Code Law §255.17 (McKinney 1980); Va Code §§18.2-344, -345 (1980).

An issue which may become relevant in jurisdictions where adultery is still a crime is the invocation of the Fifth Amendment in depositions and at trial in response to questions concerning the adultery. Where adultery is a crime it is proper for a litigant to invoke the privilege. However, a civil litigant who invokes the Fifth Amendment to prevent discovery may be subject to noncriminal sanctions, the harshest being dismissal of the suit. *See* Hackes v Hackes, 446 A2d 396, 399 (DC 1982); Mahne v Mahne, 66 NJ 53, 55, 328 A2d 225, 226 (1874).

[71] 2 C. Vernier, American Family Laws 18 (1931).

[72] *See* N. Blake, The Road to Reno 189-225 (1962). New York's strict law became a rallying point for proponents of no-fault divorce who pointed to the complicated problems of New York's ridiculously lenient annulment grounds and the increase in migratory divorce as symptoms of fault divorce's ineffectiveness. See **§§1.27-1.42** for further discussion of no-fault divorce.

[73] *See* Ala Code §30-2-1(a)(2) (1983); Alaska Stat §25.24.050(2) (1983); Ark Stat Ann §34-1202 (Supp 1983); Conn Gen Stat Ann §46b-40(c)(3) (West Supp 1984); Del Code Ann tit 13, §1505(b)(2)(1981); DC Code Ann §16-904(b)(3)(1981) (ground for limited divorce); Ga Code Ann §19-5-3(6)(1982); Idaho Code §32-604 (1983); Ill Ann Stat ch 40, §401(2) (Smith-Hurd 1980); La Civ Code Ann art 139(1) (West Supp 1984); Me Rev Stat Ann tit 19, §691(1)(A) (1981); Md Fam Law Code Ann §7-103(a)(1) (1984); Mass Ann Laws ch 208, §1 (Michi/Law Co-op 1981); Miss Code Ann §93-5-1 (1973); NH Rev Stat Ann §458:7(II)(1983); NJ Stat Ann §2A:34-2(a) (West Supp 1984-85); NM Stat Ann §40-4-1(c) (1983); NY Dom Rel Law §170(4) (McKinney 1977); ND Cent Code §14-05-03(1) (1981); Ohio Rev Code Ann §3105.01(c) (Page 1980); Okla Stat Ann tit 12, §1271 (West 1961); Pa Stat Ann tit 23, §201(a)(2) (Purdon Supp 1984-85); RI Gen Laws §15-5-2 (1981); SC Code Ann §20-3-10(1) (Law Co-op Supp 1983); SD Codified Laws Ann §25-4-2(1) (1984); Tenn Code Ann §36-4-101(3) (1984); Tex Fam Code Ann §3.03 (Vernon 1975); Utah Code Ann §30-3-1(2) (1984); Vt Stat Ann tit 15, §551(1) (Supp 1984); Va Code §20-91(1) (1983); W Va Code §48-2-4(a)(1) (Supp 1984).

criminal definition of adultery was sexual intercourse by a man, married or single, with a married woman not his wife.[74] After the Revolutionary War the definition of adultery was enlarged to include sexual intercourse by either spouse with someone other than his or her spouse.[75] However, some divorce statutes established different standards of proof for husbands and wives, requiring a wife to prove that her husband engaged in a course of conduct termed *living in adultery*, while requiring that a husband prove only a single act of adultery. However, this prejudice has been eliminated from most statutes.

The adultery ground is rarely used if other grounds are available which are less scandalous and easier to prove. Most divorce cases involving adultery are plagued by problems of evidence and proof. Adultery is usually proved by circumstantial evidence because, as one family law authority has stated, "there are seldom eyewitnesses to adultery."[76]

This almost universal resort to circumstantial evidence to prove the voluntary, intentional act of adultery has given rise to the *disposition and opportunity rule*. This rule creates a presumption of adultery where the plaintiff proves that the defendant and his or her lover, who may be named as a corespondent in the divorce action, had adulterous disposition and the opportunity to commit adultery.[77]

Evidence which proves adulterous disposition tends to reveal a romantic relationship between the defendant spouse and the paramour, for example, love letters or public displays of affection. Opportunity may be shown by proving that the defendant and corespondent were alone at night in an apartment or a hotel. Both opportunity and disposition must be proven; either aspect alone is insufficient.[78]

Certain evidence clearly proves adultery. A party who contracts a sexually transmittable disease may be guilty of adultery where the circumstances are such that the disease could not have been contracted before the marriage or from another source. Adultery may be proven where a wife becomes pregnant despite her husband's sterility or absence. Whether a party's homosexual

---

74 2 Am Jur 2d *Adultery and Fornication* §1, at 962 (1962).

75 Ohlson, *supra* note 68, at 333.

76 H. Clark, *supra* note 68, at 330.

77 *Id.*

78 *Id* asserts that "[i]n general the same type of evidence tends to prove both opportunity and disposition, such as, for example, frequent association with persons of the opposite sex at night and alone, improper familiarity, visits to hotels or apartments with the paramour and similar conduct."

The authors disagree with Clark's statement that the same type of evidence tends to prove both opportunity and disposition. The evidence which establishes disposition includes conduct such as kissing, holding hands, writing love letters, using terms of endearment and the like. But a different type of evidence proves the opportunity, such as spending the night together in an abode without others present. This latter type of evidence does not itself show disposition, while the former type does not itself show opportunity.

activity may be sufficient for the adultery ground varies from state to state.[79]

Historically, the traditional defenses of recrimination, condonation, connivance, and collusion were frequently used in divorce actions based on adultery grounds. Insanity at the time of the act is generally a good defense in an adultery action, while intoxication and polygamous beliefs are not.[80]

Adultery is not used as frequently in this era of no-fault divorce as at the height of the fault system. However, the adultery ground may still prove useful. It has been pled as a bargaining chip for settlement negotiation or on the theory that it may predispose a court toward the plaintiff. An advantage of this fault ground is that, if the evidence is available, a divorce action may be filed immediately. At worst, the action is in line for a trial date, even if it is eventually amended to a no-fault ground, which saves the waiting time required by a no-fault divorce.

In addition, many states still look to fault as a factor with respect to property distribution even where the action is based upon a no-fault ground.[81] Thus, in those states a court may properly consider the situation where a spouse dissipates marital assets in connection with adulterous activities. Although an award of alimony is not supposed to be punitive, some practitioners believe that adultery does influence such an award.

In any event, in the psychological divorce battle, wronged spouses sometimes look to the adultery ground as a way to strike back at a spouse who wishes to remarry quickly. These human reactions contribute to the continued life of the adultery ground in divorce actions.

## §1.12 —Cruelty

The evolution of the cruelty ground reflects the policy shift in divorce law from fault to no-fault. The cruelty ground became a useful judicial tool for circumventing the strict divorce statutes.

In England and the American colonies, cruelty was originally a ground only for divorce a mensa et thoro.[82] However, by 1900, most of the United States recognized cruelty as a ground for absolute divorce. Originally, a party alleging cruelty had to prove actual bodily harm as a result of the intentional physical cruelty of the guilty spouse which was extreme, repeated, barbarous, or

---

[79] *Compare* NY Dom Rel Law §170(4) (McKinney 1977) (which defines adultery as "the commission of an act of sexual or deviate sexual intercourse voluntarily performed by the defendant, with a person other than the plaintiff, after the marriage of the plaintiff and defendant,") *with* W Va Code §48-2-4(a)(4) (Supp 1984) (which includes homosexuality as a separate ground).

[80] See H. Clark, *supra* note 68, at 329; J. Madden, Handbook of the Law of Persons and Domestic Relations 264 (1931); **§§1.19-1.25.**

[81] *See* **ch 10.**

[82] H. Clark, The Law of Domestic Relations in the United States 281 (1968); M. Ploscowe, H. Foster, & D. Freed, Family Law, Cases and Materials 393 (2d ed 1972).

intolerable.[83] This strict standard may have been based on the common law notion that a husband could use force to discipline his wife.[84]

Courts decide cruelty on a case-by-case basis, and rarely have attempted to define cruelty. However, the acts judicially accepted as cruelty over the years have set the limits of the definition. Thus, in the early stages of the development of the cruelty ground, repeated direct intentional physical violence resulting in injury was the accepted case of cruelty, and remains the most obvious example today.

When the societal view of divorce began to change from the ecclesiastical notion that divorce punished the guilty spouse to the idea that divorce protected the innocent spouse, the evidentiary rules in cruelty cases were relaxed to reflect that change and to give the innocent spouse an easier escape from a harmful marriage. The effect of the cruel act on the victim became more important than the nature of the act itself. The definition of cruelty expanded to include bodily harm, threats of violence, or reasonable apprehension of bodily harm.[85] In some jurisdictions a single act became sufficient for proving cruelty, and many courts began to reject a prior requirement that the defendant's malice or intent be proven.[86]

While the judicial standards for proving cruelty were being lowered, the strict statutory language remained the same, requiring, for example *extreme cruelty*,[87] *intolerable cruelty*,[88] or *cruel and inhuman treatment calculated to impair health or endanger life*.[89] In addition, some legislatures and courts adopted mental cruelty

---

[83] The leading English case on cruelty, Evans v Evans, 1 Hag Con 35, 161 Eng Rep 466 (1790), established a definition of cruelty which has been widely cited in the United States:

> What is cruelty? . . . it is the duty of the courts. . . to keep the rule extremely strict. The causes must be grave and weighty, and such as shew an absolute impossibility that the duties of the married life can be discharged; for the duty of self-preservation must take place before the duties of marriage. . . .
> What merely wounds the mental feelings is in few cases to be admitted where they are not accompanied with bodily injury, either actual menaced. Mere austerity of temper, petulance of manners, rudeness of language, a want of civil attention and accommodation, even occasioned sallies of passion, if they do not threaten bodily harm, do not amount to legal cruelty.

1 Hag Con at 37-78, 161 Eng Rep at 467.

[84] 1 Blackstone Commentaries 445 (3d ed Cooley 1884).

[85] Levine, *Marital Cruelty: New Wine in Old Bottles*, 2 Fam LQ 296, 303 (1968).

[86] H. Clark, *supra* note 82, at 345; Levine, *Levine, supra* note 85, at 309.

[87] *See, e.g.*, Idaho Code §32-605 (1983); Me Rev Stat Ann tit 19, §619(1)(c) (1981); NH Rev Stat Ann §458:7(III) (1983); NJ Stat Ann §2A:34-2(c) (West Supp 1984-85); ND Cent Code §14-05-03(2) (1981); Ohio Rev Code Ann §3105.01(E) (Page 1980); Okla Stat Ann tit 12, §1271 (West 1961); RI Gen Laws §15-5-2 (1981); SD Codified Laws Ann §26-4-2(2)(1984).

[88] Conn Gen Stat Ann §46b-40(c)(8) (West Supp 1984).

[89] Alaska Stat §25.24.050(5) (A)(1983). *See also* Ark Stat Ann §34-1202 (Supp 1983) (cruel and barbarous treatment as to endanger life); Mass Ann Laws ch 208, §1 (Michie/Law Co-op 1981) (cruel and abusive treatment): Miss Code Ann §93-5-1 (1973)

as a divorce ground, requiring some showing of physical injury, ill health, or damaged well-being as a manifestation of that type of cruelty.[90]

These differences between statutory language and actual courtroom requirements highlighted the hypocrisy of the fault system which led to the discrediting of divorce litigation. It has been stated that many parties obtaining divorces on the cruelty ground were fabricating evidence and committing perjury.[91] In any event, cruelty became the most commonly used divorce ground in the United States. As such, it showcased a new purpose for divorce: to dissolve a marriage of no social value.[92]

---

(habitual cruel and inhuman treatment); NH Rev Stat Ann §40-4-1(B) (1983) (cruel and inhuman treatment); NY Dom Rel Law §170(1) (McKinney 1977) (cruel and inhuman treatment); W Va Code §48-2-4(a)(4) (Supp 1984) (cruel and inhuman treatment).

[90] H. Clark, *supra* note 82, at 343-44; Levine, *supra* note 85, at 307. *See also* Ill Ann Stat ch 40, §401(2) (Smith-Hurd 1980); NJ Stat Ann §2A: 34-2(c) (West Supp 1984-85); Utah Code Ann §30-3-1(7) (1984); W Va Code §48-2-4(a) (4) (Supp 1984).

[91] H. Clark, *supra* note 82, at 341, stated:

> In trial courts in uncontested cases divorces will often be granted upon evidence of cruelty which would not qualify by the standards of the reported cases. . . . In many states, especially in the West, a divorce for cruelty may be had for the asking, providing it is uncontested. Whether this condition be labelled hypocritical or sophisticated, it is a fact which must be faced by all lawyers, and ought to be made known to laymen. . . . One might therefore say that this section is devoted to the discussion of a fiction, the pretended definition of cruelty as a ground of divorce.

See Law 103 (1972), where the author described the reality of procedure in Illinois, where the courts required that two acts of violence be proven in order to constitute *extreme and repeated cruelty* under the statute:

> In order to be extreme the acts also had to result in serious discomfort to the plaintiff. So the plaintiff would be asked by her attorney: "When your husband slapped you in the face, did it cause you great pain and suffering?" "Yes." Or the plaintiff's corroborating witness, frequently her mother or her sister, could be asked: "Did you see any physical marks in the plaintiff's face?" "Yes." Rarely would any effort be made to ascertain whether the defendant had actually performed the ritual of at least two slaps. (Footnotes omitted.)

[92] See Levine, *supra* note 85, at 304, where it is maintained that cruelty cases involved an "ultimate issue for the courts. . . . [which was] the effect of the domestic transgression on the marital res itself." See also Hand v Hand, 257 Iowa 643, 651, 133 NW2d 63, 68 (Iowa 1965), where the Supreme Court of Iowa observed:

> It is the small things that are of greatest importance in life of most people; and, while some disagreements between husband and wife are to be expected, it must be concluded that even these, carried to excess so that the unhappy husband has no hope of domestic tranquility, who is constantly faced with criticisms and complaints and belittlings, may well say he is the victim of cruel and inhuman treatment. One, or two, or a few days of this might be borne; but when it continues for year after year, the constant drippings of the antagonisms may begin to wear away the rock of endurance.

## Elements of the Cruelty Ground

Courts have not attempted to define cruelty, but generally determine whether cruelty exists on a case-by-case basis. Whether the alleged cruelty is sufficient for a divorce decree is frequently the issue at a fault trial based on the cruelty ground, and it is decided by the courts on the facts and circumstances of each case. The multitude of cruelty cases has displayed a variety of fact situations which make it difficult to generalize the concept of cruelty.

The courts usually apply subjective tests in cruelty cases. Age, education, sex, and degree of refinement and sensitivity may be taken into consideration by the court. Differences in size and strength and stereotyped notions have sometimes resulted in a double standard situation where a husband has a greater burden of proof than a wife.

Repeated direct physical violence resulting in injury is the most obvious case of cruelty. This may be evidenced by beating, major or minor physical abuse, intentional communication of disease, withholding medical care, and threats of incarceration. In a state which requires a continuing course of conduct, a single act of violence is usually insufficient to constitute cruelty, especially when committed in the heat of passion, with little chance of repetition.[93] However, if the single act is very severe, and involves malice, it may be sufficient.

Cases involving sexual abuse as cruelty must clearly show that the plaintiff's health was affected. A spouse's insistence on excessive or otherwise unnatural or unreasonable sexual intercourse may constitute cruelty or indignities within the meaning of the statutes.[94] This issue has resurfaced under the term *marital rape.*[95] Persistent and unjustifiable refusal to engage in sexual intercourse has been held to constitute cruelty, indignities, and desertion.[96] Homosexuality, transvestism, and transsexualism have also been held to come within cruelty and indignities statutory provisions.[97]

Attacks on self-respect or reputation have been found to be cruelty, especially when the defendant insults the plaintiff or accuses the plaintiff of criminal behavior, adultery, or other misconduct in the presence of friends, employers, and associates.[98] It has been held that abuse to third persons, typically in-laws or children, is sufficient cruelty for divorce.[99]

---

[93] H. Clarke, Social Legislation 124 (2d ed 1968); Annot, 7 ALR3d 761, 765 (1966).

[94] H. Clark, *supra* note 82, at 346; Annot, 88 ALR2d 553, 555 (1963).

[95] *See, e.g.*, Blay-Cohen & Coster, *Marital Rape in California: For Better or For Worse*, 8 San Fern VL Rev 239 (1980); DiCarlo, *The Marital Rape Exemption in Pennsylvania: With This Ring. . . ,*" 86 Dick L Rev 79 (1981); Griffin, *In 44 States, It's Legal To Rape Your Wife*, 9 Student Law 20 (1980).

[96] H. Clark, *supra* note 82, at 346; Annot, 82 ALR3d 660 (1978). *See also* **§§1.13-1.14.**

[97] *See* Annot, 78 ALR2d 807 (1961); Annot, 82 ALR3d 725 (1978).

[98] H. Clark, *supra* note 82, at 346.

[99] *Id;* Levine, *supra* note 85, at 312; Annot, 82 ALR2d 1361 (1962).

These and other bases, which in some jurisdictions are sufficient grounds in themselves for divorce, may constitute cruelty if combined with other conduct.

## §1.13 —Personal Indignities

In 1985, Alaska, Arkansas, New Hampshire, North Carolina, Pennsylvania, and Tennessee had the personal indignities ground for absolute or limited divorce.[100] The personal indignities ground, similar to the cruelty ground, has been generally defined as "a pattern of conduct as renders the the condition of the other party intolerable and life burdensome, and from which an inference of settled hate and estrangement may be deduced."[101]

The difference between cruelty and personal indignities is that the latter requires proof of a pattern of misconduct, while cruelty may be proven by a single incident. It has been noted that personal indignities is similar in construction to mental cruelty.[102] Thus, proving indignities may require a showing of ill health. Where both cruelty and indignities are divorce grounds, proof of cruelty is more likely to be strictly limited to personal violence, while proof of personal indignities usually remains the more flexible ground.

## §1.14 —Desertion

Desertion has been known as the poor man's divorce since the days of the ecclesiastical courts in England, where parliamentary divorces, divorces a mensa et thoro, and annulments were too expensive for ordinary people.[103] Ecclesiastical law did not recognize desertion as a ground for divorce, but did provide a remedy for desertion in the suit for *restitution of conjugal rights,* an action for specific performance of the cohabitation duty of marriage.[104]

American law, while not adopting the English restitution of conjugal rights, provided desertion as a divorce ground in all states which recognized absolute

---

[100] Alaska Stat §25.24.050(5)(B)(1983); Ark Stat Ann §34-1202 (Supp 1983); NH Rev Stat Ann §458:7V (1983) ("When either party has so treated the other as seriously to injure health or endanger reason"); NC Gen Stat §50-6 (1983); Pa Stat Ann tit 23, §201(a) (6) (Purdon Supp 1984-85).

[101] Levine, *Marital Cruelty: New Wine in Old Bottles,* 2 Fam LQ 296, 307 (1968).

[102] *Id.*

[103] Foster, *Common Law Divorce,* 46 Minn L Rev 43, 54 (1961); Mueller, *Inquiry into the State of a Divorceless Society,* 18 U Pitt L Rev 545, 572-73 (1957). Foster, *supra,* at 54, notes:

> [D]esertion, self-divorce, or extra-legal divorce by ministers of dissenting sects, or according to local customs, were the ways out for the common man. It is important to note that the first metropolitan police department in the world was that established by Sir Robert Peel (hence the nickname "bobbies") in London in 1829. Before that it was relatively easy to lose one's self in London or some other urban center, and disappear without leaving a trace.

[104] J. Madden, Handbook of the Law of Persons and Domestic Relations 278 (1931); M. Ploscowe, H. Foster, & D. Freed, Family Law, Cases and Materials 434 (2d ed 1972).

divorce. Before the no-fault trend, desertion, also known as common law divorce, was among the most frequently used divorce grounds, particularly in jurisdictions where cruelty was not a ground or was strictly construed.[105] In 1985, desertion was a statutory ground for absolute or limited divorce in 29 states.[106]

The statutes use the terms *desertion, abandonment,* or*absence,* often qualifying them with adjectives such as *willful, continued, utter, malicious,* and *obstinate.*[107] In addition, most statutes provide that the desertion must continue for a certain period of time before a right of action will accrue. One year is the most common time period, although in Vermont it is seven years, in Rhode Island, five, and in Maine, the time period is three consecutive years.[108] This time period was meant in the fault system to provide assurance that the desertion was permanent and not manufactured by the parties for the purpose of divorce.[109] The statutory period must expire before the suit based on desertion may be filed.

Desertion has been defined generally as a separation voluntarily by one spouse from the other, with an intent not to resume cohabitation, for a period of time usually defined by statute, without consent of the other spouse and without justification. Each element of this definition must be proven based on the facts and circumstances of individual cases.

---

[105] *See* H. Clark, The Law of Domestic Relations in the United States 331 (1968); Note, *Domestic Relations: Divorce: Desertion: Refusal of Sexual Relations,* 10 Cornell LQ 374, 374 (1925); Note, *Constructive Desertion—A Broader Basis for Breaking the Bond,* 51 Iowa L Rev 108, 108 (1965); **§1.12.**

[106] Ala Code §30-2-1(a)(3) (1983); Alaska Stat §25.24.050(4) (1983); Ark Stat Ann §34-1202 (Supp 1983); Conn Gen Stat Ann §46-b-40-(c)(5) (West Supp 1984); Ga Code Ann §19-5-3(7) (1982); Idaho Code §32-606 (1983); Ill Ann Stat ch 40, §401(2) (Smith-Hurd 1980); Kan Stat Ann §60-1601(a)(2) (1983); Me Rev Stat Ann tit 19, §691(1)(D) (1981); Md Fam Law Code Ann §7-103(2) (1984); Mass Ann Laws ch 208, §1 (Michie/Law Co-op 1981); Miss Code Ann §93-5-1 (1973); NH Rev Stat Ann §458:7 (IX & X) (1983); NJ Stat Ann §2A:34-2(b) (West Supp 1984-85); NM Stat Ann §40-4-1(D) (1983); NY Dom Rel Law §170(2) (McKinney 1977); ND Cent Code §14-05-03(3) (1981); Ohio Rev Code Ann §3105.01(B) (Page 1980); Okla Stat Ann tit 12, §1271 (West 1961); Pa Stat Ann tit 23, §201(a)(1) (Purdon Supp 1984-85); RI Gen Laws §15-5-2 (1981); SC Code Ann §25-4-2(2) (Law Co-op Supp 1983); SD Codified Laws Ann §25-4-2(3) (1984); Tenn Code Ann §36-4-101(4) (1984); Tex Fam Code Ann §3.05 (Vernon 1975); Utah Code Ann §30-3-1(3) (1984); Vt Stat Ann tit 15, §551(4) (Supp 1984); Va Code §20-91(6) (1983); W Va Code §48-2-4(a)(3) (Supp 1984).

[107] Although historically a legal distinction existed between desertion and abandonment, these two terms are generally defined the same way in cases. See H. Clark, *supra* note 105, at 334; M. Ploscowe, H. Foster & D. Freed, *supra* note 104, at 434, where it is stated that "[a]bandonment was a term related to property and had no delictual implication as to intent. Desertion, on the other hand, required a specific intent and usually was accompanied by a qualifying adjective. . . ."

[108] See §691(1)(D) (1981); Me Rev Stat Ann tit 19, RI Gen Laws §15-5-2 (1981); Vt Stat Ann tit 15, §551(4)(Supp 1984).

[109] H. Clark, *supra* note 105, at 332; Irwine, *Mutual Desertion,* 30 Mod L Rev 46, 46 (1967).

The intent to abandon may be inferred from the withdrawal from home, the length of time away, or lack of contact between the spouses. Many statutes use the adjective *willful* to express the intent requirement. Thus, induction into the armed forces or imprisonment cannot be desertion unless the intent to abandon also exists.

The separation and the intent must coincide in order to commence the running of the statutory period. The time period must be continuous, uninterrupted by reconciliation, a good faith offer of reconciliation, or even an isolated act of cohabitation or intercourse.[110] An abandoned spouse who refuses a good faith offer of reconciliation may become the deserting spouse and the time period will commence against him or her. If a desertion is interrupted by a reconciliation, followed by a second desertion, the two periods may not be added together to produce the statutory period.[111]

An action for desertion may be defended on the basis of justification. In most states, a spouse who is justified in leaving the marital home due to the misconduct of the other spouse is not guilty of desertion. Indeed, in some jurisdictions the spouse who justifiably leaves the marital home may bring suit on the desertion ground under the doctrine of constructive desertion.[112] Some courts require that the misconduct justifying the desertion be equivalent to independent grounds for divorce, while other jurisdictions simply require that "the provoking cause be such that it is inconsistent with the marriage relationship or makes it impossible to continue cohabitation with due regard to safety, health, or self-respect."[113]

Some examples of action constituting the basis for constructive desertion include: a husband's cruelty or deliberate failure to support his wife;[114] one spouse's insistence that the couple reside with relatives, particularly if the relatives are abusive;[115] and refusal of sexual intercourse.[116] A wife's refusal to follow her husband to a new domicile may give rise to a constructive desertion situation in some states.[117]

---

[110] See H. Clark, *supra* note 105, at 333; M. Ploscowe, H. Foster, & D. Freed, *supra* note 104, at 457; Annot, 155 ALR 232 (1945); Glendening v Glendening, 206 A2d 824, 826-27 (DC 1965).

[111] In addition, previous marital litigation may not be included in computing the period of desertion for, as the United States Court of Appeals for the District of Columbia stated in Holt v Holt, 77 F2d 538, 540 (DC Cir 1935), "[t]he parties may not litigate by day and copulate by night, inter sese and pendente lite."

[112] Note, *Constructive Desertion—A Broader Basis for Breaking the Bond,* 51 Iowa L Rev 108, 113 (1965); Annot, 19 ALR2d 1428 (1951).

[113] Note, *supra* note 112, at 120.

[114] *See* Annot, 150 ALR 991 (1944).

[115] Annot, 38 ALR 338 (1925).

[116] Annot, 82 ALR3d 660 (1978). *See also* Myerberg, *Constructive Desertion in Maryland,* 10 Md L Rev 193, 233-37 (1949).

[117] *See, e.g.,* Bennett v Bennett, 197 Md 408, 79 A2d 513 (1951). However, in 1976, the Maryland legislature enacted Md Ann Code art 16, §29, which provides that the domicile of one spouse does not fix by operation of law the domicile of the other spouse.

The expansion of desertion to include the doctrine of constructive desertion was a recognition of the futility of preserving a marriage which had "deteriorated to the point that the legitimate objects of the marriage are destroyed or the purposes of the family are no longer served."[118] It had been clear that the desertion ground prompted spouses to leave their families in order to qualify for a divorce, since divorce by consent was not permitted in the fault system. Abandoned wives and children sometimes became public charges, increasing the welfare rolls and generally burdening society.[119] The no-fault trend

---

Rather, the other spouse's domicile is to be determined by reference to the same factors as in the case of any other individual. Whether the wife's failure to follow her husband constitutes a ground for divorce awaits judicial interpretation.

Statutes like these could create interesting case law in the future. For example, in Virginia, a court may not award a wife alimony if she is guilty of misconduct equivalent to divorce grounds, even if it is a divorce based on no-fault grounds. *See* McCausey v McCausey, 221 Va 500, 272 SE2d 36 (1980); Va Code §20-91(9)(a) (1983). Also in Virginia, a wife's refusal to follow her husband to another domicile would be desertion. It would be very interesting to see what a court would do in a situation where a husband moved from Maryland to Virginia, his wife refused to follow him, and he filed for divorce in Virginia on the ground of desertion. Would a Virginia court apply Maryland or Virginia law in this circumstance?

[118] Note, *supra* note 112, at 111. See also M. Ploscowe, H. Foster, & D. Freed, *supra* note 104, at 466, where the authors argue:

> From a sociological point of view, where there is desertion, or prolonged separation for that matter, almost invariably the marriage is dead and reconciliation is difficult if not impossible. Ordinarily, to deny a divorce does not save a viable marriage. . . . It seems clear that the ramifications of the desertion ground divert attention away from what should be the focal point, namely, whether or not there is a marriage to be saved or whether it is dead and legal recognition should be given to the fact.

This principle has also been noted indirectly in case law which holds that a spouse's silent acquiescence to a separation, even after initial protestations, makes that separation voluntary in nature. In Parks v Parks, 116 F2d 556 (DC Cir 1940), the United States Court of Appeals for the District of Columbia held:

> Six consecutive years of separation had elapsed. The separation was not at first voluntary on the defendant's part; when the plaintiff deserted her, she begged him not to go. But from that time on she neither asked him to return nor made any other attempt to bring about a reconciliation. . . . Desires which are not reflected in conduct have little or no social or legal significance. . . . That purpose [of the 1935 amendment of the Code which permits absolute divorce for voluntary separation from bed and board for five consecutive years without cohabitation] was to permit termination in law of certain marriages which have ceased to exist in fact.

[119] *Id* 557. Although this condensation of the law surrounding desertion cannot possibly attempt to explore the social repercussions of desertion, it is necessary to emphasize the severity of the potential problem. Watson, *The Deserted Wife and the Law*, 43 Austl LJ 450, 450 (1969), quotes from an address by Mary Lewis in 16 Soc Serv Rev 7 (1964) stating the issues as follows:

> The main problems of the deserted wife and mother are all related and can be summed up as financial, social and emotional. Her financial problems are usually very acute, especially in the early months, as she tries to budget on reduced

attempted to solve this problem with the living separate and apart ground, which legitimized cessation of cohabitation, eliminated proof of the intricate fact issues of the desertion ground such as intent, justification, and offers to reconcile, and gave greater protection to dependent spouses, who could obtain relief by immediate pendente lite actions.[120]

## §1.15 —Imprisonment or Conviction of Crime

In 1985, 26 states statutorily provided for divorce on the ground of a spouse's imprisonment or conviction of a felony or other crime.[121] This divorce ground did not exist in the ecclesiastical law or the common law. However, conviction or imprisonment as a divorce ground has been compared to the English doctrine of civil death, whereby a person sentenced to life imprisonment was stripped of all his or her civil rights.[122] While some states retain civil death provisions which might be construed to terminate a marriage without a legal procedure at an innocent spouse's option, it has been noted, and held, that invoking the doctrine of civil death is unnecessary when imprisonment grounds are statutorily provided.[123]

The specific statutory language must be studied closely, because the states approach this divorce ground in different ways. Some statutes focus on the crime. A majority of statutes require, simply, that a spouse be convicted of a felony. No further elaboration is made. A handful of states list an ambiguous

---

> income, facing high rents . . . and unpaid bills. Her social problems arise from her altered status in the community and neighbourhood. Her emotional problems are the gravest, although not always recognized as such by the persons involved. She faces loneliness, feels fearful of the future, often guilty because she has failed as a person in failing to hold her man.

43 Aust LJ at 450.

[120] *See* **§§2.07-2.11.**

[121] *See* Ala Code §30-2-1(a)(4) (1983); Alaska Stat §25.24.050(3) (1983); Ark Stat Ann §34-1202 (Supp 1983); Conn Gen Stat Ann §46(b)-40(c)(7) (West Supp 1984); Ga Code Ann §19-5-3(8) (1982); Idaho Code §32-603(6) (1983); Ill Ann Stat ch 40, §401(2) (Smith-Hurd 1980); Ind Code Ann §31-1-11.5-3(a)(2) (West Supp 1984-85); La Civ Code Ann art 139(2) (West Supp 1984); Md Fam Law Code Ann §7-103(4) (1984); Mass Ann Laws ch 108, §2 (Michie/Law Co-op 1981); Miss Code Ann §93-5-1 (1973): NH Rev Stat Ann §458(7)(IV) (1983); NJ Stat Ann §2A:34-2(g) (West Supp 1984-85); NY Dom Rel Law §170(3) (McKinney 1977); ND Cent Code §14-05-03(6) (1981); Ohio Rev Code Ann §3105.01(I) (Page 1980); Okla Stat Ann tit 12, §1271 (West 1961); Pa Stat Ann tit 23, §201(a)(5) (Purdon Supp 1984-85); SD Codified Laws Ann §24-5-2(6) (1984); Tenn Code Ann §36-4-101(6) (1984); Tex Fam Code Ann §3.04 (Vernon 1975); Wash Rev Code Ann §30-3-1(6) (1984); Vt Stat Ann tit 15, §551(2) (Supp 1984); Va Code §20-91(3) (1983); W Va Code §48-2-4(a)(2) (Supp 1984).

[122] Note, *Civil Death Statutes: Medieval Factor in a Modern World,* 50 Harv L Rev 968, 974-77 (1937).

[123] See M. Ploscowe, H. Foster, & D. Freed, Family Law, Cases and Materials 471 (2d ed 1972); Annot, 139 ALR 1308 (1942); Villalor v Bower, 70 Nev 456, 273 P2d 409 (1954); Zizzo v Zizzo, 41 Misc 2d 298, 247 NYS2d 38 (Sup Ct 1964).

definition of a crime, such as "infamous crime involving violation of conjugal duty"[124] or "offense involving moral turpitude."[125]

Other jurisdictions focus on the fact of imprisonment. For example, the Alabama statute provides for divorce when a spouse is imprisoned for two years, where the sentence is seven years or longer. Connecticut and Massachusetts statutes specify a sentence of imprisonment for life, while the Louisiana statute states that a divorce is possible if the other spouse is sentenced to death or imprisonment at hard labor.[126] It should be noted that some statutes combine both the conviction and imprisonment elements.

The statutory language has created some problems. For example, it is not clear from the statutes what the effect of a parole or pardon would be on a divorce action. It has been observed that a pardon or sentence reduction for good behavior which makes the imprisonment for less than a statutory time period is immaterial and cannot restore a guilty party to his or her marital rights.[127]

It is also unclear what the exact philosophical basis is for the divorce ground based on imprisonment or conviction. One theory is that the divorce ground is an added penalty imposed by the law upon a guilty party. Another, more viable explanation is that this ground is meant to benefit an innocent spouse whose husband or wife cannot perform his or her marital obligations, just as a deserting spouse cannot.[128] It is also a recognition that a marital relationship may be severely damaged and fragmented because of the illegal conduct of one of the spouses. But the simple fact is that imprisonment results in actual separation, and a person may not want to wait patiently on the outside until his or her spouse serves a prison sentence.

Society also has an interest in this divorce ground. The welfare of both spouses and their children must be considered. While on one hand a prisoner's rehabilitation might be harmed by divorce, the innocent spouse and children could benefit if given the opportunity to avoid the stigma of a criminal in the family and the opportunity to start a new life with another spouse and parent.[129]

## §1.16 —Insanity

The insanity ground for divorce was nonexistent in the ecclesiastical law and at common law. In the United States, there was strong objection to the insanity

---

[124] Conn Gen Stat Ann §46b-40(c)(7) (West Supp 1984).

[125] Ga Code Ann §19-5-3(8) (1982).

[126] Ala Code §30-2-1(a)(4) (1983); Conn Gen Stat Ann §46b-40(c)(7) (West Supp 1984); Mass Ann Laws ch 208, §2 (Michie/Law Co-op 1981); La Civ Code Ann art 139(2) (West Supp 1984).

[127] J. Madden, Handbook of the Law of Persons and Domestic Relations 290 (1931); *see also* Note, *Imprisonment as a Ground for Divorce - "Statutory Desertion," Judicial Improvisation, and a Call for Reform,* 23 Rutgers L Rev 389, 401 (1969).

[128] *See* Note, *supra* note 127, at 397.

[129] *Id* 403.

ground in the fault system.[130] Spousal insanity was not considered a marital wrong or a breach of the marital duty, but rather a disease or condition that hindered the performance of such duties. Thus, it was thought that the availability of insanity as a divorce ground contradicted "the traditional marriage vow 'to cherish, in sickness and in health, for better or for worse' "[131] It was feared that the acceptance of insanity, a conjugal risk, as a divorce ground might condone repudiation of marriage for any disease, especially those affecting the cohabitation aspects of marriage.[132]

Despite the negative public policy, state legislatures began adopting insanity as a ground for divorce. In 1985, 26 states had statutory provisions for divorce based on a spouse's insanity.[133] However, because of the public policy objections to the ground, including the desires to protect the rights of the insane and to prevent those with mental illnesses from becoming public charges, the insanity statutes include limitations and safeguards which are strictly construed by the courts.

Implied in these statutes is the requirement that the insanity or mental illness must be ascertained with certainty. Thus, many statutes require that the insanity be *incurable* or *permanent.* The majority of the insanity provisions specify that the person be ill, confined, or institutionalized for a certain period of time,

---

[130] See, e.g., Baker v Baker, 82 Ind 146, 146 (1882), where the Supreme Court of Indiana expressed the general thought of the time:

> Insanity is no reason for dissolving the marriage. The statute does not make it one of the grounds for divorce, and surely no principle of justice or morality will justify the severence of the marital ties for any such cause. The judgment and conscience revolt at the thought that such a terrible affliction should be deemed cause for separating the wife and the husband. Divorces are granted not because of misfortune, but because of fault. It would be a barbarous code that would allow the wife to put aside the husband because stricken by such an awful calamity as the loss of reason.

[131] M. Rheinstein, Marriage, Stability, Divorce and the Law 315 (1972).

[132] McCurdy, *Insanity as a Ground for Annulment or Divorce in English and American Law,* 29 Va L Rev 771, 804 (1943). One response to this argument is that the distinction between physical diseases and insanity warrants the different treatment in the divorce law. While disease usually affects only physical well-being, insanity alters or abolishes the normal personality.

[133] *See* Ala Code §30-2-1(a)(8) (1983); Alaska Stat §25.24.050(8)(1983); Ark Stat Ann §34-1202 (Supp 1983); Cal Civ Code §4605(2) (Deering 1984); Conn Gen Stat Ann §46b-40(c)(10) (West Supp 1984); Del Code Ann tit 13, §1505(b)(3) (1981); Fla Stat Ann §61.052(b) (West Supp 1984); Ga Code Ann §19-5-3(11) (1982); Idaho Code §32-603(7) (1983); Ind Code Ann §31-1-11.5-3(a)(4) (West Supp 1984-85); Kans Stat Ann §60-1601(a)(3) (1983); Me Rev Stat Ann tit 19, §691 (I) (1981); Md Fam Law Code Ann §7-103(6) (1984); Miss Code Ann §93-5-1 (1973); Nev Rev Stat §125.010 (1983); NJ Stat Ann §2A:34-2(f) (West Supp 1984-85); NC Gen Stat §50-5.1 (1984); ND Cent Code §14-05-03(7) (1981); Ohio Rev Code Ann §3105.01(k) (Page 1980); Okla Stat Ann tit 12, §1271 (West 1961); Pa Stat Ann tit 23,§201(b) (Purdon Supp 1984-85); SD Codified Laws Ann §25-4-18 (1984); Tex Fam Code Ann §3.07 (Vernon 1975); Utah Code Ann §30-3-1(9) (1984); Vt Stat Ann tit 15, §551(6) (Supp 1984); W Va Code §48-2-4(a)(8) (Supp 1984).

which may be anywhere from 18 months to 7 years. A frequently litigated question is the definition of confinement for statutory purposes.[134] Some of these statutes dictate that the defendant must be adjudged legally incompetent, or that physicians, psychiatrists, or other professionals must offer medical testimony to the effect that the defendant is permanently or incurably insane, which many such professionals are reluctant to do. A few statutes also provide that the party who is divorcing an insane or mentally ill spouse must continue to support that spouse.[135]

It has been noted that insanity as a ground for divorce is inconsistent with the fault grounds insofar as it may be said that it provides an escape from a marriage which is irretrievably broken due to one spouse's mental illness and confinement rather than due to fault.[136] However, besides being similar to no-fault grounds, the insanity of a spouse has interfered with no-fault *living separate and apart grounds* for divorce which require a voluntary act by both parties, a mutual purpose, or a desire by one spouse and an acquiescence by the other.[137] Under these statutes, a spouse who was insane at the time of separation would lack the capacity to form the intent to separate or to separate voluntarily. Insanity would bar divorces on this ground.[138]

In *Crittenden v Crittenden,*[139] the parties had been divorced on the *living separate and apart* ground in Virginia, which had no statutory insanity divorce ground.

---

[134] *See, e.g.,* Finklestein v Finklestein, 88 Cal App 4, 198 P2d 98 (1948) (a district court of appeal held that a woman who was "paroled" to her mother's care for a year without her husband's knowledge or consent was not confined to an institution under the California statute); Witherspoon v Witherspoon, 289 SW2d 502 (Ky 1955) (Kentucky Supreme Court held that a woman's one-year discharge to mother's care during a five-year confinement did not meet the statutory definition of confinement); Dodier v Dodier, 183 Md 413, 37 A2d 919 (1944) (Court of Appeals of Maryland held that a defendant who had been confined to an institution for many years but placed for a time in a home under the hospital's supervision was confined within meaning of the statute); Mabrey v Mabrey, 243 NC 126, 9 SE2d 221 (1955) (North Carolina Supreme Court held that an insane spouse who was allowed to leave the institution on probation two times, although never actually discharged, met the statutory confinement requirement).

[135] *See* H. Clark, Law of Domestic Relations in the United States 357 (1968); M. Ploscowe, H. Foster, & D. Freed, Family Law, Cases and Materials 463 (2d ed 1972); Dubin v Superior Court, 37 Cal 2d 343, 231 P2d 809 (1951) (where Supreme Court of California held that it was an arbitrary and unconstitutional discrimination to make continued support a condition precedent to divorce upon the insanity ground); Annot, 141 ALR 946 (1942).

[136] See M. Rheinstein, *supra* note 131, at 315, where the author noted the fact that "[m]arriage breakdown for one special reason, namely that of incurable insanity of a marriage partner, has frequently been admitted as a ground for divorce long before breakdown in general was so recognized."

[137] *See* Recent Decisions, *Divorce—Separation Without Fault—Post Nuptial Insanity—Crittenden v Crittenden,* 4 U Rich L Rev 347, 348 (1970); **§§2.07-2.11.**

[138] A spouse's insanity may be a defense to a divorce on fault grounds as well, such as desertion, cruelty, and adultery. For a discussion of insanity as a defense in divorce actions, see §1.25; Annot, 19 ALR2d 144 (1951).

[139] 210 Va 76, 168 SE2d 115 (1969).

However, the parties' separation was due to the wife's commitment to an institution. The Supreme Court of Appeals of Virginia reversed the divorce decree, holding that the *living separate and apart* ground contemplated that the spouses be "sufficiently competent to be conscious of the fact that the act of separation occurred."[140] The plaintiff, as a result of the decision, had no remedy. However, the Virginia General Assembly amended the divorce statute, removing the requirement of consciousness of separation when one party is mentally incompetent.[141]

Insanity may also be an issue where the mentally ill spouse brings the divorce action through a guardian or next friend, a procedure generally disapproved by courts,[142] and in annulment actions, where insanity is considered a proper ground because the ill person is deemed to have the capacity to neither consent nor contract.[143]

---

[140] *Id* at 78, 168 SE2d at 116.

[141] See Va Code §20-91(9)(a) (1983), which states, in part:

> §20-91. Grounds for divorce from bond of matrimony.—A divorce from the bond of matrimony may be decreed: . . .
>
> (9)(a) On the application of either party if and when the husband and wife have lived separate and apart without any cohabitation and without interruption for one year. In any case where the parties have entered into a separation agreement and there are no minor children, a divorce may be decreed on application if and when the husband and wife have lived separate and apart without cohabitation and without interruption for six months. A plea of res adjudicata or of recrimination with respect to any other provision of this section shall not be a bar to either party obtaining a divorce on this ground; nor shall it be a bar that either party has been adjudged insane, either before or after such separation has commenced, but at the expiration of one year from the commencement of such separation, the grounds for divorce shall be deemed to be complete, and the committee of the insane defendant, if there be one, shall be made party to the cause, or if there be no committee, then the court shall appoint a guardian ad litem to represent the insane defendant.
>
> (b) This subsection (9) shall apply whether the separation commenced prior to its enactment or shall commence thereafter. Where otherwise valid, any decree of divorce hereinbefore entered by any court having equity jurisdiction pursuant to this subsection (9), not appealed to the Supreme Court of Virginia, is hereby declared valid according to the terms of said decree notwithstanding the insanity of a party hereto.

[142] Annot, 6 ALR3d 681 (1966); Decisions, *Guardian may not consent to divorce in New Jersey*, 6 Mental Disability L Rep 16 (1982). *But see* Note, *Divorce—Insane Persons—Incompetent Allowed to Sue for Divorce*, 56 Harv L Rev 310 (1942); Note, *Domestic Relations—Separation—Suit by Mentally Incompetent Wife [Sengstack v. Sengstack]*, 12 Vand L Rev 493 (1959). Comment, *Divorce - Insane Spouse Allowed to Sue for Divorce*, 28 Iowa L Rev 367 (1943).

[143] *See* **§1.26;** Wrightman v Wrightman, 4 Johns Ch 343, 344-45 (NY Ch 1820); McCurdy,*Insanity as a Ground for Annulment or Divorce in English and American Law*, 29 Va L Rev 771 (1943).

## §1.17 —Habitual Drunkenness and Drug Addiction

Habitual drunkenness and drug addiction are two other statutorily created divorce grounds in the United States. In 1985, twelve states provided for both habitual drunkenness and drug addiction as grounds for divorce,[144] while eight states provided only for habitual drunkenness or habitual intemperance.[145] While *habitual drunkenness* or *habitual intemperance* are the most common statutory language for this ground, other examples include "[h]abitual intoxication [and] . . . [h]abitual drug addiction,"[146] "guilty of gross and confirmed habits caused by excessive use of addictive drugs,"[147] "[g]ross and confirmed habits of intoxication from the use of liquor and drugs,"[148] and "continued drunkenness [and] . . . the habitual, excessive, and intemperate use of opium, morphine, or chloral."[149]

While the standards of proof of these grounds vary from state to state, some generalizations can be made. The habitual drunkenness or drug addiction must be a fixed habit that occurs with considerable frequency. Occasional or moderate use of alcohol or drugs is insufficient to sustain a divorce. Some statutes state the practice must be continuous or must continue through the filing of the complaint.[150] Other states insist that the practices persist for a statutorily set time period. However, most statutes leave the matter to judicial determination through such words as *habitual* or *addicted*. It should be noted that no attempts have been made to equate this divorce ground to the medical

---

[144] *See* Ala Code §30-2-1(a)(6) (1983); Alaska Stat §§25.24.051(6) & (9) (1983); Ga Code Ann §§19-5-3(9) & (12) (1982); Ill Ann Stat ch 40, §401(2) (Smith-Hurd 1980); Me Rev Stat Ann tit 19, §691 (1981); Mass Ann Laws ch 208, §1 (Michie/Law Co-op 1981); Miss Code Ann §93-5-1 (1973); NJ Stat Ann §2A:34-2(e) (West Supp 1984-85); RI Gen Laws §15-5-2 (1981); SC Code Ann §25-4-2 (Law Co-op Supp 1983); Tenn Code Ann §36-4-101(10) (1984); W Va Code §§48-2-4(5) & (6) (Supp 1984).

[145] Ark Stat Ann §34-1202 (Supp 1983); Conn Gen Stat Ann §46(b)-40(c)(7) (West Supp 1984); Idaho Code §32-608 (1983); NH Rev Stat Ann §458:7(VII) (1983); ND Cent Code §14-05-03(5) (1981); Ohio Rev Code Ann §3105.01(H) (Page 1980); Okla Stat Ann tit 12, §1271 (West 1961); Utah Code Ann §30-3-1(5) (1984).

[146] Ga Code Ann §§19-5-3(9) & (12) (1982).

[147] Ill Ann Stat ch 40, §401(2) (Smith-Hurd 1980).

[148] Me Rev Stat Ann tit 19, §691(E) (1981).

[149] RI Gen Laws §15-5-2 (1981).

[150] In Schneider v Schneider, 142 NJ Super 512, 362 A2d 61 (1976), a Superior Court of New Jersey found a wife could use the habital drunkenness ground where the statute required that the drunkenness exist "for a period of 12 or more consecutive months subsequent to marriage and next proceding the filing of the complaint," despite the fact that the husband had stopped drinking two months before the complaint was filed. The court asked:

> Must she file her complaint while he has his glass in hand? Does she lose her cause of action because she files in the afternoon and he has not had a drink since before lunch? Certainly a reasonable time must be allowed between the separation of the parties because of the drinking problem and the actual filing of the complaint.

or psychiatric definitions of alcoholism.[151] Generally, the case law requires that the defendant must lose his or her power or will to control the appetite for liquor or drugs, and that he or she must consume large quantities to produce an intoxicated state.[152]

It has been held that the inability to attend properly to one's business may be used as evidence of habitual drunkenness, but this is not a universal holding.[153] Similarly, a case of habitual drunkenness may be proved where a habit has caused a defendant's family to suffer or has rendered his or her presence in the family "disgusting and intolerable."[154]

Some statutes expressly provide that the habit must develop after marriage. If they do not, such a requirement is usually presumed.[155] The general rule is that antenuptial knowledge of a spouse's habitual drunkenness or drug addiction precludes divorce on those grounds.[156] A spouse may also forfeit the right to divorce upon these grounds if he or she encouraged the other spouse's habit or participated in such conduct.

## §1.18 —Other Grounds

The most commonly used divorce grounds before no-fault divorce were adultery, desertion, cruelty, conviction of a crime, and habitual drunkenness.[157] Many state statutes continue to provide miscellaneous divorce grounds based on either fault or typical annulment grounds.

Some states authorize divorce on the ground of nonsupport or neglect of a spouse. These grounds have traditionally covered the situation where a husband willfully and deliberately fails to provide for his wife or family for a certain length of time. However, limiting these grounds to the wife may be suspect in light of the doctrine of mutual support, which has replaced the traditional rule in many jurisdictions that the husband must support the wife.

---

[151] See Annot, 29 ALR2d 925, 926 (1953), where it is noted:

> It is fairly clear that thus far there has been little if any attempt to relate the legal definition in any way to scientific description of alcoholism afforded by the fields of medicine and psychiatry. It is possible that traditional public policy as respects grounds for divorce might be deemed somewhat incompatible with the continued maintenance of drunkenness as a ground for divorce, if that disability were admitted as a legal matter to be a manifestation of illness rather than a moral fault.

[152] *See, e.g.*, Todd v Todd, 56 So 2d 441 (Fla 1951); Shorthose v Shorthose, 319 Ill App 355, 49 NE2d 280 (1943); Lewis v Lewis, 235 Iowa 693, 17 NW2d 407 (1945); Kessel v Kessel, 131 W Va 239, 46 SE2d 792 (1948); 24 Am Jur 2d *Divorce and Separation* §90 (1966).

[153] Annot, *supra* note 151, at 928-29.

[154] 24 Am Jur 2d *Divorce and Separation* §94 (1966).

[155] *See* Annot, 15 ALR2d 670, 677 (1951).

[156] M. Ploscowe, H. Foster, & D. Freed, Family Law, Cases and Materials 468 (2d ed 1972).

[157] M. Ploscowe, H. Foster, & D. Freed, Family Law, Cases and Materials 460 (2d ed 1972). *See also* **§§1.10-1.15, 1.17, & 2.01-2.17.**

Other miscellaneous fault-based grounds include crimes against nature,[158] homosexuality,[159] an attempt on a spouse's life,[160] and abuse of children.[161] Another ground, called the "most esoteric"[162] divorce ground by family law authorities, is procurement of divorce in another state. This ground punished those spouses who committed the matrimonial offense of migrating to another jurisdiction to obtain a divorce decree in evasion of local law.

Some divorce statutes authorize divorce on grounds which, under English ecclesiastical law, were grounds for annulment when absolute divorce did not exist. For example, some states provide that incapacity, impotence, or failure to consummate the marriage is a proper ground for divorce.[163] Bigamy, or prior existing marriage, is also a divorce ground in a handful of jurisdictions.[164] Affinity, fraud, duress, and pregnancy at the time of marriage unknown to the husband are other divorce grounds which have also been annulment grounds in American family law.[165] Rhode Island's statute includes grounds which would render the marriage void or voidable.[166]

Although the inclusion of these grounds in the divorce statutes has been criticized,[167] their availability as divorce grounds ameliorates the potential hardships caused by annulments, which may preclude alimony, create confu-

---

[158] *See* Ala Code §30-2-1(a)(5) (1983).

[159] *See* W Va Code §48-2-4(a)(4) (Supp 1984).

[160] *See* Ill Ann Stat ch 40, §401(2) (Smith-Hurd 1980); Tenn Code Ann §36-4-101(7) (1984).

[161] *See* W Va Code §48-2-4(a)(9) (Supp 1984).

[162] M. Ploscowe, H. Foster, & D. Freed, *supra* note 157, at 459. *See* Ohio Rev Code Ann §3105.01(J) (Page 1980); Okla Stat Ann tit 12, §1271 (West 1961).

[163] *See, e.g.*, Ala Code §30-2-1(a)(1) (1983); Alaska Stat §25.24.050(1) (1983); Ark Stat Ann §34-1202 (Supp 1983); Ga Code Ann §19-5-3(3) (1982); Ill Ann Stat ch 40, §401(2) (Smith-Hurd 1980); Ind Code Ann §31-1-11.5-3(a)(3) (West Supp 1984-85).

[164] *See, e.g.*, Ark Stat Ann §34-1202 (Supp 1983); Ill Ann Stat ch 40, §401(2) (Smith-Hurd 1980); Miss Code Ann §93-5-1 (1973); Ohio Rev Code Ann §3105.01 (A) (Page 1980); Pa Stat Ann tit 23, §201(a)(4) (Purdon Supp 1984-85); Tenn Code Ann §36-4-101(2) (1984).

[165] Georgia and Mississippi include affinity as a divorce ground. Fraud and duress is a proper divorce ground in Georgia, Ohio, and Oklahoma. Antenuptial pregnancy without a husband's knowledge may be found in the divorce statutes of Georgia, Oklahoma, and Tennessee. *See* Ga Code Ann §§19-5-3(1), (4), & (5) (1982); Ohio Rev Code Ann §3105.01(F) (Page 1980); Okla Stat Ann tit 12, §1271 (West 1961); Tenn Code Ann §36-4-101(9) (1984).

[166] RI Gen Laws §15-5-1 (1981).

[167] H. Clark, The Law of Domestic Relations in the United States 357 (1968), where the professor states:

> Since these matters would normally make the marriage void or at least voidable, their inclusion in a divorce statute is quite illogical. . . . The difficulty is that divorce as we know it today presupposes a valid marriage. If the plaintiff's own allegations show that there is no valid marriage, how can there be a divorce? [Footnote omitted.]

sion as to the parties' status, and perhaps result in the illegitimization of children.

## §1.19 Historical Defenses to Divorce

The public policy which favored the preservation of marriage also encouraged the defense of divorce action. The general defenses which arise in the course of any litigation are available in divorce actions. There are also special defenses reflecting the fault basis of the law and the public policy concerns protecting those likely to be adversely affected by the dissolution of the marriage, as well as society at large. The most important of these special defenses are collusion, connivance, condonation, and recrimination.[168]

Examples of recrimination can be found in both Mosaic and Roman law.[169] However, authorities maintain that the special defenses as they have existed in American law were developed by the English ecclesiastical courts contemporaneously with the development of the analogous negligence doctrines of contributory negligence and assumption of the risk.[170] It has also been asserted that these defenses and bars, which in effect precluded divorce, were created "to prevent the wife from being cast loose in a society where an unattached woman had no place."[171]

In America courts, rather than the state legislatures, were responsible for adoption of the special divorce defenses, although eventually many divorce statutes codified them. For many years judges faithfully recognized such defenses, frequently emphasizing their fault focus.[172]

---

168 *See* **§§1.20-1.24.**

169 See Moore, *An Examination of the Recrimination Doctrine,* 20 SCL Rev 685, 705 (1968), where it is stated that the doctrine of recrimination operated in Mosaic law to bar a divorce to a husband who had falsely accused his wife of unchastity. In Roman law, the recrimination doctrine influenced the court's decision on how to divide the parties' property.

170 M. Ploscowe, H. Foster, & D. Freed, Family Law, Cases and Materials 477 (2d ed 1972).

171 *Id.*

172 See, e.g., Richardson v Richardson, 114 NYS 912, 917 (1906) where a New York Supreme Court declared out of moral indignation:

> It is, of course, unnecessary to argue about the sanctity and importance of the marriage relation, and the, therefore, propriety and duty of sustaining it in all its dignity and purity. To state the proposition is to demonstrate it. The law recognizes it, and all good people know that marriage is the mother of purity and virtue and the guardian angel of the human race; that the family is the home of our best affections, and the promoter of all our best achievements. For these reasons when, as now, the moral sense of a large part of the community seems to be dulled and deadened as to the importance and sacredness of the marriage tie; when honor and truth and plighted faith are so often and readily given to the winds; when trick and device, bribery and corruption, perjury and subornation of perjury, are rampant; when men and women circumvent the law by hurrying to states where divorces are made easy, swear to "permanent residence" with

However, the no-fault movement worked to eliminate the special defenses, a task, it has been asserted, "as a practical matter [probably] . . . more important for divorce reform than modernization of divorce grounds."[173] The abolition of the defenses was the first step to easier divorce, and most states have eliminated or restricted them by statute.[174]

In states with the no-fault grounds of living separate and apart and incompatibility, the divorce defenses have little, if any, application. For example, as early as 1940, the United States Court of Appeals for the District of Columbia held that recrimination was not a defense in the case of voluntary separation from bed and board for five consecutive years without cohabitation.[175] In Colorado, where the sole divorce ground is irretrievable breakdown of the marriage, the remaining defenses in a divorce action are denial that the marriage was irretrievably broken and lack of jurisdiction.[176]

It should be noted, however, that in many jurisdictions, fault plays an important role even in divorces based on no-fault grounds. For example, in Maryland and Virginia, the courts may consider fault in awarding alimony.[177] Thus, while the parties may not use recrimination as a bar to divorce, they may use it as a bar to alimony.

The defenses to divorce in the fault system have provoked much of the criticism which spurred the no-fault trend. The following subsections will examine these special defenses in greater detail.

## §1.20 —Collusion

In England during the period of the ecclesiactical courts and the doctrine of the indissolubility of marriage, divorce by consent of the parties was

---

return tickets in their pockets, and are received back by their coteries with open arms, to presently contract other, if not always altogether untried alliances; when one state of the Union has besmirched its statute book by creating a new cause of divorce out of an act of God; when such things are openly and shamelessly done—it is time all rightminded people, the servants of the law as well as its ministers, should put up the bars against all such abominable and increasing wickedness. The law requires real, vital obedience, in all honesty and good faith, and it is not satisfied with cloaks and labels. It follows that absolute divorce should not be granted unless entitlement is fully, fairly, and clearly made out.

[173] M. Ploscowe, H. Foster, & D. Freed, *supra* note 170, at 478.

[174] See Freed & Foster, *Family Law in the Fifty States,* 16 Fam LQ 289, 320 (1983) which lists, inter alia, some examples of states which have abolished all defenses: Arizona, California, Colorado, Delaware, District of Columbia, Hawaii, Indiana, Kentucky, Minnesota, Missouri, Montana, New York (except where ground is adultery), Ohio (defenses only by case law), Oregon, Utah (none except by case law), Virgin Islands, Wisconsin.

[175] Parks v Parks, 116 F2d 556 (DC Cir 1940). *See also* Vanderhuff v Vanderhuff, 144 F2d 509 (DC Cir 1944).

[176] Colo Rev Stat §14-20-110 (1974).

[177] *See, e.g.,* Flanagan v Flanagan, 270 Md 335, 311 A2d 407 (1973); McCausey v McCausey, 221 Va 500, 272 SE2d 36 (1980).

considered an outrage and forbidden.[178] It is not surprising that the eccelesiastical courts developed the doctrine of collusion, which barred parties from obtaining a divorce when it was discovered that they had agreed to present false testimony or suppress material facts in their divorce action.[179]

The American courts, lacking precedents, adopted the collusion doctrine along with the other fault defenses and bars to divorce. In addition, the American courts broadened the scope of the doctrine to include any agreement between the parties where they endeavored to obtain a divorce by committing a fraud on the courts. Many legislatures codified the collusion bar, incorporating it into their fault divorce statutes. A few statutes still included collusion in 1985.[180]

Generally, collusion occurs in one of three ways: the parties arrange the commission of a marital offense for the purpose of obtaining a divorce, the parties introduce evidence of an offense not actually committed, or the parties suppress a valid defense to the divorce action. Mere mutual desire for a divorce is not collusion absent some fraud upon the court. While separation agreements dividing property and providing for custody on the condition of the divorce being granted are not collusive, agreements not to defend a divorce suit or agreements providing for financial reward upon one party's obtaining a divorce have been found to be collusive.[181] Agreements for future separations are also deemed contrary to public policy as fostering separations, and are unenforceable.[182] For those reasons, agreements usually included language to the effect that the agreement was not collusive and that the parties could obtain a divorce on any available ground.

Collusion is more properly referred to as a bar to divorce imposed by the court rather than a special defense. Divorcing parties rarely plead collusion as a defense, for the obvious reason that it would destroy their chances for obtaining a divorce. Collusion usually comes to a court's attention through the parties' inadvertence or the court's proving examination.[183] Collusion is

---

[178] *See* **§1.07.**

[179] This was the actual scope of the collusion doctrine in ecclesiastical law. *See* Bevan, *The Scope and Effects of Collusion* 82 LQ Rev 371, 371 (1966).

[180] *See, e.g.*, Me Rev Stat Ann tit 19, §691 (1981); RI Gen Laws §15-5-4 (1981).

[181] M. Ploscowe, H. Foster, & D. Freed, Family Law, Cases and Materials 519 (2d ed 1972); Buss v Buss 222 Ga 378, 147 SE2d 818 (1966). The recital which is now commonplace in mutual voluntary separation jurisdictions could run afoul of the collusion doctrine. See S. Green & J. Long, Marriage and Family Law Agreements (1984), which includes a sample separation agreement which states that the parties separated as a result of a mutually voluntary agreement to separate. There is danger in using the recital in jurisdictions which retain the collusion bar, although some statutes provide that the defenses do not apply in the no-fault actions. Mutual voluntary no-fault divorce provisions essentially authorize what was historically known as collusion. *See* **§§2.01-2.17.**

[182] A. Lindey, 1 Separation Agreements and Ante-Nuptial Contracts 8-6 (1983).

[183] H. Clarke, Social Legislation 130 (2d ed 1968).

infrequently uncovered in divorce litigation, as the scarcity of case law on the topic shows.[184]

When, however, collusion is discovered at the time of trial, courts may dismiss the case.[185] Courts faced with collusion subsequent to the entry of a decree either refuse to proceed or vacate the collusion-tainted decree. If the court does nothing it condones the collusion. If it vacates the decree, it creates serious status-related problems for the parties.[186]

Some measures have been developed to prevent collusive divorce.[187] As in all trials, testifying spouses must swear or affirm to tell the truth; in some states a special oath was required of the plaintiff to the effect that his or her pleadings were not collusive. The plaintiff must prove the case even though a default has been entered. Corroboration is frequently required in addition to the testimony of the parties. Many state bar associations impose severe sanctions against attorneys who participate in collusive divorces in those jurisdictions which recognize the collusion doctrine.

In theory, the doctrine of collusion serves a valid purpose in the fault system of divorce. The collusion bar prevents parties from facilitating the dissolution of marriage in a system which supports the preservation of marriage. It assures that the divorce action will be adversarial in nature, and will include the state as an interested third party. In addition, the collusion bar protects the integrity of the judicial process by punishing attempted fraud upon the court.

Because collusion is so rarely uncovered in divorce litigation, it is impossible to know how many divorces have been obtained through the collusion of the parties. Historically, prior to no-fault divorce, it may be logical to assume that many divorces were collusive. The fault grounds and defenses were considered archaic by a substantial segment of the public. Some litigants did not hesitate to perjure themselves in divorce suits, viewing divorce trials as meaningless ceremonies which unnecessarily required a great deal of time, money, and delay in securing the mutually desired termination of the marriage. The importance of collusion has been mitigated by the general acceptance and use of no-fault grounds, which in effect allow for divorce by mutual consent.

---

[184] There were no nationally reported cases on collusion from 1976 to 1981.

[185] Bradway, *Collusion and the Public Interest in the Law of Divorce*, 47 Cornell LQ 374, 374 n2 (1962).

[186] *See* Hartizan v Hartizan, 272 Ala 67, 128 So 2d 725 (1961); *see also* Note, *Domestic Relations: Judgments: Void Divorce Decrees: The Power of a Court to Vacate a Void Decree on Its Own Motion: Hartigan v Hartigan, 128 SO 2d 725 (Ala 1961)*, 47 Cornell LQ 459 (1962). In this case the parties made misrepresentations as to their domicile and were granted a decree of divorce incorporating an agreement as to alimony in Alabama in 1954. In June 1960, the husband sought to modify the decree by eliminating the alimony, and filed a petition in the court which granted the divorce. The wife appeared, and during an *off the record* discussion the circuit judge discovered the collusion. The court, on its own motion, entered a decree setting aside the 1954 decree. The Supreme Court of Alabama affirmed.

[187] Note, *Collusive and Consensual Divorce and the New York Anomaly*, 36 Colum L Rev 1121, 1125-26 (1936).

However, collusive tendencies persist even in the no-fault context. Many times the authors have listened to clients who wanted to falsely assert in pleadings and in court that they had lived in the jurisdiction for the time period required to establish a domicile, or that they had been separated for the statutory period without cohabitation. A practitioner must be alert to reject involvement in misrepresentation which corrupts the process and makes the lawyer guilty of the criminal offense of subornation of perjury.

## §1.21 —Connivance

Connivance is traditionally defined as the corrupt consenting by one spouse to a marital offense by the other.[188] It is an affirmative defense in a fault-based action, most frequently raised in actions based on adultery, although also a bar to divorce if a court discovers connivance not pleaded in the action. In ecclesiastical law connivance was a permanent bar to divorce.[189]

Connivance is based on the Latin maxim, *volenti non fit injuria,* that is, he who consents cannot receive an injury. The ecclesiastical courts interpreted the maxim as "no injury has been done, and therefore there is nothing to redress."[190] Conceptually, this maxim means that a plaintiff in a divorce case should not be allowed to complain of something to which he or she has consented. Connivance is also based on the equitable clean hands doctrine.[191]

There is a presumption against connivance. Proof of connivance must be clear and satisfactory. A distinction has been made between active connivance and passive connivance.

Active connivance, or "smoothing the path to the adulterous bed,"[192] consists of affirmative steps calculated to induce the spouse to violate the marriage contract. Hiring or otherwise inducing a detective, relative, or other agent to seduce the defendant spouse is affirmative connivance. It is affirmative connivance to spouse-swap, to expose the defendant spouse to lewd company, and to encourage the defendant spouse's lover to visit the marital home. When one spouse supplies drugs or liquor to the other who has a propensity toward drug addiction or alcoholism, it is affirmative connivance. It is also connivance to allow the defendant spouse to remarry in reliance on a divorce known by

---

[188] J. Madden, Handbook of the Law of Persons and Domestic Relations 294 (1931); H. Clark, The Law of Domestic Relations in the United States 359 (1968), where the author maintains that the adjective *corrupt* is superfluous.

[189] Note, *A Survey of the Law of Condonation, Connivance and Collusion in New England,* 35 BUL Rev 99, 113 (1955).

[190] Forster v Forster, 1 Hag Con 144, 146, 161 Eng Rep 504, 505 (1790).

[191] See Fonger v Fonger, 160 Md 610, 623, 154 A2d 443, 448 (1931) where the Court of Appeals of Maryland stated: "[t]he foundation of equitable jurisdiction is justice, and one of its greatest landmarks is that 'he who does iniquity shall not have equity,' and connivance is iniquity."

[192] Moore, *An Analysis of Collusion and Connivance Bars to Divorce,* 36 UMKC L Rev 193, 213 (1968).

plaintiff to be invalid and then to sue for divorce on the ground of adultery.[193]

Passive connivance is harder to pinpoint. When a spouse has knowledge of the other's misconduct and simply acquiesces, or refrains from taking measures to prevent or terminate the misconduct, it is sometimes considered passive connivance. However, the cases which support the doctrine of passive connivance usually assume that the aggrieved spouse was under a duty to do something about an observed marital offense and that doing nothing, he or she connived.[194] Such passive conduct may constitute condonation.[195]

It is not connivance when a spouse spies on the other for the purpose of collecting evidence. It is also not connivance when a spouse has a suspicion of a marital offense being committed but does not act on it.

The connivance defense is infrequently used in the fault system and has even less importance in the no-fault system.

## §1.22 —Condonation

Condonation occurs when a spouse who has knowledge of a marital offense committed by his or her spouse which would constitute grounds for divorce voluntarily forgives the wrongdoer by continuing or resuming marital cohabitation or by other means. Usually, condonation as an affirmative defense in a divorce action is conditioned on the fact that the offense will not be repeated.[196] Should the offense be repeated, the divorce ground is revived and the condonation is nullified.

As with the other traditional defenses, the doctrine of condonation originated in the English ecclesiastical fault-oriented divorce law, and evolved through judicial and legislative adoption into an accepted principle of American divorce law.[197] The rule in early English law was that a plaintiff could not obtain a divorce a mensa et thoro when he or she knew of the defendant's adultery and yet resumed marital intercourse with the defendant.[198] The scope of the condonation doctrine was broadened by the courts in the United States to include other marital wrongs as well.

The important elements of condonation are knowledge, forgiveness, and revival. All three elements have generated confusion in the law.

The general rule is that an innocent spouse's knowledge of the marital offense is a condition precedent to condonation. Thus, a spouse condones upon voluntarily resuming marital relations with the other spouse after, for

---

[193] *Id* 216-17.

[194] *See* Annot, 17 ALR2d 342, 355-56 (1951).

[195] *See* **§1.22.**

[196] M. Ploscowe, H. Foster, & D. Freed, Family Law, Cases and Materials 540 (2d ed 1972). The authors state that: "[t]he usual legal effect of condonation is that a spouse who has committed a capital marital wrong is placed on probationary status on the condition that he treat the party with conjugal kindness. There is a remission of the wrong provided the culprit behaves well in the future." *Id* 539-40.

[197] *Id.*

[198] H. Clark, The Law of Domestic Relations in the United States 365 (1968).

example, a series of cruel acts, after obtaining evidence that the other spouse had committed adultery, or after the other spouse has deserted the aggrieved spouse. However, courts have agreed that mere suspicion is not enough for condonation.[199]

Three knowledge standards have evolved in American case law: the *full knowledge* standard,[200] the *probable knowledge* standard,[201] and the *reasonable knowledge* standard.[202] It appears, however, that the standard of proof is less important than whether the innocent spouse *believed* that the other spouse was indeed guilty.[203] The commentators prefer a belief of guilt test to a quantum of knowledge test.[204]

Practitioners frequently find that a client has well-grounded suspicions that the spouse is involved in romantic relationships, but has no evidence to prove adultery in a court of law. In circumstances where there is suspicion without evidence, the practitioner must advise the client that there is danger of condonation. It is important to note that condonation requires a different

---

[199] Reader, *Knowledge or Belief as a Prerequisite to Condonation in the Law of Divorce,* 21 Minn L Rev 408, 408 (1936).

[200] See Day v Day, 71 Kan 385, 80 P 974, 975 (1905), where the Supreme Court of Kansas set out the full knowledge standard as follows:

> An essential element of condonation is a full knowledge by the injured spouse of the marital misconduct of the offender. If the plaintiff had only an unconfirmed suspicion that his wife had gone astray, or if he believed that the numerous acts of adultery brought to his attention were without her consent, his continuance of the marital relation might not amount to an effective forgiveness or condonation.

[201] See Connelly v Connelly, 98 Mo App 95, 71 SW 1111, 1113 (1903), where the Court of Appeals of Missouri held that "[t]here can be no condonation of the offense of a guilty spouse without probable knowledge that the offense had been committed. . . . Absolute knowledge of guilt is not essential to condonation, but the law . . . seems to require moral certainty."

[202] See Quincey v Quincey, 10 NH 272, 274 (1839), the leading case applying the reasonable knowledge standard, where the New Hampshire Superior Court of Judicature declared:

> If, having reasonable knowledge of the infidelity of his wife, and of his power to make proof of it, the husband, notwithstanding, cohabits with her as a wife, this is an implied condonation, and bars him of any right to avail himself of the mere fact of the previous adultery, as a cause of divorce. . . . But cohabitation under circumstances which excite suspicion merely, does not amount to condonation.

[203] *See* Moore, *An Examination of the Condonation Doctrine,* 2 Akron L Rev 75, 81 (1969); Regder, *supra* note 199, at 415 (where it is concluded that "[f]rom an analytical standpoint it is clear that, despite the judicial language, the motivating principle of all the cases so far discussed is that belief in guilt is a condition precedent to the condonation of the marital offense.").

[204] See, e.g., H. Clark, *supra* note 198, at 368, where the professor argues that "[t]he requirement of knowledge should and under most cases does involve proof that the plaintiff not only knew of the marital offense in the sense of possessing information that it had happened, but that he believed and emotionally accepted this information as true."

degree of proof to show knowledge of the wrongdoing than is required to establish adultery itself.

Another element of condonation is forgiveness. While some courts equate forgiveness with condonation, others define it as a state of mind implied from words or conduct.[205] Generally, the voluntary resumption of marital relations after the commission of a marital offense gives rise to a presumption of forgiveness by the innocent spouse.[206] However, some courts have held "that sexual intercourse alone occurring after the marital wrong is condonation—regardless of intent to forgive (knowledge being assumed),"[207] while most courts have decided that evidence of intent to forgive may be required in addition to proof of resumed sexual relations.[208] A small number of cases have held that an oral or written statement of forgiveness was sufficient to activate the doctrine of condonation.[209]

The state statutes also differ as to what must be done by an aggrieved spouse in order to effect a condonation. One category of statutes states that *either*

---

[205] 24 Am Jur 2d *Divorce and Separation* §208 (1966).

[206] Moore, *supra* note 203, at 86.

[207] Note, *A Survey of the Law of Condonation, Collusion and Connivance in New England,* 35 BUL Rev 99, 106 (1955). See, e.g., Huffine v Huffine, 48 Ohio Law Abstracts 430, 74 NE2d 764, 766 (1947), where a Court of Common Pleas of Ohio held:

> Not only have the courts of Ohio seemed to follow the view that a single resumption of marital intercourse shall constitute condonation, but this Court feels that such a decision is proper. During recent years, because of a liberalization of our general beliefs it has become easier for the parties to obtain a divorce. Purely as a moral proposition, this Court does not feel that parties should be allowed to maintain sexual relations and at the same time seek a divorce as the two acts are completely incompatible. The Court feels that a single voluntary act of marital intercourse, where the injured party is in full knowledge of the other party's aggressions, shall act as a condonation of all aggressions up to that time.

[208] See, e.g., Seiferth v Seiferth, 132 So 2d 471, 472-73 (Fla 1961), where a District Court of Appeal of Florida affirmed a trial court's granting of a divorce to a husband despite the wife's contention that the parties had resumed cohabitation for a period during the pendency of the suit. The court held that:

> The denial of the motion to dismiss was on a finding that the element of forgiveness, essential for condonation, was "completely lacking in the resumption of the relationship herein." The resumption of cohabitation, per se, is not necessarily condonation. It may imply a condoning, but the principal element of the defense is the freely exercised intent to forgive.

[209] In Bush v Bush, 135 Ark 512, 205 SW 895 (1918), the Supreme Court of Arkansas held that a husband's bringing his wife back to the marital home and discussing terms of reconciliation was sufficient condonation of his wife's adultery, even though he changed his mind 10 minutes after the parties had returned home, and even though there had been no resumption of marital relations. In Thompson v Thompson, 35 Nev 375, 247 P 545 (1926), the plaintiff husband countered his wife's defense of desertion to his divorce suit based on her desertion with evidence of an executed written agreement of reconciliation in which each expressly pardoned the other for all offenses. The Supreme Court of Nevada affirmed the divorce granted to the husband on the ground of his wife's desertion because of their having the reconciliation agreement, even though the couple never established marital relations afterwards.

sexual relations *or* forgiveness constitutes condonation,[210] while another requires *both* sexual relations *and* forgiveness.[211] Some statutes specify that a *resumption of cohabitation* constitutes condonation, although there is conflict as to whether this term means sexual intercourse or a relationship existing over a period of time.[212]

Forgiveness, whether express or implied, must be voluntary and not induced by fraud, duress, or fear. Courts frequently demanded greater evidence of forgiveness when the wife was the aggrieved spouse due to the wife's historical economic, physical, and emotional dependence on her husband.[213] Courts also tended to demand more evidence of forgiveness when the divorce ground relied on was a continuing transgression, such as cruelty.[214]

Condonation is impliedly conditioned upon the wrongdoer's behaving with *conjugal kindness* toward the innocent spouse.[215] If the guilty spouse later treats the aggrieved spouse with *conjugal unkindness,* the condonation is nullified and the original cause of action is revived. This is called the *revival doctrine.*

It is uncertain exactly what conjugal unkindness means, but it is clear that the offense need not be a new ground for divorce to revive previous transgressions.[216] At common law, the revival principle is not restricted by any specific time limit. However, some courts have applied the doctrine of laches or have refused to invoke the revival doctrine after an extended time period in the absence of strict statutory time limits.[217]

---

[210] *See, e.g.,* NY Dom Rel Law §171(2) (McKinney 1977).

[211] *See, e.g.,* ND Cent Code §14-05-13 (1981).

[212] *See, e.g.,* Va Code §20-94 (1983). See also Tarr v Tarr, 184 Va 443, 35 SE2d 401 (1945) where it was held that *voluntarily cohabited* should not be restricted to its literal meaning of having dwelled together under the same roof with more or less permanency, and that a single act of sexual intercourse by an innocent spouse after knowledge of the wrongdoer's transgression was sufficient to constitute condonation.

[213] *See, e.g.,* Beeby v Beeby, 1 Hagy Ecc 789, 162 Eng Rep 755 (1799); Glass v Glass, 175 Md 693, 2 A2d 443 (1938).

[214] Moore, *supra* note 203, at 92.

[215] J. Madden, Handbook of the Law of Persons and Domestic Relations 301 (1931).

[216] See M. Ploscowe, H. Foster, & D. Freed, Family Law, Cases and Materials 542 (2d ed 1972); Moore, *supra* note 203, at 99; Annot, 16 ALR2d 585 (1951); Worsley v Worsley, 2 Lee 572, 161 Eng Rep 444 (1730), where it was held that after a reconciliation, fresh acts of cruelty would revive not only previous acts of cruelty, but also previous acts of adultery.

[217] M. Ploscowe, H. Foster, & D. Freed, *supra* note 216 at 543. See Singewald v Singewald, 165 Md 136, 141, 166 A 441, 443 (1933), where the Court of Appeals of Maryland noted the implied condition in the condonation doctrine, and held:

> There must of necessity be some limitation to that rule. And where the offenses sought to be revived are so remote in point of time and the conduct of the parties has been of such a character that no rational conclusion can be reached other than that the complainant has finally and unconditionally surrendered any and all rights to complain of such offenses they may not be revived as separate and sufficient ground for divorce. . . .

See also Welch v Welch, 34 NJ Super 197, 11 A2d 793 (1955), where a Superior Court

The doctrine of condonation's conditional nature has been criticized as an obstruction to reconciliation.[218] Generally, the doctrine of condonation has lost its importance in light of the no-fault trend of divorce. As noted by one source, "condonation is conceptually wedded to a fault-oriented concept of divorce and has no relevance to the more modern, sociological view of divorce as being simply a remedy for a couple whose marriage—for whatever reason—has failed."[219]

## §1.23 —Recrimination Generally

Recrimination is another affirmative defense in a fault-oriented divorce action. Under the doctrine of recrimination, if the defendant in a complaint for divorce also pleads and proves that the plaintiff is guilty of marital misconduct, the result is that the divorce action must be dismissed. Thus, if both parties are guilty of adultery, neither is entitled to a divorce.

Recrimination is probably the most criticized concept in fault divorce.[220] Professor Homer Clark, the prominent family law authority who has called recrimination an "outrageous legal principle,"[221] incorporated criticism into his very definition of the doctrine:

> In other words, when both parties have given the clearest indication that their marriage is dead, that is precisely the point at which the law said no divorce could be granted. The doctrine was so silly and so pernicious that many courts had begun to restrict it or abolish it before the enactment of no-fault grounds for divorce.[222]

The doctrine of recrimination has its roots in Roman law. Recrimination had nothing to do with whether a divorce would be granted or denied, because in Roman law divorce was not a judicial act at all; a marriage could be dissolved by the unilateral act of either party.[223] Instead, the question of fault went to

---

of New Jersey held that there was an absolute condonation of incidents occurring in 1946 and 1948 where the parties cohabited until 1954, and the incidents were not revived by an alleged assault in 1954.

[218] Fox, *Condonation: An Obstruction to Reconciliation,* 2 Fam LQ 259 (1968); MacDougall, *Proposals to Reform the Law of Condonation,* 39 Austl LJ 295 (1966).

[219] Moore, *supra* note 203, at 107.

[220] M. Ploscowe, H. Foster, & D. Freed, Family Law, Cases and Materials 485 (2d ed 1972). These authors note that recrimination is unpopular with text authorities, but "it retains a remarkable vitality." Justice Traynor, in DeBurgh v DeBurgh, 39 Cal 2d 858, 870, 250 P2d 598, 605 (1952), in his excellent attempt to modify the doctrine of recrimination in California, noted that "[f]ew rules of law have been more widely condemned by the legal profession."

[221] H. Clark, The Law of Domestic Relations in the United States 373 (1968).

[222] H. Clark, Domestic Relations, Cases and Principles 387 (3d ed 1980).

[223] Beamer, *The Doctrine of Recrimination in Divorce Proceedings,* 10 UMKC L Rev 213, 217 (1942).

the restitution of the wife's dos, or dowry. Roman courts developed the rule that if both parties were guilty of equal wrongs:

> [n]either party should be punished. The wife should not be penalized by allowing the husband to retain a sixth part of her dowry, nor should he be punished by being compelled to make immediate restitution. The result should be the same as if neither party were at fault—the wife recovering the whole of her dowry within one year's time.[224]

The Catholic church, which had adopted the doctrine of the indissolubility of marriage, developed a limited version of the doctrine of recrimination in order to protect women and children from the perils of divorce a mensa et thoro. The Church, in its second book to the Corpus Juris Canonici, included a provision permitting a wife who is accused of adultery in a proceeding for a divorce *a mensa et thoro* to recriminate. The church thereby compelled equally guilty parties to continue to live together as man and wife. Note, however, that because an absolute divorce did not exist, recrimination was not a bar to such an action at that time.[225]

The Protestant Reformation signalled the introduction of divorce *a vinculo matrimonii,* or the absolute divorce. The doctrine of recrimination prevented an absolute divorce in the case of the adultery of both spouses.[226]

Lord Stowell (Sir William Scott) adopted the doctrine into English ecclesiastical law in his opinion in *Forster v Forster.*[227] In that "melancholy case," a husband brought a divorce action against his wife on the adultery ground, which he clearly proved. The wife brought the defense of recrimination, based upon the husband's general neglect of the wife and pursuit of young women. Scott held that the husband was barred from divorcing his wife.[228]

---

[224] Id 218-19.

[225] *Id* 222, where the author states: "So it would seem that in the canon law, the doctrine of recrimination was, at best, merely a discretionary means of requiring the guilty husband either to promote his guilty wife with separate maintenance or to permit her to remain mistress of his home."

[226] *Id* 224, which quotes the doctrine from 2 Gibson, Codex Juris Ecclesiastici Anglecani 356 (1761);

> If a person who has been convicted of adultery can prove that the same crime has been committed by the other partner in marriage, and does prove it before the partner in marriage shall have turned himself to new marriage, the blame shall fall equally upon both and equal punishment shall ensue, and firm matrimony shall remain among them as before.

[227] 1 Hag Con 144, 161 Eng Rep 504 (1790).

[228] Lord Howell traced the doctrine of recrimination in the law and then declared at 1 Hag Con at 152-53, 161 Eng Rep at 508:

> I should be inclined to hold that the general conduct of the husband, as shewn, is quite sufficient to support a plea in bar, though not sufficient to support an original accusation of adultery, For it is a principle that runs through a variety of cases that many things are good for the one purpose, though deficient for the other. The husband who enters the Court with criminal imputation on the conduct

Thus, in England, the doctrine of recrimination provided a means for the courts to require a guilty husband to support his guilty wife and to permit her to remain in his home. In a time when divorced women were social outcasts, the doctrine was a tool to prevent injustice. The doctrine also had the effect of denying the guilty parties' rights to remarry.

The American courts adopted the common law doctrine of recrimination. The broad common law rule is that a recriminatory defense may be based upon any conduct which has not been condoned and which would constitute independent grounds for divorce.[229]

Much criticism has been directed at the American judicial system's blind acceptance of the doctrine without any investigation into its development, basis, and history.[230] It is said that the courts' application of recrimination is "a sincere but misguided effort to promote morality and to protect the stability of the marriage."[231] The next section documents the role of the doctrine of recrimination in American divorce law to the present.

## §1.24 —Recrimination in American Law

Divorce in early American law was a remedy for an innocent spouse and a punishment of the guilty spouse who breached the terms of the marriage contract through marital misconduct. The vehicle used to "preserve" marriage was the fault system of divorce which made divorces difficult to obtain. Divorce was damaging to the reputation.[232] The doctrine of recrimination provided that

---

> of his wife, must purge his own conduct of all reasonable imputation of the saner nature; and if he complains of her impurities, it must be untainted by any gross impurities of his own.

229 H. Clark,*supra* note 221, at 375.

230 Beamer, *supra* note 223, at 215, is especially hard:

> [T]he courts and legislatures have shown little inclination to probe very deeply beneath the surface. They take it for granted that a principle of law, which they think has existed and been in continuous operation for almost 2000 years, has its foundation in reason and propriety; and consider it unnecessary to ascertain the social and economic effects of its application to 20th century divorces. . . .
>
> Ignoring the ecclesiastical law, one may well wonder at this point just what the basis of the doctrine of recrimination is in our modern law if it is not statutory. . . . The courts seldom venture upon any explanation of why they apply the doctrine in a particular case, but rely upon dubious precedents and content themselves with hackneyed legal rationalizations of the result.

231 M. Ploscowe, H. Foster, & D. Freed, *supra* note 220, at 487.

232 It is clear that the strategy for preservation of marriage has shifted emphasis away from individual marriages to the entire institution. Instead of forcing unhappy couples to stay together or to endure difficult divorce proceedings and potential social ostracism, the law has facilitated the exit from "holy deadlock" with the intention that couples may try the institution again without the necessity for resorting to the extramarital or nonmarital institution of cohabitation. The rise of no-fault divorce is covered in **§§2.01-2.17.** Cohabitation is treated in S. Green & J. Long, Marriage and Family Law Agreements ch 3 (Shepard's/McGraw-Hill 1984).

two spouses guilty of marital misconduct constituting independent divorce grounds could not be divorced from each other. The objective was the preservation of marriage.

The doctrine was judicially developed, and in the second half of the nineteenth century it was codified by legislatures in various states.[233] The ensuing confusion and difficulty associated with recrimination was a typical result of many rules of the fault system. The common law doctrine provided that a spouse could recriminate with any other independent ground for divorce. In individual cases, however, and in loosely worded statutes, the interpretations varied.

In some jurisdictions, recrimination could only be based on the same marital misconduct, mutual adultery being the "venerable example."[234] In others, recrimination was available when spouses were "equally at fault."[235] Still others provided for recrimination when any cause of divorce was "in bar" of the plaintiff's cause of divorce.[236] Courts frequently followed the common law, undermining the statutes. Generally, the doctrine of recrimination added an undignified uncertainty to the American fault system of divorce which emphasized the need for divorce law reform.[237]

Many explanations have been offered for the doctrine of recrimination in American divorce law. Some are based on equitable principles, a phenomenon which has troubled family law authorities who note that judicial divorce had not existed in England until 1858 and therefore did not constitute a part of equity.[238]

For example, the clean hands doctrine is the most common reason advanced in justification of recrimination.[239] One who asks for relief must come into court with clean hands innocent of any wrongdoing. The clean hands maxim was supposed to be applied at a court's discretion, was not to be imposed if it worked an inequity, and was used to embrace any type of misconduct. Recrimination, however, was not so applied. For many years the courts mechanically invoked this defense only when misconduct constituting divorce grounds could be plead, creating considerable inequity.[240]

---

[233] Beamer, *The Doctrine of Recrimination in Divorce Proceedings*, 10 UMKC L Rev 213, 215 (1942).

[234] 1 Nelson, Divorce and Annulment 358 (2d ed 1945). *See, e.g.*, Ala Code §30-2-3 (1983); Ark Stat Ann §34-1209 (Supp 1983); Ga Code Ann §19-5-4)(a)(3) & (b) (1982); NY Dom Rel Law §171(4) (McKinney 1977).

[235] Posey v Posey, 268 Ark 894, 597 SW2d 834 (1980).

[236] DeBurgh v DeBurgh, 39 Cal 2d 858, 250 P2d 598 (1952); Idaho Code §§32-611 & -613 (1983).

[237] *See* **§2.04.**

[238] H. Clark, Law of Domestic Relations in the United States 374 (1968); M. Rheinstein, Marriage Stability, Divorce and the Law 54 (1972).

[239] H. Clark, *supra* note 238, at 374.

[240] M. Ploscowe, H. Foster, & D. Freed, Family Law, Cases and Materials 487 (2d ed 1972).

The *pari delicto* policy—that parties *in pari delicto,* equally guilty or equally at fault, should be left where the court finds them—has also been used to explain the doctrine of recrimination. Another explanation for recrimination is the contract principle that relief will not be granted for mutual breach of dependent covenants.[241] In addition, several policy reasons were used to justify recrimination: that recrimination promotes marital stability by thwarting divorce; that it serves as a deterrent to immorality; that it provides financial protection for the wife; and that it prevents spouses who have failed at the marriage from contracting subsequent bad marriages.[242]

It should not be surprising that the doctrine of recrimination has been abolished in most states.[243] The advent of the no-fault divorce system has contributed to the doctrine's obsolescence.

However, before no-fault laws were enacted, the recrimination defense was eroded by statutes and case law which permitted a discretionary application of the defense,[244] and by case law which developed the doctrine of comparative rectitude.[245] This doctrine allows a court to grant a divorce to the spouse least at fault when both have shown grounds for divorce. If the parties appear to be equally at fault, a divorce will be denied.

---

[241] Moore, *An Examination of the Recrimination Doctrine,* 20 SCL Rev 685, 712-73 (1968). While this rationalization satisfied those who argued that equitable maxims should not be applied in divorce proceedings, it troubled those who argued that marriage is a status or a hybrid, and not a contract; and if it is a contract, then parties should be allowed to rescind it by mutual consent.

[242] M. Ploscowe, H. Foster, & D. Freed, *supra* note 240, at 487.

[243] See Freed & Foster, *Family Law in the Fifty States: An Overview,* 16 Fam LQ 289, 320 (1983), where the authors list some states which have abolished all traditional defenses, including Arizona, California, Colorado, Delaware, the District of Columbia, Hawaii, Indiana, Kentucky, Minnesota, Missouri, Montana, Oregon, and Wisconsin. The authors also list states which have abolished *some* of the traditional defenses, and other states which have abolished certain defenses only as to specified grounds.

> The Uniform Marriage and Divorce Act, 9A ULA 126 (1979), which establishes the irretrievable breakdown ground for divorce, also provides that "[p]reviously existing defenses to divorce and legal separation, including but not limited to condonation, connivance, collusion, recrimination, insanity, and lapse of time, are abolished." *See* **app 1-1.**

[244] *See, e.g.,* Burch v Burch, 195 F2d 799 (3d Cir 1952); Matlow v Matlow, 89 Ariz 293, 361 P2d 648 (1961); DeBurgh v DeBurgh, 39 Cal 2d 858, 250 P2d 598 (1952); Stewart v Stewart, 158 Fla 326, 29 So 2d 247 (1946); Howay v Howay, 74 Idaho 492, 264 P2d 691 (1953); Burns v Burns, 145 Mont 1, 400 P2d 642 (1964); Clark v Clark, 54 NM 364, 255 P2d 147 (1950); Pavletich v Pavletich, 50 NM 224, 174 P2d 826 (1946); Kan Stat Ann §60-1606 (1964); Miss Code Ann §93-5-3 (1972).

[245] O'Connor v O'Connor, 253 Ind 295, 253 NE2d 250 (1969); Eals v Swan, 221 La 329, 59 So 2d 409 (1952); Marr v Marr, 191 SW 2d 512 (Tex 1945); Hendricks v Hendricks, 123 Utah 178, 257 P2d 366 (1953).

## §1.25 —Miscellaneous Defenses

Other defenses against a divorce action are available in addition to the special defenses covered in the previous sections.[246] These defenses will be covered briefly because of their diminished importance in the divorce law of the United States. Not only have many fault-divorce cases become uncontested, but the rise of no-fault divorce has virtually eliminated the need for most defenses.[247] Indeed, numerous states have abolished either some or all of the traditional defenses.[248] Nevertheless, the sophisticated practitioner must be aware of all options in divorce pleadings and litigation in order to best serve his or her client.

The most common defenses emerge in the pleadings. The defendant in the action can deny the misconduct or the separation alleged as divorce grounds or assert lack of jurisdiction if the circumstances allow. In addition, if appropriate, the defendant may deny the existence of a valid marriage or plead an invalid marriage as an affirmative defense.[249] However, the defendant may be estopped from asserting the invalidity of the marriage as a defense where the defendant knew of the other spouse's prior existing marriage, where there was an attempt to assert his or her own existing marriage, where the defendant participated with the plaintiff in obtaining the prior invalid divorce decree, or where the divorce statute provided that an invalid marriage is a proper divorce ground.[250]

A prior valid divorce between the parties entitled to full facts and credit may be asserted as a defense in a divorce action.[251]

Another defense is the plaintiff spouse's antenuptial knowledge of the misconduct alleged as divorce grounds. It is generally held that the plaintiff must have had *actual knowledge* of the defendant's premarital conduct.[252]

A delay in bringing suit, absent any signs of condonation, may also be a defense or bar to divorce. Some jurisdictions have specific statutes of limitations, many of which are only applicable to actions based upon the adultery grounds.[253] It is necessary, when applying these statutes, to determine

---

246 *See* **§§1.19-1.24.**

247 *See* **§§2.02-2.05.**

248 Freed & Foster, *Family Law in the Fifty States; An Overview,* 16 Fam LQ 289, 310 (1983).

249 *See, e.g.,* Kazin v Kazin, 161 NJ Super 174, 391 A2d 536, *revd,* 81 NJ 85, 87, 405 A2d 360, 361 (1978); Panzer v Panzer, 87 NM 29, 528 P2d 888 (1974); Fuchs v Fuchs, 104 Misc 2d 1143, 429 NYS2d 982 (Sup Ct 1980).

250 *See* **§1.18.**

251 McIntire v McIntire, 130 Me 326, 155 A 731 (1931).

252 Moore, *Forgotten Defenses to Divorce Suits,* 9 J Fam L 149, 154 (1969-70).

253 *See, e.g.,* Alaska Stat §25.24.120(5) (1983) (two-year limit on the adultery ground); Ark Stat Ann §34-1208 (Supp 1983) (plaintiff must prove that the cause of divorce existed within five years of the action for divorce); Idaho Code §32-615 (1983) (divorce must be denied if action is not commenced within two years of adultery or discovery thereof, or one year after a pardon or termination of prison sentence); NY Dom Rel

when the offense occurred and consequently when the period of limitations began running. It has been noted that while in most jurisdictions application of the statute of limitations is axiomatic, in others the statute must be raised as an affirmative defense.[254] There is also a disagreement among courts whether general statutes of limitations govern divorce where no statute of limitations specifically applicable to divorce exists.[255]

The doctrine of laches has also been used by courts to bar an action for divorce.[256] The doctrine of laches is based upon the equity maxim that equity aids the vigilant and not those who slumber on their rights. Thus, if a spouse neglects to assert the right to divorce on a fault ground which, taken together with lapse of time and other circumstances, will cause prejudice when it finally is asserted, that spouse may be barred from bringing the divorce action in a court of equity.

The advantage of laches over statutes of limitations is that it is a discretionary doctrine which is applied only when the delay by the plaintiff is not reasonably justified. The factors which may be considered include the extent of the delay, the reason for the delay, the strength of the plaintiff's case, any ignorance of fact or law, a lack of funds, a desire to reconcile, or any other such justification. However, the policy underlying no-fault divorce, that marriages which are irretrievably broken are better dissolved than preserved, may run against the discretionary application of laches.[257] As a practical matter, laches is rarely successful as a defense and seldom invoked in divorce proceedings.

If a spouse committed a marital transgression while insane, the insanity may be used as a defense in the divorce action.[258] For the most part, courts have accepted the proposition that an insane person lacks the mental capacity to formulate a wrongful intent and therefore should not be held responsible for

---

Law §§171(3) & 210 (McKinney 1977) (five-year limit); Va Code §20-94 (1983) (five-year limit).

[254] H. Clark, The Law of Domestic Relations in the United States 371 (1968); M. Ploscowe, H. Foster, & D. Freed, Family Law, Cases and Materials 566 (2d ed 1972).

[255] M. Ploscow, H. Foster, & D. Freed, Family Law, Cases and Materials 566 (2d ed 1972).

[256] In Mortimer v Mortimer, 2 Hag Con 310, 313, 161 Eng Rep 753, 754-55 (1820), Lord Stowell noted that:

> The first thing which the Court looks to, when a charge of adultery is preferred, is the date of the criminal fact charged, and known by the party; because, if the interval be very long between the date and knowledge of the fact, and the exhibition of them to this Court, it will be indisposed to relieve a party who appears to have slumbered in sufficient comfort over them; and it will be inclined to infer either an insincerity in the complaint, or an acquiescence in the injury, whether real or supposed, or a condonation of it. It therefore demands a full and satisfactory explanation of this delay, in order to take it out of the reach of such interpretations.

[257] *See* **§2.05.**

[258] Moore, *supra* note 252, at 157.

his or her acts.[259] It generally has been assumed that the test for insanity at the time of the commission of the marital misconduct is a civil modification of the *M'Naghten* test.[260] It has also been held that an insane person is incapable of forming the intent to voluntarily live separate and apart under the no-fault statutes providing such a ground.[261]

These defenses clearly have lost their importance with the rise of no-fault divorce. However, especially in the jurisdictions which have hybrid divorce statutes, mixtures of fault and no-fault grounds, it may be useful for the practitioner to be acquainted with such defenses.

## §1.26 Final Comments

This chapter has painstakingly traced the development of divorce from its roots in early society. Succeeding chapters will examine its rapid transformation of recent decades which has culminated in no-fault laws and alternative dispute methods. The reason for such detailed analysis is clear: as a societal institution, divorce reflects the maturation of civilization. In addition, divorce has had a significant impact on our society, and will continue to do so.

Divorce, or dissolution as it is now called in many states, has been accepted in modern society as a means of helping people find a happier relationship instead of forcing them to remain in an unsatisfactory one. To many persons, divorce represents failure; to others, it shines as a second chance. The divorce rate, while stabilizing in the mid 1980s after skyrocketing in the previous decade, continued to hover between 40 and 50 per cent for first marriages.[262] Nevertheless, 90 per cent of all Americans were marrying and 75 per cent of divorced people remarry, confirming the strength of the institution of

---

[259] *See, e.g.*, Payton v Payton, 252 Iowa 772, 108 NW2d 358 (1961); Fuemmeler v Fuemmeler, 381 SW2d 27, 30 (Mo Ct App 1965); Manley v Manley, 193 Pa Super 252, 164 A2d 113 (1960); Popper v Popper, 388 SW2d 468 (Tex Civ App 1965).

[260] In Schuler v Schuler, 290 SW2d 192, 199 (Mo Ct App 1956), the court stated such a test:

> The mere showing of insane delusions, unrestrained impulsiveness and lack of control, psycho-neurosis, depraved character or licentious disposition is not sufficient to sustain the defense of insanity in an action of divorce. . . . The insanity "must be such as deprives the defendant's conduct of the element of willfulness and as divests the defendant of the use of his reason to the extent of his being unable to differentiate between right and wrong, or that, if capable of so differentiating, defendant must be acting by force of an irresistable impulse generated by a diseased mind and not by volition." (citations omitted.)

[261] Moore, *supra* note 252, at 161 (citing Carlson v Carlson, 198 Ark 231, 128 SW2d 242 (1939); Crittenden v Crittenden, 210 Va 76, 168 SE2d 115 (1969); **§1.16.**

[262] Family Service America, The State of Families 1984-85, at 8 (1984). This report was compiled by the Family Service America from its own data, as well as information from other sources such as the Census Bureau, Bureau of Labor Statistics, House Budget Committee, US Department of Labor, and others.

marriage. By the year 2000, it is anticipated that the marriage rate for all Americans will drop from 90 per cent to 85 per cent.[263]

A combination of factors, including higher expectations in relationships, changing life patterns, and greater longevity produced a slightly higher divorce rate for subsequent marriages. The increasingly common situation of a person marrying several times has been called *serial marriage*.[264]

Divorce spawns significant responsibilities and consequences which are being shirked and ignored, creating serious problems in present society. Divorce has contributed to the growth of single-parent families, one-third of which have cash incomes below the poverty line. Millions of children live in single-parent homes; by 1990, 30 per cent of all children will do so.[265] Growth of families headed by women, which began in the 1960s and continued in the 1970s and 1980s, has been correlated to both higher rates of marital instability and illegitimacy.[266] The epidemic noncompliance with support orders, inevitably pushing some of those families into poverty, prompted Congress to enact legislation strengthening the federal-state scheme for the enforcement of child support orders.[267]

Another problem associated with divorce which affects children is child snatching.[268] While not affecting as substantial a number of children as in the past, this violation of custody orders persists. A significant percentage of "missing children" have been abducted by a noncustodial parent, not by a child abuser as many might believe. Other children have run away from broken or malfunctioning homes.

The development of the institution of divorce has also transformed the character of spousal support, the definition of property, and the legal

---

263 *Id* 7.

264 *Id* 11. The increase in serial marriages has been attributed to significant changes in living patterns, life plans, and lifestyles emphasizing cyclical patterns alternating education, work, leisure, and marriage. As The State of Families 1984-85 maintains:

> Many marriages will successfully adapt to changing relations. Many others, however, will be ended by divorce as spouses evaluate the relationship as out of phase and obsolete, with the time ripe for new relationships with more appropriate partners. This is not to say that these divorces will be painless; the parting spouses will still experience a sense of failure and hurt that the marriage could not be made to work.

265 *Id* 10.

266 H. Ross & I. Sawhill, Time of Transition: The Growth of Families Headed By Women 25 (1975).

267 Dodson & Horowitz, *Child Support Enforcement Amendments of 1984: New Tools For Enforcement*, Monograph no 5, 10 Fam L Rep (BNA) 3051 (Oct 23, 1984) (citing 42 USC §§651-662 & The Child Support Enforcement Amendments of 1984, Pub L No 98-378, 315).

268 *See* S. Katz, Child Snatching, The Legal Response to the Abduction of Children (1981).

ramifications of remarriage. Rehabilitative and reimbursement alimony awards have replaced the traditional lifetime alimony awards in many cases.[269] Thousands of married adults are becoming former partners in an economic partnership; in the process of divorce, their property is being redefined and then divided.[270] Couples entering subsequent marriages have learned to anticipate divorce and frequently contract the consequences of dissolution in antenuptial agreements.[271]

This increase in divorce has meant that the legal system has touched more lives than ever before. As lay people develop a greater legal awareness, the practitioner's duty to educate them increases as well. It is hoped that this work will facilitate that task by providing a thorough historical and modern treatment of these topics.

Many questions remain unanswered, however. It is part of the family law practitioner's responsibility to remain open to productive answers and solutions. Divorce and dissolution, as legal processes in the 1980s, are aimed at the reasoned termination of the marital relationship. The emergence of mediation highlights the need for dialogue between divorcing couples so that they may surmount the urgency of post-termination survival with dignity, trust, sensitivity, understanding, and respect. Divorce and dissolution can be a humane process which actually creates new and exciting relationships from old.

---

[269] Ford, *Rehabilitative Alimony—A Matter of Discretion or Direction?*, 12 Fla St UL Rev 285 (1984); Meyer, Family Law—- reimbursement alimony—is a marriage of *relatively short duration where one's spouse's contributions enable the other to attain a professional degree and there are few tangible assets to distribute, a court may consider reimbursement alimony (case note) Mahony v Mahony*, 453 A2d 527 (NJ 1982), 14 Rutgers LJ 1011 (1983).

[270] See generally **ch 10.**

[271] *See* S. Green & J. Long, Marriage and Family Law Agreements 135-55 (Shepard's/ McGraw-Hill 1984).

## Appendix 1-1
## Initial Interview Form

Date: ____________

Name:

Residence address: ______________________ Birth place: ____________

Mailing address: ______________________ Birth date: ____________

Office address: ______________________ Citizenship: ____________

Residence telephone: ______________________ Domicile: ____________

Office telephone: ______________________________________________

Office hours: ______________________________________________

By whom referred: ______________________________________________

Date & place of marriage: ______________________________________________

How do names of the parties appear on the marriage license?

First marriage for both?

Date & place of other marriages/divorces, each spouse:

Does client have license for present marriage and certificates and divorce decrees for prior divorces and prior marriages, and for spouses' prior divorces?

Names, ages, and addresses of children of prior marriages:

Details of support obligations for children of prior marriages:

**Children:**

| Name | Birth Date | Birth Place | Present Age | School |
|---|---|---|---|---|
| | | | | |
| | | | | |
| | | | | |
| | | | | |

School tuition, expenses:

Physical health:

Mental health:

Names, addresses and telephone numbers of any treating physicians and specialists, if any, including psychiatrists and psychologists, of children:

History of any special problems of each child:

Date and place of separation or contemplated separation date:

Reconciliation efforts?

Any resumption of sexual relations since separation?

If separated, present custody & visitation arrangements?

History of custody and visitation arrangements:

If there have been any changes in custody or visitation arrangements, what reasons for changes?

If not separated, what does client desire for custody and visitation?

How amenable will spouse be to client's desires?

What custody & visitation discussions have already taken place:

Does client know his/her rights re custody, UCCJA, etc.?

Client's educational history:

Who paid for it?

Source of living expenses while in school:

Spouse's educational history:

Who paid for it?

Source of living expenses while in school:

Client's and spouse's present place of employment & job title, and current gross and net salary and how and when paid:

Any commission, bonus, fringe benefits?

Who pays social security?

Does client have wage stubs or other personnel documents for self?

For spouse?

Do either or both have pension rights?

Years of marriage during creditable period:

Year contributions began:

Service computation dates for civil service pension:

Is a pension plan document explaining vesting, normal retirement date, and other pertinent data available?

Any military service by either spouse?

Does it affect pension eligibility?

Any financial obligations being paid or being received as a result of prior marriages:

Does client have federal and state tax returns (joint or for self) for past 5 years? Where filed?

**Assets:**

Marital residence (description of interior and grounds):

How titled:

Date purchased:

Purchase price:

Dates and amounts of any capital improvements and documentation for each:

Mortgages:

Current payment for principal, interest, taxes & insurance (PITI):

Balance due:

Annual statement from lender?

Is settlement sheet available?

Is amortization schedule available?

Market value:

Is an MAI appraisal needed?

Any other real estate (similar data required):

Rental property?

Unimproved land?

Commercial property?

Securities:

Certificates of deposit:

Bonds:

Stocks:

Money market funds:

Pets:

Gifts to either party?

Interspousal?

From third parties?

Date:

Values:

Automobiles:

Personalty, such as furnishings, jewelry, silver, art, rugs, etc. Outstanding debts, including other mortgages, bank loans, credit cards and other consumer debts:

Insurance:

Life: list, beneficiaries, benefits, type

Health: benefits, who is covered?

Safe deposit box: where? contents?

Special information response:

Part-time income or activity:

Hobbies:

Sports:

Wills or trusts:

Any inheritances received or anticipated?

**Family loans:**

Are family loans evidenced by promissory notes?

Can family loans be traced or proved by deposits, cancelled checks?

What have loans been used for?

Any loan applications in the past five years which might have contained admissions or corroborate other financial matters?

Any lawsuits in which either party was plaintiff or defendant in recent years?

Chronological history of marriage, including places resided, jobs, and significant events in personal relationship, such as prior separations, infidelities, violence, counseling, etc:

What is client's reason for separating or consulting an attorney?

Are there grounds for divorce?

Any cohabitation with another by either spouse, past, present or contemplated?

Chronology of prior residences, with reasons for each move and financial detail:

Is there jurisdiction?

What are pertinent facts for jurisdiction?

Is litigation underway or contemplated at an early date?

How does client feel about litigation?

What is client's ultimate objective?

Is client receiving psychological or psychiatric counseling to help deal with nonlegal aspects of the problems?

Has client been informed about legal fees to be charged?

Has client signed a retainer agreement?

# 2 No-Fault Divorce Legislation



## §2.01 Historical Background

No-fault divorce did not originate in California, contrary to popular belief. In some areas, it has been possible to obtain a divorce on no-fault grounds for a hundred years or more. As early as 1850, Kentucky enacted a ground in its statute which enabled parties to divorce upon a showing that they lived "separate and apart without any communication whatever" for five years.[1]

---

[1] McCurdy, *Divorce—A Suggested Approach with Particular Reference to Dissolution for Living*

Wisconsin enacted a similar provision in 1866, and Rhode Island followed in 1893 with a ten-year separation provision.[2]

The omnibus clause was a general catchall clause in some divorce statutes which allowed the courts wide discretion in granting divorces. For example, Washington's statute for many years provided that a divorce could be granted "at the court's discretion."[3] A Connecticut statute, which was repealed in 1878, authorized divorce for "Any such misconduct as permanently destroys the happiness of the petitioner and defeats the purpose of the marriage relationship."[4]

The Virgin Islands promulgated an incompatibility ground for divorce in 1917. New Mexico added incompatibility to its statute in 1933, followed by the then United States Territory of Alaska in 1935, and Oklahoma in 1953.[5]

Despite the existence of these no-fault divorce grounds, the fault system was firmly entrenched in the public policy of America. Divorce was considered evil. Whenever a state or territory with liberal divorce grounds or residence requirements emerged as a divorce haven, such as Pennsylvania in 1840,

---

*Separate and Apart,* 9 Vand L Rev 685, 701 (1956) (citing Kentucky Laws of 1850, ch 498, 55).

[2] 2 C. Vernier, American Family Laws 70 (1931). This author noted that at the time of publication, seven states had living apart statutes: Kentucky, 5 years; Louisiana, 7 years; North Carolina, 5 years; Rhode Island, 10 years; Texas, 10 years; and Washington, 5 years. J. Madden, Handbook of the Law of Persons and Domestic Relations 291-92 (1931):

> In several states either party may obtain a divorce where they have voluntarily lived entirely separate for a certain length of time; and in some states a divorce may be granted when either party has separated from the other without his or her consent, and joined with a religious sect or society that professes to believe the marriage relation void or unlawful, and refused to cohabit with the other.

[3] M. Ploscowe, H. Foster, & D. Freed, Family Law, Cases and Materials 349 (2d ed 1972).

[4] *Id.*

[5] *See* Wadlington, *Divorce Without Fault Without Perjury,* 52 Va L Rev 32, 45, n 47-52 (1966). The incompatibility ground is discussed further in **§2.13.** It is interesting to read what Professor Madden had to say about the incompatibility ground in 1931, in J. Madden, *supra* note 2, at 65-66:

> Finally, the lay reader should note that, despite any impression to the contrary which he may have received from the readings of novels and newspapers, no statute now existing names incompatibility of temper as a cause for absolute divorce. Many, viewing divorce simply as a sociological problem, would answer that this should be done, provided incompatibility is so defined as to confine it to the situation where the parties find themselves unable to live together happily after a bona fide effort extending over a reasonable time. Seven states do this in effect by providing for a divorce where the parties live apart even voluntarily for a fixed period. However, divorce statutes are not a product of logic alone. They are a resultant of mixed elements. Religion, sentiment, logic and historical accident, all have been combined to form an inharmonious and incongruous legislative product.

Indiana in the 1850s, and Illinois in 1868, the protectors of public policy would pounce on the presiding legislature.[6]

With time, lawyers, litigants, sociologists, and governing authorities grew increasingly dissatisfied with the fault-based divorce system. Investigations, studies, and reports were conducted and published, most of which condemned fault divorce.

In 1966 the Archbishop of Canterbury's group released a study which was instituted by the Archbishop "in the hope of discovering whether a new kind of law of divorce might be devised such as would be free from the most unsatisfactory features of the present law and yet would not weaken the status of marriage in the community."[7] The study recommended that breakdown be the sole ground for divorce.

Meanwhile, in California, the Governor's Commission issued its report in 1966, which closely paralleled the Archbishop's report and recommended that the irremediable breakdown of the marriage and the insanity ground be the sole grounds for divorce for that state.

In 1969, England adopted the irretrievable breakdown ground for divorce. However, the breakdown could only be proven with evidence of the old fault grounds such as adultery and desertion. In that same year, California passed its no-fault law, as recommended by the Governor's Commission.[8] Iowa followed suit in 1970.

In August of 1970, the Uniform Marriage and Divorce Act was proposed by the National Conference of Commissioners on Uniform State Laws.[9] Its sole ground for divorce was the irretrievable breakdown of marriage. The American Bar Association approved the Act and recommended it for passage by the states on February 4, 1974.

In 1985, South Dakota became the final state in the country to enact a

---

[6] N. Blake, The Road to Reno 116 (1962). At 152, the author noted:

> The earlier divorce colonies had lasted for only brief periods of time. When local peculiarities in the law had induced eastern divorce seekers to establish residences in places like Indiana, North and South Dakota, and Utah, the result in each case had been to attract such unfavorable publicity that the conservatives mobilized their forces and obtained a change in the laws. The first state in which this familiar pattern of developments broke down was the state of Nevada.

[7] Putting Asunder: A Divorce Law for Contemporary Society, The Report of a Group Appointed by the Archbishop of Canterbury ¶45, at vii (Jan 1964).

[8] See the following articles under the heading of the Family Law Act of 1969, Divorce, California Style: Brody, *California's Divorce Reform: Its Sociological Implications,* 1 Pac LJ 233 (1970); Johnson, *The Family Law Act: A Guide to the Practitioner,* 1 Pac LJ 147 (1970); Krom, *California's Divorce Law Reform An Historical Analysis,* 1 Pac LJ 156 (1970); Walker, *Disarming the Litigious Man—A Glance at Fault and California's New Divorce Legislation,* 1 Pac LJ 182 (1970).

[9] *See* R. Levy, Uniform Marriage and Divorce Legislation: A Preliminary Analysis, (1970), which recommended, inter alia, at 7: "Of all the currently feasible alternative approaches to the grounds for divorce, the "breakdown of marriage" notion has the fewest drawbacks, and the risks the approach entails can be minimized by adding specific legislative provisions directed at those risks." See also **app 2-1.**

no-fault ground for divorce, so that all states had either no-fault grounds exclusively or a combination of fault and no-fault grounds.[10] The various grounds available in each jurisdiction will be covered in the following sections.[11]

## §2.02 —Failures of the Fault System

The rise of no-fault divorce is the story of statutory law playing "catch-up" with changing social practices. It is the tale of a rapid evolution of public policy. The no-fault movement in divorce law is a culmination of a series of changes in family law. The repercussions of the trend will be evaluated for years to come. As a result of the no-fault trend, the character of a divorce action, or dissolution as it is now more frequently called, has shifted from a guilt-oriented trauma to a financial drama.

The no-fault divorce trend emerged because the fault system of divorce was not working in many respects. Ideally, the fault system was supposed to regularize the procedure for obtaining a divorce through the codification of socially approved practices.[12] It was devised to provide a remedy where reconciliation was impossible and it was presumed to protect children.[13] Divorce law in general, and the fault system in particular, was believed to provide adequate safeguards for dividing property and for redefining the status of the parties and their children, especially as to their rights of support, inheritance, and remarriage.[14] Finally, the fault system of divorce was supposed to reduce the number of divorces or prevent divorces altogether.[15]

For many years, in the United States, public policy supported the fault system of divorce. The preservation of the family was and still is an all-important goal, and the fault system was considered a crucial enforcement mechanism in the preservation process. Societally, divorce was considered an evil and the divorce grounds took on a moral and ethical quality which existed "quite independently of their practical necessity."[16] Divorce carried the danger of job loss, social ostracism, and reputational damage. The fault system's failure to successfully perform its functions and fulfill its goals became increasingly obvious.

Procedure was regularized only within each jurisdiction. Grounds, residency requirements, and judicial attitudes differed in each state. For those who could afford to travel to a state with short residency requirements and liberal grounds

---

[10] Freed & Walker, *Family Law in the Fifty States: An Overview*, 18 Fam LQ 369, 381-82 (1985).

[11] *See* **§§2.06-2.15.**

[12] Lichtenberger, *Divorce Legislation*, in Selected Essays on Family Law 862, 862 (1950).

[13] Note, *Florida's No-Fault Divorce: Is It Really No-Fault?*, 4 Fla St UL Rev 504 (1976).

[14] Lichtenberger, *supra* note 12, at 863.

[15] *Id.*

[16] Walker, *Disarming the Litigious Man—A Glance at Fault and California's New Divorce Legislation*, 1 Pac LJ 182, 184 (1970).

and establish a residence, migratory divorce was an option for consideration.[17]

The goal of amicable dissolution was not in the least aided by the adversary system's search for truth to determine the innocent and the guilty spouse. In many cases, both parties had the same interest—to end the marriage. When a divorce was contested, the necessity of placing blame buttressed the vindictiveness of the testimony and made the truth harder to determine.

The fault system provided no mechanism for legitimate escape from marriage when both parties were at fault, or, paradoxically, when neither party was at fault.

The fault divorce in an adversarial context probably created the greatest abuses of the legal system. The vast majority of divorces based on fault grounds were uncontested.[18] This, in itself, diminished the state's role as third party to the marriage status.

In addition, contested divorces were frequently characterized by fraud, collusion, and perjury.[19] Migratory divorces, as previously mentioned, involved lying under oath or establishing a temporary domicile solely for divorce purposes. Litigants sometimes staged an event like an episode of adultery for the purpose of creating a fault ground.[20]

---

[17] Professor Rheinstein has noted, in Rheinstein, *The Law of Divorce and the Problem of Marriage Stability,* 9 Vand L Rev 633, 641 (1956): that

> In the field of divorce it can be said with equal certainty that whenever it is possible for divorce seekers to obtain divorces with some difficulty in one place and with greater ease or speed in another, cases tend to accumulate in the place of easy, and to dry up in the place of hard divorce.

[18] See Foster, *Common Law Divorce,* 46 Minn L Rev 43, 55-56 n 35 (1961), where the writer declares that "ninety odd per cent of American divorces are uncontested," noting that his figure "is an informed guess based upon experience and research but there are no statistics available to confirm or refute this estimate." See also Foster, *Current Trends in Divorce Law,* 1 Fam LQ 21, 32 (1967), where Foster quotes from the Report of the Law Commission of England: The Law Commission, Reform of the Grounds of Divorce, The Field of Choice (Nov 1966) which stated that "[s]ome 93 per cent of divorce cases are undefended, the average case takes ten minutes to try."

*See also* R. Levy, Uniform Marriage and Divorce Legislation: A Preliminary Analysis 43 (1970). This study notes some sources of objections to the matrimonial offense system, including the "increasing publicity given to the fact that approximately 90% of divorce actions are uncontested and that many of the divorces granted could not rationally be defended under the matrimonial offense theory if they were carefully examined."

[19] See Wadlington, *Divorce Without Fault Without Perjury,* 52 Va L Rev 32, 32 (1966), where the author notes that the

> imbalance between social and legal development has led in turn to certain patterns of widespread social conduct which threaten the integrity of our matrimonial courts and force many a person into antisocial behavior ranging from perjury to mock or actual adultery in order to achieve what may be a desirable social goal: divorce.

[20] *Id* 33-34, where it is noted:

> [T]he same result can often be achieved with less theatrics and more outright lying. Ordinarily this will consist of false allegations and testimony by one spouse as to nonexistent cruel acts or vicious attacks by the other. The alleged attacker

Because lawyers and judges were at times aware of the fraud, perjury, and collusion,[21] divorce procedure became subject to disrespect and disrepute and made the legal system subject to criticism.[22]

Thus, the fault system failed in several respects. In addition, the fault system had not succeeded in discouraging divorce. Divorce did not disappear. Instead, the movement toward no-fault divorce surfaced in the legal system.

## §2.03 —Societal Changes

Underlying the movement towards no-fault divorce were several changes in the makeup and attitudes of society. The no-fault trend surfaced in the 1960s as an attack on the failures of the fault system,[23] and developed out of the prevailing thought of the time.

One of the initial developments in the no-fault movement was the accusation by social scientists that the divorce laws were predicated upon inaccurate assumptions. Two of those assumptions were that strict divorce laws prevented

---

> will remain mute by prearrangement, realizing that if he were to repudiate the testimony he would end up remaining married with no avenue to dissolution.

[21] *Id* 33 n 2. See also Note, *supra* note 13, at 506-07, where it is stated:

> One widely recognized problem is the encouragement of perjury by the parties caused by the limitation of the grounds for divorce to unilateral acts of adultery. The spouse may fabricate an instance of adultery or physical abuse. While collusion between husband and wife is generally a defense to a divorce proceeding under a fault statute, it is practically impossible to prove unless one of the parties vacillates about wanting the divorce. As a practical matter, the judges and attorneys responsible for administering the system are parties to this deceit; they are generally aware of the prevalence of perjury, yet do little more than wink at its existence. This fact alone suggests that the fault system has failed. The willingness of officers of the court to countenance this hypocrisy cannot but breed disrespect for the law and the courts. [Footnotes omitted.]

In Putting Asunder: A Divorce Law for Contemporary Society, The Report of a Group Appointed by the Archbishop of Canterbury ¶41 (Jan 1964), it is stated that:

> The result is that solicitors become only too familiar with the situation in which one or the other of the parties to a marriage that has grown intolerable to both comes to ask into what category of matrimonial offense their case be fitted. Sometimes, if those concerned are not too scrupulous, one will be contrived: in either event a nonsense is made of the law.

[22] See Tenney, Jr, *Divorce Without Fault: The Next Step,* 46 Neb L Rev 24, 33 (1967), where the author summarized some of the prevailing criticisms of the day:

> Divorce law today has been labelled a "mockery" tending to "demean and abase human relations." Specific grounds for divorce are seen as "artificial," "unrealistic," and never really "quite right"; facts alleged in support of them tend often to be "trivial or fictitious." As a result of this unreality in divorce ground, the divorce process, while remaining adversary in theory and in form, devolves into a "sham battle," a "silly comic melodrama" which, because of its emphasis on technicalities dealing with effects rather than causes, breeds the "suppression of truth."

[23] *See* **§2.02.**

divorce and that liberalizing those laws would threaten marital stability. As early as 1937, one of these assumptions was being attacked by one family law authority who stated:

> An often repeated assertion is to the effect that divorce breaks up the family and robs the children of a home. The fallacy of this assumption ought to be perceived at a glance. Divorce, as we have seen, does not break up the family. The family is already broken up.[24]

Twenty years later, similar criticisms were being offered at the beginning of the no-fault trend:

> [T]he view that "divorce breeds divorce" appears to be held by a great many people. What is meant by this proposition is apparently that divorce and factual marriage breakup are identical, and that the occurrence of factual marriage breakup is furthered by the easy availability of divorce.[25]

It was emphasized that the strict divorce laws were not preventing divorce.[26] The strict laws were only making it difficult for determined spouses to obtain divorces, with disastrous results. The legitimacy of new unions formed by parties who could not remarry was prevented; desertion was indirectly encouraged; and litigants were inspired to create evidence tailored to fault grounds.

Not only were the assumptions underlying the fault divorce system being challenged, but the institution of marriage was undergoing a transformation which increased the distance between law and social reality. An impetus to this transformation was the women's movement. The role of women in society and in marriage was changing. Women joined the work force in greater numbers. Financial dependence on their husbands began to decrease, as did their time spent at home. Both the single woman status and the divorced woman status became more socially acceptable.

The function of the family and of marriage changed as schools, public entertainment, the workplace, shopping malls, and television absorbed many of the educational, consumer-oriented, and recreational functions previously performed by the family. Marriage did, "of course, [retain] that function which may be called the basic one, that of providing the cradle and the home for the newly born members of society."[27]

---

[24] Bradway, *The Myth of the Innocent Spouse,* 11 Tul L Rev 377, 382 (1937). This article is generally referred to as one of the first important writings on the failures of the fault-based system of divorce.

[25] Rheinstein, *The Law of Divorce and the Problem of Marriage Stability,* 9 Vand L Rev 633, 658-59 (1956).

[26] *Id* 654.

[27] Id 655. *See* S. Green & J. Long, Marriage and Family Law Agreements chap 1 (Shepard's/McGraw-Hill 1984).

The expectations and emphasis within the marital institution also changed, as one family law authority noted:

> On the one hand, today's emphasis is upon the privileges, rights, and satisfactions of marriage, rather than upon the duty, responsibility, and stoical acceptance of the worse with the better. This leads to a sentimental and romantic over-emphasis upon physical love which, as often as not, culminates in disillusionment, frustration, or malcontent when the honeymoon comes to an end. . . . If the pursuit of marital happiness is successful, the result is a full partnership in every sense of the term and a sharing on all levels of existence. Today we expect too much of marriage, but when those expectations are gratified, excellence has been achieved.[28]

Other notions have influenced the movement toward no-fault divorce laws. One idea is that marriage—and more importantly for the purposes of this chapter, remarriage—is a basic fundamental right which should not be denied by the unavailability of divorce.[29] Another notion tied to the increasing societal support of individual rights is that "[n]o person in our age should be chained to another in an intolerable marriage."[30]

Finally, societal attitudes toward the institution of divorce shifted. These new attitudes provided yet another argument in favor of the no-fault trend, as noted by one authority:

> Attitudes toward divorce have changed sharply in this country during the past half century. No longer is the divorcee an object of widespread social stigma, and divorce itself has assumed the role of a necessary and desirable social institution in the minds of a substantial number of our population. Unfortunately, this change in social views has not been reflected adequately in our divorce laws, which too often still mirror the idea from a much earlier day that if a marriage went "on the rocks" it must have been because of the sins of one or both spouses.[31]

## §2.04 —Prereform Changes in Law

The pressure for an easier divorce system prompted some changes within the fault system prior to statutory elimination of fault. Courts liberally interpreted and legislatures revised some grounds and defenses to compensate for the fault divorce laws then on the books. However, the mere existence of

---

[28] Foster, *Common Law Divorce,* 46 Minn L Rev 43, 49 (1961).

[29] Note, *Are Fault Requirements in Divorce Actions Unconstitutional?,* 16 J Fam L 265 (1977-78).

[30] Bodenheimer, *Reflections On the Future of Grounds for Divorce,* 8 J Fam L 179, 192 (1968).

[31] Wadlington, *Divorce Without Fault Without Perjury,* 52 Va L Rev 32, 32 (1966).

such liberal grounds and doctrines highlighted the inconsistencies and inadequacies of the fault divorce laws and further fueled the criticisms of the system.

Three significant examples of this no-fault liberalization are the rise of the insanity ground; the increased popularity of the cruelty and mental cruelty grounds; and the development of the doctrine of comparative rectitude.[32]

The insanity ground for divorce has existed in the United States since 1886.[33] It generated controversy when adopted, especially because it was inconsistent with fault divorce grounds. The insanity ground provided an escape from marriage when one spouse had been declared incurably insane for a period of time. Frequently, a period of institutional confinement was required as a prerequisite to divorce. In other words, the insanity ground allowed for a divorce when the marriage relationship was destroyed, not by the fault of one spouse, but by the condition of one spouse. Thus, insanity was, in effect, a no-fault divorce ground long before the no-fault divorce trend.

The cruelty ground became the most commonly used divorce ground within the fault system.[34] The reason for its popularity was that some courts accepted minimal evidence of cruelty as a sufficient showing for an absolute divorce. Furthermore, many courts and legislatures permitted divorces based on a mental cruelty ground. Proof of mental cruelty usually required a showing of some ill-health or physical manifestation of the cruelty. However, some courts granted absolute divorces on the basis of scanty evidence.

It became common knowledge that in many states the cruelty and mental cruelty grounds were catch all divorce grounds used to dissolve marriages.[35] These popular marital escape hatches further emphasized the need for change and reform.

The defense of recrimination, which provided that if both parties were guilty of marital misconduct, neither could obtain the divorce, has been one of the most criticized aspects of the fault-based divorce system.[36] The inherent unfairness created by the application of the defense became a rallying point for proponents of no-fault divorce. In some jurisdictions, courts attempted to mitigate the harsh results of the recrimination defense by weighing the marital offenses of each party to see if one spouse deserved divorce more than the other.

The doctrine of comparative rectitude, as it was called, was used in some jurisdictions to justify granting a divorce to the party least at fault, or in other jurisdictions, to the parties equally at fault.[37]

---

[32] *See* **§§1.12, 1.16, & 1.24.**

[33] 2 C. Vernier, American Family Laws 59-60 (1931); *see also* **§1.16.**

[34] *See* **§1.12.**

[35] *See* M. Rheinstein, Marriage Stability, Divorce and the Law 103 (1972).

[36] *See* **§1.24.**

[37] Wadlington, *Divorce Without Fault Without Perjury*, 52 Va L Rev 32, 41 (1966).

In *DeBurgh v DeBurgh*,[38] a leading case on the doctrine of comparative rectitude, the Supreme Court of California (Traynor, J.) held that a trial judge had the "duty to determine whether or not the fault of the plaintiff in a divorce action is to be regarded as 'in bar' of the plaintiff's cause of divorce based upon the fault of the defendant."[39] Major considerations governing the court's decision were to include: the prospect of reconciliation; the effect of marital conflict upon the parties; their children, and the community; and comparative guilt. If the plaintiff's marital wrongs were "in bar" of the cause of action against the defendant, a material issue to be decided upon the facts and circumstances of each case, only then could the defense of recrimination be invoked.

The language of the opinion, written in 1952, is indicative of the growing anti-fault sentiment in the legal profession. Justice Traynor noted:

> The rising divorce rate in the United States has compelled a growing recognition of marriage failure as a social problem and correspondingly less preoccupation with technical marital fault. . . . Still more striking in recognition of this trend has been the enactment of legislation in many states authorizing divorce when the spouses have lived apart for a required number of years. Marriage failure, rather than the fault of the parties, is the basis upon which such divorces are granted. [Citation omitted.] . . .
>
> It would be forward indeed for the court, when it is called upon to evaluate an alleged recriminatory defense, to ignore the growing awareness that a marriage in name only is not a marriage in any real sense.[40]

## §2.05 —Theories of Reform

There came to be general agreement in the legal profession that no-fault divorce reform was a desirable goal. It even finally appeared to be politically feasible for legislatures to enact no-fault divorce laws.[41] The next step in the reform movement was for legislatures and citizens to choose (or not to choose) a no-fault divorce law scheme which best represented their public policy preferences.

Three distinguishable theories emerged, although their premises and designs frequently overlapped. These were the therapeutic or conciliatory approach, the fault elimination theory, and a bandaid "combination" approach.

---

[38] 39 Cal 2d 858, 250 P2d 598 (1952).

[39] *Id* at 871, 250 P2d at 605.

[40] *Id* at 867-68, 250 P2d at 603 (citations omitted).

[41] See R. Levy, Uniform Marriage and Divorce Legislation: A Preliminary Analysis 11 (1970), where the author noted that "It seems clear, then, that the need for reform is urgent and the legislatures and the public may be willing to accept real reform."

The therapeutic or conciliatory approach was based on the premise that a divorce action was a sign of the deterioration of an entire family. It was thought that this family should be assisted by counseling and conciliation services to help cure and prevent the development of additional costly social evils such as desertion, mental and physical health problems, juvenile delinquency, and the continued rise of the divorce rate.[42] Any divorce should be deferred until after all possibility of reconciliation has disappeared.[43]

This approach was actualized in some states by the creation of "family courts," and in other states by the addition of counseling or conciliation services to the divorce courts.[44] Ideally, the family court would have jurisdiction over all family problems, employ professionals who could assist in the legal, mental, emotional and criminal aspects of family difficulties, and be nonpunitive and oriented to the family's best interests.[45]

The conciliatory approach provided that a couple undergo counseling, either voluntary or mandatory, after a petition for divorce had been filed. The conciliatory system and the family court system required that the court determine the "true" cause of divorce based largely on counseling, psychological, or psychiatric reports. The rule was that no divorce could be granted "unless and until the court has been satisfied that a cure is hopeless at the outset or that the continuation of a cure would be futile."[46]

The criticisms of these approaches have centered around the argument that if a couple had come as far as filing for a divorce, postfiling counseling would not fix what was most likely already a broken marriage. There were concerns that not only would compulsory treatment become an empty formality that possibly infringed on privacy rights, but that whether the counseling was compulsory or not, this system would eventually deteriorate to divorce by consent. Other critics said the migratory divorce would persist, the system

---

[42] *See* Chute, *Divorce and The Family Court,* 18 Law & Contemp Probs 49, 49 (1953).

[43] Lichtenberger, *Divorce Legislation,* in Selected Essays on Family Law 862, 870 (1950).

[44] *See* Foster, *Conciliation and Counseling in the Courts in Family Law Cases,* 4 NYUL Rev 353 (1966).

[45] *See generally* Alexander, *The Follies of Divorce—A Therapeutic Approach to the Problem,* 1949 U Ill LF 695; Alexander, *The Family Court—An Obstacle Race?,* 19 U Pitt L Rev 602 (1958). Foster, *supra* note 44, at 354. See also Chute, *supra* note 42 at 50, where the author writes:

> To understand [the causes of divorce], to adjust them, and to prevent divorce whenever it is possible and socially desirable, requires a court equipped with a specially selected judge and referees, qualified by training, experience, and personality to deal with family problems, and even more important, a court furnished with trained family counselors, social investigators, and other specialized staff. Every such court should have a counseling bureau to assist the many who will seek voluntary advice and assistance before applying for divorce. Here is where the best preventative work can be done.

[46] Rheinstein, *The Law of Divorce and the Problem of Marriage Stability,* 9 Vand L Rev 633, 638 (1956).

would be expensive, and that the viability of such services in urban areas as compared to smaller communities would be questionable.[47]

The aim of the fault elimination theory was to abolish all fault grounds and replace them with no-fault grounds such as living separate and apart for a period of years, incompatibility, registration without delay, or some form of marital breakdown.[48]

The drafters of the Uniform Marriage and Divorce Act (UMDA) followed the fault elimination theory, stating that "we should begin with the premise that real reform can be accomplished only if all grounds based on the matrimonial offense are abolished.[49] The UMDA adopted the irretrievable breakdown ground, where "[t]he legal assignment of blame is . . . replaced by a search for the reality of the marital situation: whether the marriage has ended in fact.[50]

Perhaps the most common method of implementing a no-fault scheme in the various jurisdictions was the addition of a no-fault ground to the existing fault grounds. It has been noted that this method would probably be "the least disruptive way of introducing a non-fault ground."[51] There existed a common fear or perception among many practitioners that women would lose bargaining leverage in support and property division negotiations if fault grounds were entirely eliminated. However, it was also thought that retention of fault grounds would mean that the traditional problems associated with the fault grounds would persist. Nevertheless, despite these fears and perceptions, state legislatures began to enact no-fault grounds.

The different grounds for no-fault divorce are discussed in the following sections.[52]

## §2.06 No-Fault Grounds in General

The studies and public policy shifts prompted state legislatures to enact no-fault laws in their jurisdictions. Although some states already had no-fault laws,[53] the "major breakthrough in divorce legislation in the United States"[54] occurred in July 1969 when California enacted a divorce law providing that a court could decree a dissolution of marriage or a legal separation on the ground

---

[47] Foster, *supra* note 44, at 377.

[48] Levy, *supra* note 41, at 48-49. *See also* **§§2.06-2.13.**

[49] Levy, *supra* note 41, at 48-49.

[50] Uniform Marriage and Divorce Act §305 comment, 9A ULA 91, 132-34 (1974). *See* **app 2-1.**

[51] Levy, *supra* note 41, at 89.

[52] *See* **§§2.06-2.15.**

[53] *See* **§2.04,** which notes that in 1931 seven states had living separate and apart statutes and that by 1953, Alaska, New Mexico, Oklahoma, and the Virgin Islands all had an incompatibility ground for divorce. See also Gallagher, *No-Fault Divorce in Delaware,* 59 ABAJ 873 (1973), which notes that Delaware enacted a three-year separation without cohabitation statute in 1957.

[54] Comment, *No-Fault Divorce: Modernization Long Overdue for New Jersey,* 2 Seton L Rev 63, 95 (1970).

of irreconcilable differences causing the irremediable breakdown of the marriage or incurable insanity.[55]

On July 1, 1970, the state of Iowa followed the new trend, enacting a divorce provision stating:

> A decree dissolving the marriage may be entered when the court is satisfied from the evidence presented that there has been a breakdown of the marriage relationship to the extent that the legitimate objects of matrimony have been destroyed and there remains no reasonable likelihood that the marriage can be preserved.[56]

Thus, as one commentator remarked in 1970, "the winds of change in this field [were] blowing strongly."[57] In August 1970, the National Conference of Commissioners on Uniform State Laws approved the first draft of the Uniform Marriage and Divorce Act (UMDA), and the American Bar Association approved the Act and recommended it for passage by the states in 1974.[58] The UMDA provides for divorce upon a finding that a marriage is irretrievably broken.

The 1970s became the decade of no-fault divorce. By 1985, all 50 states and the District of Columbia had adopted some form of no-fault divorce.[59]

The most common initial legislative attempt at divorce reform was to incorporate a no-fault ground into an existing fault framework.[60] Nineteen states and the District of Columbia have added a *living separate and apart* without cohabitation for a term of years ground to existing fault grounds.[61] Five states have added an *irretrievable breakdown* ground to fault grounds,[62] nine have added

---

[55] Cal Civ Code §4506 (Deering 1972).

[56] Iowa Code Ann §591.17 (West 1971).

[57] Peters, *Iowa Reform of Marriage Termination,* 20 Drake L Rev 211, 212 (1970).

[58] Uniform Marriage and Divorce Act, 9A ULA 91 (1979). *See* **app 2-1.**

[59] Freed & Walker, *Family Law in the Fifty States: An Overview,* 18 Fam LQ 367, 379 (1983).

[60] Comment, *supra* note 54, at 80.

[61] *See* Ark Stat Ann §34-1202 (Supp 1983); Conn Gen Stat Ann §46b-40(c)(2) (West Supp 1984); Hawaii Rev State §580-41 (1976); Idaho Code §32-610 (1983); Ill Ann Stat ch 40, §401(2) (Smith-Hurd 1980); La Rev Stat Ann §9:301 (West 1984); Md Fam Law Code Ann §7-103(3) (1984); Nev Rev Stat §125.010 (1983); NH Rev Stat Ann §458:7 (IX) (1983); NJ Stat Ann §2A:34-2(d) (West Supp 1984-85); NC Gen Stat §50-6 (1984); Ohio Rev Code Ann §3105.01(k) (Page 1980); Pa Stat Ann tit 23, §201(d) (Purdon Supp 1984-85); RI Gen Laws §15-5-3 (1981); SC Code Ann §20-3-10(5) (Law Co-op Supp 1983); Tex Fam Code Ann §3.06 (Vernon 1975); Vt Stat Ann tit 15, §551(7) (Supp 1984); Va Code §20-91(9)(a) (1983); W Va Code §48-2-4(a)(7) (Supp 1984). *See* **§§2.07-2.11.**

[62] *See* Ala Code §30-2-1(a)(9) (1983); Conn Gen Stat Ann 46b-40(c)(1) (West Supp 1984); Ga Code Ann §19-5-3(13) (1982); Ind Code Ann §31-1-11.5-3(a)(1) (West Supp 1984-85); Pa Stat Ann tit 23, §201(c) (Purdon Supp 1984-85); *see* **§3.12.**

a form of *irreconcilable differences,*[63] and five other states have included an incompatibility ground with their fault grounds.[64]

The majority of states which abolished all fault grounds and substituted a no-fault ground have enacted a form of the irretrievable breakdown ground.[65] Other states which abolished fault grounds have adopted the separate and apart ground, irreconcilable differences, or incompatibility as their only no-fault ground or as one of their no-fault grounds.[66] In addition, at least 11 states provide a conversion ground by which a decree for judicial separation or separate maintenance may be converted to a decree of dissolution of marriage after a certain time period.[67]

## §2.07 Living Separate and Apart Grounds

Nineteen states, the District of Columbia, and Puerto Rico include a living separate and apart ground in their dissolution and divorce statutes.[68] These grounds provide that married persons may obtain a dissolution of their

---

[63] *See* Idaho Code §32-616 (1983); Me Rev Stat Ann tit 19, §691(1)(H) (1981); Miss Code Ann §93-5-2 (Supp 1984); NH Rev Stat Ann §458:7a (1983); ND Cent Code §14-05-03(8) (1981); RI Gen Laws §15-5-3.1 (1981); Tenn Code Ann § 36-4-101(11) (1984); W Va Code §48-2-4(10) (Supp 1984). *See* **§2.12.** See also *Legislative Note,* 11 Fam L Rep (BNA) 1274 (1985), which reports that South Dakota enacted an "irreconcilable differences" ground in March, 1985.

[64] *See* Ala Code §30-2-1(a)(7) (1983); Alaska Stat §25.24.0505(5)(c) (1983); Kan Stat Ann §60-1601(a)(1) (1983); NM Stat Ann §40-4-1(A) (1983); Okla Stat Ann tit 12, §1271 (West 1961). *See* **§2.13.**

[65] *See* Ariz Rev Stat Ann §25-312(3) (Supp 1984-85); Colo Rev Stat §14-10-106(II) (Supp 1984); Del Code Ann tit 13, §1505 (1983); Fla Stat Ann §61.0502(1)(a) (West Supp 1984); Iowa Code Ann §598.5(7) (West 1981); Ky Rev Stat Ann §§403.140, .170 (Baldwin 1983); Mich Stat Ann §25.86 (Callaghan 1984); Minn Stat Ann §518.06 (West Supp 1984); Mo Ann Stat §452.305/320 (Vernon 1977); Mont Code Ann §40-4-104—107 (1983); Neb Rev Stat §42-353(7)—361 (1984); Wash Rev Code Ann §26.09.030 (Supp 1985); Wis Stat Ann §767-07 (West 1981).

[66] *See* Cal Civ Code §4506—07 (Deering 1984); DC Code Ann §16-904(a)(1) & (2) (1981); Hawaii Rev Stat §580-41 (1976); Nev Rev Stat §125.010(2) & (3) (1983); Or Rev Stat §107.025 (1983); Wyo Stat §20-2-104 (1977).

[67] Freed & Walker, *supra* note 54, at 318-19, where jurisdictions listed include: Alabama, District of Columbia, Hawaii, Louisiana, Maine, New York, North Carolina, North Dakota, Utah, Vermont, and Virginia. *See* **§2.15.**

[68] *See 1983 Survey of American Family Law,* 10 Fam L Rep (BNA) 3017, 3018 (Jan 17, 1984); Freed & Foster, *Family Law in the Fifty States, An Overview,* 16 Fam LQ 289, 317-18 (1983). These states are Arkansas (3 years); Connecticut (12 months or 18 months due to incompatibility); District of Columbia (6 months voluntary, 1 year nonvoluntary); Hawaii (2 years); Idaho (5 years); Illinois (6 months voluntary, 2 years nonvoluntary and the marriage has irretrievably broken down); Louisiana (1 year); Maryland (voluntary 1 year, nonvoluntary 2 years); Nevada (1 year); New Hampshire (2 years under special circumstances); New Jersey (18 months); North Carolina (1 year); Ohio (1 year); Pennsylvania (3 years and the marriage has irretrievably broken down); Rhode Island (3 years); South Carolina (1 year); Texas (3 years); Vermont (6 months); Virginia (1 year—6 months if there are no minor children); West Virginia (1 year).

marriage (or a divorce) upon proof that they have lived separate and apart without cohabitation for a specified period of time. The purpose of such provisions is to grant courts authority to terminate a marriage which has failed, whatever the cause of the breakdown, following elapse of the specified period.[69] The public policy implicit in these provisions suggests that it is in the best interest of society and the parties themselves if a marriage is dissolved where the husband and wife have lived apart for a period of time, with no intention of resuming marital relations.[70]

As in many areas of family law, the statutory language and requirements for separation grounds vary from state to state. The time periods of separation range from six months in the District of Columbia,[71] Illinois,[72] Vermont,[73] and Virginia,[74] to five years in Idaho.[75] Other states have time periods of one year, eighteen months, two years and three years.[76]

The statute may require that the separation be mutually voluntary. Others require only the separation, without any re- quirement of voluntariness. Some statutes make the dissolution of the marriage or the separation ground contingent upon other factors, such as existence of a written separation agreement,[77] the resolution of alimony and support claims,[78] or some finding of incompatibility or irretrievable breakdown, which creates a hybrid no-fault ground.[79] Some states have provided that a short separation period plus the filing of a separation agreement or other document settling claims between the

---

[69] M. Ploscowe, H. Foster, & D. Freed, Family Law, Cases and Materials 353 (2d ed 1972).

[70] 24 Am Jur 2d *Divorce & Separation* §142 (1966).

[71] DC Code Ann §16-904(1)(a) (1981).

[72] See FLR's 1983 Survey of American Family Law, 10 Fam L Rep (BNA) 3017 (Jan 17, 1984), note which discusses Senate Bill 189, Pub Act 83-954, amending the Illinois Marriage and Dissolution of Marriage Act (effective July 1, 1984), Ill Ann Stat ch 40, §401 (Smith-Hurd Supp 1985).

[73] Vt Stat Ann tit 15, §551(7) (Supp 1984).

[74] Va Code §20-91(9)(a) (1983).

[75] Idaho Code §32-610 (1983).

[76] The District of Columbia, Louisiana, Maryland, Nevada, North Carolina, Ohio, South Carolina, and West Virginia have 1-year time periods. Connecticut and New Jersey have 18-month living separate and apart time requirements. Those jurisdictions which have a 2-year period include Hawaii, Illinois, Maryland, New Hampshire, and Puerto Rico. Arkansas, Pennsylvania, Rhode Island, and Texas have 3-year statutory periods.

[77] *See, e.g.*, NY Dom Rel Law §170(6) (McKinney 1977); Va Code §20-91(9)(a) (1983).

[78] *E.g.*, NC Gen Stat §50-6 (1984).

[79] See Conn Gen Stat Ann §46-32(c) (West Supp 1984), which provides for dissolution upon the parties' separation of 18 months by reason of incompatibility with no reasonable prospect of reconciliation; Pa Stat Ann tit 23, §201(d)(1) (Purdon Supp 1984-85), which provides for divorce upon a 3-year separation and either an undenied allegation that the marriage is irretrievably broken or a finding by the court that the marriage is irretrievably broken. *See also* Illinois Marriage and Dissolution of Marriage Act (amendedeffective July 1, 1984), Ill Ann Stat ch 40, §401 (Smith-Hurd Supp 1985).

parties constitutes a *summary dissolution procedure,* which may be considered a trend in no-fault divorce.[80]

The issues associated with the separation ground include the voluntariness of the separation; the marking of the time period of separation; the statutory definition of separation; and the discretion of the court to award such a divorce decree. Also, courts in states with statutes that do not require evidence of voluntariness may nevertheless require evidence that the separation was intended to lead to termination of the marriage. Therefore, as discussed in the following sections, a truly "involuntary" separation may be subject to challenge in some jurisdictions.

## §2.08 —Voluntary Separation

Some *living separate and apart without cohabitation* statutes provide that the separation must be voluntary, usually on the part of both parties.[81] This voluntary separation ground is considered a no-fault ground because the parties agree to a separation leading to divorce and the divorce is based exclusively upon the fact of the separation, and not upon any fault.[82] However, it has been noted that the voluntary ground falls short of being truly no-fault because the voluntariness precludes a spouse who is at fault in the traditional sense from obtaining a divorce unless the innocent (or less guilty) spouse agrees.[83]

The most litigated element of this divorce ground is the voluntariness of the separation. Cases generally require that the separation be voluntary at the inception of the statutory period; that it continue throughout the statutory period; and that it be affirmatively proven in the divorce or dissolution proceedings.

Because the separation under a voluntary ground must be by mutual consent, abandonment or desertion by one spouse does not begin the running of the voluntary statutory time period.[84] If a spouse is insane at the inception of the separation, the requisite voluntariness is not present and a divorce on the voluntary separation ground may not be granted.[85] Similarly, a separation

---

[80] See 10 Fam L Rep (BNA), *supra* note 68, at 3018, which lists California, Colorado, Nevada, Oregon, and Washington as having enacted summary dissolution procedures in their divorce or dissolution statutes. See **§2.14** for a more detailed discussion of these procedures. See also **§2.17** for a discussion of the evolution of the separation grounds.

[81] Some jurisdictions which allow for separation by mutual consent include Arkansas, the District of Columbia, Louisiana, Maryland, and Rhode Island. The Louisiana statute has been interpreted as requiring the voluntariness of only one spouse.

[82] M. Ploscowe, H. Foster, & D. Freed, Family Law, Cases and Materials 354 (2d ed 1972).

[83] *Id.*

[84] *See* **§1.14.**

[85] *See, e.g.,* Adams v Adams, 402 So 2d 300 (La Ct App 1981); Crittenden v Crittenden, 210 Va 76, 168 SE2d 115 (1969); **§1.16.**

resulting from imprisonment or military service is sufficient for a voluntary separation only if there is evidence of such voluntariness.[86]

What actions constitute the necessary voluntariness depend upon the circumstances of each case and the applicable rules within each jurisdiction. Generally, voluntariness may be shown by establishing that the parties affirmatively agreed to the separation. The separation agreement is a useful tool with which to prove voluntariness.[87]

Since voluntariness is a state of mind and therefore subjective, it may be that the only evidence will be a party's assertion that the separation was voluntary on his or her part. Such an assertion by itself may be insufficient in the absence of corroborating circumstances. Because of potential problems of proof, the attorney might advise his or her client who wishes to voluntarily separate that a simple informal agreement to separate on a certain date, signed by both spouses, may be sufficient. It might also be helpful to the potential plaintiff to either assist the other spouse in moving out of the marital abode or have the other spouse help him or her to move.

In some jurisdictions, a separation which began over the objection of one spouse may later be converted into a voluntary separation by agreement of both parties.[88] In addition, a spouse's silent acquiescence to a separation, with a failure to affirmatively manifest any desire to continue the marriage or communicate any intention to reconcile, has been held to evince a voluntary separation.[89]

The existence of a prior divorce or separate maintenance action between the same parties is usually insufficient by itself to prove the voluntariness of a separation.[90] However, when coupled with additional facts which tend to show voluntariness, a prior lawsuit could influence a court's determination.[91] The

---

[86] See, e.g., Pierce v Gervais, 425 So 2d 922, (La Ct App 1983), where it was noted that the couple separated prior to the husband's departure to Vietnam.

[87] *See* S. Green & J. Long, Marriage and Family Law Agreements ch 4 (Shepard's/McGraw-Hill 1984). See also NY Dom Rel Law §170(b) (McKinney 1977) and Va Code §20-91(9)(a) (1983), both of which require that the spouses live separate and apart pursuant to a separation agreement in order to obtain a divorce.

[88] *See* Martin v Martin, 160 F2d 20 (DC Cir 1947); Wallace v Wallace, 290 Md 265, 419 A2d 232 (1981); Lukat v Lukat, 21 Md App 354, 359, 319 A2d 818, 821 (1974); Matysek v Matysek, 212 Md 44, 48, 128 A2d 627, 630 (1957).

[89] *See, e.g.*, Lee v Lee, 307 A2d 757 (DC 1973); Jacobson v Jacobson, 277 A2d 280 (DC 1971); Seabrook v Seabrook, 264 A2d 311 (DC 1970); Johnson v Johnson, 221 A2d 85 (DC 1966); Sykes v Sykes, 321 So 2d 805, 808 (La Ct App 1975). See also Matysek v Matysek, 212 Md 44, 47, 128 A2d 627, 629 (1957), where the Court of Appeals of Maryland noted previous Maryland cases which held that a spouse's acquiescence to what she could not prevent did not result in a voluntary situation.

[90] *See* Matysek v Matysek, 212 Md 44, 47, 128 A2d 627, 629 (1957); Brown v Brown, 71 Wis 2d 355, 238 NW2d 111 (1976).

[91] In Brown v Brown, 71 Wis 2d 355, 238 NW2d 111 (1976), the Supreme Court of Wisconsin held the fact that a wife had commenced a civil action for separate maintenance rather than a criminal action for nonsupport was not sufficient by itself to support a finding of consent to a separation by the wife. Yet when that fact was added

practitioner should be wary of a sworn pleading constituting an admission which could be used against the client in a later proceeding.

A statutory time period which begins by mutual agreement must maintain its voluntary nature. The Louisiana courts have held that a voluntary separation is not interrupted if one of the parties becomes insane or incompetent subsequent to the separation.[92]

The District of Columbia requires proof of the continuity of the voluntary nature of the separation as an essential element in the plaintiff's case. Thus, in *Lee v Lee*,[93] the D.C. Court of Appeals held that a wife who asked her husband to return home for the benefit of their child but not to resume their marriage did not destroy the voluntariness of the separation. The court stated that it was clear "that the appellant did not 'manifest' a desire to resume the marital relationship and thus did not exhibit the 'plain or open showing' that is necessary to change the characterization of the separation."[94]

The Court of Special Appeals of Maryland reached a different conclusion on similar facts and held that an attempted reconciliation by a wife which prompted her to move back to the marital home did interrupt the parties' voluntary separation despite the fact that they did not engage in sexual relations.[95] It has been noted, however, that courts generally do "not permit a token or purely strategic last-minute offer of reconciliation to interrupt the separation period."[96]

## §2.09 —Statutes Not Requiring Voluntariness

The majority of states which include a living separate and apart ground in their divorce or dissolution statutes do not require that the separation be voluntary.[97] Thus, under these statutes, it makes no difference whether the parties agreed to separate or whether the fault of one of the spouses may have contributed or directly led to the separation. It has been noted that the separation statutes which do not require voluntariness "most effectively

---

to the husband's testimony that the wife told him he could leave if he paid support; the fact that earlier actions for divorce were dismissed; and the fact that the parties remained separated for 12 years, the court concluded that the burden of proving a voluntary separation had been met.

[92] *See* Wadsworth v Wadsworth, 328 So 2d 719 (La Ct App 1976); Clark v Clark, 215 La 835, 41 So 2d 734 (1949).

[93] 307 A2d 757 (DC 1973).

[94] *Id* 759.

[95] Lukat v Lukat, 21 Md App 354, 319 A2d 818 (1974).

[96] M. Ploscowe, H. Foster, & D. Freed, Family Law, Cases and Materials 355 (2d ed 1972).

[97] *See* Freed & Foster, *Family Law in the Fifty States: An Overview*, 16 Fam LQ 289, 317-18 (1983). These jurisdictions are: Arkansas, Connecticut, the District of Columbia, Hawaii, Idaho, Maryland, Nevada, New Hampshire (under special circumstances), New Jersey, North Carolina, Ohio, Pennsylvania, Puerto Rico, Rhode Island, South Carolina, Texas, Vermont, Virginia, and West Virginia.

minimize the role of fault in determining whether a divorce should be granted."[98]

A principal legislative consideration associated with the enactment of the pure separation ground with no requirement of voluntariness was the duration of the period of separation. The no-fault theories maintained that the time period had to be long enough to manifest the breakdown of the marriage and allow the spouses to consider reconciliation.[99] However, it was thought that the time period should not be too long, for fear that spouses of broken marriages most likely would use other divorce grounds or avail themselves of migratory divorce.[100] The legislative trend in recent years has been to reduce the time periods of living separate and apart without cohabitation.[101]

The issues presented in divorce or dissolution actions upon a ground not requiring voluntariness usually focus on the definition of living separate and apart without cohabitation, including the related issue of constructive separation, and on calculation of the time period of separation.

While it is not necessary to show voluntariness under the divorce statutes requiring mere separation for the statutory period, it may not be correct to characterize them as *involuntary* separation statutes. Some courts require that at least one of the parties have an intention to live separate and apart or to end the matrimonial cohabitation, which must be present at the inception of the separation.[102] For example, in *Hooker v Hooker,*[103] the Supreme Court of Virginia affirmed a lower court's ruling that a civilian employee of the United States Army who was transferred to South Vietnam and remained away from his family for two years could not use Virginia's separate and apart ground because he had neither expressed an intent to separate nor taken any action from which such intent could be inferred. The court expressed concern that, without the intent requirement, other situations requiring extended absences

---

[98] M. Ploscowe, H. Foster, & D. Freed, Family Law, Cases and Materials 356 (2d ed 1972).

[99] *See* **§2.05.** See also **§2.17,** which discusses the proposal set out in Cochran, Jr, & Vitz, *Child Protective Divorce Laws: A Response to the Effects of Parental Separation on Children,* 17 Fam LQ 372 (1983), which maintains that a 1-year living separate and apart without cohabitation time period would give parents an opportunity to adjust and reconsider their decision as well as evince a public policy disapproval of divorce of spouses with children.

[100] M. Ploscowe, H. Foster, & D. Freed, *supra* note 98, at 358.

[101] See, e.g., La Rev Stat Ann §301 (West Supp 1983), which reduced the separation period from 2 years to 1 year; Md Ann Code art 16, §24 (Supp 1983), which reduced the separation period from 3 years to 2 years. A historical perspective of the evolution of the District of Columbia divorce statute shows how that separation period was continually reduced. *See* Green & Long, *The Real and Illusory Changes of the 1977 Marriage and Divorce Act,* 27 Cath UL Rev 469 (1978). See **§2.17** for a discussion of the shorter time requirement divorce grounds.

[102] *See, e.g.,* Myers v Myers, 62 NC App 291, 302 SE2d 476 (1983); Hooker v Hooker, 215 Va 415, 211 SE2d 34 (1975).

[103] 215 Va 415, 211 SE2d 34 (1975).

would rupen into "instant divorces" and preclude reconciliation attempts that might otherwise take place.

Thus, practitioners should not assume that every separation will satisfy a statutory living separate and apart ground, especially if neither party expressed an intention or engaged in conduct evincing an intention to terminate the marital relationship.[104] In New Jersey, it has been held that a spouse could not use a separation ground for divorce where the separation was caused by imprisonment or institutionalization of a spouse for mental illness, because divorce grounds covering those specific situations existed in the statutory scheme.[105] An Ohio Court of Appeals held that a guardian's petition for divorce on behalf of an incompetent ward, opposed by the ward's spouse, may not be granted under the no-fault statute without first determining if the ward is incompetent to testify and express intentions as to the divorce.[106]

## §2.10 —Constructive Living Apart and Separate

Most courts have interpreted the *living separate and apart* ground to mean that the spouses lived under "separate roofs" or in completely separate abodes, thus maintaining a physical separation; that they are not engaging in sexual relations, often euphemistically termed *cohabitation;* and that these circumstances continue uninterrupted for the statutory time period,[107]

---

[104] Green & Long, *The Real and Illusory Changes of the 1977 Marriage and Divorce Act,* 27 Cath UL Rev 469, 478-79 (1978).

[105] Morrison v Morrison, 122 NJ Super 277, 300 A2d 182 (1972). *Compare* NJ Stat Ann §2A-34-2(d) (West Supp 1984-85) *with* NJ Stat Ann §2A-34-2(f) & (g) (West Supp 1984-85).

[106] Boyd v Edwards, 4 Ohio App 3d 142, 149, 446 NE2d 1151, 1159, n 4 (1982) where the court, in disagreeing with the guardian's contention that the intention or volition of the spouse is irrelevant under the no-fault statute, stated:

> Not every physical separation is automatically grounds for dissolving a marriage. There may be special circumstances–outside one or both of the parties' control, for that matter–which explain why the parties have been living apart, and which do not warrant the conclusion that the marriage should be dissolved. . . . A current example would have been the "hostages" held in Iran, if their internment had lasted two years.

[107] See, e.g., Jackson v Jackson, 13 Md App 725, 732-33, 284 A2d 654, 658 (1971), where, in a case of first impression, requiring an interpretation of the legislative intent in the use of the statutory phrase *lived separate and apart,* the Court of Special Appeals of Maryland held:

> as a matter of law that the phrase "lived separate and apart" . . . requires that the parties live in completely separate places of abode during an entire five-year period prior to the institution of the suit. The provisions of [this] ground further expressly require as additional elements that there be no cohabitation between the parties during the five-year period and that both the separation and the absence of cohabitation continue without interruption for the five-year period.

See also Del Code Ann tit 13, §1505(e) (1981), which states:

> Bona fide efforts to achieve reconciliation prior to divorce, even those that

Several courts have addressed the issue of whether constructive living separate and apart satisfies a separation statute not requiring voluntariness. Underlying this issue is a public policy concern that the separation ground may discriminate against those couples who cannot afford to live in separate residences, especially in the cities where rents tend to be high.

The United States Court of Appeals for the District of Columbia established the prededent for that jurisdiction in 1946. The court held that a couple who lived in the same house but on different floors and did not eat together were entitled to a divorce under the separate and apart ground.[108] One influential factor was the husband's silent acquiescence to the circumstances. The court held that "[t]he essential thing is not separate roofs, but separate lives."[109] This was later enacted into the District of Columbia's divorce statute in 1977.[110]

In 1923 the Supreme Court of Rhode Island held that living in different apartments in the same building constituted living separate and apart.[111] In New Jersey, a Superior Court held that where a wife and husband lived in separate quarters in one building of a multiple-apartment complex, they did live "in different habitations" as required by the New Jersey divorce statute.[112]

Courts in other jurisdictions have maintained that living separate and apart implies more than living in separate rooms in the same house and abstaining from sexual intercourse.[113] The Supreme Court of Alabama held that the separate and apart grounds means "a complete cessation of all marital duties and relations in such a manner that those in the neighborhood may see that they are not living together."[114]

In fact, sometimes, even the maintenance of separate abodes has not been

---

include, temporarily, sleeping in the same bedroom and resumption of sexual relations, shall not interrupt any period of living separate and apart, provided that the parties have not occupied the same bedroom or had sexual relations with each other within the 30-day period immediately preceding the day the Court hears the petition for divorce.

[108] Boyce v Boyce, 153 F2d 229 (1946). *See also* Hawkins v Hawkins, 191 F2d 344 (DC Cir 1951).

[109] 153 F2d at 230.

[110] DC Code Ann §16-904(c) (1981).*See* Green & Long, *The Real and Illusory Changes of the 1977 Marriage and Divorce Act,* 27 Cath UL Rev 469, 479 (1978).

[111] Stewart v Stewart, 45 RI 375, 122 A 778 (1923).

[112] Ballard v Ballard, 124 NJ Super 462, 465, 307 A2d 637, 638 (1973), that:

In our present society where space is at a premium and high-rise living a commonplace, it is not at all unusual to have hundreds, even thousands of individuals living in one building with an identical address yet still living in separate dwellings while technically "under the same roof." Obviously it was not the legislative intent to impose a technicality to refuse a divorce when public policy is settled that dead marriages should be legally terminated. . . . "Habitation," as set forth in the statute, is intended to mean living separate and apart in one's own private abode and a single dwelling can house multiple abodes.

[113] *See, e.g.,* Rogers v Rogers, 258 Ala 477, 63 So 2d 807 (1953); Boyd v Boyd, 348 So 2d 121 (La Ct App 1971); Young v Young, 225 NC 340, 34 SE2d 154 (1945).

[114] Rogers v Rogers, 258 Ala 477, 479, 63 So 2d 807, 808 (1953).

sufficient under living separate and apart statutes. A Superior Court of New Jersey made such a finding in a case where a husband resided with his mother, sleeping and keeping his clothes there, but spent almost all his waking hours at the matrimonial abode.[115] Similarly, a Court of Appeals of Ohio held that where a husband moved out of the marital home and into a van on the same premises, and continued to care for his invalid wife, there was no living separately in a marital sense because his intention to cease the marital relation was not obvious.[116] It should be noted again that spouses must stop all cohabitation, including sexual relations, in order to invoke the living separate and apart statutes in the various jurisdictions.

## §2.11 —Filing Time and Judicial Discretion

The practitioner should note that in some jurisdictions the proper filing time for an action based on the separation ground has been a litigated issue. A Superior Court of New Jersey has interpreted that state's living separate and apart statute to mean that the 18-month period of separation need not immediately precede the filing of the complaint.[117] However, the court must be satisfied that there is no reasonable prospect of reconciliation, and that "the period of separation and the irreconcilability must have a nexus; the latter must flow from the former."[118]

The Maryland courts have held that the period of separation or noncohabitation must have elapsed prior to the filing of the bill.[119] A Court of Civil Appeals of Texas has held that a husband was entitled to a divorce where the parties had been living apart without cohabitation for at least three years prior to the time of trial even though they had not been living apart for three years prior to the filing of the petition pleading separation without cohabitation as the ground for divorce.[120] These cases usually turn on whether the statute includes language specifying that the separation must have run prior to the filing of the divorce or dissolution action.

A final issue associated with the living separate and apart without cohabita-

---

[115] Ellam v Ellam, 132 NJ Super 358, 333 A2d 577 (1975).

[116] Bennington v Bennington, 56 Ohio App 2d 201, 381 NE2d 1355 (1978). See also Jackson v Jackson, 13 Md App 725, 284 A2d 654 (1971), where the Court of Special Appeals of Maryland held that a couple did not live separate and apart pursuant to the Maryland statute where the husband stayed part—time with his critically injured wife in her mother's home. The facts showed that the husband slept in the basement during these times and the wife slept upstairs in a bedroom, and that the couple did not engage in sexual relations.

[117] Brittner v Brittner, 124 NJ Super 259, 306 A2d 83 (1973).

[118] *Id* at 262, 306 A2d at 85.

[119] *See* Lukat v Lukat, 21 Md App 354, 319 A2d 818 (1974); Buckheit v Buckheit, 10 Md App 526, 272 A2d 54 (1971).

[120] Teas v Teas, 469 SW2d 918 (Tex Civ App 1971).

tion ground is whether courts have discretion in granting a divorce upon proof of the separation period.

Some statutes provide that the courts have discretion to grant a divorce based upon the separation ground. For example, the Nevada statute provides that: "When the husband and wife have lived separate and apart for 1 year without cohabitation the court may, in its discretion, grant an absolute decree of divorce at the suit of either party."[121] It is generally held, however, that a court's denial of a divorce must have some basis in reason.[122]

In Idaho, where the statute states that a divorce "shall be granted on proof of the continuous living separate and apart without cohabitation"[123] for five years, the state supreme court held that a divorce must be granted where the required facts are found by the trial court, even where relief on the separation ground was not specifically requested.[124] The Supreme Court of Arkansas has similarly held that granting a divorce is mandatory under the three-year living separate and apart statute "upon proper proof, . . . upon the suit of either party, regardless of what caused the separation or who was at fault."[125]

The practitioner should examine the statute and case law in his or her jurisdiction regarding the court's discretion to grant a divorce on the separation ground.

## §2.12 Marital Breakdown Grounds

The no-fault trend embodied the notions that marriages indeed failed, and that the fault grounds of divorce, instead of being the causes of those failures, were actually the symptoms of marital breakdown.[126] Therefore, it was not surprising that many states adopted a no-fault ground based on a breakdown of the marriage relationship. The various state legislatures chose two breakdown grounds, with different statutory language and evidentiary requirements.

By 1985, 14 states had abolished all other grounds and enacted the irreconcilable differences (which have caused the irremediable breakdown of the marriage), or the irretrievable breakdown ground, while 24 states added a form of the breakdown ground to traditional fault grounds.[127] Few state

---

[121] Nev Rev Stat §125.010 (1983).

[122] Annot, 35 ALR3d 1238, 1245 (1971).

[123] Idaho Code §32-610 (1983).

[124] White v White, 94 Idaho 26, 480 P2d 872 (1971).

[125] McCormick v McCormick, 246 Ark 348, 351, 438 SW2d 23, 25 (1969).

[126] *See* **§§2.02-2.05;** M. Rheistein, Marriage Stability, Divorce, and the Law (1972); Bradway, *The Myth of the Innocent Spouse,* 11 Tul L Rev 377, 389 (1937), where the author states that "[t]he legislature has declared certain causes for divorce. The medical profession, the social workers, the psychiatrists, dealing with families, report that the legislative 'causes' of divorce are only *symptoms;* and that the real causes are such matters as unemployment, ill health, lack of self-control, jealousy, selfishness."

[127] Freed & Walker, *Family Law in the Fifty States: An Overview,* 18 Fam LQ 369, 380-81 (1985). *See also* 11 Fam L Rep (BNA) 1274 (1985). The states enacting irreconcilable

legislatures have defined *irretrievable breakdown* or *irreconcilable differences,* or provided any specific statutory guidelines or criteria for courts to use in their determination of breakdown. The Delaware statute includes the most detailed breakdown ground, providing that a marriage is irretrievably broken when characterized by a voluntary separation, a separation caused by the respondent's misconduct or mental illness, or a separation caused by incompatibility.[128]

Some statutes assume marital breakdown from the very fact of the separation of the parties.[129] Other breakdown statutes require consent of the parties. For example, the Colorado and Connecticut statutes provide that a presumption of breakdown is created, or proper evidence of a breakdown exists, if both parties stipulate that the marriage is irretrievably broken (or one party so alleges and the other does not deny it), and the parties submit an agreement as to property division, support, and custody.[130]

Still other state statutes provide that if a petition for divorce or the breakdown grounds is contested, specific statutory findings must be made before a divorce can be granted.[131] Several states require that the parties undergo some form of counseling.[132] Iowa's statute requires corroborative evidence of marital breakdown in order to prevent collusion between the parties.[133]

The determination of breakdown in most states is an important function left to the broad discretion of the court. The ambiguity of the breakdown statute

---

differences or irretrievable breakdown as the sole ground are: Arizona, California (plus mental incompetence), Colorado, Florida (plus mental incompetence), Hawaii, Iowa, Kentucky, Michigan, Minnesota, Missouri, Montana, Nebraska, Oregon, and Washington. The states which have added a breakdown ground to traditional fault grounds are Alabama, Alaska, Arkansas, Connecticut, Delaware, Georgia, Idaho, Illinois (irretrievable breakdown and 2 years living separate and apart—if both parties consent, the period becomes 6 months), Indiana, Maine, Maryland, Massachusetts (separation agreement also required), Mississippi, North Dakota, Ohio (separation agreement also required), Pennsylvania, Rhode Island, South Dakota, Tennessee, Texas, West Virginia, Wisconsin, and Wyoming.

[128] Del Code Ann tit 13, §1505 (1981).

[129] *See, e.g.,* Ill Ann Stat ch 40, §401 (Smith-Hard Supp 1985) (effective July 1984); Mass Ann Laws ch 208, §1A (Michie/ Law COOP 1981); Pa Stat Ann tit 23, §201(d)(1) (Purdon Supp 1984-85). The Uniform Marriage and Divorce Act, 9A ULA 91, 121 (1979), requires that a finding of an irretrievably broken marriage be supported by evidence that the parties have lived separate and apart for more than 180 days or that "there is serious marital discord adversely affecting the attitude of one or both of the parties toward the marriage."

[130] Colo Rev Stat §14-10-106 (Supp 1984); Conn Gen Stat Ann §46b-40 (West Supp 1984).

[131] *See, e.g.,* Ariz Rev Stat Ann §25-316 (Supp 1984-85) which states that if one party desires the allegation of an irretrievably broken marriage, the courts are to consider "all relevant factors as to the prospect of reconciliation."

[132] *E.g.,* Ariz Rev Stat Ann §25-381.09 (Supp 1984-85); Me Rev Stat Ann tit 19, §691 (1981).

[133] Iowa Code Ann §598.5 (West 1981); *In re* Marriage of Collins, 200 NW2d 886, 890 (Iowa 1972).

prompted concern that judges would either mechanically approve divorces on these grounds, or subjectively deny divorces for any reason if they happened to disapprove of divorce.[134] The courts, on the other hand, maintained that the ambiguity of the statutes evinced a legislative recognition that complex family interactions should not be constrained within strict guidelines. The flexibility of the statutes allowed the courts to give individual attention to each unique marital relationship.[135] Courts have consistently upheld the constitutionality of the breakdown statutes against attacks on the grounds of vagueness of statutory language, impairment of obligation of contract, denial of due process of law, involuntary servitude, sex discrimination, or improper delegation of legislative power.[136]

Courts have elaborated on the definition of breakdown, however. They have focused upon the ability of the parties to live together,[137] the possibility of reconciliation,[138] and the disparity of the differences between the parties.[139]

---

[134] Frank, Berman, & Mazur-Hart, *No-Fault Divorce and the Divorce Rate: the Nebraska Experience - An Interrupted Time Series Analysis and Commentary*, 58 Neb L Rev 1, 46 (1978).

[135] *Id. See, e.g.*, Riley v Riley, 271 So 2d 181, 183 (Fla Dist Ct App 1972), where the court stated:

> The Legislature has not seen fit to promulgate guidelines as to what constitutes an "irretrievably broken" marriage. It is suggested that this lack of definitive direction was deliberate and is desirable in an area as volatile as a proceeding for termination of the marital status. Consideration should be given to each case individually and predetermined policy should not be circumscribed by the appellate courts of this State.

*See also In re* Marriage of Baier, 561 P2d 20, 22 (Colo Ct App 1977); Flora v Flora, 166 Ind App 620, 337 NE2d 846, 850 (1975); Mattson v Mattson, 376 A2d 473, 475-76 (Me 1977).

[136] *See, e.g., In re* Marriage of Walton, 28 Cal App 3d 108, 104 Cal Rptr 472 (1972); *In re* Marriage of Cosgrove, 27 Cal App 3d 424, 103 Cal Rptr 733 (1972); Posada v Posada, 179 Conn 568, 427 A2d 406 (1980); Joy v Joy, 178 Conn 254, 423 A2d 895 (1979); *In re* Marriage of Franks, 189 Colo 499, 542 P2d 845 (1975); Ryan v Ryan, 277 So 2d 266 (Fla 1973); Ford v Ford, 243 Ga 763, 256 SE2d 446 (1979); Flora v Flora, 166 Ind App 620, 337 NE2d 846 (1975).

[137] *See, e.g.*, Riley v Riley, 271 So 2d 181, 184 (Fla Dist Ct App 1972) ("Before dissolution is granted, the court should be satisfied that the parties can no longer live together because their difficulties are so deep and substantial that no reasonable effort could eradicate them so as to enable the parties to live together in a normal marital relationship"); Mattson v Mattson, 376 A2d 473, 476 (Me 1977) ("Once a finding is made that there are irreconcilable differences of such a degree as to make living together intolerable in a particular case, a 'breakdown' in the marriage in legal contemplation is implicit").

[138] *See* Flora v Flora, 166 Ind App 620, 337 NE2d 846, 850 (1975) ("In every case in which irretrievable breakdown is alleged, the key issue for the court's determination is whether there exists a reasonable possibility of reconciliation and the marriage as a whole must be considered").

[139] See Mattson v Mattson, 376 A2d 473, 476 (Me 1977), where the Supreme Judicial Court of Maine noted that "[i]t seems clear that trivial or minor irreconcilable differences should not be sufficient to justify the dissolution of a marriage . . . . Such differences contemplate a greater degree of disparity between husband and wife than mere unhappiness, for which a divorce cannot be granted."

The breakdown grounds ideally require a judicial inquiry into "the state of the marriage relationship itself rather than the acts and characteristics of the parties.[140] This is a desired goal of the no-fault movement.

Nevertheless, it is possible that the breakdown grounds such as irretrievable breakdown and irreconcilable differences have in fact evolved into little more than labels indicating the wish of one or both spouses to end a marriage. It appears that divorces on such grounds are usually granted on the basis of minimal evidence rather than a detailed inquiry into the state of the marriage. However, the existence of summary dissolution grounds in several states reflects that the no-fault trend has advanced to the point where spouses may obtain the once feared "easy divorce."[141]

## §2.13 Incompatibility Grounds

The incompatibility ground was not a part of the no-fault divorce reform movement, despite some commentators' assertions to the contrary.[142] Legislatures had granted divorces on grounds which resembled incompatibility, and during the early years of this country several states had omnibus clauses in their divorce statutes which were broad enough to include incompatibility.[143]

The Virgin Islands adopted an incompatibility ground in its statute in 1921, followed by New Mexico in 1933, Alaska in 1935, Oklahoma in 1953, Nevada in 1967, Delaware in 1968, Kansas in 1969, and Alabama in 1971. Delaware has since revised its statute to provide, like Connecticut, that a decree of dissolution may be granted upon a finding of a separation caused by incompatibility.[144] Texas has a divorce ground providing for termination of a marriage "without regard to fault if the marriage has become insupportable because of discord or conflict of personalities that destroys the legitimate ends

---

[140] Frank, Berman, & Mazur-Hart, *supra* note 134, at 46. This is distinguishable from the incompatibility ground, which requires an examination of the parties' acts and characteristics. *See* **§2.13**

[141] *See* **§2.14**.

[142] *Compare* Orfield, *Divorce for Temperamental Incompatibility*, 52 Mich L Rev 659, 659 (1954), who states that "[o]ne not acquainted with American or Continental legal history might conclude that temperamental incompatibility as a ground for divorce is a novel and radical innovation," *with* Comment, *Domestic Relations: Incompatibility Divorce in Kansas—A Movement Toward No-Fault Divorce*, 14 Washburn LJ 349, 351 (1975), which notes that "[t]he modern trend is toward no-fault divorce. Incompatibility divorce is a step in this direction." (footnotes omitted); *and* M. Ploscowe, H. Foster, & D. Freed, Family Law Cases and Materials 369 (2d ed 1972), which calls incompatibility a "reform ground."

[143] C. Vernier, American Family Laws 65 (1931). See §2.01, where it is noted that an omnibus clause was a general catchall clause in some divorce statutes which allowed the courts wide discretion in granting divorces.

[144] *See* Conn Gen Stat Ann §46b-40(c)(2) (West Supp 1984); Del Code Ann tit 13, §1505(b)(4) (1981).

of the marriage relationship and prevents any reasonable expectation of reconciliation."[145]

The incompatibility ground is available in only a few jurisdictions and a large number of divorces have not been granted on that ground. It has been noted however, that the ground is heavily relied upon in those states which do recognize it.[146] The incompatibility ground is similar to the marital breakdown ground, in that both suffer from vagueness and ambiguity of terms.[147] However, the incompatibility ground focuses on the acts, characteristics, and subjective states of mind of the parties, while the marital breakdown grounds focus on the state of the relationship itself.

The topics of importance to the attorney practicing in an incompatibility jurisdiction include the definitional elements of incompatibility and the evidence necessary to prove it; the role of fault with the incompatibility ground; and the use of the defense of recrimination.

## Elements of Incompatibility

The courts generally have refused to provide an exact definition of incompatibility. Instead, incompatibility is considered on a case-by-case basis, and broad definitions have emerged in the body of incompatibility case law.

The general definition of incompatibility followed by most courts, established in the seminal decision of the Third Circuit, *Burch v Burch,*[148] has been

---

[145] Tex Fam Code Ann §3.01 (Vernon 1975). The other incompatibility statutes are Ala Code §30-2-1(a)(7) (1983); Alaska Stat §25-25-050(5)(c) (1983); Kan Stat Ann §60-1601(a)(1) (1983); Nev Rev Stat §125.010(3) (1983); NM Stat Ann §40-4-1(a) (1983); Okla Stat Ann tit 12, §1271 (West 1961); VI Code Ann tit 16, §104(8) (1964).

[146] H. Clark, The Law of Domestic Relations in the United States 349 (1968).

[147] *See* Chavez v Chavez, 39 NM 480, 487-87, 50 P2d 264, 267 (1935) (Hudspeth, J, specially concurring), which states:

> "Incompatibility" is defined by the Century Dictionary as: "The quality or condition of being incompatible; incongruity; irreconcilableness." And Webster's New International Dictionary: "Quality or state of being incompatible; inconsistency; . . . incapable of harmonious combination; incongruous; as, incompatible colors; incapable of harmonious association or acting in accord; disagreeing; as incompatible persons . . . ." Pope's Legal Definitions gives the following: "Incompatibility. The elements and qualities which may creat incompatibility between persons elude exact definition, so varied are the circumstances and so dependent is such a state of feeling upon education, habits of thought, and peculiarities of character.

[148] 195 F2d 799, 806-07 (3d Cir 1952), where Judge Maris, writing for the court, stated:

> We conclude that while incompatibility of temperament in the Virgin Islands Divorce Law does not refer to those petty quarrels and minor bickerings which are but the evidence of that frailty which all humanity is heir to, it unquestionably does refer to conflicts in personalities and dispositions so deep as to be irreconcilable and to render it impossible for the parties to continue a normal marital relationship with each other. To use the ancient Danish phrase, the disharmony of the spouses in their common life must be so deep and intense as to be irremediable. It is the legal recognition of the proposition long established in the earlier Danish law of the Islands that if the parties are so mismated that

summarized by one commentator as follows:

> First, there must be an irreconcilable conflict in personalities and dispositions. This conflict must be irremediable and must arise from deep-rooted and substantial differences. Second, the conflict must render the marriage impossible to continue. The marriage must be ended in fact; the parties, beyond reconciliation and adjustment. . . . Most courts additionally require incompatibility to be mutual and bilateral.[149]

The state of incompatibility must in fact exist, and proof of incompatibility is usually the only requirement in cases based on that ground. It has been noted that the kind of evidence which will sustain a claim of incompatibility is similar to that required for mental cruelty in less strict jurisdictions absent the necessity of showing an adverse effect upon health.[150] Particular facts or circumstances which have been considered include: general differences of interests, tasks, dispositions, morals, education, religion, intellect, emotions, attitudes and ideals; antagonistic feelings; absence of genuine love; age disparity; adultery or unfaithful conduct; financial difficulties or nonsupport; medical problems; the inability to live together or physical separation; problems with sexual relations; and verbal abuse or objectionable language.[151]

The degree of the evidence of such facts or circumstances varies with each case. It is a general rule, however, that evidence of petty quarrels or minor bickering is insufficient to constitute incompatibility. As stated by the United States Court of Appeals for the Third Circuit construing the statute of the Virgin Islands, "Combatibility,' it may be said, is not *per se* incompatibility."[152] A spouse's willingness to reconcile *may* preclude an award of divorce based upon incompatibility.[153]

---

their marriage has in fact ended as a result of their hopeless disagreement and discord the courts should be empowered to terminate it as a matter of law.

[149] Comment, *supra* note 142, at 350-51 (footnotes omitted). *See also* Del Peschio v Del Peschio, 356 F2d 402 (3d Cir 1966); Shearer v Shearer, 356 F2d 391 (3d Cir 1965), *cert denied,* 384 US 940 (1966); Phillips v Phillips, 49 Ala App 514, 274 So 2d 71, *cert denied,* 290 Ala 370, 274 So 2d 80 (1973); Bass v Bass, 437 P2d 324 (Alaska 1968); Alewine v Alewine, 3 Alaska LJ 159 (No 11 Nov 1965); LaRue v LaRue, 216 Kan 242, 531 P2d 84 (1975); Berry v Berry, 215 Kan 47, 5423 P2d 342 (1974); Lillis v Lillis, 1 Kan App 2d 164, 563 P2d 492 (1977); Poteet v Poteet, 45 NM 214, 114 P2d 91 (1941); Williams v Williams, 543 P2d 1401 (Okla), *cert denied & appeal dismissed,* 426 US 901 (1975); Waller v Waller, 439 P2d 952 (Okla 1968); Chappell v Chappell, 298 P2d 768 (Okla 1956).

[150] H. Clark, *supra* note 146, at 350.

[151] Attorneys practicing in the incompatibility states should review the case law for specific examples of conduct resulting in successful incompatibility claims. *See generally* Annot, 97 ALR3d 989, 1004-46 (1980); Comment, *supra* note 142, at 350-51.

[152] Schlesinger v Schlesinger, 399 F2d 7, 10 (3d Cir 1968).

[153] *See, e.g.,* Shearer v Shearer, 356 F2d 391 (3d Cir 1965), *cert denied,* 384 US 940 (1966); Sachs v Sachs, 155 F Supp 860 (DVI 1957), *affd on other grounds,* 265 F2d 31 (3d Cir 1959); Wright v Wright, 303 P2d 428 (Okla 1956).

Marital fault may be used as evidence of incompatibility. However, most courts in jurisdictions with this ground have held that fault is not an essential element in proving incompatibility, and, further, that fault is irrelevant to the ground.[154] In Kansas, courts will consider marital misconduct as evidence of incompatibility only if the plaintiff has engaged in misconduct in order to create the incompatibility ground.[155] In the Virgin Islands, the statute provides that a divorce may only be granted at the instance of the "injured party." Simple proof of incompatibility is sufficient to establish injury.[156]

Historically, the doctrine of recrimination has posed some problems in the incompatibility context which are no longer crucial in light of the trend toward abolishing recrimination and other divorce defenses.[157] For example, the Alaska courts have held that adultery may be pleaded as a defense to incompatibility,[158] but because incompatibility of temperament necessarily involves both parties, recrimination is not permitted as a defense.[159]

In New Mexico, after a series of cases which vacillated about whether recrimination was a proper defense in incompatibility actions, the Supreme Court of New Mexico ultimately abolished use of recrimination in divorce cases based upon the incompatibility ground.[160] Some cases have adhered to what the commentators and these authors advance as the correct view: that neither misconduct by the plaintiff nor an assessment of major blame for the marital breakdown to the defendant should be necessary to establish the incompatibility ground.[161] The court's inquiry should properly be focused on the incompati-

---

[154] Cooper v Cooper, 57 Ala App 674, 331 So 2d 689, *cert denied,* 331 So 2d 695 (Ala 1976); Berry v Berry, 215 Kan 47, 523 P2d 342 (1974); Buckner v Buckner, 95 NM 337, 622 P2d 242 (1981); Hughes v Hughes, 363 P2d 155 (Okla 1961).

[155] Comment, *supra* note 142, at 352.

[156] Burch v Burch, 195 F2d 799, 808-09 (3d Cir 1952).

[157] *See* **§§1.23-1.24; §§2.01-2.05.**

[158] Romy v Romy, 2 Alaska LJ 102 (No 7 Aug 1964).

[159] Alewine v Alewine, 3 Alaska LJ 159 (No 11 Nov 1965).

[160] In Chavez v Chavez, 39 NM 480, 50 P2d 264 (1935), a divorce action based on desertion, the Supreme Court of New Mexico held that recrimination was a proper defense in all divorce actions. In Poteet v Poteet, 45 NM 214, 114 P2d 91 (1941), the court held that it did not have to decide whether recrimination is a defense in a divorce action based solely on incompatibility, and it upheld a trial court's decision which found against the defendant on the issue of recrimination. The court abolished recrimination as an absolute defense in incompatibility cases in Pavletich v Pavletich, 50 NM 224, 174 P2d 826 (1946), reasoning that denying a divorce because of recrimination violated public policy when the parties were in fact irreconcilable.

Then, in Clark v Clark 54 NM 364, 225 P2d 147 (1950), the New Mexico court held that, while incompatibility itself might not be pleaded as a defense in an incompatibility case, courts did have the discretion to deny a divorce based upon recrimination if the plaintiff's conduct shocked the court's conscience. Later, in Garner v Garner, 80 NM 324, 512 P2d 84 (1973), the court overruled *Clark* and abolished the defense of recrimination in incompatibility actions.

[161] *See* H. Clark, *supra* note 146, at 350; M. Ploscowe, H. Foster, & D. Freed, Family Law, Cases and Materials 370 (2d ed 1972); Del Peschio v Del Peschio, 356 F2d 402 (3d Cir 1966).

bility of the parties and whether the marriage can be saved, and not on the fault of either or both parties.

## §2.14 Conversion Grounds

At least 10 states and the District of Columbia statutorily provide that a legal separation, a divorce from bed and board, or a decree of separate maintenance may be converted into an absolute divorce.[162] Conversion usually is granted after a period of living separate and apart without cohabitation. However, the statutes' requirements vary.

It is questionable whether these conversion grounds are properly categorized as no-fault. Most state statutes provide that a legal separation, limited divorce, or decree for separate maintenance may be granted upon some showing of fault of a spouse. However, almost all of the conversion provisions allow either party to apply for the conversion, thus eliminating any fault at that stage of the proceeding.[163] In effect, these grounds may simply provide for a two-step divorce procedure which is useful for clients in some situations. Some examples of these provisions follow.

The Alabama statute provides that a court can grant an absolute divorce in favor of either party when a final judgment of divorce board or of separate maintenance based upon cruelty or any cause justifying an absolute divorce has been in force and effect for more than two years.[164] The Connecticut dissolution statute provides that either party may petition the court for a decree dissolving the marriage at any time after the entry of a decree of legal separation.[165] The Connecticut courts have ruled that this provision does not involve a determination of any ground for dissolution,[166] was intended to supplement the existing dissolution grounds,[167] and is a discretionary remedy.[168]

---

[162] These jurisdictions are Alabama, Connecticut, Hawaii, Louisiana, New York, North Dakota, Tennessee, Utah, Virginia, Wisconsin, and the District of Columbia. A decree for legal separation or divorce from bed and board *(divorce a mensa et thoro)* terminates the cohabitation obligation of marriage, and does not dissolve the marriage. A decree for separate maintenance provides for a support allowance granted to one spouse while living apart from the other spouse, but does not dissolve the marriage. *See* **§3.02.**

[163] Cf DC Code Ann §16-905 (1981), which provides for the enlargement of decrees of legal separation into decrees for absolute divorce "upon application of the party to whom the decree of legal separation was granted."

[164] Ala Code §§30-2-2, 30-2-30 (1983).

[165] Conn Gen Stat Ann §46b-65(b) (West Supp 1984).

[166] Hotch v Hotch, 157 Conn 85, 249 A2d 241 (1978).

[167] Viglione v Viglione, 22 Conn Supp 65, 160 A2d 501 (Super Ct 1960); Lee v Lee, 145 Conn 355, 143 A2d 154 (1958).

[168] Marazita v Marazita, 27 Conn Supp 190, 233 A2d 145 (Super Ct 1967); Schaefer v Schaefer, 26 Conn Supp 224, 217 A2d 70 (Super Ct 1966); Viglione v Viglione, 22 Conn Supp 65, 160 A2d 501 (Super Ct 1960).

In the District of Columbia, a legal separation obtainable on the grounds of mutually voluntary living separate without cohabitation, separation without cohabitation for one year, adultery, or cruelty may be "enlarged" to an absolute divorce for the party to whom the decree was granted "if the court finds on the basis of affidavits that no reconciliation has taken place and that a separation has continued voluntarily and without interruption for a six-month period or without interruption for a period of one year."[169]

In Hawaii, where a court may decree a separation from bed and board not to exceed two years on the basis of the disruption of the marriage, the parties to such a decree may apply for a divorce if the term of separation has expired, or the separation has exceeded two years, and no reconciliation has been effected.[170]

The Louisiana statute states that either spouse may obtain a judgment of divorce if there has been no reconciliation for a period of six months or more from the date a judgment of separation from bed and board was signed.[171] The statute also clearly preserves the spouses' rights to alimony and child custody when a divorce is obtained by conversion.

In New York State, either spouse may maintain an action for divorce upon a showing that the spouses have lived separate and apart pursuant to a decree of separation for one or more years, and that the plaintiff has substantially performed all of the terms and conditions of the decree.[172] While the grounds for separation are fault-based, New York courts have held that fault may not be considered in the conversion, and that a "guilty" spouse in a separation action is not precluded from obtaining a divorce on this ground.[173] North Dakota, a separate maintenance decree may be revoked by a judge at his or her discretion and replaced by a decree of absolute divorce if the decree of separate maintenance has been in force for one year and reconciliation is improbable. The court may also render orders as to custody, property division, and support

---

169 DC Code Ann §16-905 (1981). *See also* DC Code Ann §16-904(b) (1981). It has been noted in Green & Long, *The Real and Illusory Changes of the 1977 Marriage and Divorce Act*, 27 Cath UL Rev 469, 481 (1978) that:

> This provision appears, perhaps inadvertently, to revert back to fault theories of divorce, insofar as it bars the nonmoving party from obtaining an enlargement of a legal separation and mandates that the separation shall have continued voluntarily . . . . It is expected that enlargement of legal separations may fall into disuse in view of the availability of the six-month voluntary separation and the twelve-month separation without cohabitation grounds for absolute divorce.

170 *See* Hawaii Rev Stat §§580-71, -41 (1976).

171 La Rev Stat Ann §9:302A (West Supp 1984).

172 NY Dom Rel Law §170(5) (McKinney 1977).

173 *See* Adelman v Adelman, 58 Misc 2d 803, 296 NYS2d 999 (Sup Ct 1969). The grounds for separation include cruel and inhuman treatment, abandonment, neglect and refusal of the husband to provide for the wife, adultery, and confinement to prison for three or more consecutive years. *See* NY Dom Rel Law §200 (McKinney 1977).

"as justice and the merits of the case and the circumstances of the parties shall warrant,"[174] indicating that the court may take fault into consideration.

The Tennessee Code states that a fault-based decree for a divorce from bed and board or a decree of separate maintenance may be converted to a decree for absolute divorce upon application of either party after two years without reconciliation.[175] At least one Tennessee court has held that this conversion provision in effect provides another divorce ground in that state.[176]

The Utah Code allows conversion from a decree of separate maintenance of any state to dissolution of the marriage contract when the parties have lived separate and apart for three consecutive years.[177] Virginia courts are authorized to "merge" a decree of divorce from bed and board based on fault grounds with a decree for absolute divorce upon application of either party if the parties have been living separate and apart for one year and there is no probability of reconciliation.[178] In an interesting twist, the Code provides that the injured party need not give notice of his or her application for merger unless it raises new matter. The "guilty" party, however, must give 10 days' notice. The Wisconsin Family Code states, "By stipulation of both parties, or upon motion of either party not earlier than one year after entry of a decree of legal separation, the court shall convert the decree to a decree of divorce.[179]

## §2.15 Dissolution Procedures: Simplified or Summary

A growing number of states have adopted summary or simplified procedures in their divorce or dissolution statutes. Parties who utilize these procedures may dissolve their marriages in a short period of time upon mutual consent if specific requirements are met. Usually the requirements include filing a separation agreement or affidavits by which the parties settle all custody, property division, and support claims, as well as other issues. The summary dissolution procedures have sometimes been called "paper" dissolutions.[180] These procedures may be distinguished from those under some no-fault statutes which are summary in effect due to a short waiting period between

---

[174] ND Cent Code §14-06-05 (1981).

[175] Tenn Code Ann §36-4-102(b) (1984). The grounds for divorce from bed and board include cruel and inhuman treatment as renders cohabitation unsafe and improper, indignities, abandonment, or neglect.

[176] Abney v Abney, 222 Tenn 160, 433 SW2d 847 (1968).

[177] Utah Code Ann §30-3-1(8) (1984). Utah Code Ann §30-4-1 (1984) provides that a decree of separate maintenance may be granted upon a showing of desertion, inability to support, or neglect.

[178] Va Code §20-121 (1981).

[179] Wis Stat Ann §767.09(2) (West 1981).

[180] Freed & Walker, *Family Law in the Fifty States: An Overview* 18 Fam LQ 369, 381 (1985). The jurisdictions which have enacted summary dissolution procedures include California, Colorado, Florida, Mississippi, Nevada, Ohio, Oregon, Tennessee, Virginia, and Washington.

filing and judgment.[181] The summary procedures, analogous to summary judgment, have taken different forms in the jurisdictions in which they have been adopted.

California enacted a summary dissolution procedure based upon irreconcilable differences in 1978.[182] It was available to childless couples who jointly filed a petition requesting dissolution of their marriage and attesting that specified criteria existed at a time of the filing. These criteria include: residence; short marriage (originally two years or less); limited property interests settled by an executed separation agreement; agreement that irreconcilable differences exist, that both desire a dissolution and have read the statutorily mandated dissolution brochure; and waiver of rights to spousal support, to appeal, to request findings of facts and conclusions of law, and to move for a new trial.

The California legislature designed this expedited procedure "to enable couples to obtain a divorce by filling out forms for later approval by a judge without requiring either a formal court appearance or the aid of an attorney . . . [and] to reduce congestion in the courts and make simple divorce less expensive.[183] Nevertheless, the California statute requires that the brochure, which the parties must read as part of the dissolution procedure, state that it is in the best interests of the parties to consult an attorney regarding the dissolution of their marriage.[184]

Certain criteria in the statute were found to be excessively restrictive and to fail to provide the desired judicial economy that was possible in connection with an uncontested divorce.[185] In 1980, this summary procedure was amended to extend the period of marriage duration from two to five years and raise the monetary limits placed on property interests and debts.

In 1983, two other states enacted summary dissolution procedures similar to those established in California. In 1983, the Nevada legislature approved a bill providing for summary dissolution of marriage 10 days after the filing of a joint petition setting forth specified criteria.[186] The parties must either have lived separate and apart for one year or agree that they are incompatible. The Oregon law, also effective in 1983, created summary procedures for uncontested divorces where there are no minor children; the parties have been married

---

181 *See, e.g.*, Ariz Rev Stat Ann §25-312 (Supp 1984-85); Fla Stat Ann §61.052(2)(a) (West Supp 1984); Ga Code Ann §19-5-3(13) (1982); Iowa Code Ann §598.17 (West 1981); Mass Ann Laws ch 208, §1A (Michie/Law Co-op 1981); Pa Stat Ann tit 23, §201(c) (Purdon Supp 1984-85). The summary procedure grounds may also be distinguished from New York's no-fault grounds, which provide for divorce on the parties' living separate and apart for at least one year pursuant to a filed written separation agreement or a memorandum of such agreement. *See* NY Dom Rel Law §170(6) (McKinney 1977).

182 Cal Civ Code §4450 (Deering 1984).

183 *Review of Selected 1980 California Legislation,* 10 Pac LJ 247, 443 (1978).

184 Cal Civ Code §4456(a) (Deering 1984).

185 *Review of Selected 1980 California Legislation,* 12 Pac LJ 235, 382 (1980).

186 Act of April 26, 1983, ch 175; Nev Rev Stat §§125.181-.184 (1985).

less than 10 years; neither has any interest in real property; there are no debts in excess of $15,000; the value of their personal property is less than $30,000; and the petitioner waives any rights to spousal support.[187]

Other summary procedure statutes are less detailed than the California, Nevada, and Oregon laws. In Colorado, summary dissolution by affidavit of either or both parties is permitted where the following conditions exist: there are no minor children and the wife is not pregnant, or both parties are represented by counsel and have entered into a separation agreement resolving custody and support issues; there is no genuine issue as to any material fact; and there is no marital property to be divided or the parties have entered into an agreement for the division of their marital property.[188]

Similar simplified procedures exist in Florida, Ohio, and Washington. In 1984 the Florida legislature amended Florida Rule of Civil Procedure 1.611 by adding a section entitled "Simplified Dissolution Procedure." This section permits a divorce if both parties certify under oath that there are no children of the marriage and that they have settled all property rights and joint obligations.[189] The Ohio Courts of Common Pleas may dissolve a marriage within 30 to 90 days after the filing of a petition for dissolution of marriage where both parties appear before the court and acknowledge their consensual desire for the dissolution.[190] The petition must include a separation agreement which provides for division of property and support, and, if there are minor children, for custody of the children, child support, and visitation rights. The Washington legislature enacted a law in 1983 which provides for a simplified procedure if the parties have agreed to the division of property, child custody and support, and maintenance.[191]

Mississippi and Tennessee have enacted simplified divorce procedures based upon the irreconcilable differences ground.[192] In both states, a divorce upon this ground may be granted *only* upon a joint bill of the husband and wife where they have made adequate and sufficient provision by written agreement for the custody and support of children and for the settlement of property rights between them. In Mississippi, the divorce may be granted 60 days after the filing of the petition. In Tennessee, the law distinguishes between couples with minor children, whose petition must be on file for at least 90 days before a court will hear the case, and couples without minor children, who must wait only 60 days after filing.

The Virginia Code's simplified procedure is an alternative to its nonvoluntary one-year living separate and apart ground. The statute provides: "In any

---

[187] *1983 Survey of American Family Law,* 10 Fam L Rptr (BNA) 3017, 3018 (Jan 17, 1984) [hereinafter cited as 1983 Survey].

[188] Colo Rev Stat §14-10-120.3 (Supp 1984).

[189] 1983 Survey, *supra* note 186, at 3018.

[190] Ohio Rev Code Ann §§3105.61-65 (Page 1980).

[191] 1983 Survey, *supra* note 186, at 3018.

[192] Miss Code Ann §93-5-2 (Supp 1984); Tenn Code Ann §36-801(II) (Supp 1982).

case where parties have entered into a separation agreement and there are no minor children, a divorce may be decreed on application if and when the husband and wife have lived separate and apart without cohabitation and without interruption for six months."[193]

These summary and simplified dissolution procedures appear to be an emerging trend in divorce law. Three of these "paper" divorce statutes were enacted in 1983 and one was enacted in 1984. Similar bills were considered in 1984 in the Massachusetts and Minnesota legislatures.[194] The public policy shift toward no-fault divorce and summary procedures has eroded the traditional emphasis on fault which historically continued marriages of unhappy couples.

## §2.16 The Role of the Practitioner

The wide acceptance of no-fault grounds has influenced the role of the practitioner in divorce cases. Freed, for the most part,[195] from proving the guilt or defending the innocence of a spouse, family law attorneys have shifted their attention to prompt, equitable, civil settlement of all disputes involving custody, support, and property division. Although some no-fault grounds are geared toward reducing attorney participation in divorce cases, in reality, only the nature of that participation has changed.[196] Despite the growth of "do-it-yourself" divorces and the public perception that attorneys create more problems than they solve,[197] the family law practitioner, including those who are young and inexperienced, can make an important contribution in a dissolution situation.

The dissolution of a marriage has emotional, legal, and economic consequences which should not be treated with any less formality than a business partnership dissolution. It may still be worth the cost, even where summary or

---

[193] Va Code §20-91(9)(a) (1983).

[194] *See Legislative Notes,* 10 Fam L Rptr (BNA) 1084 (Dec 6, 1984); Legislative Notes, 9 Fam L Rep (BNA) 2323 (Mar 22, 1983).

[195] In many states, fault continues to be a consideration in property division, support awards, and child custody awards. For a list of states which still consider marital fault as a factor in property distribution and support, see **§10.05**. Freed & Walker, *Family Law in the Fifty States: An Overview,* 18 Fam LQ 369, 394-95 (1985).

[196] For example, some states have enacted summary or simplified dissolution procedures, discussed in **§2.14.** It is interesting to note that, while a stated goal of the California summary dissolution procedure is to elimate the need for legal representation, see *Review of Selected 1978 California Legislation,* 10 Pac LJ 247, 443 (1978), the statutorily mandated brochure informs the parties that the retention of an attorney may be in their best interests. *See* Cal Civ Code §4456(a) (Deering 1984).

[197] See, e.g., C. Sherman, How to Do Your Own Divorce in California With the Forms You Will Need to Do It 12 (6th ed 1975), where the author, a member of the California Bar, states that "lawyers are trained as adversaries and combatants, not as counselors. It is hardly suitable that people with such an attitude toward problems should have a monopoly over all divorces."

simplified procedures will be used, for spouses to have an in-depth consultation with an experienced practitioner. It is the lawyer's duty to make the parties aware of the law, their options, alternative services, unfolding circumstances, pitfalls, and dormant situations which could erupt later on after the dissolution. Even the most sophisticated clients frequently do not know the rights and risks associated with marriage dissolution. An informed client will be in a better position to make decisions about how to proceed.

Many of the no-fault grounds, particularly the summary or simplified dissolutions, require an agreement between the parties resolving custody, support, and property issues. The competent family law practitioner can be crucial to negotiating and drafting enforceable and successful separation agreements.[198] With the significant changes in property division rules, tax laws, and child custody arrangements, the practitioner's role as drafter has become perhaps the most important and certainly the most challenging.

There exists, unfortunately, a public misconception that family law practitioners encourage litigation to further their own economic gain. However, it is these authors' observation that, generally speaking, experienced lawyers do not push their clients to litigation despite the fact that the parties' emotional postures in dissolution situations often make settlement difficult. In addition, it is very rare that a lawyer proceeds with any action without the client's approval. Most family law attorneys act responsibly and urge a negotiated resolution of problems and a dignified dissolution of marriage.

Nevertheless, sometimes it does become necessary to bring a divorce action to trial, and most no-fault actions do require an evidentiary hearing. The family law practitioner, therefore, must be familar with the procedural and evidentiary requirements for divorce or dissolution. The attorney should know the practice and policy which have evolved in his or her jurisdiction and court system regarding proof of no-fault grounds. It is desirable to know the individual views, procedure, and practice of the judge or hearing authority, who may have a unique approach to certain problems. A modern technique welcomed by some judges and practitioners is a conference call between lawyers on both sides and the judge or the judge's clerk to determine the judge's procedures as well as to resolve other issues.

When in doubt as to the evidentiary requirements in a no-fault proceeding, the family law practitioner must simply be prepared! He or she should sufficiently explore the background of the case, extensively interview and prepare the client for the hearing, and gather property documentation and certification as required by statute, such as the marriage license, voter registration, and any other evidence that goes to the matters to be proven. It is risky to proceed without this type of evidence; it is avoid a dismissal or a continuance to another date.

With proof of some no-fault grounds, the client should be asked to identify

---

[198] *See* S. Green & J. Long, Marriage and Family Law Agreements ch 4 (Shepard's/McGraw-Hill 1984).

potential corroborative witnesses. The attorney should interview these witnesses and be prepared to proffer them if necessary at the hearing. It would be imprudent to be unprepared to meet the particularized exigencies of certain courts.

## §2.17 Trends in No-Fault Divorce Law

The family law attorney must be aware that the evolution of the no-fault grounds has included distinct trends. For example, the living separate and apart ground in some states has developed from providing the dissolution only to the innocent spouse to allowing either spouse to obtain the dissolution without reference to fault.[199] Many states have shortened the term of years for which a couple must live separate and apart without cohabitation.[200] Several states have taken the additional step of including a summary dissolution procedure, by which a couple may dissolve their marriage in six months based on the filing of a joint petition, a separation agreement, or sworn affidavits which resolve all property and custody issues between the parties.[201]

The family lawyer should be aware of both the trends in divorce law and the criticisms which threaten and challenge the trends. The practitioner, through actual experience, is in a unique position to monitor the no-fault system to ensure fairness, equity, and proper adaptation of the law to changing economic and social conditions. Therefore, he or she should become informed and knowledgeable as to both trends and criticisms of divorce law.

The greatest changes occurring in family law in the 1980s do not involve the no-fault divorce grounds themselves, but the effects that the no-fault trend has had on the other aspects of divorce, particularly property division. The no-fault laws have produced a shift in emphasis from the fault aspect of divorce to the issues implicit in establishing new lives after dissolution: custody, property, and support. Thus, attorneys must endeavor to remain up-to-date on the developments in those areas.

An important study was published in 1981 by Professor Lenore J. Weitzman,

---

[199] M. Ploscowe, H. Foster, & D. Freed, Family Law, Cases and Material 355-56 (2d ed 1972), which cites Vt Stat Ann tit 15, §551(7) (1959) and Wyo Stat §20-47 (1959) as examples of the fault-based living separate and apart statutes.

[200] See, e.g., DC Code Ann §16-904 (1981), which is an amended revision of the 1965 revision which reduced the period of voluntary separation from five years to one year. *See* Green & Long, *The Real and Illusory Changes of the 1977 Marriage and Divorce Act*, 27 Cath UL Rev 469, 477 (1978). See also Bainbridge, Jr, *Legislature slowly liberalizing state divorce rules*, Baltimore Sun, May 31, 1983, at D1, col 5, which discusses the passage of Md Ann Code art 16, §25 (Supp 1983), which reduced the involuntary separation from three years to two.

[201] *See* **§2.14**.

then a sociologist at Stanford University, on the economic impact of no-fault divorce on men, women, and children.[202]

The data presented showed that most divorcing couples have a lack of substantial assets;[203] that the average alimony award is too meager to be considered bona fide means of support;[204] that the average child support award did not cover half of the cost of raising the children, thus usually placing the greater financial burden on the custodial parent;[205] and that, "for all its aims at fairness, the current laissez-faire system of divorce is taking a high economic casualty toll among women and children."[206]

While Weitzman's important conclusions and policy recommendations do not address the validity of the no-fault grounds themselves, they do focus on the repercussions of the no-fault grounds in the area of property and support. A 1983 analysis of the impact of divorce on children has, however, made proposals which challenge the wisdom of no-fault grounds which do not include a significant waiting period prior to filing for a divorce.[207]

In their article, Professor Robert F. Cochran, Jr, of Pepperdine University of Law, and Professor Paul C. Vitz, a psychologist at New York University, evaluated several studies of the effects of parental separation and divorce on children. They concluded that parental conflict leading to divorce produced substantial, negative, damaging long-term psychological effects upon children which often led to delinquency harmful to society as a whole.[208] These authors criticized the no-fault divorce system for permitting divorce on demand of either party and for influencing societal attitudes in favor of divorce, emphasizing individual parental fulfillment at the expense of children's welfare.

Contending that the law should protect the child's interest in maintaining a close relationship with both parents, Cochran and Vitz propose that one year of separation without cohabitation be the exclusive no-fault divorce ground available to married couples with children. The authors assert that the delay would give parents an opportunity to adjust and reconsider their position and also that the delay would manifest a state policy of disapproval of divorce where children are involved.[209]

---

202 Weitzman, *The Economics of Divorce: Social and Economic Consequences of Property, Alimony, and Child Support Awards*, 28 UCLA L Rev 1181 (1981). Recognizing the shift in emphasis to property and support issues, Weitzman attempted to provide in her article "more complete information to assist judges, attorneys, and divorcing couples in making economically sound decisions." *Id* 1184.

203 *Id* 1189.

204 *Id* 1225.

205 *Id* 1240.

206 *Id* 1266.

207 Cochran, Jr, & Vitz, *Child Protective Divorce Laws: A Response to the Effects of Parental Separation on Children*, 17 Fam LQ 327 (1983).

208 *Id* 342-43.

209 *Id* 342-43. In addition, Cochran and Vitz advocate laws favoring joint custody where parents request it; requiring substantial amounts of visitation in contested cases;

It is not clear that Cochran's and Vitz's proposed one-year separation ground would further the goal of protecting children and promptly resolving custody disputes. Those authors, like many other commentators, tend to denigiate spouses' attempts to help themselves and find a way to stay together. Family law practitioners know that by the time a typical client arrives for an initial interview, he or she usually has already consulted family, friends, and counselors, and frequently is in therapy.[210] Thus, Cochran's and Vitz's one-year separation ground seem to place too much significance on the waiting period, which usually will not disrupt most clients' divorce plans. In fact, instead of protecting children, the one-year waiting period may simply provide children with more time to be victims of their parents' escalating acrimony. Also, past experience has shown that increased obstacles to divorce have frequently led to migratory divorce.[211]

While Weitzman's study offers the practitioner a valuable perspective on the results of no-fault divorce, Cochran's and Vitz's article challenges the lawyer's possibly complacent acceptance of summary or simplified no-fault procedures. These are the types of studies of which the practitioner should remain especially aware.

---

establishing statutory minimum amounts of child visitation and support, and advocating the use of mediation in custody disputes. *See id* 348, 353, & 362; **§§5.01-5.13, chs 6, 7, 8 & 9.**

210 It is the ethical responsibility of the family law practitioner to ask the client, especially the client "tuned to immediacy," to investigate the possibility of reconciliation. In addition, if the client has hope of reconciliation, the responsible practitioner should strongly urge the client to make any such attempts before initiating any legal steps, which usually have a polarizing effect, tend to alienate the couple, and may make the relationship worse.

211 *See* **§§2.02, 4.19.**

## Appendix 2-1
## Uniform Marriage and Divorce Act

Relevant Sections and Comments from the Uniform Marriage and Divorce Act (UMDA), reprinted with permission from 9A ULA 96, 118-217 (1979). This Act has been printed through the permission of the National Conference of Commissioners on Uniform State Laws, and copies of the Act may be ordered from them at a cost of $2.00 at 645 North Michigan Avenue, Suite 510, Chicago, Illinois 60611, (312) 321–9710.

UNIFORM MARRIAGE AND DIVORCE ACT
1970 ACT
Amended 1971 and 1973

* * *

Part III
DISSOLUTION

301. Application of [Rules of Civil Practice] to Proceedings under this Act.
302. Dissolution of Marriage; Legal Separation.
303. Procedure; Commencement; Pleadings; Abolition of Existing Defenses.
304. Temporary Order or Temporary Injunction.
305. Irretrievable Breakdown.
306. Separation Agreement.
307. Disposition of Property.
308. Maintenance.
309. Child Support.
310. Representation of Child,
311. Payment of Maintenance or Support to Court.
312. Assignments.
313. Attorney's Fees.
314. Decree.
315. Independence of Provisions of Decree or Temporary Order.
316. Modification and Termination of Provisibns for Maintenance, Support and Property Disposition.

Part IV
CUSTODY

401. Jurisdiction; Commencement of Proceeding,
402. Best Interest of Child.
403. Temporary Orders.
404. Interviews.
405. Investigations and Reports.
406. Hearings.
407. Visitation.

408. Judicial Supervision.
409. Modification.
410. Affidavit Practice.

* * *

## Part III
## DISSOLUTION

§301. [Application of [Rules of Civil Practice] to Proceedings under this Act]

(a) The [Rules of Civil Practice] apply to all proceedings under this Act, except as otherwise provided in this Act.

(b) A proceeding for dissolution of marriage, legal separation, or declaration of invalidity of marriage shall be entitled "In re the Marriage of ________and ________." A custody or support proceeding shall be entitled "In re the (Custody) (Support) of ________."

(c) The initial pleading in all proceedings under this Act shall be denominated a petition. A responsive pleading shall be denominated a response. Other pleadings, and all pleadings in other matters under this Act, shall be denominated as provided in the [Rules of Civil Practice].

(d) In this Act, "Decree" includes "judgment."

(e) A decree of dissolution or of legal separation, if made, shall not be awarded to one of the parties, but shall provide that it affects the status previously existing between the parties in the manner decreed.

Commissioners' Note

The basic philosophy of this part of the draft is to utilize the procedural systems of the several states, so far as possible, in divorce litigation. However, in certain respects, the change from "fault" to "no-fault" basis dictates the use of terms and of procedures different from those which have become thoroughly associated with fault-orientation, in order to impress bench and bar with the break from past concepts. . . .

Subsection (b) incorporates suggestions made by several writers that substitution of a neutral case title ("In re the Marriage of ________ and ________") for the customary adversary title ("________ v. ________"), will help to reduce the hostile atmosphere of marital actions. The Act adopts this suggestion and extends it to independent custody and support proceedings. A custody or support proceeding commenced as part of a proceeding for dissolution or legal separation need not be separately entitled.

Subsection (c), like subsection (b), is intended to reduce the adversary trappings of family cases by substituting a "proceeding" for the customary "action" and denominating the pleadings "petition" and "response" rather than "complaint" and "answer. . . .

Subsection (e) emphasizes the nonadversary philosophy by providing, in accordance with the practice of some states, that decrees of dissolution or separation shall not be awarded to either party. Instead they are to specify the change in the status of the parties.

Since the Rules of Civil Practice are made applicable to proceedings under the Act, such procedural tools as discovery procedures, bills of particulars, etc., may be required in proper cases. Obviously, the nonadversary nature of the proceedings make such tools inappropriate to the issue of irretrievable breakdown and the court should not permit their use. In matters of property division, the propriety of separation or maintenance agreements, and of provision for children, these tools may be extremely useful, and are not precluded by the Act, if they are found in the state's arsenal of procedural weapons. . . .

§302. [Dissolution of Marriage; Legal Separation]

(a) The [________] court shall enter a decree of dissolution of marriage if:

(1) the court finds that one of the parties, at the time the action was commenced, was domiciled in this State, or was stationed in this State while a member of the armed services, and that the domicile or military presence has been maintained for 90 days next preceding the making of the findings;

(2) the court finds that the marriage is irretrievably broken, if the finding is supported by evidence that (i) the parties have lived separate and apart for a period of more than 180 days next preceding the commencement of the proceeding, or (ii) there is serious marital discord adversely affecting the attitude of one or both of the parties toward the marriage;

(e) the court finds that the conciliation provisions of Section 305 either do not apply or have been met;

(4) to the extent it has jurisdiction to do so, the court has considered, approved, or provided for child custody, the support of any child entitled to support, the maintenance of either spouse, and the disposition of property; or has provided for a separate, later hearing to complete these matters.

(b) If a party requests a decree of legal separation rather than a decree of dissolution of marriage, the court shall grant the decree in that form unless the other party objects. . . .

Commissioners' Comment (1973)

Subsection (a) lists the three findings that a court must make before it has jurisdiction to enter a decree of dissolution of marriage: first, it must find that one party to the marriage has established an appropriate connection with the state; second, it must find that the marriage is irretrievably broken; and finally, to the extent it has jurisdiction to do so, it must have considered and passed on the issues of custody, support, maintenance, and property disposition. If the court lacks jurisdiction to act upon any of the matters listed in subsection (a)(3), without acting upon that matter, it may enter a decree of dissolution of marriage. . . . In such a case, the court has jurisdiction only to dissolve the marriage and it may enter its decree of dissolution after making the findings set forth in subsection (a)(1) and (2).

The 90 day period of subsection (a)(1) is intended to be continuous and to apply both to domiciliaries and to members of the armed services. It may be started at any time, but it must exist at the commencement of the action and it must have been maintained for 90 days next preceding the findings by the court. . . .

Subsection (a)(2) embodies the basic shift from fault to no-fault grounds for dissolution of the marriage which is the primary object of this part of the Act. Many terms might have been used to characterize the concept. "Irretrievably broken" was chosen because this has become a term of common use in the literature of divorce reform, and so has gained a significant meaning upon which judges may rely for guidance. . . . Two guidelines are set up for evidence sufficient to support a finding that the marriage is irretrievably broken: (i) that the parties have lived separate and apart for more than 180 days next preceding the commencement of the proceeding for dissolution; (ii) that there exists "serious marital discord adversely affecting the attitude of one or both of the parties toward the marriage." These provisions satisfy the desire of those who wish to have specific guidelines to assist the court in determining what is irretrievable breakdown. At the same time, the second provision retains all the judicial discretion to weigh all the evidence bearing upon the death of the marriage which was envisioned in the original draft of this section as approved by the Conference in St. Louis in 1970. . . .

Subsection (b) means that the court may not grant a decree of legal separation over the objection of one of the parties. In cases where both parties are before the court, if one party requests a decree of legal separation and the other party requests a decree of dissolution, the court lacks jurisdiction to enter a decree of legal separation. If only one party is before the court and the court lacks personal jurisdiction over the other party, the court may enter a decree of legal separation at the petitioner's request. . . .

§303. [Procedure; Commencement; Pleadings; Abolition of Existing Defenses]

(a) All proceedings under this Act are commenced in the manner provided by the [Rules of Civil Practice].

(b) The verified petition in a proceeding for dissolution of marriage or legal separation shall allege that the marriage is irretrievably broken and shall set forth:

(1) the age, occupation, and residence of each party and his length of residence in this State;

(2) the date of the marriage and the place at which it was registered;

(3) that the jurisdictional requirements of Section 302 exist and the marriage is irretrievably broken in that either (i) the parties have lived separate and apart for a period of more than 180 days next preceding the commencement of the prbceeding or (ii) there is serious marital discord adversely affecting the attitude of one or both of the parties toward the marriage, and there is no reasonable prospect of reconciliation;

(4) the names, ages, and addresses of all living children of the marriage, and whether the wife is pregnant;

(5) any arrangements as to support, custody, and visitation of the children and maintenance of a spouse; and

(6) the relief sought.

(c) Either or both parties to the marriage may initiate the proceeding.

(d) If a proceeding is commenced by one of the parties, the other party must be served in the manner provided by the [Rules of Civil Practice] and may within [30] days after the date of service file a verified response.

(e) Previously existing defenses to divorce and legal separation, including but not limited to condonation, connivance, collusion, recrimination, insanity, and lapse of time, are abolished.

(f) The court may join additional parties proper for the exercise of its authority to implement this Act. . . .

Commissioners' Comment (1973)

Subsection (a) provides for commencement of proceedings in whatever way is required by the local practice rules or act.

Subsection (b) lists the necessary allegations of the petition. Other appropriate allegations may be included at the pleader's discretion. . . .

Subsection (c) permits joint initiation of the proceeding by both spouses, thereby shifting from the traditional doctrine of the law forbidding so-called collusive divorce. . . .

§304. [Temporary Order or Temporary Injunction]

(a) In a proceeding for dissolution of marriage or for legal separation, or in a proceeding for disposition of property or for maintenance or support following dissolution of the marriage by a court which lacked personal jurisdiction over the absent spouse, either party may move for temporary maintenance or temporary support of a child of the marriage entitled to support. The motion shall be accompanied by an affidavit setting forth the factual basis for the motion and the amounts requested.

(b) As a part of a motion for temporary maintenance or support or by independent motion accompanied by affidavit, either party may request the court to issue a temporary injunction for any of the following relief:

(1) restraining any person from transferring, encumbering, concealing, or otherwise disposing of any property except in the usual course of business or for the necessities of life, and, if so restrained, requiring him to notify the moving party of any proposed extraordinary expenditures made after the order is issued;

(2) enjoining a party from molesting or disturbing the peace of the other party or of any child;

(3) excluding a party from the family home or from the home of the other party upon a showing that physical or emotional harm would otherwise result;

(4) enjoining a party from removing a child from the jurisdiction of the court; and

(5) providing other injunctive relief proper in the circumstances.

(c) The court may issue a temporary restraining order without requiring notice to the other party only if it finds on the basis of the moving affidavit or other evidence that irreparable injury will result to the moving party if no order is issued until the time for responding has elapsed.

(d) A response may be filed within [20] days after service of notice of motion or at the time specified in the temporary restraining order.

(e) On the basis of the showing made and in conformity with Sections 308 and 309, the court may issue a temporary injunction and an order for temporary maintenance or support in amounts and on terms just and proper in the circumstance.

(f) A temporary order or temporary injunction:

(1) does not prejudice the rights of the parties or the child which are to be adjudicated at subsequent hearings in the proceeding;

(2) may be revoked or modified before final decree on a showing by affidavit of the facts necessary to revocation or modification of a final decree under Section 316; and

(3) terminates when the final decree is entered or when the petition for dissolution or legal separation is voluntarily dismissed.

Commissioners' Note

Subsection (a) permits motions for temporary maintenance and temporary support in three kinds of proceedings, (1) dissolution of marriage; (2) legal separation; and (3) independent proceedings for maintenance, support, or property disposition following an *ex parte* dissolution of the marriage granted in another, earlier proceeding. Motions for temporary custody are covered by Section 403. . . .

§305. [Irretrievable Breakdown]

(a) If both of the parties by petition or otherwise have stated under oath or affirmation that the marriage is irretrievably broken, or one of the parties has so stated and the other has not denied it, the court, after hearing, shall make a finding whether the marriage is irretrievably broken.

(b) If one of the parties has denied under oath or affirmation that the marriage is irretrievably broken, the court shall consider all relevant factors, including the circumstances that gave rise to filing the petition and the prospect of reconciliation, and shall:

(1) make a finding whether the marriage is irretrievably broken; or

(2) continue the matter for further hearing not fewer than 30 nor more than 60 days later, or as soon thereafter as the matter may be reached on the court's calendar, and may suggest to the parties that they seek counseling. The court, at the request of either party shall, or on its own motion may, order a conciliation conference. At the adjourned hearing the court shall make a finding whether the marriage is irretrievably broken.

(c) A finding of irretrievable breakdown is a determination that there is no reasonable prospect of reconciliation.

Commissioners' Note

This section, with others, embodies a new approach to dissolution of marriage. It provides that the only basis upon which a marriage may be dissolved is that a court has found that the marriage has broken down irretrievably. The traditional grounds for divorce, which assumed that one party had been at fault by committing an act giving rise to a cause of action for divorce, are abolished. The legal assignment of blame is here replaced by a search for the reality of the marital situation: whether the marriage has ended in fact. . . .

This section makes the determination of whether the marriage is irretrievably broken, in all cases, a matter for determination by the court, "after hearing," which means "upon evidence." [Citations omitted.] . . .

Subsection (b) covers the situation in which the parties are in dispute as to whether their marriage is irretrievably broken. In these circumstances, the court is directed to consider the factors relevant to marital breakdown, including the petitioner's reasons for seeking a dissolution of the marriage and the prospect that the parties may achieve a reconciliation, and to decide forthwith or at an adjourned hearing whether the marriage is irretrievably broken.

Because the defense of recrimination and other concepts associated with fault are abolished by the Act (sections 303(e) and 503), the court may not refuse to find that the marriage has broken down irretrievably merely because of petitioner's conduct during the marriage. . . .

Section 305 intentionally makes no distinction between childless marriages and those with minor children. If the parties establish that their marriage has broken down irretrievably, the court is not authorized to make a contrary finding because of the impact of a dissolution of the marriage upon the minor children. . . .

Because it is expected that the parties themselves will be the primary source of evidence as to irretrievable breakdown, the Act has eliminated any requirement of corroboration. . . .

§306. [Separation Agreement]

(a) To promote amicable settlement of disputes between parties to a marriage attendant upon their separation or the dissolution of their marriage, the parties may enter into a written separation agreement containing provisions for disposition of any property owned by either of them, maintenance of either of them, and support, custody, and visitation of their children.

(b) In a proceeding for dissolution of marriage or for legal separation, the terms of the separation agreement, except those providing for the support, custody, and visitation of children, are binding upon the court unless it finds, after considering the economic circumstances of the parties and any other relevant evidence produced by the parties, on their own motion or on request of the court, that the separation agreement is unconscionable.

(c) If the court finds the separation agreement unconscionable, it may request the parties to submit a revised separation agreement or may make orders for the disposition of property, maintenance, and support.

(d) If the court finds that the separation agreement is not unconscionable as to disposition of property or maintenance, and not unsatisfactory as to support:

(1) unless the separation agreement provides to the contrary, its terms shall be set forth in the decree of dissolution or legal separation and the parties shall be ordered to perform them, or

(2) if the separation agreement provides that its terms shall not be set forth in the decree, the decree shall identify the separation agreement and state that the court has found the terms not unconscionable.

(e) Terms of the agreement set forth in the decree are enforceable by all remedies available for enforcement of a judgment, including contempt, and are enforceable as contract terms.

(f) Except for terms concerning the support, custody, or visitation of children, the decree may expressly preclude or limit modification of terms set forth in the decree if the separation agreement so provides. Otherwise, terms of a separation agreement set forth in the decree are automatically modified by modification of the decree.

Commissioners' Note

An important aspect of the effort to reduce the adversary trappings of marital dissolution is the attempt, made by Section 306, to encourage the parties to reach an amicable disposition of the financial and other incidents of their marriage. This section entirely reverses the older view that property settlement agreements are against public policy because they tend to promote divorce. Rather, when a marriage has broken down irretrievably, public policy will be served by allowing the parties to plan their future by agreeing upon a disposition of their property, their maintenance, and the support, custody, and visitation of their children. . . .

The terms of the agreement respecting support, custody, and visitation of children are not binding upon the court even if these terms are not unconscionable. The court should perform its duty to provide for the children by careful examination of the agreement as to these terms in light of the standards established by Section 309 for support and by Part IV for custody and visitation. . . .

§307. [Disposition of Property]

(a) In a proceeding for dissolution of a marriage, legal separation, or disposition of property following a decree of dissolution of marriage or legal separation by a court which lacked personal jurisdiction over the absent spouse or lacked jurisdiction to dispose of the property, the court, without regard to marital misconduct, shall, and in a proceeding for legal separation may, finally equitably apportion between the parties the property and assets belonging to either or both however and whenever acquired, and whether the title thereto is in the name of the husband or wife or both. In making apportionment the court shall consider the duration of the marriage, and prior marriage of either party, antenuptial agreement of the parties, the age, health, station, occupation, amount and sources of income, vocational skills, employability, estate, liabilities, and needs of each of the parties, custodial provisions, whether the apportionment is in lieu of or in addition to maintenance, and the opportunity of each for future acquisition of capital assets and income. The court shall also consider the contribution or dissipation of each party in the acquisition, preservation, depreciation, or appreciation in value of the respective estates, and the contribution of a spouse as a homemaker or to the family unit.

(b) In a proceeding, the court may protect and promote the best interests of the children by setting aside a portion of the jointly and separately held estates of the parties in a separate fund or trust for the support, maintenance, education, and general welfare of any minor, dependent, or incompetent children of the parties. . . .

*Alternative B of §307*

§307. [Disposition of Property]

In a proceeding for dissolution of the marriage, legal separation, or disposition of property following a decree of dissolution of the marriage or legal separation by a court which lacked personal jurisdiction over the absent spouse or lacked jurisdiction to dispose of the property, the court shall assign each spouse's separate property to that spouse. It also shall divide community property, without regard to marital misconduct, in just proportions after considering all relevant factors including:

(1) contribution of each spouse to acquisition of the marital property, including contribution of a spouse as homemaker;

(2) value of the property set apart to each spouse;

(3) duration of the marriage; and

(4) economic circumstances of each spouse when the division of property is to become effective, including the desirability of awarding the family home or the right to live therein for a reasonable period to the spouse having custody of any children. . . .

Commissioners' Comment (1973)

Alternative A, which is the alternative recommended generally for adoption, proceeds upon the principle that all the property of the spouses, however acquired, should be regarded as assets of the married couple, available for distribution among them, upon consideration of the various factors enumerated in subsection (a). It will be noted that among these are health, vocational skills and employability of the respective spouses and these contributions to the acquisition of the assets, including allowance for the contribution thereto of the "homemaker's services to the family unit." This last is a new concept in Anglo-American law.

Subsection (b) affords a way to safeguard the interests of the children against the possibility of the waste or dissipation of the assets allotted to a particular parent in consideration of being awarded the custody or support of a child or children.

Alternative B was included because a number of Commissioners from community property states represented that their jurisdictions would not wish to substitute, for their own systems, the great hotchpot of assets created by Alternative A, preferring to adhere to the distinction between community property and separate property, and providing for the distribution of that property alone, in accordance with an enumeration of principles, resemblant, so far as applicable, to those set forth in Alternative A. . . .

§308. [Maintenance]

(a) In a proceeding for dissolution of marriage, legal separation, or maintenance following a decree of dissolution of the marriage by a court which lacked personal jurisdiction over the absent spouse, the court may grant a maintenance order for either spouse only if it finds that the spouse seeking maintenance:

(1) lacks sufficient property to provide for his reasonable needs; and

(2) is unable to support himself through appropriate employment or is the custodian of a child whose condition or circumstances make it appropriate that the custodian not be required to seek employment outside the home.

(b) The maintenance order shall be in amounts and for periods of time the court deems just, without regard to marital misconduct, and after considering all relevant factors including:

(1) the financial resources of the party seeking maintenance, including marital property apportioned to him, his ability to meet his needs independently, and the extent to which a provision for support of a child living with the party includes a sum for that party as custodian;

(2) the time necessary to acquire sufficient education or training to enable the party seeking maintenance to find appropriate employment;

(3) the standard of living established during the marriage;

(4) the duration of the marriage;

(5) the age and the physical and emotional condition of the spouse seeking maintenance; and

(6) the ability of the spouse from whom maintenance is sought to meet his needs while meeting those of the spouse seeking maintenance. . . .

Commissioners' Comment (1973)

Section 308(a) authorizes the court to order maintenance to either spouse in three kinds of proceedings: (1) dissolution of marriage; (2) legal separation; and (3) independent proceedings for maintenance following an earlier proceeding for dissolution of the marriage by a court which lacked personal jurisdiction over the absent spouse and thus could not affect maintenance [see comment to Section 302(a)]. In all three kinds of proceedings the court may award maintenance only if both findings listed in (1) and (2) are made. The dual intention of this section and Section 307 is to encourage the court to provide for the financial needs of the spouses by property disposition rather than by an award of maintenance. Only if the available property is insufficient for the purpose and if the spouse who seeks maintenance is unable to secure employment appropriate to his skills and interests or is occupied with child care may an award of maintenance be ordered.

Assuming that an award of maintenance is appropriate under subsection 308(a), the standards for setting the amount of the award are set forth in subsection 308(b). Here, as in Section 307, the court is expressly admonished not to consider the misconduct of a spouse during the marriage. Instead, the court should consider the factors relevant to the issue of maintenance, including those listed in subdivisions (1)-(6). . . .

§309. [Child Support]

In a proceeding for dissolution of marriage, legal separation, maintenance, or child support, the court may order either or both parents owing a duty of support to a child to pay an amount reasonable or necessary for his support, without regard to marital misconduct, after considering all relevant factors including:

(1) the financial resources of the child;

(2) the financial resources of the custodial parent;

(3) the standard of living the child would have enjoyed had the marriage not been dissolved;

(4) the physical and emotional condition of the child and his educational needs; and

(5) the financial resources and needs of the noncustodial parent. . . .

Commissioners' Comment (1973)

This section does not set forth the conditions under which a parent owes a duty of support to a child. . . . Rather, the intent is merely to indicate the factors which a court should consider in setting the amount of support to be paid by either the mother or the father or both. The provision authorizing an order requiring either or both parents to pay child support permits the court to order the custodial parent to contribute to the child's support as well, or to insure that property or payment set aside to the custodial parent for child support are used for that purpose. "Child" includes any child recognized by the laws of the state as "living" or "in being", and, also, a child by adoption. The section authorizes the issue of child support to be raised in independent proceedings for dissolution of marriage or legal separation. . . .

§310. [Representation of Child]

The court may appoint an attorney to represent the interests of a minor or dependent child with respect to his support, custody, and visitation. The court shall enter an order for costs, fees, and disbursements in favor of the child's attorney. The order shall be made against either or both parents, except that, if the responsible party is indigent, the costs, fees, and disbursements shall be borne by the [appropriate agency].

Commissioners' Note

This section authorizes the court to appoint an attorney to represent a minor or dependent child in a proceeding for the dissolution of marriage, legal separation, or any other proceeding which involves the child's support, custody, or visitation. The attorney is not a guardian ad litem for the child, but an advocate whose role is to represent the child's interests. . . .

§311. [Payment of Maintenance or Support to Court]

(a) Upon its own motion or upon motion of either party, the court may order at any time that maintenance or support payments be made to the [clerk of court, court trustee, probation officer] as trustee for remittance to the person entitled to receive the payments.

(b) The [clerk of court, court trustee, probation officer] shall maintain records listing the amount of payments, the date payments are required to be made, and the names and addresses of the parties affected by the order.

(c) The parties affected by the order shall inform the [clerk of court, court trustee, probation officer] of any change of address or of other condition that may affect the administration of the order.

(d) If a party fails to make a required payment, the [clerk of court, court trustee, probation officer] shall send by registered or certified mail notice of the arrearage to the obligor. If payment of the sum due is not made to the [clerk of court, court trustee, probation officer] within 10 days after sending notice, the [clerk of court, court trustee, probation officer] shall certify the amount due to the [prosecuting attorney]. The [prosecuting attorney] shall promptly initiate contempt proceedings against the obligor.

(e) The [prosecuting attorney] shall assist the court on behalf of a person entitled to receive maintenance or support in all proceedings initiated under this section to enforce compliance with the order. The person to whom maintenance or support is awarded may also initiate action to collect arrearages.

(f) If the person obligated to pay support has left or is beyond the jurisdiction of the court, the [prosecuting attorney] may institute any other proceeding available under the laws of this State for enforcement of the duties of support and maintenance.

Commissioners' Note

This section establishes a procedure for payment of support or maintenance orders through a court officer and for enforcement by the appropriate prosecuting attorney. The section . . . is intended to make use of the state's remedy of civil contempt as an effective device for the enforcement of support and maintenance. Under subsection (f), the person to whom a decree for maintenance or support is awarded also may initiate action to collect arrearages. In this action the person might be represented by personal counsel, by a legal aid society or other public agency, or, by a "friend of the court' as envisaged by the Uniform Reciprocal Enforcement of Support Act. Subsection (f) correlates this procedure with the Uniform Reciprocal Enforcement of Support Act so that enforcement can be obtained even though the obligor is beyond the jurisdiction of the court. . . .

§312. [Assignments]

The court may order the person obligated to pay support or maintenance to make an assignment of a part of his periodic earnings or trust income to the person entitled to receive the payments. The assignment is binding on the employer, trustee, or other payor of the funds 2 weeks after service upon him of notice that it has been made. The payor shall withhold from the earnings or trust income payable to the person obligated to support the amount specified in the assignment and shall transmit the payments to the person specified in the order. The payor may deduct from each payment a sum not exceeding [$1.00] as reimbursement for costs. An employer shall not discharge or otherwise discipline an employee as a result of a wage or salary assignment authorized by this section.

Commissioners' Note

This section . . . provides an additional method of assuring that obligations for support and maintenance will be met when due. The Section goes beyond existing law in authorizing an assignment of trust income as well as periodic earnings. . . . Each state should insert in the bracket the sum it deems sufficient to meet the cost to the payor of deducting the sums due from each payment. . . .

§313. [Attorney's Fees]

The court from time to time after considering the financial resources of both parties may order a party to pay a reasonable amount for the cost to the other party of maintaining or defending any proceeding under this Act and for attorney's fees, including sums for legal services rendered and costs incurred prior to the commencement of the proceeding or after entry of judgment. The court may order that the amount be paid directly to the attorney, who may enforce the order in his name.

Commissioners' Note

The purpose of this section is to authorize the payment of costs and a reasonable fee by one party to the other party's attorney if the court, after considering the financial resources available to both parties, determines the order to be necessary. The section extends authority to make several orders for costs and fees and different stages of the proceedings, and permits an attorney to enforce the order directly. . . .

§314. [Decree]

(a) A decree of dissolution of marriage or of legal separation is final when entered, subject to the right of appeal. An appeal from the decree of dissolution that does not challenge the finding that the marriage is irretrievably broken does not delay the finality of that provision of the decree which dissolves the marriage beyond the time for appealing from that provision, and either of the parties may remarry pending appeal.

(b) No earlier than 6 months after entry of a decree of legal separation, the court on motion of either party shall convert the decree to a decree of dissolution of marriage.

(c) The Clerk of Court shall give notice of the entry of a decree of dissolution or legal separation:

(1) if the marriage is registered in this State, to the [marriage license] clerk of the [county, judicial district] where the marriage is registered who shall enter the fact of dissolution or separation in the [Registry of Marriage]; or

(2) if the marriage is registered in another jurisdiction, to the appropriate official of that jurisdiction, with the request that he enter the fact of dissolution in the appropriate record.

(d) Upon request by a wife whose marriage is dissolved or declared invalid, the court may, and if there are no children of the parties shall, order her maiden name or a former name restored.

Commissioners' Note

Subsection (a) abolishes interlocutory periods in those states which have them. The decree of dissolution or separation will be effective when entered, subject to the right of appeal. . . .

Subsection (b) permits either party to a proceeding for legal separation to move, six months after entry of the decree, to convert the decree of legal separation into a decree of dissolution of marriage. The section does not authorize the court to deny the motion. . . .

Subsection (c) establishes a procedure for the registration of a decree of dissolution of marriage or of legal separation in the place where the marriage was originally registered. The purpose of this subsection is to aid in the often difficult problem of proving whether a marriage has been terminated.

Subsection (d) expressly authorizes restoration of the maiden name or any former name of a wife, upon dissolution of a marriage or declaration of its invalidity. . . .

§315. [Independence of Provisions of Decree or Temporary Order]

If a party fails to comply with a provision of a decree or temporary order or injunction, the obligation of the other party to make payments for support or maintenance or to permit visitation is not suspended; but he may move the court to grant an appropriate order.

Commissioners' Note

This section is intended to abolish self-help remedies, now all too common in family litigation, whereby one party withholds support or maintenance payments to force the other party to comply with visitation orders and vice-versa. Disputes of this kind should be settled by the court. The "he" in the last clause of the section refers to the "other party." . . .

§316. [Modification and Termination of Provisions for Maintenance, Support and Property Disposition]

(a) Except as otherwise provided in subsection (f) of Section 306, the provisions of any decree respecting maintenance or support may be modified only as to installments accruing subsequent to the motion for modification and only upon a showing of changed circumstances so substantial and continuing as to make the terms unconscionable. The provisions as to property disposition may not be revoked or modified, unless the court finds the existence of conditions that justify the reopening of a judgment under the laws of this state.

(b) Unless otherwise agreed in writing or expressly provided in the decree, the obligation to pay future maintenance is terminated upon the death of either party or the remarriage of the party receiving maintenance.

(c) Unless otherwise agreed in writing or expressly provided in the decree, provisions for the support of a child are terminated by emancipation of the child but not by the death of a parent obligated to support the child. When a parent obligated to pay support dies, the amount of support may be modified, revoked, or commuted to a lump sum payment, to the extent just and appropriate in the circumstances.

Commissioners' Note

Subsection (a) makes each installment under an order for periodic support or maintenance final and non-modifiable when it falls due. The accrued installments cannot be modified retroactively, and future installments can be modified only as to those falling due after a motion for modification has been filed. The purpose of thus making each installment final and non-modifiable when it becomes due is to give each past due installment the status of a final judgment entitled to full faith and credit in other states pursuant to the decisions of the Supreme Court. . . .

Except where the decree, incorporating the agreement of the parties, provides to the contrary [see Section 306(f)], future installments may be modified, but the person seeking modification must show that circumstances have changed since the date of the original order so that the order is unconscionable at the time the motion is made and will continue to be unconscionable unless modified. This strict standard is intended to discourage repeated or insubstantial motions for modification. . . .

Subsection (b) authorizes the parties to agree in writing or the court to provide in the decree that maintenance will continue beyond the death of the obligor or the remarriage of the obligee. In the absences of such an agreement or provision in the decree, this section sets the termination date for the obligation to pay future maintenance.

Subsection (c) is designed to permit the parties to agree in writing or the court to provide in the decree that the obligation of each parent to support the child will extend beyond the child's emancipation and to permit parents, on occasion of a legal separation or dissolution of marriage, to agree that the child support provisions of the decree will terminate upon the death of a parent who has provided for the child in his will. In the absence of such an agreement or provision in the decree, this section terminates the obligation of a parent to support a child, only upon the child's emancipation. . . .

## Part IV
## CUSTODY

§401. [Jurisdiction; Commencement of Proceeding]

(a) A court of this State competent to decide child custody matters has jurisdiction to make a child custody determination by initial or modification decree if:

(1) this State (i) is the home state of the child at the time of commencement of the proceeding, or (ii) had been the child's home state within 6 months before commencement of the proceeding and the child is absent from this State because of his removal or retention by a person claiming his custody or for other reason, and a parent or person acting as parent continues to live in this State; or

(2) it is in the best interest of the child that a court of this State assume jurisdiction because (i) the child and his parents, or the child and at least one contestant, have a significant connection with this State, and (ii) there is available in this State substantial evidence concerning the child's present or future care, protection, training, and personal relationships; or

(3) the child is physically present in this State and (i) has been abandoned or (ii) it is necessary in an emergency to protect him because he has been subjected to or threatened with mistreatment or abuse or is neglected or dependent; or

(4)(i) no other state has jurisdiction under prerequisites substantially in accordance with paragraphs (1), (2) or (3), or another state has declined to exercise jurisdiction on the ground that this State is the more appropriate forum to determine custody of the child, and (ii) it is in his best interest that the court assume jurisdiction.

(b) Except under paragraphs (3) and (4) of subsection (a), physical presence in this State of the child, or of the child and one of the contestants, is not alone sufficient to confer jurisdiction on a court of this State to make a child custody determination.

(c) Physical presence of the child, while desirable, is not a prerequisite for jurisdiction to determine his custody.

(d) A child custody proceeding is commenced in the [________] court:

(1) by a parent, by filing a petition

(i) for dissolution or legal separation; or

(ii) for custody of the child in the [county, judicial district" in which he is permanently resident or found; or

(2) by a person other than a parent, by filing a petition for custody of the child in the [county, judicial district] in which he is permanently resident or found; or

(2) by a person other than a parent, by filing a petition for custody of the child in the [county, judicial district] in which he is permanently resident or found, but only if he is not in the physical custody of one of his parents.

(e) Notice of a child custody proceeding shall be given to the child's parent, guardian, and custodian, who may appear, be heard, and file a responsive pleading. The court, upon a showing of good cause, may permit intervention of other interested parties.

Commissioners' Note

The provisions of the Act concerning custody adjudication are integrated with the provisions of the Uniform Child Custody Jurisdiction Act, promulgated by the Conference in 1968. The latter Act deals with judicial jurisdiction to adjudicate a custody case when more than one state has an interest in the litigation. The Uniform Marriage and Divorce Act governs the substantive and procedural aspects of custody adjudication once the court has decided that it can and should hear the case on the merits. . . .

The court authorized to hear custody cases has not been identified. In many states the legislature will want to consider the establishment of a Family Court for these purposes; in other states the trial court of general jurisdiction will be named.

Subsection (d) makes an important distinction between custody disputes commenced by parents and those commenced by some other person interested in a particular child. A custody proceeding is commenced automatically whenever one of the parents files for a dissolution or legal separation under Part III. Also, a parent may commence a custody proceeding without filing a petition for dissolution or legal separation. On the other hand, subsection (d)(2) makes it clear that if one of the parents has physical custody of the child, a non-parent may not bring an action to contest that parent's right to continuing custody under the "best interest of the child" standard of Section 402. If a non-parent (a grandparent or an aunt or uncle, perhaps) wants to acquire custody, he must commence proceedings under the far more stringent standards for intervention provided in the typical Juvenile Court Act. In short, this subsection has been devised to protect the "parental rights" of custodial parents and to insure that intrusions upon those rights will occur only when the care the parent is providing the child falls short of the minimum standard imposed by the community at large–the standard incorporated in the neglect or delinquency definitions of the state's Juvenile Court Act. Once a custody proceeding is commenced, the court should be able to hear the views of all interested persons; Subsection (d) therefore authorizes the judge to permit intervention by relatives who would not have been allowed to commence an action. . . .

§402. [Best Interest of Child]

The court shall determine custody in accordance with the best interest of the child. The court shall consider all relevant factors including:

(1) the wishes of the child's parent or parents as to his custody;

(2) the wishes of the child as to his custodian;

(3) the interaction and interrelationship of the child with his parent or parents, his siblings, and any other person who may significantly affect the child's best interest;

(4) the child's adjustment to his home, school, and community; and

(5) the mental and physical health of all individuals involved.

The court shall not consider conduct of a proposed custodian that does not affect his relationship to the child.

Commissioners' Note

This section, excepting the last sentence, is designed to codify existing law in most jurisdictions. It simply states that the trial court must look to a variety of factors to determine what is the child's best interest. The five factors mentioned specifically are those most commonly relied upon in the appellate opinions; but the language of the section makes it clear that the judge need not be limited to the factors specified. Although none of the familiar presumptions developed by the case law are mentioned here, the language of the section is consistent with preserving such rules of thumb. . . .

§403. [Temporary Orders]

(a) A party to a custody proceeding may move for a temporary custody order. The motion must be supported by an affidavit as provided in Section 410. The court may award temporary custody under the standards of Section 402 after a hearing, or, if there is no objection, solely on the basis of the affidavits.

(b) If a proceeding for dissolution of marriage or legal separation is dismissed, any temporary custody order is vacated unless a parent or the child's custodian moves that the proceeding continue as a custody proceeding and the court finds, after a hearing, that the circumstances of the parents and the best interest of the child requires that a custody decree be issued.

(c) If a custody proceeding commenced in the absence of a petition for dissolution of marriage or legal separation under subsection (1)(ii) or (2) of Section 401 is dismissed, any temporary custody order is vacated.

Commissioners' Note

Subsection (a) encourages trial courts to issue temporary custody orders without formal hearing whenever possible. Since the hearing itself may be a traumatic event for both parents (and therefore for their children, indirectly), the trial court is authorized to make temporary orders on the basis of affidavits alone unless one of the parties files formal objection to that procedure. In most cases, it is expected that trial judges will award temporary custody to the existing custodian so as to minimize disruption for the child. . . .

§404. [Interviews]

(a) The court may interview the child in chambers to ascertain the child's wishes as to his custodian and as to visitation. The court may permit counsel to be present at the interview. The court shall cause a record of the interview to be made and to be part of the record in the case.

(b) The court may seek the advice of professional personnel, whether or not employed by the court on a regular basis. The advice given shall be in writing and made available by the court to counsel upon request. Counsel may examine as a witness any professional personnel consulted by the court.

Commissioners' Note

This section, and the two which follow, are designed to permit the court to make custodial and visitation decisions as informally and non-contentiously as possible, based on as much relevant information as can be secured, while preserving a fair hearing for all interested parties.

The general rule is that the judge may interview the child in chambers. It is often important for the judge to discover the attitudes and wishes of the child, and there is no reason to subject the child to the formality of the courtroom and the unpleasantness of cross-examination. This provision does not require the judge to permit counsel to be present at the interview, but he must make some kind of record of the interview (using a court reporter or a tape recorder) so that counsel for all parties will have access to the substance of the interview. Similarly, the judge may call informally on experts in a variety of disciplines without subjecting them, in the first instance, to the formal hearing process.

But the experts' advice should be available to counsel for the parties so that the judge's decision will not be based on secret information; and the parties should be able to examine the expert as to the substance of his advice to the judge. . . .

§405. [Investigations and Reports]

(a) In contested custody proceedings, and in other custody proceedings if a parent or the child's custodian so requests, the court may order an investigation and report concerning custodial arrangements for the child. The investigation and report may be made by [the court social service agency, the staff of the juvenile court, the local probation or welfare department, or a private agency employed by the court for the purpose].

(b) In preparing his report concerning a child, the investigator may consult any person who may have information about the child and his potential custodial arrangements. Upon order of the court, the investigator may refer the child to professional personnel for diagnosis. The investigator may consult with and obtain information from medical, psychiatric, or other expert persons who have served the child in the past without obtaining the consent of the parent or the child's custodian; but the child's consent must be obtained if he has reached the age of 16, unless the court finds that he lacks mental capacity to consent. If the requirements of subsection (c) are fulfilled, the investigator's report may be received in evidence at the hearing.

(c) The court shall mail the investigator's report to counsel and to any party not represented by counsel at least 10 days prior to the hearing. The investigator shall make available to counsel and to any party not represented by counsel the investigator's file of underlying data, and reports, complete texts of diagnostic reports made to the investigator pursuant to the provisions of subsection (b), and the names and addresses of all persons whom the investigator has consulted. Any party to the proceeding may call the investigator and any person whom he has consulted for cross-examination. A party may not waive his right of cross-examination prior to the hearing.

Commissioners' Note

The Act steers a middle course between those courts which prohibit a custody investigation unless both parties stipulate to it and those statutes which permit the judge to order an investigation in every case. . . . But most custody dispositions are consensual decisions of the parents, and there is no reason to permit the judge to order an investigation in such cases unless one of the spouses, although agreeing to the disposition, wants some further inquiry made. . . . Similarly, in contested cases, where the judge's need for independent investigation is greatest, a custody study can be ordered even if both spouses are opposed. . . .

§406. [Hearings]

(a) Custody proceedings shall receive priority in being set for hearing.

(b) The court may tax as costs the payment of necessary travel and other expenses incurred by any person whose presence at the hearing the court deems necessary to determine the best interest of the child.

(c) The court without a jury shall determine questions of law and fact. If it finds that a public hearing may be detrimental to the child's best interest, the court may exclude the public from a custody hearing, but may admit any person who has a direct and legitimate interest in the particular case or a legitimate educational or research interest in the work of the court.

(d) If the court finds it necessary to protect the child's welfare that the record of any interview, report, investigation, or testimony in a custody proceeding be kept secret, the court may make an appropriate order sealing the record.

Commissioners' Note

This section further details procedural aspects of custody hearings. . . .

§407. [Visitation]

(a) A parent not granted custody of the child is entitled to reasonable visitation rights unless the court finds, after a hearing, that visitation would endanger seriously the child's physical, mental, moral, or emotional health.

(b) The court may modify an order granting or denying visitation rights whenever modification would serve the best interest of the child; but the court shall not restrict a parent's visitation rights unless it finds that the visitation would endanger seriously the child's physical, mental, moral, or emotional health.

Commissioners' Note

With two important exceptions, this section states the traditional rule for visitation rights. The general rule implies a "best interest of the child" standard. Although the judge should never compel the noncustodial parent to visit the child, visitation rights should be arranged to an extent and in a fashion which suits the child's interest rather than the interest of either the custodial or noncustodial parent. . . . To preclude visitation completely, the judge must find that visitation would endanger "seriously the child's physical, mental, moral, or emotional health." . . . Although the standard is necessarily somewhat vague, it was deliberately chosen to indicate its stringency when compared to the "best interest" standard traditionally applied to this problem. The special standard was chosen to prevent the denial of visitation to the noncustodial parent on the basis of moral judgments about parental behavior which have no relevance to the parent's interest in or capacity to maintain a close and benign relationship to the child. The same onerous standard is applicable when the custodial parent tries to have the noncustodial parent's visitation privileges restricted or eliminated. . . .

§408. [Judicial Supervision]

(a) Except as otherwise agreed by the parties in writing at the time of the custody decree, the custodian may determine the child's upbringing, including his education, health care, and religious training, unless the court after hearing, finds, upon motion by the noncustodial parent, that in the absence of a specific limitation of the custodian's authority, the child's physical health would be endangered or his emotional development significantly impaired.

(b) If both parents or all contestants agree to the order, or if the court finds that in the absence of the order the child's physical health would be endangered or his emotional development significantly impaired, the court may order the [local probation or welfare department, court social service agency] to exercise continuing supervision over the case to assure that the custodial or visitation terms of the decree are carried out.

Commissioners' Note

This section states an important rule designed to promote family privacy and to prevent intrusions upon the prerogatives of the custodial parent at the request of the noncustodial parent. . . . [I]n the absence of parental agreement, the court should not intervene solely because a choice made by the custodial parent is thought by the noncustodial parent (or by the judge) to be contrary to the child's best interest. . . .

Subsection (b) pursues the family privacy theme by significantly limiting the judge's authority to order supervision of the child and the custodial parent. To be sure, there are situations in which an objective umpire is needed to facilitate post-divorce adjustment to the custody and visitation decree. But in these situations both parents will usually recognize the need and agree to supervision. If the parents cannot agree to supervision, however, it should not be ordered unless the judge finds some extraordinary need for it. Thus, the provision adopts a more stringent standard than the normal "best interest" standard. . . .

§409. [Modification]

(a) No motion to modify a custody decree may be made earlier than 2 years after its date, unless the court permits it to be made on the basis of affidavits that there is reason to believe the child's present environment may endanger seriously his physical, mental, moral, or emotional health.

(b) If a court of this State has jurisdiction pursuant to the Uniform Child Custody Jurisdiction Act, the court shall not modify a prior custody decree unless it finds, upon the basis of facts that have arisen since the prior decree or that were unknown to the court at the time of entry of the prior decree, that a change has occurred in the circumstances of the child or his custodian, and that the modification is necessary to serve the best interest of the child. In applying these standards the court shall retain the custodian appointed pursuant to the prior decree unless:

(1) the custodian agrees to the modification;

(2) the child has been integrated into the family of the petitioner with consent of the custodian; or

(3) the child's present environment endangers seriously his physical, mental, moral, or emotional health, and the harm likely to be caused by a change of environment is outweighed by its advantages to him.

(c) Attorney fees and costs shall be assessed against a party seeking modification if the court finds that the modification action is vexatious and constitutes harassment.

Commissioners' Note

. . . This section is designed to maximize finality (and thus assure continuity for the child) without jeopardizing the child's interest. . . . To discourage the noncustodial parent who tries to punish a former spouse by frequent motions to modify, the subsection includes a two-year waiting period following each modification decree. During that two-year period a contestant can get a hearing only if he can make an initial showing, by affidavit only, that there is some greater urgency for the change than that the child's "best interest" requires it. . . .

Subsection (b) in effect asserts a presumption that the present custodian is entitled to continue as the child's custodian. It does authorize modifications which serve the child's "best interest;" but this standard is to be applied under the principle that modification should be made only in three situations: where the custodian agrees to the change; where the child, although formally in the custody of one parent, has in fact been integrated into the family of the petitioning parent (to avoid encouraging noncustodial kidnapping, this ground requires the consent of the custodial parent); or where the noncustodial parent can prove both that the child's present environment is dangerous to physical, mental, moral, or emotional health and that the risks of harm from change of environment are outweighed by the advantage of such a change to the child. . . .

Subsection (c) provides an additional sanction against vexatious and harassing attempts to relitigate custody.

§410. [Affidavit Practice]

A party seeking a temporary custody order or modification of a custody decree shall submit together with his moving papers an affidavit setting forth facts supporting the requested order or modification and shall give notice, together with a copy of his affidavit, to other parties to the proceeding, who may file opposing affidavits. The court shall deny the motion unless it finds that adequate cause for hearing the motion is established by the affidavits, in which case it shall set a date for hearing on an order to show cause why the requested order or modification should not be granted.

Commissioners' Note

This section establishes a procedure for seeking temporary custody or a modification of a custody decree by motion supported with affidavits. The procedure is designed to result in denial of the motion without a hearing unless the court finds that the affidavits establish adequate cause for holding a hearing. The prbcedure will thus tend to discourage contests over temporary custody and prevent repeated or insubstantial motions for modification. . . .

# 3 Other Types of Dissolution



## §3.01 Annulment

Annulment, like divorce and dissolution, is a legal process which terminates a marriage. The annulment action originated during the dominance of ecclesiastical law, as one of three lawful methods to escape the supposedly indissoluble bond of matrimony.[1] It was called the divorce *a vinculo matrimonii.* Generally, a divorce *a vinculo matrimonii* was a judicial declaration that, because of some disability or defect which existed at the time of the marriage ceremony, no valid marriage ever took place between the parties, or that no valid marriage relation ever existed between the parties.[2]

Because annulment jurisdiction was based in the ecclesiastical courts, which did not exist in the American colonies, annulment was not an action available at American common law.[3] However, some equity courts granted annulments, and eventually the state legislatures enacted annulment statutes.

Historically, the differences between annulment and divorce have been confusing and ambiguous. Many statutes authorize divorces on grounds which were grounds for a divorce a vinculo matrimonii at a time when there were no

---

[1] *See* **§1.07;** S. Green & J. Long, Marriage and Family Law Agreements 11-12 (Shepard's/McGraw-Hill 1984). The other permissible exits from marriage were the divorce *a mensa et thoro,* or the legal separation, discussed in **§3.02,** and parliamentary divorces, which were available only to the very wealthy.

[2] 4 Am Jur 2d *Annulment of Marriage* 440 (1962).

[3] *See* H. Clark, The Law of Domestic Relations in the United States 119 (1968). *See also* **§1.09;** S. Green & J. Long, Marriage and Family Law Agreements 12-13 (Shepard's/McGraw-Hill 1984).

absolute divorces.[4] Nevertheless, it continues to be useful to distinguish between annulment and divorce. An annulment action is based on an assertion that the marriage was invalid, while a divorce action is predicated on a valid marriage. The facts which establish the annulment grounds exist prior to or contemporaneously with the marriage, while divorce grounds generally arise during the marital relationship. Annulment, in theory, invalidates a marriage retroactively to the date of its inception, while a divorce terminates the relationship as of the time of the decree. Unless state statutes provide otherwise, spousal support is not granted after an annulment is issued,[5] while it is generally available in divorce actions.

As in divorce, annulment jurisdiction is premised upon the domicile of the parties.[6] The court of the state having jurisdiction to annul a marriage will, under its conflict of laws rule, refer to and apply the law of the state which determined the validity of the marriage. Annulment decrees are within the scope of the Full Faith and Credit Clause of the United States Constitution and are entitled to recognition in other states.[7]

An invalid marriage may be void ab initio, or only voidable, depending upon the nature of the invalidity. A void marriage is a nullity for all purposes, and while it is unnecessary to invoke the courts in order to restore the parties to their unmarried status, it is preferable to do so. An example of a void marriage is one where the parties marry despite the impediment of a prior existing marriage. A marriage which is void ab initio may be attacked either collaterally or directly after the death of either or both parties.

A voidable marriage is one which is legally valid for all civil purposes until and unless it is invalidated in an annulment proceeding during the lifetime of the parties. An example of a voidable marriage is one where a spouse is underage or impotent at the time of the marriage.

Annulment grounds are provided by statute and vary from state to state. Because many of these grounds are the same as grounds for divorce, it is important to note that the facts establishing such grounds must arise prior to or contemporaneously with the marriage in order to be a proper basis for an annulment.

Many annulment grounds are products of the basic common law notion that the consent of both parties is an essential element of the marriage contract.[8] Such grounds include duress inducing the marriage, non-age, mental incapaci-

---

[4] *See* **§1.25.**

[5] Many states do have such statutes. *See, e.g.*, Alaska Stat Ann §25.24.160 (1983); Cal Civ Code §§4455 & 4456 (Deering 1984); Conn Gen Stat Ann §46-55 (West 1978); NH Rev Stat Ann §458:19 (1983); NY Dom Rel Law §§236 & 237 (McKinney 1977); Or Rev Stat §§107.095 & 107.105 (1981 replacement); Wash Rev Code Ann §26.08.090 (1961).

[6] *See* **§§4.01-4.03.**

[7] H. Clark, *supra* note 3, at 1245; *see* US Const, art IV, §1.

[8] For a discussion of the consent issue as impacting parties' capacity and right to marry, see S. Green & J. Long, Marriage and Family Law Agreements ch 1 (Shepard's/McGraw-Hill 1984).

ty, and marriage-in-jest. Other grounds focus on the performance of marital obligations, such as impotence or refusal of intercourse. Still other grounds include prior existing marriage, consanguinity, and affinity. Perhaps the most important annulment ground used over the years has been fraud going to the essentials of the marriage. This ground includes: misrepresentations and unfulfilled promises concerning status or religion; secret intention not to cohabit or have children; and concealment of mental incapacity, disease, or pregnancy.[9]

The affirmative defenses to an annulment action include ratification, the clean hands doctrine, antenuptial knowledge of the impediment, res judicata, and the statute of limitations.[10] It should also be noted that the impediment to a valid marriage may be removed during the course of the marriage, resulting in putative or common law marriages in jurisdictions recognizing those marital forms. In any event, courts might grant relief to couples in annulment situations by invoking the increasingly popular remedies created for cohabitation situations.[11]

Annulment, when viewed as a declaration that a marriage never existed, in theory should also result in a declaration that the incidents of the marriage are also nonexistent. However, most states have enacted statutes legitimizing children of annulled marriages, while some jurisdictions have entirely eliminated illegitimacy as a statutory concept.[12] Legislatures in some states have also provided that dependent parties in annulment actions may be awarded support, attorneys' fees, and costs. Historically, courts, even without statutory guidance, have been willing to grant temporary alimony for wives sued by their husbands for an annulment.[13]

In 1968, before the dramatic rise of no-fault divorce, Professor Homer Clark noted in his treatise on family law that "as a method of terminating marriages, annulment is not statistically significant in most states, accounting for approximately three percent of marriage dissolution in the 1950's."[14] This statistic included the many annulments granted under New York State's liberal annulment policy which emerged as a reaction to that state's formerly strict divorce law. Since that time, New York has enacted a no-fault divorce provision, as have all other states.[15] Because divorce has become an easier procedure for

---

[9] *See* 4 Am Jur 2d *Annulment of Marriage* 447-54 (1962).

[10] H. Clark, *supra* note 3, at 130-31.

[11] *See* S. Green & J. Long, *supra* note 8, at §3.02.

[12] *See, e.g.*, Ariz Rev Stat Ann §8-601 (Supp 1982); Ind Code §31-4-1-1 (1976); Okla Stat Ann tit 10, §1.2 (West Supp 1982-83); Or Rev Stat §109.060 (1981). The DC Code Ann §16-908 (1981) states, for example: "A child born in wedlock or out of wedlock is the legitimate child of its father and mother and is the legitimate relative of its father's and mother's relatives by blood or adoption."

[13] H. Clark, *supra* note 3, at 135.

[14] *Id* 121 (citing Jacobson, American Marriage and Divorce 90 (1959)).

[15] NY Dom Rel Law §170(5)-(6) (McKinney 1977). As of 1985, all states have enacted some form of no-fault divorce. *See* **§§2.06-2.14.**

terminating a marriage, it is not necessary for couples to pursue an annulment except perhaps for religious or personal reasons. However, the practitioner should be familiar with the annulment action in his or her jurisdiction, as a possible alternative to divorce and dissolution.

## §3.02 Limited Divorce

The limited divorce is also called divorce or separation from bed and board, *divorce a mensa et thoro,* legal separation, or judicial separation. The divorce a mensa et thoro, developed by the Catholic church as a remedy for spouses in marriages where cohabitation was intolerable due to marital misconduct, terminated the parties' cohabitation obligation, provided support for the dependent spouse, preserved all other marital duties and obligations, and prohibited remarriage.[16] In the United States, many legislatures established provisions for limited divorce.[17] The action was strongly criticized by early commentators as an ineffective remedy for married couples.[18]

In 1985, 38 jurisdictions statutorily provided a form of legal separation; Alaska had limited divorce under its common law.[19] Ten states had no limited divorce statutes, while Florida, Georgia, and West Virginia abolished their partial divorce statutes.[20] The Uniform Marriage and Divorce Act provides such an action, stating that "If a party requests a decree of legal separation

---

[16] *See* **§1.07.**

[17] 2 C. Vernier, American Family Laws 343 (1931).

[18] See, e.g., 2 J. Kent, Commentaries on American Law 128 (1889), where Chancellor Kent maintained that "[t]hese qualified divorces are regarded as rather hazardous to the morals of the parties."; 1 J. Bishop, Marriage and Divorce 67 (1891), where the author stated:

> By this decree, the injured party, in mockery of redress, is kept under all the burdens of matrimony, and cut off from all its benefits. At the same time, it enables the law to put on the delusive appearance of carrying out its boast that it furnishes a remedy for every wrong. [Footnotes omitted.]

In 2 C. Vernier, American Family Laws 34 (1931), the author exclaimed:

> Such an anomalous divorce requires a degree of chastity scarcely to be expected in an ordinary mortal, for it leaves neither party free to marry again, and is no defense to a criminal charge, either or bigamy or adultery. Yet if, after the divorce, the wife has a child, it is presumed illegitimate!

[19] The jurisdictions providing a limited divorce statute in 1985 included Alabama, Arizona, Arkansas, California, Connecticut, Colorado, the District of Columbia, Hawaii, Illinois, Indiana, Iowa, Kentucky, Louisiana, Maine, Maryland, Massachusetts, Michigan, Minnesota, Missouri, Montana, Nebraska, New Hampshire, New Jersey, New Mexico, New York, North Carolina, North Dakota, Oklahoma, Oregon, Rhode Island, South Dakota, Tennessee, Vermont, Virginia, Virgin Islands, Washington, Wisconsin, and Wyoming.

[20] The 9 states with no statutory provision for divorce from bed and board in 1985 were Delaware, Idaho, Kansas, Mississippi, Nevada, Ohio, Pennsylvania, South Carolina, Texas, and Utah.

rather than a decree of dissolution of marriage, the court shall grant the decree in that form unless the other party objects."[21]

In many statutes, the limited divorce grounds are the same as the absolute divorce grounds.[22] Some limited divorce statutes set forth fault grounds. In other states, the grounds are left to the court's discretion.[23]

Each statute has its particular requirements. Some provide that the duration of the legal separation is indefinite, while others prescribe only a limited period of time. Other statutes codify the general rule that a decree of limited divorce may not be abrogated by a reconciliation and may only be revoked upon application to the court.[24] In addition, several limited divorce statutes direct that a court may not grant such a decree if one party objects or if a petition for dissolution or absolute divorce has been filed.

Since the no-fault trend has lessened the difficulty of obtaining an absolute divorce, the action for divorce from bed and board has lost much of its earlier importance. The primary function of limited divorce now is to provide a vehicle for temporary or emergency relief. In many states, an action for limited divorce may be filed when there is no matured ground for absolute divorce. This facilitates obtaining an immediate hearing to adjudicate custody, temporary support, and other issues demanding immediate attention, such as residence of the children or where they will be registered for school.

It is important to distinguish between limited divorce and separate maintenance. In an action for separate maintenance, a dependent spouse may obtain an order for spousal support. However, property may not be divided, which is a possible remedy in a limited divorce action. Unlike the limited divorce, which terminates the cohabitation obligation, the action for separate maintenance is not contingent on the separation of the parties, although it usually presumes such separation. Reconciliation will abrogate the decree for separate maintenance while it has no effect on a limited divorce decree absent judicial authority. Perhaps the most important distinction between these two actions is that separate maintenance does not require domicile, while limited divorce is usually governed by the same jurisdictional requirements as to residence as is the absolute divorce.

There are other reasons why spouses might select the limited divorce over an absolute divorce. Certain religions forbid divorce among their adherents. If the limited divorce grounds are fault-based, marital misconduct is disclosed to the judge. This alleging of fault is believed by some practitioners to increase an injured spouse's bargaining power.

---

[21] Uniform Marriage and Divorce Act §302(b), 9A ULA 91, 121 (1979). *See* **app 2-1.**

[22] The states providing identical divorce grounds for the limited and absolute actions in 1985 included Alabama, California, Connecticut, Colorado, Illinois, Iowa, Michigan, Missouri, Montana, New Hampshire, New Jersey, North Dakota, Oklahoma, South Dakota, Vermont, Virgin Islands, Washington, Wisconsin, and Wyoming.

[23] Limited divorce could be granted in 1985 at the court's discretion in Arkansas, Kentucky, Minnesota, Nebraska, and Rhode Island.

[24] *See* Annot, 35 ALR2d 707, 710 (1954).

There may be income tax and probate consequences where there is a limited divorce. Federal Income Tax Regulation §1.6013-4(a) provides that "[a]n individual legally separated from his spouse under a decree of divorce or of separation shall not be considered as married." The Uniform Probate Code §2-802(a) states:

> A person who is divorced from the decedent or whose marriage from the decedent has been annulled is not a surviving spouse unless, by virtue of a subsequent marriage, he is married to the decedent at the time of death. *A decree of separation which does not terminate the status of husband and wife is not a divorce for purposes of this section.* (Emphasis added.)

If trial of a limited divorce is not reached by the courts until after a no-fault ground has matured, then a supplemental pleading for absolute divorce may be filed by either party. The few reported cases involving legal separations or limited divorce focus on the adequacy of the support order;[25] the sufficiency of the evidence to support a decree of limited divorce;[26] and, in jurisdictions where fault grounds are provided for the action, whether the doctrine of recrimination applies.[27]

Full consideration must be given to alternatives to absolute divorce when there is either no jurisdiction or no matured ground for absolute divorce. The strategic, personal, and religious reasons for pursuing such an alternative, as well as the legal effects of an action such as a limited divorce or decree of separate maintenance, should be fully explored with the client.

---

25 *E.g.*, Reid v Reid, 244 Or 396, 418 P2d 517 (1966).

26 *E.g.*, Mercer v Mercer, 183 Neb 515, 162 NW2d 230 (1968); Melville v Melville, 29 AD2d 970, 289 NYS 2d 416 (1968); Fore v Fore, 15 NC Ct App 226, 189 SE2d 520 (1972).

27 *E.g.*, Cousin v Cousin, 327 So 2d 136 (La Ct App 1976); Kirstein v Kirstein, 7 Mich App 316, 151 NW2d 875 (1967).

# 4 Jurisdictional Issues

## §4.01 Jurisdiction Generally

Two aspects of jurisdiction are important in the divorce context. Subject matter jurisdiction establishes a court's authority to hear and determine divorce cases, to adjudge the general or abstract questions involved, and to grant the appropriate relief. Judicial jurisdiction, the authority of the court to exercise its power over persons or things, usually depends on valid service of process within a state, adherence to the statutory requirement of a long-arm statute, or proper attachment of things or property in dispute.[1]

Historically, the power to terminate marriages in England was exercised by the ecclesiastical courts, which used the *in personam* process as the basis for divorce jurisdiction.[2] Enactment of the Matrimonial Causes Act of 1958 vested all divorce jurisdiction in the civil divorce court. Previously, subject matter jurisdiction over divorce did not exist at common law. In the United States, divorce jurisdiction was not an inherent power of the courts, and until statutes and state constitutions granted courts the power to decree divorces, "the sole recourse for dissatisfied married persons was to petition the legislature or seek an annulment."[3]

Subject matter jurisdiction over divorce in this country is governed by state statutes or, in North Dakota and Texas, by constitutional provisions, which create the appropriate courts and empower them to act in divorce cases. The federal courts have no original jurisdiction over divorce.[4]

Subject matter jurisdiction is important because the state that exercises divorce jurisdiction applies its own substantive law on the question of entitlement to divorce. It also determines the applicability of the principles of res judicata and collateral estoppel, and the operation of the Full Faith and Credit Clause.

The customary basis for divorce jurisdiction in the United States has been the domicile of one or both parties.[5] The explanation for the use of domicile

---

[1] R. Leflar, American Conflicts Law 5 (rev ed 1968). *See* **§§4.05-4.07.**

[2] *See* **§1.07.**

[3] 2 C. Vernier, American Family Laws 98 (1931).

[4] It is interesting to note, however, that until the District of Columbia Court Reform and Criminal Procedure Act of 1970, Pub L No 91-358, 84 Stat 473, the federal courts exercised divorce jurisdiction in the District of Columbia. See **§§4.20-4.24** for a discussion of the domestic relations exception to federal diversity jurisdiction.

[5] In a few states, at particular times, the jurisdictional bases have included the place of the marriage and the place where the fault-oriented cause of action arose. *See* 2 C. Vernier, *supra* note 3, at 106; Md Ann Code art 16, §30 (1981) which provides that "[n]o person shall be entitled to make application for a divorce, where the causes for divorce occurred out of this State, unless the party plaintiff or defendant shall have resided within this State for one year next preceding such application." In Adams v Adams, 101 Md 506, 61 A 628 (1905), it was held that a court of equity had jurisdiction under this section, where adultery was committed in Maryland, both husband and wife being at the time nonresidents, and the wife had become a Maryland resident a few months prior to the filing of the bill. See also M. Ploscowe, H. Foster, & D. Freed, Family Law, Cases and Materials 314 (2d ed 1972), where the authors note: "At one time New York

can be traced to the *in rem* or *marital res* theory of divorce jurisdiction as developed in the late nineteenth century by Justice Story and by Joel Bishop in his influencial treatise entitled *Marriage and Divorce.*[6] This theory maintained that the state had an interest in the status of the parties, the *marital res,* over which courts had *in rem* jurisdiction at the domicile. Domicile, traditionally defined as a person's "true, fixed, permanent home, and principal establishment, and to which, whenever he is absent, he has the intention of returning,"[7] was chosen because the importance of the action of dissolving the marital relation mandated that the forum have more than a transient connection with that relationship and with the parties.

By the turn of the century, most courts in the United States accepted the in rem theory of divorce jurisdiction and held that a valid divorce could be granted regardless of the lack of in personam jurisdiction over the absentee defendant, since the marital res was before the court in the person of the plaintiff.[8] However, other states, specifically New York, Pennsylvania, and the Carolinas, rejected the marital res theory for a number of years, and required in personam jurisdiction for a divorce action.

As was inevitable, disputes arose between the states following the majority in rem theory and those in the minority regarding the recognition of divorce decrees.[9] The courts in minority jurisdictions refused to recognize out-of-state divorce decrees obtained by constructive service on residents in their jurisdictions, presumably in retaliation against those plaintiffs who evaded their laws and obtained divorces in more liberal states. The conflicts cases which resulted served to clarify the proper jurisdictional basis for divorce actions.[10]

In *Williams v North Carolina,*[11] The Supreme Court of the United States

---

Domestic Relations Law §170 (now repealed and replaced by NY Dom Rel Law §230 (McKinney Supp 1986)) included a provision that an action for divorce might be maintained where the parties were married in that state. No requirement of residence or domicile was imposed." In countries such as France, Germany, Italy, and Switzerland, the rule has been that the court of nationality had divorce jurisdiction. *See* W. Cook, The Logical and Legal Bases of Conflict of Laws 460 (1942); M. Rheinstein, Marriage Stability, Divorce, and the Law 64 (1972); **§4.02.**

[6] M. Ploscowe, H. Foster, & D. Freed, *supra* note 5, at 316.

[7] 1 J. Beale, Conflict of Laws 94 (1935) (quoting J. Story, Conflict of Laws 40 (8th ed 1883)).

[8] M. Ploscowe, H. Foster, & D. Freed, *supra* note 5, at 317.

[9] *See* **§§4.09, 4.11.** The states in the minority refused to recognize out-of-state ex parte divorces based upon constructive service on the defendant domiciled in the minority state.

[10] *See, e.g.,* Vanderbilt v Vanderbilt, 354 US 416 (1957); Sherrer v Sherrer, 334 US 343 (1948); Estin v Estin, 334 US 541 (1948); Williams v North Carolina, 315 US 226 (1945); Williams v North Carolina, 317 US 27 (1942).

[11] 317 US 287 (1942). *See* **§4.11.**

discarded the in rem and in personam labels for divorce jurisdiction.[12] The Court declared that the proper jurisdictional basis for a divorce action was the domicile of the plaintiff spouse, not necessarily because it was the location of the marital res, but because of the domicile's commanding interest in the status of its domiciliaries.[13]

While domicile is generally still recognized as a proper jurisdictional basis, along with the fulfillment of a residence requirement, the jurisdictional standards for divorce have been challenged in recent years in light of trends restricting the limits of jurisdictional due process.[14] Domicile, residence requirements, jurisdictional standards, and recognition of divorce decrees are discussed in detail in the following sections.[15]

## §4.02 Domicile

The traditional basis for divorce jurisdiction in the United States has been the domicile of one or both parties. Domicile was chosen as the jurisdictional standard for divorce because it represented a significant relationship between a state and a party on which a court could act. As noted by the Supreme Court of the United States in *Williams v North Carolina* (*Williams I*):

> Domicile creates a relationship to the state which is adequate for numerous exercises of state power. . . . Each state as a sovereign has a rightful and legitimate concern in the marital status of persons domiciled within its borders. The marriage relation creates problems of large social importance. Protection of offspring, property interests and the enforcement of marital responsibilities are but a few of the commanding problems in the field of domestic relations with which the state must deal. Thus it is plain that each state, by virtue of its command over its domiciliaries and its large interest in the institution of marriage, can alter within its own borders the marriage status of the spouse domiciled there, even though the other spouse is absent. [Citations omitted.][16]

---

[12] *Id* 297-98. In Williams v North Carolina, 325 US 226, 232 (1945) (*Williams II*), the Court acknowledged that divorce does possess characteristics of an in rem proceeding.

[13] *See* **§4.02.**

[14] *See, e.g.,* Hawkens, *The Effect of Shaffer v Heitner on the Jurisdictional Standard in Ex Parte Divorce,* 18 Fam LQ 311 (1984); Note, *Jurisdiction in the Ex Parte Divorce: Do Absent Spouses Have a Protected Due Process Interest in Their Marital Status?,* 13 Mem St UL Rev 205 (1983); Rush v Savchuk, 444 US 320 (1980); World-Wide Volkswagen Corp v Woodson, 444 US 286 (1980); Kulko v California, 436 US 84 (1978); Shaffer v Heitner, 433 US 186 (1977); Hanson v Denckla 357 US 239 (1958); **§§4.08, 4.11.**

[15] *See* **§§4.02-4.16.**

[16] 317 US 287, 298-99 (1942).

The contemporary definition of domicile is the "habitation from which a [person] has no intention of removing."[17] Domicile is classified by the method it was acquired: by origin (by birth), by choice, or by operation of law.

Domicile by choice is the most common classification in the divorce context. To acquire a domicile by choice, a party must be physically present in a jurisdiction and at the same time have the appropriate intent. This intent has been described by various courts as an intent to make a home in the jurisdiction, to remain indefinitely, to abandon a former domicile and remain in the new one, or, at the very least, not to make a home elsewhere.[18]

Sometimes, courts have difficulty in determining whether the intent exists. Self-serving testimonial declarations of intent beg the question and are insufficient. Courts examine evidence such as location of family and business, participation in community affairs, payment of taxes, voter registration, driver's license, and the like. The mere fact that a plaintiff acquired the domicile for the purpose of obtaining a divorce does not defeat the jurisdiction since the motive in and of itself in adopting a new domicile is irrelevant.

Under traditional domicile rules, the husband and wife had the same domicile. The matrimonial domicile was defined as "[t]he place where the parties last lived as husband and wife with the intent of making that place their home."[19] If a wife refused to move with her husband, she was considered a

---

[17] H. Clark, The Law of Domestic Relations in the United States 144 (1968). The traditional definition, as set out in 1 J. Beale, Conflict of Laws 94 (1935) (quoting J. Story, Conflict of Laws 40 (8th ed 1883)) is a person's "true, fixed, permanent home and principal establishment, and to which, whenever he is absent, he has the intention of returning."

[18] See, e.g., Rzeszotarski v Rzeszotarski, 296 A2d 431, 434-35 (DC 1972), which states: "The requirements for establishing domicile are: (1) physical presence, and (2) an intent to abandon the former domicile and remain here for *an indefinite period of time;* a domicile comes into being when the two elements coexist . . .' " (emphasis in original). For cases with substantially similar definitions of domicile, see Spalding v Spalding, 171 Conn 220, 368 A2d 14 (1976); Wife W v Husband W, 376 A2d 87 (Del 1977); Curran v Curran, 362 So 2d 1042 (Fla 1978); Perry v Perry, 5 Kan App 2d 636, 623 P2d 513 (1981); Delaville v Delaville, 87 Misc 2d 726, 386 NYS2d 196 (Sup Ct 1976).

[19] J. Madden, Handbook of the Law of Persons and Domestic Relations 318 (1931). The rules of coverture, the fictional unity of husband and wife at marriage, from which the domicile rules are derived, were criticized from an early time. C. Dickens, in The Adventures of Oliver Twist ch 51 (1939), included criticism of the husband and wife's legal unity:

> "It was all Mrs. Bumble. She *would* do it," urged Mr. Bumble; first looking round to ascertain that his partner had left the room.
>
> "That is no excuse," replied Mr. Brownlow. "You were present on the occasion of the destruction of these trinkets, and indeed are the more guilty of the two, in the eye of the law; for the law supposes that your wife acts under your direction."
>
> "If the law supposes that," said Mr. Bumble, squeezing his hat emphatically in both hands, "the law is a ass—a idiot. If that's the eye of the law, the law is a bachelor; and the worst I wish the law is, that his eye may be opened by experience—by experience."

deserter.[20] In addition, she had to sue for divorce at her husband's domicile, which was legally her domicile. However, if the husband deserted the wife and acquired a new domicile, the settled rule was that the wife could retain the marital domicile and bring a divorce action there. These domicile rules are obsolete; in most states a wife may establish a domicile entirely independent from that of her husband.

In addition to proving domicile, a plaintiff spouse must also fulfill a residency requirement in most jurisdictions in order to invoke the jurisdiction of a state court.[21] In fact, it is a practitioner's reality that, for the most part, simple residence is sufficient in divorce actions for a court to exercise jurisdiction.

Indeed, domicile, as the jurisdictional basis for divorce actions, has been challenged as inadequate for different reasons. Professor Helen Garfield of Indiana University Law School has argued that legal and societal trends have rendered domicile an outmoded basis for divorce jurisdiction.[22] Garfield maintains that the concept of power which elevated domicile to a constitutional requirement—that the state's interest was to preserve marriage, even against the wishes of individuals—has lost significance with the rise of no-fault divorce. In addition, the rights of individuals to be free from unwarranted interference by the state in their private affairs have been strengthened by a series of Supreme Court decisions. The weakening of the state's role and the strengthening of individual rights, Garfield has argued, should render domicile irrelevant.[23]

---

> Laying great stress on the repetition of these two words, Mr. Bumble fixed his hat on very tight, and putting his hands in his pockets, followed his helpmate down stairs.

[20] The general rule was that the husband may choose and fix the domicile of himself and his wife, if, in doing so, he acts reasonably. Thus, a wife's unjustifiable failure or refusal to accompany him to the new domicile constituted abandonment or desertion, which if continued for the statutory period, could be used as a ground for divorce against her. *See* Neville v Neville, 220 Ala 57, 124 So 107 (1929); Dobson v Dobson, 89 SW2d 932 (Ark 1936); Perry v Perry, 93 Cal App 2d 720, 209 P2d 847 (1949); Ogden v Ogden, 159 Fla 604, 33 So 2d 870 (1947); Taylor v Taylor, 195 Ga 711, 25 SE2d 506 (1943); Bateman v Bateman, 337 Ill App 7, 85 NE2d 196 (1949); Bennett v Bennett, 197 Md 408, 79 A2d 513 (1951); Fanner v Fanner, 326 Mich 466, 40 NW2d 225 (1949); Mitter v Mitter, 121 NJ Eq 52, 187 A 174 (Ct Err & App 1936); Burke v Burke, 36 Ohio App 551, 173 NE 637 (1930); Fuller v Fuller, 158 Pa Super 378, 45 A2d 231 (1946); Graves v Graves, 193 Va 659, 70 SE2d 339 (1952); Leach v Leach, 261 Wis 350, 52 NW2d 896 (1952); Annot, 29 ALR2d 474 (1953).

[21] For a discussion of residency requirements, see **§4.03.**

[22] Garfield, *The Transitory Divorce Action: Jurisdiction in the No-Fault Era*, 58 Tex L Rev 501 (1980).

[23] *Id* 503-04, where the author states:

> A critical examination of the bases of divorce jurisdiction reveals that the present rules are founded on outmoded notions of state power over individuals and state control over marriage that are incompatible with recent Supreme Court decisions affirming the constitutional rights of individuals to be free from unwarranted interference by the state in their private lives. The same concepts of state power that elevated domicile to a constitutional requirement also

Another aspect of Garfield's case against domicile as the jurisdictional basis for divorce focused on the highly mobile, present society. Persons may frequently change domiciles for reasons unrelated to divorce, and, therefore, may face difficulty when attempting to prove domicile for jurisdictional purposes.

Several legal commentators have argued that domicile as a basis for divorce jurisdiction in ex parte situations is insufficient and perhaps unconstitutional as a violation of an absent spouse's due process rights.[24] Urging the application of the minimum contacts standards developed by a series of Supreme Court decisions culminating in *Shaffer v Heitner*,[25] these writers maintain that when a court examines the relationship of the defendant, the forum, and the litigation in an ex parte divorce action, it will refuse to exercise jurisdiction as an offense to "traditional notions of fair play and substantial justice."[26] This challenge to domicile as a basis for divorce jurisdiction is further examined in the discussion of the recognition of divorce decrees.[27]

## §4.03 Residency Requirements

In 1984, the vast majority of state statutes provided durational residency requirements as the basis for divorce jurisdiction. These requirements have consistently been construed by courts to mean domicile,[28] prompting Professor Homer Clark to remark that "[i]t is odd, in view of the widespread and long-continued use of domicile as a technical legal term, that so many statutes use the term 'residence' rather than domicile as the touchstone of rights and

---

> supported a fault concept of divorce that is rapidly passing from the scene. Fault divorce in effect recognized the state's power to preserve the institution of marriage, even against the wishes of the individuals concerned. This power could be wielded only by the state presumed to have the greatest interest in the marriage—the state of domicile. Under no-fault divorce, the individuals' interests, not the state's are recognized as paramount. Domicile should have become irrelevant. (Footnotes omitted.)

[24] *See, e.g.*, Hawkens, *The Effect of Shaffer v Heitner on the Jurisdictional Standard in Ex Parte Divorces*, 18 Fam LQ 311 (1984); Comment, *The Divisible Divorce Doctrine Reexamined in Light of Shaffer v Heitner*, 51 Miss L Rev 801 (1981); Note, *Jurisdiction in the Ex Parte Divorce: Do Absent Spouses Have a Protected Due Process Interest in Their Marital Status?*, 13 Mem St UL Rev 205 (1983).

[25] 433 US 186 (1977).

[26] International Shoe Co v Washington, 326 US 310, 316 (1945).

[27] *See* **§4.11.**

[28] *See, e.g.*, Chavis v Chavis, 394 So 2d (Ala Ct App 1981); Taylor v Taylor, 168 Conn 619, 362 A2d 795 (1975); Perry v Perry, 5 Kan App 2d 636, 623 P2d 513 (1981); Carr v Carr, 46 NY2d 270, 385 NE2d 1234, 413 NYS2d 305 (1978); Raybin v Raybin, 179 NJ Super 121, 430 A2d 953 (1981); Burnworth v Burnworth, 572 P2d 301 (Okla Ct App 1977).

duties."[29] However, experienced family lawyers recognize that as a practical matter, in most divorce cases, jurisdiction is asserted on the basis of residence with little if any attention given to domicile.

Residency requirements serve as a waiting period imposed as a condition for the exercise of divorce jurisdiction. The statutory periods range from six weeks in Idaho, Nevada, and the Virgin Islands to one year in Connecticut, Louisiana, Massachusetts, Nebraska, New Hampshire, New Jersey, New York, North Dakota, Pennsylvania, Rhode Island, South Carolina, and West Virginia.[30] The trend has been to reduce the length of residence required.[31]

Indeed, most states have liberalized their jurisdiction requirements. In Arkansas, the term *residence* is defined as "actual presence," and proof of residence is considered proof of domicile.[32] The Oregon statute requires only that one party "be a resident of or be domiciled in" the state for six months prior to bringing suit.[33] To establish jurisdiction in Hawaii, a party must be "domiciled" or "physically present."[34]

The residency requirements for divorce have been challenged on constitutional grounds. In *Sosna v Iowa*,[35] Iowa's one-year residency requirement was attacked as a violation of the Equal Protection and Due Process Clauses of the Fourteenth Amendment, and as an impediment of the right to travel. The Supreme Court of the United States rejected the argument that the one-year residency requirement violated the Due Process Clause because it denied litigants the opportunity to make an individual showing of bona fide residence and, therefore, barred access to divorce court. The Court noted that proof of residence was a jurisdictional requirement in addition to domicile, and even if the appellant could make a showing of domicile, she still would not be entitled to a divorce unless she satisfied the residence requirement. This additional requirement only delayed access to the courts, and did not deprive litigants of

---

[29] H. Clark, The Law of Domestic Relations in the United States 146 (1968).

[30] Freed & Walker, *Family Law in the Fifty States: An Overview*, 18 Fam LQ 369, 384-85 (1985).

[31] *Id* 383. In 1985, the states which had a 60-day residence requirement were Arkansas, Iowa, Kansas, and Wyoming. Arizona, Colorado, Illinois, Missouri, Montana, and Utah had a 90-day requirement. In 1985, those jurisdictions requiring a six-month length of residence were Alabama, California, Delaware, Florida, Georgia, Hawaii, Indiana, Kentucky, Maine, Michigan, Minnesota, Mississippi, New Mexico, North Carolina, Ohio, Oklahoma, Tennessee, Texas, Vermont, Virginia, Wisconsin, and the District of Columbia. Alaska, Maryland, Oklahoma, South Dakota, and Washington had no durational residency requirement, but instead required either bona fide residence or domicile as the jurisdictional basis.

[32] Ark Stat Ann §34-1208.1 (1962).

[33] Or Rev Stat §107.075(2) (1983).

[34] Hawaii Rev Stat §580.1 (1976). See also **§4.02,** which discusses challenges to domicile as the jurisdictional basis for divorce. In Garfield, *The Transitory Divorce Action: Jurisdiction in the No-Fault Era,* 58 Tex L Rev 501 (1980), the author advocates the establishment of residence as the basis for divorce jurisdiction.

[35] 419 US 393 (1974).

their day in divorce court. The Court declared that the state was reasonably justified in imposing the requirement to insure that persons seeking a divorce in Iowa have significant attachments to the state, and to insulate Iowa divorce decrees from collateral attack.[36]

The Virgin Islands' divorce statute residency requirement was challenged by the court sua sponte in *Alton v Alton.*[37] The statute provided that six weeks' residence in the Virgin Islands would be prima facie evidence of domicile, and if the defendant were personally served or entered a general appearance, there would be no jurisdictional inquiry.[38]

Mrs. Alton left the marital domicile of Connecticut, and filed for a divorce six weeks and a day after her arrival in the Virgin Islands. Mr. Alton was personally served, appeared at the hearing, and did not contest the action. The commissioner recommended that a divorce be granted, but the district court judge requested further proof of domicile, and denied Mrs. Alton the divorce when she did not provide any. Mrs. Alton appealed.

The court of appeals, in an opinion by Judge Herbert F. Goodrich, held that the Virgin Islands court lacked divorce jurisdiction and that the six-week residency statute was invalid "as either an unreasonable interference by the legislative branch . . . with the exercise of the judicial power by the judicial branch or as an attempt by the legislature to convert the suit for divorce into what is in fact a transitory action masquerading under a fiction of domiciliary jurisdiction."[39]

Judge Goodrich's opinion expressed much concern over the phenomenon of migratory divorce and the problems of perjury and evasion associated with the establishment of domicile for the purpose of obtaining a "quickie" divorce. In holding that the Virgin Islands' statute conflicted with the Due Process Clauses of the Fifth Amendment and the Virgin Islands Organic Act, Judge Goodrich stated:

> Domestic relations are a matter of concern to the state where a person is domiciled. An attempt by another jurisdiction to affect the relation of a foreign domiciliary is unconstitutional even though parties are in court and neither one raises the question. The question may well be asked as to what the lack of due process is. The defendant is not complaining. Nevertheless, if the jurisdiction for divorce continues to be based on domicile, as we think it does, we believe it to be lack of due process for

---

[36] See also Makres v Askew, 500 F2d 577 (5th Cir 1974), *affg* 359 F Supp 1225 (MD Fla 1973), where the same conclusion was reached upholding the 6-month residency requirement in Florida's divorce statute.

[37] 207 F2d 667 (3d Cir 1953).

[38] Bill No 55, 17th Legislative Assembly of the Virgin Islands, passed May 19, 1953, approved May 29, 1953, amending §9 of the Divorce Law of 1944.

[39] Alton v Alton, 207 F2d 667, 673 (3d Cir 1953).

> one state to take to itself the readjustment of domestic relations between those domiciled elsewhere.[40]

While the *Alton* decision did not make a significant impact in this area,[41] the issues in the case highlight the importance of due process in the divorce context. This will be discussed further in the sections covering long-arm statutes and divisible divorce.[42]

## §4.04 Military Personnel

Some state statutes include a special provision applicable only to military personnel that provides for jurisdiction when at least one party is either domiciled in the state or stationed in the state as a member of the armed services for a required period of time.[43] For example, the District of Columbia Code states:

> If a member of the armed forces of the United States resides in the District of Columbia for a continuous period of six months during his or her period of military service, he or she shall be deemed to reside in the District of Columbia for the purposes of this section only.[44]

These statutes may not satisfy the constitutional requirement of equal protection of the law in mandating domicile for civilians while requiring mere

---

[40] *Id* 677.

[41] In Rheinstein, *The Constitutional Bases of Jurisdiction,* 22 U Chi L Rev 775, 779 (1955), Professor Max Rheinstein disputed Judge Goodrich's assumption "that a state's lack of jurisdiction to render a particular judgment necessarily has its basis in the due process clause so that every judgment rendered outside the sphere of the forum's jurisdiction is necessarily void."

Professor Rheinstein questioned the decision that the state of matrimonial domicile, Connecticut in the *Alton* case, was a "person" under the due process clause. Furthermore, Rheinstein doubted that Connecticut was even "deprived of life, liberty, or property without due process of the law." This doubt is even stronger today in light of the shift toward no-fault divorce, with its increased emphasis on individual rights, and away from fault divorce with its emphasis on the state's third-party interest.

[42] *See* **§§4.06-4.08, 4.15-4.16.**

[43] *See, e.g.,* Ariz Rev Stat Ann §25-312(1) (Supp 1984-85); Del Code Ann tit 13, §1504(a) (1981); Ga Code Ann §19-5-2 (1982); Ill Rev Stat ch 40, §401(1) (Smith-Hurd 1980); Ind Code §31-1-11.5-6(a) (1979); Kan Stat Ann §60-1603(b) (1983); Ky Rev Stat Ann §403.140(1)(a) (Baldwin 1983); Me Rev Stat Ann tit 19, §691(2) (1981); Miss Code Ann §93-5-5(a) (Supp 1984); Mo Rev Stat §452.305(1) (1977); Mont Code Ann §40-4-104(a) (1983); Neb Rev Stat §42-349 (1984); NM Stat Ann §40-4-5(C) (1983); Okla Stat tit 12, §1272 (1961); Utah Code Ann §30-3-1 (1984); Va Code §20-97 (1983); Wash Rev Code §26.09.030 (Supp 1985).

[44] DC Code Ann §16-902 (1981).

residence for members of the armed services, unless there is an exception for the military.[45]

The Uniform Marriage and Divorce Act also includes such a provision.[46] These provisions were intended to aid military personnel who are transferred frequently, usually lack the requisite intent to establish a new domicile, and often have to keep the place where they enlisted as a domicile, regardless of whether the intention to return exists. As one commentator has noted:

> In this situation and whenever, in connection with employment or otherwise, an individual must move frequently from place to place, his [or her] domicile is technical only. Domicile in these instances does not imply "a nexus between a person and place of such permanence as to control the creation of legal relations and responsibilities of utmost significance." It implies only that the person lacks the capacity to acquire a new domicile in the place where he [or she] has substantial attachments, or that he has no such attachments anywhere.[47]

The traditional rule that domicile is the primary basis of divorce jurisdiction persists. Despite the purpose of the military personnel residency provisions, some courts have insisted upon interpreting them as requiring domicile.[48]

---

[45] Case law exists which lends support to the contention that there is an equal protection exception for the military. In Taxation With Representation v Regan, 676 F2d 715 (1982), the plaintiff organization challenged the IRS's denial of tax-exempt status to it because it had failed to meet the IRS's statutory lobbying restrictions. Taxation argued that the IRS violated its equal protection rights, alleging that the IRS granted tax-exempt status to veterans' groups which had substantial lobbying activities.

The United States Court of Appeals for the District of Columbia Circuit, in an opinion by Judge Abner Mikva, held that practical application of the statute containing the lobbying restrictions resulted in disparate treatment of non-profit organization lobbying activities and, therefore, was a denial of equal protection. The Supreme Court of the United States reversed in Regan v Taxation With Representation, 461 US 540 (1983), holding that because the sections containing the IRS's statutory lobby restrictions did not employ any suspect classifications, the rational basis test was applicable instead of strict scrutiny. Justice Rehnquist, in rejecting the equal protection challenge, noted that veterans have been given numerous advantages because of their service to the country, and thus it was not irrational for Congress to subsidize the lobbying of veterans' organizations while refusing to subsidize substantial lobbying by charities generally.

The Court's reasoning in *Regan* facilitates a conclusion that a statutory difference in domicile requirements for civilians and military may be justifiable. To the authors' knowledge, there has been no challenge of the domicile requirements on an equal protection ground.

[46] Uniform Marriage and Divorce Act (UMDA) §302(a), 9A ULA 91, 121 (1979). *See* app 2-1.

[47] Garfield, *The Transitory Divorce Action: Jurisdiction in the No-Fault Era,* 58 Tex L Rev 501, 526 (1980) (footnote omitted).

[48] *See, e.g.,* Viernes v District Court, 181 Colo 284, 509 P2d 306 (1973); Lorance v Lorance, 216 Ga 754, 119 SE2d 342 (1961); Martin v Martin, 253 NC 704, 118 SE2d 29 (1961).

## §4.05 Importance of Personal Jurisdiction

A court with personal jurisdiction over both spouses in a divorce or dissolution action can validly adjudicate all issues arising out of the action and render orders entitled to full faith and credit in sister states.[49] The Supreme Court of the United States held in the two *Williams* cases[50] that an ex parte divorce decree obtained by a domiciliary of the divorcing state is entitled to full faith and credit in other states except that an absent spouse may collaterally attack such a decree on jurisdictional grounds. Subsequent cases shielded divorce decrees from collateral attacks in sister states by either spouse or third parties when both spouses had had the opportunity to litigate the jurisdiction issue. These parties were barred by the doctrine of res judicata from relitigating in the divorcing states.[51] Personal jurisdiction over both spouses in a divorce action effectively prevents collateral attack on the validity of the decree, and also precludes application of the divisible divorce doctrine.[52]

Obtaining personal jurisdiction over both spouses historically assured valid adjudication of child custody. While, traditionally, the three jurisdictional bases for custody proceedings have been the domicile of the child, the physical presence of the child, or personal jurisdiction over the parents,[53] the Supreme Court held in *May v Anderson*[54] that a court could not effectively deprive a parent of his or her right to child custody without acquiring personal jurisdiction over both parents. While the recognition of child custody decrees is always subject to the possibility of their modification due to changed circumstances, it has been noted that the Uniform Child Custody Jurisdiction Act (UCCJA)[55] assumes that *May v Anderson* permits, but does not require, recognition of custody decrees rendered without personal jurisdiction over the absent spouse.[56]

A court with personal jurisdiction over both spouses can order a party to

---

[49] US Const art IV, §1 states, "Full Faith and Credit shall be given in each State to the public Acts, Records, and Judicial Proceedings of every other State." For further discussion of the validity of foreign divorce decrees, see **§§4.09-4.14.**

[50] Williams v North Carolina, 317 US 287 (1942) (*Williams I*); Williams v North Caroline, 325 US 226 (1945) (*Williams II*). For in-depth treatment of these cases, see **§4.11.**

[51] Sherrer v Sherrer, 334 US 343 (1948); Coe v Coe, 334 US 378 (1948); Johnson v Muelberger, 340 US 581 (1951); **§§4.13-4.14.**

[52] The divisible divorce doctrine provides that a divorcing court lacking personal jurisdiction over an absent spouse may only validly terminate the marital status of the parties, and not adjudicate rights to custody, property, or spousal and child support. *See* **§§4.15-4.16.**

[53] *See, e.g.,* Judge Traynor's influential opinion in Samspell v Superior Court, 32 Cal 2d 763, 197 P2d 739 (1948); **chs 6, 7, 8 & 9.**

[54] 345 US 528 (1953).

[55] 9 ULA 116 (1979).

[56] Comment, *Long-Arm Jurisdiction in Alimony and Custody Cases,* 73 Colum L Rev 289, 316 (1973) (citing 1968 Handbook of the National Conference of Commissioners on Uniform State Laws 213).

convey property located outside the jurisdiction. In addition, personal jurisdiction is a prerequisite for judgments for temporary and permanent child support, alimony, attorneys' fees, and costs, which are entitled to full faith and credit.

Personal jurisdiction for money judgments has become necessary in light of the Supreme Court's decision in *Shaffer v Heitner*.[57] In that case, a nonresident shareholder brought a shareholder's derivative suit against the Greyhound Corporation in Delaware. Greyhound was incorporated under the laws of Delaware and its principal place of business was in Phoenix, Arizona. In order to obtain jurisdiction, Heitner had the corporation's stocks, options, and other corporate rights sequestered in Delaware. Greyhound argued that the sequestration was invalid because the ex parte action did not accord them due process and that the Delaware courts could not exercise jurisdiction because Greyhound did not have sufficient minimum contacts under *International Shoe Co v Washington*[58] to sustain jurisdiction.

The Supreme Court of the United States held that unless the defendant had other ties to the forum, a *quasi in rem* action would not support an exercise of jurisdiction if the property serving as basis for that jurisdiction was completely unrelated to the plaintiff's cause of action. The Court held that Delaware's assertion of jurisdiction over the nonresident corporation based solely on the presence of property in the state violated the Due Process Clause of the Constitution.

*Shaffer v Heitner* effectively eliminated quasi in rem jurisdiction. Thus, an important weapon for a dependent spouse seeking support and unable to obtain personal jurisdiction over the other spouse has been removed from the arsenal. A spouse who has obtained a money judgment pursuant to an ex parte divorce cannot attach the defendant spouse's property, litigate the claim, and apply the proceeds from a judicial sale of the property toward the claim if the claim was unrelated to the property and no other contacts with the forum existed.

Thus, the greatest advantage of obtaining personal jurisdiction over both spouses is that valid orders can be rendered with certainty. Finality is especially desirable in family law matters, where delicate issues such as status and support are adjudicated. Therefore, statutory mechanisms such as long-arm statutes[59] or the Revised Uniform Reciprocal Enforcement of Support Act (RURESA)[60] are very useful where one spouse has left the jurisdiction.

---

[57] 433 US 186 (1977). See also **§§4.02 & 4.11,** which discuss the effect of *Shaffer v Heitner* on domicile as the basis for ex parte divorces.

[58] 326 US 310, 316 (1945), where it was held that in order to satisfy due process, a defendant must have minimum contacts with the forum "such that the maintenance of the suit does not offend 'traditional notions of fair play and substantial justice.'"

[59] *See* **§§4.06-4.08.**

[60] 9A ULA 643 (1979).

## §4.06 Long-Arm Statutes—Application of General Statutes to Family Law Cases

A practical solution to the problem of obtaining personal jurisdiction over a nonresident spouse in family law cases is the use of long-arm statutes. Long-arm statutes are state legislative acts which provide for personal jurisdiction over nonresident persons and corporations under specific conditions enunciated in the statutes and limited by the due process requirements of the Constitution.[61]

Most long-arm statutes in this country are broad and general, providing for personal jurisdiction over non-resident defendants for causes of action arising out of the "transaction of any business," "commission of a tortious act," or "breach of contract" in a state.[62] Other, more specific provisions include causes of action arising out of contracts of insurance, ownership of real property, contracts to supply services within the state, and the like.[63] As one commentator has stated, "[t]raditional long-arm statutes are concededly not expressly designed to deal with alimony and child support actions."[64]

Efforts to apply the general long-arm statutes to family matters have met with limited success in a few states. In Illinois, an incompetent son attempted to use the long-arm statute to gain personal jurisdiction over the executor of his deceased father's estate in order to have the portion of the father's will disinheriting him declared null and void.[65] The son contended that the father's acts in Illinois, including the establishment of a marital domicile, the birth of the son, and the tortious acts of abandonment and destruction of the family unit 28 years earlier, constituted the *transaction of business* within the meaning of the state's long-arm statute. The Supreme Court of Illinois, rejecting the son's contentions, noted particularly that "[t]he suffering of the child as a consequence of the divorce is not compensable in damage."[66]

Nevertheless, in *Poindexter v Willis*,[67] the Appellate Court of Illinois upheld the use of the state long-arm statute in a paternity action where the mother contended that the alleged father in Ohio had subjected himself to the jurisdiction of the Illinois courts by committing the "tortious conduct" of failing to support his illegitimate child conceived in Illinois. The court agreed, stating:

> The word "tortious" . . . is not restricted to the technical definition of

---

[61] *See* **§4.08.**

[62] Knowles, *Expanding Jurisdiction Over Domestic Relations Causes*, 11 J Fam L 49, 59 (1971); Comment, *Long-Arm Jurisdiction in Alimony and Custody Cases*, 73 Colum L Rev 289, 297 (1973).

[63] Knowles, *supra* note 62, at 61.

[64] Comment, *supra* note 62, at 297.

[65] Mroczynski v McGrath, 34 Ill 2d 451, 216 NE2d 137 (1966).

[66] *Id* at 455, 216 NE2d at 140.

[67] 87 Ill App 2d 213, 231 NE2d 1 (1967).

> tort, but includes any act committed in this state which involves a breach of duty to another and makes the one committing the act liable to respondent in damages. Therefore, in our opinion, the failure of the father to support an illegitimate child constitutes a tortious act within the meaning of the statute and subjects him to the jurisdiction of the Illinois courts. . . .[68]

In Louisiana, an exwife attempted to use the state long-arm statute to obtain personal jurisdiction over her former husband, who was living in Texas, in order to have the amount of past due alimony under state judgment determined and made executory.[69] The plaintiff, stating that her husband had worked in Louisiana during much of the time in which the alimony went unpaid, contended that the exercise of personal jurisdiction was justified because nonpayment of alimony was "an offense or quasi offense" causing damage in Louisiana under the Louisiana long-arm statute.

The court of appeal rejected the plaintiff's argument that failure to pay alimony was equivalent to a tort in Anglo-American law. It noted that liability for alimony could only be enforced under special statutory provisions in Louisiana, and not under the general civil code rules.

In New York, it has been held that executing a separation agreement constitutes transaction of business under the state long-arm statute.[70] Yet, it appears that in absence of such an agreement, there can be no personal jurisdiction over a nonresident in matrimonial actions.[71]

These decisions have prompted one legal writer to query:

> Clearly, if the husband [who abandoned his wife] had broken his wife's leg, damaged her car, or breached a promise to support her, he would be amenable to personal jurisdiction under many statutes. Why refuse it because damage no less real is suffered as a result of a split marriage? Is it because domestic relations causes have a nominalism of rights and duties which doesn't fit into the traditional tort-contract glossary? . . .
>
> The reason that marital causes of action have not used the long-arm statutes is only one of nominalism. Domestic relations actions simply do not sound like tort or contract actions. They certainly are conceptually

---

[68] *Id* at 3.

[69] Martin v Martin, 250 So 2d 491 (La Ct App 1971).

[70] *See, e.g.*, Van Wagenberg v Van Wagenberg, 241 Md 154, 215 A2d 812, *cert denied,* 385 US 833 (1966); Zindiver v Ehrens, 34 AD2d 906, 311 NYS2d 389 (1970); Kochenthal v Kochenthal, 28 AD2d 117, 282 NYS2d 36 (1967).

[71] *See, e.g.*, Whitaker v Whitaker, 32 AD2d 595, 299 NYS2d 482 (1969); Baum v Baum, 62 Misc 2d 305, 307 NYS2d 305 (Sup Ct 1970); Inkelas v Inkelas, 58 Misc 2d 340, 295 NYS2d 35 (Sup Ct 1968).

close enough, though, for a little judicial inventiveness to include them, and they should be.[72]

## §4.07 —Domestic Relations Statutes

Since the 1960s many state legislatures have recognized that the pressing needs of family law litigation, inadequately protected by the general long-arm statutes, necessitated special long-arm provisions for family law use.[73] These provisions allow courts to exercise personal jurisdiction over nonresident spouses who formerly maintained a matrimonial domicile within the state or who have established contacts with the forum by executing a support agreement in the state. Some states have enacted flexible statutes authorizing their courts to exercise jurisdiction to the fullest extent consistent with due process requirements.[74]

One of the most restrictive of these statutes is the Wisconsin law, which provides for personal jurisdiction:

> In any action to determine a question of status . . . or in an independent action for support, alimony or property division commenced in the county in which the plaintiff resides at the commencement of the action when the defendant resided in this state in marital relationship with the plaintiff for not less than 6 consecutive months within the 6 years next preceding the commencement of the action, and after the defendant left the state and the plaintiff continued to reside in this state. . . .[75]

The *continued to reside* aspect of this statute (which is also included in domestic relations long-arm provisions in other states[76]) created problems for a wife who took her children from Wisconsin to follow her husband to Maryland, only to leave him there and return to Wisconsin less than a year later.[77] The Wisconsin court held that it did not have jurisdiction over the husband in the wife's suit for legal separation, alimony, child support, and custody. The court interpreted the statute as requiring that the wife must not have changed her domicile from Wisconsin even for a short period of time.

---

[72] Knowles, *supra* note 62, at 62.

[73] Freed & Walker, *Family Law in the Fifty States: An Overview,* 18 Fam LQ 369, 442-43 (1985), which lists the following states with specific support long-arm statutes: Alabama, Alaska, Arkansas, California, Colorado, Delaware, District of Columbia, Florida, Illinois, Indiana, Kansas, Louisiana, Maine, Maryland, Massachusetts, Mississippi, Missouri, Nevada, New Mexico, New York, Ohio, Oklahoma, Rhode Island, South Carolina, South Dakota, Texas, Utah, Virginia, Wisconsin, and Wyoming.

[74] *See, e.g.,* Cal Civ Proc Code §410.10 (Deering 1972) ("A Court of this state may exercise jurisdiction on any basis not inconsistent with the Constitution of this state or of the United States"); RI Gen Laws §9-5-33 (1970).

[75] Wis Stat Ann §801.05(11) (West 1977).

[76] *See, e.g.,* Kan Stat Ann §60-308(b)(6) (1983); Va Code §§8.01-328.1A(8) & (9) (1984).

[77] Dillon v Dillon, 46 Wis 2d 659, 176 NW2d 362 (1970).

One of the broadest statutory attempts to extend jurisdiction over an out-of-state spouse is the Oklahoma long-arm law, which provides for personal jurisdiction over a person who maintains "any other relation to this state or to persons or property including support for minor children who are residents of this state which affords a basis for the exercise of personal jurisdiction by this state consistently with the Constitution of the United States."[78] The Oklahoma Supreme Court held that this provision was constitutional in *Hines v Clendenning*.[79] One commentator has noted that this statute puts "domestic relations jurisdiction in Oklahoma on the very edge of due process and in the very forefront of reasonable accommodation to abandoned families."[80]

Generally, the domestic relations long-arm statutes are being used and are being upheld in the courts. They are primarily utilized on behalf of abandoned dependent spouses.[81]

## §4.08 —Constitutional Limits

The enactment of long-arm statutes was prompted by a judicial trend which expanded the contours of jurisdictional due process and enlarged the permissible scope of state courts' in personam jurisdiction over nonresidents. This trend peaked with the Supreme Court's enunciation of the *minimum contacts* standard in *International Shoe Co v Washington*[82] and its progeny.[83] Later Supreme Court decisions have curbed and refined the exercise of personal jurisdiction over nonresident defendants. These decisions have caused some legal writers to challenge the very basis of divorce jurisdiction.[84]

The retreat from the expansive implication of the earlier cases began in 1958 in *Hanson v Denckla*,[85] where the Supreme Court held that in order for a court to exercise personal jurisdiction over a nonresident defendant, "it is essential in each case that there be some act by which the defendant purposefully avails itself of the privilege of conducting activities within the forum State, thus

---

[78] Okla Stat Ann tit 12, §1701.03(a)(7) (West 1980).

[79] 465 P2d 460 (Okla 1970), upholding Okla Stat Ann tit 12, §1701.03(a)(7) (West Supp 1965).

[80] Knowles, *Expanding Jurisdiction Over Domestic Relations Causes*, 11 J Fam L 49, 58-59 (1971).

[81] *See* **ch 10.**

[82] 326 US 310 (1945). The standard as enunciated by the court is whether there are "sufficient contacts or ties with the state of the forum to make it reasonable and just according to our traditional conception of fair play and substantial justice to permit the state" to act. *Id* 320.

[83] Note, *Virginia's Domestic Relations Long-Arm Legislation: Does Its Reach Exceed Its Due Process Grasp?*, 24 Wm & Mary L Rev 229, 230 (1983) (citing McGee v International Life Ins Co, 355 US 220 (1957); Perkins v Benquet Consol Mining Co, 352 US 437 (1952); Travelers Health Assn v Virginia, 339 US 643 (1950)).

[84] *See* **§§4.02, 4.09 & 4.11.**

[85] 357 US 235 (1958).

invoking the benefits and protections of its laws."[86] The retreat from the expanding state court jurisdiction over nonresident defendants continued with other Supreme Court decisions, including *Shaffer v Heitner*,[87] where the Court declared that all assertions of state court jurisdiction, including in rem, must be evaluated according to the standards set forth in *International Shoe* and its progeny.[88]

Of particular interest to the family practitioner is *Kulko v Superior Court*,[89] where the Supreme Court held that a California court could not exercise personal jurisdiction through the state general long-arm statute due to paucity of contacts between the nonresident defendant and the forum. In *Kulko*, a daughter, who by her parents' separation agreement was to live with her father in New York, decided she wanted to live in California with her mother instead. Mr. Kulko provided her with the plane fare to the west coast. Two years later, the Kulkos' other child, a son, joined his mother and sister in California without the knowledge or permission of the father.

Less than one month later, the mother brought suit to gain custody of the children and increase child support, among other things.[90] Mr. Kulko appeared specially, arguing that he was a nonresident over whom the state could not properly exercise personal jurisdiction due to insufficient contacts with California. The facts showed that he had been in California twice in his life, once to marry Mrs. Kulko.

The California Supreme Court, unable to justify the exercise of personal jurisdiction over Mr. Kulko on the basis of his presence in that state, turned to the test set forth in *Hanson v Denckla*[91] and held that Mr. Kulko purposefully availed himself of the privilege of conducting activities within the forum state. Mr. Kulko's purposeful act of sending his daughter to live with her mother in California warranted exercise of personal jurisdiction over him.

The Supreme Court of the United States disagreed, holding that California's substantial interest in protecting and supporting resident children did not "make California a "fair forum," . . . in which to require [Mr. Kulko], who

---

[86] *Id* 253.

[87] 433 US 186 (1976).

[88] *Id* 212. See also World-Wide Volkswagen Corp v Woodson, 444 US 286 (1980), where the Court held that an Oklahoma court could not exercise personal jurisdiction over a New York car retailer and its wholesale distributor in a products liability action because the defendants' only contact with Oklahoma was the fact that a car they sold in New York to a New York resident became involved in an accident in Oklahoma; Rush v Savchuk, 444 US 320 (1980), where the Supreme Court held that a Minnesota court could not exercise quasi in rem jurisdiction over a nonresident defendant by attacking the contractual obligation of defendant's insurer who was licensed to do business in Minnesota.

[89] 436 US 84 (1978).

[90] 436 US at 88, where it is stated that the mother "sought to establish the Haitian divorce as a California judgment; to modify the judgment so as award her full custody of the children; and to increase [Mr. Kulko's] child support obligations."

[91] 357 US 235, 253 (1958).

derives no personal or commercial benefit from his child's presence in California and who lacks any other relevant contact with the State, either to defend a child support suit or to suffer liability by default."[92] The Court took note that California lacked a domestic relations jurisdiction statute, and that the state interest was already being served by its participation in the Revised Uniform Reciprocal Enforcement of Support Act (RURESA).

It is clear that the Due Process Clause of the Fourteenth Amendment operates as a limitation on the exercise of personal jurisdiction by the state courts over nonresident defendants. Due process requires minimum contacts between the defendant, the forum, and the cause of action. The Supreme Court decisions suggest that three broad factors should be considered in determining the limits of due process: the nature and extent of the defendant's connection with the state; the interests of the parties in having the asserted claims litigated in a particular forum; and the interests of the state in providing the plaintiff with an effective means of redress.[93] It has been noted, however, that "*Kulko* indicates the limits on long-arm jurisdiction in [family law adjudications] are narrower than many had thought desirable and possible in the light of modern social realities—a more mobile population and the greater ease of travel and communication."[94]

## §4.09 Recognition of Divorce Decrees

Under the Full Faith and Credit Clause of Article IV, Section 1 of the Constitution and the Act of Congress of 1790,[95] each state must give full faith and credit to the judgments of the courts of every other state. If these were applied literally, every decree of divorce rendered in one state would be entitled to recognition in every other state. However, each state has developed its own divorce law according to the public opinion of its citizens as interpreted by the legislature. Divorce laws in this country have ranged historically from the strict New York statute which formerly provided adultery as the only ground for absolute divorce to the liberal Nevada statute which continues to require only six weeks residence as a jurisdictional basis for its incompatibility ground.[96]

Because of the varying public policy foundations of the individual state

---

[92] Kulko v Superior Court of Cal, 436 US 84, 100-01 (1978).

[93] Note, *supra* note 83, at 247; Comment, *Long-Arm Jurisdiction in Alimony and Custody Cases,* 73 Colum L Rev 289, 295 (1973).

[94] Weintraub, *Texas Long-Arm Jurisdiction in Family Law Cases,* 32 Sw LJ 965, 982 (1978).

[95] Presently 28 USC §1738, which implements the Full Faith and Credit Clause in the following words:

> Such acts, records and judicial proceedings or copies thereof, so authenticated, shall have the same full faith and credit in every court within the United States and its Territories and Possessions as they have by law or usage in the courts of such State, Territory or Possession from which they are taken.

[96] *See* **§§1.09, 2.01-2.02.**

divorce laws, blanket recognition of divorce decrees has been a controversial idea in American family law. The public policy of our society has accorded respect for the sanctity of marriage which in turn has affected the evolution of law in this area.

The problems involved with the recognition of divorce decrees within the United States have emerged in the context of migratory divorce. Throughout the history of divorce in this country, there have always been states where "quickie" divorces were obtainable.[97] This, not surprisingly, led to the practice of migratory divorce, whereby affluent parties living in states with strict laws would travel to a state with liberal laws, sometimes called a divorce haven or mill, to obtain a divorce. These divorces have been variously called foreign, out-of-state, migratory, sister state, extraterritorial and Reno divorces.[98]

The conflicting interests among the divorce havens, the true domiciliary states, and the parties who desired quickie divorces show why a blanket recognition of sister state divorces has been resisted.

The divorce havens, financially motivated, encouraged out-of-staters to come for their divorces, supplied liberal residence requirements and divorce grounds, and rarely questioned whether the plaintiff was a bona fide domiciliary. In order to keep the business thriving, the divorce havens were strongly interested in having their divorce decrees recognized by sister states.

The true domiciliary state is traditionally considered the third party to the marriage contract.[99] As such, the state has an interest in preserving the marriages of its domiciliaries and having its laws respected, not evaded or flouted. The true domiciliary state has not been interested in recognizing a sister state decree when the parties left their true domicile in order to obtain it.[100]

The parties who obtain migratory divorces have the strongest interest in the validity and out-of-state recognition of their divorce decrees. Many of these persons remarry, and must avoid the risk of prosecution for bigamy or adultery, endless litigation by the previous spouse, or challenge by heirs at law or the Internal Revenue Service. The potential legal and emotional ramifications of

---

[97] *See* **§§1.09 & 2.01;** 2 C. Vernier, American Family Laws 107-08 (1931).

[98] K. Redder, Federal Regulation of Family Lawa 38 (1982).

[99] This traditional view has been challenged in recent years. *See* S. Green & J. Long, Marriage and Family Law Agreements ch 1 (Shepard's/McGraw-Hill 1984); L. Weitzman, The Marriage Contract (1981); Garfield, *The Transitory Divorce Action: Jurisdiction in the No-Fault Era,* 58 Tex L Rev 501, 517 (1980).

[100] See Adams & Adams, *Ethical Problems in Advising Migratory Divorce,* 16 Hastings LJ 60, 65-66 (1964), where the authors state:

> [M]any home states refuse to indulge the resulting demands for immediate divorce. . . . Other states now have laws and customs to provide divorces quickly, and with few questions asked, for out-of-state citizens. . . . The resulting stream of litigants from the strict states to Nevada, Idaho, Alabama, Arkansas, Florida, and the Virgin Islands has produced a great cleavage between state interest and party autonomy, for many home states are jealous of their role as a third party in loco parentis to every divorce suit. [Footnotes omitted.]

nonrecognition of a foreign divorce decree for those families of a subsequent marriage prompted family law authority Professor Homer Clark to declare that "it is highly desirable, if not essential, for a divorce decree to be unchallengeable in all states."[101]

The shift from fault divorce to no-fault, while reducing the number of migratory divorces, has not eliminated all the problems. Some no-fault statutes have separation periods long enough for impatient spouses to be lured to a divorce haven. In any event, the reduction of the number of migratory divorces has not reduced the importance of a valid divorce decree which would be entitled to be recognized by sister states. The situation as it exists in family law has been summarized as follows:

> Because of the strong policies reflected in the divorce laws of the differing states and the serious human and societal implications involved in the question of recognition of divorce decrees, general principles applicable to recognition of judgments, including the requirements of full faith and credit, have not always been consistently applied in this area. But what does appear to have evolved has been reliance on the "neutral" principles of full faith and credit to achieve an accommodation between conflicting policies of the involved states and the conflicting interests of the parties to the marital relationship. Under the present state of the law, *a divorce decree is seemingly entitled to recognition and may be refused recognition on the same basis as any other judgment rendered by a sister state court.*[102]

## §4.10 —Decrees Obtained in Foreign Countries

The discussion of recognition of foreign divorce decrees concentrates primarily on recognition of sister state judgments. Foreign *country* divorces do not have the res judicata finality mandated by the Full Faith and Credit Clause. They are recognized under the discretionary principle of *comity,* which has been defined by the Supreme Court of the United States as:

> [N]either a matter of absolute obligation, on the one hand, nor of mere courtesy and good will, upon the other. But it is recognition which one nation allows within its territory to legislative, executive, or judicial acts of another nation, having due regard both to international duty and convenience, and to the rights of its own citizens or of other persons who are under the protection of its laws.[103]

A court will examine the jurisdictional basis of a foreign country divorce

---

101 H. Clark, The Law of Domestic Relations in the United States 287 (1968).

102 R. Cramton & R. Sedler, Conflicts of Laws 253 (1977) (emphasis in original).

103 Hilton v Guyot, 159 US 113, 163-64 (1985). E. Stimson, Conflict of Laws 71 (1963), stated: "Writers and most courts agree that all that is meant by comity is that the state of the forum is not obliged by any superior power or force to apply foreign law."

decree according to this country's concepts of due process of law to determine whether the divorce is valid. Even if the jurisdictional basis of the foreign country divorce does conform to the due process principles developed in this country, a court will not necessarily accord recognition. As noted by the Supreme Court, a state need not give comity to a foreign country divorce "when contrary to its policy, or prejudicial to its interests."[104] Courts will evaluate public policy considerations of possible prejudice to the state, its citizens, and the parties themselves when deciding whether to recognize foreign country divorces. A list of some public policy considerations used as defenses to defeat the effects of foreign country divorces have been summarized as follows:

> (1) insufficient authentication or proof of a foreign judgment; (2) lack of finality of a foreign judgment; (3) lack of subject matter jurisdiction in the foreign forum; (4) lack of personal jurisdiction of the foreign forum; (5) insufficiency of notice or opportunity to be heard; (6) procurement of the foreign judgment by extrinsic fraud; (7) clear mistake of fact or law made by the foreign court in its judgment; and (8) the foreign judgment contravenes the public policy of the recognition forum.[105]

The recognition of foreign country divorces under the principles of comity should be contrasted with the recognition of final divorce decrees from sister states. These latter decrees must be recognized under the Full Faith and Credit Clause even though the decree may be against the public policy of the second state.

The vast majority of articles written on the effects of foreign country divorces on American domiciliaries have involved Mexican divorces. In the 1970s these divorces became less available to American citizens due to amendments to Mexican law which required aliens to become legal residents of Mexico before obtaining a divorce.[106] The Dominican Republic and Haiti have also become

---

[104] Hilton v Guyot, 159 US 113, 165 (1895).

[105] Swisher, *Foreign Migratory Divorces: A Reappraisal,* 21 J Fam L 9, 14-18 n 8 (1982-83) (citing Peterson, *Res Judicata and Foreign Country Judgments,* 24 Ohio St LJ 291, 308-10 (1963) and authorities cited therein).

[106] Swisher, *supra* note 105, at 9-10. *See, e.g.,* Clark, *Estoppel Against Jurisdictional Attack on Decrees of Divorce,* 70 Yale LJ 45 (1960); Currie, *Suitcase Divorce in the Conflict of Laws: Simon, Rosenthiel and Borax,* 34 U Chi L Rev 26 (1966); Foster, *Recognition of Migratory Divorces: Rosenthiel v Section 250,* 43 NYU L Rev 419 (1968); Garfield, *The Transitory Divorce Action: Jurisdiction in the No-Fault Era,* 58 Tex L Rev 501 (1980); Leach, *Divorce by Plane-Ticket in the Affluent Society—With a Side Order of Jurisprudence,* 14 Kan L Rev 549 (1966); Lupstein, *Recognition of Foreign Divorces: Retrospects and Prospects,* 2 Ottawa L Rev 49 (1967); Peterson, *Foreign Country Judgments and the Second Restatement of Conflict of Laws,* 72 Colum L Rev 220 (1972); Peterson, *Res Judicata and Foreign Country Judgments,* 24 Ohio St LJ 291 (1963); Phillips, *Equitable Preclusion of Jurisdictional Attacks on Void Divorces,* 37 Fordham L Rev 355 (1969); Rosenberg, *How Void is a Void Decree, or the Estoppel Effect of Invalid Divorce Decrees,* 8 Fam LQ 207 (1974); Note, *Domestic Relations—Jurisdiction—Extension of Comity to Foreign National Divorce,* 46 Tenn L Rev 38 (1978); Note, *United States*

divorce havens. In both countries domiciliary intent or meeting a residency requirement is unnecessary to procure a divorce. Therefore, judicial recognition of these judgments by courts in the United States is doubtful.

For the family law practitioner, when dealing with a client who desires a foreign country divorce, there are serious ethical considerations involved in advising, arranging, or representing clients in such a matter. As Professor Homer Clark has stated:

> A lawyer advising his client concerning the availability and effect of migratory divorces faces extremely difficult ethical problems. . . . The law in this area is in such a state of hypocrisy and dishonesty that a lawyer who gives realistic advice about migratory divorce places his professional reputation at some hazard.[107]

## §4.11 —Foreign Ex Parte Divorces

The validity and recognition of sister state or foreign divorce decrees depend upon whether domicile exists as a basis for jurisdiction and whether the divorce is ex parte or bilateral. The general rules applicable to ex parte divorces were established by a series of cases before the Supreme Court of the United States.

By the turn of this century, the Supreme Court had confirmed that a spouse could leave the matrimonial domicile, establish a new domicile, and bring an action for divorce in that domicile. In 1869, the Supreme Court established through *Cheever v Wilson*[108] that a divorce decree would be entitled to full faith and credit from sister states if the divorcing court acquired personal jurisdiction over the spouse who remained in the matrimonial domicile. However, as *Bell v Bell*[109] reflected, if neither party were validly domiciled in the divorcing state, and especially if the judgment for divorce were granted upon constructive service, the decree would not be entitled to full faith and credit.

When these cases were before the Court, marital fault still dominated the institution of divorce, and this affected the recognition of foreign divorce decrees. In *Haddock v Haddock*,[110] the Supreme Court was asked to determine the enforceability of a divorce decree where the husband had wrongfully left his wife in New York, established a domicile in Connecticut, and obtained a divorce through constructive service upon the wife, who remained domiciled in New York and did not appear in the action. The Court based its decision on the fact that the husband's departure was not justified. Although he was a bona fide domiciliary of Connecticut, New York State, as the matrimonial

---

*Recognition of Foreign Nonjudicial Divorces*, 53 Minn L Rev 612 (1969); Comment, *Mexican Divorces: Are They Recognized in California?*, 4 Cal WL Rev 341 (1968); Comment, *Mexican Divorce—A Survey*, 33 Fordham L Rev 449 (1965); Annot, 13 ALR3d 1419 (1967).

[107] H. Clark, The Law of Domestic Relations in the United States 295 (1968); **§2.02.**

[108] 76 US (9 Wall) 108 (1869).

[109] 181 US 175 (1901).

[110] 201 US 562 (1906).

domicile, was not obliged to recognize the Connecticut decree under the full faith and credit clause. *Haddock* remained the general rule for the next 36 years.[111]

In 1942 the Supreme Court decided the case of *Williams v North Carolina (Williams I),*[112] which has been called "the seminal foreign divorce case."[113] In that case, Mr. Williams and Mrs. Hendrix left their spouses in North Carolina, lived for six weeks in trailers in Las Vegas, Nevada, thus fulfilling the residency requirement in that state, and filed for divorce. Although they received notice of the Nevada actions, their spouses were not served in Nevada, did not make appearances, and did not participate in the proceedings. Williams and Hendrix married in Nevada after their divorces were finalized, and returned to North Carolina six months later.[114]

The new Mr. and Mrs. Williams were tried and convicted of bigamous cohabitation, despite their contention that the Nevada divorce decrees and marriage were valid in North Carolina as well as Nevada.[115] The Supreme Court of North Carolina affirmed the judgments of conviction on the basis of the *Haddock* case.[116]

The Supreme Court of the United States noted that North Carolina had not challenged the validity of the parties' domiciles in Nevada,[117] but instead, by relying on *Haddock,* had simply determined the divorces were not entitled to

---

[111] See M. Rheinstein, Marriage Stability, Divorce, and the Law 66 (1872), where Professor Rheinstein points out that in *Haddock:*

> The determination of the matrimonial domicile was thus made to depend on whether that party who had left the other had done so with or without just ground. A deserter should not be able to rid himself of his spouse by moving to a state of easy divorce. Hence, whenever the question arose whether or not faith and credit were due to an *ex parte* divorce obtained in a state in which only one of the spouses was domiciled, the court had to investigate whether the plaintiff had brought about the separation with or without just cause. Conceivably the Supreme Court of the United States might have to dig into that issue.

[112] 317 US 287 (1942).

[113] K. Redden, Federal Regulation of Family Laws 36 (1982).

[114] M. Rheinstein, *supra* note 111, at 67 n 55, refers to Powell, *And Repent at Leisure: An Inquiry into the Unhappy Lot of Those Whom Nevada Hath Joined Together and North Carolina Hath Put Asunder,* 58 Harv L Rev 930, 933 (1945), where it is documented that the new Mr. and Mrs. Williams returned to Pineola, population 306, which was a short distance from their original home, Granite Falls, population 2147. Both villages are located in the hill region near the Great Smoky Mountains. As Professor Rheinstein said, "Their mores were not those of Peyton Place."

[115] O.B. Williams was sentenced to prison for 3 to 10 years, and assigned to hard labor. Lillie Shaver Hendrix (the new Mrs. Williams) was sentenced to prison for 3 to 5 years, and "assigned to perform such labor as provided for women prisoners by law." State v Williams, 220 NC 445, 453, 17 SE2d 769, 774 (1941).

[116] State v Williams, 220 NC 445, 459, 17 SE2d 769, 778 (1941).

[117] In fact, the Court noted, North Carolina "admits that there probably is enough evidence in the record to require that petitioners be considered 'to have been actually domiciled in Nevada.' " Williams v North Carolina, 317 US 287, 291 (1942).

full faith and credit because the parties had wrongfully left the marital domicile. Ruling that *Haddock* was incorrectly decided, the Court established that a divorce decree validly obtained upon a proper jurisdictional basis of domicile is entitled to full faith and credit despite the facts that it was obtained with constructive service upon the other spouse, the plaintiff spouse wrongfully left the marital domicile, and the divorcing state's divorce policy conflicted with that of the matrimonial domicile.[118]

Undaunted, North Carolina again prosecuted and convicted the Williams couple, contending that they had not been bona fide domiciliaries of Nevada, that therefore the Nevada courts did not have jurisdiction to grant the divorces, and that the Nevada divorces were invalid. In *Williams II*,[119] the Supreme Court affirmed the convictions. The Court held that where a foreign state grants an ex parte divorce, a sister state may examine the validity of the plaintiff's domicile in the foreign state. If the state determines that the domicile in the foreign state is not bona fide, it is not required to give the resulting decree full faith and credit.

The result of the *Williams* cases was that a plaintiff who properly establishes a domicile in a state may validly terminate his or her marriage even upon constructive service on the absent spouse. The decree, however, is subject to attack upon jurisdictional grounds.

While these principles remain in effect, they have been challenged by legal writers who contend that domicile is an unconstitutional basis for ex parte divorce, violative of due process in light of *Shaffer v Heitner*.[120] In *Shaffer*, as stated by one such writer, the Supreme Court

> recognized that *in rem* jurisdiction was merely an elliptical reference to jurisdiction over a person's interest in a thing. A judicial proceeding *in rem* actually was a personal proceeding against the property owner, because an adverse judgment directly affected the property owner by divesting him of his rights in the property. To justify an exercise of *in rem* jurisdiction, therefore, the basis for jurisdiction must justify exercising jurisdiction over the interest of a person in his property. The standard for exercising jurisdiction over the interest of a person was the minimum contacts standard of *International Shoe*. Accordingly, the Court concluded

---

[118] *Id* 303, where the Court stated:

> When a court of one state acting in accord with the requirements of procedural due process alters the marital status of one domiciled in that state by granting him a divorce from his absent spouse, we cannot say its decree should be excepted from the full faith and credit clause merely because its enforcement or recognition in another state would conflict with the policy of the latter.

[119] Williams v North Carolina, 325 US 226 (1945).

[120] 433 US 186 (1977). *See also* **§§4.02, 4.08;** Hawkens, *The Effect of Shaffer v Heitner on the Jurisdictional Standard in Ex Parte Divorces,* 18 Fam LQ 311 (1984); Comment, *The Divisible Divorce Doctrine Reexamined in Light of Shaffer v Heitner,* 51 Miss L Rev 801 (1981); Note, *Jurisdiction in the Ex Parte Divorce: Do Absent Spouses Have a Protected Due Process Interest in Their Marital Status?,* 13 Mem St UL Rev 205 (1983).

that *"all assertions of state-court jurisdiction must be eavluated according to the standards set forth in* International Shoe *and its progeny.'*'[121]

In light of the Supreme Court's declaration, commentators have urged the application of the minimum contacts standard in ex parte divorce cases. One writer has suggested that, although the Court has refused to characterize divorce as an in rem proceeding, the divisible divorce doctrine[122] in effect creates such a proceeding "since it allows a court to assert jurisdiction over the marital status, as if it were a res, without obtaining in personam jurisdiction."[123] Application of the minimum contacts standard to the *Williams* case, it has been argued, warrants a conclusion that the Nevada court exceeded the bounds of due process when it exercised jurisdiction over the absent spouses.[124]

Generally, courts have not applied the minimum contacts standard to divorce actions subsequent to *Shaffer.*[125] It is troublesome to apply jurisdictional

---

[121] Hawkens, *supra* note 120, at 322-23 (footnotes omitted, emphasis in original). *See also* International Shoe Co v Washington, 326 US 310 (1945). It is also important to note that in Shaffer v Heitner, 433 US 186, 200 n 17 (1977), the Court used the term in rem throughout the opinion for both in rem and quasi in rem.

[122] *See* **§§4.15-4.17.**

[123] Comment, *supra* note 120, at 810.

[124] See Hawkens, *supra* note 120, at 324, where it is noted:

> The Nevada court failed to make the critical jurisdictional inquiry, namely, whether there existed a sufficient "relationship among the defendant, the forum, and litigation" to justify an assertion of jurisdiction. . . . [N]o contacts existed between the defendants and the forum. The defendants had not engaged in conduct either in Nevada or that affected Nevada. They had neither continuous nor systematic contacts with Nevada. They had not invoked the benefits and protection of Nevada's laws. Indeed, they had never set foot in Nevada. [Footnotes omitted.]

See also Comment, *supra* note 120, at 814, which states:

> The justification most often given for allowing a court to assert jurisdiction to grant a divorce when the defendant has no contacts with the forum state is the state's high interest in the marital status of its domiciliaries. Even if it is assumed that Nevada could develop such an interest in the marital status of one who has resided in the state for only six weeks, this does not justify the court's asserting jurisdiction, since the Supreme Court explicitly stated in *Kulko* [v Superior Court of California, 436 US 84 (1978)] that a state's interest in the litigation is insufficient, standing alone, to meet the standard of fairness.

[125] See *In re* Marriage of Rinderknecht, 174 Ind App 382, 367 NE2d 1128 (1977), where a Court of Appeals of Indiana applied the minimum contacts standard to a divorce action. The court decided that two different standards of contacts should govern the termination of the marital status and the adjudication of other aspects of the marriage. Thus, it held that a party's residence was sufficient contact for termination of the status because "changing of marital status in a dissolution proceeding is one of those in rem actions which, according to *Shaffer,* 'would not be affected by a holding that any assertion of state court jurisdiction must satisfy the *International Shoe* standard.' " *Id* 1135 (citation omitted).

The court declared that sufficient minimum contacts for adjudication of the incidents of marriage would always exist if the defendant was a resident of the state. If a

standards developed in cases involving corporations and businesses to actions involving marital status.

The jurisdictional standards developed in the *Williams* cases, standing alone, do appear to give an advantage to the domiciliary spouse in that this party may deprive the other spouse of constitutional rights in a migratory divorce action. However, it is important to note that the development of the divisible divorce doctrine protected the parties' custody, support, and property rights by mandating in personam jurisdiction for adjudication of those rights.[126] In view of these protections under the divisible divorce doctrine and the enactment of no-fault divorce in all 50 states and the District of Columbia, there is no longer need to return to pre-*Williams* obstacles to full faith and credit for ex parte divorce.[127]

## §4.12 —Foreign Bilateral Divorces

An ex parte divorce decree obtained by a bona fide domiciliary of the divorcing state is entitled to full faith and credit in other states.[128] Nevertheless, such a decree may be collaterally attacked in a sister state by an absent spouse on the ground that the divorcing court lacked jurisdiction because the plaintiff was not actually domiciled in the state.[129]

Different rules govern bilateral divorces. A bilateral divorce is one where both parties appear in the action in person, or where one party appears in person and the other appears through an attorney, or where one party appears in person and the other has been personally served within the state.[130] The Supreme Court of the United States established the rules in two 1948 decisions which presented the question of whether a spouse, who actually participated

---

nonresident, sufficient contacts would exist if the requirements of the domestic relations long-arm statute were met, or if the defendant appeared or refused to dispute the court's in personam jurisdiction in a timely manner. *Id* 1135-36.

[126] *See* **§§4.15-4.16.**

[127] The fact that all jurisdictions now have no-fault grounds diffuses the arguments of some commentators who urge stricter jurisdictional requirements as a means of making divorce more difficult to obtain. See, for example, Hawkens, *supra* note 120, at 329, where it is stated:

> An ex parte divorce terminates not only the marital status of the petitioning spouse, it terminates as well the marital status of the defendant spouse and thereby adversely affects fundamental rights of that spouse. The jurisdictional standard in *Williams I* . . . ignores completely the impact of the divorce decree on a relationship that has constitutionally protected aspects of liberty, association, and privacy. More important, the standard in *Williams I* ignores that the absent spouse may have a substantial interest in remaining married.

[128] Williams v North Carolina, 317 US 287 (1942).

[129] Williams v North Carolina, 325 US 226 (1945).

[130] K. Redden, Federal Regulation of Family Law 41 (1982).

in a divorce action resulting in a bilateral divorce decree, may later collaterally attack it on jurisdictional grounds.[131]

In *Sherrer v Sherrer,*[132] the wife moved from Massachusetts to Florida and filed for divorce after expiration of the 90-day residence requirement. The husband answered through an attorney, denying that the wife was a bona fide domiciliary of Florida. He appeared personally at the hearing; his attorney did not cross-examine the wife as to her allegations of domicile, nor did the attorney introduce any rebuttal evidence. The Florida court granted the divorce, and neither party appealed. The wife remarried two days after the divorce decree was entered and returned to Massachusetts.

In Massachusetts, the husband instituted an action alleging that the Florida decree was invalid, praying that he be permitted to convey some real estate (which he evidently had promised to turn over to the wife), and asking that he receive a judicial declaration that he was living apart from his wife for justifiable cause. The Massachusetts court granted the husband's request, refusing to recognize the Florida decree on the ground that the wife was never actually domiciled in Florida. The Supreme Judicial Court of Massachusetts affirmed. The Supreme Court of the United States reversed.

In *Sherrer's* companion case, *Coe v Coe,*[133] the husband instituted divorce proceedings in Nevada after the Massachusetts courts had denied him a divorce and granted his wife a decree of separate maintenance. The wife answered in the Nevada proceedings, not disputing the husband's allegation of domicile, cross-claimed for divorce, and appeared personally at the hearing, represented by counsel. The wife was actually granted the divorce; neither party appealed. The husband remarried shortly after.

In Massachusetts, the wife brought an action against her husband to find him in contempt of court for failure to make support payments and to enlarge the support award. The husband denied the separate maintenance decree was still in effect and introduced the Nevada divorce as a bar to the contempt action. A battle on appeal resulted in the Supreme Judicial Court ultimately affirming the lower court's determination that the husband was not actually domiciled in Nevada and that the Nevada court did not have jurisdiction to terminate the marriage. As in the *Sherrer* case, the Supreme Court reversed.

The Supreme Court held that the fact that the husband in *Sherrer* and the wife in *Coe* had participated in the divorce proceedings, and had had the opportunity to dispute the jurisdictional issue, precluded them on the principle of res judicata from subsequently collaterally attacking the decree based on the

---

131 Sherrer v Sherrer, 334 US 343 (1948); Coe v Coe, 334 US 378 (1948). Professor Garfield described these decisions as a retreat from the rules of the *Williams* cases. *See* Garfield, *The Transitory Divorce Action: Jurisdiction in the No-Fault Era,* 58 Tex L Rev 501, 508 (1980). Professor Rheinstein declared that *Sherrer* and *Coe* removed "the necessity of creating at least the appearance of a true change in domicile by one or the other party." *See* M. Rheinstein, Marriage Stability, Divorce and the Law 70-71 (1972).

132 334 US 343 (1948).

133 334 US 378 (1948).

jurisdictional issue. These participating parties could not attack the decrees in a sister state if they were precluded from collaterally attacking them in the divorcing state. As stated by Chief Justice Vinson in the *Sherrer* case:

> The requirements of full faith and credit bar a defendant from collaterally attacking a divorce decree on jurisdictional grounds in the courts of a sister State where there has been participation by the defendant in the divorce proceedings, where the defendant has been accorded full opportunity to contest the jurisdictional issues, and where the decree is not susceptible to such collateral attack in the courts of the State which rendered the decree.[134]

Justice Frankfurter dissented, emphasizing the importance of the matrimonial domicile's interest in divorce. He noted particularly that the Massachusetts statute included a provision invalidating migratory divorce.[135] Reviewing the

---

[134] Sherrer v Sherrer, 334 US 343, 352 (1948).

[135] *Id* 360 (citing Mass Gen Laws ch 208, §39 (Michie/Law Co-op 1932)) which stated:

> A divorce decreed in another jurisdiction according to the laws thereof by a court having jurisdiction of the cause and of both the parties shall be valid and effectual in this commonwealth; but if an inhabitant of this commonwealth goes into another jurisdiction to obtain a divorce for a cause occurring here while the parties resided here, or for a cause which would not authorize a divorce by the laws of this commonwealth, a divorce so obtained shall be of no force or effect in this commonwealth.

It should be noted that the National Conference of Commissioners of Uniform State Laws and the American Bar Association approved the Uniform Divorce Recognition Act, 9 ULA 641 (1979), but to this date only California, Nebraska, New Hampshire, North Dakota, Rhode Island, South Carolina, and Wisconsin have adopted it. Louisiana, Montana, and Washington have repealed the Act, in fact.

The Act provides that a foreign divorce will not be recognized in a state if both parties were actually domiciled in that state. It also provides:

> Proof that a person obtaining a divorce from the bonds of matrimony in another jurisdiction was (a) domiciled in this state within twelve months prior to the commencement of the proceeding therefor, and resumed residence in this state within eighteen months after the date of his departure therefrom, or (b) at all times after his departure from this state, and until his return maintained a place of residence within this state, shall be prima facie evidence that the person was domiciled in this state when the divorce proceeding was commenced.

The Commissioners' Prefatory Note, 9 ULA at 661, §2, states that the Uniform Divorce Recognition Act

> has been framed upon the theory that it is desirable to discourage rather than to encourage migration in pursuit of a divorce; that specific statutory refusal to recognize extra-state divorces obtained by domiciliaries of the state enacting the statute will reduce tourist divorce-seeking, particularly as the perils of that practice become generally recognized; and that recognition to extra-state divorces obtained by domiciliaries should be refused except as specifically required by the Constitution of the United States, since any narrower policy both would be difficult to formulate and would introduce factors so complex as to endanger the goal of uniformity.

facts in both the *Sherrer* and *Coe* cases which indicated that the divorces were fraudulently obtained, Justice Frankfurter concluded:

> But the crux of today's decision is that regardless of how overwhelming the evidence may have been that the asserted domicile in the State offering bargain-counter divorces was a sham, the home State of the parties is not permitted to question the matter if the form of a controversy has been gone through. To such a proposition I cannot assent . . . . I cannot bring myself to believe that the Full Faith and Credit Clause gave to the few States which offer bargain-counter divorces constitutional power to control the social policy governing the domestic relations of the many States which do not.[136]

It has been noted that the practical effect of the *Sherrer* and *Coe* decisions was "to curtail the scope of the second *Williams* decision, which has established the right of one state to challenge a " 'quickie' divorce decree of another."[137] Yet, it has also been observed that these decisions were probably not meant to absolutely preclude a jurisdictional challenge from a sister state.[138]

*Sherrer* and *Coe* went beyond the normal application of res judicata, and might be described more accurately in terms of collateral estoppel, because the subsequent suits were based on different causes of action that the Florida and Nevada divorce proceedings.[139] However, in *Sherrer* and *Coe* the Supreme Court ruled that the mere opportunity to litigate the jurisdictional issue in the original divorce action, whether taken advantage of or not, was sufficient to deprive the parties of the right to any later relitigation. In other words, these cases concluded that a foreign bilateral divorce in another state is immune from attack in subsequent litigation between the parties.

## §4.13 —Equitable Estoppel

The principle of equitable estoppel exists as another limit on the rule

---

136 Sherrer v Sherrer, 334 US 343, 337 (1948). See also McDonough, *Mr. Justice Jackson and Full Faith and Credit to Divorce Decrees: A Critique*, 56 Colum L Rev 860, 879 (1956), where it was noted that:

> Mr. Justice Frankfurter did not spell out the analysis by which he thought the Court could, consistently with the full faith and credit clause, permit the home state to refuse to treat the issue of jurisdiciton as res judicata if it would be so treated were a collateral attack to be made on the decree in the divorcing state. There is some indication, however, that he would simply have relied upon the Court's judicial knowledge that divorce proceedings in some states are notoriously collusive not only as to grounds but also as to jurisdiction and that the courts of such states are designedly oblivious to such collusion. . . .

137 McDonough, *supra* note 136, at 878.

138 M. Rheinstein, *supra* note 131, at 73.

139 Garfield, *supra* note 131, at 509. *See also* **§4.13**

established in *Williams II*[140] that a foreign ex parte divorce decree may be attacked on jurisdictional grounds.[141] Equitable estoppel precludes a party from asserting or denying rights, claims, or facts against another party who justifiably relied on the first party and will suffer injury if the first party is allowed to repudiate.[142] Equitable estoppel invoked in the context of recognition of divorce decrees precludes a former spouse from attacking the validity of a divorce decree if it would be inequitable to do so.[143]

This equitable estoppel principle is not governed by the Full Faith and Credit Clause of the Constitution. Thus, a sister state court is not obliged to invoke the doctrine to bar an attack on a divorce decree if the court in the divorcing state would have invoked the doctrine to bar an attack on a divorce decree. Instead, the application of equitable estoppel is determined in each case, not by the law of the state which granted the divorce, but by the law of the state in which the divorce is questioned.[144]

This equitable estoppel principle is not a function of the divorce decree, and is usually dependent upon events which may have occurred after the divorce was granted or apart from the divorce action.[145] A party may be estopped from attacking a divorce decree if such an attack would be inconsistent with prior conduct or if there has been reliance on the decree by spouses or third parties, especially if the reliance takes the form of remarriage.[146]

---

[140] Williams v North Carolina, 325 US 226 (1945).

[141] The *Williams II* rule was limited by the cases Sherrer v Sherrer, 334 US 343 (1948) and Coe v Coe, 334 US 378 (1948), discussed in **§4.12,** where the Supreme Court held that a spouse who was personally subject to the jurisdiction of a divorcing state, with an opportunity to litigate the jurisdiction issue, is barred by the Full Faith and Credit Clause from attacking the decree in a sister state if he or she would have been barred in the divorcing state under its rules of res judicata.

[142] Black's Law Dictionary 438 (5th ed 1979). Some cases which discuss and define the equitable estoppel doctrine outside the divorce decree recognition area include, e.g.: Piazza Properties Ltd v State Dept of Motor Vehicles, 71 Cal App 3d 622, 138 Cal Rptr 357 (1977); Anderson v Anderson, 59 Hawaii 575, 585 P2d 938 (1978); Colthurst v Colthurst, 265 NW2d 590 (Iowa 1978); *In re* Shaw, 615 P2d 910 (Mont 1980); Smith v Smith, 201 Neb 21, 265 NW2d 855 (1978); Thompson v Soles, 299 NC 484, 263 SE2d 599 (1980); Seagram Distillers Co v Jones, 548 SW2d 667 (Tenn Ct App 1976), *appeal dismissed,* Joseph E. Seagram & Sons v Jones, 432 US 901 (1976); Roberts v Holton City, 543 SW2d 75 (Tex 1976).

[143] Restatement (Second) Conflicts of Law §74 (1971).

[144] Restatement (Second) Conflicts of Law §74 comment (a) (1971). The comment notes that:

> Each State of the United States has been deemed free, at least within broad limits, to determine the rule's scope and effect. Whether full faith and credit requires that a person who would be estopped from attacking the divorce decree in the State of rendition must likewise be held estopped from attacking the decree in a sister State is a question that appears never to have arisen.

[145] H. Clark, The Law of Domestic Relations in the United States 297 (1968).

[146] *Id* 306-07, where Professor Clark noted:

> The arguments supporting estoppel where there has been a remarriage are so

The most obvious application of estoppel is where the divorce was obtained by the very person attempting to attack it.[147] The exceptions to this rule have involved situations where the spouse who obtained the divorce was a victim of fraud, duress, or coercion, or was in some way not responsible for his or her actions.[148]

Generally, a person is estopped from attacking a decree when he or she participated in the divorce proceeding. Participation includes an appearance as a defendant in the divorce action,[149] as well as the financing of a married woman's divorce with the intention of marrying her.[150] Some courts have held that a party's delay in attacking a decree when he or she has knowledge of the jurisdictional defect is enough to invoke the estoppel doctrine.[151] A form of reliance accepted by courts, in addition to remarriage, as a sufficient basis for application of the estoppel doctrine is the acceptance of benefits from a divorce, such as valuable consideration from a settlement agreement, or alimony.[152]

---

strong that courts have been persuaded by them even where the divorce has been judicially held invalid, or where no final divorce had occurred at the time of the second marriage, or where the divorce was by mail order, or where there was no judicial divorce at all. (Footnotes omitted, citing, inter alia, Spellens v Spellens, 49 Cal 2d 210, 317 P2d 623 (1957); Rediker v Rediker, 35 Cal 2d 796, 221 P2d 1 (1950) (dictum); Bruguiere v Bruguiere, 172 Cal 199, 155 P 988 (1916); Apelbaum v Apelbaum, 7 App Div 2d 911, 183 NYS 2d 54 (2d Dep't 1959) (applying New Jersey law); Astor v Astor, 6 Misc 2d 967, 160 NYS 2d 106 (S Ct 1957); Anderson v Anderson, 121 Utah 237, 240 P2d 966 (1952). *Contra:* Landsman v Landsman, 302 NY 45, 96 NE2d 81 (1950).]

Other cases espousing the rule that a party who relies on a divorce decree by remarrying may not subsequently attack that decree include: Mattos v Correla, 274 Cal App 3d 413, 79 Cal Rptr 229 (1969); Oakley v Oakley, 30 Colo App 292, 493 P2d 381 (1971); Clagett v King, 308 A2d 245 (DC 1973); Sandifer v Sandifer, 389 So 2d 767 (La Ct App 1980); Poor v Poor, 381 Mass 392, 409 NE2d 758 (1980); Ross v Sitner, 274 Pa Super 445, 418 A2d 490 (1980).

147 *See, e.g.*, Diehl v United States, 438 F2d 705 (5th Cir), *cert denied*, 404 US 830 (1971); Clagett v King, 308 A2d 245 (DC 1973); Clay v Clay, 353 So 2d 428 (La Ct App 1977); *In re* Proceeding for Support Under Article 4 of Family Court Act, 94 Misc 2d 59, 404 NYS 2d 515 (Fam Ct 1978).

148 *See, e.g.*, Spindel v Spindel, 283 F Supp 797 (EDNY 1968); Meyer v Meyer, 328 Ill App 408, 66 NE2d 457 (1946); Burton v Burton, 176 Okla 494, 56 P2d 385 (1936); Graham v Graham, 54 Wash 70, 102 P 891 (1909).

149 *See, e.g.*, Sherrer v Sherrer, 334 US 343 (1948); Perrin v Perrin, 408 F2d 107 (3d Cir 1969); Smith v United States, 277 F Supp 583 (D Fla 1967); Scherer v Scherer, 405 NE2d 40 (Ind Ct App 1980).

150 *See, e.g.*, Goodloe v Hawk, 113 F2d 753 (DC Cir 1940); Margulies v Margulies, 109 NJ Eq 391, 157 A 676 (1931); Kazin v Kazin, 81 NJ 85, 405 A2d 360 (1979).

151 *See* Elliot v Hardcastle, 271 Ark 90, 607 SW2d 381 (1980); Farber v Farber, 25 AD2d 850, 269 NYS2d 608 (1966).

152 *See* Greer v Greer, 77 Ariz 219, 269 P2d 718 (1954); Anderson v Anderson, 223 Ark 571, 267 SW2d 316 (1954); Oberstein v Oberstein, 217 Ark 80, 228 SW2d 615 (1950); Ellis v White, 61 Iowa 644, 17 NW 28 (1883); Watson v Watson, 49 NC App 58, 270 SE2d 542 (1980); Smoak v Smoak, 269 SC 313, 237 SE2d 372 (1977).

Estoppel is inapplicable in cases where a party has obtained a void divorce decree, has remarried and is being prosecuted for bigamy or bigamous cohabitation. The aim of the bigamy statute is to punish that type of behavior, and the state is not subjected to estoppel.[153] In addition, estoppel is usually not applied in divorce cases where neither party has relied on the divorce decree and, therefore, the declaration of the invalidity of the decree will not yield inequitable results. The classic case in which the estoppel doctrine has been rejected involves a party who, after obtaining an invalid divorce decree, brings an action for divorce attacking the previous decree, where neither spouse has remarried or made financial claims.[154]

The discretionary application of equitable estoppel in the courts of individual states has resulted in inconsistency. Accordingly, the unique facts of each case will determine the availability and applicability of equitable estoppel.

The practitioner should be mindful of certain presumptions in a collateral attack situation. There are presumptions in favor of jurisdiction in the divorcing state, in favor of the validity of the divorce judgment, and in favor of the validity of a second or subsequent marriage.

The policy behind equitable estoppel in divorce is related to these presumptions. Equitable estoppel, like the doctrine of res judicata, emphasizes the importance of the demand for finality in divorce litigation. It reflects the reluctance of courts to upset subsequent marriages with one party in good faith and in ignorance of any defect. In this respect, equitable estoppel in divorce may be distinguished from "true" equitable estoppel: courts invoking the estoppel doctrine tend to validate the current marriage relationship rather than focus on any wrongdoing of the party.

In addition, it has been noted that the doctrine of equitable estoppel represents an adherence to contemporary sociological theories of divorce and is a reflection of the no-fault spirit.[155] When courts apply the estoppel doctrine, they acknowledge that a marriage has ended in fact even though prevailing legal requirements have not been met.

## §4.14 —Third-Party Attack

Whether a third party may attack a foreign divorce decree in a sister state, on the ground that one of the parties did not establish a bona fide domicile in the divorcing state, was presented to the Supreme Court of the United States in *Johnson v Muelberger.*[156] In that case, a daughter in New York, who was sole legatee under her father's will, attacked the validity of his Florida divorce from his second wife in order to prevent his third wife from taking her statutory

---

[153] H. Clark, *supra* note 145, at 229.

[154] *See* Garman v Garman, 102 F2d 272 (DC Cir 1939); Stevens v Stevens, 273 NY 157, 7 NE2d 26 (1937); Hamm v Hamm, 30 Tenn App 122, 204 SW2d 113 (1947).

[155] H. Clark, *supra* note 145, at 303. *See also* **§2.03.**

[156] 340 US 581 (1951).

one-third of the estate. The facts showed that the father had appeared in the Florida action, and answered on the merits, without disputing jurisdiction, even though the second wife had not complied with Florida's 90-day residence requirement. He later married the third wife.

The New York trial court decided that the daughter could not attack the decree in New York because it was valid and final in Florida and could not be collaterally attacked in that state. The Appellate Division affirmed. The New York Court of Appeals reversed on the ground that the Florida judgment, which had held that there was divorce jurisdiction, bound only the parties to the action and not third parties.[157] The New York Court of Appeals interpreted Florida law as allowing the daughter to collaterally attack the decree in that state.

The Supreme Court of the United States reversed, holding that Florida did not permit a child, a stranger to the divorce proceedings, to contest her parents' divorce where the parents were barred from contesting jurisdiction by the doctrine of res judicata. Justice Reed concluded:

> In that case New York cannot permit such an attack by reason of the Full Faith and Credit Clause. When a divorce cannot be attacked for lack of jurisdiction by parties actually before the court or strangers in the rendering state, it cannot be attacked by them anywhere in the Union. The Full Faith and Credit Clause forbids.[158]

The practical effect of *Johnson v Muelberger, Sherrer v Sherrer,*[159] and *Coe v Coe*[160] made a bilateral divorce decree virtually immune from attack, except possibly by the true domiciliary state itself. Under *Johnson,* apparently, a third party would be able to attack an ex parte decree on a jurisdictional basis, since an absent spouse would also be able to attack such a decree. This conclusion is supported by the Supreme Court's decision in *Cook v Cook.*[161]

In that case, Mr. Cook sent his wife to Florida to obtain a divorce after he discovered that she was still married to her first husband at the time of their marriage. Mr. Cook married her again after the divorce.

Eventually, the couple experienced difficulties, prompting Mrs. Cook to secure a decree of separate maintenance in Hawaii. Mr. Cook retaliated by bringing an action in Vermont to have both his marriages to Mrs. Cook declared null and void on the ground that she was still married to her first husband when each marriage was contracted.

The Vermont trial court annulled the first marriage but refused to annul the second marriage, even though it found that Mrs. Cook had not been a bona fide domiciliary of Florida and had fraudulently obtained the divorce. The

---

157 *In re* Johnson's Estate, 301 NY 13, 92 NE2d 44 (1950).

158 Johnson v Muelberger, 340 US 581, 589 (1951).

159 334 US 343 (1948). *See* **§4.13.**

160 334 US 378 (1948). *See* **§4.13.**

161 342 US 126 (1951).

Supreme Court of Vermont affirmed the annulment of the first marriage and held that the second marriage was also null and void.

The Supreme Court of the United States reversed. The Court noted the general rule that jurisdiction is presumed unless disproved, and that in that particular case there was no evidence as to what took place in the Florida proceedings except that Mrs. Cook was granted a divorce.[162] That lack of knowledge let the presumption of jurisdiction stand, and precluded Cook from attacking the Florida decree.

The *Cook* case and other decisions limiting attacks on foreign divorces were criticized as facilitating migratory divorce.[163] This reaction, like Justice Frankfurter's reaction in his dissents to *Sherrer, Coe,* and *Johnson,* must be considered in the light of the time period, 1948-1951, when prevailing public policy generally condemned divorce. These so-called res judicata decisions constitute enforcement of the Full Faith and Credit Clause rather than condonation of mutual consent divorce. The importance of the finality of a divorce decree outweighed concern that spouses were frequently colluding in order to divorce in the strict fault-based system.

## §4.15 Divisible Divorce Doctrine

The interest of the state of domicile over the marital status of its bona fide domiciliaries was developed in the in rem or marital res theory of divorce jurisdiction,[164] and strengthened by a series of Supreme Court cases, particu-

---

[162] *Id* 127-28, where Justice Douglas stated:

> So far as we know, the issue of domicile was contested, litigated and resolved in petitioner's favor. If the defendant spouse appeared in the Florida proceedings and contested the issue of the wife's domicile, Sherrer v Sherrer, . . . or appeared and admitted her Florida domicile, Coe v Coe, . . . or was personally served in the divorce State, Johnson v Muelberger, . . . he would be barred from attacking the decree collaterally; and so would a stranger to the Florida proceedings, such as respondent, unless Florida applies a less strict rule of *res judicata* to the second husband than it does the first. . . . On the other hand, if the defendant spouse had neither appeared nor been served in Florida, the Vermont court, under the ruling in *[Williams II],* could reopen the issue of domicile. (Citations omitted.)

[163] See, e.g., McDonough, *Mr. Justice Jackson and Full Faith and Credit to Divorce Decrees: A Critique,* 56 Colum L Rev 860, 879 (1956), where the author declared:

> The practical meaning of the *res judicata* decisions is that if both spouses want a divorce which they cannot get at home (and can afford it) they can, through expertly guided albeit collusive and perjurious machinations in a "divorce-mill" state, obtain a divorce decree which the full faith and credit clause makes invulnerable for all practical purposes with nothing lost save honor.

[164] According to the in rem or marital res theory of divorce jurisdiction, as developed in the late nineteenth century, a domiciliary state had a strong interest in the status of the parties, the marital res, over which the courts had in rem jurisdiction at the domicile. *See* **§4.01.**

larly *Williams v North Carolina (Williams I)*,[165] which held that an *ex parte* divorce obtained by a bona fide domiciliary was entitled to full faith and credit in the sister states.

Conflicting interests may arise between the domicile state and the state of the new residence when one spouse obtains a migratory divorce. An attempt to balance public policy, state interests, and due process considerations in the ex parte divorce situation produced the divisible divorce doctrine. According to this doctrine, a divorcing court which lacks personal jurisdiction over an absent spouse may validly terminate the marital status of the parties, but may not adjudicate rights to custody, property, or spousal and child support.[166]

The Supreme Court first enunciated the divisible divorce doctrine in *Estin v Estin*.[167] In that case, Mrs. Estin obtained a decree of separation and permanent alimony in New York in 1943, a year after her husband had left her. In 1945 Mr. Estin was granted an ex parte divorce in Nevada based on constructive service on Mrs. Estin, who did not appear in the action. The decree made no provisions for alimony, though the Nevada court had been advised of the New York decree. Mr. Estin ceased making alimony payments, and Mrs. Estin brought an action for arrears in New York.

Mr. Estin appeared in the New York action and moved to eliminate the alimony provisions of the separation decree, arguing that the Nevada decree was recognizable under *Williams I*, and that under New York law, a divorce terminated a support order. The trial court denied the motion and granted Mrs. Estin a judgment for the arrears. The Appellate Division and the New York Court of Appeals affirmed.

The Supreme Court of the United States approached the case by analyzing the conflicting interests of the two states involved. The divorcing state had an interest in the integrity of marriage, the legitimacy of offspring, and the prevention of bigamy, which necessitated application of the Full Faith and Credit Clause to its divorce decrees. The former marital domicile, on the other hand, had an interest in preventing the abandoned spouse from becoming a public charge, which weighed against the recognition of a foreign decree which would terminate that spouse's support.

The Court reconciled these conflicting interests by holding that an ex parte termination of the marital status did not necessarily result in the termination of all legal incidents of the marriage. The Court characterized Mrs. Estin's New York judgment as a property interest which could not be affected by the Nevada

---

[165] 317 US 287 (1942). While the Court in *Williams I* refused to classify divorce as an in rem action, its holding was based upon the idea that the marital res follows a spouse from state to state. *See* **§§4.02, 4.11.**

[166] Thus, the existence of the divisible divorce doctrine heightens the importance of personal jurisdiction in divorce actions. *See* **§4.05.** It has been argued that domicile as the jurisdictional basis for an ex parte divorce is unconstitutional as a violation of due process, and that termination of the marital status should be equally jurisdictionally protected as are rights to custody, support, and property. *See* **§4.11.**

[167] 334 US 541 (1948).

court without personal jurisdiction over Mrs. Estin.[168] Since the divorce was granted with jurisdiction based upon Mr. Estin's domicile with constructive service upon Mrs. Estin, New York was required to give full faith and credit to Nevada's termination of the marital status of the parties, but was not required to recognize that part of the decree which affected Mrs. Estin's property interests. In his opinion, Justice Douglas concluded:

> The result in this situation is to make the divorce divisible—to give effect to the Nevada decree insofar as it affects marital status and to make it ineffective on the issue of alimony. It accommodates the interests of both Nevada and New York in this broken marriage by restricting each state as to the matters of her dominant concern.[169]

In *May v Anderson*,[170] the Supreme Court held that an Ohio court was not obligated by the Full Faith and Credit Clause to recognize a Wisconsin ex parte divorce decree which awarded the custody of children to a father on the jurisdictional basis of the children's technical statutory domicile with their father in Wisconsin. Citing *Estin*, the Court held that the Wisconsin court was powerless to enter a constitutionally enforceable custody order without personal jurisdiction over the mother, because "[r]ights far more precious to appellant than property rights will be cut off if she is to be bound by the Wisconsin award of custody."[171]

The Supreme Court's next confrontation with the divisible divorce doctrine, *Vanderbilt v Vanderbilt*,[172] involved the situation where Mrs. Vanderbilt in New York instituted an action for support *after* her husband had obtained an ex parte divorce in Nevada. The New York court, finding that the Nevada decree was valid, nevertheless ordered Mr. Vanderbilt to make support payments under a provision of New York law which specifically enabled a court to award support

---

[168] *Id* 548, where the Court stated:

> The property interest which [the New York decree] created was an intangible, jurisdiction over which cannot be exerted through control over a physical thing. Jurisdiction over an intangible can indeed only arise from control or power over the persons whose relationships are the source of the rights and obligations.

[169] *Id* 533. Justice Jackson, in a strong dissent, declared at *id* 554:

> The Court reaches the Solomon-like conclusion that the Nevada decree is half good and half bad under the full faith and credit clause. It is good to free the husband from the marriage; it is not good to free him from its incidental obligations. Assuming the judgment to be one which the Constitution required to be recognized at all, I do not see how we can square this decision with the command that it be given *full* faith and credit. (Emphasis in original.)

[170] 345 US 528 (1953). See **§4.05** for a discussion of the importance of personal jurisdiction in such situations. *See also* **chs 6, 7, 8 & 9.**

[171] *Id* 533.

[172] 354 US 416 (1957).

to a wife who had been constructively served and did not appear in an ex parte divorce action.[173]

The Supreme Court of the United States held that the Nevada court could not extinguish Mrs. Vanderbilt's property rights without having obtained personal jurisdiction over her. Thus, the New York court was not obligated by the Full Faith and Credit Clause to give that part of the decree recognition.[174]

In *Simons v Miami Beach First National Bank,*[175] the issue was whether a valid Florida ex parte divorce, obtained without personal jurisdiction over the wife, terminated the wife's right to dower where the husband had made support payments under a New York separation decree until his death. The Court held that the New York decree did not preserve any dower interest for the wife, and that since dower does not survive a divorce decree under Florida law, the denial of dower by the Florida courts did not violate the Full Faith and Credit Clause of the Constitution.

## §4.16 —Utility

The divisible divorce doctrine was strongly criticized by dissenters in cases which created the doctrine.[176] One commentator noted in 1980 that "[d]ivisible divorce may be an untidy or even an unwielding concept, but only because it accurately reflects the complexity of the human relationship to which it applies."[177]

Whether or not it reflected reality, the divisible divorce doctrine proved useful in both a societal and a legal context. The doctrine was developed during the time when migratory divorce was a serious societal problem. By requiring that the litigation over custody, property, and support issues take place only in the forum having personal jurisdiction over the absent spouse, the divisible divorce doctrine eliminated much of the financial incentive for supporting spouses to leave the marital domicile and obtain migratory divorces. It also dampened the financial motivation for the absent spouse to relitigate the jurisdiction issue at a later time.

Perhaps most importantly, the divisible divorce doctrine successfully thwart-

---

[173] *Id* 418 (citing Gilbert-Bliss' NY Civ Prac Law, vol 6A, §1170-b (1956 Supp)). Historically, New York was a strict divorce law state, providing adultery as the only divorce ground for decades, and jealously defending against migratory divorce. Hypocritically, it also had the most lenient annulment statute in the country. *See* **§§2.02, 3.01.**

[174] In his dissent, Justice Frankfurter criticized the Court for "turning the constitutional law of marital relations topsy-turvy," *id* 425, and argued that the marital relation, as a personal claim or obligation, was as worthy of protection as alimony.

[175] 381 US 81 (1965).

[176] *See, e.g.*, the dissents in Estin v Estin, 334 US 541 (1948); Vanderbilt v Vanderbilt, 354 US 416 (1957).

[177] Garfield, *The Transitory Divorce Action: Jurisdiction in the No-Fault Era,* 58 Tex L Rev 501, 512 (1980).

ed potential due process arguments by absent spouses. The severing of the property and support aspects of divorce from the status aspects tended to protect spouses' custody, support, and property rights from deprivation without due process of law.[178] The Supreme Court managed to solve the problem through the divisible divorce doctrine without expressly holding that a foreign court's adjudication of a spouse's custody, support, and property rights, absent personal jurisdiction over that spouse, was a violation of due process.

## §4.17 —Bifurcation of Action

The divisible divorce doctrine established the possibility of spouses litigating the termination of the marital status in one jurisdiction while litigating the incidents of the divorce in another jurisdiction.[179] However, it is also possible to divide the divorce action within a single jurisdiction. In some states courts will bifurcate a dissolution action so that the issue of termination of marital status is separated from other issues.

Bifurcation may be either statutory or judicially created. The Uniform Marriage and Divorce Act (UMDA) provides that a court may enter a decree or dissolution if "the court has considered, approved, or provided for child custody, the support of any child entitled to support, the maintenance of either spouse, and the disposition of property; *or has provided for a separate, later hearing to complete these matters.*"[180] The Illinois statute permits a court to reserve determination of custody, support, and property division in appropriate circumstances.[181] The California Civil Code expressly reserves jurisdiction for a later determination of division of property,[182] and this reservation of jurisdiction has been judicially expanded to include other issues as well.[183] In

---

[178] *Id* 510-11, where the author notes:

> The divisible divorce cases also answered in advance the due process arguments the absent spouse might have raised as a result of the *Williams I* requirement that states give full faith and credit to *ex parte* decrees. If courts had applied *Williams I* to adjudications of support and property rights, the absent spouse could have argued persuasively that this deprived him of property rights without due process. . . . With the absent spouse's property and custody rights protected, the only deprivation of which he could complain would be the alteration of his marital status *in absentia.* It seems unlikely, however, that the right to remain married to an unwilling spouse rises to the dignity of a due process right. [Footnotes omitted.]

[179] *See* Vanderbilt v Vanderbilt, 354 US 416 (1957); May v Anderson, 345 US 528 (1953); Estin v Estin, 334 US 541 (1948); **§§4.15-4.16.**

[180] Uniform Marriage and Divorce Act §302(a)(4), 9A ULA 91, 121 (1979); *see also* **app 2-1.**

[181] Ill Ann Stat ch 40, §401(3) (Smith-Hurd 1980).

[182] Cal Civ Code §4800(a) (Deering 1984).

[183] *See In re* Marriage of Fink, 54 Cal App 3d 357, 126 Cal Rptr 626 (1976).

Florida, courts have authorized bifurcation of a dissolution.[184]

Some jurisdictions allowing bifurcation are restrictive in its application while others utilize it broadly. It is likely that the results of bifurcation in particular states have influenced the courts. For example, in California and Washington, community property states, real property retains its marital character after the marital status is terminated and until it is equally divided between the spouses. In Florida and Maryland, among other common law states recognizing bifurcation, property held as tenants by the entireties becomes property held as tenants in common upon termination of marital status.

The strongest policy arguments favoring bifurcation of dissolution actions have been provided by the California and Washington courts. In these jurisdictions, under their no-fault laws, the state's interest has shifted from preserving unworkable marriages to promptly terminating them.[185] In addition, the Washington courts, at least, have found unpersuasive the arguments against bifurcation, the "parade of horribles," as one judge has called them,[186] and have maintained that problems such as the loss of property rights and extended litigation exist in dissolution actions even without the bifurcation issue.[187]

The Florida and Illinois courts, on the other hand, are persuaded that bifurcation should not be used except under appropriate circumstances. The strongest policy arguments for avoiding bifurcation center on the achievement of finality, promotion of judicial economy, and avoidance of multiple litigation and complications which can result from the entry of partial judgments. The

---

[184] In Hyman v Hyman, 310 So 2d 378, 379 (Fla Dist Ct App 1975), the court declared:

> It is uncontested that a court may reserve jurisdiction to determine child custody, support, and alimony. . . . We rule that a Trial Court may enter an interlocutory order granting a dissolution of marriage and therein reserve jurisdiction to later determine property rights.

*See also* Ellett v Ellett, 94 Nev 34, 573 P2d 1179 (1978); *In re* Marriage of Hermsen, 27 Wash App 318, 617 P2d 462 (1980).

[185] See Hull v Superior Court, 54 Cal 2d 139, 147-48, 352 P2d 161, 166, 5 Cal Rptr 1, 6 (1960), where the court stated:

> The divisible divorce is more than a jurisdictional concept. Severance of a personal relationship which the law has found to be unworkable and, as a result, injurious to the public welfare is not dependent upon final settlement of property disputes. Society will be little concerned if the parties engage in property litigation of however long duration; it will be much concerned if two people are forced to remain legally bound to one another when this status can do nothing but engender additional bitterness and unhappiness.

[186] *In re* Marriage of Hermsen, 27 Wash App 318, 617 P2d 462, 466 (1980).

[187] *Id*, where the Court of Appeals of Washington acknowledged, however:

> The important right to a prompt dissolution without regard to fault is not absolute. It may conflict with other rights such as the right to the just and equitable distribution of property and liabilities guaranteed by [the statute]. Upon a showing that interim protective orders will not prevent a denial of this or some other significant right, the court may require the resolution of all issues in one decree.

Supreme Court of Illinois has listed the potential complications of a bifurcated judgment, including that:

> The court could likely be required to adjudicate marital property rights that have become entangled with the supervening rights of third parties, including subsequent spouses. Additionally [bifurcation] . . . would complicate, rather than simplify, matters with respect to the rights of a surviving spouse in the event of an intervening death. Other complications that can ensue . . . include the loss of ability to file joint income tax returns, the loss of medical insurance coverage, and the loss of marital property treatment for property accumulated during the intervening period between the entry of the judgment of dissolution and the final disposition of property rights.[188]

There are several reasons why parties may move for or stipulate to bifurcation of their dissolution,[189] based on preference, timing, necessity, or litigation strategy. One or both parties may wish to remarry.[190] Bifurcation is useful to delay litigation over support and property issues where a dependent spouse is unable to obtain personal service on an elusive supporting spouse or where the supporting spouse is temporarily unable to provide such support. Bifurcating an action to force the dissolution of the marital status may be important where one spouse is deliberately frustrating efforts to dispose of the case.[191]

The practical and legal considerations regarding bifurcation are discussed in the next section.[192]

## §4.18 —Bifurcation Practice Considerations

The family law practitioner will be aware of the ramifications of bifurcation of a dissolution action. These must be fully explained to the client so that an informed decision on bifurcation may be made.[193]

---

188 *In re* Marriage of Cohen, 93 Ill 2d 190, 199, 443 NE2d 541, 545 (1982).

189 Miller, *Bifurcation of Dissolution of Marriage Actions, Part One,* 55 Fla BJ 755, 757 n 1 (1981). Here the author notes that there are no reported cases where a court has failed to approve the parties' stipulation to bifurcation, which leads him to the conclusion that stipulations to bifurcation will be approved by a court.

190 California courts have held that freedom to remarry is a sufficient reason for bifurcation, *In re* Marriage of Fink, 54 Cal App 3d 357, 126 Cal Rptr 626 (1976), while Florida courts have held that it is not. *See* Claughton v Claughton, 393 So 2d 1061 (Fla 1980).

191 *See, e.g.,* Behar v Southeast Banks Trust Co, NA, 374 So 2d 572 (Fla Dist Ct App 1979), *rehg denied,* 379 So 2d 202 (Fla 1980); Chayka v Chayka, 361 So 2d 430 (Fla Dist Ct App 1978); *In re* Marriage of Cohen, 93 Ill 2d 190, __, 443 NE2d 541, 543 (1982); Ellett v Ellett, 94 Nev 34, 573 P2d 1179 (1978).

192 *See* **§4.18.**

193 For an excellent discussion of these legal and practical ramifications, see Miller,

First, it is important to know whether the jurisdiction permits bifurcation, what standard is used to determine whether such a bifurcation should be granted, and whether the individual judges generally grant motions to bifurcate. In these days of crowded court calendars, judges may not appreciate the continuing reappearance of a case. A judge may be unable to reach the case where numerous other cases are awaiting their first and perhaps final hearing.

Bifurcation is costly; it requires more preparation than one dissolution hearing or trial. In addition, it runs against the general policy of settling all aspects of a case as soon as possible.

The practitioner must be aware that bifurcation may affect the negotiating process. Where one party desires bifurcation in order to remarry,[194] for example, the attorney for the other spouse may use that urgency as leverage in negotiating a separation agreement, especially in a jurisdiction where remarriage is an insufficient basis for bifurcation.

Generally, the delay between termination of status and adjudication of property rights is a time period full of potential problems. The fact of entry of a divorce decree may result in change of the character of the marital property by operation of law. There is always the possibility that the parties' property may be encumbered by liens, the Internal Revenue Service, or third-party debtors enforcing their rights. There are daily changes in the value of an asset. One spouse may dispose of property to prevent the other from receiving any of it, perhaps in violation of a court's injunction.

One or both spouses may die before property rights are adjudicated. If one spouse remarried before death, two surviving spouses may fight over the same property.

There are other disadvantages to bifurcation. The dependent spouse ordinarily loses medical insurance, which could profoundly affect an ill spouse. In some states the basis for spousal support changes when a dependent spouse remarries. For example, in Florida, "upon remarriage the wife is barred from recovering periodic alimony or lump sum alimony 'which is predicated on need,' "[195] although she may still be awarded a lump sum award based upon an equitable share of assets during marriage.

The parties' circumstances may have changed significantly between the time when the marriage is terminated and the time when the property and support issues are adjudicated. Obviously, such changes affect the computation of a spousal support award. For example, if a supporting husband remarries and adopts his new wife's children before any support is awarded to the first wife

---

*Bifurcation of Dissolution of Marriage Actions, Part One,* 55 Fla BJ 755 (1981); Miller, *Bifurcation of Dissolution of Marriage Actions, Part Two,* 55 Fla BJ 831 (1981); **§4.17.**

[194] Miller, *Part One, supra* note 193, at 756, where the author claims that "The basic motive for bifurcation is often the husband's desire to remarry."

[195] Miller, *Part Two, supra* note 193, at 832 (quoting from Claughton v Claughton, 362 So 2d 752 (Fla Dist Ct App 1974)). For a discussion of support, *see* **ch 10.**

and the children, a court must consider the husband's new support obligations. It is probable that the first wife and the children would have received more had the dissolution not been bifurcated. Even though the husband who remarried would most likely come back to court eventually to request a modification of the support award based on a change of circumstances, as a practical matter, parties do not return for modification immediately after the dissolution. This means that the first wife would benefit from higher support payments for a longer time.

There is yet another consideration where there is remarriage before support issues are litigated. It has been suggested that a custodial parent who remarries may receive less child support than he or she would obtain as an unmarried custodial parent, "notwithstanding the obvious response that the new [spouse] has no legal obligation (absent adoption proceedings) to another [person's] children."[196] The family law practitioner needs to be aware of multiple factors when considering and advising bifurcation as an alternative in a dissolution action, including the informed wishes of the client.

## §4.19 Advising Clients About Migratory Divorce

The principal motives for pursuing an out-of-state divorce have included taking advantage of more liberal divorce laws, avoiding the exposure of intimate marital history in a local court, and, of course, obtaining a divorce quickly, frequently in order to remarry. The growth of no-fault divorce has largely eliminated the need to pursue foreign divorces. Nevertheless, there may be circumstances in which a client desires a divorce immediately. For example, one might want to marry a military or corporate person who must soon move out of the state for employment reasons. The practitioner then must decide to what extent he or she may ethically advise the client about migratory divorce.

The lawyer has the duty to competently advise the client on any question which the client poses. Thus, "[i]t is not, it is believed, professionally improper for a lawyer to advise a local client that by going to another state the client may take advantage of its more liberal divorce laws."[197] However, the attorney should not arrange, participate in, or encourage the client to obtain a migratory divorce, especially if the lawyer knows the client intends to return immediately after the decree is granted. An attorney cannot properly counsel a client to deceive or perpetrate a fraud upon any court, whether of his or her own or another state.

The ethical opinions and case law on advising a client about migratory divorce are dated and, therefore, of questionable applicability. In 1932, the American Bar Association Committee released Opinion No. 84 which precludes attorneys from advising their clients to obtain out-of-state divorces if

---

[196] Miller, *Part Two, supra* note 193, at 832; *see also* **ch 10.**

[197] Drinker, *Problems of Professional Ethics in Matrimonial Litigation,* 66 Harv L Rev 443, 454 (1953).

they know that the clients intend to return to their original domicile after procuring their divorces.[198] In 1942 the ABA Committee declared that any lawyer involvement in the procurement of illegal Mexican divorces for New York residents was unethical and illegal.[199] In New York and New Jersey, some attorneys were disbarred for obtaining Mexican "mail order" divorces.[200]

Two commentators remarked in 1964 that:

> Many American cases, as well as opinions of bar association ethics and grievance committees have commented upon the ethical duty of the family lawyer in migratory divorce. Many of these expressions of judicial and professional opinion date from before World War II, and changed social attitudes toward divorce havens weakened their authority. Others . . . represent more recent judicial pronouncements which circumscribe very strictly the lawyer's ethical duty in migratory divorce. In almost every state the bar association grievance and ethics committees are generally composed of the more conservative lawyers in the community, who are frequently associated with firms which avoid family law problems as "messy" and unbecoming of the profession. The existing opinions, while significant as the only extant formal expression of the views of the organized bar, must, therefore, be taken with salt sufficient to counteract their frequently impractical loftiness (footnotes omitted).[201]

This comment shows that not only is migratory divorce a dated issue, but even much of the writing on the issue is behind the times. The family law bar has developed and diversified since 1964, when the previously quoted article was written. Statistics published in a 1983 survey of the American Bar Association's Family Law Section reveal that during the preceding two and a half years, the section's membership had jumped from 6,000 to nearly 15,000![202] Twenty-six per cent of the membership were women, and 59 per cent had been in practice for 10 years or less. A majority of the family law attorneys surveyed work in relatively small firms. Many of the leading family law litigators are sole practitioners. However, preeminent firms are also becoming involved in family law.

A lawyer who informs a client about the divorce law in another state should make it clear to the client whether he or she is licensed to practice in that

---

[198] Note, *The Role of the Lawyer in Divorce: Some Ethical Problems*, 21 U Pitt L Rev 720, 727 (1960).

[199] ABA Opinions 248 (1942).

[200] *In re* Cohen, 10 NJ 601, 93 A2d 4 (1952); *In re* Esquitol, 285 AD 138, 136 NYS2d 133 (1954); *In re* Anonymous, 274 AD 89, 80 NYS2d 75 (1948) (the court here denied a motion for an order adjudging an attorney guilty of professional misconduct due to the "novelty" of the situation of procurement of a Mexican "mail order" divorce).

[201] Adams & Adams, *Ethical Problems Advising Migratory Divorce*, 16 Hastings LJ 60, 67-68 (1964).

[202] Smith & Troha, *A Survey of the Membership of the ABA Section of Family Law*, 17 Fam LQ 225, 233 (1983).

jurisdiction.[203] The client must be informed of the risks and legal ramifications of migratory divorce. These consequences are discussed in the previous sections.[204]

Although bigamy prosecutions have not been reported in migratory divorce cases in recent years, it is important for the practitioner to inform the client of that possibility. Were a divorce decree to be denied recognition, irreparable problems could result with subsequent spouses' property and inheritance rights. In short, advise the client to proceed with the utmost caution, if at all.

The wise practitioner will not arrange "quickie" ex parte divorces in foreign jurisdictions. If the client desires the immediacy of a migratory divorce, the lawyer should advise him or her to "cut the cord" with the home state and establish a new domicile in the divorcing state to avoid raising the question of domicile at a later time. The client should be advised to terminate the lease or sell the house, and resign from employment or at least take a leave of absence. In the new state, he or she should get a driver's license, register to vote, and apply for work.

The practitioner is faced with a dilemma when approached by a client who wishes to obtain a migratory divorce. The safer route would be to recommend that the client obtain a divorce in the matrimonial domicile or decline the case entirely. If the client is determined to seek a divorce in a more favorable jurisdiction, then the client should be referred to an attorney in the foreign jurisdiction for competent advice.

## §4.20 Domestic Relations Exception to Federal Diversity Jurisdiction

Generally, federal courts refuse to exercise diversity jurisdiction over cases which involve domestic relations issues such as divorce, alimony, or child custody. This *domestic relations exception* has no express constitutional or statutory basis. It is a judicially implied limitation on federal diversity jurisdiction, along with a similar exception for probate matters. The domestic relations exception has evolved unevenly from a murky historical basis.

Writings on the domestic relations exception inevitably conclude with frustrated criticism of the application of the exception.[205] It is clear that federal

---

[203] Adams & Adams, *supra* note 201, at 60, 68. The authors state that "a clear labelling of his status as a non-practitioner there, coupled with an outline of the sources used, plus a caveat that more conclusive and up-to-date information may be available from a member of the other state's bar, ought to satisfy his ethical duty."

[204] *See* **§§4.05-4.16.**

[205] *See, e.g.*, 13 C. Wright, A. Miller, & E. Cooper, Federal Practice and Procedure §3609 (1975); Vestal & Foster, *Implied Limitations on the Diversity Jurisdiction of Federal Courts*, 41 Minn L Rev 1, 23-26 (1956); Comment, *Enforcing State Domestic Relations Decrees in Federal Courts*, 50 U Chi L Rev 1357 (1983); Note, *The Domestic Relations Exception to Diversity Jurisdiction*, 83 Colum L Rev 1824 (1983); Note, *Federal Jurisdiction of "Domestic Relations" Cases*, 7 J Fam L 309 (1967). *See also* Phillips, Nizer, Benjamin, Krim & Ballon

courts have no original jurisdiction to grant divorces in the 50 states.[206] However, when faced with actions incidental to a divorce, such as enforcement of support decrees, federal courts have inconsistently and unpredictably applied the domestic relations exception to federal diversity jurisdiction.

The primary focus of this section is the domestic relations exception in relation to divorce, and, peripherally, alimony and custody.[207] Because of the serious challenges to the accuracy of the historical basis of the exception, a detailed discussion of the origins of the exception is included in the general discussion of the exception's application.

## §4.21 —Historical Background

Diversity jurisdiction was established in the Constitution and further developed by Congress.[208] The domestic relations exception to diversity jurisdiction was created by the judiciary. However, inconsistent application and rationalization of the exception by the federal courts over the years have produced uncertainty as to the scope and the purpose of the doctrine; increased federal presence in the area has fostered challenges to the exception's utility.[209]

The existence of an exception is generally attributed to dictum in the Supreme Court's 1859 decision in *Barber v Barber*.[210] In that case a wife domiciled in New York sued her husband in a Wisconsin federal court for enforcement of a New York decree for divorce a mensa et thoro and alimony. Judgment was entered for the wife. The Supreme Court of the United States affirmed the judgment as a proper exercise of federal jurisdiction by the district court.

The Court was careful to state that the suit was not one asking for an allowance of alimony. The Court disclaimed "altogether any jurisdiction in the

---

v Rosenstiel, 490 F2d 509 (2d Cir 1973); Spindel v Spindel, 283 F Supp 797 (EDNY 1968).

[206] This rule does not apply in the territories, and, prior to 1956, did not apply to the District of Columbia. In that year Congress enacted a compromise bill, an Act to Establish a Domestic Relations Branch in the Municipal Court for the District of Columbia, Pub L No 486, Chap 204, 70 Stat 111 (1956) which created a Domestic Relations Branch of what was then the Municipal Court of the District of Columbia. This marked the end of the exercise of federal jurisdiction over domestic matters in the district. Family law jurisdiction is set forth in DC Code Ann §11-1101 (1981). For a brief article on this transfer of jurisdiction, see Meyers, *Washington's New Domestic Relations Tribunal*, 6 Cath UL Rev 139 (1957).

[207] There will be no discussion of the domestic relations exception in relation to other family matters, such as illegitimacy, torts, or the like.

[208] The Constitution broadly provides in art III, §2, that "[t]he Judicial Power shall extend . . . to Controversies . . . between Citizens of different States." In the Act of Sept 24, 1789, §11, Stat 73, 78, inferior courts were authorized to decide "suits of a civil nature at common law or in equity," when a minimum sum in controversy was alleged.

[209] *See also* **§4.22.**

[210] 62 US (21 How) 582 (1859).

courts of the United States upon the subject of divorce, or for the allowance of alimony, either as an original proceeding in chancery or as an incident to divorce *a vinculo* or to one from bed and board."[211]

This language has been frequently cited as establishing the domestic relations exception to federal diversity jurisdiction. However, the rationale for the exception derived from the three-pronged *Barber* dissent. The dissent (Chief Justice Taney, and Justices Daniel and Campbell) maintained that it was impossible for diversity jurisdiction to exist in *Barber,* because the parties' marital status had not been terminated and, therefore, they were still one person under the doctrine of coverture.[212] Declaring that it was not within the design, operation and competence of the federal courts to "assume to regulate the domestic relations of society,"[213] the dissent concluded that because the English civil courts had no power over divorce or alimony, neither did the courts of the United States, which exercised jurisdiction "the same in nature and extent as the jurisdiction of England, whence it is derived."[214]

In 1890 the Court decided another case using language which, along with *Barber,* has been consistently cited as authority for the domestic relations exception to federal diversity jurisdiction. Ironically, the Court did not even consider whether a domestic relations exception existed in *In re Burrus.*[215] The Supreme Court held in that case that a district court did not have the power to issue a writ of habeas corpus to restore an infant to the custody of his father from the custody of his grandparents. The Court ruled that the right of child custody was unaffected by federal law, because "[t]he whole subject of domestic relations of husband and wife, parent and child, belongs to the laws of the States and not to the laws of the United States."[216] In *Burrus,* the Supreme Court was discussing the limits of the power of the federal government to enact substantive law in the area of domestic relations. In fact, the Court reserved the question of exercising federal jurisdiction over custody disputes.[217]

---

[211] *Id* 584.

[212] This rationale appeared frequently in early cases. However, the power of this argument has diminished in light of the fact that the common law rule that the wife's domicile followed her husband, used to defeat diversity jurisdiction in early cases, has been relaxed in all jurisdictions to the point where a wife may establish her own domicile for good reason. *See* Note, *Federal Jurisdiction of "Domestic Relations" Cases,* 7 J Fam L 309, 309 n 4 (1967) (citing Bowman v Bowman, 30 F 845 (CCND Ill 1887); Druen v Druen, 247 F Supp 754 (D Colo 1965); Garberson v Garberson, 82 F Supp 706 (ND Iowa 1949)).

[213] Barber v Barber, 62 US (21 How) at 602.

[214] *Id* 592 (quoting Livingston v Story, 34 US (9 Pet) 632 (1835)). The historical accuracy of this rationale has been challenged with examples from English case law where English courts exercised jurisdiction over domestic matters. *See* Note, *The Domestic Relations Exception to Diversity Jurisdiction,* 83 Colum L Rev 1824, 1835-39 (1983); Spindel v Spindel, 283 F Supp 797, 802-03 (EDNY 1968), and cases cited therein.

[215] 136 US 586 (1890).

[216] *Id* 593-94.

[217] *Id* 596, where the Court stated, "But whether the diverse citizenship of parties

Courts frequently have cited *Barber* and *Burrus* as authority for the existence of the domestic relations exception to diversity jurisdiction. Two cases brought before the Supreme Court of the United States in 1899 and 1906 further clarified the power of federal courts to act on domestic relations causes. *Simms v Simms*[218] an appeal from a judgment of the Supreme Court of the Territory of Arizona, had affirmed an alimony award. *De La Rama v De La Rama*[219] involved the appeal of a judgment from the Supreme Court of the Philippines which had reversed a lower court decree granting a wife a divorce, division of property, and support.

The Supreme Court of the United States acknowledged that there is a domestic relations exception. Nevertheless, in both cases, the Court affirmed the exercise of divorce jurisdiction by the federal territorial courts. The Court exercised appellate jurisdiction over the divorce decrees of the territorial courts and in *De La Rama* actually reviewed adultery evidence in detail in affirming the trial court's divorce award to the wife.

The "most extreme case"[220] involving the federal courts' jurisdiction over divorce is *Ohio ex rel Popovici v Agler.*[221] In that case the wife had originally brought a divorce action against her husband, the vice-consul of Roumania, in federal district court, where it was dismissed because of lack of jurisdiction under the domestic relations exception.[222] The wife then brought an action in a state court in Ohio, where the court granted an order for temporary alimony over the husband's jurisdictional objection. The Supreme Court of Ohio denied the vice-consul's petition for a writ of prohibition to restrain the state court proceeding, and the Supreme Court of the United States granted certiorari.

The vice-consul claimed the federal courts had exclusive jurisdiction over all actions against foreign consuls.[223] In his opinion affirming denial of the writ, Justice Holmes held that in light of the historical basis of the domestic relations exception, there was no other conclusion except that such "[s]uits against consuls and vice consuls must be taken to refer to ordinary civil proceedings."[224]

---

contesting this right to the custody of the child, could, in the courts of the United States, give jurisdiction to those courts to determine that question, has never been decided by this court that we are aware of. Nor is it necessary to decide it in this case. . . ."

218 175 US 162 (1899).

219 201 US 303 (1906).

220 C. Wright, Handbook of the Law of Federal Courts 97 (2d ed 1976).

221 280 US 379 (1930).

222 Popovici v Popovici, 30 F2d 185 (ND Ohio 1927).

223 US Const art III, §2; 28 USC §1351.

224 Ohio *ex rel* Popovici v Agler, 280 US 379, 382-84 (1930). Justice Holmes stated that:

> [The Constitution and the statutes] do not affect the present case if it be true as

It is important to note that Congress has never disapproved the judicially developed domestic relations exception. In addition, in 1948, when Congress changed the wording of the diversity statute from "suits of a civil nature at common law or in equity" to "all civil actions,"[225] it did not intend any substantive change in limitation of jurisdiction.[226] This response "may be considered a sign of Congressional concurrence in the Supreme Court's construction excluding competence to grant divorces."[227]

## §4.22 —Supporting Rationales

Generally, federal courts have adopted two methods for invoking the domestic relations exception to diversity jurisdiction, each method supported by accompanying rationales. Some courts have taken an expansive view of the exception, asserting that federal courts are barred from hearing all actions involving "domestic relations."[228] These federal courts declare that they lack the power to hear such cases, based on the historical rationale that the ecclesiastical courts' jurisdiction over divorce did not extend to the federal courts in the United States. This approach may leave untouched an important federal question or legal issue unrelated to the domestic character of the case.

Other federal courts have invoked the abstention doctrine as a means to refuse to hear cases with family law issues.[229] Under this doctrine, a federal court may decline to exercise its jurisdiction under exceptional circumstances.[230] These courts examine the merits of the case and refuse to grant relief if circumstances warrant refusal.

---

> has been unquestioned for three-quarters of a century that the Courts of the United States have no jurisdiction over divorce. If when the Constitution was adopted the common understanding was that the domestic relations of husband and wife and parent and child were matters reserved to the States, there is no difficulty in construing the instrument accordingly and not much in dealing with the statutes. 'Suits against consuls and vice-consuls' must be taken to refer to ordinary civil proceedings and not to include what formerly would have belonged to the civil courts.

[225] Act of June 25, 1948, §1, 62 Stat 930 (codified at 28 USC §1332).

[226] Spindel v Spindel, 283 F Supp 797, 801 (EDNY 1968). In fact, the change was made simply to conform to the Federal Rules of Civil Procedure.

[227] *Id.*

[228] *Id* 806 (citing Albanese v Richter, 161 F2d 688 (3d Cir), *cert denied,* 332 US 782 (1947); Bercovitch v Tanbum, 103 F Supp 62 (SDNY 1952); Linscott v Linscott, 98 F Supp 802 (SD Iowa 1951); Garberson v Garberson, 82 F Supp 706 (ND Iowa 1949)). *See also* Csibi v Fustos, 670 F2d 134 (9th Cir 1982); Sutter v Pitts, 639 F2d 842 (1st Cir 1981); Gargallo v Gargallo, 472 F2d 1219 (6th Cir), *cert denied,* 414 US 805 (1973).

[229] *See, e.g.,* Firestone v Cleveland Trust Co, 654 F2d 1212 (6th Cir 1981); Phillips, Nizer, Benjamin, Krim & Ballon v Rosenstiel, 490 F2d 509 (2d Cir 1973); Kilduff v Kilduff, 473 F Supp 873 (SDNY 1979); *In re* Freiberg, 262 F Supp 482 (ED La 1967); Brandtscheit v Britton, 239 F Supp 652 (ND Cal 1965); Abdul-Rahman Omar Adra v Clift, 195 F Supp 857 (D Md 1961).

[230] *See* C. Wright, Handbook of the Law of Federal Courts 218 (2d ed 1976), where it is noted that the abstention doctrine is invoked:

The most common reason asserted for refusing to exercise jurisdiction is the strong interest of the state in the domestic matters of its citizens.[231] Federal court abstention avoids intrusion on this interest and avoids entangling the federal courts in continuing jurisdiction due to the possibility of modifying state decrees. Modification would necessarily include a hearing on domestic matters similar to the state court hearing. This exercise of federal jurisdiction would be no less an intrusion on the state interest.[232] Courts must avoid incompatible state and federal decrees.

Deference to state courts has also been justified in the federal judiciary by the declaration that state courts have greater competence in handling family matters, particularly where the state system has access to conciliation, mediation, and social services.[233] Finally, some federal courts have reasoned that if they were allowed to hear domestic relations cases and retain continuing jurisdiction, it would cause further congestion of their already crowded dockets.[234]

Needless to say, many of the rationales given to support the domestic relations exception have been disputed, and other policy considerations favoring elimination of the exception have been proposed. These challenges to the exception are discussed in a subsequent subsection.[235]

---

> (1) to avoid decision of a federal constitutional question where the case may be disposed of on questions of state law; (2) to avoid needless conflict with the administration by a state of its own affairs; (3) to leave to the states the resolution of unsettled questions of state law; and (4) to ease the congestion of the federal court docket.

[231] *See, e.g.*, Solomon v Solomon, 516 F2d 1018, 1025 (3d Cir 1975); Phillips, Nizer, Benjamin, Krim & Ballon v Rosenstiel, 490 F2d 509, 516 (2d Cir 1973); Walker v Walker, 509 F Supp 853 (ED Va 1981). Nevertheless, it may be argued that in light of the rise of no-fault divorce, this state interest has been weakened and overshadowed by the rights of individuals. *See* **§§2.03, 4.11.**

[232] Lloyd v Loeffler, 694 F2d 489, 492 (7th Cir 1982); Thrower v Cox, 425 F Supp 570, 573 (DSC 1976). See also Comment, *Enforcing State Domestic Relations Decrees in Federal Courts,* 50 U Chi L Rev 1357 (1983), which discussed the reluctance of federal courts to enforce state domestic relations decrees because of a desire to avoid complicated investigations into domestic conditions. The comment states:

> No court has articulated the connection between enforcement of state decrees and the investigations they are said to entail. The essential link appears to be the modifiability of most decrees. A federal court that modified a state decree when enforcing it would indeed be required to make the same detailed investigations involved in an original decree.

[233] *Id* 1358. *See, e.g.*, Lloyd v Loeffler, 694 F2d 489, 491 (7th Cir 1982); Csibi v Fustos, 670 F2d 134, 137 (9th Cir 1982); Walker v Walker, 509 F Supp 853 (ED Va 1981).

[234] See, e.g., Thrower v Cox, 425 F Supp 570, 573 (DSC 1976) where the court declared that allowing federal courts to hear domestic relations cases would "greatly increase the workload of an already burdened court system."

[235] *See* **§4.24.**

## §4.23 —Federal Jurisdiction in Family Matters

Generally, it may be said that federal courts refuse to make determinations of child custody; are wary of enforcing custody or visitation arrangements; do not grant divorces; and will not award family support in direct actions. Yet, there have been instances in which federal courts have exercised jurisdiction over cases involving family matters. These courts have explained their refusal to invoke the domestic relations exception in several ways.

Federal courts have decided domestic relations issues in some cases where those issues are ancillary to the cause of action. For example, in a diversity action initiated by an alleged widow against the administratix of her putative husband's estate, the validity of the marriage was challenged. The Court of Appeals, Third Circuit, in retaining jurisdiction over the case, declared that "[t]he fact of marriage is a necessary issue in this suit of plaintiff; but the purpose of the suit is, not to establish the marriage, but to determine the rights to the property. . . ."[236]

Federal courts have also been more willing to hear cases involving enforcement of a support award. This willingness has been supported by the historic fact that English courts of equity have enforced support awards.[237] Federal courts generally limit enforcement to the extent of the amount due. In an action brought by a former wife against her exhusband for alimony and child support arrearages, a district court rejected defendant's argument that the domestic relations exception should be applied. The court stated:

> What is presented is simply a dispute between two persons, who for over nine years have been divorced and living apart and between whom there have been no domestic relations, as to whether there has been compliance with two contracts existing between them.[238]

Federal courts have also exercised jurisdiction in contract cases with domestic relations components. Federal courts have heard cases alleging that a former spouse fraudulently induced the plaintiff into entering into a

---

[236] Oxley v Sweetland, 94 F2d 33, 35 (3d Cir 1938). See also Barnett v United States, 82 F2d 765, 769 (9th Cir), *cert denied*, 299 US 546 (1936), where the government sought to have an Indian ward's marriage declared void in a suit to recover monies that had been held for the ward by the government and were later fraudulently procured from him. The court based jurisdictiion on the fact that the United States was a party, and declared the marriage void, stating that "the remedy sought by the government herein was ancillary to the main purpose of the action."

[237] 13 C. Wright, A. Miller, & E. Cooper, Federal Practice and Procedure §3609 (1975) (citing Sutton v Leib, 342 US 402 (1952); Sistare v Sistare, 218 US 1 (1910); Barber v Barber, 62 US (21 How) 582, 590-91 (1859); Cain v King, 313 F Supp 10 (D La 1970); Gonzales v Gonzales, 74 F Supp 883 (D Pa 1947).

[238] Zimmerman v Zimmerman, 395 F Supp 719, 721 (ED Pa 1975). *See also* Davis v Davis, 452 F Supp 44 (ED Pa 1978) (suit for default in alimony and support payments; no mention of domestic relations exception); Hemphill v Hemphill, 398 F Supp 1134 (ND Ga 1975) (arrears of alimony due under agreement incorporated into divorce decree).

separation agreement and obtaining a divorce.[239] The United States District Court of the Eastern District of New York exercised jurisdiction over an exwife's suit against her exhusband to enforce a state court judgment for $10,785 awarded to her for unpaid alimony under the parties' separation agreement.[240] The court disagreed with the exhusband's argument that the domestic relations exception should apply. It noted that the plaintiff's claim did not involve domestic relations, but was in fact an action to recover damages for breach of contract between parties who were not husband and wife and had not in fact been married for nearly 10 years.

There have been federal cases involving family law issues where the domestic relations exception was not even mentioned. The United States Court of Appeals, Third Circuit, in determining whether the plaintiff was a widow for the purposes of receiving social security benefits, reviewed New Jersey divorce law and held that the petitioner did have widow status based on her reconciliation with the deceased during the statutory three-month waiting period before the New Jersey divorce became final.[241] In *Jones v Jones*,[242] a district court in New York enforced a separation agreement involving a support arrangement without noting the domestic relations exception. The Court of Appeals, Ninth Circuit, in *Commissioner v Eccles*,[243] affirmed a decision of the Tax Court holding that a taxpayer was entitled to file a joint income tax return for the tax year preceding his final divorce despite an interlocutory decree which had been entered during that tax year.

Finally, some courts have shown a willingness to separate domestic relations issues from other legal issues and exercise jurisdiction over cases which would have been excluded under an expansive view of the domestic relations exception. For example, some federal courts have distinguished between actions for enforcement of custody decrees and actions for tort damages in child-snatching cases. These courts, while refusing to exercise jurisdiction to enforce the custody decrees, have nevertheless exercised jurisdiction over the tort claims. This separation of issues has been called "[p]erhaps the most significant development"[244] in federal enforcement of state domestic relations decrees.

---

[239] *See, e.g.*, Cohen v Randall, 137 F2d 441 (2d Cir), *cert denied*, 320 US 796 (1943); McNeil v McNeil, 78 F 834 (ND Cal 1897), *affd*, 170 F 289 (9th Cir 1909); Holm v Shelinsky, 388 F2d 54 (2d Cir 1968); Block v Block, 196 F2d 930 (7th Cir 1952); Schoonover v Schoonover, 172 F2d 526 (10th Cir 1949).

[240] Richie v Richie, 186 F Supp 592, 594 (EDNY 1960). *See also* Crouch v Crouch, 566 F2d 486 (5th Cir 1978); Korby v Erickson, 550 F Supp 136 (SDNY 1982). For a discussion of federal jurisdiction over palimony disputes, see S. Green & J. Long, Marriage and Family Law Agreements §3.12 (Shepard's/McGraw-Hill 1984).

[241] Legory v Finch, 424 F2d 406 (3d Cir 1970).

[242] 242 F Supp 979 (SDNY 1965).

[243] 208 F2d 796 (9th Cir 1953).

[244] Comment, *Enforcing State Domestic Relations Decrees in Federal Courts*, 50 U Chi L Rev 1357, 1363 (1983).

One such case is *Bennett v Bennett*,[245] where a divorced father brought an action seeking monetary relief against his former wife for kidnapping the parties' child in violation of a state custody decree. The United States Court of Appeals for the District of Columbia Circuit observed that "[a] federal court should not . . . avoid all diversity cases having intrafamily aspects,"[246] and exercised federal jurisdiction over the plaintiff's tort claim for money damages. Nevertheless, it held that the district court did not have jurisdiction to give injunctive relief in the case. In similar cases, however, the Sixth Circuit rejected jurisdiction over either claim, and the First Circuit abstained from taking jurisdiction.[247] Because of the split in the circuits on this matter, the Supreme Court is bound to revisit the domestic relations exception.

## §4.24 —Challenges

The domestic relations exception to federal diversity jurisdiction is an embattled concept in family law with an uncertain future. The stability of the exception has been continually undermined by inconsistent application as well as by a general increased federal presence in family law, most obviously with legislative action in the areas of child support, child-snatching, and pension rights.[248] The domestic relations exception has been attacked generally, its rationales have been challenged, and new approaches have been suggested by commentators.

Commentators are critical of the concept of a broad domestic relations exception to diversity jurisdiction, suggesting that courts improperly base their decisions on whether to invoke the exception based solely on the relationship of the parties involved.[249] It has been urged that the courts should examine the nature of the cause of action, rather than the parties' relationship:

> If it is purely an action concerning a right to recover a judgment because of some contractual, quasi-contractual, or tortious wrong that has been committed, the federal court should not decline jurisdiction. The federal courts should refuse to exercise jurisdiction in domestic cases only where a problem of status arises. Where only property rights are involved, jurisdiction should be taken.[250]

---

245 682 F2d 1039 (DC Cir 1982).

246 *Id* 1042. *See also* Lloyd v Loeffler, 694 F2d 489 (7th Cir 1982).

247 *See* Gargallo v Gargallo, 472 F2d 1219 (6th Cir), *cert denied*, 414 US 805 (1973); Sutter v Pitts, 639 F2d 842 (1st Cir 1981).

248 See discussions of the various federal laws in **chs 6-10.**

249 Vestal & Foster, *Implied Limitations on the Diversity Jurisdiction of Federal Courts*, 41 Minn L Rev 1, 29 (1956); Note, *The Domestic Relations Exception to Diversity Jurisdiction*, 83 Colum L Rev 1824, 1828-29 (1983).

250 Vestal & Foster, *supra* note 249, at 31.

This recommendation seems inadequate, however, since questions of property rights may be intertwined with issues of status. Another commentator has proposed a test which requires a court to look to the nature of the action rather than labeling the matter "domestic" based on the parties involved:

> The proposed test has two elements. The first involves federal-state relations, and addresses the appropriateness of federal courts' entertaining diversity suits where state law compels state courts to act as third parties to the proceedings. The second element invokes the traditional case or controversy requirement of article III of the Constitution, and excludes diversity cases that do not meet this standard. Such an application of this common jurisdictional requirement to the domestic relations area is new, and long overdue.[251]

The practical result of the application of this proposed test would effectively deny federal jurisdiction to many divorce cases in the no-fault context, due to a lack of controversy. Custody cases similarly would be rejected on the ground of the state's parens patriae role.

Some of the support for the exception has been challenged as well. It has been argued that the state's interest in family law litigation is protected by the *Erie* doctrine. In *Erie Railroad v Tompkins*,[252] the Supreme Court held that a federal diversity court must apply the same substantive law as would the highest court in the state in which it sits. This requirement avoids conflict between federal and state family litigation.

More recently, the state interest has been weakened in the family law area. The use of no-fault divorce signaled an increased emphasis on spouses' private rights to decide to terminate marriage. The federal government has taken an important role in family law in the 1980s, as mentioned earlier in this section, arguably undermining the significance of the role of the state in domestic relations.

It has been argued that federal courts do not have expertise in family law matters only because the exception has denied the courts the opportunity to hear such cases.[253] Federal courts clearly possess competence in family law matters, as evinced by the cases involving domestic relations issues which federal courts *have* heard.[254]

Militating in favor of the exercise of federal diversity jurisdiction in family cases is the apprehension of local bias that gave rise to diversity jurisdiction. Also, there is concern that the exception may bar a federal court from hearing important federal questions or crucial issues which are arising with greater

---

[251] Note, *supra* note 249, at 1852 (footnote omitted).

[252] 304 US 64 (1938).

[253] Note *supra* note 249, at 1849.

[254] *See* **§4.24.**

frequency in family law cases.[255] The inconsistent application of the domestic relations exception tends to undermine the integrity of the federal system.

This area of the law is, from a nationwide perspective, in a general state of disarray. Family law practititioners would be well-advised to conduct a thorough research of the law in their jurisdictions before attempting to bring a domestic relations action in federal court. However, they should not be discouraged from doing so because of the scarcity of family law cases which have succeeded in the federal courts. The impact of family law in current society, the expansive trends in the exercise of federal jurisdiction in cases involving important family law issues, and the enlarged federal presence in family law through federal legislation indicate that selective use of federal jurisdiction is a potential alternative for the practitioner.

[255] Note, *supra* note 249, at 1848.

# 5 Nonadversarial Divorce



## Introduction

### §5.01 The Nonadversarial Trend

Within the fault system, divorce was often an intense confrontation. An innocent spouse was required to prove that the other spouse was guilty of marital misconduct in order to "win" a divorce. The doctrines of collusion, connivance, and recrimination were developed to prevent spouses from amicably agreeing to divorce and to insure that divorces were not granted where both spouses were guilty of marital wrongs.[1] Courts awarded spousal support and divided property based on the parties' guilt or innocence.[2] The attorney's role was to win the battle by proving the opposing spouse's fault.

The process of fault divorce placed little, if any, emphasis on the privacy and emotional well-being of the parties. Frequently, intimate marital discord was revealed on the public record as a party testified to the other spouse's adultery, cruelty, or other fault. In addition, divorced persons carried the social and moral stigma of marital failure.

The enactment of no-fault grounds was the first step toward nonadversarial divorce. These grounds were designed in part to minimize conflicts in the termination process. Instead of proving that one party was guilty of destroying the marriage, spouses only had to demonstrate that they were living separate and apart, that they were incompatible, or that their marriage was over in fact in order to obtain a divorce.

While no-fault grounds have initiated a nonadversarial trend in divorce, they have not been entirely successful in producing conflict-free dissolutions, for several reasons. First, these grounds have been incorporated into an adversarial system whose procedure is structured for battle.[3] Second, a majority of state codes have retained fault grounds, which loom as a threatening option in each divorce case. In addition, fault remains a consideration in many jurisdictions for child custody, support, and property division determinations.

But most importantly, as experienced practitioners know, people in the process of divorce have the need to express the failure, anger, sadness, and disappointment that accompanies marital dissolution. The legal aspect of dissolution often becomes the arena within which spouses fulfill this need to express negative emotions. Family law practitioners, frequently accused of fueling the adversarial nature of dissolution by urging their clients to strive for the best financial resolution while supposedly ignoring their emotional needs and those of their children,[4] are in fact many times used by the clients to try

---

[1] *See* **§§1.19-1.25.**

[2] In some states, this is still true despite the enactment of no-fault grounds. *See* **ch 10.**

[3] Pearson & Thoennes, *Mediating and Litigating Custody Disputes: A Longitudinal Evaluation,* 17 Fam LQ 497, 498 (1984), where the authors state:

> Court congestion is not the only problem with the adversarial system. . . . According to one writer, the adversarial model increases trauma and escalates conflict. Another . . . argues that the adversarial system encourages "dog and cat fights" that run counter to the best interests of the child. . . . Others feel that adversarial interventions foster low commitment to the eventual agreement and fail to enhance the cooperative, communication and problem-solving skills of the parties. Still others fault the coercive nature of adjudication as well as the "twin dragons" of cost and delay. (Footnotes omitted.)

[4] See Note, *Non-Judicial Resolution of Custody and Visitation Disputes,* 12 UCD L Rev 582, 585 (1979), which states that "children's emotional trauma is intensified by the uncertainty of lengthy legal proceedings which too often result in a custody or visitation plan tailored to the wishes of their competing parents rather than their own needs and

to win both emotional and legal battles which emanate from marital breakdown.

As no-fault divorce became an acceptable method for terminating marital status, the number of divorces skyrocketed, adding to the congestion of the already-crowded court calendars. Critics quickly earmarked the weaknesses, failures, and disappointments of dissolution, many of which were common to other types of judicial actions as well. The process itself in some jurisdictions was complex and riddled with delay. A general perception that dissolution did not accord enough attention to the emotional well-being of the spouses and their children developed as society's psychological awareness increased.

The criticism of no-fault divorce produced the same results as did the criticism of fault divorce: a search for better alternatives and solutions to the problems.[5] The path taken in this search has focused on reduction of the adversarial nature of divorce. This has become the nonadversarial trend which has grown in the 1980s.

## §5.02 The Search for New Solutions

It has been noted that "[n]o-fault legislation reflects a preference for private ordering over public name calling, for resolution over retribution."[6] Those who have explored the problems of no-fault divorce have attempted to find answers which are consonant with the spirit of the no-fault trend. The search has focused on a nonadversarial approach to marriage dissolution which would provide a more constructive means to settle disputes and dissipate emotionally charged controversy before involving the courts.

Some divorcing parties are avoiding or curtailing their use of attorneys, which may be indicative of a desire to avoid an adversarial divorce. There has been an increase in pro se divorces and a rise in self-help alternatives for

---

wishes." *See also* Winks, *Divorce Mediation: A Nonadversary Procedure for the No-Fault Divorce,* 19 J Fam L 615, 622-25 (1980-81). The author, who was a recent law school graduate before publication of the article, paints a particularly harsh and unflattering picture of family law practitioners:

> Adversary lawyers may reinforce the conflict between the parties and create obstacles to settlement. The lawyer may volunteer criticism of the absent spouse or justify extreme positions as a prelude to compromise. Some attorneys recommend tactics almost guaranteed to generate ill will; running up big bills, concealing financial records. . . .
>
> Where the differences between the parties cannot be resolved through the negotiation of their attorneys, classic divorce strategy calls for each attorney to threaten to go all the way to trial, set a court date, and tell the judge more time is needed to settle. (Footnotes omitted.)

[5] *See* **§5.02.**

[6] Winks, *Divorce Mediation: A Nonadversary Procedure for the No-Fault Divorce,* 19 J Fam L 615, 615 (1980-81).

divorcing people.[7] Many parties try to proceed with either one attorney representing one spouse, or with dual representation, where one attorney representing both spouses. While some aspects of the decision to use one attorney may be reasonable for reducing costs and avoiding conflict and acrimony, one-sided counseling inadequately represents the parties' rights. Dual representation is also ethically dangerous and widely discouraged by state bar associations.[8]

An important recent movement toward nonadversarial divorce has been the increasingly popular use of extrajudicial dispute resolution methods which have been invoked to avoid conflict. Two of these methods which are discussed in greater detail in later sections are arbitration and mediation.[9]

Arbitration is a method of dispute resolution which is invoked on the parties' agreement to provide a solution or remedy when the parties are deadlocked on an issue arising in negotiation, mediation, or enforcement of a separation agreement or divorce decree. It is most frequently used to resolve child custody and visitation disputes. Arbitration resembles the adversarial court system in that an independent person or entity hears evidence and renders a decision to which the parties have agreed to be bound. Arbitration is based on the consent of the spouses, but still retains adversarial characteristics.

Divorce mediation encourages spouses to solve their own problems and determine the parameters of their agreement, thus avoiding traditional divorce battles. Mediation, which gathered popularity on the crest of the no-fault wave in the late 1970s and early 1980s, has attracted significant attention and controversy.[10]

Nonadversarial approaches to divorce and increased use of alternative methods of dispute resolution in the context of divorce are important trends in family law which cannot be ignored by the practitioner. While such approaches may prove to be failed fads in the long run, they may also very well become tomorrow's tradition.

---

[7] *Id* 625, which notes, inter alia, "In Los Angeles County in 1977, more than one in four divorces were filed in propria persona; ten years before, the proportions were one in a thousand."

[8] *Id* 627. While some courts and state bar associations have given indirect approval to dual representation, see 1 Colo Law 59 (May 1972), Op 47, Feb 26, 1972, *cited in* O. Maru, Supplement to Digest of Bar Association Ethics Opinions No 8000 (1975); Brossie v Stocton, 105 Ariz 574, 468 P2d 933 (1970); Klemm v Superior Court, 75 Cal App 3d 893, 142 Cal Rptr 509 (1977); Halvorsen v Halvorsen, 3 Wash App 827, 479 P2d 161 (1970), these authors highly recommend that attorneys avoid the dangers which potentially accompany such representation. *See also* S. Green & J. Long, Marriage and Family Law Agreements chs 4 & 6 (Shepard's/McGraw-Hill 1984).

[9] *See* **§§5.03-5.13.**

[10] For a very small example, see the side-by-side articles in the *Family Advocate:* Pearson & Thoennes, *Mediation & Divorce, The Benefits Outweigh the Costs,* 4 Fam Advoc 26 (Winter 1982); Crouch, *Mediation & Divorce, The Dark Side Is Still Unexplored,* 4 Fam Advoc 27 (Winter 1982).

# Arbitration

## §5.03 Arbitration Generally

Arbitration is a method of alternative dispute resolution which, although used primarily to resolve controversies in the labor, commercial, and international fields, has been utilized to some extent in the process of marriage dissolution.[11] Arbitration resembles the adversarial judicial process in that the parties to a dispute present their cases to an impartial decision-maker for resolution.

There is an important distinction between arbitration and the judicial system, however. Arbitration is premised on the voluntary agreement and cooperation of the parties as an attempt to avoid the traditional adversarial forum. The parties, in their separation or mediation agreement, include provisions for arbitration. These provisions specify the issues which are arbitrable, the identity and number of arbitrators, and the method of choosing the arbitrators. In an arbitration, the parties also agree to be bound by the arbitrator's decision.

Because arbitration is premised on the idea that the arbitrator derives his or her authority from the agreement and may not exceed the scope of that authority,[12] the parties' definition of arbitrable issues is very important. The parties can agree to limit the arbitration to specific disputes, to disputes which arise under particular terms of the agreement, or to any dispute arising under the contract. The American Arbitration Association (AAA), a nonprofit independent agency which administers arbitrations throughout the United States, recommends that the following broad clause be included in separation agreements in order to avoid resorting to the courts when the parties disagree on the arbitrability of an issue:

> Any controversy arising out of or relating to this agreement, or the breach thereof, shall be settled by arbitration in accordance with the Rules of the American Arbitration Association. Both parties agree to abide by

---

[11] While these authors do not know of any survey of broad statistical analysis of divorcing or divorced couples who have resorted to arbitration, circumstantial evidence indicates that the number is probably small. A. Lindey, 1 Separation Agreements and Ante-Nuptial Contracts §29 (rev ed 1983); S. Green & J. Long, Marriage and Family Law Agreements Appendices 1-4 (Shepard's/McGraw-Hill 1984), both suggest that family practitioners advise their clients about the arbitration alternative when drafting family law agreements.

Spencer & Zammit, *Mediation-Arbitration: A Proposal for Private Resolution of Disputes Between Divorced or Separated Parents,* 1976 Duke LJ 911, 920 n 31, reports that there were only 39 domestic relations arbitrations at the New York Regional Office of the American Arbitration Association during 1973 and 1974.

[12] Spencer & Zammit, *supra* note 11, at 921.

> the terms of the award rendered by the Arbitrator(s) and judgment upon the award may be entered in any court having jurisdiction thereof.[13]

If, during the course of mediation, settlement negotiation, or actual performance of contractual obligations, an arbitrable dispute arises, a spouse may invoke arbitration by serving the other with an informal demand for arbitration which must also be filed with the AAA if the spouses have agreed to operate under its rules.[14] Arbitration may be had before a single arbitrator, either chosen by the parties or appointed by a court or an independent agency; an impartial tripartite board appointed under the AAA procedure;[15] or a panel

---

[13] American Arbitration Association, Family Dispute Services 305 (1977). A. Lindey, *supra* note 11, at §29-5, includes the following bracketed provisions, which have been added to the AAA's recommended standard form in light of Bowmer v Bowmer, 67 AD2d 8, 414 NYS2d 340 (1979), *affd,* 50 NY2d 288, 406 NE2d 760, 428 NYS2d 902, (1980), which held that the parties' general arbitration clause in their separation agreement was insufficient for arbitration of the husband's claim for downward modification of his support obligation:

> Any controversy or claim arising out of or relating to this contract, or the breach thereof, [including any and all controversies as to the upward or downward modifications of the support provisions of this agreement, or any other disputed issues relating to the modification or enforcement of this agreement,]. . . .

See also S. Green & J. Long, Marriage and Family Law Agreements 382 (Shepard's/McGraw-Hill 1984), where the authors recommend the inclusion of the following clause in separation agreements:

> In the event of any dispute over the terms of this Agreement [or in the event of any dispute between the parties as to any matter], either party may invoke binding arbitration by notifying the American Arbitration Association in writing of the issue to be arbitrated with a copy to the other party at his or her last known address. The party invoking arbitration shall provide the American Arbitration Association with a copy of this Agreement and pay to the American Arbitration Association the fees it requires in order to proceed with the arbitration. The arbitrator shall be selected and the arbitration shall be conducted in accordance with the rules of the American Arbitration Association. The arbitrator shall decide the issues submitted by each party but shall be limited by the terms of this Agreement [or shall not be limited by the terms of this Agreement] and the arbitrator shall determine how the expense of the arbitration proceeding shall be apportioned between the parties.

(Comment: The high cost af litigation and the delay inherent in court proceedings make arbitration an attractive alternative. The parties may wish to utilize the alternative language in brackets in order to authorize an arbitrator to consider matters not contemplated by the parties in their Agreement but which have later surfaced as disputed issues. . . .)

[14] Spencer & Zammit, *supra* note 11, at 922.

[15] *Id,* where the authors describe the AAA procedure:

> The AAA selection process is designed to minimize the possibility of disagreement. On receipt of a demand for arbitration, the AAA sends each party a list of possible arbitrators drawn from its domestic relations panel, along with an abbreviated description of each arbitrator's background. Each party then excises the names of those individuals deemed unsatisfactory and numbers the others in order of preference. The arbitrator with the lowest combined number is the one selected. (Footnotes omitted.)

consisting of two designees appointed by the parties, and a third chosen by either the two designees or an outside agency.[16]

The arbitrators hear the dispute and render a decision, by which the parties have agreed to be bound. Despite that agreement, spouses may attack the arbitration process by maintaining that an issue is not arbitrable, questioning the validity of the arbitrator clause in the preliminary agreement, or disputing the enforceability of the award.[17] If a spouse argues against the arbitrability of an issue, the arbitrator must make a finding of jurisdiction. If arbitrability is challenged in the courts, the arbitrator having made a finding, the court determines whether the parties intended the particular controversy to come within the scope of the arbitration agreement.[18]

Consider the advantages of an arbitration arrangement. The existence of an arbitration clause in a separation or mediation agreement itself may serve as a deterrent to using the process and, thus, an incentive for parties to settle issues between themselves.[19] Arbitration clauses are also useful for providing a mechanism with which to manage future problems not evident or imminent at the time of entering into a separation agreement.[20]

There are also practical advantages to arbitration. The hearings are private and informal. The parties may choose arbitrators who are professionally qualified to deal with a particular dispute. For example, if the controversy centers on finances, the parties could choose an accountant, an actuary, or a tax specialist to arbitrate their dispute. The arbitration process is much faster

---

[16] A. Lindey, *supra* note 11, at §29-2. This volume also includes examples of clauses designating the number of arbitrators and the ways the parties will choose such arbitrators.

[17] Meroney, *Mediation and Arbitration of Separation and Divorce Agreements,* 15 Wake Forest L Rev 467, 483 (1979); **§5.04.**

[18] Comment, *The Enforceability of Arbitration Clauses in North Carolina Separation Agreements,* 15 Wake Forest L Rev 487, 489 (1979) (citing, inter alia, Sperling v Sperling, 26 AD2d 827, 274 NYS2d 107 (1966) (dictum); Sheets v Sheets, 22 AD2d 176, 254 NYS2d 320 (1964); Lipschutz v Gutwirth, 304 NY 58, 106 NE2d 8 (1952)). See also Spencer & Zammit, *supra* note 11 at 921, n 34, where the authors note that "where there is disagreement as to whether a particular issue is arbitrable, the question is normally resolved by a court," (citing Uddo v Toarmine, 21 AD2d 402, 405, 250 NYS2d 645, 647 (1964)).

[19] See Coulson, *Family Arbitration-An Exercise in Sensitivity,* 3 Fam LQ 22, 29 (1969), where the author, a longtime president of the American Arbitration Association, stated "a binding arbitration clause as to custody and visitation has a psychological effect on the parents which often makes it possible for the parties to settle their controversy under the benevolent influence of a prompt terminal procedure."

[20] See A. Lindey, *supra* note 11, at §29-3, where the author stated that in some situations:

> [A] simple expedient is not to try to resolve the problem immediately but to leave it to arbitration when it actually arises. This does not necessarily mean that a clash is being postponed. It may well be that when the question does present itself, perhaps years after the execution of the agreement, there has been a complete change in the temper and attitude of the parties. Moreover, the question may be such as will be resolved or rendered academic by the lapse of time.

than the overburdened court system, and usually costs far less than contested litigation.

Of course, there are also disadvantages to arbitration. In a marital breakdown characterized by bitterness and mutual harassment, arbitration may become just another means for the parties to continue their battle.[21] Arbitrators are not bound by the same principles of substantive law and rules of evidence that apply to the courts. This eliminates the judicial protections of precedent, procedural rules, and enforcement sanctions available to the parties in court proceedings.[22]

Arbitrators sometimes are drawn from panels of practicing attorneys and lay persons inexperienced at practicing impartiality. There is no right to appeal an arbitration award, although its validity may be challenged on narrow grounds in a court proceeding. As discussed in the following section, courts sometimes refuse on public policy grounds to be bound by child custody arbitration awards and occasionally reject arbitration awards involving spousal support.[23]

## §5.04 Enforcement of Arbitration Agreements and Awards

The critical difficulty of arbitration is judicial enforcement. Enforcement problems arise where one party challenges the validity of an arbitration clause in a mediation or separation agreement, or one party challenges the enforceability of an arbitration award. While a majority of states have arbitration statutes which mandate enforcement of such clauses and awards by providing for limited judicial review and substantial judicial deference to them, courts have been reluctant to relinquish the role as parens patriae in family law arbitration matters.[24]

Case law involving arbitration of family disputes is scarce, perhaps due to the infrequency of such arbitrations or possibly due to the success of such arbitrations.[25] Nevertheless, some general rules may be quickly summarized.

---

[21] *Id.*

[22] *Id* §29-1; Comment, *supra* note 18, at 492 n 48, which notes that freedom from substantive law and rules of evidence may also be viewed as an advantage.

[23] *See* **§5.04.**

[24] Spencer & Zammit, *Mediator-Arbitrator: A Proposal for Private Resolution of Disputes Between Divorced or Separated Parents,* 1976 Duke LJ 911, 925, where the authors note that under the arbitration statutes, many of which are modeled after the Unif Arbitration Act, 7 ULA (1978) (which was approved by the National Conference of Commissioners on Uniform State Laws and the American Bar Association in 1955), arbitral awards may be vacated only on very limited grounds such as procurement by corruption, fraud, or undue means; evident partiality or misconduct by the arbitrators; and the arbitrators' exceeding their powers.

[25] Meroney, *Mediation and Arbitration of Separation and Divorce Agreements,* 15 Wake Forest L Rev 467, 483 (1979), where the author states:

Clauses providing for the arbitration of disputes concerning spousal support generally have been enforced by the courts.[26] There has been a growing tendency of courts to recognize arbitration of child support issues, although the courts reserve the power to closely review and scrutinize such agreements, as they do all agreements relating to the welfare of children.[27] Arbitration of child custody and visitation disputes has not been generally accepted by courts but is viewed as an impermissible infringement on the courts' parens patriae powers.[28] In a view not shared by a majority of courts, a New York Supreme Court declared that "[there seems to be no clear and valid reason why the arbitration process should not be made available in the area of custody and incidents thereto, i.e., choice of schools, summer camps, medical and surgical expenses, trips and vacations."[29]

Arbitration awards based on enforceable arbitration agreements are upheld unless they violate statutory guidelines regarding the fairness of the arbitration, the authority of the arbitrators, and, of course, public policy considerations.[30] Awards usually will not be vacated for mistake of law or fact, but may be

---

> Many of the decisions [in the arbitration of family disputes] are old and possibly would not be followed by courts today. The most recent decisions have come from New York, which has both a family court system and a modern arbitration statute. Despite its limitations, this family arbitration case law is the best indication of how courts throughout the United States will respond to the arbitration of separation and divorce agreements today. (Footnotes omitted.)

[26] *See In re* Mesmer's Estate, 94 Cal App 97, 270 P 732 (1928); Sokolsky v Sokolsky, 59 AD 600, 398 NYS2d 161 (1977); Hirsch v Hirsch, 37 NY2d 312, 33 NE2d 371, 372 NYS2d 71 (1975); Swartz v Swartz, 42 AD2d 254, 374 NYS2d 857 (1975); Annot, 18 ALR3d 1264 (1968).

[27] A. Lindey, Separation Agreements and Ante-Nuptial Contracts 29-18-20 (rev 3d ed 1983) (citing Schneider v Schneider, 17 NY2d 123, 16 NE2d 318, 269 NYS2d 107 (1966); Adams v Rhoades, 56 Misc 2d 249, 288 NYS2d 710 (NY Fam Ct 1969).

[28] 1 A. Lindey, Separation Agreements and Ante-Nuptial Contracts 29-29-20 (rev 3d ed 1983) (citing People *ex rel* Herzog v Morgan, 287 NY 317, 39, NE2d 255 (1942); Nestel v Nestel, 38 AD2d 942, 331 NYS2d 241 (1972); Agur v Agur, 32 AD2d 16, 1298 NYS2d 772 (1969), *appeal dismissed,* 27 NY2d 643, 261 NE2d 903, 313 NYS2d 866, (1970); Michelman v Michelman, 5 Misc 2d 570, 135 NYS2d 608 (Sup Ct 1954); *In re* Hill, 199 Misc 1035, 104 NYS2d 755 (Sup Ct 1951).

[29] Sheets v Sheets, 22 AD2d 176, 177, 254 NYS2d 320, 323 (1964). In Friedberg v Friedberg, 23 Misc 2d 196, 201 NYS2d 606 (Sup Ct 1960), the court did, in fact, compel arbitration of a dispute concerning the education of the parties' son, distinguishing it from *Michelman v Michelman,* 5 Misc 2d 570, 135 NYS2d 608 (Sup Ct 1954), by stating that only the selection of a school and payment of tuition were involved, and not custody or visitation rights.

[30] AAA General Counsel's Annual Report, Arbitration & the Law, 1982, 15-16 (1983), reports the case Sobel v Sobel, NYLJ, May 12, 1982, at 11, col 1 (Sup Ct 1982):

> The Sobels submitted to arbitration the question of a breach of their separation agreement, pursuant to a provision in that agreement. The husband sought a cancellation of alimony arrears and a release of future child support obligation because the wife had removed the children from the country for seven years, and, upon return, had frustrated the husband's visitation attempts for another four years. The arbitrator awarded the wife alimony arrears and future child support,

modified by the courts on the grounds of miscalculation of figures, an evident mistake, and imperfection in the form of the award.[31]

The practitioner should be prepared to discuss with a client the possibility of including an arbitration clause in a separation agreement as an alternative to litigation when problems arise in the course of mediation or negotiation, or after the divorce. While the arbitrability of matters relating to children and actual awards involving children are always subject to the review of the courts, arbitrations involving support are generally upheld. Thus, in the settlement of property and support disputes of divorcing couples, arbitration provides a cheaper, faster, and more private resolution of controversy than the court system.

## Mediation

### §5.05 Introduction to Mediation

Mediation is the emerging current in the nonadversarial trend in divorce. Mediation provides a means by which a husband and wife may negotiate the conditions of divorce with each other, assisted by a trained mediator, whose background is typically law, therapy, or social services. In successful mediation the mediator is an impartial third person who wins the trust of both spouses, and determines what issues are disputed. The mediator obtains an amicable agreement by clarifying priorities, facilitating communication, exploring areas of compromise, and helping the spouses to overcome or compromise any rigid or irrational bargaining positions. The goal of mediation is to help the spouses arrive at a settlement in which they have both fully participated. This agreement

---

contingent on her compliance with a visitation program to be worked out between the parties. In the event they were unable to agree within three months, the matter was to be resubmitted to the arbitrator for a binding decision on the terms and conditions of the visitation program. The parties did not reach agreement and the husband sought to have the arbitrator modify the award, but the arbitrator had died. The husband, therefore, crossmoved to vacate the award when his wife petitioned for confirmation. The court agreed with the husband that, because the award was not "final and definite," as required by the New York Civil Practice Law & Rules §7511(b)(iii), it could not be confirmed. Moreover, the court noted that the wife's removal of the children violated the state's public policy and, therefore, a confirmation of the arbitral award "would encourage a violation of the public policy of this state, that is, to allow both parents to be with their children and for the children to be nurtured and guided by their father." The court then remanded the case to a new arbitrator for a determination of future child support and visitation rights.

[31] Comment, *The Enforceability of Arbitration Clauses in North Carolina Separation Agreements,* 15 Wake Forest L Rev 487, 491 (1979).

must be fair to both parties and approved by them as appropriate to their interests and those of their family.[32]

Mediation is a direct response to the criticisms of the adversarial system. Highly praised by its proponents, and warily eyed by its opponents, in 1985 divorce mediation was still relatively new and developing.[33] Several models have been designed, each striving to reduce conflict between the divorcing parties and promote agreement without judicial involvement.

The asserted advantages of a successful divorce mediation are impressive: it minimizes the impact of divorce on children; promotes family privacy; preserves the self-worth of the spouses; encourages client participation and self-determination; establishes new relationships based on cooperative communication; lessens the financial and emotional costs of divorce; reduces lawyer time spent to obtain a final divorce; minimizes state interference in the dissolution; eases the burden of litigation on the courts; and produces agreements which are respected by the parties. Mediation has been used to resolve labor and commercial disputes, as well as a wide variety of other disputes. In the context of divorce, however, mediation has generated much controversy.

When divorce mediation debuted as an alternative to the adversarial system, the response was emotionally charged. Lawyers derided mediation as antilawyer, and mediation advocates accused lawyers of overprotecting their livelihood and high fees. As mediation attracted interest and established a foothold in the process of marriage dissolution, closer examination prompted concern over some serious unanswered questions and troublesome problems.[34] Some aspects of the controversy included the protection of divorcing spouses in

---

[32] Pickrell & Bendheim, *Family Disputes Mediation—A New Service for Lawyers and Their Clients,* 15 Ariz BJ 33, 34 (Oct 1979).

[33] Gold, *Mediation in the Dissolution of Marriage,* 36 Arb J 9, 10 (Sept 1981). The author, a marriage and family therapist and the director of the Family Mediation Center in Portland, Oregon, stated:

> Theoretically, this new area of practice seems most closely allied with the principles of conflict resolution and the practices of psychotherapy. It is generally broader in its conceptualization than the application of the mechanics of dispute resolution and while it is therapeutic, it is not psychotherapy. This means that the goals are greater than the efficient resolution of the dissolution conflicts and less than curative of emotional ills.

As a new system, it can be viewed as an interfacing of legal and psychological structure.

[34] *See, e.g.,* Crouch, *Mediation & Divorce, The Dark Side is Still Unexplored,* 4 Fam Advoc 27 (Winter 1982); Crouch, *Divorce Mediation and Legal Ethics,* 16 Fam LQ 219 (1982); Harbinson, *Family Law—Attorney Mediation of Marital Disputes and Conflict of Interest Considerations,* 60 NCL Rev 171 (1981); Levy, *Comment on the Pearson-Thoennes Study and Mediation,* 17 Fam LQ 525, 529-33 (1984); Meroney, *Mediation and Arbitration of Separation and Divorce Agreements,* 15 Wake Forest L Rev 467 (1979); Silberman, *Professional Responsibility Problems of Divorce Mediation,* 16 Fam LQ 107 (1982); Winks, *Divorce Mediation: A Nonadversary Procedure for the No-Fault Divorce,* 19 J Fam L 615 (1980-81); Zumeta, *Mediation as an Alternative to Litigation and Divorce,* 62 Mich BJ 434, 437 (1983).

mediation, the competence of mediators and their roles, ethical considerations for attorneys involved in the mediation process, confidentiality of the sessions, the extra layer mediation added to the divorce process, and the actual success of mediation.

The few studies conducted which examined results of mediation acknowledged the necessity for further research.[35] Despite this lack of knowledge of the actual benefits and drawbacks of divorce mediation, and despite the problems associated with it, mediation continues to grow as an alternative to litigation. In 1980, California made such mediation mandatory for contested custody and visitation issues.[36] It was reported in 1983 that 23 states offered court-connected counseling and mediation services.[37] Many private mediators practice throughout the country.

The American Bar Association (ABA) has acknowledged the importance of the nonadversarial trend by forming a Special Committee on Alternative Means of Dispute Resolution, which serves as a focal point for resources information in the field of dispute resolution, including divorce mediation.[38] The Family Law Section of the ABA, which includes a Mediation and Arbitration Committee, has adopted Standards of Practice for Family Mediators which have been "promulgated as a service to the matrimonial practice community."[39]

Thus, it appears that divorce mediation is here to stay. It is imperative that the problems associated with the process be recognized and resolved. The promulgation of mediation standards is but one step. Mediation, despite its potential for fashioning beneficial divorce agreements and custody arrangements, is not for everyone. As one writer has maintained:

> For many couples, the traditional adversary system is clearly necessary

---

[35] *See* Bahr, *Mediation is the Answer,* 4 Fam Advoc 32, 32 (Winter 1982) ("Very little systematic evaluation of these [mediation] services has been conducted to date. . . . More research is clearly needed to help guide policy agreements in this field"); Pearson & Thoennes, *Mediating and Litigating Custody Disputes: A Longitudinal Evaluation,* 17 Fam LQ 497, 500 (1984) ("Despite its growing popularity and use, there have been few studies to empirically assess mediation. Many theoretical and practical issues have yet to be addressed"). *See also* **§4.21.**

[36] Freed & Foster, *Family Law in the Fifty States: An Overview,* 16 Fam LQ 289, 295-96 (1983) (citing Divorce Mediation Research Project, Directory of Mediation Services (1982)). These states are: Arizona, California, Connecticut, Delaware, Florida, Hawaii, Illinois, Indiana, Kentucky, Maine, Massachusetts, Michigan, Minnesota, Missouri, Montana, Nebraska, Ohio, Oklahoma, Oregon, Texas, Virginia, Washington, Wisconsin.

[37] Cal Civ Code §4607 (Deering 1984).

[38] This Committee has compiled a Dispute Resolution Program Directory (1981); a Selected Bibliography of Alternative Methods of Dispute Settlement (updated May 1982) and a Panel Discussion Series, Alternative Dispute Resolution: Bane or Boon to Attorneys (Topic 1—1982), in addition to publishing Dispute Resolution, a quarterly update bulletin on developments in the field.

[39] Loeb, *Introduction to the Standards of Practice for Family Mediators,* 17 Fam LQ 451, 453 (1984). *See* **app 5-1.**

and desirable, for example, where one or both parties cannot negotiate for themselves; where the power imbalance is too great; where the issues are too complex; where the parties are simply unable or unwilling to come to an agreement.[40]

There have been excessive claims that mediation is "good" while the traditional adversarial approach to divorce is "bad." In actual practice, peppered by a multitude of variables, the difference between the two processes may not be so great. As Professor Robert J. Levy, in reviewing one mediation study, has observed:

> [R]eal world complexities make irrelevant any research based on the simplistic notion that divorce cases can be dichotomized into "traditional adversarial" and "mediation" groups. Every lawyer who has labored in the dissolution vineyard knows that no two divorce cases or divorce clients are identical–either financially or psychologically. . . .
>
> No one should dispute the claim that lawyers' values differ. . . . As with lawyers, so with divorcing clients. . . . Despite all these variations–from year to year and jurisdiction to jurisdiction, something like 85 to 90 percent of divorce cases are *settled* by the spouses and the lawyers prior to trial These cases are, in some significant sense, not adversarial at all. [Emphasis in original.][41]

A basic knowledge of divorce mediation as an alternative to litigation is essential to fully advise clients about its possible use. It is also important for attorneys who have clients in mediation, or who are mediators themselves, to be aware of the ethical pitfalls associated with mediation. The summary of issues provided here should be supplemented by the experience of others in addition to the multitude of books and articles written on the topic.[42]

---

[40] Zumeta, *supra* note 34, at 435.

[41] Levy, *supra* note 34, at 529-30.

[42] *See* F. Bienenfield, Child Custody Mediation, Techniques for Counselors, Attorneys and Parents (1983); O. Coogler, Structured Mediation in Divorce Settlement (1978); J. Haynes, Divorce Mediation, A Practical Guide for Therapists and Counselors (1981); H. Irving, Divorce Mediation: A Rational Alternative to the Adversary System (1981); Buser, *Your Role As A Mediator,* 13 Idaho Trial Law 4 (1983); Crouch, *Mediation & Divorce, The Dark Side is Still Unexplored,* 4 Fam Advoc 27 (Winter 1982); Crouch, *Divorce Mediation and Legal Ethics,* 16 Fam LQ 219 (1982); Gaughan, *Taking a Fresh Look at Divorce Mediation,* 17 Trial 39 (1981); Gold, *Mediation in the Dissolution of Marriage,* 36 Arb J 9 (Sept 1981); Harbinson, *supra* note 34, at 171 (1981); Meroney, *Mediation and Arbitration of Seperation and Divorce Agreements,* 15 Wake Forest L Rev 467 (1979); Silverman, *supra* note 34 at 107 (1982); Winks, *supra* note 34, at 615 (1981); Zumeta, *supra* note 34, at 434 (1983), and many others.

## §5.06 Approaches to Mediation

Because divorce mediation was still a developing discipline in 1985, there was, as noted by one specialist "no unifying theory, no unifying model, only an emerging body of knowledge."[43] Nevertheless, different approaches to divorce mediation have been developed in both court-connected and private mediation services. These approaches have been categorized into two basic schools of thought: *structured mediation* and *comprehensive mediation*.[44] These schools in turn have been divided into separate models identified by the number and educational background of the mediators. Each of these models possesses such individualized characteristics that there will be no attempt to describe all the variations here.

An acknowledged pioneer of divorce mediation is O.J. Coogler, a lawyer-psychologist who founded the Family Mediation Association in 1974. His structured mediation model is the best known approach to divorce mediation.[45] *Structured* is an appropriate label. The mediator, who is usually a family counselor educated in a behavioral science, is trained to conduct the mediation within a set of private rules based on Coogler's theory, divorce laws, and property laws. The parties, by written contract, agree to follow specific rules, including submitting a complete financial statement, meeting with the mediator on a fixed schedule, and agreeing to submit any impasse to arbitration.[46]

The structured mediation program consists of four to six two-hour-long sessions with both parties and the mediator present. When a mediated agreement has been reached, an "impartial advisory attorney" selected from a panel of attorneys provided by the mediation center is called in "to answer any legal questions that have been raised, to 'finalize' the tentative agreement that has been reached and to draft the formal settlement agreement."[47] The impartial advisory attorney is a distinguishing characteristic of Coogler's approach, and the attorney's role, particularly drafting the separation agreement for both parties and explaining its terms to each, has raised questions which will be discussed in the next sections.[48]

Comprehensive mediation provides greater flexibility than structured

---

[43] Gold, *Mediation in the Dissolution of Marriage,* 36 Arb J 9, 10 (1981). O. Coogler, Structured Mediation in Divorce Settlement 79 (1978), states "Marital mediation is an art in its early stages of development."

[44] Coombs, *Noncourt-Connected Mediation and Counseling in Child-Custody Disputes,* 17 Fam LQ 469, 471 (1984) (footnote omitted). However, Professor Coombs also notes that "[f]rom these two basic approaches, a variety of programs has developed adopting concepts from each and intermingling them to the point where it is no longer possible to pigeonhole most mediation programs as belonging to one school or the other." *Id* 472.

[45] *See* O. Coogler, Structured Mediation in Divorce Settlement (1978).

[46] Coombs, *supra* note 44, at 471; Silberman, *Professional Responsibility Problems of Divorce Mediation,* 16 Fam LQ 107, 135 (1982).

[47] Silberman, *supra* note 46, at 135.

[48] *See* **§§5.08-5.13.**

mediation. It does not follow an elaborate set of rules or require that the parties sign a contract with an arbitration clause. Comprehensive mediation allows individual meetings with the mediator if useful. The spouses are encouraged to retain their own attorneys to provide legal guidance.[49]

Mediation has been categorized also by the identity, number, and educational background of the mediators. There are the lawyer-mediator, the mental health professional-mediator, and the interdisciplinary co-mediation team models.[50] Each type differs according to the mediator, presenting advantages and disadvantages.

The attorney-mediator knows the law and may be familiar with the types of agreements acceptable to local judges. It is questionable whether an attorney-client privilege exists when a lawyer serves as mediator. However, the attorney-mediator faces a risk of ethics code violations and may experience difficulty putting aside his or her adversarial training during the process of mediation.[51]

By virtue of their training, mental health professional-mediators take a different approach to mediation. Accustomed to dealing with emotional crises, "the mental health professional may focus more heavily on preserving the integrity of the individuals or on evaluating individual needs than the lawyer-mediator, who might instead concentrate primarily on the legal ramifications. . . ."[52] This expertise in emotional behavior is advantageous where couples are genuinely restructuring their relationship to continue their roles as parents. However, the mental health professional often lacks knowledge of the legal consequences of divorce and may risk unauthorized practice of the law. In addition, there may be no confidentiality privilege for the mediation process, unless there is any contractually created confidentiality. It is uncertain whether such confidentiality agreements would be honored in court, however.

The interdisciplinary co-mediation team, which usually includes a lawyer and a mental health professional, frequently a male and a female, "offers disputing couples an approach which recognizes the fusion of numerous legal and emotional issues in the divorce process."[53] A male/female team can provide the divorcing parties a model of how a couple can work together with mutual respect.

Yet, the same problems which confront the individual attorney and mental health professional mediators also confront the team. In addition, the lawyer is faced with other possible ethical violations, including assisting a lay person in practicing law; practicing law in association with or in partnership with a

---

[49] Coombs, *supra* note 44, at 472.

[50] *Id* 472, 476, 485.

[51] *See* **§§5.08-5.12.**

[52] Coombs, *supra* note 44, at 476.

[53] *Id* 489.

nonlawyer; fee-splitting; and working for clients of a law employer.[54] It is also believed that spouses working with an interdisciplinary team are less likely to consult independent counsel following mediation, compounding these dangers.[55]

After investigating the types of mediation available in his or her community, the attorney will be able to advise interested clients and responsibly refer them to mediation services. Many bar associations, in addition to the American Bar Association, have committees on alternative dispute resolution which are a source of information for the practitioner.[56]

## §5.07 Overview of a Typical Mediation

While all mediations are not the same, due to differences in individual spouses, mediators, and problems presented for resolution, it is possible to present a general overview of a typical mediation. The director of the Family Mediation Center in Portland, Oregon, claims that a mediation follows four steps: assessment and direction; prenegotiation; active negotiation; and formulating the agreement.[57] The co-director of the Ann Arbor, Michigan Mediation Center offers the following outline of a typical mediation in a private mediation setting:

> 1. The couple meets with the mediator, who explains the mediation process and its use of outside experts. It is stressed that the mediation process is one of cooperation, mutual problem-solving, and respect for each other's problems and needs.
>
> The parties explain their situation, what they hope to achieve in mediation and any problems or issues they foresee.
>
> The mediator then sets up a tentative timetable. If the parties and the mediator agree that mediation is for them, the parties will sign a mediation agreement. This agreement usually sets out the mediation process ground rules and often includes an agreement that the process

---

[54] *See* Silberman, *supra* note 46, at 129-30 (citing American Bar Foundation, Annotated Code of Professional Responsibility, Canon 3, EC 3-8, DR 3-102 & 3-103 (1979)). *See also* **§§5.09-5.12.**

[55] *Id* 135.

[56] *See, e.g.*, Committee on Alternative Dispute Resolution and Litigation Economics, Litigation Division, District of Columbia Bar, Alternative to Litigation (1985). The authors of this pamphlet maintain that:

> Despite general acceptance in certain specialized fields, [alternative dispute resolution] tends to be avoided by the litigating bar. Lawyers are creatures of habit. Skilled in using existing tools to achieve innovative results, they feel uncomfortable about handling new tools to achieve traditional results.

*Id* 1.

[57] Gold, *Mediation in the Dissolution of Marriage*, 36 Arb J 9, 12-13 (Sept 1981).

is confidential, that the mediator will not be called as a witness by either party and that there will be full disclosure of assets by both parties.

2. The mediator meets with each party separately to make sure that each party will be able to carry on negotiations, and to find out more about their individual goals and needs. The mediator may also assist them in setting personal directions in which they may need to go, such as career counseling, personal therapy, or obtaining personal counsel. The mediator does not give legal advice in these sessions.

3. For the third session the parties are asked to bring financial information and to fill out financial data and budget forms, in order to assess the property in question and the need for support or alimony.

Finances are usually important even where the only issue between the parties is custody. . . .

When all the information-gathering is complete, the couple begins to sort out issues and reach agreements on them. Often the mediator will try to deal first with a relatively easy issue, in order to help the couple feel confident about their ability to negotiate; then the mediator builds on that success for the more difficult issues.

4. There usually are two to four more sessions in which the couple work through the issues. Experts are brought in where necessary, such as a pension valuation specialist, a tax specialist, or a child psychiatrist. Some mediators bring in children routinely; others rarely do so. . . .

The last steps of mediation tend to be unique to each mediation organization. In some an attorney for the organization will advise the parties and/or draft the agreement and file the divorce for the parties. As discussed below, this procedure has been criticized by some state and local bar ethics committees.

In other organizations the attorneys for the parties (or for one of the parties) will draft the agreement and file the divorce.

Of course, some clients wish to file their own divorce. Ethical questions and general prudence lead many mediation organizations to strongly encourage clients to consult their own attorneys during mediation and after the agreement is signed.[58]

## §5.08 Ethical Considerations

The Code of Professional Responsibility provides "an inspirational guide to the members of the profession and . . . a basis for disciplinary action when the conduct of a lawyer falls below the required minimum standards. . . ."[59] It was drafted to provide guidance in an adversarial system. While recognizing that

---

[58] Zumeta, *Mediation as an Alternative to Litigation in Divorce,* 62 Mich BJ 434, 436-37 (1983).

[59] American Bar Foundation, Annotated Code of Professional Responsibility 2 (1979). All references to the Code are from this edition [hereinafter cited as Code].

lawyers may serve as "impartial arbitrators or mediators,"[60] the Code does not define those terms or list the roles and responsibilities involved. Ethical Consideration 5-20 states that an attorney who does act as an arbitrator or mediator should not represent any of the parties involved thereafter.

Other than those specific references, the Code does not address nonadversarial proceedings directly. Guidance must be extrapolated from the principles of the Code.[61] One writer has noted that possible ethical violations in the divorce mediation process exist only because "the Code was written for a traditional adversary process, and a non-adversary process simply does not fit into its assumptions."[62]

In 1981, the Kutak Commission completed a final draft of the Model Rules of Professional Conduct as "a comprehensive rethinking of the ethical premises and problems of the profession of law."[63] The Model Rules provided, inter alia, that a lawyer could act as an "intermediary" if he or she fully disclosed to the clients all implications and reasonably believed that the matter could be resolved on terms compatible with the clients' best interests.[64] Once again, the

---

[60] See Code at 223, EC 5-20, which provides:

> A lawyer is often asked to serve as an impartial arbitrator or mediator in matters which involve present or former clients. He may serve in either capacity if he first discloses such present or former relationships. After a lawyer has undertaken to act as an impartial arbitrator or mediator, he should not thereafter represent in the dispute any of the parties involved.

[61] Opinion 80-23, Association of the Bar of the City of New York, 7 Fam L Rep (BNA) 3097 (Oct 13, 1981).

[62] Zumeta, *Mediation as an Alternative to Litigation in Divorce,* 62 Mich BJ 434, 439 (1983).

[63] Proposed Final Draft, Model Rules of Professional Conduct, American Bar Association Commission on Evaluation of Professional Standards i (May 30, 1981). All references to the Model Rules are from this edition.

[64] See *Id* 113, Rule 2.2, which provides:

> (a) A lawyer may act as intermediary between clients if:
>
> (1) The lawyer discloses to each client the implications of the common representation, including the advantages and risks involved, and obtains each client's consent to the common representation;
>
> (2) The lawyer reasonably believes that the matter can be resolved on terms compatible with the clients' best interests, that each client will be able to make adequately informed decisions in the matter and that there is little risk of material prejudice to the interest of any of the clients if the contemplated resolution is unsuccessful; and
>
> (3) The lawyer reasonably believes that the common representation can be undertaken impartially and without improper effect on other responsibilities the lawyer has to any of the clients.
>
> (b) While acting as intermediary, the lawyer shall explain fully to each client the decisions to be made and the considerations relevant in making them, so that each client can make adequately informed decisions.
>
> (c) A lawyer shall withdraw as intermediary if any of the clients so request, if the conditions stated in paragraph (a) cannot be met or if in the light of subsequent events the lawyer reasonably should know that a mutually advantageous resolution cannot be achieved. Upon withdrawal, the lawyer shall not continue to represent any of the clients unless doing so is clearly compatible with the lawyer's responsibilities to the other client or clients.

absence of a specific recognition of the divorce mediation process left a series of unanswered questions concerning the ethical considerations involved in divorce mediation.

These questions are different depending upon the role of the attorney and the model of mediation used. Generally, court-connected mediation services have not been challenged on ethical grounds and will not be discussed here. A body of ethics associated with divorce mediation has developed as a result of attorneys' inquiries into the appropriateness of mediation "which is not court-referred and which takes place independently and preliminary to any traditional legal processes."[65] The answers to these inquiries—opinions of ethics committees of several bar associations—are the clearest source of guidance for the practitioner contemplating participation in divorce mediation. Supplementing the Code, the Model Rules, and the ethics opinions are a few law review articles which usefully discuss and evaluate the ethical implications of divorce mediation.[66] To guide mediators, the Family Law Section of the American Bar Association adopted Standards of Practice for Family Mediators, reproduced in Appendix 5-1.[67]

The ethical considerations of divorce mediation are subtle and complex. The practitioner who is involved with mediation must be clear on his or her role, the ethical considerations involved, and the malpractice pitfalls of this nonadversarial approach to divorce. Linda J. Silberman, Professor of Law at New York University School of Law, has suggested that because of the uncertainty in this area, "perhaps what is needed is more serious reflection on how those ethical responsibilities can be met within the structure of individual mediation programs."[68]

## §5.09 —Conflict of Interest

The Code of Professional Responsibility provides that a lawyer can represent "multiple clients if it is obvious that he can adequately represent the interest of each and each consents to the representation after full disclosure of the possible effects of such representation. . . ."[69] The Model Rules of Professional

---

[65] Silberman, *Professional Responsibility Problems of Divorce Mediation,* 16 Fam LQ 107, 109 (1982).

[66] *See, e.g.,* Crouch, *Mediation & Divorce, The Dark Side is Still Unexplored,* 4 Fam Advoc 27 (Winter 1982); Crouch, *Divorce Mediation and Legal Ethics,* 16 Fam LQ 219 (1982); Harbinson, *Family Law - Attorney Mediation of Marital Disputes and Conflict of Interest Considerations,* 60 NCL Rev 171 (1981); Silberman, *Professional Responsibility Problems of Divorce Mediation,* 16 Fam LQ 107 (1982); Zumeta, *Mediation as an Alternative to Litigation in Divorce,* 62 Mich BJ 434, 437 (1983).

[67] *Standards of Practice for Family Mediators,* 17 Fam LQ 461 (1984), found in **app 5-1.**

[68] Silberman, *supra* note 65, at 108.

[69] American Bar Foundation, Annotated Code of Professional Responsibility 225 (1979) [hereinafter cited as Code]. DR 5-105(c). The Disciplinary Rule, in its entirety, provides:

Conduct advise the lawyer not to undertake the permitted "common representation" of clients "between whom litigation is imminent or who contemplate contentious negotiations . . . [or] if the relationship between the parties has already assumed definite antagonism."[70] Traditionally, representing both the wife and husband in a divorce action has been prohibited. It has been held that the conflicts inherent in divorce are such that it is never appropriate to represent both spouses.[71]

With the advent of no-fault divorce, the rule has been slightly relaxed: an attorney may draft a separation agreement and appear in court proceedings as the representative of one spouse if both parties have given their informed and written consent.[72] The Arizona and Virginia Bar Ethics Committees[73] and a

---

> DR 5-105 Refusing to Accept or Continue Employment If the Interests of Another Client May Impair the Independent Professional Judgment of the Lawyer.
>
> (A) A lawyer shall decline proffered employment if the exercise of his independent professional judgment in behalf of a client will be or is likely to be adversely affected by the acceptance of the proffered employment, or if it would be likely to involve him in representing differing interests, except to the extent permitted under DR 5-105(c).
>
> (B) A lawyer shall not continue multiple employment if the exercise of his independent professional judgment in behalf of a client will be or is likely to be adversely affected by his representation of another client, or if it would be likely to involve him in representing different interests, except to the extent permitted under DR 5-105(c) (footnotes omitted). In the situations covered by DR 5-105 (A) and (B), a lawyer may represent multiple clients if it is obvious that he can adequately represent the interests of each and if each consents to the representation after full disclosure of the possible effect of such representation on the exercise of his independent professional judgment on behalf of each.

[70] *See* Rule 2.2, Proposed Final Draft, Model Rules of Professional Conduct, American Bar Association Commission on Evaluation of Professional Standards 113 (May 30, 1981).

[71] Opinion 80-23, Association of the Bar of the City of New York, 7 Fam L Rep (BNA) 3097, 3098 (Oct 13, 1981).

[72] See Code at 222, EC 5-16, which states:

> In those instances in which a lawyer is justified in representing two or more clients having differing interests, it is nevertheless essential that each client be given the opportunity to evaluate his need for representation free of any potential conflict and to obtain other counsel if he so desires. Thus before a lawyer may represent multiple clients, he should explain fully to each client the implications of the common representation and should accept or continue employment only if the clients consent. If there are present other circumstances that might cause any of the multiple clients to question the individual loyalty of the lawyer, he should also advise all of the clients of those circumstances. (Footnotes omitted.)

See also Silberman, *Professional Responsibility Problems of Divorce Mediation,* 16 Fam LQ 107, 110 (1982) (citing OSBA Ethics Comm, OSBA Rep 780 (Opi 30) (May 1975)), in which the Ohio State Bar Ethics Committee

> ruled that although dual "representation" would not adequately protect the parties' rights, a single lawyer could draft a separation agreement so long as (A) the lawyer represented one of the parties and the second party (1) was fully

California Court of Appeal[74] have allowed dual representation in exceptional circumstances.

Yet, the Code also permits the attorney to act as "an impartial arbitrator or mediator," without defining those terms or delineating rules and responsibilities. Thus, as the Code stands, a lawyer is not supposed to represent a husband and wife in a divorce action, and yet may act as mediator. These conflicting principles raise important ethical considerations Few matters which arise in divorce mediation are dealt with in a relaxed manner and without some confrontation. All aspects in a divorce have legal implications. The questions revolve around the lawyer's rendering of a legal opinion or giving advice so as to "represent" the position of a spouse.

Generally, the fact that an attorney-mediator is capable of giving impartial legal advice is seen as an advantage in the divorce mediation field.[75] Nevertheless, there has been concern that an attorney-mediator cannot remain impartial in divorce mediation when rendering advice and drafting agreements, particularly in light of his or her advocacy training.[76]

---

> aware that (s)he was not being represented and (2) was given full opportunity to get independent counsel, and (B) both parties gave written consent to the arrangement–which was contained or attached to the separation agreement.

[73] Silberman, *supra* note 72, at 110-11 (citing Ariz State Bar Assn Comm dn Legal Ethics, Op No 76-25 (Nov 25, 1976); Va State Bar Assn Comm on Legal Ethics, Informal Op No 296 (1977)).

[74] Klemm v Superior Court, 75 Cal App 3d 893, —, 142 Cal Rptr 509, 573 (1977), where the court stated:

> Finally, as a caveat, we hasten to sound a note of warning. Attorneys who undertake to represent parties with divergent interests owe the highest duty to each to make a full disclosure of all facts and circumstances which are necessary to enable the parties to make a fully informed decision regarding the subject matter of the litigation, including the areas of potential conflict and the possibility and desirability of seeking independent legal advice. . . . Failing such disclosure, the attorney is civilly liable to the client who suffers loss caused by lack of disclosure. . . . In addition, the lawyer lays himself open to charges, whether well-founded or not, or unethical and unprofessional conduct.

[75] Zumeta, *Mediation as an Alternative to Litigation in Divorce,* 62 Mich BJ 434, 439 (1983), where the author declares:

> It is important for attorneys to be involved in mediation. Attorneys can make sure that legal issues are addressed in mediation. In addition, many attorneys want to be involved in non-adversary divorce procedures. Finally, many attorneys would make excellent mediators.

[76] See Crough, *Divorce Mediation and Legal Ethics,* 16 Fam LQ 219, 226 (1982), where the author asks:

> [Does attorney-mediation] include advice that benefits one party to the detriment of the other? Presumably so. The question that naturally arises is what happens when the attorney-mediator sees one party being "disadvantaged." in negotiations. If the mediator cannot advise one party to break off mediation without hurting the interests of the one who is gaining by mediation, then a real conflict of interests problem seems to arise. Obviously the definitions of benefit and detriment in this context are infinitely debatable and presumably framed by the

Bar ethics committees have managed to avoid these dangers, reluctantly permitting mediation by an attorney-drafter by stating that the mediator is not representing anyone and, therefore, has no conflict of interest.[77] A prerequisite to this "nonrepresentative" role is that the attorney-mediator must advise the parties that he or she is not representing either party and, therefore, has no duty of partisan loyalty.

In one of the first malpractice actions against a lawyer-mediator, the plaintiff-wife claimed that the defendant was negligent, alleging that he failed to inquire into the financial state of the husband and to advise her as to the husband's finances. Neither did he negotiate for a better settlement for the wife nor counsel the wife that she would do better if she litigated. In sum, the wife declared that the mediator did not fully and fairly advise her of all her rights.[78] The defendant asserted that because he acted as a mediator, it was improper for him to advocate the rights of either party. Unfortunately, the Missouri Court of Appeals did not reach the question of whether such actions were appropriate functions of an attorney-mediator, choosing instead to focus on the absence of plaintiff's damages.[79]

The Oregon Bar Committee approved the position of the Boston Bar which permitted attorney mediation as long as the mediator was not representing either party, and imposed four prerequisites appropriate for mediation:

> The lawyer (1) must clearly inform the parties that (s)he represents neither and they must both consent; (2) can give legal advice only to both parties in the presence of each other; (3) can draft the proposed

---

> preliminary assumption that a fair, comprised and conflict-avoiding settlement is the desire of both.

See also Silberman, *supra* note 72, at 114, who notes that the Wisconsin State Bar Committee (Wis State Bar Assn Comm on Professional Ethics, Ops E-79-2 (Jan 1980) refused to permit a lawyer to offer a mediation service in which he proposed to educate the parties as to their legal rights, mediate, draft the agreement, and process the divorce through the courts. The Committee maintained that the attorney's proposal went beyond the role of impartial mediator as provided in the Code of Professional Responsibility (EC 5-20), and also thought that the education aspect was suspect because the divorcing parties would most likely perceive the attorney in his advocate role.

[77] *See* Silberman, *supra* note 72, at 111-12 (citing Boston Bar Assn Comm on Ethics, Op No 78-1 (1978) & Oregon Bar Assn Comm on Legal Ethics, Proposed Op No 70-46 (Apr 2, 1980)). *See also* Op 80-23, Association of the Bar of the City of New York, 7 Fam L Rep (BNA) 3097, 3098 (Oct 13, 1981).

[78] Lange v Marshall, 622 SW2d 237 (Mo Ct App 1981).

[79] *Id* 239, where the court stated:

> There is no evidence in the record that had the defendant done the things plaintiff contends he did not do, that these items of expense would not have been incurred in order for plaintiff to achieve the settlement she considered proper. There is no evidence that [the husband] would have voluntarily agreed to a settlement acceptable to the plaintiff had defendant done the things he admittedly did not do. If anything the evidence is to the contrary.

> agreement but must advise and encourage the parties to seek independent legal counsel; and (4) must not represent either or both parties in a later legal proceeding.[80]

The New York City Bar reluctantly permits lawyers to serve as mediators in a nonrepresentative capacity only when it is clear to the lawyer-mediator that the issues are not particularly complex and that the parties fully understand the mediator's role and consent to the procedure.[81] However, the Washington State Bar Committee and the New Hampshire Ethics Committee relied on Disciplinary Rule 5-105 in deciding that a lawyer's participation as a mediator is unethical because it directly conflicts with counsel's ability to adequately represent the interests of each party.[82]

---

[80] Silberman, *supra* note 72, at 112 (citing Ore Bar Assn Comm on Legal Ethics, Proposed Op No 74-46 (Apr 2, 1980)).

[81] Opinion 80-23, Association of the Bar of the City of New York, *supra* note 77, at 3099-100, where the Committee established the following conditions:

> To begin with, the lawyer may *not* participate in the divorce mediation process where it appears that the issues between the parties are of such complexity or difficulty that the parties cannot prudently reach a resolution without the legal advice of separate and independent legal counsel.
>
> If the lawyer is satisfied that the situation is one in which the parties can intelligently and prudently consent to mediation and the use of an impartial legal adviser, then the lawyer may undertake these roles provided the lawyer observes the following rules:
>
> First, the lawyer must clearly and fully advise the parties of the limitations on his or her role, and specifically, of the fact that the lawyer represents neither party and that, accordingly, they should not look to the lawyer to protect their individual interests or to keep confidences of one party from the other.
>
> Second, the lawyer must fully and clearly explain the risks of proceeding without separate legal counsel and thereafter proceed only with the consent of the parties and only if the lawyer is satisfied that the parties understand the risks and understand the significance of the fact that the lawyer represents neither party.
>
> Third, a lawyer may participate with mental health professionals in those aspects of mediation which do not require the exercise of professional legal judgment and involve the same kind of mediation activities permissible to lay mediators.
>
> Fourth, lawyers may provide impartial legal advice and assist in reducing the parties' agreement to writing only where the lawyer fully explains all pertinent considerations and alternatives and the consequences to each party of choosing the resolution agreed upon.
>
> Fifth, the lawyer may give legal advice only to both parties in the presence of the other.
>
> Sixth, the lawyer must advise the parties of the advantages of seeking independent legal counsel before executing any agreement drafted by the lawyer.
>
> Seventh, the lawyer may not represent either of the parties in any subsequent legal proceedings relating to the divorce.
>
> Underlying these guidelines is the requirement that the lawyer's participation in the mediation process be conditioned on *informed* consent by the parties.

[82] Silberman, *supra* note 72, at 113 (citing Wash State Bar Assn Code of Professional Responsibility Comm, Informal Op, Item 385 (Feb 20, 1980), and NH State Bar Assn

The attorney who acts as an advisor to one party of the mediation has no conflict of interest, but the lawyer's participation in the process as advisor of one of the parties may actually thwart the goals of mediation by introducing adversarial elements. As commentators have stated:

> There is also the dilemma created when independent advice is sought regarding the financial terms of a mediated agreement. The mediation service tells the client to consult his or her attorney, and the latter is presented with the problem of accepting, rejecting, or modifying the mediated agreement. An attorney who does not check out the financial and economic facts behind the agreement may risk a malpractice action, but if he does check out the facts, he may upset the agreement and the mediation may have been a waste of time and money.[83]

Insisting that mediating parties retain their own individual attorneys may serve "to generate public suspicion that the real motivation is the legal profession's self-interest."[84] Nevertheless, the attorney's duty to protect a client overrides the risk of confirming a public perception that the legal profession foments antagonism and litigation to collect fees. It is far more important to encourage mediating clients to obtain representation to safeguard their interests.

## §5.10 —Conflict of Interest in Structured Mediation

The conflict of interest issue also arises in the *structured mediation* model, which provides for an *impartial advisory attorney* to give the parties legal advice and draft the separation agreement after mediation. The Coogler system[85] contemplates that the attorney, with the other party's informed consent, will represent only one party in the divorce proceeding subsequent to the successful mediation process.

The Maryland State Bar Association was asked to rule on the propriety of a lawyer's participation on the board of the Family Mediation Association (FMA) in the capacity of impartial advisory attorney. While not directly forbidding such participation, the Maryland Committee on Ethics emphasized the conflict of interest dangers.[86] Citing a previous opinion which had expressed the belief that it was impossible for an attorney to represent both

---

Ethics Comm (Mar 16, 1982); 8 NH L Weekly 385 (1982)). DR 5-105 provides, inter alia, that a lawyer may represent multiple clients only if it is obvious that the lawyer can adequately represent the interests of each client with independent judgment after full disclosure of the possible effect of such representation.

[83] Freed & Foster, *Family Law in the Fifty States: An Overview,* 16 Fam LQ 289, 296 (1983).

[84] Crouch, *supra* note 76, at 234.

[85] *See* **§5.06.**

[86] *An Informal Ethics Opinion,* 14 Md BJ 8 (Jan 1981).

a husband and wife in a divorce action, the Committee nevertheless acknowledged that successful mediation may bring about a "no-contest" situation which could make the advisory attorney's participation proper. This situation would have to be determined on a case-by-case basis, however.[87] It was also noted that the lawyer who undertakes multiple representation must virtually guarantee the satisfaction of all clients and be legally and financially responsible to all the clients for any damage caused by disloyalty.

The Committee enlightened the profession on the distinction between an impartial arbitration or mediation and a "representing" attorney:

> In the former situation the attorney-client relationship would not necessarily exist and, while honesty would remain a fundamental duty regardless of the role, loyalty would not. The attorney-mediator, like the lay mediator in the same role, has no particular right or duty to give legal advice to the participants nor have the participants, upon hearing such gratuitous advice, received "legal representation."[88]

The New York City Bar Committee on Professional and Judicial Ethics ruled that a lawyer may participate in a nonprofit organization's mediation program which uses the structured mediation approach. This participation was possible only:

> if the lawyer advises the parties of the limitations of his or her role, explains the risks of proceeding without counsel, and obtains "informed" consent of all parties, and if the issues are not of "such complexity or difficulty that the parties cannot prudently reach a resolution of the conflict without the advice of separate and independent legal counsel."[89]

## §5.11 —Unauthorized Practice of Law

Some attorneys are affiliated with mediation organizations, and act as mediators or impartial attorney-advisors. These attorneys must insure that lay mediators with whom they are associated are not practicing law. Canon 3 of the Code of Professional Responsibility establishes the lawyer's duty to assist

---

[87] *Id* 9, where the Committee also stated:

> There are at least two specific conditions which must exist for a lawyer to attempt to serve as an Impart [Impartial?] Advisory Attorney:
>
> (1) The possibility of adjusting the client's interests must be *strong*.
>
> (2) There must be little likelihood that any of the clients will be significantly prejudiced if the contemplated adjustment of interests is unsuccessful.

[88] *Id* 9-10.

[89] Opinion 80-23, Association of the Bar of the City of New York, 7 Fam L Rep (BNA) 3097, 3097 (Oct 13, 1981).

in preventing the unauthorized practice of law.[90] Disciplinary Rule 3-101(A) states, "A lawyer shall not aid a non-lawyer in the unauthorized practice of law." It is improper for an attorney to participate in a mediation program where nonlawyers are engaged in the unauthorized practice of law.

Other Code provisions balance the principles of preventing the unauthorized practice of law and maintaining professional independence.[91] Ethical Consideration 3-8 provides that lawyers should not practice law in association with laymen nor should they split fees with laymen. Disciplinary Rule 3-103 states that a lawyer shall not form a partnership with a nonlawyer if any of the activities of the partnership consist of the practice of law.

The practitioner must determine what constitutes the unauthorized practice of law in the divorce mediation process. The Maryland Bar Ethics Committee has stated that "[i]t is possible for a mediator, or a family mediation center to engage in the practice of law by applying general legal principles to the specific problems of his, her, or its clients."[92] No other sources serve to clarify the definition of unauthorized practice of law in the context of divorce mediation. Ethical Consideration 3-5 of the Code states:

> It is neither necessary nor desirable to attempt the formulation of a single, specific definition of what constitutes the practice of law. Functionally, the practice of law relates to the rendition of services for others that call for the professional judgment of a lawyer. The essence of the professional judgment of the lawyer is his educated ability to relate the general body and philosophy of law to a specific legal problem of a client; and thus, the public interest will be better served if only lawyers are permitted to act in matters involving professional judgment. Where this professional judgment is not involved, non-lawyers, such as court clerks, police officers, abstracters, and many governmental employees, may engage in occupations that require a special knowledge of law in certain areas. But the services of a lawyer are essential in the public interest whenever the exercise of professional legal judgment is required. (Footnote omitted.)

In an influential opinion, the Association of the Bar of the City of New York's Committee of Professional and Judicial Ethics assumed that it was possible for lay mediators to participate in divorce mediation without exercising legal

---

[90] American Bar Foundation, Annotated Code of Professional Responsibility (1979). All references to the Code in this section are from this edition. It should be noted at the outset that it is generally agreed that the Kutak Commission's Proposed Final Draft of The Model Rules of Professional Conduct does not adequately address the problems discussed here in the divorce mediation context. *See* Crouch, *Divorce Mediation and Legal Ethics,* 16 Fam LQ 219; Silberman, *Problems of Divorce Mediation,* 16 Fam LQ 107, 144 (1982).

[91] *See* **§5.12.**

[92] *An Informal Ethics Opinion,* 14 Md BJ 8, 8 (Jan 1981).

judgments or practicing law, but did not elaborate.[93] The North Carolina State Bar Unauthorized Practice of Law Committee decided that a nonprofit structured mediation organization was practicing law by requiring its clients to sign a contract agreeing to abide by the rules of the organization and to submit any unresolved disputes to binding arbitration.[94] The North Carolina Committee maintained that the preparation of this contract and the explanation of its implications were tasks reserved for attorneys.

One rationale supporting the principle that a lawyer should prevent the unauthorized practice of law is that the public must be protected from the lay person who attempts to exercise legal judgment or render legal opinions. It has been argued, however, that divorce mediation simply requires that the mediator inform the parties of the fairly straightforward legal issues so that "one can imagine a well-trained group of mediators (in the manner of paraprofessionals) acquiring the necessary expertise" to be able to inform the parties without actually practicing law.[95]

Nevertheless, nonlawyer mediators frequently assist in the development of the parties' separation agreement, and may actually draft such an agreement. Professor Linda J. Silberman of the New York University Law School suggests that these mediators may use an argument advanced by insurance companies, real estate brokers, and accountants that any legal advice given or legal instruments prepared during mediation are only "incidental" to their profession and as such fall outside the unauthorized practice prohibition.[96] There has been no substantial guidance in this area.

## §5.12 —Lawyer Independence

The Code of Professional Responsibility summarizes the issue in Ethical Consideration 5-24:

> Although other innovations in the means of supplying legal counsel may develop, the responsibility of the lawyer to maintain his professional independence remains constant, and the legal profession must insure that changing circumstances do not result in loss of professional independence of the lawyer.[97]

---

[93] Opinion 80-23, Association of the Bar of the City of New York, 7 Fam L Rep (BNA) 3097, 3100 (Oct 13, 1981).

[94] Silberman, *supra* note 90, 16 Fam LQ at 126 (citing NCSBA Unauthorized Practice of Law Comm (Oct 1980)).

[95] *Id* 124.

[96] *Id* 125.

[97] American Bar Foundation, Annotated Code of Professional Responsibility (1979). All references to the Code in this section are from this edition. [hereinafter cited as Code]. *See generally* Canon 5, Code at 187, and all accompanying Ethical Considerations and Disciplinary Rules. Canon 5 is: A Lawyer Should Exercise Independent Judgment on Behalf of a Client.

This issue becomes important in divorce mediation with the relationship between the impartial advisory attorney and the mediation organization, the method of solicitation, and the method of payment. As Disciplinary Rule 5-107(B) states: "A lawyer shall not permit a person who recommends, employs, or pays him to render legal services for another to direct or regulate his professional judgment in rendering such legal services."

An attorney advisor, whether acting impartially or as an advocate for one of the parties, must be free to form an independent relationship with the parties. The Maryland Ethics Committee has concluded that it was improper for a structured mediation program to appoint an attorney to assist a husband and wife when they failed to select an attorney from the program's panel.[98] The Committee stated that this procedure:

> creates a situation where the attorney who is attempting to balance the rights of two individuals was not chosen for the task by either. In the absence of consent, no attorney-client relationship can develop; and the attorney, who derives his authority from the clients and not from the center, is powerless to act as lawyer for the couple.[99]

This independent relationship of advisor includes the duty to promote the interests of the clients over the success of the mediation. This may place the attorney in the unhappy situation of recommending that the couple cease mediation. In addition, the practice which has developed in divorce mediation is that an attorney bills separately for the services rendered, and should be paid by the mediating couple or by the individual party. The more independence an advisor attorney exercises, the better. The State of Virginia Ethics Committee approved lawyer participation on an advisory attorney panel of a mediation program where the lawyers drafted the separation agreement at the conclusion of the couple's negotiations, did not share fees with the mediation program, and were not individually referred by the program, but simply included in a list of approved panel members.[100]

The independence concern also underlies the issue of solicitation. "Consumerism of legal services" took on new meaning in the 1980s, and for many lawyers divorce mediation has been a new source of business. The attorney who desires to create a mediation service or participate in an existing program must be wary of the traditional, complicated guidelines enunciated in the Code of Professional Responsibility.

Disciplinary Rule 2-103, which is reproduced in its entirety in the footnote due to its importance and complexity, generally prohibits lawyers from

---

[98] An Informal Ethics Op, 14 Maryland BJ 8, 10 (Jan 1981).

[99] *Id.*

[100] Informal Ethics Op No 400, Sept 18, 1979, 7 Fam L Rep (BNA) 288 (Jan 27, 1981).

soliciting employment or requesting or permitting an organization to recommend or promote the use of his or her services.[101] A primary concern

---

[101] Code at 66-67, DR 2-103 Recommendation of Professional Employment, provides:

(A) A lawyer shall not, except as authorized in DR 2-101(B), recommend employment as a private practitioner, of himself, his partner, or associate to a layperson who has not sought his advice regarding employment of a lawyer.

(B) A lawyer shall not compensate or give anything of value to a person or organization to recommend or secure his employment by a client, or as a reward for having made a recommendation resulting in his employment by a client, except that he may pay the usual and reasonable fees or dues charged by any of the organizations listed in DR 2-103(D).

(C) A lawyer shall not request a person or organization to recommend or promote the use of his services or those of his partner or associate, or any other lawyer affiliated with him or his firm, as a private practitioner, except as authorized in DR 2-101, and except that

(1) He may request referrals from a lawyer referral service operated, sponsored, or approved by a bar association and may pay its fees incident thereto.

(2) He may cooperate with the legal service activities of any of the offices or organizations enumerated in DR 2-103 (D)(1) through (4) and may perform legal services for those to whom he was recommended by it to do such work if:

(a) The person to whom the recommendation is made is a member or beneficiary of such office or organization; and

(b) The lawyer remains free to exercise his independent professional judgment on behalf of his client.

(D) A lawyer or his partner or associate or any other lawyer affiliated with him or his firm may be recommended, employed or paid by, or may cooperate with, one of the following offices or organizations that promote the use of his services or those of his partner or associate or any other lawyer affiliated with him or his firm if there is no interference with the exercise of independent professional judgment in behalf of his client:

(1) A legal aid office or public defender office:

(a) Operated or sponsored by a duly accredited law school.

(b) Operated or sponsored by a bona fide nonprofit community organization.

(c) Operated or sponsored by a government agency.

(d) Operated, sponsored, or approved by a bar association.

(2) A military legal assistance office.

(3) A lawyer referral service operated, sponsored, or approved by a bar association.

(4) Any bona fide organization that recommends, furnishes or pays for legal services to its members or beneficiaries provided the following conditions are satisfied.

(a) Such organization, including any affiliate, is so organized and operated that no profit is derived by it from the rendition of legal services by lawyers, and that, if the organization is organized for profit, legal services are not rendered by lawyers employed, directed, supervised or selected by it except in connection with matters where such organization bears ultimate liability of its member or geneficiary.

(b) Neither the lawyer, nor his partner, nor associate, nor any other

underlying this rule is that a lawyer must remain free to exercise independent professional judgment on behalf of a client.

Nevertheless, this prohibition is lifted if the organization falls within the exceptions enunciated in DR 2-103, the person to whom the recommendation is made is a member or beneficiary of the organization, and the lawyer retains independence. Other considerations are that the organization should be nonprofit, it should not have been created by lawyers in order to increase business, and the organization's primary purpose should not be procurement of legal work for attorneys. In short, there is limited room for attorney participation in mediation services and the attorney must be sensitive to solicitation issues.

The ethics committees of the Bars of the City of New York[102] and the Commonwealth of Virginia[103] have ruled that a lawyer's participation on a

---

lawyer affiliated with him or his firm, nor any non-lawyer, shall have initiated or promoted such organization for the primary purpose of providing financial or other benefit to such lawyer, partner, associate or affiliated lawyer.

(c) Such organization is not operated for the purpose of procuring legal work or financial benefit for any lawyer as a private practitioner outside of the legal services program of the organization.

(d) The member or beneficiary to whom the legal services are furnished, and not such organization, is recognized as the client of the lawyer in the matter.

(e) Any member or beneficiary who is entitled to have legal services furnished or paid for by the organization may, if such member or beneficiary so desires, select counsel other than that furnished, selected or approved by the organization for the particular matter involved; and the legal service plan of such organization provides appropriate relief for any member or beneficiary who asserts a claim that representation by counsel furnished, selected or approved would be unethical, improper or inadequate under the circumstances of the matter involved and the plan provides an appropriate procedure for seeking such relief.

(f) The lawyer does not know or have cause to know that such organization is in violation of applicable laws, rules of court and other legal requirements that govern its legal service operations.

(g) Such organization has filed with the appropriate disciplinary authority at least annually a report with respect to its legal service plan, if any, showing its terms, its schedule of benefits, its subscription charges, agreements with counsel, and financial results of its legal service activities or, if it has failed to do so, the lawyer does not know or have cause to know of such failure.

(E) A lawyer shall not accept employment when he knows or it is obvious that the person who seeks his services does so as a result of conduct prohibited under this Disciplinary Rule. (Footnotes omitted.)

[102] Opinion 80-23, Association of the Bar of the City of New York, 7 Fam L Rep (BNA) 3097, 3101 (Oct 13, 1981).

[103] Informal Ethics Op no 400, Sept 18, 1979, 7 Fam L Rep (BNA) 288, 288-89 (June 27, 1981).

panel of impartial advisory attorneys in a structured mediation program is ethical as long as the requirements of DR 2-103 are met. The New York City Bar's Committee on Professional and Judicial Ethics concluded that mediating couples were beneficiaries of the mediation program under DR 2-103(C) and (D), and, therefore, the lawyers could accept fees from those couples.

A later opinion by the New York City Committee reaffirmed that a lawyer may cooperate in a legal referral service only in the limited circumstances set forth in DR 2-103(C) and (D).[104] The committee rejected a proposed for-profit mediation program that would include a central referral system for financial mediation, therapy, and legal counsel which would provide separate billing for each service.

Commentary on the possible ethical problems posed by the lawyer's participation with divorce mediation has noted the frustrating ambiguity of the guidance of the Code, Model Rules, and ethical opinions. Professor Silberman of New York University Law School encourages ethics committees to permit experimentation in divorce mediation,[105] while attorney Richard E. Crouch advocates drafting of a special rule tailored specifically to the lawyer participating in the divorce mediation process which would both establish the procedure of mediation and outline steps necessary for an ethically safe mediation.[106] Already, the parameters of ethical participation by lawyers in the divorce mediation process are being formed, and should continue to develop as divorce mediation matures as an alternative to traditional adversarial litigation.

## §5.13 Additional Considerations

Several other issues relating to divorce mediation have received some attention in legal literature. These focus primarily on divorce mediation as an alternative legal service for the "consumer" client.

An initial concern is the competence of mediators, many of whom are professionals who mediate in addition to their traditional legal or mental health work. While most mediators have professional training in law, therapy, or social service, anyone can represent himself or herself to the public as a divorce mediator, regardless of training and experience. The "profession" of mediation has no established educational prerequisites, licensing procedures, or

---

[104] Opinion No 82-30, Association of the Bar of the City of New York, Committee on Professional and Judicial Ethics, Oct 27, 1983, 10 Fam L Rep (BNA) 1057 (Nov 22, 1983).

[105] Silberman, *Professional Responsibility Problems of Divorce Mediation,* 16 Fam LQ 107, 144 (1982).

[106] Crouch, *Divorce Mediation and Legal Ethics,* 16 Fam LQ 219, 248-50 O 982).

Some "essentials of honest and safe mediation" as suggested by Mr. Crouch include, inter alia, a preliminary written contract embodying all warnings, waivers, and informal consents, additional warnings repeated in person, exclusions from subsequent representation by the lawyer-mediator, and instructions to the parties about the advantages of independent legal counsel for each party.

policing policies. There exists a legitimate concern that mediating couples may be vulnerable to mediators who abuse the system.

The Family Law Section of the American Bar Association has provided some guidance with its adoption of Standards of Practice for Family Mediators.[107] The National Center for Family Studies at the Catholic University of America in Washington, D.C., was the first educational institution in this country to offer a postgraduate certificate program in family mediation. The purpose of that program, as stated in the brochure, "is to equip professionals with the information, skills, and experience necessary to engage in the process of mediation responsibly and with excellence."[108] Other mediation courses and training programs are offered around the country, but none was regulated by any governmental authority or bar group as of 1985. While state bar associations have been encouraged to provide family law attorneys with some mediation training, and ethics committees have been encouraged to provide greater flexibility for lawyers participating in the mediation process,[109] it remains to be seen whether any such actions will be taken.

Additional considerations which have emerged include the confidentiality of the mediation process and the possibility that a mediator may not be able to neutralize the power imbalance between the divorcing parties. The confidentiality issue has been handled through evolving practice. Generally, the mediator agrees not to voluntarily disclose any information obtained in mediation without the prior consent of both parties. The couple, in turn, agrees in writing not to call the mediator as a witness in any subsequent legal action or require the mediator to disclose any statements made in mediation to any third parties.[110] It is thought that having these agreements will encourage

---

[107] *See* Loeb, *Introduction to the Standards of Practice for Family Mediators,* 17 Fam LQ 451 1984; **app 5-1.**

[108] The brochure continues:

> The program of studies during the first year consists of introductory seminars in foundational theories of marital and family systems, theory and practice of conflict resolution, legal issues in family mediation, family finances, and a survey of family therapy theories (see inside course descriptions). Participants with adequate backgrounds may qualify out of one or more of these seminars by examination, provided they select other suitable electives.
>
> The program of studies during the second year combines seminars in the advanced theory and practice of family mediation with a supervised field placement. Placement settings may include court-connected mediation services, hospitals, neighborhood centers and juvenile detention centers.

[109] Bahr, *Mediation is the Answer,* 4 Fam Advoc 32, 35 (Winter 1982).

[110] *See* Pickrell & Bendheim, *Family Disputes Mediation—A New Service for Lawyers and Their Clients,* 15 Ariz BJ 33 (Oct 1979) and 15 Ariz BJ 34 (Dec 1979), for an example of an "Agreement in Mediation" which provides in clause 6:

> 6. The parties further agree that none of the materials, statements or information shall be used by either party, nor shall the Mediator's suggestions be offered into evidence nor shall the Mediator be called by either party to testify; nor shall any Court take judicial notice of any of the foregoing information, in the event the parties are unable to negotiate an amicable

divulgence of information which otherwise might not have been disclosed because of the informal atmosphere of the mediation process.[111]

Concern has been expressed that the mediator's prejudices might unfairly influence a mediation or that "imperfect human mediators, stepping into a god-like role in the process [may be] deceived into allowing, and even contributing to, the unconscionable exploitation of the weaker by the dominant party."[112] This is one of the pitfalls of divorce mediation. On the other hand, the problem of professional competence and integrity exists in every profession.

Will divorce mediation live up to its lofty promises of a cheaper, faster, more satisfying route to marriage dissolution than the courts? Two studies conducted in the early 1980s reached similar conclusions after exploring that question.[113]

While conceding that more research is imperative, these studies agreed that divorce mediation more frequently leads to stipulations about custody and visitation arrangements, modest financial savings for the divorcing couple and the public sector, and a lower rate of relitigation. Perhaps the most important conclusion was that the majority of the mediating couples reported satisfaction with their final agreements. Nevertheless, another question remains: how can full and fair mediation be provided in the absence of a practicing lawyer's advice as to each party's rights and the legal ramifications involved? Also, one might ponder whether these clients would have reached a negotiated settlement through legal counsel without mediation.

It will be interesting to monitor the further developments of the divorce mediation field. Despite controversial beginnings, divorce mediation has established a place in the no-fault dissolution process.

---

> out-of-court settlement and it is necessary that the matter be tried at some future time before a Court of competent jurisdiction.

111 This is a disputed point. Some think that the informality of mediation encourages truth-telling, while others think that the lack of an enforcement mechanism such as the crime of perjury actually reduces the tendency to tell the truth.

112 Crouch, *Divorce Mediation and Legal Ethics,* 16 Fam LQ 219, 240 (1982). See Winks, *Divorce Mediation: A Nonadversary Procedure for the No-Fault Divorce,* 19 J Fam L 615, 643-44 (1980-81), where the author notes:

> Mediation is appropriate for clients who have already achieved some independence and have relatively equal bargaining positions. Ideally, both parties will be assertive, although self-esteem even for the initiator of the divorce may be hard to come by during this stage in the process. . . . [W]hen trust has been seriously eroded, no agreement can be worked out.

113 *See* Bahr, *Mediation is the Answer,* 4 Fam Advoc 32 (Winter 1982); Pearson & Thoennes, *Mediating and Litigating Custody Disputes: A Longitudinal Evaluation,* 17 Fam LQ 497 (1984).

# Appendix 5-1
# ABA Standards of Practice for Mediators

These standards are reprinted with permission from 17 Fam L Q 455-60 (1984). The American Bar Association's Section of Family Law approved the Standards at its 1984 annual meeting in Chicago, Illinois.

## Standards of Practice for Family Mediators

### Preamble

For purposes of these standards, family mediation is defined as a process in which a qualified person helps family members resolve their disputes in a consensual and informed manner. It is essential to this process that the mediator be qualified and impartial; that the participants reach decisions voluntarily; that their decisions be based on sufficient factual data; and that each participant understands the information upon which decisions are reached. While family mediation may be viewed as an alternative means of conflict resolution, it shall not be a substitute for the benefit of independent legal advice.

### Standards

I. *The mediator has a duty to define and describe the process of mediation and its cost before reaching an agreement to mediate.*

Specific Considerations

A. Before the actual mediation sessions begin, the mediator shall conduct an orientation session to give an overview of the process and to assess the appropriateness of mediation for the participants. Among the topics covered, the mediator shall discuss the following:

1. The mediator shall define the process in context so that the participants understand the differences between mediation and other means of conflict resolution available to them. In defining the process, the mediator shall also distinguish it from therapy or marriage counseling.

2. The mediator shall obtain sufficient information from the participants so they can mutually define the issues to be resolved in mediation.

3. The mediator and the participants shall agree upon the duties and responsibilities that each is accepting in the mediation process. The participants should understand that either of them or the mediator has the right to suspend or terminate the process at any time.

4. The mediator shall assess the ability and willingness of the participants to mediate. The mediator shall also assess his or her own ability and willingness to undertake mediation with these particular participants and the issues to be mediated. This is a continuing duty.

5. The mediator shall explain the fees for mediation and reach an agreement with the participants for payment. It is inappropriate for a mediator to charge a contingency fee or to base the fee on the outcome of the mediation process.

6. The mediator shall inform the participants that each should employ independent legal counsel for advice throughout the mediation process. In the event the mediator is a lawyer, the lawyer-mediator shall inform the participants that the lawyer-mediator cannot represent either or both of them in a marital dissolution or in any legal action.

7. The mediator shall discuss the issue of separate sessions and shall reach an understanding with the participants as to whether and under what circumstances the mediator may meet alone with either of them or with any third party.

II. *The mediator shall not voluntarily disclose any information obtained through the mediation process without the prior consent of both participants.*

Specific Considerations

A. At the orientation session the parties should agree in writing not to require the mediator to disclose to any third party any statements made in the course of mediation. The mediator shall inform the participants that the mediator will not voluntarily disclose to any third party any of the information obtained through the mediation process.

B. The mediator shall inform the participants of the mediator's inability to bind third parties to an agreement not to disclose in the absence of any absolute privilege.

C. At this orientation session, the mediator must discuss with the participants the potential outcome of their disclosure of facts to each other during the mediation process.

III *The mediator has a duty to be impartial.*

Specific Considerations

A. A lawyer-mediator shall not represent either party during or after the mediation process in any legal matters. In the event the mediator has represented one of the parties beforehand, the mediator shall not undertake the mediation.

B. A mediator who is a mental health person shall not provide counseling or therapy to either party or both during or after the mediation process. If the mediator has provided marriage counseling to the participants, or therapy to either of them beforehand, the mediator shall not undertake the mediation.

C. The mediator shall disclose to the participants any biases relating to the issues to be mediated both in the orientation session and also before those issues are discussed in mediation.

D. Impartiality is not the same as neutrality. While the mediator must be impartial as between the mediation participants, the mediator shaould be concerned with fairness. The mediator has an obligation to avoid an unreasonable result.

E. The mediator has a duty to promote the best interest of the children. The mediator also has a duty to assist parents to examine the separate and individual needs of their children and to consider those needs apart from their own desires for any particular parenting formula. If the mediator believes that any proposed agreement between the parents does not protect the best interests of the children, the mediator has a duty to inform them of this belief and its basis.

F. The mediator shall not communicate with either party alone or with any third parties to discuss mediation issues without the prior consent of the mediation participants.

IV. *The mediator has a duty to assure that the mediation participants make decisions based upon sufficient information and knowledge.*

Specific Considerations

A. The mediator shall assure that there is full financial disclosure, evaluation, and development of relevant factual information in the mediation process, such as each would reasonably receive in the normal discovery process.

B. In addition to requiring this disclosure, evaluation and development of information, the mediator shall promote the equal understanding of such information before any agreement is reached. This consideration may require the mediator to recommend that either or both obtain expert consultation in the event that it appears that additional knowledge or understanding is necessary for balanced negotiation.

C. The mediator who is a lawyer may define the legal issues. The lawyer-mediator shall not direct the decision of the mediation participants based upon the lawyer-mediator's interpretation of the law as applied to the facts of the situation. The mediator shall endeavor to assure that the participants have a sufficient understanding of appropriate statutory and case law as well as local judicial tradition, before reaching an agreement by recommending to the participants that they obtain independent legal representation during the process. This recommendation shall be made whether or not the mediator is a lawyer. If the participants or either of them choose to proceed without independent counsel the mediator shall warn them of the risk involved in not being represented including the possibility that any agreement they submit to a court may be rejected as unreasonable in light of both parties' legal rights or may not be binding on them.

V. *The mediator has a duty to suspend or terminate mediation whenever continuation of the process would harm or prejudice one or more of the participants.*

Specific Considerations

A. If the mediator believes that the ability or willingness of either of the participants to meaningfully participate in the process is lacking the mediator has a duty to suspend or terminate the process.

B. If the mediator believes that the agreement being approached is unreasonable, the mediator has a duty to suspend or terminate the process.

C. The mediator should assure that each person has had the opportunity to fully understand the implications and ramifications of all options available.

D. The mediator shall inform the participants that emotions play a part in the decision-making process. The mediator shall attempt to elicit from each of the participants a confirmation that each understands the connection between one's own emotions and the bargaining process.

E. The mediator has a duty to assure a balanced dialogue and must attempt to diffuse any manipulative or intimidating negotiation techniques utilized by either f the participants.

F. If the mediator has suspended or terminated the process, the mediator should suggest that the participants obtain additional professional services as may be appropriate.

VI. *The mediator has a continuing duty to advise each of the mediation participants to obtain legal review prior to reaching any agreement.*

Specific Considerations

A. Each of the mediation participants should have independent legal counsel before reaching final agreement. The mediator shall recommend that the participants obtain legal advice at the beginning of the mediation process and before the participants have reached any accord to which they have made an emotional commitment. In order to promote the integrity of the process, the mediator shall not refer either of the participants to any particular lawyers. When an attorney referral is requested, the parties should be referred to a Bar Association list if available. In the absence of such a list, the mediator may only provide a list of qualified family law attorneys in the community.

B. The mediator shall obtain an agreement from the participants in the orientation session as to whether and under what circumstances the mediator may speak directly and separately with each of their lawyers during the mediation process.

C. The mediator shall obtain an agreement from the husband and the wife that each lawyer, upon request, shall be entitled to review all the factual documentation provided by the participants in the mediation process.

D. Any agreement which is prepared in the mediation process should be separately reviewed by independent counsel for each participant before it is signed. While the mediator cannot insist that each participant have separate counsel they should be discouraged from signing any agreement which has not been so reviewed.

## The Standards of Practice for Family Mediators: An Individual Interpretation and Comments

Thomas A. Bishop*

---

* Member, Mediation and Arbitration Committee, Section of Family Law, ABA, engaged in private practice of law in New London, Connecticut. The comments expressed herein are those of the authors, as a member of the Mediation and Arbitration Committee and do not necessarily reflect the views of the Mediation and Arbitration Committee as a whole or the Section of Family Law.

## Introduction

Setting standards for an activity can serve a variety of purposes and may have a range of effects. If done by an authority, it may constitute rule making and be coercive. If promulgated by a representative body, standards may serve an advisory and educational purpose. Standards which are both proscriptive and prescriptive may provide a model or a norm for the conduct of the activity.

In adopting, in principle, these Standards of Practice, the Family Law Section of the American Bar Association has acknowledged to its peer constituents, and to the larger community, that there is an ethical dimension to the practice of mediation. Without either advocating or sanctioning the practice for lawyers, the Section has said that there are certain qualities of conduct for mediators which it believes should be part of an ethical practice; similarly, the Section has expressed its view that there are certain limitations to permissible mediator behavior. In the absence of direct rule-making authority, it is the hope of the Section that the publication of these standards and the debate which may ensue will assist mediators to find ethical modes of practice, and will also serve to illuminate areas of concern for the protection of the public.

# 6 Introduction to Child Custody



## §6.01 Child Custody Generally

Modern child custody law reflects changes in society's view of children. Recent developments in custody are attributed to a shift in legal focus from rights of the parents to the welfare of children. This shift has been a product of the changing values of our society with respect to children as persons, their rights and their relationships to their parents.

Historically, children were considered the property of their father in part because of their value as workers in an agrarian society. Only the emergency of a new societal value, that children deserved a *childhood,* was powerful enough to loosen the father's possessory stronghold in child custody situations in this century.

The further maturation of society produced the concept of the nuclear family, and the emergence of the mother as the nurturing parent. Child custody law reflected this new maternal role, and the practice of awarding custody to divorced mothers replaced any former rights of the father.

The *maternal preference* or *tender years doctrine* was relied upon by courts for many years in deciding custody cases. Only when the mother was deemed *unfit* could the father have a chance of retaining custody of his children since the mother by definition was a nurturing parent and the father was the breadwinner.

However, the same societal forces which influenced the shift from fault to no-fault divorce, as well as that shift itself, began to influence the child custody awards. The acceptance of failure of marriages as an unfortunate fact rather than an immoral act to be discouraged by the courts, the powerful influence of the women's movement, and the expansion of a gender-neutral approach in the law diminished preference for the mother as custodian, absent unfitness. In addition, the idea that children, as human beings, possessed rights and that their welfare is the primary concern of the courts in custody disputes, replaced old values and presumptions. The *best interests of the child doctrine* became a reality and the new foundation of custody decisions. Legislatures began including specific factors to be expressly considered by judges when making custody decisions.

In the early 1970s, the focus on the best interests of the children resulted in a controversial doctrine which, while a powerful trend in custody law, has yet to be approved by the society, legal profession and mental health profession at large. Recognizing that the optimum postdivorce situation for children is to have the benefit of *both* their parents, some legislatures and judges have mandated joint custody, which, although available in many forms, generally requires both parents to be involved in coparenting after divorce.

Joint custody supposes that parents can resolve their differing views in the best interests of their children. While the doctrine of joint custody is a product of the changing society, it is also continuing to influence the behavior of parents because it exists as a symbol of postdivorce cooperation. Also, it imposes a duty of coparenting and the cessation of disruptive conduct.

In child custody cases, the family law practitioner must often expand the role of advocate for the client to include the role of protector of children. Lawyers should counsel their clients in the child's best interests and try to avoid the damaging child custody battle. Even where joint custody is favored by law or public policy, the lawyer should not necessarily advocate it if it appears it will not serve the children's best interests.

The lawyer must explore the client's situation individually as to the potential success of various custodial arrangements. Here, as much as anywhere in family law, the lawyer must artfully disinter the past, illuminate the present, and discern the future, counseling the parent-client to be ever-mindful that spousal wrath and difficulties are always secondary to the child's best interests in the continuous love and guidance of both parents albeit divorced.

This difficult task requires experience and compassion as well as knowledge of the law on the part of the family lawyer who has a unique responsibility to be more than a lwayer in representing a client in a child custody case.

## §6.02 Historical Overview

Child custody law is directly linked to a society's perception of its institutions of marriage, divorce, and family, and of the individual roles of parents and children. While there is not an abundance of evidence pertaining to child custody upon divorce in many early societies, there is information about family interactions which provides an understanding of custody situations. An historical overview of child custody shows the practitioner the basis of today's custody trends, and how custody law has developed from a property theory to an area of law stressing sensitivity to human rights.

In the early patriarchal and agricultural societies of the Hebrews, Greeks,

Romans, and Anglo-Saxons, children were considered to be property of their father, who exercised significant power over them and usually retained them upon a divorce.[1] In these early societies, children were frequently important as commercially valuable workers whose labor could be transferred and sold. A child was primarily a financial asset to the father.[2]

A well-documented example of this patriarchal authority is the Roman father, whose *patria potestas* was so strong that it nearly equaled his power over his slaves.[3] He could beat his children, banish them from the country, sell them into slavery, marry them to a partner of his choice, divorce them against their wishes, and even put them to death without state interference. The legal identity of the father and son were merged; they could not contract with each other, and any property acquired by the son became the father's. Religion provided the only checks on the father's patria potestas.[4]

The severity of the father's power over his children in the Hebrew, Greek, and Roman societies eased as the cultures developed. During the early Christian era, the rabbis began to favor the mother in child custody decisions, perhaps to offset the harshness of the husband's absolute right to divorce. By the close of the third century A.D., rabbis from Palestine and Babylon developed the rules that a divorced mother could keep her daughters permanently and her son until his sixth year. The father was liable for support for his son while he remained with his mother, and his daughter until her marriage. If the mother declined custody for whatever reason, the father was bound to take the children.[5]

The Greek father's power over his children declined markedly during the rule of Solon, who became chief magistrate of Athens early in the sixth century

---

[1] See **§§1.02-1.09** for a history of the law of divorce which serves as a supplement to the information presented herein. See also S. Green & J. Long, Marriage and Family Law Agreements 3-13 (Shepard's/McGraw-Hill 1984), for a comparable history of marriage.

[2] S. Katz, When Parents Fail: The Law's Response to Family Breakdown 4 (1971).

[3] Couch, *Women in Early Roman Law,* 8 Harv L Rev 39, 41 (1895), where the author quotes St. Paul in *Gal* 4:1 when stating:

> In ancient times, the father's control over his children, i.e., the *patria potestas,* was probably so nearly assimilated to the power of the master over the slave that it would be difficult to say wherein a child's position was superior to a slave's. "The heir, as long as he is a child, differeth nothing from a slave, though he be lord of all." (Footnote omitted.)

[4] Couch, *supra* note 3, 42, where it is noted that:

> A man who sold his married son was given over to the infernal gods. When a father contemplated the death of a child, he was required to summon a council of its blood relatives, maternal as well as paternal, to whom he was to submit the question of the child's death. But the power of the council was merely advisory. If the father had the hardihood to brave public opinion and to defy religious excommunication, he could in no way be prevented from even the severest exercise of his paternal power.

[5] W. Goodsell, A History of Marriage and the Family 85 (1934).

B.C.[6] Among Solon's legal reforms was a law forbidding Greek fathers from selling their children. It has been noted that there is little evidence of Greek child custody law.[7]

The gradual diminishing of the Roman father's power over his children was spurred by "the silent operation of refined manners and cultivated morals."[8] In the fourth century A.D., that silent operation was codified by two edicts of Emperor Constantine which outlawed infanticide and the sale of children into slavery. Emperor Justinian (483-565A.D.), primarily responsible for the drafting of the *Corpus Juris Civilis,* proclaimed that the patria potestas was inhuman and enacted laws which punished fathers who left their infants to die and which provided that sons could independently acquire and hold property.[9]

There is little record of child custody law in Anglo-Saxon history. However, among the Germanic tribes, the great family, or *sib,* was the source of private law which exercised authority over each household as well as over its individual members. The sib as a whole could protect a child even from its father, whose power over his children, or *mund,* was limited compared to the Roman father's patria potestas.

The law of the sib did provide that if the father died before the children reached majority—an age which varied among the different tribes—the father's sib acted as guardian of the widow and children, and controlled the children's property until they attained majority.[10] An eighth-century Anglo-Saxon law mandated that the actual control of the children be given to the mother:

> If a ceorl [freeman] and his wife have a child between them and the ceorl die,, let the mother have her child and feed it; and let VI shillings be given her for its fostering, a cow in the summer and an ox in winter; and let the kindred take care of the homestead until it be of age.[11]

It is probable that similar arrangements were made upon divorce.

## §6.03 —Common Law

Practitioners are well aware of the impact that the English common law has had on the development of American law. Thus, it is important to review the development of child custody law in England. The common law of custody followed the Roman model: children were considered the property of the

---

[6] *Id.*

[7] See A. Harrison, The Law of Athens, Family and Property 44 (1968), where the author states, "The rules affecting the children of divorced parents are obscure from lack of evidence."

[8] 2 J. Kent, Commentaries on American Law 204 (1873).

[9] *Id* 205.

[10] W. Goodsell, *supra* note 5, at 192.

[11] Young, *Anglo-Saxon Family Law,* in Essays in Anglo-Saxon Law 180 (A. Adams ed 1876).

father, who had the paramount right to their care, custody, maintenance, and nurture.[12] The father's right was supplemented by the fact that the mother, as a married woman, had no rights at law, and no control over the father's power.[13] In feudal times, "custody was automatically an incident of guardianship of lands and only gradually came to be regarded as a trusteeship with responsibilities toward the child."[14]

Until the nineteenth century, there were few situations in which any court would interfere with the father's right to custody of his children. Sometimes children were denied access to life with a potentially better custodian because of the father's superior right.[15]

Even an adulterous father retained his right to custody of his children at common law. In *Ball v Ball*,[16] a mother who had divorced her husband in the ecclesiastical courts on the ground of adultry petitioned the Vice-Chancellor's Court to gain custody of her 14-year-old daughter.[17] The court dismissed her petition as Vice-Chancellor Hart clearly articulated the established rule:

> Some conduct, on the part of the father, with reference to the management and education of the child, must be shewn to warrant an interference with his legal right; and I am bound to say that, in this case, there does not appear to me to be sufficient [misconduct] to deprive the father of his common law right to the care and custody of his child.[18]

The right of the father to custody at common law was so absolute that courts

---

[12] See R. Gottesman, The Child and The Law 135 (1981), where the author notes:

> As with most areas of American jurisprudence, child custody law evolved from English common law tradition. This tradition comprised much of the feudal value structure in which men owned and controlled virtually everything. Child custody was an incident of ownership of lands and chattel. . . .

[13] 1 J. McCahey, M. Kaufman, C. Kraut, & J. Zett, Child Custody and Visitation Law and Practice 1-14 (1983) [hereinafter cited as 1 J. McCahey]; Foster & Freed, *Child Custody*, 39 NYU L Rev 423, 423-24 (1964); Note, *The Tender Years Presumption in Missouri: A Judicial Anachronism*, 23 St Louis ULJ 697, 699 (1979).

[14] Foster & Freed, *supra* note 13, at 423.

[15] 1 J. McCahey, *supra* note 13 at 1-10. See also W. Weyrauch & S. Katz, American Family Law in Transition 495 (1983), where the authors state:

> Today's conceptions of child custody, as they in fact operate within the courts, cannot be understood without considering the historical importance of marriage for property and the rules governing succession upon death. Paternal power over children as the future heirs of property was essential to this system. Property itself was perceived in terms of relationships between persons. Yet, since they were subject to parental dominion, some of the persons–children–themselves acquired some of the characteristics of property, or chattels.

[16] 2 Sim 35, 2 Eng Rep 703 (1827).

[17] "Custody issues were heard either in law courts in habeas corpus proceedings or by petition to the Chancellor, rather than in the ecclesiastical courts in matrimonial proceedings." Foster & Freed, *supra* note 13, at 423.

[18] 2 Sim at 36-37, 2 Eng Rep at 704.

lacked jurisdiction even to grant the mother access if the father refused it. The court in *Ball v Ball* was petitioned for a right to access by the mother as an alternative to custody. Although the vice-chancellors were tempted to grant the innocent mother access to her daughter, they refrained, noting that there existed no "case similar to this, which would authorize making the order sought, in either alternative."[19] The sole check on the father's right was the court's ability to act as parens patriae, representing the king's power to care for infants.

Nevertheless, some fathers did lose custody of their minor children in England. A famous case involved the poet, Percy Bysshe Shelley, who deserted his wife after three years of marriage to live with another woman.[20] His wife returned to her father's house with their children where she raised them until her death three years later. During those years, Shelley had published a work, *Queen Mab,* in which he expressed his atheistic beliefs.

Upon his wife's death, Shelley demanded the return of his children so that he could raise and educate them. The combination of Shelley's desertion, adultery, and atheism was more than sufficient for the Court of Chancery to override Shelley's custodial right. As the Lord Chancellor declared:

> This is a case in which, as the matter appears to me, the father's principles cannot be misunderstood, in which his conduct, which I cannot but consider as highly immoral, has been established in proof, and established as the effect of those principles: conduct, nevertheless, which he represents to himself and others, not as conduct to be considered as immoral, but to be recommended and observed in practice, and as worthy of approbation. . . . I cannot, therefore, think that I should be justified in delivering over these children for their education exclusively, to what is called the care to which Mr. S. wishes it to be intrusted. . . .[21]

In fact, Shelley's loss was an isolated instance at that time. Because the duty to support was an aspect of custody, it was also impractical to award custody to anyone other than the father unless the child had property of his or her own or unless the proposed custodian had made some financial arrangements to provide for the child, a difficult task for a woman, who had no significant rights at common law.[22]

In 1839, Parliament enacted "An Act to amend the Law relating to the Custody of Infants,"[23] which provided that a mother might be awarded custody

---

[19] *Id* at 37, 2 Eng Rep at 704.

[20] Shelley v Westbrooke, 1 Jac 266, 37 Eng Rep 850 (1817).

[21] *Id* at 267, 37 Eng Rep at 851.

[22] Foster & Freed, *supra* note 13, at 424. *See also* **§10.02.**

[23] Talfourd's Act, 2 & 3 Fict, ch 54 (1839), which stated in part:

> [I]t shall be lawful for the Lord Chancellor . . . upon hearing the Petition of the Mother of any Infant or Infants being in the sole Custody or Control of the Father thereof . . . if he shall see fit, to make Order for the Access of the Petitioner to

of a child under seven years of age by the Court of Chancery, and that she might be granted access to her children in the custody of the father as a court saw fit. The Infants Custody Act of 1873[24] amended the Act of 1839 and provided not only that a court could award a mother custody of children under sixteen, but that a court could award a mother custody despite the fact that she had committed adultery. In 1886, the Guardianship of Infants Act[25] designated the mother as proper guardian upon the father's death, and gave both parents equal right to the custody of and access to their children. The decision was to be made "having regard to the welfare of the infant, and to the conduct of the parents, and to the wishes as well of the mother as of the father."

The modern view of child custody law in England is found in the Guardianship of Infants Act of 1925.[26] This Act memorialized the notion that the welfare of the child is the "paramount consideration" in custody proceedings and could not be diminished by the rights or wishes of the parents.

The development of custody law in the United States parallels the development in England, except that fathers apparently never had as absolute a right to custody in the United States as in England.[27] The development of American child custody law is discussed in subsequent chapters.[28]

---

> such Infant or Infants, at such Times and subject to such Regulations as he shall deem convenient and just; and if such Infant or Infants shall be within the Age of Seven Years, to make Order that such Infant or Infants shall be delivered to and remain in the Custody of the Petitioner until attaining such Age. . . .

[24] 36 & 37 Vict, ch 12 (1873).

[25] 49 & 50 Vict, ch 27 (1886).

[26] 15 & 16 Geo 5, ch 49 (1925).

[27] A. Haralambie, Handling Child Custody Cases 3 (Shepard's/McGraw-Hill 1983). *See* **§7.04.**

[28] *See* **chs 7-9.**

# Part Two

# Child Custody

# 7 Bases and Theories for Child Custody Decisions



## §7.01 Introduction

Professor Homer Clark, writing in 1968, noted that *custody* is rarely defined, and is an ambiguous concept because it represents a complex intersection of rights and obligations.[1] In its broadest sense, custody refers to the relationship which exists between parents and children in a normal, ongoing family. Tainted by elements of possession, custody is based on the parents' claim to their children created by the biological "blood-tie."[2] In modern society, this claim is legally confirmed by a birth certificate.

The parents' natural custodial rights have been explained in many ways over the years. Historically, children were viewed as the property of the father, a

---

[1] H. Clark, The Law of Domestic Relations in the United States 573 (1968).

[2] J. Goldstein, A. Freud, & A. Solnit, Beyond the Best Interests of the Child 16 (1973). [hereinafter cited as J. Goldstein].

valuable source of labor which could be sold if necessary or desirable.[3] The idea of "childhood" did not exist in premodern society. As noted by one legal historian, children were distinguished from adults principally by their dependence, and were cast into adult roles as soon as they were able to function without the constant supervision of an adult.[4]

In the sixteenth and seventeenth centuries, the ideas emerged that childhood was a distinctive stage of life and that children should be segregated and educated to prepare them for their future roles as adults in society. It is maintained that this discovery was "in part cause and in part consequence of yet another idea: that of the private conjugal family."[5] Parents began to take a responsible interest in the upbringing of their children as the extended family faded in light of the growth of an industrial urban society. Parental right to custody was defended because of parents' "natural affection" for their children. Natural affection existed because of the biological bond; it was thought that biological parents would naturally feel the strongest bond with their children.[6] Such concepts fueled the notion that fit parents had the right to raise their children.[7]

While most historians agree that the family's structure shifted from a powerful patriarchy to a set of interpersonal relationships founded on mutual affection, companionship, and understanding, they have disagreed over the chronology and causes of the shift. The time periods of the shift have been designated as the seventeenth, eighteenth, and nineteenth centuries. The attributed sources of the notions of childhood and the modern family have included: capitalism; the evolution of social class; ideas of individualism; the impact of industrialization; and the development of personality theory.[8] These

---

[3] *See* **§§6.02-6.03.**

[4] Zainaldin, *The Emergence of a Modern American Family Law: Child Custody, Adoption, and the Courts, 1796-1851,* 73 NW UL Rev 1038, 1047 (1979). In this recommended article, Professor Jamil S. Zainaldin quotes D. Hunt, Parents and Children in History 33-34 (1970) (citing P. Aries, Centuries of Childhood: A Social History of Family Life 9, 128 (1962)):

> As soon as the child could live without the constant solicitude of his mother, his nanny, or his cradle-rocker, he belonged to adult society. On the other hand, the infant still requiring this attention . . . was treated by grown-ups with "indifference." Too fragile as yet to take part in the life of adults, the infant simply "did not count."

[5] Zainaldin, *supra* note 4, at 1048.

[6] S. Katz, When Parents Fail: The Law's Response to Family Breakdown 4 (1971).

[7] These rights were expressed as a constitutionally protected freedom by the United States Supreme Court in a series of cases. *See, e.g.,* Quilloin v Wolcott, 434 US 246, 255 (1978); Smith v Organization of Foster Families; 431 US 816 (1977); Wisconsin v Yoder, 406 US 205 (1972); Stanley v Illinois, 405 US 645 (1972); Prince v Massachusetts, 321 US 158 (1943); Pierce v Society of Sisters, 268 US 510 (1925). *See also* **§7.02.**

[8] Zainaldin, *supra* note 4, at 1049-50. Professor Zainaldin cites P. Aries, Centuries of Childhood: A Social History of Family Life 114-19, 129-31 (1962); E. Shorten, The Making of the Modern Family 255-68 (1976); L. Stone, The Family, Sex and Marriage in England, 1500-1800, at 147-81 (1977); De Mause, *Our Forebears Made Childhood A Nightmare,* 1975 *Psychology Today* 850.

sources—undoubtedly accompanied by other factors, the growth of psychology and of cause-and-effect—have influenced the legal system's interaction with children. One aspect of the interaction was the promulgation of legislation to prevent the industrial exploitation of children and to mandate a minimum level of education. Another aspect involved the interference by the state with its *parens patriae* power. The state changed its basis for making custody decisions from a preference for paternal custody to a standard which favored the best interests of the child.[9]

Child custody matters are sometimes raised in the context of parental failure, where, upon proof of parental abuse, neglect, or unfitness, the state assumes custody and may terminate parental rights.[10] The vast majority of child custody matters, however, are raised in the context of divorce, where, absent any agreement, the state, acting through its judicial machinery, places the child in a custodial arrangement upon breakdown of a marriage.

The theories which judges follow in making custody decisions vary. Two prominent family law authorities have maintained that:

> The facts of the individual case—whether a parent or an outsider asserts rights, whether distribution of assets after dissolution of marriage or neglect is involved—may determine what particular historical style is activated for purposes of allocating power over the child.[11]

However, generally, the legal theories involved emanate from three areas: a residual property influence which permeates child custody law;[12] the psychoanalytic literature which awakened the legal profession to the notion of the "psychological parent,"[13] and the evolution of marriage away from status and toward contract and partnership.[14]

---

In N. Postman, The Disappearance of Childhood (1984), it is argued that childhood, which is a social artifact, and not a biological category, is being eroded by the "uncontrollable information" of television programming. According to Postman, the very conception of childhood is based on secrets from which the child is excluded. The long periods of education necessary to teach the child such secrets sets him or her apart from adults. This differentiation, Postman argues, is being destroyed by electronic media, which provide the same information to both child and adult.

[9] *See* **§§6.02-6.03, 7.03-7.10.** *See also* 1 J. McCahey, M. Kaufman, C. Kraut, & J. Zett, Child Custody and Visitation Law and Practice 1-22 to -23 (1983).

[10] *See* S. Green & J. Long, Marriage and Family Law Agreements 295-302 (Shepard's/McGraw-Hill 1984).

[11] W. Weyrauch & S. Katz, American Family Law in Transition 497 (1983).

[12] *Id* 496, where the authors note that while judges never say the words *adverse possession,* they hesitate to disrupt the status quo of a child's life and change custody when the child has been residing with one parent for an extended period of time.

[13] *See* J. Goldstein, *supra* note 2.

[14] *See* W. Weyrauch & S. Katz, *supra* note 11, at 497, where the authors state:

> Yet if the courts increasingly treat marriage as a partnership—that is, as a co-ownership for profit between parties presumed to be equal who deal with each other at arm's length—then children acquire new and sometimes contradictory

This chapter addresses custody matters associated with divorce rather than with parental neglect proceedings. In such cases, it is important that the practitioner become conversant with the facts of the case and aware of the predilections of the local judges in custody matters. It is well-known among experienced family law practitioners that "[r]egardless of what the law or weight of expert opinion says, the decision in a custody case often will boil down to what is in the heart of the trial judge who hears the case."[15]

Most parties avoid the uncertainty of judicial decision by fashioning their own custody and visitation agreements, which are ritualistically incorporated into the divorce decree.[16] Such agreements also reduce the probability that the parties will resort to the appeals process.

Of the small number of contested cases which are adjudicated, only a small percentage are appealed.[17] The rate of reversal in child custody cases is low,[18] and more likely than not can be attributed to the deference given to the trial judge's application of the criteria established by statute and case law. In a majority of cases, state appellate courts affirm a trial court's decision unless it is a "clear abuse of discretion" or is "against the manifest weight of the evidence."[19]

Nevertheless, new aspects of child custody law have emerged in the 1970s and 1980s, and undoubtedly will continue to appear as society advances and progresses. For the practitioner, custody becomes yet another area of family law—along with divorce, cohabitation, reproductive technology, property definition and division, and others—which requires a constant monitoring of new developments.

## §7.02 By Agreement of the Parties

The trial court, exercising its parens patriae power, may after hearing enter a custody order at its discretion despite any agreement by the parties. In fact, however, most custody arrangements are fashioned by the divorcing parties, often with assistance of their counsel, and usually these amicable arrangements are approved by the court.[20] The family law practitioner should make every effort to negotiate a workable custody agreement acceptable to both parties.

---

characteristics. They are "assets" of the marriage to be fought over in case of dissolution. . . .

[15] Atkinson, *Criteria for Deciding Child Custody in the Trial and Appellate Courts,* 18 Fam LQ 1, 16 (1984).

[16] *See* **§7.02.**

[17] W. Weyrauch & S. Katz, *supra* note 11, at 505.

[18] Atkinson, *supra* note 15, at 39, Table C, which shows that the total reversals of awards to fathers and mothers was 17.6% in 1982.

[19] *Id* 40.

[20] *See* A. Haralambie, Handling Child Custody Cases 39 (Shepard's/McGraw-Hill 1983); W. Weyrauch & S. Katz, American Family Law in Transition 505 (1983).

The advantages of a negotiated agreement over contested custody litigation are great.

State interference is minimized because judges are likely to approve the parents' decision upon a review of appropriate factors. The parties' privacy rights are thus preserved.[21]

Parties who participate in the formulation of their family law agreements are generally more satisfied and more likely to comply with the terms than parties who must accept the rulings of the courts.[22] This is particularly true with child custody and visitation, an area where the divorcing parties possess unique knowledge about themselves and their children which is pertinent to custody and visitation decisions.

The process of negotiation enables the parties to communicate their emotions, specify their needs and wants, and feel that they make a difference in the solution of their problems. Parties are better able to live with custody and visitation terms which they themselves have helped to craft. These voluntary agreements usually obviate resort to the appeals process.

Most importantly, the children's best interests are served because they are shielded from the turmoil and damage associated with contested custody trials. In adversarial battles, children frequently become pawns in the dispute or the targets for parental frustration and hostility.[23]

Despite the parens patriae power, it has been argued that there exists a "fundamental right of parents to determine custody without state intervention."[24] This argument is premised upon the twentieth-century movement towards recognition of family rights to privacy and the extension of due process

---

[21] See J. Goldstein, A. Freud, & A. Solnit, Beyond the Best Interests of the Child 7-8 (1973), where the authors exhibit their lack of confidence in the judicial process as a means of protecting the best interests of children:

> To safeguard the right of parents to raise their children as they see fit, free of government intrusion, except in cases of neglect and abandonment, is to safeguard each child's need for continuity. This preference for minimum state intervention and for leaving well enough alone is reinforced by our recognition that law is incapable of effectively managing, except in a very gross sense, so delicate and complex a relationship as that between parent and child.

*See also* Developments, *The Constitution and the Family,* 93 Harv LRev 1156, 1323 (1980)

[22] In S. Green & J. Long, Marriage and Family Law Agreements 114, 210, 213 (Shepard's/McGraw Hill 1984), the advantages of negotiated family law agreements are discussed.

[23] See J. Wallerstein & J. Kelly, Surviving the Breakup (1980), the product of a 5-year study of children of divorced parents which documents extensive emotional and psychological damage. Such evidence of harm to children could lead to the conclusion that in some custody situations, where neither party is less fit to have custody, an arbitrary decision is less harmful than a protracted battle for custody. On the other hand, it would be appalling in our society to choose something as serious as a child's custodian by the flip of the coin rather than by a deliberate process.

[24] *See* Berdon, *Child Custody Litigation: Some Relevant Considerations,* 53 Conn BJ 279, 282 (1979). The author, Robert I. Berdon, is a judge of the Supreme Court of the State of Connecticut.

and equal protection safeguards to families. It is useful to examine the relevant language in support of the notion of such a fundamental right.

In 1923, the Supreme Court of the United States declared in *Meyer v State of Nebraska* that "[w]ithout doubt, [the liberty protected by the Fourteenth Amendment] denotes . . . the right of the individual to marry, establish a home and bring up children . . . "[25] This declaration was reaffirmed in 1925 in *Pierce v Society of Sisters,* where the Supreme Court stated that "the child is not the mere creature of the State; those who nurture him and direct his destiny have the right, coupled with the high duty, to recognize and prepare him for additional obligations."[26] Both of these cases involved the parents' right to educate their children as they saw fit.

In the 1943 case of *Prince v Massachusetts,*[27] the Court held that a statute which prohibited minors from vending newspapers, magazines, and the like did not violate the religious freedom of a Jehovah's Witness guardian and minor who were distributing religious literature on the street, nor was it violative of equal protection of the laws. The language relevant to a parent's right to determine custody without state intervention is:

> It is cardinal with us that the custody, care and nurture of the child reside first in the parents, whose primary function and freedom include preparation for obligations the state can neither supply nor hinder. . . . And it is in recognition of this that these decisions have respected the private realm of family life which the state cannot enter.[28]

In *Stanley v Illinois,*[29] the Court held unconstitutional a statute which denied an unmarried father a pretermination hearing before the state assumed custody of his children after the death of the mother. The Court took into consideration the fact that such a hearing was provided for married and divorced parents and for unwed mothers. The Court noted that Stanley's private interest in raising his children "undeniably warrants deference and, absent a powerful countervailing interest, protection."[30] Most importantly, however, the Court recog-

---

[25] Meyer v State of Nebraska, 362 US 390, 399 (1923). The Court held that a state law forbidding the teaching of a foreign language to any student before successful completion of the eighth grade invaded the liberty protected by the Fourteenth Amendment.

[26] Pierce v Society of Sisters, 268 US 510, 535 (1925). Here, the Court invalidated a law which precluded parents from sending their children to private schools.

[27] 321 US 158 (1943).

[28] *Id* 166. It is important to note, however, on the same page of the decision, the Court also declared: "But the family itself is not beyond regulation in the public interest. . . . And neither rights of religion nor rights of parenthood are beyond limitation. Acting to guard the general interest in youth's well-being, the state may restrict the parent's control. . . ."

[29] 405 US 645 (1972).

[30] *Id* 651. The Court continued:

> The Court has frequently emphasized the importance of the family. The rights

nized Stanley's rights despite the absence of a marriage. This would emphasize that a parent's right to custody is a broad one, which exists after a marriage is terminated by divorce, dissolution, or annulment, and exists even if there is no marriage.

In *Moore v City of East Cleveland*,[31] the Supreme Court held unconstitutional a zoning ordinance limiting the occupancy of a dwelling to a "family." Family was defined in the ordinance so that a grandmother could not live with her grandsons. The Court in effect declared that the government could not so interfere with family living arrangements absent important governmental interests which are served by the government's action. The Court noted that it "has long recognized that freedom of personal choice in matters of marriage and family life is one of the liberties protected by the Due Process Clause of the Fourteenth Amendment."[32] In *Smith v Organization of Foster Families*,[33] decided the same year as *Moore*, the Court articulated a distinction between the rights of natural parents and those of foster parents. In relevant language, Justice Stewart declared in a concurring opinion:

> If a State were to attempt to force the breakup of a natural family, over the objections of the parents and their children, without some showing of unfitness and for the sole reason that to do so was thought of to be in the children's best interest, I should have little doubt that the State would have intruded impermissibly on "the private realm of family life which the state cannot enter."[34]

Based upon the Supreme Court's enunciation of protected liberties, it is arguable that, absent parental unfitness or evidence of neglect, the State may not interfere with a divorcing couple's custody and visitation decisions. As a judge has maintained, "it should be recognized by the state that just because the jurisdiction of the courts has been invoked to dissolve their marriage, parents are not to be deprived of their constitutional rights to rear their children in a manner they deem best."[35]

Thus, the trial court in an uncontested custody case has both the duty to be aware of neglect and an obligation to insure that parents have knowingly consented to a proposed agreement. Frequently, the only way a judge may ascertain the reality of the situation in an uncontested case is to be sensitive to signals in testimony which suggest that there exists a dangerous situation

---

to conceive and raise one's children have been deemed "essential," Meyer v Nebraska, 262 US 390, 399 (1923), "basic civil rights of man," Skinner v Oklahoma, 316 US 535, 541 (1942), and "[r]ights far more precious . . . than property rights," May v Anderson, 345 US 528, 533 (1953).

31 431 US 494 (1977).

32 *Id* 499 (citing Cleveland Bd of Educ v La Fleur, 414 US 632, 639-40 (1974)).

33 431 US 816 (1977).

34 *Id* 862-63.

35 Berdon, *supra* note 24, at 285.

for the child, notwithstanding the appearance of wholesome environment. This sensitivity, or "listening ear," is usually cultivated over years of presiding over custody cases, and consists of the judge's intuition braced by judgment and experience. Should any signals appear, judges in many jurisdictions order social service investigations of the family background as it impacts on the child or order a psychiatric evaluation of the parents and child. If the investigation or evaluations prove inconclusive, excellent. If they substantiate judicial suspicions, then the court can fashion a remedy to benefit the entire family. The parens patriae power remains at a judge's disposal as a safeguard to protect the best interests of the child, and the family relationship as a whole, and not as a weapon to destroy the rights of the parents.

## §7.03 Best Interests of the Child Standard

The prevailing view and the unifying principle dominating modern child custody law focus on the premise that a court must award custody so as to promote the involved child's best interests.[36] Nearly every custody case in the twentieth century contains language to that effect, and the vast majority of states have codified the *best interests of the child* standard in their domestic relations statutes.[37]

In divorce-related custody cases, the trial court applies the standard when comparing conflicting prayers for custody. Some state statutes provide guidelines for the application; others do not; and no statute limits the court's consideration.[38] The court must evaluate pertinent factors in each case with a view to their consequences for the child's happiness and future. The court must consider all circumstances rather than relying exclusively on one factor. Relevant criteria include: characteristics and physical well-being of the child and parents;[39] the needs of the child; the home environments of the parents, including neighborhood, schools, friends, peer groups, and recreational resources; the ability of each parent to provide for the material, social, moral,

---

[36] *See* H. Clark, The Law of Domestic Relations in the United States 572 (1968); M. Ploscowe, H. Foster, & D. Freed, Family Law, Cases and Materials 882 (2d ed 1972). This view was codified in England in the Guardianship of Infants Act of 1925, 15 & 16 Geo 5, ch 49; *see* **§6.03.** The best interests standard is established in the Uniform Marriage and Divorce Act §402; *see* **app 1-2.**

[37] Freed & Walker, *Family Law in the Fifty States: An Overview,* Table IX (presented to the American Bar Association Aug 5, 1984).

[38] *Id.* States with statutory custody guidelines include: Alaska, Arizona, California, Colorado, Connecticut, Delaware, District of Columbia, Florida, Georgia, Hawaii, Illinois, Indiana, Iowa, Kansas, Kentucky, Michigan, Minnesota, Mississippi, Missouri, Montana, Nebraska, North Dakota, Ohio, Oklahoma, Oregon, Pennsylvania, Rhode Island, Texas, Utah, Vermont, Virginia, Washington, Wisconsin, and Wyoming. *See* **§8.02.**

[39] The term *parents* is used for convenience, since custody battles upon divorce generally occur between the mother and the father. It is noted, however, that such situations might involve grandparents, other relatives, and even unrelated third parties.

religious, educational, physical and emotional needs of the child; the preference of the child; the wishes of the parents, the significance of emotional and psychological ties; and other factors unique to the individual case.

Thus, the trial court has broad discretion in deciding where a child will live upon the divorce of his or her parents. Needless to say, this discretionary power has disturbed some commentators, who have described the best interests of the child standard as "indeterminate and speculative,"[40] requiring the court to act "in a vague, discretionary manner"[41] when making life-directing decisions. However, the flexibility of the standard insures that each case will receive individual attention and that custody law will reflect the constant change of societal values.[42] It is the imperative role of the attorneys in custody cases to educate the judge by providing an in-depth and accurate picture of what is in the child's best interests.[43] As one of the leading cases in the District of Columbia dealing with judicial discretion in custody matters observed:

> Out of a maze of conflicting testimony, usually including what one court called "a tolerable amount of perjury," the judge must make a decision which will inevitably affect materially the future life of an innocent child. In making his decision, the judge can obtain little help from precedents or general principles. Each case stands alone. After attempting to appraise and compare the personalities and capabilities of the two parents, the judge must endeavor to look into the future and decide that the child's best interests will be served if committed to the custody of the father or mother. He starts with the premise, as did the trial judge here, that the best interests of the child would be served by living in a united home with the affection, companionship and care of both father and mother, but that possibility has been eliminated before the case reaches

---

[40] W. Weyrauch & S. Katz, American Family Law in Transition 506 (1984). Professors Weyrauch and Katz assert, in fact, that "the standard is not applied to bring about a result, but merely serves as a convenient and useful justification for a decision reached on another level."

[41] R. Gottsman, The Child and the Law 140 (1981). This type of criticism has also been directed at no-fault divorce grounds such as irreconcilable differences and irretrievable breakdown of the marriage. *See* **§2.12.**

[42] The greatest examples of this phenomenon are the works by Joseph Goldstein, Anna Freud, and Albert J. Solnit, Beyond the Best Interests of the Child (1973) and Before the Best Interests of the Child (1979). The authors emphasize the importance of the *psychological parent,* who may or may not be the biological parent, in determining the best interests of the child. Their conclusions and emphasis drew attention to the fact that the biological parent does not necessarily have a good relationship with the child, which knocked a hole in the long-standing idea that the biological parent always had a "natural affection" for the child. Thus, the psychological relationship between the custodian and child increased in importance.

The authors also suggest a replacement for the best interests standard, the "least detrimental alternative."

[43] See **§§8.01-8.15.** for discussion of factors to be considered in the presentation of a custody case.

> the judge. So, the question for him is what is best for the child within the limitations presented. When the judge makes his decision, he has no assurance that his decision is the right one. He can only hope that he is right. He realizes that another equally able and conscientious judge might have arrived at a different decision on the same evidence.[44]

It might be said that the best interests of the child standard has either specifically produced or in some way influenced almost every aspect of child custody law. It has spawned offshooting presumptions, including the tender years doctrine; the preference of parents over nonparents; the avoidance of sibling-splitting; and, most recently, the flowering presumption favoring joint custody.[45] The Uniform Child Custody Jurisdiction Act (UCCJA) and the Parental Kidnapping Prevention Act (PKPA), among other legislation involving child custody, were enacted for the very purpose of protecting the best interests of the child.[46]

The best interests of the child standard, as developed by the judiciary,[47] has evolved to guide the courts and now provides the focus of the child custody proceeding. Under the standard's influence, the role of the court in custody litigation has shifted from a restricted private dispute settlement function to that of child protection, which, while increasing the responsibility of courts, including the requirement of detailed fact finding to justify the determination, has served to promote what is most beneficial for the child, the family, and, ultimately, society.

## §7.04 —Historical Development

The best interests standard does not have a static history. Its development, in fact, has encompassed the extremes of rigid and flexible application. Because it is a sweeping standard, the best interests of the child doctrine will continue to evolve as a reflection of the changing attitudes of society.

In the United States, courts did not blindly follow the strict common law rule that the father had an absolute right to custody of his minor children upon a divorce. Instead, American courts recognized early in dicta that the welfare of the child was the most compelling consideration.[48] Some of these courts were

---

[44] Coles v Coles, 204 A2d 330, 332 (DC 1964).

[45] *See* **§§7.05, 8.06, ch 9.**

[46] *See* UCCJA §1, 9 ULA 111 (1979), PKPA, 28 USC §1738A.

[47] *See* **§7.04.**

[48] J. Madden, Handbook of the Law of Persons and Domestic Relations 371 (1931) (citing inter alia, Wadleigh v Newhall, 136 F 941 (1905); Saunders v Saunders, 166 Ala 351, 52 So 310 (1910); Cowls v Cowls, 8 Ill (3 Gilm) 435, 44 Am Dec 708 (1846); Dumain v Gwynne, 92 Mass (10 Allen) 270 (1865); Corrie v Corrie, 42 Mich 509, 4 NW 213 (1880); Ward v Ward, 34 Tex Civ App 104, 77 SW 829 (1903); Jensen v Jensen, 168 Wis 502, 170 NW 735 (1919)). *See also* Comment, *The Custody of Children,* 2 Ind LJ 325, 325 (1926); **§6.03.**

guided by statutes empowering them to order custody as was "necessary and proper," "just and proper," or "expedient," while others received no statutory direction and relied upon their equitable powers.[49]

Despite the judicial enunciation of a compelling concern for a child's welfare, courts in the nineteenth century subordinated this concern to the presumption that a fit father was entitled to the custody of his children upon divorce.[50] Thus, the early best interests of the child standard was in fact a parental fitness test favoring the father. The limited judicial inquiry focused upon the relative innocence of the father in the divorce, and not the circumstances relevant to a child's well-being.[51]

In the midnineteenth century, the emergence of the postindustrial revolution nuclear family brought about a shift in society's perception of children.[52] The view that children were vulnerable, impressionable persons whose early upbringing would affect their future development slowly gained recognition in the law in the form of the maternal preference or tender years doctrine.[53] This doctrine required the placement of young children, particularly girls, with the mother, who, until the later part of the twentieth century, remained at home while the father worked outside the home.

The chipping away of the common law presumption favoring the father seems to have been accelerated by judicial reliance on cases which ruled against fathers in custody disputes with third persons. In these cases, like the oft-cited *Chapsky v Wood*,[54] courts invoked a best interests test in which they exercised far greater discretion than they did in custody disputes related to divorce, and they strictly emphasized the welfare of the child as controlling.[55] This increased

---

[49] 2 C. Vernier, American Family Laws 191-212 (1931).

[50] W. Tiffany, Handbook on the Law of Persons and Domestic Relations 247 (1896), where the often-cited author observed:

> Generally, in this country, the courts of law, as well as those of equity, while acknowledging the general rule that the father, and on his death the mother, is entitled to the child's custody, modify the rule to a greater or less extent by adopting the equitable principle that this right must yield to considerations affecting the well-being of the child.

[51] See Uviller, *Rather's Rights and Feminism: The Maternal Presumption Revisited,* 1 Harv Women's LJ 107, 112-13 (1978), where the author maintains that even the worst paternal unfitness rarely resulted in a maternal custody award:

> because a father denied custody had no obligation to support children of whose "services" he was deprived. Given the almost total financial dependence of women upon their husbands, separated or divorced mothers were unable to support their children and were thus constrained from seeking custody from even the most unfit fathers.

[52] *See* **§7.03.**

[53] *See* **§§7.05-7.11.**

[54] 26 Kan 650 (1881).

[55] *See* W. Tiffany, Handbook on the Law of Persons and Domestic Relations 249 (1896) (citing inter alia, *Ex parte* Murphy, 75 Ala 409 (1883); Washaw v Gimble, 50 Ark 351, 7 SW 389 (1888); Gibbs v Brown, 68 Ga 803 (1881); *In re* Smith, 13 Ill 138 (1851); Bryan v Lyon, 104 Ind 227, 3 NE 880 (1885); Bonnett v Bonnett, 61 Iowa 199, 16 NW

discretion, arising out of third-party custody disputes, overflowed to custody disputes between parents, as the advent of the tender years doctrine had the courts examining more factors in determining the child's best interests, including parental conduct, the age of the children, and sexual roles.[56]

While the tender years doctrine mitigated the common law presumption favoring the father, it, too, became a best interests of the child test which focused upon the fitness of the parent—specifically, the mother—rather than the needs of the child. For much of the twentieth century, placing children with their mothers was nearly universally considered to be in the child's best interests.

Not surprisingly, further developments in the increasingly urbanized society spawned more changes in both the statutory expression of the best interests of the child standard and its judicial application. A number of factors have contributed to the shift of the best interests standard away from parental presumptions of the past and toward an application wherein the child's welfare is the central focus: the imposition of a child support obligation upon both parents; the increase of women in the work force, the burgeoning influence of psychological theory, the popularization of the ideas of sexual equality and gender neutrality; the enactment of state equal rights amendments; the reaction of fathers to the maternal preference doctrine; and the advocacy of children's rights.

The tender years doctrine has been abolished by statute or case law in many jurisdictions.[57] Child custody statutes specifically empower courts to evaluate the child's best interests in determining custody, many of them supplying a list of factors for courts to consider in the process.[58] The current trend toward a presumption in favor of joint custody stands as a marker of the progression of the development of the best interests standard.[59]

The breadth of the best interests of the child doctrine and the ever-increasing changes in our society insure that the standard will continue to develop. As noted by one writer: "There is room for optimism that all the thought and discussion presently underway will ultimately produce a legal mechanism which, with minimal interference, does the most good for the family, especially the children."[60]

---

91 (1883); Corrie v Corrie, 42 Mich 509, 4 NW 213 (1880); McShan v McShan, 56 Miss 413 (1879); Sturtevant v State, 15 Neb 459, 19 NW 617 (1884); Waldron's Case, 13 Johns 418 (NY 1816); Gishivila v Dodez, 4 Ohio St 615 (1855); *Ex parte* Schumpert, 40 SC (6 Rich) 137 (1853).

[56] 1 J. McCahey, M. Kaufman, C. Kraut, & J. Zett, Child Custody and Visitation Law and Practice 1-15 (1983).

[57] *See* **§§7.08-7.10.**

[58] *See* **§§7.03, 8.02.**

[59] *See* **ch 9.**

[60] R. Gottesman, The Child and the Law 144-45 (1981). Cf Mnookin, *Child-Custody Adjudication: Judicial Functions in the Face of Indeterminacy*, 39 Law & Contemp Probs 226 (1975), in which the author maintains that the best interests standard is usually

## §7.05 Maternal Preference and the Tender Years Doctrine or Presumption

The maternal preference, or the tender years doctrine or presumption,[61] originated as an exception to the common law rule that a fit father was entitled to the custody of his children after a divorce. It was considered that the best interests of a child of tender years are served by placing the child in the custody of the mother. Because of strong judicial adherence to the maternal preference, the doctrine became an independent principle in the twentieth century. The rush of societal changes which has so dramatically altered family law has also toppled the tender years doctrine, although it lingers on in some states. Nevertheless, it is a reality that in the vast majority of custody actions, the mother obtains custody of the children.

The origin of the tender years doctrine in the United States has been traced to an 1813 Pennsylvania case, *Commonwealth v Addicks*,[62] where a father was attempting to gain the custody of his two daughters from the mother by a writ of habeas corpus. The court, influenced by the father's desertion of the family four years earlier, ordered that custody remain with the mother, despite the fact that the mother's adultery had been the ground for the parties' divorce. The court stated:

> We cannot avoid expressing our disapprobation of the mother's conduct, although so far as regards her treatment of the children, she is in no fault.

---

indeterminate and speculative because existing psychological theories do not allow confident predictions of the effects of alternative custody dispositions and because society lacks a clear-cut consensus about what values should comprise the determination of what is "best."

[61] In research, the authors have found no clear distinctions among *maternal preference, the tender years doctrine* and *the tender years presumption.* Only one source attempted to make any such distinction, stating, "As a corollary to the maternal preference rule, a larger number of courts have recognized the 'tender years doctrine' which provides that the preference for the mother carries the greatest weight when the child is in infancy. . . ." Annot, 70 ALR3d 262, 269-70 (1976).

Historically, it appears that the tender years doctrine was the first to emerge, since courts (and the English Parliament by statute) awarded young children to mothers as an exception to the presumption favoring a fit father, beginning in the early 19th century. However, in the United States, the upper limit of the tender years has never been specifically settled, and usually was only vaguely defined as the "onset of adolescence." This seems to leave one only with a *maternal preference.*"

One lawyer has observed that a majority of the interspousal custody disputes involve children under the age of 9, so that an arbitrary confinement of tender years to children under 13 or 14 would have virtually no impact upon most actions. *See* Klaff, *The Tender Years Doctrine: A Defense,* 70 Cal L Rev 335, 354 (1982). This thought, combined with the fact that since 1968, 90% of custody awards have been to mothers, has prompted the authors also to ignore any distinctions outside the procedural one associated with *tender years presumption,* and to use the terms *maternal preference* and *tender years doctrine* interchangeably.

[62] 5 Binn 520 (Pa 1813). See Klaff, *supra* note 61 at 340, which dated the introduction of the tender years doctrine in American law.

> They appear to be well taken care of in all respects. It is to *them*, that our anxiety is principally directed; and it appears to us, that considering their tender age, they stand in need of that kind of assistance, which can be afforded by none so well as a mother.[63]

The industrial revolution made fathers into wage earners outside the home, leaving mothers in charge of the home and the children. In the nineteenth century, it was the wives who customarily filed for and were awarded divorces as the innocent parties.[64] Viewing guilt in divorce proceedings as evidence of parental unfitness, courts began to award custody to mothers in greater numbers.

The tender years doctrine became stronger in the law. Several states were influenced by the English statute which codified the doctrine in 1839.[65] In 1859, Kansas provided a model for many other states by establishing in its constitution that the mother and father, for all purposes, had equal rights to the custody of their children.[66] By the end of the nineteenth century, the American judiciary had invoked the doctrine to such an extent that Tiffany

---

[63] 5 Binn at 521 (emphasis in original). However, the two daughters in this case were later returned to their father because of the mother's adultery. *See* Commonwealth v Addicks & Lee, 2 Serg & Rawle 174 (Pa 1815).

[64] Mnookin, *Child-Custody Adjudication: Judicial Functions in the Face of Indeterminacy*, 39 Law & Contemp Probs 226, 235 (1975). Fault has played a role in the development of the maternal preference. As noted in the text, the fact that children were placed with innocent mothers accelerated the rise of the preference. With time, the rule was developed that even if a father obtained a divorce, the mother might still retain custody if her fault did not reflect on her fitness to raise the child of tender years. *See* Solly v Solly, 384 So 2d 208 (Fla Dist Ct App 1980); Cleeton v Cleeton, 383 So 2d 1231 (La 1980); Swain v Swain, 43 Md App 622, 406 A2d 680 (1979); Yates v Yates, 284 So 2d 46 (Miss 1973); Lockard v Lockard, 193 Neb 400, 227 NW2d 581 (1975); Pendergraft v Pendergraft, 23 NC App 307, 208 SE2d 887 (1974); Tapal v Tapal, 448 SW2d 560 (Tex Civ App 1969); Wendland v Wendland, 29 Wis 2d 145, 138 NW2d 185 (1965). The emergence of no-fault divorce prompted concern that custody would become the new battleground, and that some fathers who formerly would have acquiesced to their wives retaining custody would now contest custody as a method of obtaining leverage in settlement negotiations. In addition, in some states, custody is the only area where any evidence of fault is admissible. *See*, Cal Civ Code §4509 (Deering 1984). One study conducted in California reported that between 1968 and 1972, there was no increase in the percentage of fathers who requested sole custody. *See* Weitzman & Dixon, *Child Custody Awards: Legal Standards and Empirical Patterns for Child Custody, Support and Visitation After Divorce*, 12 UCD L Rev 473, 488-89 (1979).

[65] Roth, *The Tender Years Presumption in Child Custody Disputes*, 15 J Fam L 423, 429 (1976-77) (citing 1860 NJ Laws, ch 157, at 437 as one example of a state which followed Talfourd's Act, An Act to Amend the Law Relating to the Custody of Infants, 2 & 3 Vict, ch 54 (1831)).

[66] *Id* (citing Kan Const art 15, §6, and the Oregon statute of 1880 and the Pennsylvania statute of 1895, *quoted in* 1 G. Abbott, The Child and the State 75 (1949), as examples of statutes following the Kansas pattern and establishing equal rights to custody for both parents).

included a discussion of the doctrine in his famous treatise on domestic relations in 1896.[67]

In the twentieth century, the tender years doctrine was elevated to an express preference for the fit mother as custodian of her children, particularly young children, after a divorce. This was not because of statutes, however. Most custody statutes enacted in this century have favored the best interests of the child standard for determining custody, or provided that both parents have equal right to custody or that neither parent is to be preferred.[68] Only a few statutes expressly favored one parent over another.[69]

Many courts ignored the statutes calling for equal rights in parents to custody, and overwhelmingly invoked the presumption that placing children in the custody of the fit mother upon divorce was indeed in the children's best interests.[70] As two writers have acknowledged:

---

[67] W. Tiffany, Handbook on the Law of Persons and Domestic Relations 250-51 (1896), where it is stated:

> A child of very tender years needs the care and attention of a mother, and even were she to desert the father, without any fault on his part, the child would not be taken from her, at least until it has reached an age when the father can properly care for it. It can only be in such cases as this, where the child, from its extreme youth or sickness, needs a mother's care, that the court can deprive the father of the right to the child's custody, where the father . . . is in every way a fit person to have the charge of it. . . .

[68] Roth, *supra* note 65, at 430-31, and statutes cited therein. *See also* **§7.09.**

[69] *Id* 432, where the author notes that before their respective amendments in 1972 and 1973, California and Arizona's statutes stated:

> As between parents adversely claiming the custody or guardianship, neither parent is entitled to it as of right, but, other things being equal, if the child is of tender years, it shall be given to the mother. If the child is of an age requiring education and preparation for labor or business, then to the father. Cal Civ Code §318, repealed 1972 Cal State ch 1007 at 1855; Ariz Rev Stat Ann §14-846, amended 1973 Ariz L 1973 ch 139 §2.

[70] *Id* 432-34 n 38 (citing inter alia) Davis v Davis, 255 Ala 488, 51 So 2d 876 (1951); Sheridan v Sheridan, 466 P2d 821 (Alaska 1970); Grimditch v Grimditch, 71 Ariz 198, 226 P2d 489, *modified on other grounds*, 71 Ariz 237, 226 P2d 142 (1951); Disheroon v Disheroon, 211 Ark 519, 201 SW2d 17 (1947); Green v Green, 139 Colo 551, 342 P2d 659 (1954); L'Marian v L'Marian, 14 Conn Supp 306 (County Ct 1946); Doane v Doane, 330 So 2d 753 (Fla Dist Ct App 1976); Brashear v Brashear, 71 Idaho 158, 228 P2d 243 (1951); Nye v Nye, 411 Ill 408, 105 NE2d 300 (1952); Cramer v Cramer, 185 NW2d 787 (Iowa 1971); Patton v Patton, 215 Kan 377, 524 P2d 709 (1974); Hinton v Hintan, 377 SW2d 88 (Ky 1964); Hudson v Hudson, 295 So 2d 92 (La Ct App), *writ denied*, 295 So 2d 446 (La 1974); Kirstukas v Kirstukas, 14 Md App 190, 286 A2d 535 (1972); Eisel v Eisel, 261 Minn 1, 110 NW2d 881 (1961); Brown v Brown, 237 Miss 83, 112 So 2d 556 (1959); Horst v McLain, 466 SW2d 187 (Mo Ct App 1971); Trudge v Trudge, 134 Mont 174, 329 P2d 225 (1958); Adams v Adams, 86 Nev 62, 464 P2d 458 (1970); Esposito v Esposito, 41 NJ 143, 195 A2d 295 (1963); Garner v Stone, 85 NM 716, 516 P2d 687 (1973); Sheil v Sheil, 29 AD2d 950, 289 NYS2d 87 (1968); Riggs v Riggs, 69 Ohio App 263, 124 NE2d 835 (1954); Kuykendall v Kuykendall, 290 P2d 128 (Okla 1955); Spriggs v Carson, 229 Pa Super 9, 323 A2d 273 (1974); Loebenberg v Loebenberg, 85 RI 115, 127 A2d 500 (1956); Pullen v Pullen, 253 SC 123, 169 SE2d

> The result was a consistent pattern of decisions which both justified and further reinforced the maternal presumption. . . . Eventually, the belief that the mother was the natural and proper custodian of her children became so widely assumed that it was rarely questioned and even more rarely challenged.[71]

## §7.06 —Rationales

Although the tender years doctrine became ingrained in the judicial and societal belief system in the early twentieth century, courts offered few explanations for its use. The initial rationale given by some courts, termed the "divine right" theory by one writer,[72] is actually quite poetic.

For example, in 1921 the Supreme Court of Wisconsin declared:

> For a boy of such tender years nothing can be an adequate substitute for mother love–for that constant ministration required during the period of nurture that only a mother can give because in her alone is duty swallowed up in desire; in her alone is service expressed in terms of love. She alone has the patience and sympathy required to mold and soothe the infant mind in its adjustment to its environment.[73]

In that same year, the Supreme Court of Iowa noted:

> A court is naturally inclined to give to the mother the custody of her children of tender years. This tendency is well-founded. It is a recognition that, other conditions being equal, the mother is God's own institution for the rearing and upbringing of the child. It puts a premium on child culture in the hands of an expert.[74]

---

376 (1969); Hershey v Hershey, 85 SD 85, 177 NW2d 267 (1970); Graham v Graham, 140 Tenn 328, 204 SW 987 (1918); Erwin v Erwin, 505 SW2d 370 (Tex Ct App 1974); Cox v Cox, 532 P2d 994 (Utah 1975); Rowlee v Rowlee, 211 Va 689, 179 SE2d 461 (1971); Bjorneby v Bjorneby, 56 Wash 2d 561, 354 P2d 384 (1960); Funkhouser v Funkhouser, 158 W Va 964, 216 SE2d 570 (1970); Farwell v Farwell, 33 Wis 2d 324, 147 NW2d 289 (1967); Butcher v Butcher, 363 P2d 923 (Wyo 1961).

Cases representative of the abandonment of the tender years doctrine are cited and discussed in **§7.07.**

[71] Weitzman & Dixon, *Child Custody Awards: Legal Standards and Empirical Patterns for Child Custody, Support, and Visitation After Divorce,* 12 UCD L Rev 473, 480 (1979).

[72] Roth, *The Tender Years Presumption in Child Custody Disputes,* 15 J Fam L 423, 436 (1976-77); *see also* Weitzman & Dixon, *Child Custody Awards: Legal Standards and Empirical Patterns for Child Custody, Support, and Visitation After Divorce,* 12 UCD L Rev 473, 480 (1979).

[73] Jenkins v Jenkins, 173 Wis 592, ___, 181 NW 826, 827 (1921).

[74] Hines v Hines, 192 Iowa 569, ___, 185 NW 91, 92 (1921). *See also* Washburn v Washburn, 49 Cal App 2d 581, 584, 122 P2d 96, 100 (1942) ("It is not open to question, and indeed it is universally recognized, that the mother is the natural custodian of her young. This view proceeds on the well-known fact that there is no satisfactory substitute for a mother's love"); Bath v Bath, 150 Neb 591, 602, 35 NW2d 509, 515 (1949) ("it is clear that generally the love, solicitude, and devotion of a mother cannot be replaced

Other courts emphasized that the maternal preference was a product of the laws of nature. An Idaho court maintained that the tender years doctrine "arises out of the very nature and instincts of motherhood," while New Jersey and Maryland courts respectively referred to the preference as the result of an "inexorable natural force," and a "primordial" maternal tie.[75] As they continued to affirm the tender years doctrine over time, courts actually justified its application by declaring that it was part of tradition and "the wisdom of the ages."[76]

The rise of psychology initially served to support the maternal preference. Many judges dabbled in what one writer has called "wool-sack psycho-sociology,"[77] offering such explanations for the preference as:

> Mother love is a dominant trait in even the weakest of women, and as a general thing surpasses the paternal affection for the common offspring, and, moreover, a child needs a mother's care even more than a father's. For these reasons courts are loathe to deprive the mother of the custody of her children, and will not do so unless it is shown clearly that she is so far an unfit and improper person to be intrusted with such custody as to endanger the welfare of the children.[78]

Psychologists, child development specialists, and social scientists provided further support for the tender years doctrine, stating that women were uniquely suited for the child-rearing task, both biologically and psychologically, while men were not.[79]

In the 1970s and 1980s, the tender years doctrine was attacked and abolished in most jurisdictions, despite arguments that its mere existence kept the

---

by another, and is worth more to a child of tender years than all other things combined. A child should not be deprived of necessary and wholesome influences which spring from these characteristics of a mother if it can be reasonably avoided").

[75] Weitzman & Dixon, *supra* note 72, at 480 (citing Kreiger v Kreiger, 59 Idaho 301, 81 P2d 1081, 1083 (1938); Kirstukas v Kirstukas, 14 Md App 190, 196, 286 A2d 535, 538 (1972); Wojnarowicz v Wojnarowicz, 48 NJ Super 349, 353, 137 A2d 618, 620 (Super Ct Ch Div 1958)).

[76] Weitzman & Dixon, *supra* note 72 at 480 (citing Commonwealth *ex rel* Lucas v Kreischer, 450 Pa 352, __, 299 A2d 243, 245 (1973); Cox v Cox, 532 P2d 994, 996 (Utah 1975)).

[77] Roth, *supra* note 72, at 436.

[78] Freeland v Freeland, 92 Wash 482, __, 159 P 698, __ (1916).

[79] Weitzman & Dixon, *supra* note 72, at 481 (citing inter alia, J. Bowlby, Child Care and the Growth of Love 21 (1965); J. Levine, Who Will Raise the Children: New Options for Fathers (and Mothers) 41 (1976); Watson, *The Children of Armageddon: Problems of Custody Following Divorce,* 21 Syracuse L Rev 55, 82 (1969); Wortis, *The Acceptance of the Concept of the Maternal Role by Behavioral Scientists: Its Effects on Women,* 41 Am J Orthopsychology 733-46 (1971); Bettelheim, *Fathers Shouldn't Try to Be Mothers,* Parent Magazine, Oct 1956, at 124-25, *cited in* J. Levine, Who Will Raise the Children: New Options for Fathers (and Mothers) 22 (1976).

number of contested cases to a minimum.[80] In the midst of the attack, new support for the doctrine appeared in legal commentary.[81] The central argument behind the contemporary support for the doctrine is that women overwhelmingly have remained the primary caretakers of their children, and that the maternal preference should exist as a recognition of that fact and as protection against the separation of the mother and child. The presumption would serve, then, to shield a mother from a father who would pursue custody out of vindictiveness or for economic gain. These assertions have been augmented by studies reporting the damaging effects of maternal deprivation upon children and studies documenting the surprisingly low amount of involvement by fathers in the day-to-day life of their children.[82] In addition, it has been argued that in situations where the father is the primary caretaker, this interpretation of the presumption will serve to protect the father's greater demands for custody.[83]

As all experienced practitioners know, mothers obtain custody of their children in the vast majority of cases. However, to attribute maternal custody primarily to the tender years doctrine is inaccurate.

Most dissolution cases are amicably settled, and the custody issue is resolved between the parties, usually in favor of the mother. It has been noted that 90 per cent of all custody arrangements are finalized without a court order, and that "parents making private agreements may give more weight to the maternal preference than the courts traditionally have done."[84]

In contested cases, custody is frequently not an issue because it has been settled by the parties, again usually in favor of the mother. In contested custody disputes, the typical facts are that the father leaves the family, only to return a few months or years later to request custody of their children. It has been consistently reported that courts give custody of children to their mothers in

---

[80] *See* **§§7.08-7.10.**

[81] *See* Katz, *The Maternal Preference and the Psychological Parent: Suggestions for Allocating the Burden of Proof in Custody Litigation,* 53 Conn BJ 343, 347 (1979); Klaff, *The Tender Years Doctrine: A Defense,* 70 Cal L Rev 335, 343-48 (1982); Leonard & Provence, *The Development of Parent-Child Relationships and the Psychological Parent,* 53 Conn BJ 320, 326 (1979); Morris, *A Developmental Approach to Child Custody,* 53 Conn BJ 330, 333 (1979); Okpaku, *Psychology: Impediment or Aid in Child Custody Cases?,* 29 Rutgers L Rev 1117, 1121-22 (1976); Uviller, *Fathers' Rights and Feminism: The Maternal Presumption Revisited,* 1 Harv Women's LJ 107, 121 (1978); Watson, *The Children of Armageddon: Problems of Custody Following Divorce,* 21 Syracuse L Rev 55, 70 (1969).

[82] *See* Klaff, *supra* note 81, at 345-47 (citing inter alia: S. Frasberg, Every Child's Birthright: In Defense of Mothering (1977); M. Klaus & J. Kennell, Maternal Infant Bonding (1976); R. Spitz, The First Year of Life (1965); Nagera, *Children's Reactions to the Death of Important Objects,* 25 Psychoanalytic Study of the Child 360, 369 (1970); Rebelsky & Hanks, *Fathers' Verbal Interaction with Infants in the First Three Months of Life,* 42 Child Dev 63 (1971).

[83] Klaff, *supra* note 81, at 347.

[84] Jones, *The Tender Years Doctrine: Survey and Analysis,* 16 J Fam L 695, 696 (1977-78) (citing Marschall & Gatz, *The Custody Decision Process: Toward New Roles for Parents and the State,* 7 (NC Cent LJ 50, 54-60 (Fall 1975)).

90 per cent of divorce cases.[85] It is these cases where the maternal preference may be significant.

It is true that there are more fathers actively involved in raising their children in our society. However, because those numbers are still very small, there has not been a dramatic increase of paternal custody awards.

## §7.07 —Application

The tender years doctrine has been judicially applied in several ways. The most extreme version of the tender years doctrine entitles the mother to custody unless she is shown to be unfit.[86] This application comes close to an irrebuttable presumption; the preference for the mother is strong and the burden for proving her unfitness is heavy regardless of the fact that the father is better suited to care for the children. Fathers are rarely able to meet this burden and mothers are invariably awarded custody when this version of the doctrine is applied. It has been argued that this traditional "unfitness test" is "insufficiently child protective" because it emphasizes the mother's fault in the divorce and not the reasons behind her actions or her actual caregiving ability.[87] Practitioners are aware that parents in the divorce situation, while experiencing difficulties between themselves, often maintain good relationships with their children.

Another application of the tender years doctrine involved the best interests of the child standard. This "more moderate approach makes a maternal preference one factor among many, while allowing the preference to be overcome by a showing that it would be in the child's best interest to award custody to the father even though the mother is a fit parent."[88] Thus, a father who was his child's primary caretaker could presumably overcome the presumption without any showing that the mother was unfit.

The third version of the tender years doctrine resulted in an application of

---

[85] *See* Drinan, *The Rights of Children in Modern American Family Law,* 2 J Fam L 101, 102 (1962); Roth, *supra* note 72, at 423, Weitzman & Dixon, *supra* note 72, at 484. Note, *Measuring the Child's Best Interests—A Study of Incomplete Considerations,* 44 Den LJ 132 (1967).

[86] *See, e.g.,* Dalton v Dalton, 214 Kan 805, 522 P2d 378 (1974); Whatley v Whatley, 312 So 2d 149 (La Ct App 1975); Sistrunk v Sistrunk, 245 So 2d 845 (Miss 1971); Peavey v Peavey, 85 Nev 571, 460 P2d 110 (1969); MP v SP, 169 NJ Super 425, 404 A2d 1256 (Super Ct App Div 1979); JB v AB, 242 SE2d 248 (W Va 1978).

[87] Klaff, *The Tender Years Doctrine: A Defense,* 70 Cal L Rev 335, 349 (1982).

[88] *Developments in the Law, The Constitution and the Family,* 93 Harv L Rev 1156, 1333 (1980). *See, e.g.,* Turner v Turner, 46 Ala App 350, 242 So 2d 397 (1970); DuPont v DuPont, 59 Del 206, 216 A2d 674 (1966); Rzeszotarski v Rzeszotarski, 296 A2d 431 (DC 1972); Patton v Armstrong, 16 Ill App 3d 881, 307 NE2d 178 (1974); Sharp v Sharp, 491 SW2d 639 (Ky 1973); *In re* Marriage of Barr, 579 SW2d 833 (Mo Ct App 1979); Di Biano v Di Biano, 105 NJ Super 415, 252 A2d 735 (1969); Bingham v Bingham, 575 P2d 703 (Utah 1978).

the maternal preference "all other things being equal."[89] Courts used the preference as a tiebreaker in cases where both parents were found to be equally fit. In a similar vein, as an alternative, the authors of *Beyond the Best Interests of the Child* suggested that a flip of the coin, or lottery, be used to choose the custodial parent when the parents are "equally suitable in terms of the child's most immediate predictable needs."[90] This apparently callous approach would be offensive to most people.[91]

Besides these three approaches and the relevant statutes, there are two other factors which influence judicial application of the tender years doctrine: age and sex of the children. Some courts adhere to the rule that the tender years presumption carries the greater weight when the child is in infancy, and declines in importance as the child grows older, when more weight is given to the preference of the child.[92] It has been noted that the maternal preference carries greater weight when the minor children are female.[93]

The practitioner should be aware that it has not always been possible to determine which maternal preference application courts have used. In some jurisdictions, the law is undecided because of inconsistent decisions within the state.[94] As one author points out: "What actually happens in court or in the mind of the judge is not necessarily as clear cut as the above rules of presumption indicate."[95]

## §7.08 —Decline

In the 1970s, support for the maternal preference in the law was eroded by what has been called "a formal insistence on a neutral application of the best-interests standard."[96] Provoked by changes in societal attitudes, psycho-

---

[89] Jones, *The Tender Years Doctrine: Survey and Analysis,* 16 J Fam L 695, 700 (1977-78) (citing *Patton v Patton,* 215 Kan 377, 524 P2d 709 (1974); Cox v Cox, 532 P2d 994 (Utah 1975)). *See also* Glasgow v Glasgow, 426 P2d 617 (Alaska 1967); Barrett v Barrett, 94 Idaho 64, 480 P2d 910 (1971); Cooke v Cooke, 21 Md App 376, 319 A2d 841 (1974); Moore v Moore, 222 Va 153, 183 SE2d 172 (1971).

[90] J. Goldstein, A. Freud, & A. Solnit, Beyond the Best Interests of the Child 63 (1973).

[91] Mnookin, *Child-Custody Adjudication: Judicial Functions in the Face on Indeterminacy,* 39 Law & Contemp Probs 226, 290-91 (1975). The question remains: is it any less offensive to apply the maternal preference, "all other factors being equal?"

[92] *See* Annot, 70 ALR3d 262, 287-90 (1976).

[93] *Id* 292-93.

[94] *Id* 284-87, discussing Louisiana, Missouri, and Pennsylvania.

[95] R. Gottesman, The Child and the Law 137 (1981).

[96] Mnookin, *Child-Custody Adjudication: Judicial Functions in the Face of Indeterminacy,* 39 Law & Contemp Probs 226, 235 (1975). The best interests of the child standard, while enunciated in American case law for nearly 200 years, has received greatest attention and adherence in the last two decades. *See* **§§6.03-7.04.** This standard's philosophy was eloquently summarized by Justice Cardozo in Finlay v Finlay, 240 NY 429, 433-34, 148 NE 624, 626 (1925) (citations omitted):

> The Chancellor in exercising his jurisdiction upon petition does not proceed upon

logical theories, and marital roles, this "formal insistence" has been evinced by gender-neutral custody statutes, state equal rights amendments, and case law abolishing the maternal preference on statutory, policy, and constitutional grounds.

A combination of social forces accelerated the decline of the tender years doctrine. The rise of no-fault divorce reduced the difficulty of dissolving a marriage and resulted in more people obtaining divorces. The women's movement promoted an expanded view of the role of women in society, and prompted them to enter the labor force in great numbers. In addition, society's conception of appropriate sexual roles was changing, and gender neutrality became an important issue. Fathers began exercising and receiving recognition of their parental rights.[97]

It became clear that it was essential for courts to consider the roles of the parents during the marriage and the reality of the family's post divorce life instead of relying upon traditional sentimental notions of motherhood. A sociological "role analysis" of family members in 1967 noted that the traditional role of wife as mother was in fact commingled with her emerging roles as companion to her husband and as partner contributing to the economic support of the family.[98] Psychological works such as *Beyond the Best Interests of the Child*[99] distinguished between biological parent and psychological parent, noted that mothering is a gender-neutral function, and advocated in custody

---

> the theory that the petitioner, whether father or mother, has a cause of action against the other or indeed against anyone. He acts as *parens patriae* to do what is best for the interest of the child. He is to put himself in the position of a "wise, affectionate, and careful parent" . . . and make provision for the child accordingly. . . . He is not adjudicating a controversy between adversary parties to compose their private differences. He is not determining rights "as between a parent and a child," or as between one parent and another. . . . Equity does not concern itself with such disputes in their relation to the disputants. Its concern is for the child.

[97] See Weitzman & Dixon, *Child Custody Awards: Legal Standards and Empirical Patterns For Child Custody, Support and Visitation After Divorce,* 12 UCD L Rev 473, 501 (1979), where the authors state that a "new legal era" of "equal rights for fathers" probably began with the Supreme Court's decision in Stanley v Illinois, 405 US 645 (1972), which held that a presumption that an unwed father is an unfit parent is unconstitutional as a denial of both due process and equal protection. Media attention focused on fathers who attempted to get custody of their young children, and fathers' rights groups were springing up all over the country.

[98] Note, *Measuring the Child's Best Interests—A Study of Incomplete Considerations,* 44 Den LJ 132, 138 (1967).

[99] J. Goldstein, A. Freud, & A. Solnit, Beyond the Best Interests of the Child (1973); Katz, *The Maternal Preference and the Psychological Parent: Suggestions for Allocating the Burden of Proof in Custody Litigation,* 53 Conn BJ 343 (1979); Leonard & Provena, *The Development of Parent-Child Relationships and the Psychological Parent,* 53 Conn BJ 320 (1979); Morris, *A Developmental Approach to Child Custody,* 53 Conn BJ 330 (1979); Okpaku, *Psychology: Impediment or Aid in Child Custody Cases?,* 29 Rutgers L Rev 1117 (1976). One court has used this reasoning to justify the application of the maternal preference, stating that the preference is based "upon the acts of motherhood—not the fact of motherhood." *See* Garrett v Garrett, 464 SW2d 740, 742 (Mo Ct App 1971).

disputes that a child should be placed with the primary caretaker in order to insure a continuity of care.

Perhaps the reality of post divorce life will continue to shatter traditional notions of motherhood. It has been noted that courts award mothers custody of their children in 90 percent of child custody cases, and that probably a similar percentage of mothers gain custody through private agreements.[100] Only a small percentage of wives receive alimony, and many custodial mothers have had difficulty enforcing child support awards. In fact, one study has shown that the post divorce income of men is substantially higher than that of their former wives.[101]

Thus, many mothers upon the dissolution of their marriages are forced to find employment, and thereby adjust their custodial role to include the role of provider, which may or may not affect the child-caring abilities that courts have assumed could only be provided by the traditional mother.[102] It is interesting to note, however, that in response to a hypothetical question, 75 percent of attorneys surveyed in a 1979 study predicted that a working mother who attended "women's liberation meetings at night" would receive custody of her children in a custody dispute.[103] As one writer has observed, post divorce life for a custodial parent may be difficult no matter which parent has assumed the role:

> After divorce, the pressures on the single parent are to act as both a father and a mother, and at the same time the single parent's psychological, financial, and physical resources are subject to an extra tax as a result of

---

[100] *See* Drinan, *The Rights of Children in Modern American Family Law*, 2 J Fam L 101, 102 (1962); Roth, *The Tender Years Presumption in Child Disputes*, 15 J Fam L 423, 423 (1976-77); Weitzman & Dixon, *Child Custody Awards: Legal Standards and Empirical Patterns for Child Custody, Support, and Visitation After Divorce*, 12 UCD L Rev 473, 484 (1979); Note, *supra* note 98, at 132.

[101] Weitzman & Dixon, *The Alimony Myth: Does No-Fault Divorce Make a Difference?*, 14 Fam LQ 141, 175 (1980). *See also* **ch 10.**

[102] Note, *supra* note 98, at 145. The author also cites two cases where a mother lost custody of her children upon her husband's remarriage because he offered them a home with a woman to care for the children while the natural mother was forced to work and spend time away from her children: Wood v Wood, 207 Cal App 2d 33, 24 Cal Rptr 260 (1963); Thalassinos v Thalassinos, 77 NYS2d 311 (Sup Ct 1947), *affd*, 274 AD 807, 81 NYS2d 155 (1948). This point is also discussed in Bazemore v Davis, 394 A2d 1377, 1381 (DC 1978).

[103] *See* Weitzman & Dixon, *supra* note 100, at 473 (1979), which continues:

> Thus it would seem that most attorneys do not think that judges view women who work as inadequate or neglectful mothers.
>
> In explaining their predictions, most of the attorneys said that the mother's "job was irrelevant if she provided care for the children." The next most common explanation was that the new case presented "no evidence that she was not a good mother . . . the *quality* of the mothering was most important." The third most common reason was that the presumption in favor of the mother was still effective. None of the attorneys referred to the husband in responding to the revised case. *Id* 513-15 (footnotes omitted, emphasis in original).

> the loss of a companion and co-bearer of responsibility. The situation has been characterized as "psychological overload." To date, there is no evidence to support a conclusion that a "psychologically overloaded" mother is preferable to a "psychologically overloaded" father.[104]

These societal, psychological, and role model changes were expressed in the law by the enactment of gender neutral statutes, state equal rights amendments, and case law specifically abolishing the maternal preference.

## §7.09 —Legislative Action

It may certainly be said that the persistence of the maternal preference in custody actions is not the fault of state legislatures. The vast majority of custody statutes are based on a best interests of the child standard and provide that both natural parents have an equal right to custody of their children upon divorce.[105] In some states, custody statutes were amended or repealed to abolish presumptions favoring a particular parent.[106]

The legislative trend in the 1980s favors joint custody or a presumption of joint custody, another step away from maternal preference.[107] Custody laws in several states have been influenced by equal rights amendments, which require equal treatment of the sexes.[108]

While legislative action was the initiating force in the decline of the tender years doctrine, many courts continued to implement presumptions in favor of mothers as custodians in a majority of cases despite the statutes.[109] As two

---

[104] Roth, *supra* note 100, at 454-55 (footnotes omitted).

[105] These states include: Alabama, Alaska, Arizona, Arkansas, California, Colorado, Connecticut, Delaware, District of Columbia, Florida, Georgia, Hawaii, Idaho, Illinois, Indiana, Iowa, Kansas, Kentucky, Louisiana, Massachusetts, Minnesota, Montana, Nevada, New Hampshire, New York, North Carolina, North Dakota, Ohio, Oklahoma, Oregon, Pennsylvania, South Dakota, Tennessee, Texas, Virginia, Washington, West Virginia, Wisconsin, Wyoming.

[106] *See, e.g.*, Ariz Rev Stat Ann §25-332 (1976) (replacing §14-846 in 1974); Cal Civ Code §4600 (Deering 1984) (amended in 1972); Fla Stat Ann §61.13(2) (West Supp 1984) (amended in 1971); Neb Rev Stat §42-364(2) (1978) (amended in 1974); Okla Stat Ann tit 30, §11 (West 1955) (repealed 1983); Or Rev Stat §107.105(1)(a) (1981) (amended in 1971); Utah Code Ann §30-3-10 (Supp 1983) (amended 1977).

[107] States which provide for joint custody or for a presumption of joint custody include: Alaska, Arizona, California, Colorado, Connecticut, Delaware, Florida, Hawaii, Idaho, Illinois, Iowa, Kansas, Kentucky, Louisiana, Maine, Massachusetts, Michigan, Minnesota, Mississippi, Montana, Nevada, New Hampshire, New Jersey, New Mexico, New York, North Carolina, Ohio, Oregon, Pennsylvania, Texas, and Wisconsin.

[108] States which have enacted state ERAs include: Alaska, Colorado, Connecticut, Hawaii, Illinois, Louisiana, Maryland, Massachusetts, Montana, New Hampshire, New Mexico, Pennsylvania, Texas, Utah, Virginia, Washington, Wisconsin, and Wyoming.

[109] *See* Roth, *The Tender Years Presumption in Child Custody Disputes,* 15 J Fam L 423, 432-34 n 38 (1976-77); *see also, e.g.*, Smith v Smith, 172 Colo 516, 474 P2d 619 (1970); Ryg v Kerkow, 296 Minn 265, 207 NW2d 701 (1973); Ettinger v Ettinger, 72 NM 300, 383 P2d 261 (1963).

family law authorities have stated: "One of the amazing things about the tender years doctrine is that it has often persisted even in the face of 'equalization' statutes or state Equal Rights Amendments (ERA)."[110] But ultimately, the force primarily responsible for the rejection of the maternal preference in the law was the same force that carved the preference into stone at the beginning of the twentieth century: the state courts.

## §7.10 —Judicial Rejection

Courts have abolished the tender years doctrine in a majority of jurisdictions for several compelling reasons.

Many courts have followed their statutes and state constitutions in rejecting the maternal preference. Thus, when legislatures specifically abolished the doctrine, repealed language which had provided for the preference, or established an equal right to custody for both parents, the judiciary has enforced the law.[111] In a few states, courts have held that the tender years doctrine violates state equal rights amendments and, thus, is not supported by the law.[112]

In other jurisdictions, courts have rejected the maternal preference independently of any legislative action.[113] The driving force behind this trend has been

---

[110] Foster & Freed, *Life With Father: 1978*, 11 Fam LQ 321, 332 (1978).

[111] *See, e.g.*, Anderson v Anderson, 121 Ariz 405, 407, 590 P2d 637, 640 (1973); *In re* Marriage of Carney, 24 Cal 3d 725, 598 P2d 36, 157 Cal Rptr 383, (1979); Anderson v Anderson, 289 So 2d 463 (Fla Ct App 1974); *In re* Marriage of Meyers, 387 NE2d 1360 (Ind Ct App 1979); McAndrews v McAndrews, 39 Md App 1, 382 A2d 1081 (1978); Arnold v Arnold, 95 Nev 951, 604 P2d 109 (1979); Korkrow v Korkrow, 191 Neb 657, 217 NW2d 89 (1974); Starkeson v Starkeson, 119 NH 78, 397 A2d 1043 (1979); *In re* Marriage of Van Dyke, 48 Or App 965, 618 P2d 465 (1980). At least two courts have held that state statutes specifically forbidding any preference based solely upon sex were not inconsistent with the rule that, other things being equal, custody should be awarded to the mother. *See* Petersen v Petersen, 296 Minn 147, 206 NW2d 658 (1973); Scolman v Scolman, 66 Wis 2d 761, 226 NW2d 388 (1975).

[112] *See, e.g.*, King v Vancil, 34 Ill App 3d 831, —, 341 NE2d 65, 69 (1975) (tender years doctrine violates Ill Const, art I, §18); Commonwealth *ex rel* Weber v Weber, 272 Pa Super 88, 414 A2d 682, 684 (1979); Commonwealth *ex rel* Spriggs v Carson, 470 Pa 290, 299-300, 368 A2d 635, 639 (1979) (tender years presumption violates P Const art 1, §28). *Cf* Cox v Cox, 532 P2d 994, 996 (Utah 1975) (state ERA "does not mean that the law must pretend to be unaware of and blindly ignore obvious and essential biological differences"). *See also* Cooke v Cooke, 21 Md App 376, 319 A2d 841 (1974) (court declined to consider argument that tender years presumption violated ERA because it was not raised below).

[113] *See, e.g.*, Devine v Devine, 398 So 2d 697 (Ala Ct App 1981); Johnson v Johnson, 564 P2d 71 (Alaska), *cert denied*, 434 US 1048 (1977); Rayer v Rayer, 32 Colo 400, 404, 512 P2d 637, 640 (1973); Bazemore v Davis, 394 A2d 1377 (DC 1978); Turoff v Turoff, 56 Hawaii 51, 527 P2d 1275 (1974); *In re* Marriage of Bowen, 219 NW2d 683 (Iowa 1974); *In re* Marriage of Estelle, 592 SW2d 277, 278 (Mo Ct App 1979); *In re* Marriage of Markegard, 616 P2d 323 (Mont 1980); State *ex rel* Watts v Watts, 77 Misc 2d 178, 350 NYS2d 285 (Fam Ct 1973).

judicial insistence on a more thorough application of the best interests of the child standard. In light of accumulating evidence that the tender years presumption was based on unwarranted assumptions, courts have declared that invoking the presumption is inconsistent with and obscures the "basic tenet in all custody cases,"[114] the best interests of the children. It was thought that the tender years doctrine had been used to save time and avoid fact finding "at the price of tremendous legal and logical confusion, and accompanied by an intolerable risk of unnecessary error."[115] In addition, with the maternal preference in many jurisdictions, the father had to introduce evidence of the mother's deficiencies in order to gain custody of his children, which discouraged harmony between the parties and prompted ill-feeling.[116] Such a vague and destructive standard was not an effective tool with which to make important human decisions.[117] Thus, courts demanded full consideration of a variety of factors under the best interests standard, relegating the tender years presumption to one factor to be considered or a tie-breaking factor, or rejecting its consideration altogether.

The strengthening of the best interests standard at the expense of the maternal preference was propelled by judicial recognition that one premise of the preference was based on outdated social stereotypes. Courts began to take note that the function of "mothering," or the acts of motherhood, not the fact of motherhood, could be performed by either parent.[118] As a result, the

---

[114] *In re* Marriage of Bowen, 219 NW2d 683, 688 (Iowa 1974).

[115] Bazemore v Davis, 394 A2d 1377, 1382 (DC 1978). Similar criticisms of the use of presumptions have occurred in legal commentary and in other case law. See, *e.g.*, Foster & Freed, *Life With Father: 1978,* 11 Fam LQ 321, 337 (1978), where the authors state:

> The law's use of fictions and substantive rules of law disguised as presumptions is probably as old as our art and craft. These fictions and rules have been useful devices to avoid difficult fact-finding and provide a means of adapting the law to a myriad of unforeseeable circumstances so that the law may appear to be what it is not: secure and certian.

See also Stanley v Illinois, 405 US 645, 656-57 (1972), where, invalidating a presumption that an unwed father is an unfit parent, Justice White declared:

> Procedure by presumption is always cheaper and easier than individualized determination. But when, as here, the procedure forecloses the determinative issues of competence and care, when it explicitly disdains present realities in deference to past formalities, it needlessly risks running roughshod over the important interests of both parent and child.

[116] Bazemore v Davis, 394 A2d 1377, 1382 n 6 (DC 1978); Braiman v Braiman, 44 NY2d 584, 378 NE2d 1019, 407 NYS2d 449 (1978).

[117] Bazemore v Davis, 394 A2d 1377, 1383 (DC 1978), where the court cited Lemay v Lemay, 109 NH 217, 218, 247 A2d 189, 191 (1968), when stating: "As one court has aptly noted, magic formulas have no place in decisions designed to salvage human values."

[118] A particularly strong discussion of this point may be found in State *ex rel* Watts v Watts, 77 Misc 2d 178, 181, 350 NYS2d 285, 288-90 (Fam Ct 1973), where it is stated:

> Apart from the question of legality, the "tender years presumption" should be discarded because it is based on outdated social stereotypes rather than

maternal preference has been replaced in most of the recent custody decisions by a preference for the primary caretaker or psychological parent.

Finally, a small number of courts have held that the tender years presumption violates the Equal Protection Clause of the Constitution.[119] Other courts have held that the presumption is constitutional, or have declined to consider the constitutional question.[120] The Supreme Court of the United States has not confronted this issue.

## §7.11 —Constitutionality

In *State ex rel Watts v Watts,*[121] Judge Sybil Hart Kooper of the Family Court of the City of New York held that under the Supreme Court's decision in *Frontiero v Richardson,*[122] the deferential treatment based on sex created by the tender years presumption was "suspect" and, therefore, subject "to the strictest judicial scrutiny."[123] Noting that classifications subject to strict scrutiny under the Fourteenth Amendment must serve a compelling state interest in order to pass constitutional muster, Judge Kooper declared that the best interests of the child, while a potential compelling state interest, was not served by the application of the tender years presumption which was based on outdated stereotypes of parental roles. There was, therefore, no justification for differentiating between parents on the basis of sex by invoking the maternal preference. The court held that application of the presumption denied the father equal protection of the law under the Fourteenth Amendment.

The Supreme Court of Alabama held in *Devine v Devine*[124] that the tender years presumption represented an unconstitutional gender-based classification discriminating solely on the basis of sex between fathers and mothers in custody proceedings. In a detailed opinion, the Alabama court reviewed the historical development of the maternal preference, and its contemporary

---

> on rational and up-to-date consideration of the welfare of the children involved. . . .
>
> Eminent psychologists and anthropologists, including Margaret Mead, have also acknowledged and asserted that both female and male parents are equally able to provide care and perform child-rearing functions.

*See also* Johnson v Johnson, 564 P2d 71 (Alaska), *cert denied,* 434 US 1048 (1977); Bazemore v Davis, 394 A2d 1377 (DC 1978); *In re* Marriage of Bowen, 219 NW2d 683 (Iowa 1974).

[119] *See, e.g.,* Devine v Devine, 398 So 2d 686 (Ala 1981); State *ex rel* Watts v Watts, 77 Misc 2d 178, 350 NYS 2d 285 (Fam Ct 1973).

[120] *See, e.g., In re* Marriage of Bowen, 219 NW2d 683 (Iowa 1974); Gilbert v Gilbert, 166 Mont 312, 533 P2d 1079 (1975); Gordon v Gordon, 577 P2d 1271 (Okla), *cert denied,* 439 US 863 (1978).

[121] 77 Misc 2d 178, 350 NYS2d 285 (Fam Ct 1973).

[122] 411 US 677 (1973).

[123] State *ex rel* Watts v Watts, 77 Misc 2d 178, ___, 350 NYS2d 285, 290 (Fam Ct 1973).

[124] 398 So 2d 686 (Ala 1981).

status. The court examined the tender years presumption in light of a series of decisions from the Supreme Court of the United States which had scrutinized gender-based classifications under the Equal Protection Clause of the Fourteenth Amendment.[125] The Alabama court stressed the Supreme Court's criticism of reliance on stereotypical notions for administrative convenience; adherence to sexual characterizations which bear no relationship to ability to perform or contribute; and broad gender-based distinctions between parental relations.

Concluding that the tender years presumption imposed legal burdens on individuals based on sex, the Alabama court, like the *Watts* court, held that the tender years doctrine is not substantially related to the significant state interest of providing for the best interests of the children. According to the court, this was true because, inter alia, "the tender years presumption rejects the fundamental proposition asserted in *Caban* that 'maternal and paternal roles are not invariably different in importance.' "[126]

The cases which have upheld the constitutionality of the tender years doctrine have done so for different reasons. In *Cooke v Cooke,*[127] the Court of Special Appeals of Maryland, while not squarely presented with the issue of whether the maternal preference violated the equal rights of the parents, nevertheless discussed it. The court declared that, because the rights of the parties in a custody case are subordinated to the best interests of the child, proper application of the maternal preference neither denies nor abridges the rights of either party. As the court stated, "[t]he 'self-evident truth' of equality of creation of all persons was not meant to describe human congenital endowments, but rather their political and legal rights."[128]

In *Gordon v Gordon,*[129] the Supreme Court of Oklahoma, declaring that gender is not a "suspect" classification for equal protection purposes, held constitutional that state's statutory maternal preference custody provision. The court

---

[125] The court examined Orr v Orr, 440 US 268 (1977) (statutory scheme imposing a support duty on husbands and none on wives establishes a classification based upon sex subject to scrutiny under the Fourteenth Amendment and unconstitutional); Reed v Reed, 404 US 71 (1971) (mandatory provision of the Idaho probate code giving preference to men over women when persons of equal entitlement applied for appointment as administrator of a decedent's estate forbidden by the Equal Protection Clause of the Fourteenth Amendment); Frontiero v Richardson, 411 US 677 (1973) (striking down a federal statutory scheme which extended a "presumption of dependency" to spouses of male members of military, but not to spouses of female members); Caban v Mohammed, 441 US 380 (1979) (holding that a New York adoption law which permitted an unwed mother, but not an unwed father, to block the adoption of their minor child simply by withholding consent violated the Equal Protection Clause).

[126] Devine v Devine, 398 So 2d 686, 698 (1981) (citing Caban v Mohammed, 441 US 380, 389 (1979)).

[127] 21 Md App 376, 319 A2d 841 (1974).

[128] *Id* at 379, 319 A2d at 843 (footnote omitted).

[129] 577 P2d 1271 (Okla 1978).

relied on *Craig v Boren,*[130] in which the Supreme Court of the United States fashioned a "middle-tier" standard of equal protection review for certain classifications such as gender, requiring that such classifications "must serve important governmental objectives and must be substantially related to the achievement of those objectives."[131]

The Oklahoma court maintained that the tender years presumption met the test established in *Craig v Boren:*

> We believe that consideration of the cultural, psychological and emotional characteristics that are gender related make this custodial preference one of "those instances where the sex-centered generalization actually [comports] to fact." [Citation omitted.] . . .
>
> If the legislature should determine that our contemporary social structure demands a change in the traditional family roles that have been part of our culture since its beginning, they may enact legislation reflecting that change. Meanwhile, the expression of those roles as embodied in [the statute] is not unconstitutional.[132]

In *In re Marriage of Bowen,*[133] the Supreme Court of Iowa found it unnecessary to decide the constitutionality of the maternal preference because it rejected it as an unjustified a priori principle.

Two commentators have offered further constitutional arguments pertaining to the tender years doctrine which have not appeared in the courts. One author argues that the constitutional attack on the presumption as a gender-based classification is misplaced because, in fact, the presumption is based upon continuity of care, and not mere gender.[134] Taking a different side, another writer suggests, in addition to the fact that the doctrine denies fathers equal protection of the laws, the existence of the tender years presumption violates a child's right to a proceeding where the adversary process is not distorted by such a presumption.[135]

---

130 429 US 190 (1976).

131 *Id* 197.

132 Gordon v Gordon, 577 P2d 1271, 1277 (Okla 1978).

133 219 NW2d 683 (Iowa 1974).

134 Klaff, *The Tender Years Doctrine: A Defense,* 70 Cal L Rev 335, 360 (1982).

135 Roth, *The Tender Years Presumption in Child Custody Disputes,* 15 J Fam L 423, 440 (1976-77).

# 8 Factors Considered in Awarding Custody



## §8.01 Introduction

When awarding custody in a divorce action, the court looks at a variety of factors to determine what is in the child's best interests. These factors are, in many states, catalogued in the custody statutes as guides which manifest the expressed intent of the legislature. Custody statutes do not limit the scope of the court's consideration to the statutory checklist, however. The family law practitioner should introduce other relevant evidence which pertains to the child's welfare for the court's review.

Any survey of statutes, authorities, commentaries, and cases reveals a long list of factors to be considered in a custody case, and this book is no exception. Relevant criteria include: the child's wishes; the parents' wishes; the child's relationship with parents, siblings, and other significant persons; the child's adjustment to school, home, and community; the mental and physical health of the parties; the conduct of the parties if relevant; the child's needs and the parents' ability and desire to provide for them, specifically: love, affection, guidance, education, neighborhood, food, clothing, medical care, etc.; home atmosphere; financial circumstances; stability and continuity; and whatever other factors are important to the particular case.

Generally, the threshold issue is a determination of the needs of the child and the desire and ability of each parent to meet those needs.[1] The court then compares the alternative environments offered by the individual parents.

Because a child does not live in a vacuum, the practitioner must not consider the factors as existing in a vacuum. Attorneys should realize that judges do not make their custody decisions on the basis of an isolated factor.

Relevant factors in a child custody case interact with each other. They vary in weight and importance. Some will have more influence than others; at times, only the aggregate influence will make the difference. A good judge will analyze each factor according to its actual impact on the welfare of the child and it is incumbent, therefore, that the lawyer present the full picture to the judge.

Thus, the practitioner must know the factors which may be specified in the custody statute in his or her jurisdiction. In addition, counsel will, of course, review case law to discover which factors have carried weight in previous cases. However, the primary source of factors for each custody action will be the parties involved. Interviews with clients, family members, and witnesses focusing on the custody question will begin to uncover what factors are important in a presentation of the child's best interests. Frequently, in these interviews, the questions arise spontaneously, and usually center on the child's daily life, school, extracurricular activities, physical and mental health, and relationship with the parents. Sometimes it is necessary for lawyers to see the child for informational purposes, even though most lawyers and judges have deep reservations about using children as adverse witnesses. While these interviews may be a source of valuable information, practitioners should proceed cautiously when dealing with children.[2]

Some of the more important factors in determining the child's best interests are discussed in the remainder of this chapter.

---

[1] A. Haralambie, Handling Child Custody Cases 24 (Shepard's/McGraw-Hill 1983).

[2] *See, e.g.,* Jordan, When in Doubt, Keep Child Out, 6 Fam Advoc 16 (Spring 1984); Wood, The Child as Witness, 6 Fam Advoc 14 (Spring 1984).

## §8.02 Statutory Factors

In 1984, 34 state statutes provided guidelines for a judicial determination of a child's best interests in a custody case.[3] Half of those statutes included the factors set forth in §402 of the Uniform Marriage and Divorce Act (UMDA),[4] which provides:

> The court shall determine custody in accordance with the best interest of the child. The court shall consider all relevant factors including:
>
> (1) the wishes of the child's parent or parents as to his custody;
>
> (2) the wishes of the child as to his custodian;
>
> (3) the interaction and interrelationship of the child with his parent or parents, his siblings, and any other person who may significantly affect the child's best interest;
>
> (4) the child's adjustment to his home, school, and community; and
>
> (5) the mental and physical health of all individuals involved.
>
> The court shall not consider conduct of a proposed custodian that does not affect his relationship to the child.[5]

Many other statutes, while not containing the exact language of the UMDA, nevertheless have similar statutory factors. For example, several statutes provide that courts consider the preference of the child if the child is of sufficient age, intelligence, understanding, experience, and capability to express a preference.[6] The New Mexico statute requires a court to consider the child's preference if 14 years of age or older, while the Georgia law gives a child of that age or older the right to select the parent with whom to live, which is a controlling factor unless the parent is unfit.[7] The Maryland statute permits a child who is 16 years or older and who is subject to a custody order or decree to file a petition to change custody.[8]

---

[3] Freed & Walker, *Family Law in the Fifty States: An Overview* Table IX (Aug 5, 1984).

[4] §402, 9A ULA 96, 198 (1979). *See* **app 1-2.**

[5] Statutes which contain the same factors as the UMDA include: Ariz Rev Stat Ann §25-332 (Supp 1983-84); Colo Rev Stat §14-10-124 (Supp 1984); Del Code Ann tit 13, §722 (1981); DC Code Ann §16-911 (1981); Idaho Code §32-717 (1983); Ill Ann Stat ch 40, §602 (Smith-Hurd 1980); Ind Code Ann §31-1-11.5-21 (Burns 1976); Kan Stat Ann §60-1610 (1983); Ky Rev Stat Ann §403.270 (Baldwin 1983); Me Rev Stat Ann tit 19, §752 (Supp 1984-85); Mo Ann Stat §452.375 (Vernon Supp 1984); Mont Code Ann §40-4-2.2 (1983); NM Stat Ann §40-4-9 (1983); Vt Stat Ann tit 15, §652 (Supp 1984); Wash Rev Code Ann §26.09.190 (Supp 1984-85); Wis Stat Ann §767.24 (West 1981).

[6] Cal Civ Code §4600 (Deering 1984); Conn Gen Stat Ann §46b-56 (West Supp 1984); Fla Stat Ann §61.13(3)(i) (West Supp 1984); Hawaii Rev Stat §571-46(3) (Supp 1983); La Civ Code Ann art 146 C(2)(i) (West Supp 1984); Me Rev Stat Ann tit 19, §752(5)(c) (Supp 1984-85); Mich Stat Ann §25.312(3)(i) (Callaghan Supp 1984); Minn Stat Ann §518.17(1)(b) (West Supp 1984); Neb Rev Stat §41-364(1)(b) (1978); Nev Rev Stat §125.480 (1983); ND Cent Code §14-09-06.2(9) (1981); Okla Stat Ann tit 12, §1277.1 (West Supp 1984-1985). *See* **§8.10.**

[7] *See* NM Stat Ann §40-4-9(B) (1983); Ga Code Ann §19-9-1(a) (Supp 1984).

[8] Md Fam Law Code Ann §9-103 (1984).

The love, affection, and other emotional ties existing between the parents and child is a criterion in some states,[9] while the "capacity and disposition of the parties involved to give the child affection and guidance"[10] is included in other statutes. Another UMDA-like provision is the "home, school and community record of the child,"[11] which is included in a handful of state statutes.

Many custody statutes focus on the stability and permanence of the child's home or the need for stability and continuity of a child's relationships.[12] The Maine statute considers the length of time that the child has been under the actual care and control of any person other than a parent.[13] Another common best interest factor is the parents' willingness and ability to meet the child's needs, whether general, physical, emotional, mental, religious, material, or medical.[14]

An increasing number of statutes have placed importance on the desire, willingness, and ability of each parent to allow, facilitate, or encourage an open and ongoing relationship, or the sharing of love, affection, and contact, between the child and the noncustodial parent.[15] In fact, the California and Florida legislatures have codified such a goal as the policy of the state.[16]

---

[9] *See* Fla Stat Ann §61.13(3)(b) (West Supp 1984); La Civ Code Ann art 146 C(2)(a) (West Supp 1984); Me Rev Stat Ann tit 19, §752(5)(B) (Supp 1984-85); Mich Stat Ann §25.312(3)(a) (Callaghan Supp 1984); ND Cent Code §14-09-06.2(1) (1981); Or Rev Stat §107.137(1)(a) (1983). *See* **§8.11.**

[10] *See* La Civ Code Ann art 146 C(2)(b) (West Supp 1984); Me Rev Stat Ann tit 19, §752(5)(F) (Supp 1984-85); Mich Stat Ann §25.312(3)(b) (Callaghan Supp 1984); Minn Stat Ann §518.17(1)(h) (West Supp 1984); ND Cent Code §14-09-06.2(2) (1981).

[11] Fla Stat Ann §61.13(3)(h) (West Supp 1984); La Civ Code Ann art 146 C(2)(h) (West Supp 1984); Me Rev Stat Ann tit 19, §752(5)(G) (Supp 1984-85); Mich Stat Ann §25.312(3)(h) (Callaghan Supp 1984); ND Cent Code §14-09-06.2(8) (1981).

[12] *See* Fla Stat Ann §61.13(3)(d) & (e) (West Supp 1984); Idaho Code §32-717 (1983); Kan Stat Ann §60-1610 (1983); La Civ Code Ann art 146 C(2)(d) & (e) (West Supp 1984); Me Rev Stat Ann tit 19, §752(5)(E) (Supp 1984-85); Mich Stat Ann §25.312(3)(d) & (e) (Callaghan Supp 1984); Minn Stat Ann §518.17(1)(f) (West Supp 1984); ND Cent Code §14-09-06.2(4) & (5) (1981). *See* **§8.03.**

[13] Me Rev Stat Ann tit 19, §752(5)(D) (Supp 1984-85). *See* **§8.03.**

[14] *See* Alaska Stat §25.24.156 (1984); Fla Stat Ann §61.13(3)(c) (West Supp 1984); Kan Stat Ann §66-1610 (1983); La Civ Code Ann art 146 C(2)(b) & (c) (West Supp 1984); Mich Stat Ann §25.312(3)(c) (Callaghan Supp 1984); Minn Stat Ann §518.17(1)(h) (West Supp 1984); Mo Ann Stat §452.375 (Vernon Supp 1984); ND Cent Code §14-09-06.2(3) (1981); Va Code §20-107.2(1)(d) (Supp 1984). *See* **§8.11.**

[15] Alaska Stat §25.24.150 (1984); Ariz Rev Stat Ann §25-332 (Supp 1983-84); Cal Civ Code §4600(b)(1) (Deering 1984); Colo Rev Stat §14-10-124(1)(f) (Supp 1984); Fla Stat Ann §61.13(3)(a) (West Supp 1984); La Civ Code Ann art 146(2)(j) (West Supp 1984); Me Rev Stat Ann tit 19, §752(5)(H) (Supp 1984-85); Mo Ann Stat §452.375 (Vernon Supp 1984); Pa Cons Stat Ann §1004 (Purdon Supp 1984-85).

[16] Cal Civ Code §4600(a) (Deering 1984); Fla Stat Ann §61.13(2)(b)1 (West Supp 1984).

A few states focus on the character of the parents. Alabama's statute requires the court to regard "the moral character and prudence of the parents,"[17] while Florida, Louisiana, and North Dakota, which have very similar statutes, include the parents' "moral fitness" as a factor for judicial consideration.[18] Idaho's statute calls for a review of the "integrity of all individuals involved."[19] The Wyoming legislature provided that the court must consider "the relative competency of both parents."[20] Still other statutes include the capacity or ability of the parents to perform their child care functions.[21] The Wisconsin law stresses the availability of public or private child care services as a factor to be considered in awarding child custody upon divorce.[22] The Maine statute also includes the following provisions:

> J. Methods for assisting parental cooperation and resolving disputes and each parent's willingness to use those methods;
> K. The effect on the child if one parent has sole authority over the child's upbringing.[23]

Alabama and Indiana are the only states which still consider age and sex of the children a factor in determining the best interests of the child.[24] Maine and Virginia call for consideration of the child's age, and Virginia also includes the parents' ages as factors.[25]

Remaining miscellaneous factors include: the causes of dissolution if relevant;[26] the distance between the respective residences of the parties;[27] the child's cultural background;[28] those facts which directly affect the well-being

---

17 Ala Code §30-3-1 (1983). *See* **§8.11.**

18 Fla Stat Ann §61.13(3)(f) (West Supp 1984); La Civ Code Ann art 146 (2)(f) (West Supp 1984); ND Cent Code §14-09-06.2(6) (1981). *See* **§8.11.**

19 Idaho Code §32-717 (1983).

20 Wyo Stat §20-2-113(a) (1977).

21 *See, e.g.*, Me Rev Stat Ann tit 19, §752(5)(I) (Supp 1984-85); Mo Ann Stat §451.375 (Vernon Supp 1984); Va Code §20-107.2(1)(e) (Supp 1984). *See* **§8.05.**

22 Wis Stat Ann §767.24 (West 1981).

23 Me Rev Stat Ann tit 19, §752(5)(j) & (K) (Supp 1984-85).

24 Ala Code §30-3-1 (1983); Ind Code Ann §31-1-11.5-21 (Burns 1976).

25 Me Rev Stat Ann tit 19, §752(5)(A) (Supp 1984-85); Va Code §20-107.2(1)(a) & (e) (Supp 1984).

26 Conn Gen Stat Ann §466-56 (West Supp 1984); Minn Stat Ann §518.17(1) (West Supp 1984).

27 La Civ Code Ann art 146(C)(2)(k) (West Supp 1984).

28 La Civ Code Ann art 146(C)(2)(i) (West Supp 1984). *See* **§8.09.**

of the child;[29] and the threat or incidence of physical violence.[30] The District of Columbia custody statute is unique in that it requires determination of custody "without conclusive regard to the race, color, national origin, political affiliation, sex, or sexual orientation, in and of itself, of a party."[31]

It is also important to note that an increasing number of custody statutes include provisions covering joint or shared custody. These will be discussed in subsequent sections.[32]

While the statutory list of factors is an excellent starting point for the practitioner in the preparation of child custody cases, greater emphasis has been placed on some of the elements, such as status quo, keeping siblings together, the fitness or lifestyles of the parents, race, religion, and others. Some of these factors are discussed in the following sections.[33]

## §8.03 Status Quo

Maintaining the status quo, which provides continuity, stability, or permanence in a child's life, is probably the most important factor in a custody case. Indeed, one group of authors has suggested that the principle that the best interests of children are served by keeping them in an already established environment or stable relationship is so strong that it approaches the level of presumption in child custody law.[34] Consciously or not, judges will give significant weight to the stability factor before uprooting or severing a child from a parent, friends, neighborhood, or school.

It is possible that favoring the status quo in custody cases emanates from the historical property roots of the parent-child relationship.[35] As two prominent family law authorities have noted:

> The longer the custodian succeeds in maintaining possession of the child, regardless of bad faith, the more will contemporary law be inclined to leave the child for its own sake where it was found. While parental rights may have been weakened, the principle of "the best interests of the child" may have inadvertently brought about a result that sometimes resembles acquisition of title in real property by adverse possession.[36]

---

[29] Alaska Stat §25.24.150 (1984); Mass Ann Laws ch 208, §31 (Michie/Law Co-op Supp 1984).

[30] Ill Ann Stat ch 40, §602 (Smith-Hurd 1980).

[31] DC Code Ann §16-911(5) (1981). *See* **§§8.07-8.10.**

[32] *See* **§§9.08-9.09.**

[33] *See* **§§8.03-8.16.**

[34] 2 J. McCahey, M. Kaufman, C. Kraut, D. Gaffner, M. Silverman, & J. Zett, Child Custody and Visitation Law and Practice 10-4 (1983). Many statutes provide that stability, permanence, and continuity must be considered by the court. *See* **§8.02.**

[35] See **§6.02** for a discussion of the historical proprietary aspects of the parent-child relationship.

[36] W. Weyrauch & S. Katz, American Family Law in Transition 496 (1983).

The importance of stability, continuity of environment, and relationships for a child has also been supported by psychiatrists, psychologists, and health professionals who warn against aggravated disruption in the life of a child of divorcing parents.

Judicial consideration of status quo as one aspect in determining the best interests of a child necessarily requires an analysis of interrelated factors. Thus, for example, a court will note which party has had de facto or temporary custody, or custody pendente lite; which party is the primary caretaker or parent; whether either party will keep the marital home or remain in the same neighborhood; the child's performance in school and interaction with peers; the economic feasibility of maintaining the status quo; and the mental and physical stability of the parties.

Factors which courts have specifically considered as important to maintaining the status quo in a child's life include: the stability of the parents' lives;[37] the stability of each parent's home, particularly if the child can stay in the same neighborhood and schools;[38] and the effect of joint custody on that stability.[39]

In addition, other factors reviewed in a best interests determination will be evaluated in terms of their effect on continuity and stability. Courts consider the impact on a child's life of a new marriage or nonmarital cohabitation relationship, the separation of siblings, presence of stepsiblings, or the removal

---

[37] *See, e.g.*, Anderson v Anderson, 121 Ariz 405, 590 P2d 944, 946 (1979) (the court noted that "[t]he total evidentiary picture showed substantially more stability in the life situation of appellee than in that of appellant," where the mother was working long nights, attending school, and participating in other activities which kept her away from home, and the father had daytime jobs and free time to spend with the children).

[38] *See* Johnson v Johnson, 395 So 2d 1043 (Ala Civ App 1981); Campbell v Campbell, 668 SW2d 580 (Mo Ct App 1984); Cole v Cole, 274 SC 449, 265 SE2d 669 (1980).

[39] *See* Elebash v Elebash, 450 So 2d 1268, 1270 (Fla Dist Ct App 1984), where the court overturned the parties' separation agreement which provided that the children's actual physical residence would alternate between the parties every other weekday and weekend. The trial court had found, and the court of appeals agreed, that such an arrangement "deprives [the children] of that stability, security, and comfort which is so necessary in the lives of young children and which is associated with the home and the order and discipline of one single authority."

See also Utley v Utley, 364 A2d 1167, 1170 (DC 1976) where the District of Columbia Appeals held:

> Generally, divided custody of a child of tender years is not favored . . . (citations omitted). Perhaps the reason for this is that an orderly, meaningful, and reasonably secure family life is crucial during the formative years of a child's life. A happy and normal family life is often impossible of accomplishment when a child of tender years is subjected to the frustrating experience of divided custody, especially when in the process he is shifted from home to home, from city to city, or from one family environment to another.

Joint custody is discussed further in **§§9.01-9.16.**

of a child from the jurisdiction. In short, it is essential to consider the introduction of anything which alters or varies the child's norm.

Experience produces a valuable sensitivity to situations which are potentially disruptive to stability in a child's life. The practitioner may enhance and sharpen personal sensitivities and skills by introspectively reflecting on personal experience impacting on healthy and ideal relationships in his or her own life or the lives of others. This process heightens the awareness of the lawyer to potentially disruptive situations and stimulates the inquiry necessary to assist in developing an understanding of the needs of parent and child.

Minimizing disruption in a child's life in the midst of a divorce is a universally accepted goal in family law litigation.

## §8.04 Temporary Custody or Custody Pendente Lite

In many cases, particularly where both parents are fit custodians and enjoy healthy relationships with their children, the party who obtains temporary custody or custody *pendente lite* has the edge in the final determination of child custody. That the child has remained in de facto custody of one parent since separation is frequently the deciding factor in cases because the courts recognize the importance of maintaining stability and continuity in a child's life.[40]

Thus, the practitioner plays an important role with initial advice to a parent about custody. Some parents who are contemplating divorce want to take time to establish themselves in a career or to recover emotionally, and may wish to relinquish the child temporarily to the other spouse. No matter how justifiable the reasons are that influence a parent to decline custody, even if those reasons are beyond the person's control, the overwhelming probability is that that parent, whatever sex, will not regain custody absent some compelling reason. The practitioner must inform the client that the scenario presented in the movie *Kramer vs Kramer* is not what usually happens in real life.[41]

---

[40] *See, e.g., In re* Marriage of Weidner, 338 NW2d 351, 359 (Iowa 1983) ("Although the issue is close, we concur in the trial court's decision that Betsy should be the sole custodian. The children have been physically in her custody more frequently than in Marvin's and she has maintained a good home for them under sorely trying circumstances . . ."); Neis v Neis, 3 Kan App 589, 599 P2d 305, 309 (1979) ("The court especially noted that the children had been in a stable environment since their mother had relinquished custody . . . and that it would be in the best interests of the children to remain with their father"); Spohrer v Spohrer, 428 So 2d 1350, 1354 (La Ct App 1983) ("Our courts have recognized that stability of a child's environment is so crucial that even de facto custody (as here) should not be altered without compelling reasons"); *In re* Matter of Tuttle, 62 Or App 281, 660 P2d 196, 199 (1983) ("it is likewise relevant that the mother has had custody of the children since the parties' separation in January, 1982"). *See* **§8.03.**

[41] In that movie, the mother left her husband and child to "find herself." The father restructured his entire life in order to accommodate caring for the child. When she

Where the parent seeks to regain custody, the court will consider the fact that that parent left the child, and investigate the extent of involvement that parent had in the youngster's life during the absence. Custody will almost always be awarded to the parent who has maintained a close and continuing relationship with the child; removing the child from the parent who has been living with the child might well result in psychological harm to the youngster.

The advice of the lawyer immediately after separation can be the crucial influence in the outcome of the custody case. Failure to move quickly and take determinative steps early in the case may result in the parent's loss of custody simply due to circumstances and passage of time. While these authors do not countenance procedural stalling in a custody case, it is acknowledged that in the vast majority of cases, the parent who obtains custody after separation will probably be awarded permanent custody of the child.

As the Supreme Court of Appeals of West Virginia has stated:

> A few comments are also necessary regarding the proper consideration to be given to the length of time that a parent has enjoyed temporary custody. Voltaire once noted that there is nothing so permanent as a temporary relationship. In cases where temporary custody extends for a period of several years it would be unwise and detrimental to the *child's* best interests to transfer custody unless there is a change of circumstance that makes it in the child's best interest to effect a change. Indeed, we believe that after a sufficient lapse of time it is usually in the best interest of the child to award permanent custody to the custodial parent if the disabled parent has not sought a hearing. In recognizing this fact, however, we do not mean to condone a system in which one parent deliberately delays adjudication of permanent custody to enhance his or her likelihood of getting custody.
>
> Finally, judges may not always believe it is possible to make a definitive judgment on the comparative fitness of parents. In such cases, the fact that one parent has maintained custody of a child for a substantial period should weigh heavily in that parent's favor.[42]

Temporary custody or custody pendente lite does not always work in favor of the custodian, however. This is true in cases where the temporary custodian is guilty of neglect or has created an environment which endangers a child.[43]

---

returned some time later, the mother went to court in order to regain custody of her son. She won, but ultimately let the father (as the psychological parent) keep their child. This result is not what happens in most jurisdictions.

[42] JEI v LMI, 314 SE2d 67, 72 (W Va 1984) (emphasis in original). It might be true that there is a certain sexism or prejudice against mothers who give up custody of their children. Clearly, it has not been traditional until recently for both spouses to live independent lives. Men have long been expected to give priority to a career outside the home, women, inside the home. A mother's reason for leaving a child do not always receive the same acceptance as a father's.

[43] *See, e.g., In re* Marriage of Renow, 624 P2d 365, 366 (Colo Ct App 1981); Anderson

## §8.05 Primary Caretaker

One of the most important factors considered in a child custody determination is the primary caretaker, particularly if the child is under age 10.[44] Such works as *Beyond the Best Interests of the Child*[45] emphasized the importance of the parent's involvement in a child's daily life and needs for physical care, nourishment, comfort, affection, and stimulation. This involvement builds a psychological relationship within which a child can grow up feeling valued and wanted. Psychological studies show that disruption of this relationship can lead to serious damage to the child's personality.[46]

Judicial recognition of the importance of the primary caretaker has mushroomed in the 1980s.[47] Courts now favor awarding custody to the parent most intimately involved in the daily life and care of the child.[48] The primary caretaker is usually what has been called the *psychological parent.* This is the parent who has a close relationship with the child, is experienced in meeting the child's needs, and has demonstrated a commitment to caring for the child which, barring contrary evidence, is likely to continue.[49] Thus, awarding the

---

v Anderson, 240 Ga 795, 242 SE2d 593 (1978); *In re* Marriage of Beitz, 683 P2d 485, 488 (Mont 1984); Auffhammer v Auffhammer, 101 AD2d 929, 475 NYS2d 649 (App Div 1984).

[44] Atkinson, *Criteria for Deciding Child Custody in Trial and Appellate Courts,* 18 Fam LQ 1, 16 (1984).

[45] J. Goldstein, A. Freud, & A. Solnit, Beyond the Best Interests of the Child 17-20 (1973).

[46] *Id* 18, where the authors state: "Where there are changes of parent figure or other hurtful interruptions, the child's vulnerability and the fragility of the relationship become evident. The child regresses along the whole line of his affections, skills, achievements, and social adaptations."

[47] Several factors contributed to the recognition, including: the diminished importance of fault in divorce actions; the concomitant rise of the importance of the best interests of the child; the decline of the maternal preference; and the increased interest of fathers in parenting. In Atkinson, *supra* note 44, at 16, the author notes that in 1982, 14 appellate court opinions from 12 states discussed the primary caretaker factor, including: Alaska, Delaware, Florida, Illinois, Iowa, Louisiana, Minnesota, Montana, North Dakota, Pennsylvania, Utah, and West Virginia.

[48] The parent may be the primary caretaker and awarded the child even if that parent is employed or will become employed outside the home after the divorce. *See* **§8.12;** Lipsey v Lipsey, 450 So 2d 1075 (Ala Civ App 1984); Gatrix v Gatrix, 652 P2d 76 (Alaska Ct App 1982); Agudo v Agudo, 411 So 2d 259 (Fla Dist Ct App 1982); Bankston v Bankston, 355 So 2d 58 (La Ct App 1978); Berndt v Berndt, 292 NW2d 1 (Minn 1980); Leach v Leach, 660 SW2d 761 (Mo Ct App 1983); Dodd v Dodd, 93 Misc 2d 641, 403 NYS2d 401 (1978); *In re* Maxwell, 8 Ohio App 3d 302, 456 NE2d 1218 (1982); Van Dyke v Van Dyke, 48 Or App 965, 618 P2d 465 (1980); Commonwealth *ex rel* Jordan v Jordan, 302 Pa Super 421, 448 A2d 1113 (1982).

[49] Atkinson, *supra* note 44 at 17 (citing Commonwealth *ex rel* Jordan v Jordan, 302 Pa Super 421, 448 A2d 1113, 1115 (1982)).

child to the primary caretaker also furthers important objectives such as maintaining stability and continuity in a child's life.[50]

Most states include the primary caretaker factor as only one of many to be considered in a custody determination. In West Virginia, however, there exists a judicially created presumption in favor of the person who was the primary caretaker "before the domestic strife giving rise to the proceeding began," where the children are of tender years.[51] The Minnesota Supreme Court has issued strong language favoring custody awards to primary caretakers, stating that "[t]he intimacy of the relationship between parent and child to be assumed under such circumstances should not be disrupted without strong reasons which relate specifically to the parent's capacity to provide and care for the child."[52] It is important to note that where both parents share in caring for the child, application of a preference without consideration of other factors may be unfair.[53]

There is no general rule to determine who is a child's primary caretaker. A multitude of factors are considered. Most courts would be inclined to examine which parent was the primary caretaker at the time of divorce, thus acknowledging that the caretaker parent may change from the situation during the marriage to the time of litigation.[54] The court looks to the present and to the foreseeable future in determining child custody. Therefore, it is important to note that as he or she grows older, a child advances through states of psychological development within which needs change. The nature of caretaking when a child is an infant, and requiring daily constant attention, is different from when a child is an adolescent, and requiring discipline, friendship, and guidance. A child may develop psychological relationships with others during these stages, or may rebel against the parent who is present every day. Therefore, it is important that the attorney present each custody case based on the specific facts and circumstances involved.

---

[50] *See* **§8.03.**

[51] Garska v McCoy, 278 SE2d 357, 362-63 (W Va 1981), where the Supreme Court of Appeals of West Virginia held:

> Therefore, in the interest of removing the issue of child custody from the type of acrimonious and counter-productive litigation which a procedure inviting exhaustive evidence will inevitably create, we hold today that there is a presumption in favor of the primary caretaker parent, if he or she meets the minimum, objective standard for being a fit parent . . . regardless of sex. Therefore, in any custody dispute involving children of tender years it is incumbent upon the circuit court to determine as a threshold question which parent was the primary caretaker parent before the domestic strife giving rise to the proceeding began.

[52] Berndt v Berndt, 292 NW2d 1, 2 (Minn 1980). *See also In re* Marriage of Weatherly, 330 NW2d 890, 892 (Minn 1983).

[53] The adoption of a primary caretaker presumption has in fact been criticized as "wooden" and possibly a denial of due process. *See* Atkinson, *supra* note 44, at 18.

[54] J. Goldstein, A. Freud, & J. Solnit, *supra* note 45, at 51. See also Hawaii Rev Stat §571-46(2) (1976), which states, "Any person who has had de facto custody of the child

In every case, the family practitioner should gather probative evidence as to who is the primary caretaker. A checklist including graphic examples evincing the role of the primary caretaker should be prepared in contested custody cases for use in interviews, at depositions, in interrogatories, and at trial. The Supreme Court of Appeals of West Virginia has provided a useful list of "obvious criteria" for a court to examine when deciding which parent is the primary caretaker, including:

> performance of the following caring and nurturing duties of a parent: (1) preparing and planning of meals; (2) bathing, grooming and dressing; (3) purchasing, cleaning, and care of clothes; (4) medical care, including nursing and trips to physicians; (5) arranging for social interaction among peers after school, i.e., transporting to friends' houses or, for example, to girl or boy scout meetings; (6) arranging alternative care, i.e., babysitting, day-care, etc.; (7) putting child to bed at night, attending to child in the middle of the night, waking child in the morning; (8) disciplining, i.e., teaching general manners and toilet training; (9) educating, i.e., religious cultural, social, etc.; and, (10) teaching elementary skills, i.e., reading, writing and arithmetic.[55]

Judges may not have the personal experience in which to develop an understanding of parent and child relationships on a daily basis. The attorney can demonstrate the specific relationship for the court by making an inquiry into customary parent-child activities in open court. For example, when there is an emergency or when the child is injured, to whom does the child turn? When something exciting happens at school, in whom does the child confide? These are questions relevant to the primary caretaker issue which the attorney should ask during preparation and presentation of the case so that the judge may look at the same factors.

## §8.06 Separating Siblings: Split Custody

Split custody involves awarding sole custody of one or more children to one parent and sole custody of the remaining child or children to the other parent.[56] Generally, split custody is not favored by the courts, which follow the widely held reasoning that siblings should be kept together so they may enjoy the normal condition of childhood in growing up as brothers and sisters.

While one group of authors has suggested that there exists a presumption against separating siblings,[57] it is more correct to state that there is a preference and strong public policy favoring keeping siblings together after their parents'

---

in a stable and wholesome home and is a fit and proper person shall prima facie be entitled to an award of custody."

[55] Garska v McCoy, 278 SE2d 357, 363 (W Va 1981).

[56] A. Haralambie, Handling Child Custody Cases 31 n 81 (Shepard's/McGraw-Hill 1983).

[57] 2 J. McCahey, M. Kaufman, C. Kraut, D. Gaffner, M. Silverman, & J. Zett, Child Custody and Visitation Law and Practice §10-4 (1983) (hereinafter cited as J. McCahey).

divorce.[58] Thus, the general rule in most states is that, absent exceptional circumstances or clear and compelling reasons, children of divorced parents should not be separated.[59] This is not an absolute rule, however, since it is governed by the guiding principle of the best interests of the children, as are all aspects of child custody cases. Thus, split custody decrees are not a per se abuse of discretion, and will be upheld if there is substantial evidence to support the award, and overturned if the award is against the weight of the evidence or erroneously declares or applies the law.

Separating siblings has been justified for several reasons, many of which once again highlight the interrelation of factors considered in a determination of a child's best interests. Some siblings have been separated when one child was the natural child of one parent, while the other child was the natural child of both parents.[60] Such a separation was justified by one court which noted that the child who was not the natural child of both parents required the stability and continuity supplied by his natural parent.[61] However, there have been cases where all children have been awarded to one parent so that the siblings might stay together, even where that party was not the natural parent of some of the children.[62]

An influential factor in split custody situations is the preference of the children. Many states statutorily provide that a court should consider a child's preference if the child is of suitable age, maturity, and intelligence,[63] and generally most courts will consider the child's wishes in the absence of statutory mandate. In split custody cases, a child's preference to be separated will usually prevail when combined with other factors, such as a gap between the siblings' ages,[64] a child's special and healthy relationship with one parent,[65] or a parent's

---

[58] In fact, one court has placed the policy against separating siblings under its "family solidarity doctrine." *See* Gilcrense v Gilcrense, 438 So 2d 658 (La Ct App 1983). See also J. McCahey *supra* note 57, at §10-4, where the authors have noted that some courts have described keeping the siblings together "a moral duty." The Minnesota Supreme Court has, in fact, termed a decree of split custody "unfortunate." *See* Schultze v Schultze, 226 Minn 205, 208, 123 NW2d 118, 121 (1963).

[59] *See, e.g.*, Collier v Collier, 384 So 2d 697 (Fla Dist Ct App 1980); Bezou v Bezou, 436 So 2d 592 (La Ct App 1981); Dutton v Dutton, 668 SW2d 585 (Mo Ct App 1984); Atwood v Atwood, 664 SW2d 673 (Mo Ct App 1984); Zuniga v Zuniga, 664 SW2d 810 (Tex Ct App 1984); Annot, 98 ALR2d 926 (1964).

[60] *See, e.g., In re* Marriage of Larkin, __ Ind App __, 462 NE2d 1338 (Ind Ct App 1984); Bezou v Bezou, 436 So 2d 592 (La Ct App 1981); Chambard v Chambard, 348 NW2d 821 (Minn 1984).

[61] *See* Chambard v Chambard, 348 NW2d 821, 823 (Minn 1984); **§8.03.**

[62] Tardzer v Tardzer, 441 So 2d 934 (Ala Civ App 1983).

[63] See **§8.02** for a review of statutory factors in a best interests of the child determination. *See also* **§8.11.**

[64] *See, e.g.*, Walls v Walls, 227 Ark 191, 297 SW2d 648 (1957); Brown v Brown, 409 So 2d 1133 (Fla Dist Ct App 1982); *In re* Marriage of Larkin, __ Ind App __, 462 NE2d 1338 (Ind Ct App 1984); *In re* Neff, 193 NW2d 82 (Iowa 1971); Bezou v Bezou, 436 So 2d 592 (La Ct App 1983).

[65] Atwood v Atwood, 664 SW2d 673 (Mo Ct App 1984).

difficulty in properly parenting one or more of the children.[66] The children's preferences weigh heavily with appellate courts where the siblings were split against their wishes for no compelling reasons.[67]

The separation of siblings should only be ordered by a court for reasons which, when considered together, indicate that it is in the best interests of the children to do so. Courts are sometimes more willing to order split custody when the visitation schedule provides the siblings with ample time to be together.[68] In addition, it is important to note that the preference for keeping siblings together is considerably less persuasive where custody was split initially and a modification of the custody award to bring the siblings back together is sought years later.[69]

Therefore, absent extraordinary circumstances, the practitioner should not encourage the client to pursue a split custody arrangement.

## §8.07 Religion

Religious freedom is one of the most fervently protected liberties in this country. The First Amendment, applicable to the states through the Fourteenth Amendment, provides in pertinent part that "Congress shall make no law respecting an establishment of religion, or prohibiting the free exercise thereof. . . ." The Establishment Clause of the First Amendment guarantees government neutrality in matters touching upon religion, and prohibits the establishment of any religion by the government; the Free Exercise Clause recognizes the individual's liberty in religious matters. While the freedom to believe is absolute, the freedom to act is subject to regulation for society's protection. However, action associated with religious belief may be regulated for "only the gravest abuses, endangering paramount interests."[70]

In this society based on religious liberty, it is not surprising that religion is sometimes a difficult issue in child custody cases. The questions involving religion in custody disputes focus on whether, and to what extent, religion may be considered in a judicial analysis of a child's best interests without infringing any constitutional rights. Another issue involves the enforceability of agree-

---

[66] *See, e.g.*, Hild v Hild, 221 Md 349, 157 A2d 442 (1960); Hornbeck v Hornbeck, 316 Mich 208, 25 NW2d 171 (1946); Zuniga v Zuniga, 664 SW2d 810 (Tex Ct App 1984).

[67] *See, e.g.*, *In re* Marriage of Mihalovich, 659 SW2d 798 (Mo Ct App 1983); Boroff v Boroff, 197 Neb 641, 250 NW2d 613 (1977); *In re* Marriage of Moe, 66 Or App 947, 676 P2d 336 (1984). In the latter two cases, the appellate court held that the trial court's placing the daughter with the mother for no reason except a maternal preference was an abuse of discretion.

[68] *See, e.g., In re* Marriage of Larkin, 462 NE2d 1338 (Ind App 1984); Atwood v Atwood, 664 SW2d 673 (Mo Ct App 1984) (brother and sister would see each other every weekend and for eight weeks in the summer).

[69] *See In re* Marriage of Scott, 31 Or App 975, 571 P2d 1281 (1977).

[70] Sherbert v Verner, 374 US 398, 406 (1963).

ments between the parents or court orders as to the religious education of the child.

At least five state statutes provide that courts may consider religion in custody determinations.[71] It is fair to say that even in states where custody statutes are silent on religion, courts consider religion generally when evaluating home environments, educational opportunities, status quo, and the child's wishes.[72] For example, courts often favor the continuation of religious training as promoting the welfare of children, and, after evaluating the child's own preferences and involvement in religion, may award the child to the parent better able to satisfy the actual, demonstrated religious needs of that child.[73]

Some appellate courts have upheld custody awards where the trial court considered that one parent was religious while the other one was not.[74] However, it has been held that the Establishment Clause of the First Amendment prevents a court from preferring the religion of one parent over that of another when awarding child custody.[75]

The Supreme Court of the United States has decided that the Free Exercise Clause of the First Amendment protects parents' interests in the religious

---

[71] *See* Alaska Stat §25.24.150(c)(1) (1983) ("The court shall consider (1) the physical, emotional, mental, religious and social needs of the child"); Hawaii Rev Stat §571-46(5) (1976) ("The court may hear the testimony of any person or expert . . . [whose] testimony is relevant to a just and reasonable determination of what is to be the best physical, mental, moral, and spiritual well-being of the child . . ."); Mich Stat Ann §25.312(3)(6) (Callaghan 1984); Minn Stat Ann §518.17(h) (West Supp 1984), expressing it similarly ("The capacity and disposition of the parties to give the child love, affection, and guidance, and to continue educating and raising the child in his culture and religion or creed, if any"); Wis Stat Ann §767.24(2)(c) (West 1981) ("The child's adjustment to the home, school, religion, and community").

[72] Annot, 66 ALR2d 1410, 1414-15 (1959), where it is stated, with cited cases as supporting authority:

> Even in the absence of any particular issue as to whether a child should be raised in one religion or another, the courts in awarding custody have referred, in passing, to the good religious standing or qualifications of the custodian chosen, or to the facts that one choice or another would best promote the child's religious or spiritual welfare or that in the home chosen the child would have superior facilities for church attendance or religious training.

*See also* Annot, 22 ALR4th 971, 987-90 (1983).

[73] *See, e.g.*, Bonjour v Bonjour, 592 P2d 1233 (Alaska 1979); Allison v Ovens, 4 Ariz App 496, 421 P2d 929 (1966); T H, 102 NJ Super 38, 245 A2d 221 (1968), *affd*, 110 NJ Super 8, 264 A2d 244 (1970); Martin v Martin, 308 NY 136, 123 NE2d 812 (1954).

[74] *See, e.g.*, Plum v Plum, 252 Ark 340, 478 SW2d 882 (1972); *In re* Marriage of Ford, 91 Ill App 3d 1066, 47 Ill Dec 541, 415 NE2d 546 (1980); *In re* Marriage of Moorhead, 224 NW2d 242 (Iowa 1974); Dean v Dean, 32 NC App 482, 232 SE2d 470 (1970); Crounse v Crounse, 207 Va 524, 151 SE2d 412 (1966).

[75] *See, e.g.*, Smith v Smith, 90 Ariz 190, 367 P2d 230 (1961); McLaughlin v McLaughlin, 20 Conn Supp 278, 132 A2d 420 (1957); Compton v Gilmore, 98 Idaho 190, 560 P2d 861 (1977); Harris v Harris, 343 So 2d 762 (Miss 1967); Angel v Angel, 2 Ohio Op 2d 136, 140 NE2d 86 (1956). *See also* Scanlon v Scanlon, 29 NJ Super 317, 102 A2d 656 (1954); *cf* Commonwealth *ex rel* Derr v Derr, 148 Pa Super 511, 25 A2d 769 (1942).

upbringing of their children.[76] This topic may be a source of disagreement between divorcing parents requiring delicate judicial action. Generally, courts have not specifically enforced antenuptial agreements requiring that the children be raised in a particular faith where such enforcement would not be in the best interests of the child.[77] Yet, divorcing parents may contract to raise their children in observance of a particular religious lifestyle,[78] and courts sometimes impose terms or conditions in the custody award which pertain to the religious upbringing of the child.[79] In Florida, it has been held that when parents disagree about the religious upbringing of their child, a court may properly order that a child continue a particular religious training because of that state's *shared parental responsibility* act, which directs courts to require shared parental responsibility in all cases unless detrimental to the child.[80]

At least one court has urged that any inquiry into the parents' religious practices should be avoided in the same manner as courts avoid constitutional questions, and that courts should make "a preliminary determination of the child's best interest, *without giving any consideration to either parent's religious practices,* in order to ascertain which of them is the preferred custodial parent"

---

[76] Wisconsin v Yoder, 406 US 205 (1971), where the Supreme Court held, after an investigation of the history, tradition, and beliefs of the Amish people, and after a balancing of the Amish claims and the state's compelling reasons, that the First and Fourteenth Amendments prevented the state of Wisconsin from forcing the Amish respondents to attend formal high school to the age of 16, contrary to their religious beliefs. Among the pertinent discussion was a reference to Pierce v Society of Sisters, 268 US 510 (1925), in which the Supreme Court held that the state could not compel parents to send their children to public schools instead of private schools. The Court, in *Wisconsin* stated, "However read, the Court's holding in *Pierce* stands as a charter of the rights of parents to direct the religious upbringing of their children." 406 US at 233.

[77] *In re* Marriage of Wolfert, 42 Colo App 433, 598 P2d 524 (1979); McLaughlin v McLaughlin, 20 Conn Supp 278, 132 A2d 420 (1957); Annot, 12 ALR 1153 (1921).

[78] See, e.g., Perlstein v Perlstein, 76 AD2d 49, 429 NYS2d 896 (1980), where the parents had contracted to raise their child as an Orthodox Jew and the custodial mother subsequently abandoned practically all the ritualistic and fundamentalistic aspects of that religion. The New York Supreme Court remanded the case for a new trial in which the mother was required to carry the burden of proving that the observance of the religious guidelines as enumerated in the separation agreement were detrimental to the child's welfare. *See also* Butler v Butler, 132 So 2d 437 (Fla Dist Ct App 1961); Stern v Stern, 40 Ill App 2d 374, 188 NE2d 97 (1963); Wagshal v Wagshal, 249 Md 143, 238 A2d 903 (1968). *Contra* Stanton v Stanton, 213 Ga 545, 100 SE2d 289 (1957); Call v Call, 250 Iowa 1175, 98 NW2d 335 (1959); O'Neill v O'Neill, 45 Misc 2d 1, 255 NYS2d 776 (Sup Ct 1965).

[79] *See, e.g.,* Sullivan v Sullivan, 141 Conn 235, 104 A2d 898 (1954); Reace v Reace, 39 Ill App 3d 496, 350 NE2d 143 (1976); Hodge v Hodge, 186 So 2d 748 (Miss 1966); DiCroce v DiCroce, 27 Misc 2d 1035, 209 NYS2d 624 (Sup Ct 1961); Weiss v Weiss, 53 Misc 2d, 262, 278 NYS2d 61 (Sup Ct 1967). *Contra* Wilhelm v Wilhelm, 504 SW2d 699 (Ky Ct App 1973); Paolella v Phillips, 27 Misc 2d 763, 209 NYS2d 165 (Sup Ct 1960).

[80] Vasquez v Vasquez, 443 So 2d 313 (Fla Dist Ct App 1983); *see also* **§9.12.**

(emphasis in original).[81] While many courts do consider religion in their best interests analysis, the majority rule is that religion cannot be the determinative factor in the custody award.[82] It has been held in many states that a trial court may not refuse to award a child to an otherwise fit parent simply because of that parent's unorthodox beliefs.[83]

In many states, specific rules regarding consideration of religion in custody cases have developed in the case law. For example, in New York, courts will consider religion in a custody dispute:

> when a child has developed actual religious ties to a specific religion and those needs can be better served by one parent than the other . . . , when a religious belief violates a State statute . . . , and when a religious belief poses a threat to a child's well-being.[84]

A series of cases involving parents with unorthodox beliefs, a surprising number of them Jehovah's Witnesses, have produced narrow rulings in custody cases which parallel rulings involving religion generally. These cases, with minor variations, have held that evidence of a parent's religious practices is inadmissible unless the proponent of such evidence establishes that those practices will harm or endanger the child's well-being.[85] The variations in these

---

[81] Osier v Osier, 410 A2d 1027, 1029 (Me 1980).

[82] *See, e.g.,* Quiner v Quiner, 59 Cal Rptr 503 (1967); *In re* Marriage of Short, 675 P2d 323 (Colo Ct App 1983); *In re* Marriage of Grandinette, 342 NW2d 876 (Iowa Ct App 1983); Jackson v Jackson, 181 Kan 1, 309 P2d 705 (1957); Osier v Osier, 410 A2d 1027 (Me 1980); Aldous v Aldous, 99 AD2d 197, 473 NYS2d 61 (1984); Dean v Dean, 32 NC App 482, 232 SE2d 470 (1977); Stone v Stone, 16 Wash 2d 315, 133 P2d 526 (1943). If there is ample evidence supporting a custody award to one parent, that award will not be vacated even if the court's consideration of religion was impermissible. *See* Aldous v Aldous, 99 AD2d 197, 473 NYS2d 61 (1984).

[83] *See, e.g.,* Johnson v Johnson, 564 P2d 71 (Alaska), *cert denied,* 434 US 1048 (1977); *In re* Marriage of Urband, 678 Cal App 3d 796, 137 Cal Rptr 433 (1977); Quiner v Quiner, 59 Cal Rptr 503 (1967); *In re* Marriage of Short, 675 P2d 323 (Colo Ct App 1983); Stone v Stone, 16 Wash 2d 315, 133 P2d 526 (1943). In Smith v Smith, 90 Ariz 190, 367 P2d 230, 233 (1961), the Supreme Court of Arizona addressed this issue, elaborately noting:

> We are not unaware that deviation from the normal often brings ridicule and criticism. We reject, however, the notion that it is necessarily the basis for implanting neuroses. Criticism is the crucible in which character is tested. Conformity stifles the intellect[,] fathering decadency. New ideas are the rungs upon which mankind supports itself in the long climb to perfection. It is sufficient to say until then, man's personality is not to be warped into a universal mold. A judgment supported only by the tenuous trends of a possible neurosis derived from deviation in normal activities will not withstand the thrust of constitutional guarantees.

[84] Aldous v Aldous, 99 AD2d 197, 473 NYS2d 61 (1984) (citations omitted).

[85] *See, e.g.,* Smith v Smith, 90 Ariz 190, 367 P2d 230 (1961); *In re* Marriage of Urband, 68 Cal App 3d 796, 137 Cal Rptr 443 (1977); Quiner v Quiner, 59 Cal Rptr 509 (1967); *In re* Marriage of Short, 675 P2d 323 (Colo Ct App 1983); *In re* Marriage of Hadeer,

cases center on the harm or endangerment element. As noted by the Court of Appeals of Washington:

> Cases involving religion as an aspect of custody dispute generally comport with the language of *Wisconsin v Yoder* [406 US 205 (1972)], regarding a showing that the parental decisions will jeopardize the child's health or safety. The showing that must be made and the test involved in the determination of when jeopardy must arise are, however, subject to significant dispute.[86]

One line of cases holds that, because of the danger of infringement of First Amendment rights, the evidence in a child custody case involving religion must establish that there is a substantial probability of harm, or that actual impairment of the child's well-being exists because of a parent's religious practices.[87] The less rigid test employed by other courts requires a showing that a parent's religious practices could be reasonably considered dangerous to a child, or that such practices will pose a reasonable and substantial likelihood of immediate or future impairment.[88]

It is obvious that different states, by statute and case law, place different emphasis on religion as an issue in child custody cases. In addition, the constitutional issue is constantly lurking in the background. For an excellent review of custody cases involving religious issues, *see* Annot, 22 ALR 4th 971 (1983).

## §8.08 Race

Since the Supreme Court's decision in *Loving v Virginia*,[89] which struck down miscegenation statutes as a violation of equal protection and due process, there has been a steady increase in the number of interracial marriages.[90] It has been argued that the disturbing and pervasive racial prejudice which persists in this country means that interracial couples and their children will endure extraordinary tension and unique pressures both during marriage and upon divorce.[91]

---

27 Wash App 566, 619 P2d 374 (1980); Welker v Welker, 24 Wis 2d 570, 129 NW2d 134 (1964).

[86] *In re* Marriage of Hadeen, 27 Wash App 566, 619 P2d 374, 380 (1980).

[87] *See, e.g.*, Quiner v Quiner, 59 Cal Rptr 503 (1967); *In re* Marriage of Short, 675 P2d 323 (Colo Ct App 1983).

[88] *See, e.g.*, Clift v Clift, 346 So 2d 419 (Ala Civ App 1977); Staply v Staply, 15 Ariz App 64, 485 P2d 1181 (1971); *In re* Marriage of Hadeen, 27 Wash App 566, 619 P2d 374 (1980); Welker v Welker, 24 Wis 2d 570, 129 NW2d 134 (1964).

[89] 388 US 1 (1967). *See* S. Green & J. Long, Marriage and Family Law Agreements ch 1 (Shepard's/McGraw-Hill 1984).

[90] Note, *Custody Disputes Following the Dissolution of Interracial Marriage: Best Interests of the Child or Judicial Racism,* 19 J Fam L 97, 100-01 (1980-81).

[91] *Id* 102.

Custody battles resulting from the breakup of interracial marriages and from custodial spouses' interracial remarriages have produced "unique challenges to the wisdom of the courts."[92]

Generally, race or culture becomes a difficult issue in two fact patterns. One common scenario involves parents of different races or cultures battling for the custody of their children who may or may not physically resemble one parent. In the other repeated fact pattern, the custodial parent remarries someone of a different race, precipitating a modification proceeding by the noncustodial parent.

Courts have responded to the issue of race as a factor in the best interests analysis in two ways. Some courts have decided that racial differences are not relevant to a custody award, while others have held that race is one of many factors that a court may consider in its deliberations, although race may not be the determinative factor in awarding custody.[93] Nevertheless, some courts have been accused of perpetuating prejudices in custody cases.[94]

In several cases courts have held that racial considerations were not, at least under the circumstances presented, relevant in deciding which parent was best suited to have custody of the children. The Pennsylvania courts have consistently held that problems related to racial identity are inapplicable in custody proceedings.[95] For example, in *Commonwealth ex rel Lucas v Kreischer,*[96] the white custodial mother remarried a black man, prompting her white former husband to take the children of the first marriage away from her and institute an action to change custody. The trial court, which acknowledged that both parents were fit, awarded the children to the father based on the size and rural location of the father's residence and the possibility that the children would be the victims of the "almost universal prejudice and intolerance of interracial

---

[92] *Id* 103.

[93] Annot, 10 ALR4th 796, 798-99 (1981).

[94] *See, e.g.,* Grossman, *A Child of a Different Color: Race as a Factor in Adoption and Custody Proceedings,* 17 Buffalo L Rev 303, 326 (1968) (author declares that there exists a "reluctance on the part of many judges to allow a white child to grow up with a Negro stepfather"); Note, *supra* note 90, at 105 (author states, "This discussion of biracial custody cases begins, then, with the logical presumption that judges are not more or less prejudiced than anyone else. Add . . . the fact that judges are granted a great deal of discretion in resolving custody disputes and one begins to understand the potential misuse of race as a decisionmaking factor . . ."); Comment, *Child Custody—Interracial Marriage May Be Considered in Framing Custody Modification Orders—Niles v Niles, 299 So2d 162 (Fla 2d Dist Ct App 1974),* 3 Fla St UL Rev 195, 290 (1975) (declaring "[C]ourts now tend to reason that, because our society has not yet overcome racial prejudice, children raised in interracial homes will inevitably be exposed to detrimental pressures").

[95] Milligan v Davison, 244 Pa Super 255, 367 A2d 299 (1976); Commonwealth *ex rel* Meyers v Meyers, 468 Pa Super 134, 360 A2d 587 (1976); Commonwealth *ex rel* Lucas v Kreischer, 450 Pa Super 352, 299 A2d 243 (1973).

[96] 450 Pa Super 352, 299 A2d 243 (1973).

marriage."[97] In reversing the award to the father, the Supreme Court of Pennsylvania noted that there was no evidence that the children had any problems arising out of the mother's second marriage. It adopted language from a dissenting opinion below, which stated: "In a multi-racial society such as ours racial prejudice and tension are inevitable. If . . . children are raised in a happy and stable home, they will be able to cope with prejudice and hopefully learn that people are unique individuals who should be judged as such."[98]

In addition to the state courts which have held that race has no relevance in custody proceedings,[99] the Supreme Court of the United States held in *Palmore v Sidoti*[100] that changing custody from a white mother (remarried to a black man) to the white father, based on possible future social stigmatization of the child, was a violation of equal protection. The Supreme Court stated:

> The question, however, is whether the reality of private biases and the possible injury they might inflict are permissible considerations for removal of an infant child from the custody of its natural mother. We have little difficulty concluding that they are not. The Constitution cannot control such prejudices but neither can it tolerate them. . . . The effects of racial prejudice, however real, cannot justify a racial classification removing an infant child from the custody of its natural mother found to be an appropriate person to have such custody.[101]

---

[97] *Id* 245.

[98] *Id* 246.

[99] *See, e.g.*, Murphy v Murphy, 143 Conn 600, 124 A2d 891 (1956) (custody of daughter changed to father where mother married a black dentist; court held that the trial court did not even consider race in the modification award, looking only at the fact that the mother was excommunicated from the church, did not provide her child with religious education, and alienated her parents from the child); Stingley v Wesch, 77 Ill App 2d 472, 222 NE2d 505 (1966) (court held that the race of a child's stepfather was not significant in a case where a custodial mother's mother was attempting to obtain custody of her grandchild); Potter v Potter, 372 Mich 637, 127 NW2d 320 (1964) (held that trial court did not even consider race when it changed custody from mother who married a black surgeon and left the state in violation of a divorce decree to the father); *In re* H, 305 NE2d 815 (1973) where court held that a mother did not forfeit the custody of her illegitimate child because of her marriage to a black man. In relevant language, the Court of Common Pleas of Ohio stated:

> Irrespective of the chances for success or failure of bi-racial or other "mixed" marriages and in spite of abounding prejudice of all kinds (racial, ethical, and religious) the American "melting pot" will continue to bring about the marital union of persons of different racial, religious and cultural backgrounds. *The law wisely does not and should not interfere with this process.*

*Id* 819 (emphasis added).

[100] 466 US 429 (1984).

[101] *Id* 433 (footnotes omitted). See also Beazley v Davis, 92 Nev 81, 545 P2d 206 (1976), where the Supreme Court of Nevada remanded a case where the mother was denied a change of custody solely on racial considerations. The trial court relied on the fact that the children involved were children of an interracial marriage and strongly

Other state courts have held that race is a factor which may be considered in a custody determination.[102] An often-cited case is *Fountaine v Fountaine,*[103] where a white mother appealed an order denying a change of custody from the black father, a convicted rapist who had been awarded the children upon the divorce because the mother had had no means to provide for them. The trial court, noting that the mother had subsequently married a white man and moved into an interracial neighborhood, declared that but for the color of the children, who resembled their black father, it would have awarded the children to the mother. The Appellate Court of Illinois held that the trial court abused its discretion by basing its decision solely on race, but in remanding, declared that race was a relevant consideration which could not "overweigh all other considerations and be decisive of the question."[104]

The District of Columbia statute provides that a court may decide custody issues "without *conclusive* regard to the race, color, national origin, political affiliation, sex, or sexual orientation, in and of itself, of a party."[105] One commentator has argued that the *Fountaine* rule, and presumably, the District of Columbia statute, fall short of equal protection requirements and has proposed an alternative: "To satisfy equal protection requirements, then, the rule should be that an interracial environment is relevant to a change-of-custody determination only to the extent that it has produced specific racial abuse affecting the specific child."[106]

---

resembled their black father. The white mother remarried a white man, and sought to regain custody of her children. The Nevada Supreme Court stated that "[i]n the absence of a showing that race in custody proceedings is necessary to the accomplishment of a permissible State Policy, such a consideration would constitute an impermissible discrimination in violation of the Fourteenth Amendment." *Id* 208.

[102] *See, e.g.,* White v Appleton, 53 Ala App 702, 304 So 2d 206 (1974); Goldman v Hicks, 241 Ala 80, 1 So 2d 18 (1941) (court held that a divorced mother's remarriage to a man of the "Jewish race" did not create a condition rendering her unfit or unsuitable to have custody of her child); Niles v Niles, 299 So 2d 162 (Fla Dist Ct App 1974); Langir v Langir, 2 Ill App 3d 544, 276 NE2d 822 (1971); *In re* Marriage of Kramer, 297 NW2d 359 (Iowa 1980); Tucker v Tucker, 14 Wash App 454, 542 P2d 789 (1975). The *Tucker* case is interesting because the black father who wanted custody of his children who resembled him relied on Ward v Ward, 36 Wash 2d 143, 216 P2d 755 (1950), where the court awarded black children to their black father instead of their white mother stating, "These unfortunate girls, through no fault of their own, are the victims of a mixed marriage and a broken home. They will have a much better opportunity to take their rightful place in society if they are brought up among their own people." *Id* 756. The *Tucker* court refused to follow the *Ward* decision, stating "We believe that the [Supreme Court of Washington] would specifically overrule the unfortunate language upon which the father relies if the issue was again before the court." 542 P2d at 791.

[103] 9 Ill App 2d 482, 133 NE2d 532 (1956).

[104] *Id* 535.

[105] DC Code Ann §16-911(a)(5) (1981).

[106] Comment, *supra* note 94, at 299. The author continues

> Such a rule would also satisfy due process requirements. The Fountaine rule arguably interferes with fourteenth amendment liberties to "marry, establish a home and bring up children," since the rule may discourage parents with custody

It is obvious that there are sensitivities where race is considered in an award of child custody. The majority of courts give weight to the race factor, whether stated or unstated. However, it is important that race not be the deciding factor in a best interest analysis.

## §8.09 Culture

In custody disputes between parents of differing cultural backgrounds, courts must again take care not to favor one culture over another in making the award, just as courts must not favor one race or religion over another race or religion.[107] Only two state statutes list culture as a factor to be considered in a custody award.[108] Some courts have held that culture or, more specifically, cultural dissimilarity may be considered in a best interests analysis.[109]

One example of a custody case where culture was an issue was *Carle v Carle*,[110] where the Supreme Court of Alaska reversed an award of custody of a child to the mother and remanded the case for further proceedings. Both parents were Alaskan Indians, and their financial and employment situations forced them to leave their child with members of their extended family, both during the marriage and after their divorce. The custody dispute arose when the mother, who was involved with a nonnative whom she planned to marry, wanted to take the child away from the native extended family to Juneau. The trial court considered many factors in its deliberations, including "whether this child is to be reared in a Native culture in a village or in the Anglo-Saxon culture in a developed community."[111] The trial court decided that because the village way of life was succumbing to modern urban society, the child would probably thrive better with its mother in Juneau.

The Supreme Court of Alaska held that consideration of that cultural factor was "utilization of impermissible criteria,"[112] and stated:

> We think it is not permissible, in a bicultural context, to decide a child's custody on the hypothesis that it is necessary to facilitate the child's adjustment to what is believed to be the dominant culture. . . . Here the differing lifestyles flowing from the two cultures have significance in

---

> of their children from entering into interracial marriages, and may deprive parents who have already entered into such marriages of custody.

*Id* 300.

[107] 2 J. McCahey, M. Kaufman, C. Kraut, D. Gaffner, M. Silberman, & J. Zett, Child Custody & Visitation Law and Practice §10-48 (1983). *See* **§§8.07-8.08.**

[108] *See, e.g.*, Ill Ann Stat ch 40, §602 (Smith-Hurd 1980); Minn Stat Ann §518.17(i) (West Supp 1984).

[109] *See, e.g.:* Carle v Carle, 503 P2d 1050 (Alaska 1972); *In re* Marriage of Mahalingan, 21 Wash App 228, 584 P2d 971 (1978).

[110] 503 P2d 1050 (Alaska 1972).

[111] *Id* 1054.

[112] *Id* 1055.

determining which parent could provide the best possible parent-child relationship. In such circumstances, we deem it inappropriate to decide the custody issue on the basis of cultural assumptions which are not borne out by the record.[113]

Thus, with the cultural factor, as with all factors in child custody cases, the focal point is the impact on the welfare of the child.

## §8.10 Preference of the Child

The child, as the subject of the custody dispute, has significant immediate and lasting interests in the decision reached by the court.[114] The child's preference is usually considered in a custody determination, not because the child has a legal right to have his or her wishes granted,[115] but because such consideration promotes a custody decree based on the child's best interests. Indeed, experienced attorneys, judges, and mental health specialists generally agree that a child does not always express his or her preference on sound grounds; that children do not always mean what they say or say what they mean. Psychotherapists point out, moreover, that determination of a child's preferences is a delicate and sometimes difficult task.

Case law on the child's preference in custody actions exists in almost every state, the earliest of which dates back over 150 years.[116] Consideration of the preference has been an exercise in broad judicial discretion. Over the years courts have developed standards as to the admissibility and weight of the wishes of the child, some of which have been incorporated into modern custody statutes.

The universal rule is that the child's preference in a custody dispute is not

---

[113] *Id.*

[114] These interests, in order of importance to the child, include: physical, emotional, and psychological well-being; continuing relationships with noncustodial parent and other family members; continuing access to friends, neighborhood, school, and social activities; support factors, including tuition, camp, lessons, allowances, and other special costs. Overall, children need a quick and harmonious resolution of custody disputes. *See* Note, *Lawyering for the Child: Principles of Representation in Custody and Visitation Disputes Arising from Divorce.* 87 Yale LJ 1126, 1129-34 (1978).

[115] Cf Ga Code Ann §19-9-1(a) (Supp 1984), which provides, "In all such cases in which the child has reached the age of 14 years, the child shall have the right to select the parent with whom he desires to live." Advocates of children's rights may very well argue that a child of a certain age does have a right to choose which parent with whom he or she shall live.

[116] Siegal & Hurley, *The Role of the Child's Preference in Custody Proceedings,* 11 Fam LQ 1, 1 (1977) (citing Smith v Smith, 6 Me 462 (1830); Foster v Alston, 4 Miss (6 Howard) 155 (1842); Marshall v Reams, 32 Fla 499, 14 So 95 (1893)). *See also* early cases cited in Annot, 4 ALR3d 1396 (1965).

controlling, but is subordinated to the best interests of the child.[117] Courts, in a procedure which has evolved through the years, make a preliminary admissibility determination based upon whether the child is of sufficient age, maturity, and mental capacity to make an informed and intelligent choice.[118] Some courts have arbitrarily established that children of certain ages are unable to make a rational choice,[119] while others examine the particular characteristics of the individual child before them.[120]

Custody statutes provide different standards for admissibility of evidence of the child's preference. A number of statutes codify the common law rule, providing that courts consider the preference of the child if the child is of sufficient age, intelligence, understanding, experience, and capability to express that preference.[121] Oklahoma's law is purely discretionary, in that a court may consider an expression of preference by the child in determining custody but only after finding that the child's choice will serve its best interests.[122] Without the benefit of a preliminary finding as to capacity to choose, some statutes mandate that considerable weight be given to the child's

---

[117] *See, e.g.,* Livengood v Sechler, 382 So 2d 567 (Ala Civ App 1980); *In re* Marriage of Hopson, 110 Cal App 3d 884, 168 Cal Rptr 345 (1980); Garvey v Garvey, 383 So 2d 1172 (Fla Dist Ct App 1980); Cope v Cope, 98 Idaho 920, 576 P2d 201 (1978); Rizzo v Rizzo, 95 Ill App 3d 636, 420 NE2d 555 (1981); *In re* Marriage of Burham, 283 NW2d 269 (Iowa 1979); Schramm v Simpson, 343 So 2d 423 (La Ct App 1977); Albright v Albright, 437 So 2d 1003 (Miss 1983); Krohn v Krohn, 217 Neb 148, 347 NW2d 869 (1984); Mayer v Mayer, 150 NJ Super 556, 376 A2d 214 (1977); Sooy v Sooy, 101 AD2d 287, 475 NYS2d 920 (1984); Campbell v Campbell, 63 NC App 113, 304 SE2d 262 (1983); *In re* Marriage of Moe, 66 Or App 947, 676 P2d 336 (1984); Commonwealth *ex rel* Pierce v Pierce, 493 Pa 292, 426 A2d 555 (1981); Jasper v Jasper, 351 NW2d 114 (SD 1984).

[118] Siegal & Hurley, *supra* note 116, at 2.

[119] *See, e.g., In re* Marriage of Cavitt, 564 SW2d 53 (Mo Ct App 1978) (an 8-year-old child usually cannot have a rational basis for a preference as to which parent should have custody); *In re* Marriage of Tweeten, 172 Mont 404, 563 P2d 1141 (1977) (unnecessary for trial court to interview 3-year-old child as to preference); Feltman v Feltman, 99 AD2d 540, 471 NYS2d 619 (1984) (child of 11 is not mature enough to intelligently weigh factors necessary to make a wise choice as to his or her custody).

[120] Siegal & Hurley, *supra* note 116, at 2 (citing Ross v Pick, 199 Md 341, 86 A2d 463, 469 (Md 1952); Aske v Aske, 233 Minn 540, 542, 47 NW2d 417, 419 (1951)).

[121] *See* Cal Civ Code §4600 (Deering 1984); Conn Gen Stat Ann §466-56 (West Supp 1984); Fla Stat Ann §61.13(3)(i) (West Supp 1984); Hawaii Rev Stat §571-46(3) (Supp 1984); La Civ Code Ann art 146 C(2)(i) (West Supp 1984); Me Rev Stat Ann tit 19, §752(5)(c) (Supp 1984-85); Mich Stat Ann §25.312(3)(i) (West Supp 1984); Minn Stat Ann §518.17(1)(b) (Callaghan Supp 1984); Neb Rev Stat §41-364(1)(b) (1978); Nev Rev Stat §125.480 (1983); ND Cent Code §14-09-06.2(9) (1981).

[122] Okla Stat Ann tit 12, §1277.1 (West Supp 1984-85). See also Hester, *Expression of Preference By Children In Child Custody Disputes in Oklahoma,* 51 Okla BJ 3097, 3097 (1980), where it is noted that "it is not mandatory that the court listen to the preference of the child or conduct any inquiry into the child's preference . . . the expression of preference is never binding upon the court, it becomes a factor to be taken into consideration when reaching a final decision."

preference if the child is at least age 12 in Texas, and 14 in both Georgia and New Mexico.[123]

The majority of states which include consideration of the child's preference in custody actions have patterned their legislation after the Uniform Marriage and Divorce Act (UMDA).[124] The UMDA provides in §402 that a "court *shall* consider all relevant factors including: . . . the wishes of the child as to his custodian" (emphasis added). While the language appears to mandate judicial consideration of the child's wishes, some courts have held otherwise. This has generated uncertainty as to the admissibility of the preference under these statutes. An Appellate Court of Illinois held in *DeFranco v DeFranco*[125] that the "seemingly mandatory" language of the child custody statute patterned after the UMDA did not alter the common law rule providing for consideration of a child's wishes only if sufficiently mature and intelligent. In *In re Marriage of Tweeten,*[126] the Supreme Court of Montana held that a trial court's discretionary refusal to ascertain the wishes of a three-year-old child was not in error. A Missouri Court of Appeals, without even considering the language of its UMDA-like custody statute, held that it was proper for a trial court to forgo consideration of the wishes of the children, aged six and four, particularly because "the children were confused and unsure about what was going on between the parents."[127] Clearly, some courts in states which have adopted UMDA provisions are continuing to make discretionary preliminary determinations as to the admissibility of a child's preference.

Since a child's statements in this regard are relevant as to the child's state of mind, rather than for the truth of the matter asserted, there is no reason to exclude as hearsay a witness's testimony about a child's expressed preference.[128] The credibility of the witness may be a factor in determining what

---

[123] Ga Code Ann §19-9-1(a) (Supp 1984); NM Stat Ann §40-4-9(B) (1983); Tex Fam Code Ann §14.07(a) (Vernon 1975).

[124] §402(2), 9A ULA 96, 198 (1979). *See* **app 1-2.** *See also* Ariz Rev Stat Ann §25-332 (Supp 1983-84); Colo Rev Stat §14-10-124 (Supp 1984); Del Code Ann tit 13, §722 (1981); DC Code Ann §16-911 (1981); Idaho Code §32-717 (1983); Ill Ann Stat ch 40, §602 (Smith-Hurd 1980); Ind Code Ann §31-1-11.5-21 (Burns 1976); Kan Stat Ann §60-1610 (1983); Ky Rev Stat Ann §403.270 (Baldwin 1983); Me Rev Stat Ann tit 19, §752 (Supp 1984-85); Mo Ann Stat §452.375 (Vernon Supp 1984); Mont Code Ann §40-4-2.2 (1983); Vt Stat Ann tit 15, §652 (Supp 1984); Wash Rev Code Ann §26.09.190 (Supp 1984-85); Wis Stat Ann §767.24 (West 1981). *See also* **§8.02.**

[125] 67 Ill App 3d 760, 384 NE2d 997 (1979).

[126] 563 P2d 1141 (Mont 1977). *See also In re* Marriage of Hickey, 689 P2d 1222 (Mont 1984).

[127] Johnson v Johnson, 526 SW2d 33, 35 (Mo 1975).

[128] *See* Fed R End 803, which states:

> The following are not excluded by the hearsay rule, even though the declarant is available as a witness: . . .
>
> (3) *Then existing mental, emotional or physical condition.* A statement of the declarant's then existing state of mind, emotion, sensation, or physical condition (such as intent, plan, motive, design, mental feeling, pain and bodily health), but not including a statement of memory or belief to prove the fact

weight to give to that preference when the child is not available for cross-examination and is not interviewed by the judge. A child's state of mind may be unduly influenced by a parent, has little durational quality, and may be altered several times during litigation. As long as a judge is sensitive to these factors, there should be no problem with admitting such evidence.

The weight to be given to the wishes of a child is determined on a case-by-case basis. Generally, the closer to maturity the child is, the greater the weight given to the preference as to a custodian. Strong preferences of insistent children must be considered as a practical matter, but not necessarily accepted without balancing other, more important factors. Courts realize that older children are able to make more rational decisions, and that it is difficult to enforce a custody decree against the wishes of a mature child, even where the decree is in the child's best interest.[129]

The child's preference will carry less weight when prompted by immature desires for less discipline, increased vacation time, or other such reason. In addition, if recognized as such, courts will discount the child's wishes where they are affected by parental manipulation such as enticement, coaching, or encouraging negative feelings against the other parent.[130] A child's preference is usually an insufficient basis by itself for a modification of a custody award.[131]

Psychiatric testimony based on interviews with the child and both parents and based on standard psychological testing are frequently a better source of information as to a child's true preference than a child's stated preference. The authors of this work, who have combined experience as a judge in custody cases and as practitioners, agree with the prevailing psychiatric view that a young child usually should not be asked to make a choice and that a young child's

---

remembered or believed unless it relates to the execution, revocation, identification, or terms of declarant's will.

[129] *See, e.g.*, Poesy v Bunney, 98 Idaho 258, __ 561 P2d 400, 404 (1977), where the court declared:

> The desire of the child becomes particularly important as the child grows older and more intelligent. With age comes an increased capacity on the part of the child to evaluate his own circumstance and determine what living situation is optimal. Also, with age comes a decreased ability to impose a custody order on a child which is contrary to the desires of the child.

*See also* Jines v Jines, 63 Ill App 3d 564, 380 NE2d 440 (1978); SM v SJ, 143 NJ Super 379, 363 A2d 353 (1976); Com *ex rel* Husack v Husack, 273 Pa Super 192, 417 A2d 233 (1979); Siegal & Hurley, *supra* note 116, at 9.

[130] Siegal & Hurley, *supra* note 116, at 14 (*citing* Tarling v Tarling, 8 Cal Rptr 621 (1960); Wallis v Wallis, 235 Md 33, 200 A2d 164 (1964); Neal v Medcalf, 244 SW2d 666 (Tex 1951)). *See also* Taylor v Schilt, 292 So 2d 47 (Fla Dist Ct App 1974); *In re* Marriage of B__A__S__, 541 SW2d 762 (Mo Ct App 1976); *In re* Marriage of Campbell, 599 SW2d 256 (Mo Ct App 1980); Fleharty v Fleharty, 202 Neb 245, 274 NW2d 871 (1979); Jordan v Corley, 220 NW2d 515 (ND 1974); Smith v Smith, 261 SC 41, 198 SE2d 271 (1973).

[131] *See, e.g.*, Wilson v Condra, 255 So 2d 702 (Fla 1971); Abbott v Abbott, 40 Ill App 3d 348, 352 NE2d 404 (1976); Curylo v Curylo, 104 Mich App 340, 304 NW2d 575 (1981). *Contra* Dailey v Dailey, 146 Ohio St 93, 64 NE2d 246 (1945); Frates v Frates, 135 Wash 567, 238 P 573 (1925).

preferences and other criteria for determining his or her best interest should be determined indirectly and subtly. Examples from professional experiences include the following situations.

In one case, a teen-age girl came to see her mother's lawyer to tell him that she and her brother would rather reside with their mother and the younger siblings, but that they had decided to testify that they preferred to live with their father, because otherwise he would not give them money for college.

Several other cases involved children who preferred a mentally ill parent with whom there was a symbiiotic pathological relationship. This intense expression of preference is well-known to mental health specialists, who use the term *splitting* to describe the child who incorrectly but sincerely believes one parent is all bad and the other is without fault. Sometimes a child expresses a preference for a rejecting or even an abusing parent, because, the psychotherapists tell us, the child is confident in the love and constancy of the well parent but fears loss of the rejecting, abusing, or ill parent.

But even when there is little or no pathology, determining a child's preference is fraught with difficulty. A child who chooses is frequently guilt-ridden; as a result, the choice may be the result of the guilt feelings. A child was asked by her aunt, with whom she lived, whether she preferred to remain with the aunt or reside with the widowed father. The child's tears and indecision were interpreted by the aunt as embarrassed preference to return to the father, whereas the contrary was the true state of the feelings of the child, who preferred to remain with the aunt but felt guilty over rejecting the father.

These examples suggest that neither the lawyer nor the judge should ask a child directly to choose between parents and that a child's preferences should be determined insightfully with professional help. For these reasons, a lawyer representing a parent desirous of seeking custody should urge the parent to consult a child psychotherapist concerning the minor's best interest before deciding to proceed with the custody action. Psychologists and social workers have devised techniques such as the "desert island" and "the baby bird falling from the nest" stories to learn indirectly with which parent the child is most strongly aligned. It is most important to determine whether the child is able to withstand the pressures and trauma of a custody battle which is so often harmful to a child.

## §8.11 Parent-Related Factors

Statutory criteria frequently include consideration of characteristics, qualities, and circumstances of the parents.[132] The Uniform Marriage and Divorce Act (UMDA) at §402 (3) and (5) mandates analysis of "the interaction and interrelationships of the child with his parent or parents" and "the mental and physical health of all parties involved."[133] Other statutes include such

---

[132] *See* **§§8.01-8.02.**

[133] Uniform Marriage and Divorce Act (UMDA) §402(3) & (5), 9A ULA 966, 198 (1979). *See* **app 1-2.**

parent-related provisions as: the "capacity and disposition of the parties involved to give the child affection and guidance,"[134] the "moral fitness"[135] or "moral character and prudence of the parents,"[136] and the causes of dissolution, if relevant.[137]

While the statutes provide guidelines, the cases reveal the specific parental lifestyles, actions, characteristics, and circumstances which have been considered in custody decisions. These include activities which consume time away from the child, such as employment, career-related activities, education, hobbies, and social pursuits.[138] The financial circumstances of the parents have been examined in some cases.[139] A parent's homosexuality, nonmarital relationship, marital misconduct, physical, mental, or emotional fitness, inadequacy, and misconduct toward the child are important factors in custody decisions.[140]

Child custody law in the 1980s continues to emphasize the best interests of the child.[141] Thus, parent-related factors should be considered as to their impact on the child's best interests. It is a long-settled rule that a custody proceeding should not discipline one parent for any shortcomings as a spouse or reward a parent for perceived mistreatment by the other parent. Nevertheless, for different reasons, custody disputes are generally viewed as, and sometimes are, adversarial battlegrounds where parents' rights and parental factors dominate any consideration of the best interests of the child.

Notwithstanding the rise of no-fault divorce, fault continues to be a factor considered in custody cases in most states, where the fault is alleged to be relevant to the child's welfare. Some divorcing couples, consciously or not, utilize custody litigation to vent hostilities toward each other.[142] Practitioners

---

[134] *See, e.g.*, La Civ Code Ann art 146c(2)(b) (West Supp 1984); Me Rev Stat Ann tit 19, §752(5)(F) (Supp 1984-85); Mich Stat Ann §25.312(3)(b) (Callaghan Supp 1984); Minn Stat Ann §518.17(1)(h) (West Supp 1984); ND Cent Code §14-09-06.2(2) (1981).

[135] Ala Code §30-3-1 (1983).

[136] Fla Stat Ann §61.13(3)(f) (West Supp 1984); La Civ Code Ann art 146(2)(f) (West Supp 1984); ND Cent Code §14-09-06.2(6) (1981).

[137] Conn Gen Stat Ann §466-66 (West Supp 1984); Minn Stat Ann §518.17(1) (West Supp 1984).

[138] *See* **§8.12.**

[139] *See* **§8.12.**

[140] It should be noted that judicial investigation of behavior of parents has been criticized as an invasion of their constitutional rights to privacy and to the exercise of free speech, religion, association and travel. *See* Comment, *Child Custody: Best Interests of Children vs Constitutional Rights of Parents,* 81 Dick L Rev 733 (1977).

[141] *See* **§7.03.**

[142] However, it is interesting to note a study by sociologists Lenore J. Weitzman and Ruth B. Dixon, which showed that the California no-fault law, which does allow fault to be considered in custody determinations, had no significant impact on custody requests. This prompted the sociologists to conclude, contrary to their initial prediction, that parents were not necessarily resorting to custody litigation to confront their spouses with fault-based accusations. *See* Weitzman & Dixon, *Child Custody Awards:*

know that it is not necessarily that one parent deliberately sets out to create hostility, but that the parent believes passionately that those actions or beliefs *are* in the best interests of the child. Often, a parent becomes so immersed in these emotional convictions as to the child's well-being that he or she loses perspective necessary for the child's welfare and is prevented from taking reasonable positions. It is difficult, in the midst of a custody dispute, for attorneys to expect parents to distance themselves from their beliefs. That is one reason why impartial adjudicators are necessary.

Most contested custody cases involve the fitness of the potential custodians. Indeed, fitness may be a proper issue; parents have a right to express their personal moral views. Unfortunately, however, fitness is sometimes at issue in cases where fathers are attempting to gain custody. Attacking a mother's fitness is often favored as a means to overcome implicit maternal preference in some courts, even where the tender years doctrine has been statutorily repealed or judicially overruled.[143] Yet, while fitness used to be an either/or issue, child custody litigation has evolved to the point that parental fitness usually is considered as only one of many factors.[144] When troublesome problems, such as religion or sexual activity are raised in contested cases, the emphasis should be on "appropriateness" rather than "fitness."

Attorneys have been accused of losing their objectivity in custody disputes and "converting the courtroom into a battleground for blood-letting between the parties."[145] Lawyers must avoid adopting the emotional attitude of the parent and parroting the parent's belief. While advocacy is important, it is also the attorney's responsibility to give the client a dispassionate look into the future, and not to implant the hostility of the parties in the case. Some may criticize this approach as psychological or moral rather than advocacy for the client. However, in the long run, it is the professional duty of the family lawyer

---

*Legal Standards and Empirical Patterns for Child Custody, Support, and Visitation After Divorce,* 12 UCDL Rev 473, 487-88 (1979).

[143] In Weitzman & Dixon's study, *id* 508-09, the sociologists asked family law attorneys in San Francisco and Los Angeles the following question: "Under what conditions do you think a husband is likely to get custody of a preschool child today?" In response, 77% of the attorneys' factors focused on the behavior of the mother, 7% on the father, and 17% on the child!

Earlier, the authors had noted:

> One explanation for the enduring maternal preference is that judges are still following the traditional standard: most judges, having spent the major portion of their legal careers in an era in which a mother's special nurturing abilities were unquestioned, may still be reluctant to "take little children away from their mothers." These judges may themselves believe that mother custody is in the child's best interest.

*Id* 504 (footnote omitted).

[144] *See* **§§8.01-8.15.**

[145] Brown, *Good Lawyers Needn't Be Gladiators,* 6 Fam Advoc 5 (Fall 1984). The author is the presiding judge of the Domestic Relations Division of the Superior Court for Maricopa County, Arizona.

to combine forceful advocacy of the client's rights with an objective view of the future of the child's family.

Fortunately, parent-related factors are more frequently being considered in light of their effect on the child and in conjunction with other factors. Per se rules as to the negative impact of adultery, nonmarital cohabitation, and homosexuality are slowly being replaced by the more reasonable rule that each factor in each case must be viewed in the context of its effect on the child.

## §8.12 —Employment and Financial Circumstances

The employment and financial circumstances of the parents are considered in custody decisions, but usually in terms of their impact on the child's best interests in relationship to other factors such as the primary caretaker, stability, and continuity.[146] Rarely, if ever, is the employment or financial situation of a parent the deciding factor in a custody award.

Courts sometimes favor as custodial parent the person having the less time-consuming or more flexible job than the other parent, particularly when it is the parent with more free time who has assumed the role of primary caretaker. In *Keramida v Zachmanoglou,*[147] an Indiana Court of Appeals affirmed an award of a child to a father where his $50,000-a-year job provided a flexible work schedule, allowing him to spend time with the child and assume the household chores. The mother's $25,000-a-year position with the Indianapolis Department of Public Works demanded much of her time and required a significant commute. The Supreme Court of South Dakota affirmed a custody award to a father, a teacher, where it was shown that he had always been more involved in the daily care of the children than the mother, who had pursued an education in medicine and was subsequently involved in a stressful and time-consuming medical practice.[148]

The importance of stability frequently influences cases involving employment or financial situations. In *McLeod v McLeod,*[149] a Louisiana Court of Appeals reviewed a mother's career as a professional singer in Las Vegas in affirming an award of custody to a father. The court noted that the mother's job was transitory, and required her to work nights and frequently be on the road. The child had continuously stayed with the father, who lived with his

---

[146] *See* **§§8.03 & 8.05.**

[147] __ Ind App __, 470 NE2d 769 (1984). See also *In re* Marriage of Bolin, 336 NW2d 441 (Iowa 1983), where, in a modification proceeding from joint custody to sole custody, one of the influential factors was that the mother's employment was sufficiently flexible to permit her to spend extra time with her son.

[148] Saint-Pierre v Saint-Pierre, 357 NW2d 250 (SD 1984). The court was quick to state, "In reaching this conclusion, we wish to make crystal clear that we are in no way intimating that a woman who pursues a separate career, whether it be in medicine, law, education, business, or any other vocation, forfeits her right to the custody of her minor children." *Id* 255.

[149] 434 So 2d 1238 (La Ct App 1983).

parents in a stable home. In a 1983 case, the Supreme Court of Illinois affirmed a custody award to the mother, who had remarried, was not employed and could care for the child, and had had continuous custody over the two years of separation.[150] Although the father maintained a home in Illinois and made arrangements for the care of the child, he was employed five days a week in Kentucky in a job that was to last several more months.

The fact that a custodial mother has to work and place her child in some kind of out-of-home care has been treated differently by the courts. In a 1951 California case, a mother who did not receive alimony found it necessary to board her child full-time. A district court of appeal reversed a lower court's modification of the custody award from the mother to the father. The court declared that:

> Plaintiff did what any other working mother would have done under similar circumstances. The fact that a divorced working mother is impelled by circumstances to relinquish the physical care of her child when boarding him is not, in itself, indicative of a relinquishment of her power of supervision over her child.[151]

Similarly, a waitress mother who worked a split shift and often left the child overnight with a babysitter was not required to give up the child to the husband in *In re Neff*.[152] The award to the mother was affirmed even though her custody was a split custody situation, the other two children residing with the father. Both the trial court and the appellate court were influenced by the fact that all the children were doing well in their respective homes.

Generally, a parent's financial situation is more properly considered when awarding support rather than custody.[153] As the Supreme Court of Wisconsin has aptly stated:

> Basing custody award on the relative affluence of one of the parents would in effect discriminate against women in violation of the [statutory] provision . . . that "the court . . . shall not prefer one potential custodian over the other on the basis of the sex of the custodian." Such a consideration will discriminate not only against women who work inside the home full time fulfilling the important, traditional role of homemaker

---

150 *In re* Marriage of Olson, 96 Ill 2d 432, 451 NE2d 825 (1983). See also *In re* Marriage of Guyer, 238 NW2d 794 (Iowa 1976), where, during the marriage, both parties had worked on a garbage truck and left their child with the father's parents. When the parties separated, the child stayed with the father and his parents. While the mother found another job and made plans to place him in a day care center, the court awarded the child to the father, to avoid disruptions in the child's life. The court observed that even during the marriage, the wife worked against the husband's wishes.

151 Sorrells v Sorrells, 105 Cal App 2d 465, —, 234 P2d 103, 108 (1951).

152 193 NW2d 82 (Iowa 1971).

153 *See* **ch 10.**

but also against women who work outside the home and generally have less earning power than men.[154]

However, there are cases in which courts have based custody awards on the economic circumstances of the parties. In *Clift v Clift,*[155] a mother's appeal of a custody award to the father, both the trial and appellate courts considered the mother's unemployment, and concluded that if she obtained a position she would be compelled to work away from the child. Thus, she had an uncertain future. The father, on the other hand, had a relatively stable income as a farm manager, a job which allowed him to spend 75 per cent of his time with the child and save for his child's future. The Court of Civil Appeals of Alabama decided that those factors were sufficient to rebut the maternal preference.

In *Calhoun v Calhoun,*[156] a mother challenged a custody award to the father, alleging that "poverty is not a valid basis for depriving a mother, who is otherwise fit, of the custody of her children."[157] However, the mother's mental instability, along with the fact that the children had always lived with the father, influenced the court's decision. Yet, the court stated:

> [I]t is clear that Geraldine's only source of financial means to provide and maintain a home for herself and the children would be whatever can be squeezed from Darrell, and his income is not enough to stand it. Her own prospects of supplementing that source of revenue are, at present, speculative and remote. It seems inevitable that she and the children would wind up in the home of her parents and other children. Their life would be a constant battle in the court house to force Darrell to provide funds, transportation and medical treatment for the children . . . that he now provides voluntarily.[158]

## §8.13 —The Homosexual Parent

One troublesome factor in child custody disputes, whether involving initial placement, visitation, or modification, is a parent's homosexuality. As with other nonstatutory factors, a parent's homosexual lifestyle is considered and weighed as to the child's best interests at the court's discretion, creating the typical concern that a judge may be influenced by personal opinions.[159] However, where one parent is homosexual, this concern is heightened by the

---

[154] Gould v Gould, 116 Wis 2d 493, __, 342 NW2d 426, 42 31 n 2 (1984) (citing Weitzman, *Economics of Divorce: Social and Economic Consequences of Property, Alimony, and Child Support Awards,* 28 UCLA L Rev 1181 (1981)).

[155] 346 So 2d 429 (Ala Civ App), *cert denied sub nom Ex parte* Clift, 346 So 2d 439 (Ala 1977).

[156] 559 SW2d 721 (Ky 1977).

[157] *Id* 722.

[158] *Id* 723.

[159] *See* **§7.03.**

stigma, fear, and ignorance about homosexuality in our society.[160] There have been reported cases where the custodial choice or visitation schedule was based on broad declarations of unproven beliefs, unsupported by evidence or written findings.[161] As a result, a special expertise for practitioners has emerged in this area, involving negotiation and litigation strategies which emphasize settlement, low client profile, and use of experts to provide information and evaluation of the impact of homosexuality on a child in a heterosexual society.[162]

Until the 1970s and 1980s, there was minimal documentation of custody cases involving homosexual parents, presumably because few such parents discussed their sexual preference and to protect the privacy of the parties.[163] However, it has been noted that the historical approach to such cases was that homosexual parents were unfit as a matter of law to assume custody of a child.[164] This rule was supported by the fact that homosexuals as well as adulterors violated state criminal laws.[165]

The per se unfitness rule was first struck down in *Nadler v Superior Court.*[166] In that case, a California District Court of Appeal held that a trial court failed to exercise its discretion when it found that a lesbian mother was unfit as a matter of law to have custody of her five-year-old daughter. The court ruled that the trial court should have considered the mother's homosexuality as only one factor in awarding the child.

---

[160] Hitchens & Price, *Trial Strategy in Lesbian Mother Custody Cases: The Use of Expert Testimony,* 9 Golden Gate UL Rev 451, 452 (1978-79) ("Homophobia, like racism and sexism, pervades our society and is just recently being examined and challenged as an irrational basis of widespread discrimination" (footnotes omitted)); Hunter & Polikoff, *Custody Rights of Lesbian Mothers: Legal Theory and Litigation Strategy,* 25 Buffalo L Rev 691, 694 (1976) ("homosexuality is often viewed as immoral or unhealthy"); Comment, *Burdens on Gay Litigants and Bias in the Court System: Homosexual Panic, Child Custody, And Anonymous Parties,* 19 Harv CR-CL L Rev 497 (1984) ("Despite the influence of the gay rights movement in recent years, few would deny that there remains much hostility toward gays in our society. Much of this hostility stems from widespread ignorance" (footnotes omitted).

[161] *See* Comment, *Custody: Lesbian Mothers in the Courts,* 16 Gonz L Rev 147, 148-52 (1980) (citing interalia, Shuster v Shuster, 90 Wash 2d 626, 585 P2d 130 (1978)); Comment, *supra* note 160, at 516 (citing JLP(H) v DJP, 643 SW2d 865, 869 (Mo Ct App 1982); NKM v LEM, 606 SW2d 179, 186 (Mo Ct App 1980)); Comment, *The Law and the Problem Parent: Custody and Parental Rights of Homosexual, Mentally Retarded, Mentally Ill and Incarcerated Parents,* 16 J Fam L 797, 799 (1977-78) (citing J. Noble & W. Noble, The Custody Trap 138-39 (1975)).

[162] *See especially* Hitchens & Price, *supra* note 160, at 471-478; Hunter & Polikoff, *supra* note 160, at 715-732.

[163] Comment, *Bezio v Patenaude, The "Coming Out" Custody Controversy of Lesbian Mothers in Court,* 16 New Eng L Rev 331 (1981).

[164] Comment, *supra* note 161, at 154.

[165] *See, e.g.,* Chaffin v Frye, 1 Fam L Rep (BNA) 2308 (Cal Ct App 1975); Roe v Roe, 11 Fam L Rep (BNA) 1155, 1156 (Va 1985).

[166] 255 Cal App 2d 523, 63 Cal Rptr 352 (1967).

The general rule which has emerged in some states is that "sexual orientation per se, without a showing of adverse effect upon the child, does not justify denying a gay parent custody or reasonable visitation rights."[167] In one such case, a Superior Court of New Jersey has held:

> The right of a parent, including a homosexual parent, to the companionship and care of his or her child, insofar as it is for the best interest of the child, is a fundamental right protected by the First, Ninth and Fourteenth Amendments to the United States Constitution. That right may not be restricted without a showing that the parent's activities may tend to impair the emotional or physical health of the child.[168]

While this general rule requiring a showing of adverse effect is fair, some courts have narrowed its application in different ways. After enunciating the general rule, courts sometimes simply have presumed that living with a homosexual parent is not in the child's best interests. For example, in *Bezio v Patenaude,*[169] the Supreme Judicial Court of Massachusetts held that a trial court's denial of a lesbian mother's petition to remove her children's guardian and regain custody was not supported by adequate findings as to the fitness of the mother. The trial judge had concluded that the mother's household was unstable, prompting the appellate court to state that "[i]n the absence of evidence suggesting a correlation between the mother's homosexuality and her fitness as a parent we believe that the judge's finding that a lesbian household would adversely affect the children to be without basis in the record."[170]

Other courts have also concluded that a child's relationship with a homosexual parent is inherently damaging to the child. The Missouri Court of Appeals has concluded in one case that a "father's acknowledgment that he was living with an avowed homosexual certainly augurs for potential harm to the child that the trial court was perfectly competent to assess,"[171] and in another custody action, that while "the child at this time age 10 shows no ill

---

[167] Comment, *supra* note 160, at 520, n 80 (citing Nadler v Superior Court, 255 Cal App 2d 523, 63 Cal Rptr 352 (1967); DH v JH, 418 NE2d 286 (Ind Ct App 1981); Bezio v Patenaude, 381 Mass 563, 410 NE2d 1207 (1980); MP v SP, 169 NJ Super 425, 432, 404 A2d 1256, 1260 (1979); Doe v Doe, 222 Va 736, 748, 284 SE2d 799, 806 (1981); *In re* Marriage of Cabalquinto, 100 Wash 2d 325, 669 P2d 886 (1983)). *See also* Gay v Gay, 149 Ga App 173, 253 SE2d 846 (1979); Hall v Hall, 95 Mich App 614, 291 NW2d (1980); DiStefano v DiStefano, 60 AD2d 976, 401 NYS2d 636 (1978); A v A, 15 Or App 353, 514 P2d 358 (1974); *In re* Breisch, 290 Pa Super 404, 434 A2d 815 (1981); Kallas v Kallas, 614 P2d 641 (Utah 1980).

[168] *In re* JS & C, 129 NJ Super 486, __ 324 A2d 90, 92 (1974), *affd,* 142 NJ Super 499, 362 A2d 54 (1976).

[169] 381 Mass 563, 410 NE2d 1207 (1980).

[170] *Id* at __, 410 NE2d at 1216.

[171] JLP(H) v DJP, 643 SW2d 865, 869 (Mo Ct App 1982).

effects from her present environment . . . [t]he court does not need to wait, though, till the damage is done."[172]

Other courts have restricted the custodial and visitation rights of homosexual parents, especially if they are in a practicing sexual relationship. Commentators have argued that the per se unfitness rule has been modified in some jurisdictions to hold that homosexual couples are harmful per se to children.[173] In *A v A*,[174] a mother who had no contact with her children for nearly ten years after divorcing the father attempted to modify custody on the ground that the father was homosexual, because his business partner had lived with the father and children for two years. The trial court, while refusing to modify the custody award, placed certain conditions on the father's custody "designed to safeguard the home environment against possible pernicious influences."[175] This included forbidding any man from living in the house, even though there was no evidence that the welfare of the children was being adversely affected. The Oregon Court of Appeals affirmed, and additionally required that the father's custody be placed under supervision of juvenile authorities.[176] In *Roe v Roe*[177] the Supreme Court of Virginia changed custody after six years from the father to the mother, because the father was living with a male lover. The court held:

> The father's continuous exposure of the child to his immoral and illicit relationship renders him an unfit and improper custodian as a matter of law . . . we have no hesitancy in saying that the conditions under which this child must live daily are not only unlawful but also impose an intolerable burden upon her by reason of the social condemnation to them, which will inevitably afflict her relationship with her peers and the community at large. The father's unfitness is manifested by his willingness

---

[172] NKM v LEM, 606 SW2d 179, 186 (Mo Ct App 1980). *See also In re* Jane B, 85 Misc 2d 515, 380 NYS2d 848 (1976).

[173] Comment, *supra* note 160, at 535; Hunter & Polikoff, *supra* note 160, at 705, where the authors state, "In effect, such courts have simply inched beyond the point of treating the status of lesbianism as per se unfitness to the point of treating the *practice* of lesbianism as per se unfitness." (Emphasis in original.)

[174] 15 Or App 353, 514 P2d 358 (1973), *rehg denied,* 15 Or App 353, 515 P2d 730 (1973).

[175] *Id* at ___, 514 P2d at 359.

[176] See also *In re* JS & C, 129 NJ Super 486, 324 A2d 90 (1974), *affd,* 142 NJ Super 499, 362 A2d 54 (1976), where a father, who was extremely active in the homosexual community, had his visitation rights limited. His children's overnight stay was eliminated. He was forbidden to have male guests when the children were with him, and he was also prevented from taking his children to any homosexual rallies. The court was influenced by the facts that the father had headed national gay organizations, participated in homosexual business ventures, and cohabited with his lover in an apartment building populated primarily by homosexuals. *See also* Irish v Irish, 102 Mich App 75, 300 NW2d 739 (1980); NKM v LEM, 606 SW2d 179 (Mo Ct App 1980); Jacobson v Jacobson, 314 NW2d 78 (ND 1981); MJP v JGP, 640 P2d 966 (Okla 1982); Hunter & Polikoff, *supra* note 160, at 697-705, and cases cited therein.

[177] 11 Fam L Rep (BNA) 1155 (Va 1985).

> to impose this burden upon her in exchange for his own gratification.[178]

Commentators have suggested that courts may be misguided by hidden assumptions that exist at large in society.[179] Two such assumptions are that homosexuals are more likely to molest their children[180] and that children of such parents are more likely to become homosexual.[181] Another frequent, more legitimate concern is that children of homosexual parents will incur psychological damage as a result of confronting the social stigma attached to homosexuality.[182] Nevertheless, as commentators have argued, a nexus test would provide a safeguard for such situations.

Such a test would require a court to find a nexus between the parent's homosexuality and an adverse effect on the child, which is similar to the tests which have emerged in custody cases involving race and parental misconduct.[183] Other recommendations such as an increased use of psychological

---

[178] *Id* 1156 (citations omitted).

[179] *See, e.g.,* Comment, *supra* note 160, at 526-28, 531-34; Comment, *supra* note 161, 16 J Fam L at 799; Comment, *supra* note 163, at 353; Comment, *Doe v Doe: Destroying the Presumption That Homosexual Parents are Unfit—The New Burden of Proof,* 16 U Rich L Rev 851, 854 (1982).

[180] See, e.g., *In re* JS & C, 129 NJ Super 486, 324 A2d 90, 96 (1974), where one expert, contradicted by two other experts, testified that it was possible that the children "could be exposed to overt or covert seduction."

[181] See Hitchens & Price, *supra* note 160, at 456, where the authors discuss the expert testimony offered at trial in two cases:

> In the *Nadler* case, there was expert testimony that the children would be more likely to seek a heterosexual relationship if they were with a heterosexual parent. . . . This testimony was in no way substantiated by empirical research or professional studies. . . .
>
> *In re Nicholson* is a lesbian mother custody case that was lost by the mother specifically because she would not be providing a heterosexual role model. (Footnotes omitted.)

[182] Compare Doe v Doe, 16 Mass App Ct 499, 452 NE2d 293, 296 (1983), where the court stated "the trial judge specifically found, and we think this is an important fact, that David 'has not been tormented by his friends in regard to his mother's lifestyle,' " with MP v SP, 169 NJ Super 425, 404 A2d 1156, 1263 (1979) where the court declared:

> If defendant retains custody, it may be that because the community is intolerant of her differences these girls may sometimes have to bear themselves with greater than ordinary fortitude. But this does not necessarily portent that their moral welfare or safety will be jeopardized. It is just as reasonable to expect that they will emerge better equipped to search out their standards of right and wrong, better able to perceive that the majority is not always correct in its moral judgments, and better able to understand the importance of conforming their beliefs to the requirements of reason and tested knowledge, not the constraints of currently popular sentiment or prejudice.

See also Judge Ard's dissent, where it is stated: "Children should not be victims of an avant garde tolerance that does not represent the thinking of a vast majority of society." *Id* 1270.

[183] *See* Note, *In the "Best Interests of the Child: and the Lesbian Mother: A Proposal for Legislative Change in New York,* 48 Alb L Rev 1021, 1024 (1984); Comment, *supra* note 160, at 523; Comment, *supra* note 163, at 348. *See also* **§§8.08 & 8.14.**

evidence and complete written recording of judicial findings would help to insure that a parent's homosexuality would have no presumptive effect unless proven by concrete, not speculative, evidence that it harms the child.

Because this is a burgeoning area of custody law with many more reported cases existing than cited here, it is suggested that interested practitioners consult the more complete works which are available.[184]

## §8.14 —Parental Misconduct

In the fault system of divorce, courts were inclined to award the custody of children to the innocent party on the theory that they would probably receive better treatment from the parent who had kept the marital vows than from the one who had broken them.[185] A few statutes entitling an innocent party to child custody on divorce or annulment still existed in 1985.[186]

Nevertheless, with some significant exceptions,[187] courts refrained from mechanically awarding custody to the innocent parent. Guided by the best interests of the child standard, and for a long time strongly influenced by the maternal preference, courts developed the rule that marital fault, parental misconduct, or parental immorality were factors to be considered to the extent that they reflected on the parent's fitness to have custody, and were not automatic bars to a custody award.[188]

While no-fault divorce removed the consideration of misconduct from the award of divorce or dissolution in most states, it has not precluded such an evaluation from the award of custody. Some state statutes include moral fitness, the threat or incidence of physical violence, or the relevant causes of dissolution as factors to be reviewed in an action for child custody.[189] A growing number of states statutorily provide that fault may not be considered in a dissolution action except if relevant to child custody or the parent-child relationship.[190]

---

[184] R. Actenberg, Sexual Orientation and the Law (1985).

[185] J. Madden, Handbook of the Law of Persons and Domestic Relations 317 (1931); 2 J. McCahey, M. Kaufman, C. Kraut, D. Gaffner, M. Silverman, & J. Zett, Child Custody and Visitation Law and Practice 10-64 (1983); Caldwell v Caldwell, 141 Iowa 192, 119 NW 599 (1909).

[186] *See, e.g.*, Ga Code Ann §19-9-1(a) (Supp 1984); Mass Laws Ann ch 208, §31 (West Supp 1984); Wyo §20-2-113(b) (1977).

[187] The most notable exceptions, discussed in this section, have been adultery, and, more recently, nonmarital cohabitation. *See also* **§§8.09, 8.13.**

[188] *See* Annot 23 ALR3d 6, 17 (1964).

[189] *See* Ala Code §30-3-1 (1983) ("moral fitness"); Conn Gen Stat Ann §466-66 (Supp 1984); Fla Stat Ann §61.13(3)(f) (West Supp 1984); Ill Ann Stat ch 40, §602 (Smith-Hurd 1980) ("The physical violence or threat of physical violence"); La Civ Code Ann art 146(2)(f) (West Supp 1984); Minn Stat Ann §518.17(1) (West Supp 1984) ("The causes of dissolution, if relevant"). ND Cent Code §14-09-06.2(6) (1981) ("Moral character and prudence").

[190] *See, e.g.*, Cal Civ Code §4509 (Deering 1984); Colo Rev Stat §14-10-121 (Supp 1984); Ill Ann Stat ch 40, §602(b) (Smith-Hurd 1980); Ky Rev Stat Ann §403.270

Case law to the same effect exists in some states as well.[191] Nearly all custody statutes permit the introduction of any relevant evidence under the best interests of the child standard.

Many examples of parental misconduct as a factor exist, in far more cases than can be cited here. In addition, the practitioner must keep in mind that parental misconduct may be aggravated or mitigated by other factors such as continuity, stability, the primary caretaker, the preference of the child, emotional illness, or unfitness of the other parent. Some of the more common types of parental misconduct influencing custody decisions include cruelty,[192] child abuse,[193] violent temper,[194] alcohol or drug abuse,[195] criminal acts,[196]

---

(Baldwin 1983); Minn Stat Ann §518.17 (West Supp 1984); Or Rev Stat §107.137 (1983); SD Comp Laws Ann §29.09.150 (1984); Wash Rev Code Ann §26.09.190 (Supp 1984-85). See also Krug v Krug, 647 SW2d 79 (Ky 1983), where the Supreme Court of Kentucky held that when the misconduct of a proposed custodian is alleged as a factor under that state's statute, the evidence of such misconduct may be heard and received without any prerequisite proof that it adversely affects the child. The court must decide whether the misconduct has affected, or is likely to affect, the child adversely, and professional testimony to adverse effects is not absolutely necessary. *See also In re* Marriage of Marks, 96 Ill App 3d 360, 420 NE2d 1184 (1981).

[191] *See, e.g.,* Harris v Harris, 240 Ga 276, 240 SE2d 30 (1977); Meyers v Meyers, 51 Ill App 3d 830, 366 NE2d 1114 (1977); *In re* Marriage of Carmack, 550 SW2d 815 (Mo Ct App 1977), JB v AB, 242 SE2d 248 (W Va 1978).

[192] *See, e.g.,* Modling v Modling, 45 Ala App 493, 232 So 2d 673 (1970); Watson v Watson, 271 Ark 294, 608 SW2d 44 (1980); Weaver v Weaver, 238 Ga 101, 230 SE2d 886 (1976); Hughes v Hughes, 463 A2d 478 (Pa Super 1983); Kelly v Kelly, 679 SW2d 458 (Tenn Ct App 1984).

[193] *See, e.g.,* Galeano v Galeano, 444 So 2d 658 (La Ct App 1983) (presumption of joint custody of young daughter successfully rebutted by evidence that father had sexually abused older daughter); Dixon v Dixon, 67 NC App 73, 312 SE2d 669 (1984) (appellate court overturned trial court's award of child to mother on the basis of overwhelming evidence that mother had continuously abused child). *See also* Horton v Horton, 519 P2d 1131 (Alaska 1974); Lenderman v Lenderman, 588 SW2d 707 (Ark Ct App 1979); Masterson v Masterson, 40 Ill App 3d 201, 351 NE2d 888 (1976); Irwin v Irwin, 678 SW2d 861 (Mo Ct App 1984); Smith v Smith, 246 Pa Super 607, 371 A2d 998 (1977); Cooper v Cooper, 673 SW2d 152 (Tenn Ct App 1984).

[194] *See, e.g.,* Lake v Robertson, 452 So 2d 376 (La Ct App 1984); *In re* Carpenter, 96 AD2d 607, 464 NYS2d 606 (1983); Salisbury v Salisbury, 657 SW2d 761 (Tenn Ct App 1983).

[195] *See, e.g.,* Weaver v Weaver, 238 Ga 101, 230 SE2d 886 (1976); Krug v Krug, 647 SW2d 79 (Ky 1983); *In re* Marriage of Rysterski, 655 SW2d 102 (Mo Ct App 1983); *In re* Carpenter, 96 AD2d 607, 464 NYS2d 606 (1983); Kelly v Kelly, 679 SW2d 458 (Tenn Ct App 1984).

[196] *See, e.g.,* Krug v Krug, 647 SW2d 79 (Ky 1983) (mother, who had previously been married to a convict, wrote bad checks); Lake v Robertson, 452 So 2d 376 (La Ct App 1984) (wife hid a convicted felon and fired a pistol); Bourlon v Bourlon, 670 P2d 1004 (Okla Ct App 1983) (mother secured alcohol and drugs for local teenagers and brought home unprescribed drugs from the VA hospital); Kelly v Kelly, 679 SW2d 458 (Tenn Ct App 1984) (mother assaulted husband with a pistol).

abandonment or neglect of children,[197] and even parental teachings.[198] In West Virginia, where there is a presumption in favor of the primary caretaker, the rule is that the primary caretaker must be fit.[199] That a parent snatched a child may or may not be considered in the custody award.[200] Past misconduct should only be considered if it adversely affects the child's welfare, but it is sometimes reviewed without such a finding.[201]

Generally, the drift has been away from showing that one parent is immoral, has a bad character, is guilty of marital misconduct, or is unfit. Unless the evidence proves an adverse effect on the child or the parent-child relationship, in most states it will be inadmissible. In states where a presumption for joint custody exists, the importance of fitness has decreased because it is no longer necessary to prove which parent is *more* fit to have custody.[202] Finally, it is in the child's best interest to avoid confrontations on parental fitness unless vital to the child's welfare.

## Nonmarital Sexual Conduct

By far the most frequently litigated parental misconduct issue is the nonmarital sexual conduct of a parent, whether adultery or nonmarital cohabitation.[203] Historically, the adultery of a mother automatically precluded her from obtaining the custody of her children. While that view remains the

---

[197] *See, e.g.*, Hattrick v Hattrick, 2 Ala App 539, 295 So 2d 260 (1974); Caraway v Caraway, 321 So 2d 405 (La Ct App 1975); J-A-F v P-J-F, 552 SW2d 739 (Mo Ct App 1977); Garner v Stone, 85 NM 716, 516 P2d 687 (1973); Baker v Rose, 28 Ohio Misc 200 (1970); Bevis v Bevis, 254 SC 345, 175 SE2d 398 (1970); Kelly v Kelly, 679 SW2d 458 (Tenn Ct App 1984); TCB v HAB, 317 SE2d 174 (W Va 1984). A parent who defaults in the divorce action may forfeit the right to custody, *see* Harris v Harris, 240 Ga 276, 240 SE2d 30 (1977); Farley v Farley, 172 Ind App 120, 359 NE2d 583 (1977). In addition, an uncaring attitude of a parent may weigh heavily in a custody award. See *In re* Marriage of Brogder, 344 NW2d 273 (Iowa Ct App 1983), where the Iowa Court of Appeals reversed an award of custody to the father where the father failed to pay child support until he was held in contempt of court, attempted to have a lien on the wife's household possessions foreclosed while the children were living with her, and supplied the wife and children with an old unsafe truck for transportation.

[198] In *In re* Marriage of Brand, 123 Ill App 3d 1047, 79 Ill Dec 483, 463 NE2d 1037 (1984), the court decided that the facts that the father told his son he need not obey the law and the father's general disdain for the law as evinced by his actions in court could affect the father's relationship with the boy and were properly considered in the custody decision.

[199] Gibson v Gibson, 304 SE2d 336 (W Va 1983). *See also* **§8.05.**

[200] *See* Witmayer v Witmayer, 320 Pa Super 372, 467 A2d 371 (1983).

[201] *See, e.g.*, Bergan v Bergan, 42 Ill App 3d 740, 356 NE2d 673 (1976); In the Interest of Mann, 293 NW2d 185 (Iowa 1980); Lake v Robertson, 452 So 2d 376 (La Ct App 1984); Berndt v Berndt, 292 NW2d 1 (Minn 1980); *In re* Leskovitch, 253 Pa Super 349, 385 A2d 373 (1978); Allen v Allen, 78 Wis 2d 263, 254 NW2d 244 (1977).

[202] Note, *Louisiana's New Joint Custody Law*, 43 La L Rev 759, 767 (1983).

[203] See **§8.13.** for a discussion of a parent's homosexual conduct in a custody award. The cohabitation of a parent is more frequently considered in a modification action as a change of circumstances.

rule in a few states, courts vary in their approaches to an adultery or nonmarital cohabitation situation, and are influenced by mitigating or aggravating circumstances.[204] Some general approaches will be outlined here.

It is undisputed that the 1960s and 1970s brought a wave of change through the Western world which challenged conventional moral standards and created uncertainty in the area of sexual behavior. One result of the change was an increased acceptance of, and participation in, nonmarital cohabitation.[205] The destigmatization of nonmarital sexual behavior has influenced many courts in custody disputes as well as many litigants, who sometimes have ignored the moral issue and concentrated on the financial aspect of nonmarital cohabitation.[206]

The rules in such cases are inextricably linked to the facts of each case. The majority rule in the country is that adultery or cohabitation is one factor to be considered in a custody decision, and is insufficient to deprive a parent of custody unless it is shown to have an adverse effect upon the child.[207] Examples of adverse effects upon children include: child's inability to get along with adulterous or cohabiting parent or that parent's lover; a child's sudden display of symptoms of psychological disturbance, or dramatic drop in performance at school, or a definite distortion of the child's moral perception.[208] Many courts assume that where the sexual conduct occurs in the presence of the child,

---

[204] *See* Bergman, *Custody Awards: Standards Used When the Mother Has Been Guilty of Adultery or Alcoholism,* 2 Fam LQ 384 (1968); Foster & Freed, *Child Custody,* 39 NYU L Rev 423, 429-31 (1964); Lauerman, *Nonmarital Sexual Conduct and Child Custody,* 46 U Cin L Rev 647 (1977); Note, *Custody and the Cohabiting Parent,* 20 J Fam L 697 (1981-82); Annot, 23 ALR3d 6 (1969).

[205] *See* S. Green & J. Long, Marriage and Family Law Agreements ch 3 (Shepard's/McGraw-Hill 1984).

[206] Note, *supra* note 205, at 698 n 6, citing several cases where there were attempts to modify or terminate a cohabiting parent's alimony, but no attempt to change custody: McAnerney v McAnerney, 165 Conn 277, 334 A2d 437 (1973); McRae v McRae, 381 So 2d 1052 (Miss 1980); Wertlake v Wertlake, 137 NJ Super 476, 349 A2d 552 (Super Ct App Div 1975); Grossman v Grossman, 128 NJ Super 193, 319 A2d 508 (Super Ct Ch Div 1974); Wright v Wright, 284 SE2d 625 (W Va 1981). *See also* J. Green, J. Long, & R. Murawski, Marriage and Family Law Agreements §§3.24A-.24E (Shepard's/McGraw-Hill Supp 1985).

[207] Lauerman, *supra* note 204, at 658 calls this the *direct adverse impact* approach. *See e.g., In re* Marriage of Gonzales, 116 Cal App 3d 556, 172 Cal Rptr 179 (1981); Claughton v Claughton, 344 So 2d 944 (Fla Dist Ct App 1977); Burris v Burris, 70 Ill App 3d 503, 388 NE2d 811 (1979); *In re* Marriage of Brogden, 344 NW2d 273 (Iowa Ct App 1983); *In re* Marriage of Kramer, 297 NW2d 354 (Iowa 1980); Davis v Davis, 280 Md 119, 372 A2d 231 (1977); Fastracht v Fastracht, 616 SW2d 98 (Mo Ct App 1981); DiStefano v DiStefano, 60 AD2d 976, 401 NYS2d 636 (1978); Witnayer v Witnayer, 476 A2d 371 (Pa Super Ct 1983); Hanks v Hanks, 296 NW2d 523 (SD 1980); Krueger v Stevens, 244 NW2d 763 (SD 1976).

[208] Lauerman, *supra* note 204 at 660-63 (citing inter alia, Moore v Smith, 255 Ark 249, 499 SW2d 634 (1973); *In re* Marriage of Bower, 219 NW2d 683 (Iowa 1973); S v J, 81 Misc 2d 828, 367 NYS2d 405 (Sup Ct 1975); Calbertson v Calbertson, 91 Nev 230, 533 P2d 768 (1975); Repetti v Repetti, 1 Fam L Rep (BNA) 2739 (NY Sup Ct 1975)).

the child will be harmed.[209] However, one writer has asserted that it is very difficult to ascertain whether a child is being adversely affected by a parent's cohabitation rather than the trauma associated with divorce, losing a parent to visitation, or moving after a separation.[210]

Few courts still hold that an adulterous parent is unfit for custody as a matter of law.[211] Nevertheless, in many states courts will presume that a parent should not be awarded custody if he or she is living in an open adulterous relationship (cohabiting), does not plan to marry that lover, is involved with a married person, or has a pattern of continuous, promiscuous, or outrageous sexual behavior.[212] Similarly, the presumption may be outweighed by mitigating circumstances such as remarriage, intention to remarry, discreet conduct without the knowledge of the children, or termination of the conduct or relationship.[213] Finally, an isolated act of adultery rarely precludes an award of custody.[214]

---

[209] *See, e.g., In re* Marriage of Grandinetti, 342 NW2d 876 (Iowa Ct App 1983); Rising v Rising, 608 SW2d 510 (Mo App 1981); Witmayer v Witmayer, 467 A2d 371 (Pa Super 1983); Wolff v Wolff, 349 NW2d 656 (SD 1984); Haskell v Haskell, 279 NW2d 903 (SD 1979).

[210] Note, *supra* note 204, at 713, where the author also comments:

> It is crucial that courts understand what effect a custodial parent's cohabitation has on a child. . . . Unfortunately, this information is unavailable. There are no definitive psychological studies on this issue . . . [because] [w]idespread cohabitation is a recent development, and its spectacular growth was not predicted. Furthermore, studies to determine the effect of one variable on a human population are invariably confounded by conditions which cannot be controlled.

[211] *See, e.g.,* James v James, 456 So 2d 829 (Ala Civ App 1984); Cleeton v Cleeton, 369 So 2d 1072 (La Ct App 1979), *affd* 383 So 2d 1231 (La 1980); Keyes v Keyes, 252 Miss 138, 171 So 2d 489 (1965); Brown v Brown, 218 Va 196, 237 SE2d 89 (1977).

[212] *See, e.g.,* Rippon v Rippon, 64 Ill App 3d 4654, 381 NE2d 70 (1978); Sherman v Sherman, 441 So 2d 469 (La Ct App 1983); McCurdy v McCurdy, 369 So 2d 1216 (La Ct App 1979); LFH v RLH, 543 SW2d 520 (Mo Ct App 1976); Hicks v Hicks, 214 Neb 588, 334 NW2d 807 (1983); *In re* Carpenter, 96 AD2d 607, 464 NYS2d 606 (1983); Bourlon v Bourlon, 670 P2d 1004 (Okla Ct App 1983); JB v AB, 242 SE2d 248 (W Va 1978).

[213] See, for example, three different cases in Louisiana: Lingenfelter v Ligenfelter, 384 So 2d 523 (La Ct App 1980) (fact that mother had an affair with former employer before final divorce did not render her "morally unfit" to have custody of her five-year-old son where she had terminated the affair and there was no indication that any immoral acts occurred in the presence of the son); Ingram v Ingram, 382 So 2d 980 (La Ct App 1980) (holding that a custody award to father on bases of mother's adultery was in error in light of fact mother was pri-primary caretaker and no adultery had occurred in presence of the children); Coltharp v Coltharp, 368 So 2d 793 (La Ct App), *writ denied,* 370 So 2d 578 (La 1979) (holding that it was not an abuse of discretion to award custody of sons to father where father and sons resided with father's girlfriend for 10 months, particularly because father married the girlfriend as soon as he secured divorce from the son's mother).

[214] *See, e.g.,* Etheridge v Etheridge, 375 So 2d 474 (Ala Civ App 1979); Fouchi v Fouchi, 391 So 2d 1352 (La Ct App), *writ refused,* 396 So 2d 918 (La 1980); JB v AB, 242 SE2d 248 (W Va 1978).

It is important to emphasize that the competence of the parent in caring for the child and the overall character of the parent-child relationship overshadow parental misconduct in most cases. While misconduct of the parent is a weighty consideration, the courts will usually balance it with an abundance of other factors which appear in each custody case.

## §8.15 —Mental and Physical Health

The Uniform Marriage and Divorce Act (UMDA),[215] and state statutes patterned after it,[216] provide that "the mental and physical health of all individuals involved" is a relevant factor in a child custody decision. Similar statutory provisions exist in other states as well.[217] Parental mental and physical health are unquestionably important as they relate to a parent's ability to care for, guide, and teach a child, as well as fully participate in the child's life.

Courts have long recognized that parental mental and emotional health are appropriate criteria in determining the best interests of the child.[218] It has been noted that these appear as factors in initial custody determinations nearly twice as frequently as in modification cases, presumably because the condition has been longstanding and perhaps even contributed to the breakup of the marriage.[219] In cases where serious mental or emotional problems exist, as where a parent has been hospitalized or has attempted suicide, courts will

---

[215] Uniform Marriage and Divorce Act (UMDA) §402, 9A ULA 96, 198 (1979). *See also* **§8.02.**

[216] Statutes which contain the same factors as the UMDA include: Ariz Rev Stat Ann §25-332 (Supp 1983-84); Colo Rev Stat §14-10-124 (Supp 1984); Del Code Ann tit 13, §722 (1981); DC Code Ann §16-911 (1981); Idaho Code §32-717 (1983); Ill Ann Stat ch 40, §602 (Smith-Hurd 1980); Ind Code Ann §31-1-11.5-21 (Burns 1976); Kan Stat Ann §60-1610 (1983); Ky Rev Stat Ann §403.270 (Baldwin 1983); Me Rev Stat Ann tit 19, §752 (Supp 1984-85); Mo Ann Stat §452.375 (Vernon Supp 1984); Mont Code Ann §40-4-2.2 (1983); NM Stat Ann §40-4-9 (1983); Vt Stat Ann tit 15, §652 (Supp 1984); Wash Rev Code Ann §26.09.190 (Supp 1984-85); Wis Stat Ann §767.24 (West 1981).

[217] *See, e.g.,* Fla Stat Ann §61.3(3)(g) (West Supp 1984); La Civ Code Ann art 146(2)(g) (West Supp 1984); ND Cent Code §14-09-06.2(7) (1981).

[218] *See, e.g.,* Makar v Makar, 398 So 2d 717 (Ala Civ App 1981); Ridgeway v Ridgeway, 180 Conn 533, 429 A2d 801 (1980); Critchlow v Critchlow, 347 So 2d 453 (Fla Dist Ct App 1975); Sims v Sims, 171 Ga App 99, 318 SE2d 805 (1984); *In re* Marriage of Meyers, 180 Ind App 284, 387 NE2d 1360 (1979); *In re* Marriage of Kramer, 297 NW2d 359 (Iowa 1980); *In re* Marriage of Smith, 269 NW2d 406 (Iowa 1978); Richard v Richard, 359 So 2d 696 (La Ct App), *writ denied,* 360 So 2d 798 (La 1978); Angelone v Angelone, 9 Mass App 728, 404 NE2d 672 (1980); *In re* Marriage of RR, 575 SW2d 766 (Mo Ct App 1978), Leigh v Leigh, 66 AD2d 735, NYS2d 320 (1978); *In re* Marriage of Buiner, 27 Or App 703, 556 P2d 1377 (1976); Hall v Mason, ___ Pa Super ___, 462 A2d 843 (1983); Born v Born, 614 SW2d 49 (Tenn Ct App 1981); Pfeifer v Pfeifer, 62 Wis 2d 417, 215 NW2d 419 (1974). For older cases, see Annot, 74 ALR2d 1073 (1963).

[219] Atkinson, *Criteria for Deciding Child Custody in the Trial and Appeallate Courts,* 18 Fam LQ 17, 24 (1984).

award the children to the healthy parent or even a third party.[220] However, courts have not developed the rule, as they have in parental misconduct cases,[221] that a direct adverse impact upon the children must be proven before denying an unstable parent custody. Thus, some custody awards have been made to parents without an examination of the effect of the unstable parent upon the child.[222]

In many cases where the mental or emotional health of a potential custodian is at issue, the parties and children may undergo professional psychiatric or psychological examination, voluntarily or by court order. The report of the mental health professional may provide evidence of any adverse effects on the child if custody were awarded to an unstable parent. One issue which is frequently litigated is whether a court may order such examinations, either under a specific procedural rule or at the decision of the court.[223]

Like all factors in child custody decisions, the mental and emotional health of the parents are weighed in light of other factors in each case, resulting in a variety of decisions which defy simple generalizations. For example, in a Massachusetts case, a mother who had been voluntarily hospitalized for short periods of time because of emotional problems was granted custody of her children because she had been their primary caretaker and they had lived with

---

[220] *See, e.g.*, Makar v Makar, 398 So 2d 717 (Ala Civ App 1981) (wife had attempted suicide by taking an overdose of pills and then shot herself in the chest, custody awarded to father); *In re* Marriage of Meyers, 180 Ind App 284, 387 NE2d 1360 (1979) (award of custody to mother reversed because she had attempted suicide three times and had been hospitalized for treatment of breakdowns); *In re* Marriage of Smith, 269 NW2d 406 (Iowa 1978) (custody awarded to father's brother where brother had had custody for an extended period of time, father would have kept child with brother anyway for child care, and mother was unstable, had threatened to commit suicide, and was hysterical in court); Richard v Richard, 359 So 2d 696 (La Ct App), *writ denied*, 360 So 2d 198 (La 1978) (award to father where mother had been hospitalized). *Cf* Sims v Sims, 171 Ga App 99, 318 SE2d 805 (1984) (custody awarded to mother because of presumption favoring natural parent despite the fact that mother had left children with their grandmother for years while she worked out emotional problems).

[221] *See* **§8.14.**

[222] *See, e.g.*, Richard v Richard, 359 So 2d 696 (La Ct App), *writ denied*, 360 So 2d 198 (La 1978) (while there were no written reasons for custody award to father rather than mother, who had been hospitalized four years earlier, appellate court affirmed); Pfeifer v Pfeifer, 62 Wis 2d 417, 215 NW2d 419 (1974) (custody of children, who had been living with the mother for one year before the divorce with no adverse effects, was awarded to father in light of the mother's "infantile immaturity" as evinced by mentioning suicide, taking diet pills to get high, stating she was losing her mind, and threatening to kill her husband).

Of course, many courts do examine the adverse impact upon the child. *See* Ridgeway v Ridgeway, 180 Conn 533, 429 A2d 801 (1980) (court noted that children were upset after visits from mother who thought she was being "monitored," and psychiatrist expressed concern that she would hurt herself and her children); *In re* Marriage of Bainer, 27 Or App 703, 556 P2d 1377 (1977) (court noted that the juvenile counselor's child custody study demonstrated problems in the wife's relationship with the children and the effect her illness could have on her caretaking ability).

[223] *See* Annot, 99 ALR3d 268 (1980) and cases cited therein.

her.[224] Yet, in Pennsylvania, an award of custody to the father was affirmed because of the mother's emotional instability and suicide attempt despite the fact that the mother had retained custody of the children for the year after the separation and the father was involved in a nonmarital cohabitation relationship.[225] The mental and emotional health factors are so important that appellate courts have remanded cases where evidence of instability was not evaluated by the trial court.[226] Courts are reluctant to dismiss prior mental instability as a past condition unrelated to present fitness.[227]

The physical health of the parents has been an issue more in modification cases than in initial custody decisions.[228] However, the general rules gleaned from those cases are equally applicable in initial decisions. A parent's sickness or physical handicap does not render him or her an unfit custodian per se, but must be considered as to its effect on the parent-child relationship. Thus, in *In re Marriage of RR,*[229] the Missouri Court of Appeals held that there was no evidence for the trial court's finding that the children would be emotionally damaged if they lived with their father, who was confined to a wheelchair with multiple sclerosis.

*In re Marriage of Carney,*[230] a change of custody action, is a leading case in this area. The Supreme Court of California overturned a trial court's change of custody from the father, who, after five years as custodian, had become a quadriplegic in a jeep accident a year earlier. The court did this even though the mother had had little communication with her sons. The court stated the appropriate balancing test:

> In all cases the court must review the handicapped person as an individual and the family as a whole. To achieve this, the court should inquire into the person's actual and potential physical capabilities, learn how he or she has adapted to the disability and manages its problems, consider how the other members of the household have adjusted thereto, and taken into account the special contributions the person may make to the family despite—or even because of—the handicap. Weighing these and all other relevant factors together, the court should then carefully determine

---

[224] Angelone v Angelone, 9 Mass App 728, 404 NE2d 672 (1980).

[225] Hall v Mason, 316 Pa Super 160, 462 A2d 843 (1983); **§8.14.**

[226] *See, e.g.,* Critchlow v Critchlow, 347 So 2d 453 (Fla Dist Ct App 1977); Leigh v Leigh, 66 AD2d 735, 411 NYS2d 320 (1978).

[227] *In re* Marriage of Myers, 180 Ind App 284, 387 NE2d 1360 (1979) (dissent noted that mother had not been under treatment for 2-1/2 years); Pfeifer v Pfeifer, 62 Wis 2d 417, 215 NW2d 419 (1974) (mother had written letters threatening suicide, and stating that she was losing her mind at the time of the divorce).

[228] *See* Annot, 3 ALR4th 1044 (1981).

[229] 575 SW2d 766 (Mo Ct App 1978).

[230] 24 Cal 3d 725, 598 P2d 26, 157 Cal Rptr 383 (1979).

whether the parent's condition will in fact have a substantial and lasting adverse effect on the best interests of the child.[231]

In chastising the trial court for assuming that the father could not have a normal relationship with his sons, Justice Mosk eloquently capsulated the meaning of being a parent:

> Contemporary psychology confirms what wise families have perhaps always known—that the essence of parenting is not to be found in the harried rounds of daily carpooling endemic to modern surburban life, or even in the doggedly dutiful acts of "togetherness" committed every weekend by well-meaning fathers and mothers across America. Rather, its essence lies in the ethical, emotional, and intellectual guidance the parent gives to the child throughout his formative years, and often beyond. The source of this guidance is the adult's own experience of life, its motive power is parental love and concern for the child's well-being, and its teachings deal with such fundamental matters as the child's feelings about himself, his relationships with others, his system of values, his standards of conduct and his goals and priorities in life. Even if it were true, as the court herein asserted, that William cannot do "anything" for his sons except "talk to them and teach them, be a tutor," that would not only be "enough"—contrary to the court's conclusion—it would be the most valuable service a parent can render. Yet his capacity to do so is entirely unrelated to his physical prowess: however limited his bodily strength may be, a handicapped parent is a whole person to the child who needs his affection, sympathy, and wisdom to deal with the problems of growing up. Indeed, in such matters his handicap may well be an asset: few can pass through the crucible of severe physical disability without learning enduring lessons of patience and tolerance.
>
> No expert testimony was necessary to establish these facts.[232]

## §8.16 Consideration of the Factors

Custody trials are frequently harmful to children. Their interests are best served when parents reach agreement as to their custody and support without resort to the courts. Judges generally approve custody agreements without judicial investigation, recognizing that cooperative parents are better able to determine the best interests of their children than courts or government agencies.

Unfortunately, there are parents who cannot agree about child custody. Some of these parents turn to mediation to fashion a workable agreement.[233]

---

[231] *Id* 598 P2d at 42, 157 Cal Rptr at 389 (footnote omitted).

[232] 598 P2d at 44, 157 Cal Rptr at 391.

[233] *See* **§§5.05-5.13.**

Other parents, whether acting out of good intentions, fear, or hostility, enlist the aid of the family law practitioner to negotiate an agreement or obtain custody through litigation. The attorney, then, has the unrivaled task of balancing the interests of the child, the client, and the family's future.

Preparation for a custody case necessarily involves consultation of statutes and case law to determine what factors a court will consider when making an award.[234] It also demands the attorney's sensitivity, compassion, and dispassionate ability in evaluating the children's needs and the parties' rights. Nevertheless, strategy in presentation of the case will ultimately depend upon the interrelated circumstances of each unique case.

One major change in custody law over the years has been the shift in focus from parental fault to the best interests of the child.[235] At one time courts generally awarded the child to the innocent party in divorce, considering that marital fault rendered a parent unfit. Now the courts evaluate a variety of criteria in order to determine where the child will fare better after the dissolution. Thus, while courts formerly denied custody of the child to a parent guilty of adultery, nonmarital cohabitation, or active homosexuality, they now examine the evidence for any adverse impact on the child. In the absence of actual proof of harm, there is no presumption arising from the parent's sexual activity or orientation in most jurisdictions.

The important factor in most custody cases, but often unarticulated, is continuity or *status quo*.[236] Judges are loathe to uproot a child from the stability and continuity of a primary caretaker parent, friends, neighborhood, school, or church without concrete evidence that the child is being harmed in the existing situation. Mental health professionals generally favor status quo for the same basic reasons: continuity and stability. For this reason, among others, temporary custody is an advantage in a custody battle.[237] Experienced lawyers are keenly aware that the more protracted the "temporary" custody, the greater the likelihood that that custodian will become the permanent custodian.

It is the current trend in custody cases throughout the United States to provide for maximum access to both parents, whether by "liberal" visitation or joint custody arrangement.[238] Joint custody is both enthusiastically praised and vigorously opposed by parents, the mental health community, and the legal profession. A majority of states authorize joint custody by statute, insuring its place in modern custody law.

It has been observed countless times that the Solomon-like custody award is one of the most difficult judgments a court must make. In a custody trial, a judge can only briefly review and instantly glimpse a microcosm of the entire

---

[234] *See* **§§8.01-8.15**

[235] *See* **§§7.03-7.04.**

[236] *See* **§8.03.**

[237] *See* **§8.04.**

[238] *See* **ch 9.**

lives of the child and parents. The judge must evaluate future variables, predict unknowns, and render a decision which will profoundly affect the future lives of children and their parents as well as those children's children. It is difficult to know exactly how the judge has considered each factor. It is usually impossible to know what, if any, influence the judge's personal opinions and experiences have had on the case. Experienced custody trial lawyers say that it is important to know one's judge.

Child custody following divorce is a difficult and emotionally trying area of family law. The statutory factors and those deemed relevant in case law serve to guide attorneys and judges involved in custody cases. These criteria, and their application, continue to reflect the values of an ever-changing society.

## §8.17 Types of Custody Awards

Child custody is another aspect of family law which constantly adapts to societal change. Postdivorce custody awards reflect the attitudes and lifestyles of the times. In agrarian English society, where children were considered the property of their father, the law provided a nearly irrefutable presumption that the father was entitled to custody, with no right of access for the mother.[239] In urbanized, postindustrial America, where most fathers were breadwinners outside the home and mothers were housewives responsible for raising the children, the law supplied the maternal preference, insuring that mothers received custody in 90 per cent of divorces.[240]

Sole custody emerged as the product of those times, and remains the most common form of custody approved by the courts. A parent receiving sole custody is entitled to physical custody, the daily companionship of the child, and is responsible for making the controlling decisions in the child's life. The noncustodial parent has rights to visitation, usually consisting of short time periods, and may only minimally participate in important decisions in the child's life and upbringing unless greater participation is authorized by informal agreement or court order.[241]

For many years, the only alternatives to sole custody awards upon divorce were split custody, divided custody, and placement with third parties.[242] None were favored by the courts. Split custody, the awarding of sole custody of one or more children to one parent and custody of the remaining child or children to the other parent, was disapproved as damaging to healthy, desirable sibling relationships. Placement with third parties has always been made more difficult

---

[239] *See* **§6.03.**

[240] *See* Drinan, *The Rights of Children in Modern American Family Law,* 2 J Fam L 101, 102 (1962); Roth, *The Tender Years Presumption in Child Disputes,* 15 J Fam L 423 (1976-77); Weitzman & Dixon, *Child Custody Awards: Legal Standards and Empirical Patterns for Child Custody, Support, and Visitation After Divorce,* 12 UCD L Rev 473, 484 (1979).

[241] Folberg & Graham, *Joint Custody of Children Following Divorce,* 12 UCD L Rev 523, 526 (1979).

[242] See **§8.06** for a discussion of split custody.

by an acknowledgment of the rights of natural parents as well as a presumption in their favor.

Divided custody, also called joint custody, shared custody, split custody, and alternating custody,[243] is an arrangement whereby each parent lives with the child for part of the year with reciprocal visitation rights reserved to the other. Each parent exercises exclusive control over the child when in his or her custody. After near-absolute judicial prohibition of divided custody at the beginning of the century, courts began to make such awards under custody statutes authorizing custody decisions "as the case may warrant," or as "is necessary and proper," or as the children's "spiritual as well as other interests may require."[244]

Nevertheless, judicial acceptance of this precursor of modern joint custody, divided or alternating custody, has been limited. Courts feared that the "shifting of the child from one parent to the other would create instability for the child, who would have no real home, fixed environment, or permanent associations."[245] This has been particularly true where the parents' homes are far apart.[246] Other judicial concerns have included the child's confusion about parental authority and discipline, the resurrection of old marital problems by continued bickering over custody and visitation and efforts to prejudice the child against the other parent, and the child using the parents against each other.[247] In addition, courts have held that in most cases, young children are best left in the sole custody of one parent.[248]

Courts have upheld divided custody awards in special circumstances, after balancing the advantages of access to both parents with the possible instability and confusion.[249] However, frequently these awards resembled sole custody with liberal visitation for the noncustodial parent.

The divided custody cases brought greater attention to the equal rights possessed by both parents to the custody of their children. It was, however, the tumultuous, significant, and swift social changes of the 1960s, 1970s, and 1980s

---

243 This ambiguity of terms his created confusion which writers advocating joint custody as a viable option have attempted to erase. *See* **§9.02.**

244 Note, *Divided Custody of Children After Their Parents Divorce,* 8 J Fam L 58, 63 n 25, 26 (1968) and statutes cited therein.

245 Folberg & Graham, *supra* note 241, at 526; Note, *supra* note 244, at 64-65.

246 Thus, divided custody has been awarded where the parents' home environments were similar and in close proximity. *See* Mansfield v Mansfield, 230 Minn 574, 42 NW2d 315 (1950) (eight miles apart); Lutker v Lutker, 230 SW2d 177 (Mo Ct App 1950) (same city); Grant v Grant, 286 SW2d 349 (Tenn Ct App 1954) (close enough for easy transfer).

247 *See, e.g.,* Phillips v Phillips, 153 Fla 133, 13 So 2d 922 (1943).

248 Folberg & Graham, *supra* note 241, at 527, Note, *supra* note 244, at 67, n 48, noting that of the cases cited in the article, 13 denied divided custody of children under six and 5 cases allowed divided custody of children six or older.

249 *See, e.g.,* Maxwell v Maxwell, 351 SW2d 192 (Ky 1961); Davis v Davis, 354 SW2d 525 (Mo Ct App 1962); Muller v Muller, 180 Va 259, 49 SE2d 349 (1948); Reynolds v Reynolds, 45 Wash 2d 394, 275 P2d 421 (1954).

which shattered the foundations of the reign of sole custody. The women's movement, the sexual revolution, and technological advancements spurred recognition of equal rights, a flow of women into the marketplace, a redefinition of sexual roles with recognition of fathers as child caretakers, and the universal acceptance of no-fault divorce.

From this societal flux emerged the concept of joint custody, as distinguished from existing divided custody arrangements. The new concept of joint custody, sparked by grass roots campaigns by fathers interested in participating in custody and parents who had already established a form of joint custody, separated the concept of custody into two parts: physical custody, or the companionship and actual presence of the child, and legal custody, or the legal control over the child and the ability to make decisions about the child's life. Joint custody, which is the trend in child custody law, is discussed in detail in the next chapter.[250]

---

[250] *See* **ch 9.** It should be noted that custody law is continually evolving, and one area that some would like to see changed is the actual language associated with custody law. See Elkin, *The Language of Family Law is the Language of Criminal Law,* 13 Conciliation Courts Review iii, v (Sept 1975), where the author states: "We need family law words that will help society reform its current thinking as well as develop new attitudes, traditions and customs regarding divorcing families."

## Appendix 8-1
## The Parent Locator Service, 42 USC §653

§653. Parent Locator Service

(a) The Secretary shall establish and conduct a Parent Locator Service, under the direction of the designee of the Secretary referred to in section 452(a) [42 USCS §652(a)], which shall be used to obtain and transmit to any authorized person (as defined in subsection (c)) information as to the whereabouts of any absent parent when such information is to be used to locate such parent for the purpose of enforcing support obligations against such parent.

(b) Upon request, filed in accordance with subsection (d) of any authorized person (as defined in subsection (c)) for the most recent address and place of employment of any absent parent, the Secretary shall, notwithstanding any other provision of law, provide through the Parent Locator Service such information to such person, if such information—

(1) is contained in any files or records maintained by the Secretary or by the Department of Health, Education and Welfare; or

(2) is not contained in such files or records, but can be obtained by the Secretary, under the authority conferred by subsection (e), from any other department, agency, or instrumentality, or the United States or of any State.

No information shall be disclosed to any person if the disclosure of such information would contravene the national policy or security interests of the United States or the confidentiality of census data. The Secretary shall give priority to requests made by any authorized person described in subsection (c)(1).

(c) As used in subsection (a), the term "authorized person" means—

(1) any agent or attorney of any State having in effect a plan approved under this part [42 USCS §§651-660], who has the duty or authority under such plans to seek to recover any amounts owed as child and spousal support (including, when authorized under the State plan, any official of a political subdivision);

(2) the court which has authority to issue an order against an absent parent for the support and maintenance of a child, or any agent of such court; and

(3) the resident parent, legal guardian, attorney, or agent of a child (other than a child receiving aid under part A of this title [42 USCS §§601-610]) (as determined by regulations prescribed by the Secretary) without regard to the existence of a court order against an absent parent who has a duty to support and maintain any such child.

(d) A request for information under this section shall be filed in such manner and form as the Secretary shall by regulation prescribe and shall be accompanied or supported by such documents as the Secretary may determine to be necessary.

(e) (1) Whenever the Secretary receives a request submitted under subsection (b) which he is reasonably satisfied meets the criteria established by subsections (a), (b), and (c), he shall promptly undertake to provide the information requested from the files and records maintained by any of the departments, agencies, or instrumentalities of the United States or of any State.

(2) Notwithstanding any other provision of law, whenever the individual who is the head of any department, agency, or instrumentality of the United States receives a request from the Secretary for information authorized to be provided by the Secretary under this section, such individual shall promptly cause a search to be made of the files and records maintained by such department, agency, or instrumentality with a view to determining whether the information requested is contained in any such files or records. If such search discloses the information requested, such individual shall immediately transmit such information to the Secretary, except that if any information is obtained the disclosure of which would contravene national policy or security interests of the United States or the confidentiality of census data, such information shall not be transmitted and such individual shall immediately notify the Secretary. If such search fails to disclose the information requested, such individual shall immediately so notify the Secretary. The costs incurred by any such department, agency, or instrumentality of the United States or if any State in providing such information to the Secretary shall be reimbursed by him. Whenever such services are furnished to an individual specified in subsection (c)(3), a fee shall be charged such individual. The fee so charged shall be used to reimburse the Secretary or his delegate for the expense of providing such services.

(f) The Secretary, in carrying out his duties and functions under this section, shall enter into arrangements with State agencies administering State plans approved under this part for such State agencies to accept from resident parents, legal guardians, or agents of a child described in subsection (c)(3) and, after determining that the absent parent cannot be located through the procedures under the control of such State agencies, to transmit to the Secretary requests for information with regard to the whereabouts of absent parents and otherwise to cooperate with the Secretary in carrying out the purposes of this section.

(Aug. 14, 1935, c. 531, Title IV, Part D, §453, as added Jan. 4, 1975, P.L. 93-647, Part B, §101(a), 88 Stat. 2353; Aug. 13, 1981, P.L. 97-35, Title XXIII, Subtitle A, ch 2, §§2332(c), 2333(c), 95 Stat. 862, 863; Sept. 3, 1982, P.L. 97-248, Title I, Subtitle E, §171(b)(2), 96 Stat. 401.)

# 9 Joint Custody



## §9.01 The Rise of Joint Custody

Child custody disputes increased dramatically as the number of divorces skyrocketed in the no-fault era.[1] The predominant judicial disposition has continued the traditional sole custody, with the mother retaining exclusive control over the child, subject to the father's rights of visitation.

There are many problems with this traditional system. Mothers are often overburdened with the responsibilities historically assumed by both parents. Fathers are often relegated to an artificial weekend fun role absent parental authority, which strains their relationship with their children and is a contributory cause of termination of visitation and support. Some parents have resorted to child snatching in defiance of judicial decisions. Courts, flooded with custody cases, are painfully aware that protracted custody disputes are often harmful to the children. In addition, there have been legal developments, societal forces and new psychological knowledge prompting examination of the inadequacies of the traditional system and exploration of alternatives, among them the concept of joint custody.

Two legal developments particularly influential in the rise of joint custody have been the strengthening of the best interests standard and the enactment of gender-neutral legislation. The best interests of the child standard demands a judicial analysis of a variety of factors unique to each custody case, thereby reducing judicial adherence to superficial presumptions such as the maternal preference and the culpability doctrine.[2] Gender neutrality, as evinced by state equal rights amendments, alimony statutes, and laws requiring both parents to contribute to child support, has also decreased reliance on traditional sex roles.

Profound societal changes in recent decades have placed traditional families under stress. The women's movement saw a record number of mothers entering the work force. It has become acceptable for fathers to perform child-rearing tasks traditionally performed exclusively by the mother. Raising children has slowly begun to be considered a sex-neutral occupation, reflected in the language of such provisions as the *primary caretaker* performs the *mothering* or *parenting* function. Fathers have demanded greater involvement in their children's lives, and now request custody more frequently upon the dissolution of marriage.[3] Traditional sole custody runs counter to this societal flow by perpetuating the mother's role as a stay-at-home housewife and the father's role as the uninvolved sole breadwinner.

Psychological studies of what had long been assumed to be the inherent trauma of divorce showed that some of the trauma could be tied to external variables, such as the adjudication process and the structure of the custodial

---

[1] Trombetta, *Joint Custody: Recent Research and Overloaded Courtrooms Inspire New Solutions to Custody Disputes,* 19 J Fam L 23, 224 (1980-81), where the author notes that in 1960 courts decided the custody of over 400,000 children, while in 1970 the number doubled to 800,000. *See also* **§§2.02-2.05.**

[2] *See* **§§7.03-7.11.** The culpability doctrine, discussed in **§8.14,** requires courts to deny custody of the child to the guilty parent in the divorce action.

[3] *See, e.g.,* Yenkel, *Families: Fighting For Father's Rights,* Wash Post, Jan 13, 1982, at B5, col 1.

arrangement.[4] Some damaging symptoms are said to be traceable to the sole custody arrangement. Children were found to experience loss and abandonment due to the noncustodial spouse's absence.[5] Parent deprivation studies established that children experienced adverse effects associated with parental absence such as antisocial behavior, negative changes in IQ and achievement test scores, and problems with sexual identification.[6] In addition, it was shown that both parents suffered loss, dependency, guilt, anxiety, and depression previously unrecognized and perceived to be associated with divorce. Noncustodial parents especially experienced loss of their children, familiar activities, and habit systems.[7] The parents and children's experiences affected the enduring strength of their relationships, which were strained by the classic stages of mourning associated with divorce: denial, anger, depression, and resolution.[8]

Researchers were "finding that the key variable affecting satisfactory adjustment of children following divorce is the extent of continuing involvement by both parents in child rearing."[9] It was concluded that the traumatic impact of divorce on children could be decreased by parents cooperating and continuing their parental roles. Mediation and joint custody were offered as potential alternatives to litigation and the sole custody arrangement.

---

[4] Trombetta, *supra* note 1, at 216.

[5] J. Wallerstein & J. Kelly, Surviving the Breakup: How Children and Parents Cope With Divorce (1980); Schwartz, *Toward a Presumption of Joint Custody,* 18 Fam LQ 225 230 (1984) (citing Jellinek & Slovik, *Current Concepts in Psychiatry; Divorce: Impact on Children,* 305 New Eng J Med 557 (Sept 3, 1981)); Trombetta, *supra* note 1, at 217.

[6] *See, e.g.,* Miller, *Joint Custody,* 13 Fam LQ 345, 358 (1979) (citing D. Lynn, The Father: His Role in Child Development 279 (1974); Derdeyn, *A Consideration of the Legal Issues in Child Custody Contests,* 33 Archives Gen Psychiatry 165, 168 (1976); Santrock, *Effects of Father Absence on Sex-Typed Behavior in Male Children: Reason for the Absence and Age of Onset of the Absence,* 130 J Genetic Psychology 3, 8 (1977); Santrock, *Relation of Type and Onset of Father Absence to Cognitive Development,* 43 Child Dev 445 (1972); Trombetta, *supra* note 1, at 218-19 (citing Bach, *Father-Fantasies and Father-Typing in Father-Separated Families,* 17 Child Dev 63 *passim* (1946)); J. Grief, Fathers, Children and Joint Custody, 6-8 (1978) (paper presented at the Annual Meeting of the American Orthopsychiatric Association, San Francisco); E. Hetherington, M. Cox, & R. Cox, Family Interaction and the Social, Emotional and Cognitive Development of Children Following Divorce 22 (May 17-20, 1978) (paper presented at Symposium on The Family: Setting Priorities, Washington, D.C.); Sears, *Doll-Play Aggression in Normal Young Children: Influence of Sex, Age, Sibling Status, Father's Absence,* 6 Psych Monographs 65 (1951).

[7] Trombetta, *supra* note 1, at 220-21.

[8] Schwartz, *supra* note 5, at 228

[9] Folberg & Graham, *Joint Custody of Children Following Divorce,* 12 UCD L Rev 523, 535 (1979) (citing Hetherington, Cox & Cox, *Divorced Fathers,* 25 Fam Coordinator 417, 425-26 (1976); Wallerstein & Kelly, *The Effects of Parental Divorces: Experiences of the Child in Later Latency,* 46 Am J Orthopsychology256 (1976); Wallerstein & Kelly, *The Effects of Parental Divorce: Experiences of the Preschool Child,* 14 J Am Acad Child Psych 600 (1975); Wallerstein & Kelly, *The Effects of Parental Divorce: The Adolescent Experience,* in 3 The Child in His Family (E. Anthony & C. Koupernik eds 1974); Wallerstein, *Children Who Cope in Spite of Divorce,* 1 Fam Advoc 2 (1978)).

Legal writers began advocating joint custody, pointing out additional inadequacies of the sole custody system, including its inflexibility in light of the family's changing needs and its ineffectiveness at reducing parental hostilities.[10]

Finally, states began to enact joint custody laws. In 1979, only Iowa, Maine, North Carolina, Oregon, and Wisconsin had joint custody laws. By 1985, 30 states included some joint custody provision in their custody laws.[11] Joint custody has had a meteoric rise as a national family law trend.

## §9.02 Definition of Joint Custody

The term *custody* is rarely defined. It embraces a variety of child-associated rights and obligations shared by parents during a marriage and adjusted by the parents themselves or by a court upon dissolution of the marriage. *Joint custody* describes a type of custody arrangement after divorce which has gained increased recognition and acceptance in the 1980s. However, the *term* joint custody preceded today's *concept,* a factor contributing to the reasons why the concept of joint custody has been confusing and its definition elusive.

Confusion surrounds joint custody primarily because many terms have been used to describe postdivorce custody arrangements, alternatives to traditional sole custody, where parents share in the responsibility for the child.[12] At times, these terms have overlapped. For example, the Superior Court of Pennsylvania stated in one case that the labels *shared custody* and *joint custody* were "synonymous and interchangeable."[13] In *DeForest v DeForest,*[14] the parties, in their separation agreement, described as *joint custody* an arrangement whereby the child spent half of the year and seven weeks of each summer with each parent, while the Supreme Court of North Dakota labeled it *split* or *alternating custody.*

The ambiguity of terminology has been compounded by the fact that some courts in the past have approved custodial arrangements whereby physical custody and parental responsibility were shared without using any term to describe them.[15] In addition, lawyers and courts who label traditional sole

---

[10] Miller, *supra* note 6, at 355.

[11] *See* **§9.03.**

[12] In Miller, *Joint Custody,* 13 Fam LQ 345, 360, n 79 (1979) the author states:

> I have encountered at least fifteen terms used to refer to various alternatives to sole custody: joint legal custody, joint physical custody, alternating custody, split custody, managing conservatorship, possessory conservatorship, equal custody, shared custody, partial custody, custody "given to neither party to the exclusion of the other," temporary custody, shifting custody, and concurrent custody.

[13] Smith v Smith, 307 Pa Super 544, 453 A2d 1020, 1022 n 3 (1982). *See* **§8.17.**

[14] 228 NW2d 919, 922 (ND 1975).

[15] Bratt, *Joint Custody,* 67 Kent LJ 272, 283-84, n 50 (1978-79) (*citing* Hockensmith v Hockensmith, 151 KY 90, 151 SW2d 37 (1941); Riggins v Riggins, 216 KY 280, 287 SW2d 715 (1926); Baer v Baer, 235 Mo App 537, 51 SW2d 873 (1932); Zinni v Zinni,

custody arrangements joint custody in separation agreements or decrees as a placebo for a noncustodial parent further complicate the language of custody.[16]

A definition of joint custody is elusive because the term has been used to describe a broad variety of situations. There has been no uniform application of joint custody. No single arrangement results when an award of joint custody is made. Joint custody varies according to the requirements, desires, and characteristics of each family which adopts this arrangement. As stated by two writers, "No one model is adequate to describe the possibilities opened by joint custody arrangements to post-divorce families. . . ."[17]

It is, therefore, most accurate to say that joint custody is a concept which is implemented in various ways. The essence of joint custody is the participation of both parents in the child's life after divorce or dissolution. Each parent assumes equal responsibility for the physical, emotional, and moral development of the child and shares in major decisions affecting the child's life.[18] As noted by one commentator:

> The decision making process thus approximates that of an intact nuclear family. Parents with joint custody make joint decisions on all matters having a significant impact on their children's lives. Such matters include the upbringing, education, religion and financial support of the children. Also included would be medical and psychological help, if necessary, school vacations and trips, summer camp, and extra curricular activities and associations.[19]

In addition, joint custody presumes that the child has substantial interaction with both parents.

There are two components of joint custody, which are used separately or together in a joint custody arrangement. Physical custody is the actual time parents share with the child, the companionship, and the day-to-day upbringing. Contrary to popular belief, joint custody arrangements usually do not divide physical custody on a 50-50 basis. Sometimes, children spend a majority of time with one parent, while spending a weekday night and alternating weekends with the other parent.[20]

---

103 RI 417, 238 A2d 373 (1968); Grant v Grant, 39 Tenn App 539, 286 SW2d 349 (1954); Brock v Brock, 123 Wash 450, 212 P 550 (1923).

[16] *See In re* Marriage of Jenks, 55 Or App 824, 640 P2d 1032 (1982), where the Court of Appeals of Oregon held that a joint custody decree whereby the mother had physical custody subject to reasonable visitation rights was an inappropriate characterization of the arrangement, and modified the decree to award custody to the wife.

[17] Grote & Weinstein, *Joint Custody: A Viable and Ideal Alternative* 1 J Divorce 43, 45 (1977).

[18] Axelrod, Everett, & Haralambie, *Joint Custody* in A. Haralambie, Handling Child Custody Cases 50 (Shepard's/McGraw-Hill 1983).

[19] Miller, *supra* note 12, at 360 (footnote omitted).

[20] See, e.g., the examples of custody agreements, including the model used by the Northern California Mediation Center in Custody: Litigation or Liberation, The Case for Joint Custody (Section of Family Law of the ABA 1985).

The other component of joint custody has been designated *legal custody*. This is the shared authority and decision-making function. While in sole custody, split custody, and divided custody arrangements, the parent with physical custody has legal custody, in joint custody situations both parents retain it, which makes it the distinguishing feature of joint custody.

The arguments for and against joint custody, the statutory approach, and the case law involving joint custody are discussed in the following sections.[21]

## §9.03 Arguments for and Against Joint Custody

A review of arguments for and against joint custody reveals why the concept has generated controversy. Generally, the inspiring policy and goals of joint custody conflict with, or are undermined by, the practical realities of making the arrangement work successfully in daily post divorce life.

The leading argument favoring joint custody is that it is not sole custody.[22] As the criticism of sole custody has increased, joint custody looms larger as a possible alternative. Whether it will succeed as such remains to be seen.

The most obvious and important advantages of joint custody derive from the fact that a joint custody arrangement most nearly approximates an intact family. Children maintain relationships with both parents. They continue contact with their extended families. Usually, children spend more time with a joint custodial father than they might have spent with a noncustodial father or perhaps even a nondivorced father. This continued access to both parents after a divorce ensures that the children have both sexes as role models, and are exposed to different lifestyles, people, and relationships.

Another argument for joint custody is that it is flexible and adaptable to each individual family and the changing needs, circumstances, and relationships of that family. Assuming familial cooperation, the joint custody arrangement can be adjusted to compensate for changing schools, shifting role models as the children mature, and modifying parental career plans.

Supporters of joint custody contend that it creates an incentive for parental cooperation by fostering an atmosphere of detente rather than hostility.[23] The sharing of legal custody, it is argued, gives both parents a sense of dignity and self-worth not felt by noncustodial parents in sole custody arrangements. This, in turn, may prompt increased involvement by both parents with the child, with time and money, relieving the oppressive sole parenting burden experienced by some custodial parents.

Another significant argument favoring joint custody is that it decreases the likelihood of default on child support payments because bitterness over the custody decision is reduced and parental involvement in the children's lives is

---

[21] *See* **§§9.03-9.15.**

[22] Miller, *Joint Custody,* 13 Fam LQ 345, 361 (1979).

[23] Folberg & Graham, *Joint Custody of Children Following Divorce,* 12 UDC L Rev 523, 560-61 (1979).

increased.[24] Also, there is some evidence for concluding that joint custody decrees are rarely modified.[25]

The primary argument against joint custody has been that it creates instability for children, who need continuity, certainty, and a secure environment. Children whose physical custody is shared by both parents may become confused about lifestyle, rules, authority, and even socioeconomic conditions. These children may develop discipline problems or feel that they live at "daddy's house" or "mommy's house," never their own.

Another concern is whether parents whose marriage failed can communicate and cooperate to the degree necessary for a successful joint custody arrangement and not use their children as weapons and spies in parental conflict. Many lawyers are teaching their clients the principles of *coparenting*,[26] reminding them that very small things begin to become symbolic in a shared parenting arrangement.

Joint custody may cause needless tensions due to logistical and administrative difficulties. At which house should the pets, bicycles, sports equipment, dollhouses, and other important personal effects be located? These are things which are not easily carried back and forth each time the children change residences. Which parent will attend school conferences, plays, and other activities? Does it work to have both parents there, particularly when one or both have remarried? All the family members in a joint custody arrangement must work together to adjust and adapt to changing conditions such as shifting role models, increasing children's independence, parental remarriage, and relocation, all of which create the potential for modification to sole custody.

A disadvantage of joint custody is that it is more expensive than sole custody. Joint custody, particularly where physical custody is shared, requires duplication of housing expense, toys, clothing, and travel. Some lawyers have cited unexpected financial difficulty as a factor frequently leading to the failure of joint custody agreements.[27] It is questionable whether joint custody is a viable option for anyone but those who are amiably disposed to its concept. Joint custody requires an ability to compromise and determination to work daily and energetically to insure the elasticity of the arrangement.

It should be noted that the authors of *Beyond the Best Interests of the Child*[28] do not support the concept of joint custody, favoring instead an arrangement whereby one parent, usually the psychological parent, retains legal and physical

---

[24] *Id* 564; Miller, *supra* note 22, at 105 (citing Stack, *Who Owns the Child? Divorce and Child Custody Decisions in Middle Class Families,* 23 Soc Prob 505, 512 (1976)).

[25] Folberg & Graham, *supra* note 23, at 572-73, where the author makes such an argument based on the spirit of joint custody agreements, the estimation of a California commissioner, the opinion of a published attorney who has secured joint custody decrees for many of his clients, and the general practice of including a provision in joint custody agreements for periodic review by the parties.

[26] *See* **chs 7, 8, & 9.**

[27] Patterson, *The Added Cost of Sharing Lives,* 5 Fam Advoc 10, 11 (Fall 1982).

[28] J. Goldstein, A. Freud, & A. Solnit, Beyond the Best Interests of the Child 38 (1973).

custody, without any legally enforceable rights of visitation to the other. Goldstein, Freud, and Solnit declared:

> Children have difficulty in relating positively to, profiting from, and maintaining the contact with two psychological parents who are not in positive contact with each other. Loyalty conflicts are common and normal under such conditions and may have devastating consequences by destroying the child's positive relationships to both parents.[29]

One final argument against joint custody is that it may be used by parents and judges to avoid exploring all issues and reaching an ultimate decision about custody. Parents who cannot totally sever their relationship or agree to custody may use joint custody as an alternative. A judge presented with a parental agreement to a joint custody arrangement is likely to find that it is in the best interests of the child and does not merit further consideration since, at least as to this important matter, there is agreement. Of course, agreement eliminates a custody contest at trial. Joint custody is a solution which seems to serve a child's best interests better than an arbitrary or difficult award of sole custody.

## §9.04 A Review of State Joint Custody Laws—Alaska, California, Colorado, Connecticut, Delaware, and Florida

The meteoric rise of joint custody as a viable alternative to sole custody is directly attributable to state legislatures, which were prodded to action by grass roots groups of parents, legal and mental health professionals, and others. In 1979, only five states had joint custody statutes.[30] By 1985, thirty states had some statutory provision for joint custody and most state legislatures had seriously considered the issue.[31] The trend in the law favors joint custody, but, not surprisingly, the various states have adopted different approaches to it in their statutes.

The Alaska statute provides that a court may award "shared custody" if it is determined to be in the best interests of the child after a consideration of

---

[29] *Id.*

[30] *See* Folberg & Graham, *Joint Custody of Children Following Divorce*, 12 UCD L Rev 523, 542-44 (1979). The states were Iowa, Maine, North Carolina, Oregon, and Wisconsin. This article was published just as the California joint custody bill, which went into effect in 1980, was signed into law.

[31] Freed & Walker, *Family Law in the Fifty States: An Overview*, 18 Fam LQ 369, 434-35 (1985). The states providing for joint custody include: Alaska, California, Colorado, Connecticut, Delaware, Florida, Hawaii, Idaho, Illinois, Indiana, Iowa, Kansas, Kentucky, Louisiana, Maine, Massachusetts, Michigan, Minnesota, Mississippi, Missouri, Montana, Nevada, New Hampshire, New Mexico, North Carolina, Ohio, Oklahoma, Oregon, Pennsylvania, Texas, and Wisconsin. Selected statutes are included in **app 9-1**.

the same factors relevant to an award of sole custody.[32] The legislative intent, expressly stated in the law, is to assure that the child has frequent and continuing contact with each parent to the maximum extent possible.

In California, there is a presumption affecting the burden of proof that joint custody is in a minor child's best interests where the parents agree.[33] Joint custody may be ordered at the court's discretion upon application of one parent, and a court must state reasons for granting or denying the joint custody request. The California law is rich in definitions and particulars, requiring that a court specify circumstances under which the consent of both parents is necessary for the exercise of legal control, for example.

The Colorado joint custody provision is also a detailed statute.[34] It defines joint custody as an order of *legal custody* to both parents. This law specifically states that such an order does not eliminate the duty of child support and lists issues which a parent- or court-formulated plan must address. The parents must agree to such a plan for joint custody to be ordered.

In Connecticut, a court may "assign the custody of any child to the parents jointly . . . according to its best judgment upon the facts of the case and subject to such conditions and limitations as it deems equitable."[35] There also exists a presumption affecting the burden of proof that joint custody is in the child's best interests where the parents agree to such an arrangement, similar to the California rule. The Connecticut definition of joint custody is *joint legal custody.*

The Delaware Code provides that parents have joint legal custody of their children until and unless changed by agreement or court order.[36] This has been interpreted by at least one family law authority as providing for joint custody.[37] It has been reported that Delaware courts have ordered joint custody even over the objection of one parent.[38]

In 1982, the Florida legislature overturned long-standing case law forbidding joint custody by enacting the Shared Parental Responsibility Act.[39] This law establishes the public policy encouraging parents to share the rights and responsibilities of child rearing by providing that courts are to order shared parental responsibility unless such an order would be detrimental to the child.

---

[32] Alaska Rev Stat Ann §25.20.060(c) (1983). The use of the term *shared custody* adds to the multitude of names for a joint custody situation. *See* **§9.02.**

[33] Cal Civ Code §4600.5 (Deering 1984). See **app 9-1,** where this statute is included in its entirety.

[34] Colo Rev Stat §14-10-123.5 (Supp 1984). *See also* **app 9-1.**

[35] Conn Gen Stat Ann §46b-56(a) (West Supp 1985).

[36] Del Code Ann tit 13, §701 (1981).

[37] Freed, *Joint Custody Laws: An Analysis And Comparative Study,* 9 Fam L Rep (BNA) 4025 (1983); Letter from Doris Jonas Freed, Chair, Research Committee, Family Law Section, ABA, to John V. Long, Esquire (Jan 10, 1985) (including a list of states having joint custody laws).

[38] Freed & Foster, *Divorce in the Fifty States: An Overview as of August 1, 1981,* 7 Fam L Rep (BNA) 4049, 4065 (1981).

[39] Fla Stat Ann §61.13(2)(b)-(3) (West Supp 1985). *See also* **app 9-1.**

Evidence of spousal abuse and the expressed desires of the parents are among the factors to be considered along with the usual factors considered in an initial custody award. In addition, the statute allows the court to divide between the parents the different aspects of the child's life such a physical residence, education, and medical and dental care.

## §9.05 —Hawaii, Idaho, Illinois, Indiana, Iowa, Kansas, and Kentucky

In 1980, the Hawaii custody law was amended to include joint custody as an alternative to sole custody, awarded according to the best interests of the child.[40] Hawaii, unlike Colorado and Connecticut,[41] defines joint custody as including both legal and physical custody, although providing that joint legal custody may be awarded without joint physical custody.

Idaho is yet another state providing joint custody as a mechanism to assure children of continuing and frequent care by and contact with both parents.[42] The Idaho Code establishes a presumption that joint custody is in the best interests of the child, absent a preponderance of evidence to the contrary. Defining both joint legal and physical custody, and providing that a court can award either or both, the Idaho statute nevertheless requires that physical custody be shared in such a way as to insure frequent and continuing contact.

The Illinois courts may award joint legal custody, joint physical custody, or both pursuant to a specific plan if the parties agree to joint custody and to the terms of the plan, and if it is determined that the arrangement is in the child's best interests.[43] In Indiana, legal custody may be awarded jointly if in the child's best interests.[44] The statute includes a list of primary considerations in making such an award, among them the fitness of the parents, their willingness and ability to communicate and cooperate, and geographic proximity.

The Iowa law allows for joint legal custody but not joint physical custody.[45] Nevertheless, the best interests of the child analysis includes consideration of "the opportunity for maximum continuous physical and emotional contact possible with both parents, unless direct physical or significant emotional harm may result from this contact."[46] Iowa courts can assign joint custody even where the parents do not agree, must cite clear and convincing evidence if denying joint custody pursuant to a list of statutory factors, and may require

---

[40] Hawaii Rev Stat §571.46 (Supp 1984); Hawaii Rev Stat §571.46.1 (Supp 1984).

[41] *See* **§9.04.**

[42] Idaho Code §32-717B (1983). Other states with this stated policy are Alaska, California, Florida, Iowa, Louisiana, Michigan, Mississippi, Missouri, Montana, New Mexico, and Pennsylvania.

[43] Ill Ann Stat ch 40, §603.1 (Smith-Hurd Supp 1985).

[44] Ind Code §31-1-11.5-21(f) & (g) (Supp 1984-85). *See also* **app 9-1.**

[45] Iowa Code Ann §§598.21 & .41 (West Supp 1985). *See also* **app 9-1.**

[46] Iowa Code Ann §598.21(6) (West Supp 1985).

the parties to participate in custody mediation counseling to determine whether joint custody is in the child's best interests.

The Kansas joint custody law, enacted in 1983, also distinguishes between joint legal and physical custody and allows for the award of either or both if in the best interests of the child.[47] The court, in its discretion, may require the parents to submit a joint custody plan, and it must include on the record specific findings of fact justifying the denial of joint custody. The Kansas statute also allows for *divided custody,* which is actually *split custody,* to be awarded in exceptional cases.

The Kentucky custody statute broadly provides that the "court may grant joint custody to the child's parents if it is in the best interests of the child."[48]

## §9.06 —Louisiana, Maine, Massachusetts, Michigan, Minnesota, and Mississippi

The Louisiana custody statute has been twice amended to accommodate the joint custody trend.[49] In 1979, the statute was changed to provide an order of preference for custody awards in the best interests of the child. The first preference is for joint custody, to be detailed by a plan of implementation prepared by one or both parents which must allocate both the time periods of physical custody and the authority, privileges, and responsibilities of legal custody, and address other considerations listed in the statute. This section of the law also specifically dictates that joint custody does not eliminate responsibility for child support.

The Louisiana legislature's 1983 amendment established a rebuttable presumption that joint custody is in the best interests of a minor child. However, joint custody cannot be awarded if both parents agree to sole custody. The presumption may be rebutted with evidence that joint custody is not in the best interests of the child according to broad statutory standards. The law defines joint custody to include physical custody, and it encourages that custody be shared so as to assure a child of frequent and continuing contact with both parents.[50]

Maine's Parenting of Children statute avoids traditional custody terminology.[51] Courts in that state may award *allocated, shared,* or *sole parental rights and responsibilities* which are defined in the statute and include, *inter alia:* primary physical residence, parent–child contact, support, education, religious up-

---

[47] Kan Stat Ann §60-1610(a)(4)(A) (1983).

[48] Ky Rev Stat Ann §403.270(3) (Baldwin 1983).

[49] La Civ Code Ann art 146 (West Supp 1985). *See also* **app 9-1.**

[50] La Civ Code Ann art 146 (I) (West Supp 1985) also provides that a court may require, on its own motion or the motion of either party, the parties to mediate their differences. See **§§5.05-5.13;** for an overview of mediation.

[51] Me Rev Stat Ann tit 19, §752 (Supp 1984-85). The spirit of this law may be found in the stated legislative findings and purpose, which provide that mediated resolutions of disputes between parents are in the best interests of minor children. *See* **app 9-1.**

bringing, and travel boundaries. Parents agreeing to share rights and responsibilities should be allowed to do so, unless the court indicates substantial evidence against a shared award.

The Massachusetts law specifically provides that parents retain shared legal custody of their children upon commencement of a divorce action unless there is evidence presented and written findings made that shared custody would not be in the best interests of the child *and* the parents do not have a history of being able and willing to cooperate in matters concerning the child.[52] The statute requires that within 30 days of the entry of a temporary custody order the parents submit to the court in writing a plan setting forth the details of the shared legal custody. This plan must include procedures for resolving any dispute between parents with respect to child-raising decisions and duties.

The shared legal custody plan must be reviewed by a Massachusetts court within one year of the date of its adoption if a hearing on the merits has not been held within that time. At the hearing on the merits, the court determines whether the plan is in the child's best interests and whether the parents have carried out the plan according to the best interests of the child. If so, the parents' shared legal custody is to continue.

The joint custody provision of the Michigan Child Custody Act requires the court to consider joint custody at the request of either parent and to state reasons for granting or denying the request.[53] The court determines whether joint custody is in the child's best interests by considering the statutory factors used for initial custody placement,[54] as well as whether the parents will be able to cooperate and generally agree about important child-related decisions. If the parents agree on joint custody, the court shall award it unless there is clear and convincing evidence that it is not in the best interests of the child in the record. Michigan's statute defines joint custody as including both physical and legal custody. The custody order may allocate specific time periods for physical custody or may provide that physical custody is to be shared in a manner to assure the child continuing contact with both parents.

The Minnesota statute was amended in 1981 to include two subdivisions addressing joint custody.[55] The first subdivision provides definitions of *legal* and *joint legal custody, physical* and *joint physical custody,* and *custodial parent.* Another subdivision includes factors to be considered in a joint custody situation, in addition to the factors applicable to the best interests of the child. These include the ability of parents to cooperate in the rearing of their children, methods for resolving disputes regarding the child and the parents' willingness

---

[52] Mass Gen Laws Ann ch 208, §31 (West Supp 1985). Shared legal custody is defined as "a continued mutual responsibility and involvement by both parents in decisions regarding the child's welfare in matters of education, medical care, emotional, moral and religious development."

[53] Mich Stat Ann §25.312(6a) (Callaghan 1984); Wilcox v Wilcox, 108 Mich App 488, 310 NW2d 434 (1981).

[54] *See* Mich Stat Ann §25.312(3) (Callaghan 1984); **§8.02.**

[55] Minn Stat Ann §§518.003(3) & .17(2) (West Supp 1985).

to use these methods, and whether it would be detrimental to the child if one parent were to have sole authority over the child's upbringing.[56]

The Mississippi Code lists the custody options acceptable in that state: physical and legal custody to both parents jointly; physical custody to both parents jointly and legal custody to either parent; and physical and legal custody to both parents jointly and physical custody to either parent; and physical and legal custody to either parent.[57] The statute defines these terms, and provides that *joint custody* means both joint physical and legal custody. Establishing a presumption that joint custody is in the best interests of the child when the parents agree, the statute also gives the court discretion to award joint custody upon the application of one or both parents, as well as to require the parents to submit a plan for the implementation of the custody order.

## §9.07 —Missouri, Montana, Nevada, New Hampshire, New Mexico, and North Carolina

In Missouri, a court may award joint legal custody, joint physical custody, or both to parents.[58] These terms are defined in the statute, and joint physical custody must be shared so as to assure the child frequent and continuing contact with the parents. The Missouri law specifically provides that a plan setting forth the terms of joint custody must be included in the decree and that an award of joint custody does not preclude an award of child support.

In 1981 the Montana legislature, in a declaration of legislative intent, established a public policy favoring frequent and continuing contact of a minor child with separated divorced parents and encouraged these parents to share the rights and responsibilities of child rearing to effect the policy.[59] The law gives the Montana courts the authority to award joint custody according to the child's best interests, with *joint custody* encompassing both legal and physical custody. As in many states, the Montana courts require a plan of implementation from the parents and that a court state its reasons in any decision refusing to award joint custody.

Nevada is another state where a presumption affecting the burden of proof exists that joint custody is in the child's interests where the parents agree.[60] Joint legal custody may be awarded separately from physical custody where there is parental agreement. The court must state its reasons for any denial of a joint custody request.

New Hampshire extends the presumption favoring joint legal custody where

---

[56] Minn Stat Ann §518.17(2)(a)-(c) (West Supp 1985).

[57] Miss Code Ann §93-5-24 (Supp 1984).

[58] Mo Rev Stat §452.375 (Supp 1985).

[59] Mont Code Ann §40-4-222 (1983). *See also* Mont Code Ann §§40-4-223 & 224 (1983).

[60] Nev Rev Stat §§125.490 & .510 (1983).

parents agree to situations where one parent applies for joint legal custody.[61] A court in that state can award joint physical custody as it deems most conducive to the benefit of the children. A court declining to enter an award of joint legal custody must state reasons for doing so.

The New Mexico custody law states that a court "should first consider an award of joint custody" of a child if it is in the child's best interests in any proceeding where custody is at issue.[62] Joint custody is defined as encompassing joint legal custody and, if joint physical custody is not shared, as assuring frequent and continuing parent and child contact.

North Carolina law provides broadly that "[a]n order for custody of a minor child may . . . if clearly in the best interest of the child, provide for custody in two or more [persons, agencies, organizations, or institutions], at such times and for such periods as will in the opinion of the judge best promote the interest and welfare of the child."[63]

## §9.08 —Ohio, Oklahoma, Oregon, Pennsylvania, Texas, and Wisconsin

In Ohio, if both parents request joint custody, they must file a plan delineating their exercise of joint care, custody, and control of their children.[64] The statutory definition of joint custody centers on the plan,[65] which should include provisions for physical living arrangements, child support obligations, medical and dental care, school placement, and the like. Obtaining an order for joint custody involves traveling a procedural path with the plan.

A court reviews the plan to determine whether it is in the child's best interests. If it is, the plan is approved. If it is not, the parents may make appropriate changes to meet the court's objections. A court deciding that a new or amended plan is still not in the child's best interests may then reject the request for joint custody.

An approved plan is incorporated into a provisional joint custody decree which grants the parents provisional joint care, custody, and control of the child. This decree may be modified in the best interests of the child any time within 60 days of its issuance and may be terminated upon the motion of either parent or the court within 90 days. A provisional plan which survives these time

---

[61] NH Rev Stat §458.17 (II) (1983).

[62] NM Stat Ann §40-4-9.1 (1978).

[63] NC Gen Stat §50-13.2(b) (1984).

[64] Ohio Rev Code Ann §§3109.04, 3109.041 (Page Supp 1984).

[65] See Ohio Rev Code Ann §3109.04(f) (Page Supp 1984), which states:

> "Joint custody" or "joint care, custody and control," as used in the Revised Code, means that the parents share, in the manner set forth in the parents' plan for joint custody that is approved by the court, all or some of the aspects of physical and legal care, custody, and control of their children.

periods becomes final on the ninetieth day after the date of its issuance without need for further action.

Oklahoma law also requires that separating or divorcing parents requesting joint custody, whether separately or together, file their plans for the exercise of joint care, custody, and control of their child.[66] In addition, these parents must file a signed affadavit to the effect that they agree to the plan and will abide by its terms. In Oklahoma, joint custody encompasses legal and physical custody. A distinguishing feature of this law is that it provides that a court may appoint an arbitrator, "a disinterested person knowledgeable in domestic relations law and family counseling,"[67] to resolve disputes between the joint custodians. If a parent refuses to consent to arbitration, the court may terminate the joint custody decree.

The Oregon custody statute is a simple one, stating that a court may provide "[f] or the care, custody, support and maintenance of the minor children of the marriage by one party or jointly and for the visitation rights of the parent or parents not having custody of such children."[68]

In contrast, the Pennsylvania General Assembly enacted a detailed shared custody statute, introduced by a declaration of policy and purpose to assure reasonable and continuing parent-child contact and the parental sharing of the rights and responsibilities of child rearing.[69] The definitions section supplies meanings for legal, physical, and shared custody. A Pennsylvania court may award shared custody as in the child's best interests upon application of one or both parties, when the parties agree, at its discretion. The court may require the parents to attend counseling sessions and submit an implementation plan for shared custody. Judicial denial of joint custody requires a statement of reasons for denial on the record.

The Texas law, to promote amicable settlement of divorces and separations, allows parents to enter into written agreements providing for "conservatorship and support of the child, and appointment of joint managing conservators."[70]

The family code in Wisconsin lists the types of custody awards allowed by law. The second type on the list is the joint custody arrangement, if both parties agree and if in the best interests of the child.[71] The Wisconsin definition of joint custody is "that both parties have equal rights and responsibilities to the minor child and neither party's rights are superior."[72] In addition, the statute provides that legal custody of a child may be awarded.

---

[66] Okla Stat Ann tit 12, §1275.4 (West Supp 1984-85).

[67] *Id.*

[68] Or Rev Stat §107.095(1)(b) (1983).

[69] Pa Stat Ann tit 23, §§1001-1005, 1011 (Purdon Supp 1985).

[70] Tex Fam Code Ann §1406(a) (Vernon Supp 1985).

[71] Wis Stat Ann §767.23(1)(b) (West Supp 1984-85).

[72] *Id.*

## §9.09 Joint Custody Statutes—Types

The preceding statutory review reveals the different types of joint custody laws as well as common provisions possessed by many of them.[73] While an additional analysis of case law is essential for thorough understanding,[74] a summary of statutory types and provisions offers useful information to practitioners involved in joint custody cases.

One way to categorize joint custody statutes is by the role played by parental agreement. This is where the statutes vary widely.

The simplest type of statute, called "joint custody as an option"[75] by one lawyer, is a sweeping provision that joint custody may be awarded at a court's discretion. These laws may include joint custody definitions or policy declarations, but usually provide no judicial guidance or limits other than the best interests of the child standard, and any statutory factors accompanying that standard.[76] The statutes have no rules about parental agreement, which frees courts to award joint custody even against the parents' wishes. Alaska, Hawaii, Kentucky, Missouri, Montana, North Carolina, Oregon, and Pennsylvania have this general type of statute.[77] Michigan and Minnesota also have "joint custody as an option" statutes, but these laws include three additional factors to guide the court.[78]

Another type of joint custody statute allows for such awards only when the parents agree and joint custody is determined to be in the best interests of the child. It has been noted that these laws are the best joint custody legislation because they are "based on what many experts have found to be true–agreement of the parties is prerequisite to a workable joint custody arrangement."[79]

Typically, the parental agreement is evinced by a written instrument or plan developed by the parents, court, or both which describes the terms of the arrangement. States predicating joint custody awards upon the agreement of

---

[73] *See* **§§9.04-9.08.**

[74] *See* **§§9.11-9.15.**

[75] Schulman, *Who's Looking After the Children?*, 5 Fam Advoc 31 (Fall 1982).

[76] See **§8.02** for a discussion of statutory factors important to the best interests of the child standard. These factors are equally applicable in the joint custody situation.

[77] Alaska Stat §25.20.060(c) (1983); Hawaii Rev Stat §§571.46, .46.1 (Supp 1985); Ky Rev Stat Ann §403.270(3) (Baldwin 1983); Mo Rev Stat §452.375 (Supp 1985); Mont Code Ann §§40-4-222 to -224 (1983); NC Gen Stat §50-13.2(b) (1984); Or Rev Stat §107.095(1)(b) (1983); Pa Stat Ann tit 23, §1005 (Purdon Supp 1985). It should be noted that Delaware's statute, while providing that both parents are "joint natural custodians of their minor child," does not expressly delegate power to Delaware courts to award joint custody. *See* **§9.04;** Del Code Ann tit 13, §701 (1981).

[78] Mich Stat Ann §25.312(6a) (Callaghan 1984); Minn Stat Ann §518.17(2) (a-c) (West Supp 1985).

[79] Schulman, *supra* note 75, at 32.

both parties include Colorado, Illinois, Ohio, Texas, and Wisconsin.[80] In Indiana, while it is not absolutely necessary that the parents agree to joint custody, the courts are directed to "consider it a matter of primary, but not determinative importance that the persons awarded joint custody have agreed to an award of joint legal custody."[81]

It has been noted that problems can arise under this legislation.[82] A parent who does not believe joint custody is in the child's best interests may be forced into accepting an agreement out of fear of losing sole custody in a contested trial. There are no statutes which require that parental joint custody agreement be made knowingly and voluntarily by the parties.

In other states, parental agreement is more powerful, giving rise to a presumption that joint custody is in the best interests of the child. California, Connecticut, Kansas, Maine, Mississippi, and New Hampshire so provide in their custody laws.[83]

Some state legislatures fully embraced the joint custody trend either by requiring that courts give preference to joint custody arrangements over all others or by establishing an absolute presumption that joint custody is in the best interests of the child. State statutes listing joint custody as first preference include Louisiana, Mississippi, and New Mexico.[84] States which established a pure presumption in all custody cases are Florida and Idaho, while in Iowa and New Hampshire the presumption is triggered by one or both parents requesting joint custody.[85] These statutes promote joint custody as appropriate

---

[80] Colo Rev Stat §14-10-123.5(5) (Supp 1984); Ill Ann Stat ch 40, §603.1(a) (Smith-Hurd Supp 1985); Ohio Rev Code Ann §3109.04 (Page Supp 1984); Tex Fam Code Ann §1406(a) (Vernon Supp 1985); Wis Stat Ann §767.23(1)(b) (West Supp 1984-85).

[81] Ind Code §31-1-11.5-21(g) (Supp 1984).

[82] Schulman, *supra* note 75, at 32.

[83] Cal Civ Code §4600.5(a) (Deering 1984); Conn Gen Stat Ann §46b-56a(b) (West Supp 1985); Kan Stat Ann §60-1610(a)(3)(A) (1983); Me Rev Stat Ann tit 19, §752(b) (Supp 1984-85); Miss Code Ann §95-3-24(4) (Supp 1984); NH Rev Stat Ann §458.17(II) (1983).

[84] La Civ Code Ann art 146(1) (West Supp 1985); Miss Code Ann §95-3-24(1) (Supp 1984); NM Stat Ann §40-4-9.1 (1978).

[85] Fla Stat Ann §61.13(2)(b)(2) (West Supp 1985) ("The court shall order that the parental responsibility for a minor child be shared by both parents unless it finds that shared parental responsibility would be detrimental to the child"); Idaho Code §32-717B(4) (1983) ("Absent a preponderance of the evidence to the contrary, there shall be a presumption that joint custody is in the best interests of a minor child or children"); Iowa Code Ann §598.41(2) (West Supp 1985) ("On the application of either parent, the court shall consider granting joint custody in cases where the parties do not agree to joint custody. If the court does not grant joint custody . . . (it) shall cite clear and convincing evidence . . . that joint custody is unreasonable and not in the best interest of the child . . ."); La Civ Code Ann art 146(c) (West Supp 1985) ("There shall be a rebuttable presumption that joint custody is in the best interest of a minor child"); NH Rev Stat Ann §458:17 (II)(b) (1983) ("In the making of any order relative to such custody there shall be a presumption, affecting the burden of proof, that joint legal custody is in the best interests of a minor child: . . . (b) Upon application of either parent for joint legal custody, in which case it may be awarded in the discretion of the courts").

for all cases, and contradict the heart of the best interests standard, which is to insure that custody decisions are made on a case-by-case analysis of unique factors. The assumption that joint custody is appropriate or workable in all cases is unrealistic.[86] Provisions common to many of these joint custody statutes are discussed in the following section.[87]

## §9.10 Common Provisions

Certain provisions are common in the joint custody legislation, highlighting trends, the role of the practitioner in joint custody cases, and potential pitfalls.

The majority of joint custody laws have either a requirement or an option for a court-ordered plan, drafted by the parents, the court, or both, which details the specifics of the joint custody arrangement. It is important that the practitioner, as negotiator and drafter of joint custody plans, be familiar with the issues and information necessary to be included in such plans.[88]

Another common provision is for the assurance of continuity and frequent parent-child contact, which has been elevated to expressed legislative declaration in some states. These "friendly parent"[89] provisions carry the danger of encouraging bad faith requests for custody. For example, a parent who does not think joint custody is in a child's best interests in a friendly parent state may be perceived to be uncooperative and run the risk of losing custody of the child. This parent may feel pressured enough by that prospect to agree to joint custody or bargain away other rights in exchange for sole custody. A parent desiring sole custody in a state with a frequent and continuing contact standard must be prepared to produce evidence as to why joint custody is not in a child's best interests and to introduce a visitation plan which does promote contact with the other parent.[90]

Several joint custody laws mandate that a court state reasons for denying a joint custody request. This may encourage courts to prefer joint custody over sole custody and carries an assumption that joint custody is appropriate in all or most cases.[91] A fairer alternative, already existing in some states, would be to require courts to issue a statement of reasons for *all* awards.

Some joint custody legislation specifies that joint custody does not abrogate the duty of child support. This provision addresses the fear that a dependent spouse may be financially disadvantaged by a joint custody award by insuring that a court will allocate sufficient support for the child.

---

[86] Schulman, *supra* note 75, at 34. *See also* **§9.16.**

[87] *See* **§9.10.**

[88] *See* **app 9-1,** & S. Green & J. Long, Marriage and Family Law Agreements app 3 (Shepard's/McGraw-Hill 1984).

[89] Schulman, *Who's Looking After the Children?,* 5 Fam Advoc 31, 35 (Fall 1982).

[90] A. Haralambie, Handling Child Custody Cases 54 (Shepard's/McGraw-Hill 1983).

[91] Schulman, *supra* note 89, at 43.

A few state legislatures used the enactment of joint custody laws as an opportunity to statutorily provide for mediation or alternative dispute resolution. Thus, the joint custody trend supported the mediation trend.[92] In fact, the Maine legislature declared as public policy that mediation of parental disputes is in the best interests of the child.[93]

A number of joint custody statutes provide a standard for modification or termination of joint custody orders which is different from the modification standard for sole custody.[94] These statutes provide that, upon the motion of either parent or the court, a joint custody order may be modified or terminated if in the best interests of the child. In addition, a handful of statutes state that any custody order may be modified to joint custody at any time. This is yet another implied preference for joint custody over sole custody.

## §9.11 Case Law

The state legislatures, while providing a powerful push toward the use of joint custody, have certainly not been solely responsible for the trend. Joint custody law has been, and continues to be, developed and refined by the courts, at both trial and appellate levels.

Courts have played different roles in the joint custody movement. In some states where no specific joint custody statute exists, courts have decided whether they had the authority to order such arrangements.[95] In jurisdictions with joint custody laws, courts have interpreted them, enunciating and enlarging the standards and factors to be considered in the cases.[96] In addition, the judiciary has performed its tasks of evaluating facts and circumstances of individual cases to award or deny joint custody, to modify or reject modification of joint custody, and to determine whether the trial court's action should be affirmed or reversed at the appellate level.[97]

Whether guided by statutes or case law, courts have worked cooperatively with parents, fashioning joint custody agreements which further the best interests of all the parties.

## §9.12 —Authorizing Joint Custody

Some state courts have established their authority to award joint custody in the absence of a statute directly addressing the joint custody issue. In Maryland, the Court of Special Appeals decided that a chancellor could award joint custody of children to both parents even where they were involved in a "bitter,

---

92 *See* **§§5.05-5.13.**

93 Me Rev Stat Ann tit 19, §752 (Supp 1984-85).

94 *See* **§9.15.**

95 *See* **§§9.12-9.13.**

96 *See* **§9.14.**

97 *See* **§9.15.**

intense, and sometimes violent struggle over the control of the custody and lives of their children."[98] The court, adopting the position previously developed in an opinion by the state attorney general,[99] derived the authority from two sections of the Maryland Code. It decided that the statute's broad authorization to award custody did not preclude a joint custody order, and that another section, maintaining that parents were natural joint custodians of their children, supported the joint custody concept.[100] The court declared that joint custody could be awarded without the parents' agreement, but in another case cautioned that such an award could be inappropriate where the parents were not dedicated to and able to carry out the joint custody arrangement.[101]

In New York, joint custody bills were twice vetoed by the governor in the early 1980s on the ground that they put the agreement of the parents ahead of the best interests of the children.[102] Nevertheless, the New York courts, which had not hesitated to infer the power to give joint custody to both parents from the New York Custody Law, continued to do so.[103] There has been no uniform application of the term *joint custody* in that state, and no single arrangement has resulted when a joint award is made. In addition, the New York courts have refined their power to award joint custody, holding, for example, that joint custody "is encouraged primarily as an alternative for relatively stable amicable parents behaving in mature civilized fashion and should not be imposed upon embattled parents because it can only enhance familial chaos."[104]

Similarly, the Supreme Court of New Jersey held that the broad language of the custody statute included authorization for joint custody, particularly when coupled with the legislative declaration that parents involved in custody controversies are granted equal rights and responsibilities regarding the care,

---

[98] Kerns v Kerns, 59 Md App 87, 474 A2d 925, 926 (1984).

[99] Opinion no 83-024 (June 2, 1983); 68 op Atty Gen ____(1983).

[100] Kerns v Kerns, 59 Md App 87, 474 A2d 925, 927 (1984) (citing Md Ann Code art 72A, §1 (1983).

[101] Taylor v Taylor, 60 Md App 268, 482 A2d 164 (1984).

[102] See Freed & Foster, *Family Law in the Fifty States: An Overview,* 16 Fam LQ 289, 292-94 (1982), where Governor Hugh Carey is quoted as saying: "Currently, there is no legal bar in New York State to joint custody. §240 of the Domestic Relations Law provides that "in all cases there shall be no prime facie right to the custody of the child in either parent."

[103] Dodd v Dodd, 93 Misc 2d 641, 644, 403 NYS2d 401, 403 (Sup Ct 1978) (citing NY Dom Rel Law §240 (McKinney 1977) and Perrotti v Perrotti, 78 Misc 2d 131, 355 NYS2d 68 (Sup Ct 1974); Woicik v Woicik, 66 Misc 2d 357, 321 NYS2d 5 (Sup Ct 1971); Ross v Ross, 4 Misc 2d 399, 149 NYS2d 585 (Sup Ct 1956); R v R, 91 Misc 2d 792, 399 NYS2d 93 (Tram Ct 1977); Krois v Krois, NYLJ 10-14-77, 1977, at 13, col 5; Levy v Levy, NYLJ 1-29-76, 1976, at 11, col 3; Schack v Schack, NYLJ 8-21-74, 1974, at 15, col 8.

[104] Braiman v Braiman, 44 NY2d 584, 378 NE2d 1019, 1021, 407 NYS2d 449, 451, (1978). *See also* Reed v Reed, 93 AD2d 105, 462 NYS2d 73 (1983).

nurture, education, and welfare of their children.[105] Declining to create a presumption favoring joint custody, the court elaborated upon factors to be considered when awarding joint custody, maintaining "that the necessary elements will coalesce only infrequently."[106] The New Jersey courts then described a guideline to be followed in such cases. The threshold question was whether a sufficient parent-child relationship existed so that the child would benefit from joint custody. If so, the focus was shifted to the parents: their fitness, willingness to accept custody, and degree of cooperation.

The New Jersey Supreme Court encouraged trial courts to award joint legal custody where joint physical custody was not feasible. The considerations surrounding joint physical custody include: financial status of the parties, proximity of their homes, and demands of parental employment. Joint custody law, as crafted by the judiciary in New Jersey, is that it is not necessary for the parties to agree to joint custody for such an award to be ordered.

The Supreme Court of Utah, acknowledging lack of statutory authority either permitting or prohibiting a joint custody arrangement, held that Utah courts had the power to award joint custody under its broad custody statute.[107] The court appeared to require parental cooperation and agreement as prerequisites to a joint custody award.[108]

Other courts have also authorized joint custody awards in absence of a specific statute.[109]

## §9.13 —Disapproving Joint Custody

Only a few courts have expressly disapproved of joint custody absent a statute.[110]

---

[105] Beck v Beck, 86 NJ 480, __, 432 A2d 63, 65 (1981). The court continued:

> Although not an explicit authorization of joint custody, this clearly related statute indicates a legislative preference for custody decrees that allow both parents full and genuine involvement in the lives of their children following a divorce. This approach is consonant with the common law policy that "in promoting the child's welfare, the court should strain every effort to attain for the child the affection of both parents rather than one." Turney v Nooney, 5 NJ Super 392, 397, 69 A2d 342 (App Div 1959).

[106] 432 A2d at 71.

[107] Lembach v Cox, 639 P2d 197, 200 (Utah 1981).

[108] *Id* 200, where the court stated:

> The trial court found, based upon testimony and argument, that a joint custody arrangement is not appropriate for parents who cannot cooperate with each other. . . . The fact that the mother and father could not negotiate a joint custody arrangement demonstrates the inappropriateness of ordering joint custody. It was not an erroneous application of a legal standard.

[109] *See, e.g.*, Freitag v Freitag, 318 NW2d 760 (ND 1982); Zinni v Zinni, 103 RI 417, 238 A2d 373 (1968).

[110] More courts have disapproved of divided custody. *See* **§8.06.** In the District of Columbia, Utley v Utley, 364 A2d 1167 (DC 1976), is sometimes interpreted as a

In a 1984 Nebraska case,[111] a father who was not awarded sole custody of his children urged the state supreme court to adopt the concept of joint custody, particularly where both parents were found to be fit and proper persons to have custody. The court rejected the father's request, stating:

> We believe, however, that [joint custody] arrangements must be reserved for the most rare of cases, i.e., where in the judgment of the trial court the parents are of such maturity that the arrangement will not operate to allow the child to manipulate the parents or confuse the child's sense of direction. A collateral question exists as to why those most ideal of parents, who would satisfactorily cope with the conflicts inherent in a joint custody arrangement, came to be divorced in the first instance. . . . We are not prepared to reject the concept of joint custody, but are not prepared to state that it should be a regular tool in the remedies of the district court.[112]

The premier example of disapproval of joint custody is the oft-cited Vermont case, *Lambra v Lambra.*[113] There, the parties appealed an award of joint custody which the trial court had adopted verbatim in the order from the recommendation of an attorney representing the children, without making any findings of fact on the children's best interests. The Supreme Court of Vermont, defining joint custody as joint *legal* custody, noted the special problems which might erupt in a joint custody arrangement, including degree of cooperation between parents unable to agree on custody, confusion to the children, and lack of a stable home life where the children are exposed to separate households and routines.

After evaluating these problems, the court held that:

> [J]oint custody should only be decreed in cases where there is a finding of extraordinary circumstances. Joint custody is rarely the best solution to a custody dispute from the child's point of view. . . .
>
> We do not hold that joint custody is against the best interests of the child as a matter of law. *We rather presume that this is so,* and require a finding

---

disapproval of joint custody. However, the arrangement of which the District of Columbia Court of Appeals disapproved was a divided custody situation, where the child was to be in the physical custody of one parent for a month, then in the custody of the other for the next month. In fact, the trial court never discussed joint legal custody, and the appeals court expressly stated: "Generally, *divided custody* of a child of tender years is not favored." *Id* 1170 (emphasis added). Nevertheless, the court of appeals indicated that had there been any exceptional circumstances or compelling reason why the custody arrangement could reasonably have been in the best interests of the child, it might have been affirmed.

[111] Tremble v Tremble, 218 Neb 118, 352 NW2d 599 (1984).

[112] *Id* 601.

[113] 136 Vt 529, 394 A2d 1139 (1978).

> of some special circumstance indicating that such disposition would serve the child's best interests to overcome the presumption.[114]

Despite the presumption against joint custody, the Supreme Court of Vermont enunciated several factors to be considered in making a determination on joint custody. These include fitness of parents, parental cooperation, age of the child, distance between the houses, frequency of transportation, and the fair proportion of each parent's custodial time.

It should be noted that joint custody was expressly disapproved by some state courts before joint custody was authorized by statute.[115]

## §9.14 —Interpreting Joint Custody Statutes

Another role of the courts in the joint custody trend has been to interpret the joint custody statutes, thereby further developing the law.

In *In re Marriage of Wood,*[116] the Court of Appeal of California, Fifth Circuit, was presented with the opportunity to interpret the language of the state's joint custody statute.[117] The court answered the question of whether judicial findings were required upon modification of sole custody to joint custody in the negative, declaring that the statute mandating reasons when a court denied joint custody, or modified or terminated joint custody, did not apply. The court responded to the mother's contention, supported by case law, that joint custody could not be awarded absent parental agreement by identifying the statutory language which allowed such an award. The court pointed out that the mother's cited authority was pre-joint custody law, and that "[i]n adopting or amending statutes, the legislature is presumed to have acted with knowledge of existing domestic judicial decisions and to have enacted or amended statutes in light of such decisions. . . ."[118]

In *Malchiodi v Malchiodi,*[119] a District Court of Appeal of Florida curtly held that the state's Shared Parental Responsibility Act[120] had no retroactive application to child custody judgments which became final prior to the effective date of the Act. In another short decision, the Texas Court of Appeals interpreted the custody statute in overturning a trial court's appointment of

---

[114] *Id* 1142 (emphasis added).

[115] *See* Elebash v Elebash, 450 So 2d 1268 (Fla Dist Ct App 1984); Scott v Scott, 401 So 2d 819 (Fla Dist Ct App 1981); Bienvenu v Bienvenu, 380 So 2d 1164 (Fla Dist Ct App 1980).Wood v Wood, 400 SW2d 431 (Mo Ct App 1976).

[116] 141 Cal App 3d 671, 190 Cal Rptr 469 (1983). *See also* Wilcox v Wilcox, 108 Mich App 488, 310 NW2d 434 (1981).

[117] Presently Cal Civ Code §4600.5 (Deering 1984).

[118] *In re* Marriage of Wood, 141 Cal App 3d 671, 683, 190 Cal Rptr 469, 477 (1983).

[119] 431 So 2d 301 (Fla Dist Ct App 1983). *See also* Vazquez v Vazquez, 443 So 2d 313, *review denied* 451 So 2d 851 (Fla 1983).

[120] Fla Stat Ann §61.13(2)(b) (West Supp 1985).

a husband and wife as joint conservators.[121] After reviewing the statutory language, the court held that a trial court could appoint one conservator, but joint conservatorship was solely a product of parental agreement.

It should be noted that the judiciary and the legislature sometimes work together, influencing each other while creating law. A powerful example of this influence is found in Iowa joint custody law. In *In re Burham,*[122] the Supreme Court of Iowa reviewed a joint custody award to see if it was in the best interests of the Burham children, in light of the then-recent legislation permitting joint custody awards. In deciding that such an arrangement was not workable in the case at bar, the court provided tests for appropriateness taken from opinions and commentaries to assist Iowa courts in applying the new law.[123] Similar versions of these tests were later added to an amended joint custody law.[124]

Four years later, the Supreme Court of Iowa was again to decide whether a trial court's award of joint custody was in the child's best interests.[125] Once again, the court interpreted the statute, this time focusing on the factors added to the law after the *Burham* decision. The court stated:

> We would be remiss if we did not mention and correct certain misconceptions counsel and trial courts have concerning joint custody. None of the eight factors which judges must weight in the balance are conditions precedent to a joint custody determination. The trial court should consider and express itself in writing on those factors among the eight listed which are pertinent in disputed cases, but there is no magic number of the factors which, when satisfied, will mandate a decision for

---

[121] Coles v Coles, 676 SW2d 226 (Tex Ct App 1984).

[122] 283 NW2d 269 (Iowa 1979).

[123] *Id* 274, which includes:

(1) Is each parent fit and suitable as a custodial parent?

(2) Do the parents agree to joint custody, or is one or both opposed?

(3) Have the parents demonstrated that they are able to communicate and give priority to the child's welfare such that they are capable of reaching shared decisions in the child's best interests?

(4) Is there geographical proximity such that there will be no substantial disruption of the child's schooling, association with friends, religious training, or other routines?

(5) Is there similarity in the environment of each parent's home, or will the child be confronted with vastly different or potentially disruptive environmental changes?

(6) Is there any indication that the psychological and emotional needs and development of the child will suffer due to a particular joint custodial arrangement?

(7) Are the work hours and routines of both parents such that child care will be suitable with either parent?

(8) Is joint custody in accord with the child's wishes and does he or she not have strong opposition to such an arrangement?

[124] Iowa Code Ann §598.41 (West Supp 1985). *See* **app 9-1.**

[125] *In re* Marriage of Weidiner, 338 NW2d 351 (Iowa 1983).

or against joint custody. The quality of the total family custodial setting rather than a given quantity of the listed factors should be determinative on the issue of joint custody.[126]

## §9.15 —Awarding, Denying, and Reviewing Joint Custody

Perhaps the most crucial function of the courts in the custody process following marriage dissolution is making the final decision as to which parent shall retain custody. This is important both at the trial and appellate level. The number of cases dealing with joint custody is growing, particularly at the appellate level. Because custody cases are unique, their precedental value is limited. However, the cases serve as a guide for the practitioner to the issues, facts, and circumstances which may be important in joint custody cases.

In California, it was held that an award of joint legal custody was not an abuse of discretion where the parents lived 700 miles apart, the mother had previously interfered with the father's visitation rights, and the parents could not get along.[127] Florida courts disapprove of frequent exchanges of physical custody and depriving children of necessary stability, security, and comfort.[128] In Louisiana, where the statute provides a list of factors to be used to rebut the presumption favoring joint custody,[129] a court of appeal held that a father introduced sufficient evidence to rebut the presumptions in an arrangement whereby the child would be with each parent in alternating weeks, and when school began, the child would stay with the mother during the week and with the father on weekends, holidays, and for two summer months.[130] The evidence weighed included the distance between the two parents' homes, the disruptive frequent traveling required, which would upset the child's stability and continuity, and the mother's attempt to undermine the child's respect and love for the father.

The Minnesota Supreme Court held that yearly rotations in a joint custody arrangement were no different from frequent modifications of an award which, absent extraordinary circumstances, did not serve the involved children.[131] The court reiterated what it saw as the important factors in the case: the ability of the parents to cooperate and the desirability of maintaining continuity.

Although not rejecting a court-approved stipulation granting the parties joint custody of their children, the Supreme Court of Montana remanded one

---

[126] *Id* 358.

[127] *In re* Marriage of Wood, 141 Cal App 3d 671, 190 Cal Rptr 469 (1983).

[128] *See* Elebash v Elebash, 450 So 2d 1268 (Fla Dist Ct App 1984); Frey v Wagner, 433 So 2d 60 (Fla Dist Ct App 1983).

[129] La Civ Code Ann art 146(c)(2) (West Supp 1985).

[130] Bishop v Bishop, 457 So 2d 264 (La Ct App 1984). *See also* Hatchett v Hatchett, 449 So 2d 626 (La Ct App 1984); Peters v Peters, 449 So 2d 1372 (La Ct App 1984).

[131] Heard v Heard, 353 NW2d 157 (Minn 1984).

case to the district court for an additional hearing to determine whether the children's interests were being served by a joint custody arrangement where the geographic distance between the parents was fostering antagonism between the parents.[132]

The New Hampshire Supreme Court affirmed an award of sole custody to the mother in one case where the father was granted almost as much time in visitation as the mother had, thus assuring the child would maintain a relationship with both parents.[133] The court noted that it was not compelled to award joint custody in every case.

The numerous joint custody cases in New York provide practitioners in that state with an abundance of guidance, or, at least, information about New York joint custody law. *Braiman v Braiman*[134] held that joint custody was a rare custodial alternative never to be used where the parents were incapable of cooperating. In *Bazant v Bazant*[135] the court held that an award of joint custody to parents was appropriate despite the geographic distance between the one parent in Buffalo and the other in Saskatchewan, Canada, and the fact that there was some animosity between the parents. An award of joint custody of an 18-year-old child to both parents was found to be unwarranted where the mother had expressed no desire for custody and the child was capable of choosing with which parent he wanted to live.[136] Oregon courts have stressed cooperation between the parents in case law.[137]

The practitioner reviewing case law in his or her jurisdiction should pay attention to issues which arise repeatedly in the joint custody cases such as parental cooperation, geographical proximity, and, of course, continuity and stability for the children.

## §9.16 When Joint Custody Is Appropriate

Experienced family law practitioners know that marriage dissolution is traumatic for families, inspiring hostility, anger, grief, and other powerful emotions. Yet, there exists this movement in the law toward joint custody, a concept founded on cooperation, agreement, and understanding. Creating a joint custody agreement from a broken marriage might be compared to fitting

---

[132] Quinn v Quinn, 622 P2d 230 (Mont 1981).

[133] Starkeson v Starkeson, 119 NH 78, 397 A2d 1043 (1979).

[134] 44 NY2d 584, 378 NE2d 1019, 407 NYS2d 449 (1978).

[135] 439 NYS2d 521 (1981).

[136] Hoffman v Hoffman, 68 AD2d 806, 413 NYS2d 719 (1979). See also Bergson v Bergson, 68 AD2d 931, 414 NYS2d 593 (1977), which involved custody of a 15-year-old where the parents were so bitter and lacking in cooperation that an award of joint custody was impossible.

[137] *See, e.g., In re* Marriage of Clement, 52 Or App 101, 627 P2d 1263 (1981); *In re* Marriage of Handy, 44 Or App 225, 605 P2d 738 (1980); *In re* Marriage of Bohn, 43 Or App 561, 603 P2d 781, *modified,* 288 Or 697, 607 P2d 1375, *on remand,* 45 Or App 623, 609 P2d 390 (1979).

a square peg into a round hole. Although frequently it is claimed that joint custody agreements grow stronger over time after the dissolution turmoil has faded and adjustment crises have been overcome, how can a lawyer tell in the midst of the trauma that joint custody is the alternative to pursue for the client? After all, if joint custody is successful, the entire family benefits greatly. If it fails, the cost is very ominous: potential psychological problems, particularly for the children, severely damaged relationships, and further litigation.

There are some conditions conducive to a joint custody arrangement of which the practitioner should be aware. It should be noted that these conditions are irrelevant to strategy decisions which ignore the best interests of the child.[138] These conditions are discussed in case law and articles, and have been incorporated into some joint custody statutes.[139]

An initial condition for successful joint custody is that both parents be *fit.* This means that they should be both physically and psychologically capable of fulfilling the role of parent, making rational child-rearing decisions, and providing love and care to their children.

Parental cooperation is an essential condition; judges have awarded or denied joint custody based solely on the presence or absence of it.[140] Cooperation implies that the parents agree to the joint custody arrangement, share some child-rearing philosophies, and have a moderate degree of trust in and respect for each other. The parents must show willingness to make decisions together in the best interests of the child.

Another important condition is honest parental communication. Problems will arise which will require discussion for resolution. It will be necessary for parents to talk about all aspects of the arrangement, from logistics, to travel, to purchases, to education, to health and beyond.

Of course, the parents must be willing to continue their active involvement in raising their child. Joint custody should be the custodial alternative which would disrupt the parent-child relationship the least.

Other factors which are helpful, but not absolutely necessary, for joint custody are: flexible work schedules, as workaholics do not make good joint custodians; similar homes offered by each parent; sufficient financial means; and geographic proximity.

Practitioners can recognize the poor candidates for joint custody. They are parents who do not communicate or cooperate; they are actively litigating for the custody of their children. These parents are fighting for custody for reasons not related to the benefit of the child, such as vengeance, guilt, an opportunity

---

[138] An example of such a strategy decision is discussed in **§9.09.**

[139] *See e.g.,* A. Haralambie, Handling Child Custody Cases §5.06 (Shepard's/McGraw-Hill 1983); Folbert & Graham, *Joint Custody of Children Following Divorce,* 12 UCD L Rev 523, 579 (1979); Gardner, *Joint Custody Is Not For Everyone,* 5 Fam Advoc 7, 9 (Fall 1982); Miller, *Joint Custody,* Fam LQ 345, 370-72 (1979); Ind Code §31-1-11.5-21(g) (Supp 1984); Iowa Code Ann §598.41 (West Supp 1985); *In re* Marriage of Burham, 283 NW2d 269, 274 (Iowa 1979); **§9.15.**

[140] *See* **§9.15.**

to shift responsibility, or a stronger negotiating position. As one child psychiatrist has noted:

> Joint custody is a terrible compromise for warring parents. When recommended in such situations, what may actually result is a *no-custody* arrangement that merely is called joint custody. Neither parent has power or control, and the children find themselves in a no-man's land exposed to their parents' crossfire and available to both as weapons. The likelihood of children developing a psychological problem in such a situation is practically 100 percent.[141]

Because conflict is so prevalent in dissolutions, it is important that parents have an ability to move beyond marital conflict, or sever marital issues from child-related ones, in order to prevent contamination of their parenting of their child.

## §9.17 The Role of the Lawyer

The family law practitioner has important tasks in a joint custody case: defining joint custody for the client; ascertaining whether such an arrangement is appropriate for the family; influencing the client's behavior and approach to coparenting; and negotiating and drafting an agreement.

It is important to define joint custody for the client, who may hold the popular belief that joint custody is 50-50 division of physical custody in a state where only joint legal custody is allowed. Then, the practitioner should ask questions to discern whether negotiating joint custody is appropriate.

Has the client been actively involved in the child's life? Has the client participated in raising the child, performing such tasks as feeding, bathing, taking the child to school, the doctor's, a friend's? Does the client want joint custody? What are the client's needs and concerns? Do the parties have a history of cooperation in the marriage? Why does the other spouse want joint custody? What are the other spouse's needs and concerns? Do the parties communicate with each other? Have third parties influenced the client's desire for joint custody?

In cases involving joint custody, the lawyer has the opportunity to be a teacher. Persuading the client to acknowledge the other spouse's emotional needs can teach the client empathy for that other spouse, which is an important building block for a successful joint custody arrangement. The lawyer should teach the client that joint custody is something to *do* and not to *get,* so that the client will increase any participation in the child's life, open communication with the other spouse, and practice flexibility. The lawyer must also insure that the client accepts responsibility for the joint custody arrangement. For example, a common problem occurs where a parent who has less custodial time

---

[141] Gardner, *supra* note 138, at 9.

with the children cannot take the children as planned. That parent must find an appropriate solution to the problem, and not simply call the other parent and cancel the custodial time. The parent must respect the other parent's need for independence and make arrangements to accommodate the plan, like finding a sitter for the children.

A client interested in joint custody should be advised to work out a custodial routine with the other parent immediately and follow it, even if the parents are still living together. This creates regularity, fosters stability, minimizes hostility, and nurtures trust. The lawyers should also encourage the client to resolve all conflicts with the spouse as a means to strengthen the joint custody arrangement. This has the added advantage of reducing client reliance on the lawyer and enhances the client's independence in life.

The lawyers representing the parents can also contribute to the success of the joint custody arrangement by establishing some ground rules for negotiation. The lawyers can agree to separate the negotiations about custody from the negotiations about money, with a commitment to be fair about the child support. In addition, the lawyers can agree to a conflict resolution process such as mediation, if it would help the case, as well as agree to a mental health process, if it seems warranted. A planning session between the two lawyers can clarify common interests and bargaining positions.

A useful tool in establishing a joint custody schedule is a two- or four- way conference call, involving both parents and their lawyers. A goal for this type of conference is to get very specific about day-to-day events. It is often useful to encourage the parents to meet weekly or monthly in neutral territory, such as a coffee shop or park, to work out any glitches in the system. Once again, in joint custody communication is the key.

## §9.18 —Drafting the Agreement

Ideally, the joint custody agreement should be drafted and included in the total marital settlement contract after the parents have established a joint custody routine between themselves. In this situation, the parents probably will have experienced the reality of day-to-day living with joint custody, including the exchange of the child and other logistical maneuvers, as well as the need for constant communication and cooperation between them. Thus, they will have an informed idea of the topics to include in the agreement.

As joint custody grows more popular as an alternative to sole custody and more joint custody agreements are drafted, certain clauses are being commonly included, tailored to the specific circumstances. These clauses do not necessarily follow the order in which they are discussed here.

The typical joint custody agreement opens with the declaration of the parents' agreement to joint custody, which may acknowledge the parents' love for their children and their equal desires to fully participate in the life of the children. The parameters of joint legal custody should be detailed, including parental involvement in decisions regarding the child's health, welfare, education, and upbringing. A clause requiring equal access to all records might be included, whether or not provided for by statute. The agreement could state specifically that the parents will consult frequently in an effort to mutually agree on the decisions which confront them. A useful clause allows each parent to make unilateral decisions in emerging situations.

The agreement should cover the arrangements for physical custody, primary residence, and nonresidential parent access in detail. Thus, agreements typically establish the weekly time periods to the hour, as well as the division of holidays, birthdays, Mother's and Father's Days, and summer vacation. A plan for the exchange of the child may also be included. Some parents have found that school is an effective neutral exchange area which also insures continuity in the child's life. If necessary, a clause stating that both parents are entitled to attend special activities in which the children are involved such as school programs, religious activities, sports events, and the like may be placed in the contract. This type of clause may satisfy parents eager to retain maximum access to their child's life.

Sometimes the parents may want to contractually provide that they will encourage the child's love and affection for both of them, or in the negative, will not attempt to estrange the child from the other parent. It is commonly provided that each parent will inform the other of the child's whereabouts, the details of any vacation plans, including addresses and telephone numbers, or of any illness or accident befalling the child.

Probably the most important part of a joint custody agreement deals with the possibility of the removal of the child from the state due to one's parent's change of residence. This subject should be discussed by the parties, who must be made aware of future problems. An initial resolution of the difficulty might be to include a *notice requirement* mandating that the parents notify each other even of the possibility of a change in residence out of the state. One example of such a clause is:

> *Notice of Moving.* Neither parent shall move from the city of Boise without first giving sixty (60) days advance written notice by certified mail to the other person so that adequate adjustments can be made concerning visitation, custody, support, and the costs and expenses of sharing transportation concerning visitation with the child should the move actually take place.
>
> If the parties cannot reach a voluntary agreement concerning the change of residence by one or both of them, this will give the court adequate time to make a ruling on those circumstances which may differ from what is contemplated herein because of the proposed move.[142]

The agreement may provide a mechanism for handling other future problems as well, particularly serious physical or emotional problems of the children, physical or emotional disability or impairment of either parent,

---

[142] Buser, *A Typical Joint Custody Agreement,* 5 Fam Advoc 26, 28 (Fall 1982).

remarriage or cohabitation by a parent, and changes in the children's needs as they mature.

A joint custody agreement may also detail any financial arrangements associated with the sharing of custody. For example, the parties may establish an account into which they deposit a monthly amount for the expenses of the children. The agreement may simply provide that each parent will be responsible for the expenses of the child while in that parent's custody, or a child support payment may be given to a dependent spouse. The agreement may also include provisions on day care, babysitting, allowance, or travel expenses.

A joint custody agreement may provide for mediation, and should include some language on jurisdiction, modification, and renegotiation. Any other clauses appropriate to the circumstances of the parties should be added as well.

# Appendix 9-1
# Selected State Joint Custody Statutes

## Cal Civ Code §4600.5 (Deering 1984)

### §4600.5 (Joint Custody)

(a) There shall be a presumption, affecting the burden of proof, that joint custody is in the best interest of a minor child where the parents have agreed to an award of joint custody or so agree in open court at a hearing for the purpose of determining the custody of a minor child of the marriage.

(b) Upon the application of either parent, joint custody may be awarded in the discretion of the court in other cases. For the purpose of assisting the court in making a determination whether an award of joint custody is appropriate under this subdivision, the court may direct that an investigation be conducted pursuant to the provisions of Section 4602.

(c) Whenever a request for joint custody is granted or denied, the court, upon the request for any party, shall state in its decision the reasons for granting or denying the request. A statement that joint physical custody is, or is not, in the best interest of the child shall not be sufficient to meet the requirements of this subdivision.

(d) For the purposes of this part:

(1) "Joint custody" means joint physical custody and joint legal custody.

(2)"Joint custody" means that a child shall reside with and under the supervision of one parent, subject to the power of the court to order visitation.

(3) "Joint physical custody" means that each of the parents shall have significant periods of physical custody. Joint physical custody shall be shared by the parents in such a way so as to assure a child of frequent and continuing contact with both parents.

(4) "Sole legal custody" means that one parent shall have the right and the responsibility to make the decisions relating to the health, education, and welfare of a child.

(5) "Joint legal custody" means that both parents shall share the right and the responsibility to make the decisions relating to the health, education, and welfare of a child.

(e) In making an order of joint legal custody, the court shall specify the circumstances under which the consent of both parents is required to be obtained in order to exercise legal control of the child and the consequences of the failure to obtain mutual consent. In all other circumstances, either parent acting alone may exercise legal control of the child. An order of joint legal custody shall not be construed to permit an action that is inconsistent with the physical custody order unless the action is expressly authorized by the court.

(f) In making an order of joint physical custody, the court shall specify the right of each parent to the physical control of the child in sufficient detail to enable a parent deprived of that control to implement laws for relief of child snatching and kidnapping.

(g) In making an order for custody with respect to both parents, the court may award joint legal custody without awarding joint physical custody.
(h) In making an order of joint physical custody or joint legal custody, the court may specify one parent as the primary caretaker of the child and one home as the primary home of the child, for the purposes of determining eligibility for public assistance.
(i) Any order for joint custody may be modified or terminated upon the petition of one or both parents or on the court's own motion if it is shown that the best interests of the child require modification or termination of the order. The court shall state in its decision the reasons for modification or termination of the joint custody order if either parent opposes the modification or termination order.
(j) Any order for the custody of a minor child of a marriage entered by a court in this state or any other state may, subject to the jurisdictional requirements set forth in Sections 5152 and 5163, be modified at any time to an order of joint custody in accordance with the provisions of this section.
(k) In counties having a conciliation court, the court or the parties may, at any time, pursuant to local rules of court, consult with the conciliation court for the purpose of assisting the parties to formulate a plan for implementation of the custody order or to resolve any controversy which has arisen in the implementation of a plan for custody.
(1) Notwithstanding any other provision of law, access to records and information pertaining to a minor child, including but not limited to medical, dental, and school records, shall not be denied to a parent because such parent is not the child's custodial parent.

**Colo Rev Stat §14-10-123.5 (Supp 1984).**

**14-10-123.5 Joint custody.** (1) For the purposes of this article, "joint custody" means an order awarding legal custody of the minor child to both parties and which provides that all decisions regarding the health, education, and general welfare of the child shall be made jointly. The order may designate one party as a residential custodian for the purpose of determining the legal residence of the child and may provide that, under emergency circumstances, it is sufficient for one party to sign legal releases or to take any other necessary measures.

(2) Joint custody shall not eliminate the duty of child support ordered pursuant to section 14-10-115, nor shall joint custody alone constitute grounds for modification of a support order. In making the determination of child support, the court may consider, in addition to the factors specified in section 14-10-115, the ability of each party to maintain adequate housing for the child and may order modified support payments to continue from one party to the other during a period when the child is not residing in the home of the payee.

(3) In order to implement joint custody, both parties may submit a plan or plans for the court's approval. If no plan is submitted or if the court does not approve a submitted plan, the court, on its own motion, shall formulate a plan

which shall address and resolve, where applicable, the parties' arrangements for the following:

(a) The location of both parties, the period of time during which each party will have physical custody of the child, and the legal residence of the child;

(b) The child's education;

(c) The child's religious training, if any;

(d) The child's health care;

(e) Finances to provide for the child's needs;

(f) Holidays and vacations; and

(g) Any other factors affecting the physical or emotional health and well-being of the child.

(4) The court may order mediation to assist the parties in formulating or modifying a plan or in implementing a plan specified in subsection (3) of this section any may allocate the cost of said mediation between the parties.

(5) The final plan specified in subsection (3) of this section shall be jointly agreed by the parties.

(6) Any provisions relating to joint custody in this article shall apply only to an order of joint custody entered on or after July 1, 1983.

(7) Notwithstanding any other provisions of law to the contrary, access to information pertaining to a minor child, including but not limited to medical, dental, and school records, shall not be denied to the noncustodial parent.

**Fla Stat Ann §61.13(2)(b)-(3) (West Supp 1985).**

. . . .

(2)(b) 1. The court shall determine all matters relating to custody of each minor child of the parties as a part of any proceeding under this chapter in accordance with the best interests of the child and in accordance with the Uniform Child Custody Jurisdiction Act. It is the public policy of this state to assure each minor child frequent and continuing contact with both parents after the parents have separated or dissolved their marriage and to encourage parents to share the rights and responsibilities of child-rearing. Upon considering all relevant factors, the father of the child shall be given the same consideration as the mother in determining custody without regard to the age of the child.

2. The court shall order that the parental responsibility for a minor child be shared by both parents unless it finds that shared parental responsibility would be detrimental to the child. The court shall consider evidence of spouse abuse as evidence of detriment to the child. If the court determines that shared parental responsibility would be detrimental to the child, it may order sole parental responsibility. If the court finds that spouse abuse has occurred between the two parties, it may award sole responsibility to the abused spouse and make such arrangements for visitation as will best protect the child and abused spouse from further harm.

a. "Shared parental responsibility" means that both parents retain full parental rights and responsibilites with respect to their child and requires both parents to confer so that major decisions affecting the welfare of the child will be determined jointly. In ordering shared parental responsibility, the court may consider the expressed desires of the parents and may grant to one party the ultimate responsibility over specific aspects of the child's welfare or may divide those aspects between the parties based on the best interests of the child. When it appears to the court to be in the best interests of the child, the court may order or the parties may agree how any such responsibility will be divided. Such areas of responsibility may include primary physical residence, education, medical and dental care, and any other responsibilities which the court finds unique to a particular family and/or in the best interests of the child.

b. "Sole parental responsibility" means that responsibility for the minor child is given to one parent by the court, with or without rights of visitation to the other parent.

c. The court may award the grandparents visitation rights of a minor child if it is deemed by the court to be in the child's best interest. Grandparents shall have legal standing to seek judicial enforcement of such an award. Nothing in this section shall be construed to require that grandparents be made parties or given notice of dissolution pleadings or proceedings, nor shall such grandparents have legal standing as "contestants" as defined in s. 61.1306. No court shall order that a child be kept within the state or jurisdiction of the court solely for the purpose of permitting visitation by the grandparents.

3. Access to records and information pertaining to a minor child, including but not limited to medical, dental, and school records, shall not be denied to a parent because such parent is not the child's primary residential parent.

(3) For purposes of shared parental responsibility and primary physical residence, the best interests of the child shall be determined by the court's consideration and evaluation of all factors affecting the best welfare and interests of the child, including, but not limited to:

(a) The parent who is more likely to allow the child frequent and continuing contact with the nonresidential parent.

(b) The love, affection, and other emotional ties existing between the parents and the child.

(c) The capacity and disposition of the parents to provide the child with food, clothing, medical care or other remedial care recognized and permitted under the laws of this state in lieu of medical care, and other material needs.

(d) The length of time the child has lived in stable, satisfactory environment and the desirability of maintaining continuity.

(e) The permanence, as a family unit, of the existing or proposed custodial home.

(f) The moral fitness of the parents.

(g) The mental and physical health of the parents.

(h) The home, school, and community record of the child.

(i) The reasonable preference of the child, if the court deems the child to be of sufficient intelligence, understanding, and experience to express a preference.

(j) Any other factor considered by the court to be relevant to a particular child custody dispute.

**Ind Code §31-1-11.5-21(f) and (g) (Supp 1984-1985).**

. . . .

(f) The court may award legal custody of a child jointly if the court finds that an award of joint legal custody would be in the best interest of the child. As used in this section "joint legal custody" means that the persons awarded joint custody will share authority and responsibility for the major decisions concerning the child's upbringing, including the child's education, health care, and religious training. An award of joint legal custody does not require an equal division of physical custody of the child.

(g) In determining whether an award of joint legal custody would be in the best interest of the child, the court shall consider it a matter of primary, but not determinative importance that the persons awarded joint custody have agreed to an award of joint legal custody. The court shall also consider:

(1) the fitness and suitability of each of the persons awarded joint custody;

(2) whether the persons awarded joint custody are willing and able to communicate and cooperate in advancing the child's welfare;

(3) the wishes of the child and whether the child has established a close and beneficial relationship with both of the persons awarded joint custody;

(4) whether the persons awarded joint custody live in close proximity to each other and plan to continue to do so; and

(5) the nature of the physical and emotional environment in the home of each of the persons awarded joint custody.

**Iowa Code Ann §598.41 (Supp 1985)**

**598.41. Custody of Children**

1. The court, insofar as is reasonable and in the best interests of the child, shall order the custody award, including liberal visitation rights where appropriate, which will assure the child the opportunity for the maximum continuing physical and emotional contact with both parents after the parents have separated or dissolved the marriage, unless direct physical harm or significant emotional harm to the child is likely to result from such contact with one parent, and which will encourage parents to share the rights and responsibilities of raising the child. The court shall consider the denial by one parent of the child's opportunity for maximum continuing contact with the other parent, without just cause, a significant factor in determining the proper custody arrangement. Unless otherwise ordered by the court in the custody decree, both parents shall have legal access to information concerning the child, including but not limited to medical, educational and law enforcement records.

2. On the application of either parent, the court shall consider granting joint custody in cases where the parents do not agree to joint custody. If the court does not grant joint custody under this subsection, the court shall cite clear and convincing evidence, pursuant to the factors in subsection 3, that joint custody is unreasonable and not in the best interest of the child to the extent

that the legal custodial relationship between the child and a parent should be severed. Before ruling upon the joint custody petition in these cases, the court may require the parties to participate in custody mediation counseling to determine whether joint custody is in the best interest of the child. The court may require the child's participation in the mediation counseling insofar as the court determines the child's participation is advisable.

The costs of custody mediation counseling shall be paid in full or in part by the parties and taxed as court costs.

(3) In considering what custody arrangement under subsection 2 is in the best interests of the minor child, the court shall consider the following factors:

a. Whether each parent would be a suitable custodian for the child.

b. Whether the psychological and emotional needs and development of the child will suffer due to lack of active contact with and attention from both parents.

c. Whether the parents can communicate with each other regarding the child's needs.

d. Whether both parents have actively cared for the child before and since the separation.

e. Whether each parent can support the other parent's relationship with the child.

f. Whether the custody arrangement is in accord with the child's wishes or whether the child has strong opposition, taking into consideration the child's age and maturity.

g. Whether one or both the parents agree or are opposed to joint custody.

h. The geographic proximity of the parents.

4. Subsection 3 shall not apply when parents agree to joint custody.

5. Joint legal custody does not require joint physical care. When the court determines such action would be in the child's best interests, physical care may be given to one joint custodial parent and not to the other. If one joint custodial parent is awarded physical care, the court shall hold that parent responsible for providing for the best interests of the child. However, physical care given to one parent does not affect the other parent's rights and responsibilities as a legal custodian of the child. Rights and responsibilities as legal custodian of the child include, but are not limited to, equal participation in decisions affecting the child's legal status, medical care, education, extracurricular activities, and religious instruction.

6. When the parent awarded custody or physical care of the child cannot act as custodian or caretaker because the parent has died or has been judicially adjudged incompetent, the court shall award custody including physical care of the child to the surviving parent unless the court finds that such an award is not in the child's best interests.

**La Civ Code art 146 (Supp 1985)**

**Art. 146. Custody of children pending the litigation**

A. If there are children of the marriage whose provisional custody is claimed by both husband and wife, the suit being yet pending and undecided, custody shall be awarded in the following order of preference, according to the best interests of the children:

(1) To both parents jointly. The court shall, unless waived by the court for good cause shown, require the parents to submit a plan for implementation of the custody order, or the parents acting individually or in concert may submit a custody implementation plan to court prior to issuance of a custody decree. A plan of implementation shall allocate the time periods each parent shall enjoy physical custody of the children and the legal authority, privileges and responsibilities of the parents. The plan may also include such considerations as the following:

(a) Designation of the child's legal domicile.

(b) Rights of access and communication between the respective parents and the child or children.

(c) Child support. (i) An award of joint custody shall not eliminate the responsibility for child support. Each parent shall be responsible for child support based on the needs of the child and the actual resources of each parent. If a parent would otherwise be unable to maintain adequate housing for the child and the other parent has sufficient resources, the court may order modified support payments for a portion of housing expenses even during a period when the child is not residing in the home of the parent receiving support. An order of joint custody, in and of itself, shall not constitute grounds for modifying a support order . . .

(d)Any other matter deemed in the best interest of the child or children.

(2) To either parent. In making an order for custody to either parent, the court shall consider, among other factors, which parent is more likely to allow the child or children frequent and continuing contact with the noncustodial parent, and shall not prefer a parent as custodian because of that parent's sex or race. The burden of proof that joint custody would not be in a child's best interest shall be upon the parent requesting sole custody.

(3) If to neither parent, the person or persons in whose home the child has been living in a wholesome and stable environment.

(4) To any other person or persons deemed by the court to be suitable and able to provide an adequate and stable environment.

B. Before the court makes any order awarding custody to a person or persons other than a parent without the consent of the parents, it shall make a finding that an award of custody to a parent would be detrimental to the child and the award to a nonparent is required to serve the best interest of the child. Allegations that parental custody would be detrimental to the child, other than a statement of that ultimate fact, shall not appear in the pleadings.

C. There shall be a rebuttable presumption that joint custody is in the best interest of a minor child.

(1) However, the parents may agree to an award of custody to one parent.

(2) The presumption in favor of joint custody may be rebutted by a showing that it is not in the best interest of the child, after consideration of evidence introduced with respect to all of the following factors:

(a) The love, affection, and other emotional ties existing between the parties involved and the child.

(b) The capacity and disposition of the parties involved to give the child love, affection, and guidance and to continue the education and raising of the child in his religion or creed, if any.

(c) The capacity and disposition of the parties involved to provide the child with food, clothing, medical care, and other material needs.

(d) The length of time the child has lived in a stable, satisfactory environment, and the desirability of maintaining continuity.

(e) The permanence, as a family unit, of the existing or proposed custodial home or homes.

(f) The moral fitness of the parties involved.

(g) The mental and physical health of the parties involved.

(h) The home, school, and community record of the child.

(i) The reasonable preference of the child, if the court deems the child to be of sufficient age to express a preference.

(j) The willingness and ability of each of the parents to facilitate and encourage a close and continuing parent-child relationship between the child and the other parent.

(k) The distance between the respective residences of the parties.

(l) Any other factor considered by the court to be relevant to a particular child custody dispute. However, the classification of persons according to race is neither relevant nor permissible.

(3) For the purpose of assisting the court in making a determination whether an award of joint custody is appropriate, the court may direct that an investigation be conducted.

D. For purposes of this Article, "joint custody" shall mean the parents shall, to the extent feasible, share the physical custody of children of the marriage. In making an award of physical custody, the court shall consider, among other things, the factors enumerated in Paragraph (C)(2). Joint custody shall also mean that the parents shall enjoy the natural cotutorship of such children in accordance with Article 250, subject to the plan of implementation effected pursuant to Paragraph A of this Article. Physical care and custody shall be shared by the parents in such a way as to assure a child of frequent and continuing contact with both parents. An award of joint custody obligates the parties to exchange information concerning the health, education, and welfare of the minor child; and unless allocated, apportioned, or decreed, the parents or parties shall confer with one another in the exercise of decision-making rights, responsibilities, and authority.

E. Any order for joint custody, or any plan of implementation effected pursuant to Paragraph A of this Article, may be modified or terminated upon the petition of one or both parents or on the court's own motion, if it is shown that the best interest of the child required modification or termination of the order. The court shall state in its decision the reasons for modification or termination of the joint custody order if either parent opposes the modification or termination order.

F. Any order for the custody of a minor child of a marriage entered by a court in this state or in any other state, subject to jurisdictional requirements, may be modified at any time to an order of joint custody in accordance with the provisions of this Article.

G. A custody hearing may be held in private chambers of the judge.

H. In a custody or visitation proceeding, an evaluation may be ordered on the motion of either party. The evaluation shall be made by a mental health professional agreed upon by the parties or selected by the court. The court may apportion the costs of the investigation between the parties and shall order both parties and the children to submit to and cooperate in the evaluation, testing, or interview by the mental health professional. The mental health professional shall provide the court and both parties with a written report. The mental health professional shall serve as the witness of the court subject to cross-examination by either party. For the purposes of this Article, "mental health professional" means a psychiatrist or a person who possesses a Master's degree in counseling, social work, psychology, or marriage and family counseling.

I. In any custody or visitation proceeding, the court, on its own motion or the motion of either party, may require the parties to mediate their differences. The court may apportion the costs of the mediation between the parties. The mediator may be selected by the parties or, upon their failure to agree upon a mediator, may be selected by the court. The mediation shall be conducted and the mediator shall be qualified in accordance with R.S. 9:351 et seq.

J. Notwithstanding any other provision of law, access to records and information pertaining to a minor child, including but not limited to medical, dental, and school records, shall not be denied to a parent because the parent is not the child's custodial parent.

**Me Rev Stat Ann tit 19, §752 (Supp 1984-1985).**

**§752. Parenting of children; change of names; compulsory process; support and maintenance**

1. Legislative findings and purpose. The Legislature finds and declares as public policy that encouraging mediated resolutions of disputes between parents is in the best interest of minor children.

2. Definitions. As used in this section, unless the context otherwise indicates, the following terms have the following meanings.

A. "Allocated parental rights and responsibilities" means that responsibilities for the various aspects of a child's welfare are divided between the parents, with the parent allocated a particular responsibility having the right to control that aspect of the child's welfare. Responsibilities may be divided exclusively or proportionately. Aspects of a child's welfare for which responsibility may be divided include primary physical resident, parent-child contact, support, education, medical and dental care, religious upbringing, travel boundaries and expenses and any other aspect of parental rights and responsibilities. A parent allocated responsibility for a certain aspect of a child's welfare may be required to inform the other parent of major changes in that aspect.

B. "Child support" means money to be paid directly to a parent or to another person or agency awarded parental rights and responsibilities with respect to a child for the support of a child and may include the provision of health or medical insurance coverage for a child.

C. "Shared parental rights and responsibilities" means that most or all aspects of a child's welfare remain the joint responsibility and right of both parents, so that both parents retain equal parental rights and responsibilities and both parents must confer and make joint decisions regarding the child's welfare.

D. "Sole parental rights and responsibilities" means that one parent is granted exclusive parental rights and responsibilities with respect to all aspects of a child's welfare, with the possible exception of the right and responsibility for support.

3. Jurisdiction. The court making an order of nullity or of divorce may make an order awarding parent rights and responsibilities with respect to a minor child of the parties.

4. Mediation. Prior to a contested hearing under this chapter where there are minor children of the parties, the court shall refer the parties to mediation. Any agreement reached by the parties through mediation on any issue shall be reduced to writing, signed by the parties and presented to the court for approval as a court order. When agreement through mediation is not reached on any issue, the court must determine that the parties made a good faith effort to mediate the issue before proceeding with a hearing. If the court finds that either party failed to make a good faith effort to mediate, the court may refer the parties back to mediation.

5. Best interest of the child. The court, in making an award of parental rights and responsibilities with respect to a minor child, shall apply the standard of the best interest of the child. In applying this standard, the court shall consider the following factors:

A. The age of the child;

B. The relationship of the child with the child's parents and any other persons who may significantly affect the child's welfare;

C. The preference of the child, if old enough to express a meaningful preference;

D. The duration and adequacy of the child's current living arrangements and the desirability of maintaining continuity;

E. The stability of any proposed living arrangements for the child;

F. The motivation of the parties involved and their capacities to give the child love, affection and guidance;

G. The child's adjustment to the child's present home, school and community;

H. The capacity of each parent to allow and encourage frequent and continuing contact between the child and the other parent, including physical access;

I. The capacity of each parent to cooperate or to learn to cooperate in child care;

J. Methods for assisting parental cooperation and resolving disputes and each parent's willingness to use those methods;

K. The effect on the child if one parent has sole authority over the child's upbringing; and

L. All other factors having a reasonable bearing on the physical and psychological well-being of the child.

6. Order. The order of the court shall award allocated parental rights and responsibilities, shared parental rights and responsibilities or sole parental rights and responsibilities, according to the best interest of the child. Where the parents have agreed to an award of shared parental rights and responsibilities or so agree in open court, the court shall make that award unless there is substantial evidence that it should not be ordered. The court shall state in its decision the reasons for not ordering a shared parent rights and responsibilities award agreed to by the parents. . . .Every final order issued under this section shall contain:

A. A provision for child support or a statement of the reasons for not ordering child support; and

B. A statement that each parent shall have access to records and information pertaining to a minor child, including but not limited to, medical, dental and school records, whether or not the child resides with the parent, unless that access is found not to be in the best interest of the child or that access is found to be sought for the purpose of causing detriment to the other parent. If that access is not ordered, the court shall state in the order its reasons for denying that access. . . .

**Ohio Rev Code Ann §3109.04 (Page Supp 1984).**

**§3109.04 Custody.**

(A) Upon hearing the testimony of either or both parents and in accordance with sections 3109.21 to 3109.36 of the Revised Code, the court shall decide to whom the care, custody, and control of the children shall be given. The court may grant the care, custody and control of the children to either parent or, if a request is made in accordance with division (D) of this section, to the parents jointly. The court shall take into account that which would be in the best interest of the children. . . .

The court shall not grant joint care, custody, and control of the children to the parents unless they request the grant of joint care, custody, and control pursuant to division (D) of this section. . . .

The court may order that the parents have joint care, custody, and control of the children only if both parents request joint custody and file a plan for joint custody pursuant to division (D) of this section and if joint custody is in the best interest of the children. Upon the filing of a plan requesting the joint care, custody, and control of the children, the court shall review the parents' plan for joint custody to determine if the plan is in the best interest of the children.

If the court determines that the plan is in the best interest of the children, the court shall approve the plan. If the court determines that the plan or any part of the plan is not in the best interest of the children, the court shall require the parents to make appropriate changes to the plan to meet the court's objections to the plan. If changes to the plan are made to meet the court's objections, and if the new plan is in the best interest of the children, the court shall approve the plan. If changes to the plan are not made to meet the court's objections, or if the parents attempt to make changes to the plan to meet the court's objections, but the court determines that the new plan or any part of the new plan still is not in the best interest of the children, the court may reject the parent's request for joint care, custody, and control of the children and proceed as if the request has not been made. A plan approved by the court under this division shall be incorporated into a provisional joint care, custody, and control of the children. The provisional custody decree granting the parents the provisional joint custody decree shall clearly state that it is provisional, that it may be modified at any time prior to sixty days after the date of its issuance, and that it is subject to termination at any time prior to ninety days after the date of its issuance upon motion of either parent or, in certain situations, upon motion of the court itself, that if either parent or the court itself makes such a motion, the court is required to terminate the provisional joint custody decree and proceed as if no request for joint custody ever had been made, and that if neither parent nor the court itself makes such a motion prior to the expiration of the ninety-day period, the provisional joint custody decree immediately and without need for further action become final on the ninetieth day after the date of its issuance, subject to modification or termination authorized by this section. Any such provisional joint custody decree shall be appended to, but shall be separate and independent from and shall not affect the final decree of dissolution, divorce, separation, annulment, or alimony arising out of the action out of which the question of care, custody, and control arose. . . .

(B)(2) In addition to the modification authorized under division (B)(1) of this section:

(a) Joint custodians may modify the terms of the plan for joint care, custody, and control approved by the court and incorporated by it into the joint custody decree. Modifications may be made under this division, in relation to final decree, at any time, and in relation to a provisional decree, at any time prior to sixty days after the date of issuance of the provisional decree. The modifications to the plan shall be filed with the court, and the court shall include them in the plan, unless they are not in the best interest of the children, in which case the court may reject the modifications. Modifications submitted by the joint custodians shall be effective upon their inclusion by the court in the plan. A modification to a provisional plan made under this division does not affect or extend the ninety-day period during which the provisional plan may be terminated upon motion of either parent or the court itself.

(b) The court may modify the terms of the plan for joint care, custody, and control approved by the court and incorporated by it into the joint custody decree upon the request of one or both of the joint custodians. Modifications may be made under this division, in relation to a final decree, at any time, and in relation to a provisional decree, at any time prior to sixty days after the date of issuance of the provisional decree. The court shall not make any modification to the plan, unless the modification is in the best interest of the children and the joint custodians agree to the modifications. A modification to a provisional plan made under this division does not affect or extend the ninety-day period during which the provisional plan may be terminated upon motion of either parent or the court itself.

The court shall terminate a provisional joint custody decree if either parent or the court itself makes a motion to terminate the provisional decree at any time prior to ninety days after the date of its issuance. The court itself may make a motion to terminate a provisional decree only if it has reason to believe that the plan incorporated into the provisional decree is not in the best interest of the children and that it cannot be modified so as to be in the best interest of the children or if it has reason to believe that joint custody itself is not in the best interest of the children. If the court has reason to believe that the plan incorporated into the provisional decree is not in the best interest of the children but that it can be modified so as to be in the best interest of the children, the plan may be modified in accordance with division (B)(2)(a) or (b) of this section regardless of whether the sixty-day period that normally applies in relation to modification of provisional decrees under those divisions has expired. If a provisional decree is terminated under this division, the court shall proceed in accordance with division (B)(2)(e) of this section. If neither parent nor the court itself makes a motion to terminate a provisional decree prior to the expiration of the ninety-day period, the provisional decree immediately and without need for further action shall become final on the ninetieth day after the date of its issuance, subject to modification and termination authorized by this section.

(d) The court may terminate a prior final joint custody decree upon the request of one or both of the joint custodians or whenever it determines that joint custody is not in the best interest of the children. If modification of the terms of the plan for joint care, custody, and control approved by the court and incorporated by it into the final joint custody decree is attempted under division (B)(2)(a) of this section and the court rejects the modifications, it may terminate the final joint custody decree if it determines that joint custody is not in the best interest of the children. If the court proposes a modification to a final joint custody decree under division (B)(2)(b) of this section and the joint custodians do not agree to the modification, the court may terminate the final joint custody decree if it determines that joint custody is not in the best interest of the children.

(e) Upon the termination of a provisional joint custody decree or a prior final joint custody decree under division (B)(2)(c) or (d) of this section, the court shall proceed and issue a modified decree for the care, custody, and control of the children under the standards applicable under division (A) of this section as if no decree for joint care, custody, and control had been granted and as if no request for joint care, custody, and control had ever been made.

(C) In determining the best interest of a child pursuant to this section, whether on an original award of custody or modification of custody, the court shall consider all relevant factors, including:

(1) The wishes of the child's parents regarding his custody;

(2) The wishes of the child regarding his custody if he is eleven years of age or older;

(3) The child's interaction and interrelationship with his parents, siblings, and any other person who may significantly affect the child's best interest;

(4) The child's adjustment to his home, school, and community;

(5) The mental and physical health of all persons involved in the situation.

(D) The parents of any child may request the court to grant them joint care, custody, and control of the children in a proceeding held pursuant to division (A) of this section. If a request for joint care, custody, and control is made, the parents making the request shall file with the court a plan for their exercise of joint care, custody, and control of the children. The plan shall be filed with the petition for dissolution of marriage, if the question of care, custody, and control arises out of an action for dissolution of marriage, or, in other cases, at a time at least thirty days prior to the hearing on the issue of the care, custody, and control of the children. A plan for joint custody shall include provisions covering all factors that are relevant to the care, custody, and control of the children, including, but not limited to provisions covering factors such as physical living arrangements, child support obligations, provision for the children's medical and dental care, school placement, and visitation.

(E) If an appeal is taken from a decision of a court that grants custody or modifies a prior custody decree, the court of appeals shall give the case calendar priority and handle it expeditiously.

• (F) "Joint custody" or "joint care, custody, and control," as used in the Revised Code, means that the parents share, in the manner set forth in the parents' plan for joint custody that is approved by the court, all or some of the aspects of physical and legal care, custody, and control of their children.

# Part Three

## Division of Property

# 10 Division of Property

## §10.01 Introduction

Historically, in the traditional fault system of divorce, the central issue involved the moral fault and responsibility of the parties in ending the marriage.[1] Once fault was established, property division and alimony awards predictably favored the innocent spouse as punishment of the guilty spouse.

The rise of no-fault divorce[2] shifted the issue from establishing the grounds for ending the marriage to determining the economic consequences of that termination. In their efforts to minimize the acrimony and because of a widespread perception of perjury and fraud as associated with divorce, the no-fault reformers in many states eliminated good behavior in the marriage as leverage for a financial reward or reduced fault to a mere discretionary factor in property division.[3] This change in divorce law, when combined with other legal and societal movements, irrevocably changed the nature of divorce.

The women's movement, which arose simultaneously with the no-fault trend, challenged traditional mores, opened career opportunities for women, and decreased dependence of women on the traditional breadwinning man. The movement toward gender neutrality in the law, spurred by the women's movement, encouraged the continued independence of women by abolishing the assumption that husbands were responsible for the support of their former

---

[1] *See* **§§1.10-1.25.**

[2] *See* **§§2.02-2.17.**

[3] See Freed & Walker, *Family Law in the Fifty States: An Overview,* 18 Fam LQ 369, 394-96 (1985), which provides the following information: states regarding fault as a discretionary factor in property distribution and for maintenance awards include Alabama, Connecticut, the District of Columbia, Florida, Georgia, Hawaii, Idaho, Kentucky, Louisiana, Maryland, Massachusetts, Michigan, New York, North Carolina, North Dakota, Pennsylvania, Rhode Island, South Carolina, Texas, Vermont, Virginia, West Virginia (fault excluded only for property division, not alimony), and Wyoming. States with property and maintenance standards which are silent regarding fault include Arizona, Kansas, Montana, Oklahoma, Pennsylvania, and Utah. States expressly or implicitly excluding marital fault from consideration include California, Colorado, Delaware, Illinois, Iowa, Maine, Minnesota, Nevada, New Hampshire, New Jersey, New Mexico, Oregon, Tennessee, Washington, West Virginia (fault excluded only for property division), and Wisconsin.

wives. Instead, the old assumption was replaced by the goal of economic independence for women after divorce. Expected to be self-supporting, wives are more often awarded rehabilitative, compensatory, or other short-term alimony based upon their contributions and needs and the husband's ability to pay, or, more frequently, are awarded no alimony at all.[4]

Without the predictable economic consequences of traditional fault divorce or the assumption that the husband must support the former wife upon divorce, the financial focus of no-fault divorce has been property division. The result has been a rapid transformation in the law of property division in the 1970s and 1980s. This transformation has affected the principles by which the property is divided as well as the definition of marital property itself.

For example, many states have adopted the concept of equitable distribution,[5] which requires that courts consider each party's contribution to the acquisition of property in the marriage when ordering its division. In addition, many states are creatively expanding the definition of marital property to increase the amount to be divided. Most importantly, this expansion has included *career assets,* defined by sociologist Lenore J. Weitzman as "a large array of specific assets such as pension and retirement benefits, a license to practice a profession or trade, medical and hospital insurance, and entitlements to company goods and services."[6]

It is these career benefits which are the focal point of this chapter. Not intended as a thorough examination of the law of property division upon divorce, this chapter nevertheless provides an historical perspective to document the shift in emphasis in marital property law and the concomitant creation of new marital property.

## §10.02 History—Property Rights During Marriage

At common law, an unmarried woman was legally competent to own property, although her right to inherit it was limited. She could enter into some contracts, but her ability to contractually dispose of property was restricted. She could sue or be sued in her own name, but could not serve on a jury, vote, hold public office, or make a will legally disposing of her property.[7]

Upon marriage, a woman's meager property rights became subordinate to

---

[4] See also L. Weitzman, The Divorce Revolution 144 (1985) where the author states:

> In reality, however, alimony has always been awarded to a small percentage of divorced women. In 1968 for example, under the traditional divorce law, our research shows that less than 20 percent of the divorced wives in California were awarded alimony. Nor does California appear to be unique: only 14 percent of the divorced wives in a census survey said they were awarded alimony. [Footnotes omitted.]

[5] *See* **§10.07.**

[6] L. Weitzman, *supra* note 4, at 11.

[7] *See* H. Clark, Law of Domestic Relations 219 (1968); Chused, *Married Women's Property Law: 1800-1850,* 71 Geo LJ 1359, 1366-67 (1983).

her husband's due to the doctrine of coverture. This doctrine provided that, upon marriage, the husband and wife became one person, the husband.[8]

The husband, upon marriage, became entitled to possession of all of the wife's personalty, whether acquired before or after marriage. If he actually took possession, it became his property; if he did not, title remained in the wife.[9] He could, if he wished, dispose of it without her consent. If the husband died intestate, the wife's chattels passed to his personal representative. The exception to this common law rule was that the wife's necessary clothing and her *paraphernalia* (her "jewels, trinkets and ornaments of the person") reverted to her upon the death of her husband.[10]

A married woman's real property continued to be titled in her name after marriage. Nevertheless, her husband was entitled to exclusive use of her land, and to all of its income or profits. He could convey this interest in his wife's property without her consent, but she could not convey the land without his.[11] If she did convey the land, her proceeds would be treated as personalty, and subject to possession by her spouse.[12]

If a child were born to the marriage, the husband became a *tenant by the curtesy* of the wife's real property. Thus, he was entitled to the use of her land for his lifetime, if his wife predeceased him.[13] This was true even if the child predeceased him, or he remarried.

If the couple had no children, and the woman died during her husband's lifetime, all of her property passed to him in any case, as she could have no other intestate successor. She could not make a will disposing of property without her husband's consent, and even if he gave it, he could revoke it at any time up to probate.[14] If the wife outlived her husband, her property passed by rule of intestate succession which generally favored the oldest male child, or male collaterals.

By the late thirteenth century, a corresponding right of dower began to

---

[8] W. Blackstone, Commentaries on the Laws of England 442 (Cooley 3d ed 1884). Professor Homer Clark says of Blackstone's observation that:

> Such a notion may have been both useful and comforting as a summary of the legal situation in a less sophisticated age, but it hardly accounts for the rules which gave the husband extensive rights in his wife's property and which deprived her of power to contract or to engage in litigation. A realist might be pardoned for thinking that the rules were the result of male economic, social and legal power.

H. Clark, *supra* note 7, at 219. *But see* **§10.06.**

[9] Blackstone adds that once the husband took possession of the wife's personalty, and title to it vested in him, while he lived title could never again revest in the wife. 2 W. Blackstone, Commentaries on the Laws of England 433 (Cooley 3d ed 1884).

[10] 2 F. Pollock & F. Maitland, The History of English Law 402 (1895).

[11] *Id* 405-06.

[12] J. Madden, Handbook of the Law of Persons and Domestic Relations 93-94 (1931).

[13] This appears to have been based on the theory that parents should support children, and the husband should have the use of the wife's land for that purpose. It is also one of the reasons why a wife could not dispose of her property by will.

[14] F. Pollock & F. Maitland, *supra* note 10, at 402.

develop for surviving wives. Dower entitled the widow to a life estate in one-third of all her husband's land, held in fee at any time during the marriage. This included any property that the husband once owned, but which he had conveyed before his death. In effect, dower prevented the husband from conveying good title to land unless his wife formally waived her rights in it.[15] Dower did not entitle the widow to any of her husband's personalty, although eventually statutes were enacted which entitled her to a one-third share, or one-half if there were no children.[16]

Prior to the seventeenth century, no method existed for a married woman to hold any property not subject to the possession of her husband. Eventually, the idea developed that the best interests of women and society in general would be served by the establishment of some system whereby women could control and convey their own property.[17] To that end, the English courts of equity developed the concept of a wife's *separate estate* which softened the harsh treatment of married women at common law.

To create a wife's separate estate, the court imposed a trust upon the husband in favor of his wife, composed of her real and personal property. Those assets were regarded as her own separate estate. She was entitled to the use of and income from that property, and could convey it by deed or by will, make contracts, and sue or be sued with respect to it. This system was more widely adopted in England than in America.[18]

By the mid-to-late nineteenth century, most American jurisdictions had enacted statutory reforms to remove some of the legal disabilities of married women. Early changes gave women the right to dispose of property by will and to enter into contracts as if they were not married.[19] Because American courts did not develop concepts such as the English courts' separate estate in equity, it was necessary for state legislatures to take action to ameliorate the discrimination against married women at common law. The legislative action was a reflection of the rapid changes in American society at that time. The Industrial Revolution drew more women into the labor force. These women began to earn money and actually acquired property.

Although the married women's property acts differed from state to state, most of the laws enacted in the 1800s defined separate property as anything a woman owned before marriage, as well as that which she personally acquired during coverture. The statutes allowed women to convey both personal and

---

[15] *Id* 419-20. See S. Green & J. Long, Marriage and Family Law Agreements 109-11 (Shepard's/McGraw-Hill 1984), for a discussion of jointure, which existed as an effective method of barring dower.

[16] J. Madden, *supra* note 12, at 121-22.

[17] 1 J. Schouler, Marriage, Divorce, Separation and Domestic Relations §247 (6th ed 1921).

[18] H. Clark, *supra* note 7, at 221-22.

[19] Chused, *supra* note 7, at 1366-67.

real property.[20] Most states allowed women to manage and control their separate property.[21] Dower and curtesy were almost universally abolished in favor of statutory shares for spouses.[22]

Most of the nineteenth century statutes gave married women the right to sue and be sued without having to be joined by their husbands, although there were usually some restrictions on interspousal lawsuits.[23] Under these statutes, married women were generally as free to contract with their husbands as with third persons.[24]

## §10.03 —Property Rights upon Divorce

Historically, when marriage was considered an indissoluble union, divorces were infrequent.[25] For that reason, property division as a part of divorce was rarely discussed. Rules of property division received little attention at early common law because title to virtually all the wife's personalty vested in the husband upon marriage and remained in him upon divorce.[26] A divorced woman was legally entitled only to her necessary clothing and her *paraphernalia.* Divorce did not affect a husband's rights in his own property. The result in common law states was that at divorce, the husband retained almost all marital property. In community property jurisdictions, property division was based upon the principle of partnership in marriage and an undivided one-half interest of each spouse in the community property.[27]

An important change accompanied the passage of the married women's property acts in the common law jurisdictions in the late 1800s. These acts gave wives the right to own separate property. A spouse's rights in the real property of the other depended upon the marital relationship. Upon divorce, the spouse became entitled to immediate possession of his or her own real property. From this rule developed the *title theory,* which required courts in common law jurisdictions to award property to that spouse in whose name the property was titled. While a court could divide property titled in the names of both spouses, it could not divide property titled in one spouse's name except under certain conditions. A court of equity could compel a husband to reconvey his wife's

---

[20] H. Clark, *supra* note 7, at 222-25.

[21] J. Madden, *supra* note 12, at 117-18.

[22] 3 C. Vernier, American Family Laws 351-55 (1935). These reforms actually came a little later. Dower and curtesy still existed in limited forms in a few states well into the twentieth century.

[23] H. Clark, *supra* note 7, at 225-28. For example, interspousal tort suits were barred in nearly all states. Suits upon interspousal contracts were viewed with suspicion because of the possibility of undue influence.

[24] J. Madden, *supra* note 12, at 137.

[25] *See* **§§1.06-1.09.**

[26] E. Peck, The Law of Persons and of Domestic Relations §69 (1930).

[27] *See* **§10.06.**

lands if he obtained title to them during the marriage.[28] The court could also order him to compensate her for waste committed on her land while it was under his control.[29]

Divorce laws enacted in both common law and community property jurisdictions in the late nineteenth century predicated property division upon the fault of the parties in contributing to the divorce.[30] Often under such statutes an *innocent* spouse could be given some portion of the *guilty* spouse's land as punishment of the guilty spouse's behavior.[31] This rule tended to temper the harshness of the title theory when the husband, in whose name the property was titled, was the guilty spouse. The division of property under fault rules was at the discretion of the court; in rare cases, one spouse could be awarded all of the other's property.[32] Most of these property division statutes which allowed courts to consider fault applied equally to husbands and wives. Few of these statutes provided for distribution of marital assets based upon the needs of either party. Where children were involved, some statutes gave courts the discretion to set aside some of the spouses' property for the benefit of the children.

Contingent interests such as dower and curtesy terminated upon divorce. However, some statutes preserved the wife's right to dower where she obtained a divorce through the misconduct of her husband.[33] There did not seem to be any corresponding protection of the husband's right to curtesy. Curtesy in some states depended upon the birth of issue to a marriage and was intended to allow a widower to provide for his children as well as his own needs.

The parties' rights to an intestate share of the other's property also ended with divorce.

## §10.04 Definitions of Marital Property

Before a court can distribute a divorcing couple's property, it must first determine what property may be divided. By 1985 most state legislatures had

---

[28] 3 C. Vernier, American Family Laws 215 (1935).

[29] H. Whitney, Marriage and Divorce: The Effect of Each on Personal Status and Property Rights 317 (1873).

[30] T. D. Woolsey, Divorce and Divorce Legislation 117 (1882). In 1985, courts in the following states could consider fault as a factor in property division: Alabama, Connecticut, the District of Columbia, Florida, Georgia, Hawaii, Idaho, Kentucky, Louisiana, Maryland, Massachusetts, Michigan, New York, North Carolina, North Dakota, Pennsylvania, Rhode Island, South Carolina, Texas, Vermont, Virginia, and Wyoming. *See* Freed & Walker, *Family Law in the Fifty States: An Overview,* 18 Fam LQ 369, 394-96 (1985).

[31] Tillery v Tillery, 115 Kan 81, 222 P 100 (1924); Gains v Gains, 19 SW 929 (Ky 1892); West v West, 2 Mass 223 (1806); Wetmore v Wetmore, 5 Or 470 (1875); Donovan v Donovan, 20 Wis 586 (1966).

[32] Wuest v Wuest, 17 Nev 217, 30 P 886 (1882); Young v Young, 23 SW 83 (Tex Civ App 1893).

[33] J. Schouler, Divorce Manual §193 (1944).

codified a definition of *marital property* which generally included all property acquired by either spouse during the marriage, except property acquired by gift or inheritance. This section briefly summarizes the evolution of definitions of marital property in common law jurisdictions.[34]

Historically, marital property was limited to jointly titled property, or assets in which both spouses had some equitable interest under common law principles. A handful of states which continue to have no statutory definition of marital property adhere loosely to this common law interpretation. In 1985, only Mississippi technically remained a *title* jurisdiction, in that courts awarded to each spouse only those assets actually titled in his or her name. Nevertheless, even in Mississippi, the harsh consequences of the application of the historic title theory of property division, which was once the law of the overwhelming majority of states, has been mitigated by case law. Mississippi courts now look at the monetary and nonmonetary contributions of both spouses to the acquisition of assets in order to determine division, a development which was part of the equitable distribution trend in common law jurisdictions.[35]

Florida, Georgia, and South Carolina, which long adhered to the title theory, usually avoided the theory's pitfalls by finding a *resulting trust* or a *special equity* favoring the nontitled spouse.[36] This enabled courts in those states to treat assets as marital property, regardless of how they were titled.

In other jurisdictions, courts and legislatures creatively expanded traditional notions of marital property, looking beyond bare title to ownership of assets at divorce to determine equitable distribution. A major influence for statutory change in marital property law was the Uniform Marriage and Divorce Act (UMDA),[37] approved by the National Conference of Commissioners on Uniform State Laws in 1971. The UMDA drafters proposed the then-novel premise that "(t)he distribution of property upon the termination of marriage should be treated, as nearly as possible, like the distribution of assets incident to the dissolution of a partnership."[38]

With property division, as with dissolution, the aim of the UMDA was elimination of fault. At the time the UMDA was approved, there remained resistance to the idea of no-fault divorce.[39] This was partly attributable to a perception that the threat of litigation over fault grounds often provided an innocent spouse with his or her only means of leverage for an equitable alimony award on property settlement. The loss of that leverage urgently crystallized

---

[34] For a brief discussion of community property, see **§10.06.**

[35] *See* Reeves v Reeves, 310 So 2d 1300 (Miss 1982).

[36] *See* Canarkis v Canarkis, 382 So 2d 1197 (Fla 1980); Stokes v Stokes, 246 Ga 765, 273 SE2d 169 (1981); Parrott v Parrot, 278 SC 60, 292 SE2d 182 (1982).

[37] 9A ULA 93 (1973); **app 1-2.**

[38] *Id* 9A ULA at 93.

[39] *See* **§§2.01-2.05.**

the need for a fair system of defining and dividing marital property in no-fault divorce.[40]

As originally adopted in 1971, the UMDA included a section defining marital property which expanded and clarified the definition of separate property. Section 307 provided that separate property was:

1. Property acquired by gift, bequest, devise, or descent
2. Property acquired in exchange for property acquired before the marriage or in exchange for property acquired by gift, bequest, devise or descent
3. Property acquired by a spouse after a decree of legal separation
4. Property excluded by valid agreement of the parties
5. The increase in value of property acquired before the marriage[41]

---

[40] See L. Weitzman, The Divorce Revolution (1985), which contends that no-fault divorce has resulted in devastating economic consequences for women and children.

[41] §307, 9A ULA 143-44 (1971, superseded 1973). The revised §307 included alternatives A and B, which provide:

Alternative A of §307

§3.07 [Disposition of Property]

(a) In a proceeding for dissolution of a marriage, legal separation, or disposition of property following a decree of dissolution of marriage or legal separation by a court which lacked personal jurisdiction over the absent spouse or lacked jurisdiction to dispose of property, the court, without regard to marital misconduct, shall, and in a proceeding for legal separation may, finally equitably apportion between the parties the property and assets belonging to either or both however and whenever acquired, and whether the title thereto is in the name of the husband or wife or both. In making apportionment the court shall consider the duration of the marriage, and prior marriage of either party, antenuptial agreement of the parties, the age, health, station, occupation, amount and sources of income, vocational skills, employability, estate, liabilities, and needs of each of the parties, custodial provisions, whether the apportionment is in lieu of or in addition to maintenance, and the opportunity of each for future acquisition of capital assets and income. The court shall also consider the contribution or dissipation of each party in the acquisition, preservation, depreciation, or appreciation in value of the respective estates, and the contribution of a spouse as homemaker or to the family unit.

(b) In a proceeding, the court may protect and promote the best interests of the children by setting aside a portion of the jointly and separately held estates of the parties in a separate fund or trust for the support, maintenance, education, and general welfare of any minor, dependent, or incompetent children of the parties.

Alternative B of §307

§307. [Disposition of Property]

In a proceeding of dissolution of the marriage, legal separation, or disposition of property following a decree of dissolution of the marriage or legal separation by a court which lacked personal jurisdiction over the absent spouse or lacked jurisdiction to dispose of the property, the court shall assign each spouse's separate property to that spouse. It also shall divide community property, without regard to marital misconduct, in just proportions after considering all relevant factors including:

This early version of §307 established a presumption that property acquired by a couple during a marriage was marital property, regardless of how title was held. This presumption was rebuttable by showing that the property was acquired by one of the five methods listed above. Section 307 was ultimately revised. Few states actually adopted it. However, some states enacted statutes patterned after the original §307, or which define marital property in a substantially similar manner.[42]

## §10.05 Uniform Marital Property Act

In 1983, the National Conference of Commissioners on Uniform State Laws approved the Uniform Marital Property Act (UMPA).[43] This act was proposed to standardize the miscellany of property division laws employed by states. According to the Commissioners:

> This Act is a property law. It functions to recognize the respective contributions made by men and women during a marriage. It discharges that function by raising those contributions to the level of defined, shared, and enforceable property rights at the time the contributions are made.[44]

The UMPA creates these "defined, shared, and enforceable property rights" by designating two classes of property: individual and marital.[45] All property

---

(1) contribution of each spouse to acquisition of the marital property, including contribution of a spouse as homemaker;

(2) value of the property set apart to each spouse:

(3) duration of the marriage; and

(4) economic circumstances of each spouse when the division of property is to become effective, including the desirability of awarding the family home or the right to live therein for a reasonable period to the spouse having custody of any children.

These alternative sections were added to accommodate the view that a divorce court should have power to distribute *all* property (including separate assets) and not just marital property. Alternative A has been adopted in Montanà, and Alternative B has been adopted in Arizona and Kentucky, with some variations.

[42] *See, e.g.,* Alaska Stat §25.24.160(6) (1983); Me Rev Stat Ann tit 19, §722A (1981), which parallel the UMDA almost exactly, and Ill Ann Stat ch 40, §503 (Smith-Hurd 1980), and Mo Rev Stat §452-330 (1984), which are similar.

[43] Uniform Marital Property Act (UMPA), 9A ULA 21 (Supp 1986).

[44] *Id* 19, prefatory note (Supp 1984).

[45] UMPA §4. Classification of Property of Spouses

(a) All property of spouses is marital property except that which is classified otherwise by this [Act].

(b) All property of spouses is presumed to be marital property.

(c) Each spouse has a present undivided one-half interest in marital property.

(d) Income earned or accrued by a spouse or attributable to property of a spouse during marriage and after the determination date is marital property.

(e) Marital property transferred to a trust remains marital property.

of either spouse is presumed to be marital property.[46] This presumption aids in the classification of assets. Property is classified by the type or character of the property, or the name in which title is held.[47]

The UMPA defines marital property as all property acquired by either spouse during marriage, which is not individual property. The definition of individual property includes all property acquired at any time by gift or inheritance. In addition, assets exchanged for individual property, personal injury awards, and items so designated by a valid marital property agreement are classified as individual property.[48]

The UMPA property classification section gives to each spouse a "present undivided one-half interest" in all marital property.[49] This means that marital property is created as assets are acquired by a couple, and not simply when the parties divorce and attempt to divide their assets. The UMPA system of property classification is designed to provide guidelines for the management and control of property *during* marriage, as well as for the disposition of property at divorce. Property management rights are based upon the form in which title to property is held. If one spouse alone holds title to an asset, then

---

(f) Property owned by a spouse at a marriage after the determination date is individual property.

(g) Property acquired by a spouse during marriage and after the determination date is individual property if acquired:

(1) by gift or a disposition at death made by a third person to the spouse and not to both spouses;

(2) in exchange for or with the proceeds of other individual property of the spouse;

(3) from appreciation of the spouse's individual property except to the extent that the appreciation is classified as marital property under Section 14;

(4) by a decree, marital property agreement, written consent, or reclassification under Section 7(b) designating it as the individual property of the spouse;

(5) as a recovery for damage to property under Section 15, except as specifically provided otherwise in a decree, marital property agreement, or written consent; or

(6) as a recovery for personal injury except for the amount of that recovery attributable to expenses paid or otherwise satisfied from marital property.

(h) Except as provided otherwise in this [Act] the enactment of this [Act] does not alter the classification and ownership rights of property acquired before the determination date.

(i) Except as provided otherwise in this [Act] and to the extent it would affect the ownership rights of the spouse that existed in the property before the determination date, during marriage the interest of a spouse in property owned immediately before the determination date is treated as if it were individual property.

[46] UMPA, 9A ULA 27, §4(b) (Supp 1984).

[47] *Id* 27-28, §4 comment. However, there are specific guidelines for life insurance policies, based on when the policy was issued and on the source of premium payments (*see* UMPA §12), and for deferred employment benefits, based on when the benefits were earned (*see* UMPA §13).

[48] *Id* 27, §4(g).

[49] *Id* §4(c).

he or she has the sole right of control over it; if the spouses hold title jointly, they must both participate in property management.[50]

In 1983, Wisconsin became the first state to enact a marital property law based on the UMPA.[51] The UMPA has been considered, but not adopted, by the legislatures of Colorado, Illinois, Indiana, Michigan, and Missouri.[52]

Most states which adopted no-fault divorce in the 1970s also altered their marital property laws at that time.[53] The marital property statutes of many states now resemble the property provisions of the Uniform Marriage and Divorce Act (UMDA).[54] The UMPA definition of marital property is similar to that of UMDA, although UMPA goes much farther in the area of property management and control. Consequently, some states which followed the UMDA scheme of property classification may be reluctant to enact UMPA-type legislation simply because it would not significantly change the definition of marital property for divorce purposes. This may also be true in community property states, which already recognize the interests of both spouses in community assets.[55] Unless a state finds attractive UMPA's non-divorce oriented provisions concerning management and control of property during marriage, it may have no incentive to change.

## §10.06 Community Property

In contrast to the common law states are the eight states which operate under the community property system. In Arizona, California, Idaho, Louisiana, Nevada, New Mexico, Texas, and Washington, marital property is characterized as either separate or community property *at the time of acquisition.* This concept of marital property based on time of acquisition created an important distinction pursued as an improvement on the historic common law marital property scheme by the drafters of the Uniform Marital Property Act.[56]

The community property laws vary from state to state, but generalizations

---

[50] *Id* 30-31, §5. It should be noted that the management and control provisions, which are based upon title, do not determine *ownership* of property. All spousal property is still presumed to be marital, regardless of how title is held.

[51] Wis Stat Ann §766 (West Supp 1984). The Wisconsin Uniform Marital Property Act (WUMPA) was effective January 1, 1986.

[52] Winter, *UMPA Fights for Recognition,* 70 ABA J 76 (June 1984).

[53] *See* **§10.03.**

[54] Uniform Marriage and Divorce Act (UMDA), 9A ULA 91 (1973). *See also* Ark Stat Ann §34-1214 (Supp 1983); Colo Rev Stat §14-10-113 (1973 & Supp 1984); Ill Ann Stat §403.190 (Smith-Hurd 1983); Me Rev Stat Ann, tit 19, §722-A (1981); Minn Stat Ann §518.54 (West Supp 1984); Mo Rev Stat §452-330 (1977 & Supp 1984); NY Dom Rel Law §236-B (McKinney Supp 1977-84); NC Gen Stat §50-20 (Supp 1983); Pa Stat Ann tit 23, §401 (Purdon Supp 1984); RI Gen Laws §15-5-16.1 (1981 & Supp 1984); Tenn Code Ann §36-4-121 (1984); Va Code §20-107.3 (1983 & Supp 1984); W Va Code §48-2-1 (Supp 1984).

[55] Winter, *supra* note 52, at 79.

[56] Uniform Marital Property Act, 9A ULA 21, 23 (Supp 1984). *See* **§10.05.**

can be made. *Separate property* in community property jurisdictions is that property obtained prior to the marriage, acquired during the marriage by gift, bequest, devise, or descent, or earned from increases from any separate property, such as rents, issues, and profits. All property acquired during the marriage is presumed to be *community property,* giving rise to a present, vested one-half undivided ownership by each spouse. The husband and wife also possess certain management rights and duties, which differ among the community property states.[57]

It has been noted that the policy of community property is one of equality of property rights between spouses, with the system's cardinal principles based upon the separate identity of each spouse, as opposed to the common law doctrine of the merger of the identity of the wife into that of the husband.[58] The community property system has always encompassed what was later achieved by equitable distribution in the common law states, namely, a division of property established upon the principle of partnership in marriage.

The origins of the community property systems in the United States, derived from the Napoleonic Code, can be traced to Spanish, Mexican, and French influences which began during the exploration and colonization of the New World.[59] The strength of the historic precedent varies among the states. Arizona courts have held, for example, that California and Texas law is more influential in interpreting the community property statute than is the Spanish Legal Code.[60] New Mexico courts, on the other hand, continue to look to the civil law of Spain and Mexico for interpretations and definitions.[61]

While there exists a rebuttable presumption that property acquired during the marriage is community property, the spouses may change the character of

---

[57] At one time, management rights were vested in the husband. In 1967, the community property states began a reform, completed in 1980, that eliminated explicit sex discrimination in the laws respecting management. *See* W. Reppy, Jr. & C. Samuel, Community Property in the United States 7 (1982).

[58] Vaughn, *The Policy of Community Property and Inter-Spousal Transactions,* 19 Baylor L Rev 20, 34 (1967).

[59] *Id* 36, where the author states:

> Community of property was continued in the western states after the end of the Spanish and Mexican domination only because the factors which originally precipitated it were closely approximated. The women worked side by side by their husbands to provide the necessities of life for the family. When the husband was away for one reason or the other the wife was head of the family: she cared for the family, fed the livestock, tended the crops and in all ways participated with her husband as an equal worker attempting to see that their marital partnership prospered and succeeded. The system was continued among those not native to it to protect the wife and secure to her that to which she was entitled.

*See also* I. Baxter, Marital Property 111-16 (1978) for a detailed analysis of the historical basis of community property in the United States.

[60] Guerin, *Transmutation and Commingling of Community Property* 3, 3-4, in Transmutation of Community Property During Marriage, His, Hers or Ours (Presented by the Section of Family Law of the ABA 1985).

[61] McDonald v Senn, 53 NM 198, 204 P2d 990 (1949).

their property after marriage by agreement, gift, commingling, or their actions. *Transmutation* is the term used to describe arrangements between spouses to convert property from one characterization to another.

The spouses can contract either before or after marriage to alter their community property rights. They may agree to use community funds to create other forms of joint ownership or to designate one spouse's earnings as separate. The husband and wife might also vary the usual equal division of property upon divorce in their separation agreement.

Gifts effectively rebut the community property presumption. For example, if a husband shows that the shares of stock titled in his name were a gift from his wife, then they are deemed separate property.

Commingling occurs when separate and community property are mixed to the extent that each loses its individual character or identity. If the confusion is not extensive and the property's origin can be traced, then the presumption that the commingled property is community may be rebutted.

With transmutation of property, whether by written agreement, gift, commingling, or some other action of the parties, the important consideration is the intent of the husband and wife. In most jurisdictions, a high standard of proof is imposed on the party attempting to show transmutation.

There are other trouble spots in the community property scheme of which the family lawyer should be aware upon divorce. In some states, property cannot be classified as community until there is a valid marriage. Fraud is a danger because in most community property states both spouses must join in the execution of any deed or in any transaction involving guaranty, idemnity, or suretyship.[62] Conflicts of law become important where the spouses acquire property in one jurisdiction and transfer it to a jurisdiction possessing a different marital property scheme.[63]

For the purposes of this chapter, it is important to note that in virtually all community property states, employee benefits such as qualified pension or profit-sharing plans, whether or not vested, are community property. Thus, to

---

[62] Wiley & Rosepink, *When What You Own Depends on Where You Live,* 2 Fam Advoc 20, 23 (Winter 1980). This fine article gives some examples of fraud:

> If a husband purchases a life insurance policy on his life, pays for it with community funds, and without his wife's consent, makes his mother the beneficiary, in some states he is considered to have defrauded his wife, who gains an absolute right to half the proceeds on the husband's death. . . .
>
> As another example, suppose the husband owns an apartment house as separate property and he uses community funds to pay for improvements to the building. If the wife does not consent, there has been a fraud on her rights. Although the husband's separate property is not as a result converted into community property, the wife's interest is protected by giving the community a lien on the building to the extent of the community contribution.

[63] *Id* 22-23, 44-45.

the extent that the interest is acquired during the existence of the community, each spouse will be entitled to one-half of that interest.[64]

## §10.07 Equitable Distribution

Historically, courts in common law jurisdictions distributed assets upon divorce based on title. Except in the rare cases where resulting or constructive trust theories were successfully asserted, no equitable interest was recognized for the non-title holding spouse.[65] In contrast, in community property states, courts considered marriage as an economic partnership from the beginning and treated all property accumulated during the marriage as a vested one-half interest of each spouse.[66]

The advent of no-fault divorce produced both an increase in the number of divorces and a shift in emphasis from fault in the divorce to the economic circumstances of the dissolution. The inequity of the title theory of property distribution became more evident as a result of this combination of factors together with the fact that more women were working making financial contributions to the marriage in addition to their domestic contributions.

Although some common law states had modified their marital property systems before the no-fault divorce change, the majority of those jurisdictions instituted marital property reform in the 1970s by adopting some form of equitable distribution.[67] As described by eminent family law authorities, the doctrine of equitable distribution:

> permits a spouse who has made a material economic contribution toward the acquisition of property, which may be titled in the other spouse, to claim an equitable interest in such property. The economic contributions made by both spouses during the marriage are weighed against the net assets that are available at the time of divorce. In computing the value of any asset, the indebtedness owed against such asset would ordinarily be deducted from its fair market value.[68]

Almost all the common law jurisdictions in the United States have adopted some form of equitable distribution to facilitate the division of property upon divorce.[69] The equitable distribution laws are not uniform, however. Some are as simple as a legislative directive to the courts that the property be divided

---

[64] *See* **§§10.11-10.24.**

[65] *See* **§10.03.**

[66] *See* **§10.06.**

[67] Freed, *Equitable Distribution as of December 1982,* 9 Fam L Rep (BNA) 4001 (Monograph No 1, 1983).

[68] Freed & Walker, *Family Law in the Fifty States: An Overview,* 18 Fam LQ 369, 392 (Winter 1985).

[69] *Id.* As of 1985, 42 common law property states had given courts the equitable power to distribute property upon divorce. Mississippi was the sole remaining title theory state, although recent judicial decisions may indicate a swing toward equitable distribution.

equitably at divorce; other statutes are specific as to what property may be divided, in what proportions, and as to the factors a court may or must consider in making its distribution. In Maryland, for example, the courts have no power to change title to an asset, but can only make a "marital award" to adjust the equities in marital property regardless of title.

The area of greatest difference among equitable distribution states concerns the classes of property that can be divided upon divorce. Fifteen states allow all property to be considered.[70] Twenty-six jurisdictions provide that courts may only divide *marital property,* with some variations.[71] Marital property is defined in these equitable distribution jurisdictions by much the same rules as those found in the community property states. Accordingly, only property acquired during the marriage can be divided, excluding property acquired before the marriage, property covered by a valid separation agreement, or, in some states, property received by gift or inheritance.[72]

An increasing number of states recognize nonmonetary contributions of a spouse when dividing property.[73] This recognition is not limited to equitable distribution states. Some nonmonetary contributions include services rendered as homemaker, parent, or contributor to family well-being. Other nonmonetary factors focus on the economic rehabilitation of the supported spouse, such as the periods of unemployment due to homemaker services which have affected that spouse's earning capacity or the time needed for job training.

Many equitable distribution statutes enumerate specific criteria relevant to

---

[70] *Id* 390-91. These states are: Connecticut, Florida, Hawaii, Indiana (court must consider whether property was acquired prior to marriage or by inheritance or gift); Kentucky (gifts and inheritances are excluded); Iowa (excludes gifts and inheritances unless injustice would result); Massachusetts (court has discretion to invade gifts and inheritances); Michigan, Montana, Pennsylvania (gifts and inheritances are excluded); Rhode Island, South Dakota, Utah, Vermont, and Wyoming.

[71] *Id.* These jurisdictions are: Alabama (unless separate property is used for the common benefit of both parties), Alaska (except where equity demands the inclusion of property acquired prior to marriage), Colorado (except as to increase in value), Delaware, Georgia, Illinois, Kentucky, Maine, Maryland, Minnesota, Missouri, Nebraska, New Hampshire, New Jersey, New York, North Carolina, North Dakota, Ohio, Oklahoma, Oregon, South Carolina (became an equitable distribution state by court decision, not by statute), Tennessee (except as to increase in value), Virginia, West Virginia, Wisconsin, and the District of Columbia.

[72] *Id.* Gifts and inheritances are excluded from marital property and property division in Alabama, Colorado, Illinois, Kentucky, Maine, Maryland, New Jersey, Ohio, Tennessee, Virginia, Wisconsin, and the District of Columbia. Interspousal gifts are not considered *gifts* in some states.

[73] *Id* 394-95. These states include Alaska, Arizona, California, Colorado, Connecticut, Delaware, the District of Columbia, Florida, Georgia, Illinois, Indiana, Iowa, Kansas, Kentucky, Maine, Maryland, Massachusetts, Minnesota, Mississippi, Missouri, Nebraska, New Hampshire, New Jersey, New Mexico, North Carolina, North Dakota, Ohio, Oregon, Pennsylvania, Rhode Island, South Carolina, South Dakota, Tennessee, Vermont, West Virginia, Wisconsin, and Wyoming.

division of property.[74] According to Professors Doris Freed and Thomas Walker, these statutory criteria often include:

1. Length of marriage
2. Age, health, and station in life of the parties
3. Occupation(s) of the parties
4. Amount and sources of income
5. Vocational skills
6. Employability
7. Estate, liabilities, and needs of each party and opportunity of each party for further acquisition of capital assets and income
8. Contribution or dissipation by each party in acquisition, preservation, appreciation, or dissipation of marital property, including services as a homemaker
9. The loss of inheritance or pension rights
10. The need of a custodial parent to occupy or own the marital residence, and its effects
11. Whether the property distribution is in lieu of, or in addition to, maintenance
12. Tax consequences of property division[75]

Marital fault and economic fault remain considerations in a majority of states.[76]

Equitable distribution was developed in part to compensate an innocent spouse for the loss of an important negotiating leverage, marital fault. Nevertheless, there have been indications that these property division statutes do not necessarily yield equitable results. In Professor Lenore Weitzman's documentation of her 10-year sociological research on no-fault reform, *The Divorce Revolution: The Unexpected Social and Economic Consequences for Women and*

---

[74] *Id.* These states include Alaska, Colorado, Connecticut, Delaware, the District of Columbia, Florida, Georgia, Illinois, Indiana, Iowa, Kentucky, Maine, Maryland, Massachusetts, Minnesota, Missouri, Montana, Nebraska, New Jersey, New York, Ohio, Oregon, Pennsylvania, Rhode Island, South Carolina, Tennessee, Vermont, Virginia, West Virginia, and Wisconsin.

[75] Freed & Walker, *Family Law in the Fifty States: An Overview,* 18 Fam LQ 369, 393-94 (Winter 1985).

[76] *Id* 394-95. Fault may be considered in Alabama, Connecticut, Florida, Georgia, Hawaii, Idaho, Kentucky, Louisiana, Maryland, Massachusetts, Michigan, New York, North Carolina, North Dakota, Pennsylvania, Rhode Island, South Carolina, Texas, Vermont, Virginia, Wyoming, and the District of Columbia. Economic misconduct may be considered in Arizona, California, Colorado, Connecticut, Delaware, Florida, Kansas, Maine, Minnesota, Montana, Pennsylvania, South Dakota, Texas, Washington, West Virginia, and the District of Columbia.

*Children in America,*[77] the author exposes an area of inequity in property division. Noting that the most important economic factor for contemporary families is the earning capacity of the breadwinner spouse rather than accumulation of property, Weitzman maintains that, when the tangible assets are divided upon divorce, the spouse with the lesser or impaired earning capacity, typically the wife, is the loser. This problem is compounded in many divorces where the wife is not awarded support, the family home is sold to satisfy the equal or equitable property division, and the wife is awarded child custody and inadequate child support.[78]

One attempt to remedy this inequity has evolved naturally from the concept of equitable distribution as well as from community property theory. This attempt, the focus of this chapter, has been to increase the pool of marital property to be divided upon divorce, with particular attention to career assets, such as retirement benefits and pensions, licenses to practice a profession, medical insurance, and entitlements to company goods and services. These assets, more common in most marriages than an abundance of real property or other investment property, have been categorized as marital property in case law around the country. This categorization has not been without criticism. Nevertheless, the trend is toward recognition of these assets as marital property because of the same social awareness of the joint efforts of the partnership of marriage which produced the equitable distribution concept. Issues of classification of property, valuation, and division continue to dominate dissolution negotiation and litigation. For a more complete review of equitable distribution, see L. J. Golden's *Equitable Distribution of Property* (Shepard's/McGraw-Hill 1983).

## §10.08 Pensions

Divorcing parties frequently discover that their most valuable assets, if not their only assets, are the family home and their retirement benefits, particularly pension rights.[79] A pension is generally considered deferred income which, if earned during the marriage, is now treated as marital property.[80] While community property states began to address the issue of whether pension

---

[77] L. Weitzman, The Divorce Revolution: The Unexpected Social and Economic Consequences for Women and Children in America (1985).

[78] *Id* 12, where Professor Weitzman concludes:

> The result is often hardship, impoverishment, and disillusionment for divorced women (and their children). This research shows that, on the average, divorced women and their minor children in their households experience a 73 percent decline in their standard of living the first year after divorce. Their former husbands, in contrast, experience a 42 percent rise in their standard of living.

*See also* **§§10.01, 10.03.**

[79] Foster & Freed, *Spousal Rights in Retirement and Pension Benefits,* 16 J Fam L 187, 189 (1977-78).

[80] See **§10.09,** which discusses the development of pensions as marital property.

rights constitute a marital asset as early as 1941,[81] equitable distribution jurisdictions have dealt with the issue only in the 1970s and 1980s.[82] As of 1985 nearly all community property states and a majority of common law states required division of pension as marital property at divorce.[83]

Simply stated, a pension is "an arrangement whereby an employer can provide retirement benefits for employees in recognition of their services to the company before their retirement."[84] Pension plans vary widely in the ways they are established and organized.[85] Nevertheless, there are common elements in pension plans, including eligibility and participation requirements, normal retirement dates, benefit provisions, and vesting requirements. Some of these factors, such as participation and vesting standards, are prescribed for private pension plans by the Employee Retirement Income Security Act of 1974 (ERISA).[86]

In most plans, an employee must meet some age or length of service requirements (e.g., 24 years old with one year of service) before becoming eligible to participate in the plan.[87] No plan may require that an employee work for more than one year, or attain an age greater than 25, before becoming eligible for coverage.[88] There may also be a maximum age at which employees may join, although this limit is often waived for long-term employees when a new pension plan is started.[89]

The normal retirement date, the designated age at which an employee may retire and receive full pension benefits, is usually age 65. Many plans also provide for an early retirement date, but these often require long-term employment. For example, an employee might retire at 55, after 30 years of service. When an employee elects to take early retirement, pension benefits are less than if he or she had waited until the normal retirement date.[90]

Most pension plans provide for benefits from the normal retirement date

---

[81] See, e.g., French v French, 17 Cal 2d 776, 112 P2d 235 (1941), holding that nonvested pension rights are not property, but a mere expectancy, and thus not a community asset subject to division. This is no longer the law of California.

[82] Note, *Pensions as Marital Property: Valuation, Allocation, and Related Mysteries,* 16 Creighton L Rev 743 (1983).

[83] Freed & Walker, *Family Law in the Fifty States: An Overview,* 18 Fam LQ 369, 424-26 (Winter 1985).

[84] F. Pomeranz, G. Ramsey, & R. Steinberg, Pensions: An Accounting and Management Guide 5 (1976) [hereinafter cited as F. Pomeranz].

[85] *See* **§10.10.**

[86] ERISA's labor provisions have been codified at 29 USC §1001 *et seq.* Its tax provisions amend scattered sections of the IRC of 1954.

[87] F. Pomeranz, *supra* note 84, at 8.

[88] 29 USC §1052.

[89] The Conference Board, Financial Management of Company Pension Plans 13 (1973).

[90] F. Pomeranz, *supra* note 84, at 8.

until the employee's death.[91] Some plans provide payments beyond the life of the employee, in the form of benefits to a surviving spouse.[92] In order to secure survivor's benefits, the employee receives reduced benefits at retirement to fund the continued payment of benefits to the survivor for his or her lifetime.[93] Under the terms of the Retirement Equity Act of 1984 (REA), discussed in greater detail in later sections, the participant may not opt out of survivor coverage without the written consent of his or her spouse.[94]

Other benefits commonly provided by pension plans are death benefits (paid to the employee's spouse in the event of the employee's death before retirement), and disability benefits. Pension benefits paid for a disability occurring before retirement are usually smaller than normal benefits because payments begin earlier and are expected to last longer.[95]

A pension is vested when the employee's right to receive benefits is nonforfeitable, and not contingent on his or her continuing in the same employment until retirement.[96] In the past, most pension plans did not provide for vesting of employer contributions until the normal retirement date.[97] ERISA has established statutory vesting requirements for private pension benefits derived from employer contributions.[98] All plans must provide that employer contributions be vested in accordance with one of three alternative vesting schedules.[99] The three alternatives differ in the amount of time required for vesting and the amount of contributions which become vested, but all three require 100 per cent vesting of employer contributions after 10 to 15 years.[100] The benefits attributable to employee contributions (if any) must be fully and immediately vested when contributed.[101] This means that the employee is entitled to the return of all such contributions upon death or termination of employment before retirement.

## §10.09 —History

Secure income after retirement has long been a concern of society. The

---

[91] *Id.*

[92] See **§10.10** for a discussion of the methods by which the amount of the benefit is determined. This discussion is limited to the *types* of benefits offered by most plans.

[93] F. Pomeranz, *supra* note 84, at 10.

[94] Retirement Equity Act of 1984 §103. *See also* **§10.23.**

[95] The Conference Board, *supra* note 89, at 16.

[96] F. Pomeranz *supra* note 84, at 8-9. *See also* **§10.11.**

[97] D. McGill, Fundamentals of Private Pensions 131-32 (3d ed 1975).

[98] Neal, *An Analysis of Newly Established Vesting Requirements Under Pension Reform,* 41 J Taxation 258, 259-60 (1974). *See also* **§10.11.**

[99] ERISA, 29 USC §1053.

[100] Neal, *supra* note 98, at 260. *See* **§10.11.**

[101] ERISA, 29 USC §1053.

traditional, historical methods used to provide for retirement have been private savings, investments, pensions, and other retirement benefits.[102]

In ancient times, the Roman military offered old age benefits to soldiers who had long and faithfully served the Empire.[103] Medieval trade guilds established a system by which to care for craftsmen whose productivity had been impaired because of age or infirmity.[104] In nineteenth—century Europe, it was common for government workers to receive a small stipend upon retirement.[105]

The first private pension plan originated in the United States in 1875.[106] Most of the early pension plans in this country were established by railroad, banking, and public utility companies. With the Industrial Revolution and the growth of large-scale manufacturing concerns employing thousands of workers, old age pensions became more common.[107]

In the early twentieth century, American trade unions began to establish pension plans independently of employers. Early union welfare programs offered pensions, disability and unemployment pay, and death benefits for the widows and orphans of members. These plans were generally established as inducements for new members. They were financed usually by membership dues.[108] In the early twentieth century, state and federal governments began to establish pension plans for their workers.[109]

During World War II, wage increases were prohibited under a national wartime policy against inflation. Employers created new pension plans in order to attract employees to whom they could not offer wage increases.[110] Unions negotiated pensions and other fringe benefits in lieu of prohibited inflationary wage increases. As a result, the number of pension plans more than tripled during World War II, and the number of employees almost doubled.[111] Another wage stabilization program implemented during the Korean War produced similar results.

After World War II, employers began to resist union bargaining for pension

---

[102] E. Allen, J. Melone, & J. Rosenbloom, Pension Planning 1 (3d ed 1976) (hereinafter cited as E. Allen].

[103] Eckstein, *The History of the Law of Pensions, Together With a Summary of the Pension Laws of the United States* in The Johnson Prize Essays 2-3 (G. Pepper ed 1890).

[104] Note, *The Employee Retirement Income Security Act of 1974: Policies and Problems,* 26 Syracuse L Rev 539, 542 n 9 (1975).

[105] E. Allen, *supra* note 102, at 1.

[106] Note, *supra* note 104, at 542 n 7, where it states that the American Express Company's plan, begun in 1875, provided a lump sum payment to workers who attained age 60 with 20 years of continuous service.

[107] E. Allen, *supra* note 102, at 2-3.

[108] Note, *supra* note 104, at 542 n 9.

[109] *Id* n 10, where it is noted that by 1935, one-half of the states had pension programs for public employees which included strict residence requirements and provided minimal benefits.

[110] Bureau of National Affairs, Pensions and Profit Sharing 206 (3d ed 1964).

[111] C. Dearing, Industrial Pensions 37 (1954).

benefits. But in 1948, the National Labor Relations Board ruled that employers were required by the National Labor Relations Act, as amended by the Taft-Hartley Act,[112] to negotiate with unions on pensions. In *Inland Steel Co v United Steelworkers of America (CIO)*,[113] the employer had wanted to change certain provisions of the company's pension plan without bargaining with the union. The United States Court of Appeals, Seventh Circuit, held, however, that pension plans were subject to mandatory collective bargaining. The court concluded that pensions are both deferred compensation and a condition of employment within the meaning of the Act, like seniority provisions and vacation periods. Since management could not unilaterally make changes in wages or working conditions,[114] it was also required to bargain with the collective representative over pensions.

The purpose of the Taft-Hartley Act was to foster labor peace by means of fair and orderly interaction between labor and management.[115] To that end, the Act encouraged the formation of pension plans. Contributions to pension plans constitute an exception to the criminal prohibition against employer payments to a union or union official. Pension funds are required to be held in a trust administered jointly and equally by employer and union representatives who serve as trustees.[116]

Other than these provisions in the National Labor Relations Act as amended by the Taft-Hartley Act, there was little regulation or public supervision of pension funds until the close of the 1950s. Allegations of corruption in pension plan investments and administration prompted Congress to pass the Landrum-Griffin Act in 1959.[117] Aimed at correction of mismanagement in pension funds, this Act instituted federal regulation of pension plans, requiring, inter alia, that trustees of pension and welfare plans file reports open to public inspection.[118]

All these factors were a part of the active growth of pension plans. By the

---

[112] Labor-Management Relations Act of 1947, 29 USC §§141-187.

[113] 77 NLRB Dec (CCH) (1948).

[114] Inland Steel Co v National Labor Relations Bd, 170 F2d 247, 251 (7th Cir 1948), *cert denied,* 336 US 960 (1949).

[115] 29 USC §141(b). The purpose is stated in this section as follows:

> It is the purpose and policy of this chapter, in order to promote the full flow of commerce, to prescribe the legitimate rights of both employees and employers in their relations affecting commerce, to provide orderly and peaceful procedures for preventing the interference by either with the legitimate rights of the other, to protect the rights of individual employees in their relations with labor organizations whose activities affect commerce, to define and prescribe practices on the part of labor and management which affect commerce and are inimical to the general welfare, and to protect the rights of the public in connection with labor disputes affecting commerce.

[116] 29 USC §186.

[117] Labor-Management Reporting and Disclosure Act of 1959, as codified in scattered sections of 29 USC.

[118] T. R. Brooks, *Toil and Trouble: A History of American Labor,* 288 (1971).

1970s, pensions had become such an integral aspect of the national economy that the 90-day wage-price freeze between August 15 and November 12, 1971, included pension contributions.[119] By 1975, private pension plans, with fund assets valued at close to $180 billion, provided for almost 44 per cent of all privately employed individuals.[120] In 1980 it was reported that private and public sector pension funds exceeded $550 billion, owned 20 per cent of all publicly and privately financed securities in the United States, and were larger than the combined gross national products of Great Britain and France.[121] Those numbers continued to grow in 1985.

Prior to 1974, there were a considerable number of state and federal regulations governing the administration and operation of pension funds.[122] However, this historical period has been called the "decades of relative quiet"[123] compared to the period since the passage of the Employee Retirement Income Security Act of 1974 (ERISA).[124] ERISA will be discussed later.[125]

## §10.10 —Characterization of Plans

Pension plans can be characterized by different aspects and qualities. For example, they may be defined by the method by which they are established, the source of their funding, and the technique used to determine costs and calculate benefits.

A *conventional* or *voluntary* plan is a pension plan established unilaterally by an employer or a small group of employers for the benefit of the employees.[126] A *negotiated* plan is one established as a part of a total compensation package (including wages and other benefits) in a collective bargaining agreement. Negotiated plans often follow a pattern, in terms of costs and benefits, within

---

[119] Note, *supra* note 104, at 543 (citing Economic Stabilization Act of 1970, Pub L No 91-379, 84 Stat 796).

[120] E. Allen *supra* note 102, at 1.

[121] Leonard, *Older Women and Pensions: Catch 22,* 10 Golden Gate UL Rev 1191 (1980) (citing Rifkin & Barber, *American Workers Own $550 Billion,* in Retirement Income: A Report from the Pension Rights Center (1979).

[122] Note, *supra* note 104, at 543-44 (citing IRC of 1954, §401(a)-(f) (empowering the IRS to grant or disallow *qualified* status to plans, thereby affecting their eligibility for tax advantages); Welfare and Pension Plan Disclosure Act (WPPPA), 29 USC §§301-309 (1970), *repealed,* ERISA, §111, 29 USC §1031 (Supp 1975); Labor-Management Reporting and Disclosure Act (LMRDA) (Landrus-Griffin Act), 29 USC §§401-531 (1970)).

[123] Smith, *New Rules, New Burdens,* 8 Fam Advoc 4 (Fall 1985).

[124] ERISA's labor provisions have been codified at 29 USC §1001 *et seq,* while its tax provisions amend scattered sections of the IRC of 1954.

[125] *See* **§§10.10, 10.11.**

[126] F. Pomeranz, G. Ramsay, & R. Steinberg, Pensions: An Accounting and Management Guide 5 (1976) (hereinafter cited as F. Pomeranz].; E. Allen, J. Melone, & J. Rosenbloom, Pension Planning 1 (3d ed 1976) [hereinafter cited as E. Allen].

a particular industry or group of affiliated employers.[127] Most negotiated plans are established by groups of employers in an industry or several related industries.

Pension plans which are characterized by their source of funding are classified as *noncontributory* and *contributory*. In a *noncontributory* plan, the employer makes contributions to the pension fund without deducting any amount from the employee's wages. Thus, the employee is not taxed for these contributions when they are made. A *contributory* plan requires either voluntary or involuntary contributions from the employees, in addition to employer contributions. Generally, contributory plans yield greater overall benefits unless the employer in a contributory plan chooses to make smaller contributions and provide for the same benefits as if the plan were noncontributory.

Whether a plan is noncontributory or contributory often depends upon the abilities of the employer and employee to pay the cost of the pension benefits.[128] As might be expected, this issue is frequently the subject of collective bargaining negotiations in which employers favor contributory plans and employees favor noncontributory plans.

The two principal types of pension plans are *defined contribution* and *defined benefit* plans, which are distinguished by their approaches to determining costs of the plan and calculating benefits for the participants.[129] In a *defined contribution* plan, the pension benefits are based on the money paid *into* the plan. In a *defined benefit* plan, the cost of the plan is based on the amount of money ultimately paid *out*.

The *defined contribution* plan does not provide a fixed benefit, but, rather, the benefit is based on a fixed contribution. The amount of the contribution (from the employer, the employee, or both) is usually stated as a percentage of the employee's wages, though some plans base it on hours worked or on production (such as per piece manufactured or per ton loaded). In a *unilateral* or *voluntary* plan, especially if it is noncontributory, the determination of this percentage is at the discretion of the employer. In *negotiated* plans, where pension benefits are a vital part of the total compensation package, the percentage and source of contributions are usually bargained for by the parties and specified in a legally binding collective bargaining contract between the employer and employees.[130]

The combined employer and employee contributions are either credited to an account for each employee, or, more commonly, paid as a monthly premium toward the purchase of an annuity contract. An annuity contract (usually purchased from an insurance company) is a promise to provide a series of annual or monthly payments after retirement, for the lifetime of the participant.

---

[127] F. Pomeranz, *supra* note 126, at 43-44. See **§10.08** for a brief discussion of the history of these negotiated plans.

[128] E. Allen, *supra* note 126, at 56-57.

[129] W. Greenough & F. King, Pension Plans and Public Policy 176-77 (1976).

[130] E. Allen, *supra* note 126, at 10-11.

The annuity may also provide other benefits, such as disability payments or a survivor's annuity.[131]

The contributions to the plan are usually the same for any employee, regardless of age, sex, length of service, or anticipated retirement date. However, the cost of the annuity will vary according to these same factors.[132] Therefore, the benefits received by similarly situated employees may be quite different. This inequity, along with the fact that until the employee actually retires, the precise benefit can only be estimated, may be one of the reasons why the *defined contribution* approach is used in relatively few private pension plans. It is frequently utilized by smaller employers, partnerships, and nonprofit organizations.[133]

The *defined benefit* approach is used in about 70 per cent of the pension plans in the United States.[134] The benefits in a defined benefit plan are established before retirement by one of four kinds of formulas. The contributions vary according to the cost of the benefits chosen.

Most formulas provide a benefit that is based on length of service or earnings history or both.[135] The *flat amount* formula, a feature of older negotiated plans, provides a flat monthly benefit to all employees who meet basic eligibility requirements, ignoring distinctions such as age, length of service, or compensation level.[136] This formula produces inequitable results, and is, therefore, no longer used in current plans.[137]

A *percentage of earnings* formula is widely used today in plans which cover salaried employees. The pension benefit is simply a percentage of the employee's wages, generally ranging between 20 and 40 per cent of earnings. The earnings upon which the percentage is calculated may be a career average, or may be based on earnings in the final years of employment (which produce a higher benefit).[138]

The *flat sum per year of service* formula is another way to calculate benefits in *defined benefit* plans. Under this formula a predetermined sum is multiplied by years of service to yield the monthly payment.[139] For example, an employee could receive a flat $10 times 30 years of service and have a pension of $300 per month.

Many pension plans use a *percentage of earnings* formula which also includes calculations based upon *years of service.* A percentage of earnings (usually

---

131 D. McGill, Fundamentals of Private Pensions 118-19 (3d ed 1975).

132 E. Allen, *supra* note 126, at 35-36.

133 W. Greenough & F. King, *supra* note 129, at 177-78.

134 D. McGill, *supra* note 131, at 98.

135 D. McClanahan, Pension Plans and Pension Funding (The Actuarial Basis), Simplified for Non-Actuaries 195-96 (1980).

136 The Conference Board, Financial Management of Company Pension Plans 13 (1973).

137 E. Allen, *supra* note 126, at 37.

138 F. Pomeranz, *supra* note 126, at 9.

139 E. Allen, *supra* note 126, at 9.

between 1 and 2 percent) is multiplied by the number of years the employee participated in the pension plan.[140] Thus, an employee with 30 years of employment, who earned an average of $800 per month under a plan providing 1-1/2 per cent of compensation for each year of service, would receive a pension of $360 per month.

One final way of characterizing pension plans is by eligibility for favorable tax treatment. A *qualified* pension plan under the Internal Revenue Code[141] must be operated exclusively for the benefit of employees and their beneficiaries, must not discriminate, either in terms of benefits or contributions, in favor of highly placed or highly compensated employees, and must be in writing. The plan assets, once contributed, must be unavailable to the employer. Benefits must be definitely determinable and the employee's right to receive them must vest according to statutory standards.[142] Employer contributions in a *qualified* plan are deductible as a business expense and not included in the employee's preretirement income. In addition, the investment income from qualified plans is not taxed.[143]

## §10.11 —Employee Retirement Income Security Act of 1974

Prior to the 1970s, there was little government supervision of employee pension plans.[144] However, there were substantial problems, often resulting in workers not receiving their benefits, which revealed a need for some regulation. The primary problems involved inadequate vesting, insufficient funding, and irresponsibility of plan fiduciaries.[145] To remedy the inequities created by these problems, Congress enacted the Employee Retirement Income Security Act of 1974 (ERISA).[146]

*Vesting* has been defined as "the nonforfeitable right or interest which an employee acquires in his pension fund—that is, a right to receive amounts credited to his account in the event that he leaves or loses his job prior to retirement."[147] Before the enactment of ERISA, private pension plans

---

[140] The Conference Board, *supra* note 136, at 15.

[141] IRC §§401-404.

[142] The employer has the option of selecting one of three applicable standards: vesting of all accrued benefits after ten years of employment; progressive vesting over five to ten years based on percentage of benefits; and progressive vesting based on both age and length of service.

[143] D. McGill, *supra* note 131, at 135-38.

[144] *See* **§10.08.**

[145] Note, *The Employee Retirement Income Security Act of 1974: Policies and Problems,* 26 Syracuse L Rev 539, 546 (1975).

[146] The Employee Retirement Income Security Act of 1974 contains both labor and tax provisions. ERISA's labor provisions have been codified at 29 USC §1001 *et seq.* Its tax provisions amend scattered sections of the IRC of 1954.

[147] Note, *supra* note 145, at 546 n 47.

generally adhered to strict vesting standards in order to promote long, loyal employee-employer relationships and to reduce the administrative costs of pension plans. The existence of these standards and the mobility of the American work force resulted in substantial pension forfeitures.[148]

ERISA, which covers all employee benefit plans excluding government plans, church plans, and others,[149] provides maximum participation requirements and minimum vesting requirements. Thus, no plan may require as a condition of participation that an employee complete a period of employment extending beyond the age of 25, or the date of one year of service.[150] The participation requirements of ERISA also specify the conditions for excluding an employee on the basis of age.[151] ERISA provides three alternative vesting formulas for employer contributions, since employee contributions must be fully and immediately vested when contributed. One formula provides simply that a participant must be 100 per cent vested after ten years of service.[152] Another formula is a graded schedule where a participant becomes 25 per cent vested after five years of employment, 5 percent vested in each of the next five years, and 10 per cent vested in each of the remaining five years.[153] Finally, the *rule of 45* formula provides that a worker with at least five years of service must become 50 per cent vested when the sum of the worker's age plus years of employment equals 45, with an additional 10 per cent for each of the next five years.[154]

---

[148] *Id* 547, where it is noted:

> A Senate subcommittee investigation of 87 selected plans representing more than $16 billion in pension fund assets, or 20 percent of the total invested pension assets in the United States in 1970, found that 51 of the plans studied required 11 or more years for vesting. As a result of their long vesting requirements, these 51 plans paid benefits to a mere five percent of all departing participants since 1950. In the 36 plans which required 10 years or less for vesting, only 16 percent of all departing participants over the 20-year span received pension benefits.

[149] Other exclusions from ERISA's coverage are plans maintained solely to comply with applicable workers' compensation, unemployment compensation, or disability insurance laws, plans maintained outside of the United States primarily for the benefit of persons substantially all of whom are nonresident aliens, and unfunded excess benefits plans.

In the experience of one of the authors, another excluded class from ERISA's coverage is pension plans of international agencies which are geographically located in the United States. The International Monetary Fund and the World Bank have taken the position that they are governmental plans and are thus excluded from ERISA's coverage. *See* 29 USC §1003(b)(3), (4), & (5).

[150] 29 USCA §1052(a)(1)(A). However, §1052(a)(1)(B)(1) provides that if the plan requires, as a condition for participation, that the employee work for three years, then the pension must be fully vested at that time.

[151] 29 USCA §1052(a)(2).

[152] 29 USC §1053(a)(2)(A).

[153] 29 USC §1053(a)(2)(B).

[154] 29 USC §1053(A)(2)(C); Note, *supra* note 145, at 551.

A serious pre-ERISA problem was that some pension plans were inadequately funded, being required only to fund the amount of past service liabilities, or, in the case of qualified pension plans, to fund the amount of currently created liabilities and the interest on unfunded past liabilities. This level of funding precluded the reduction or eventual elimination of such accrued liabilities. When pension plans terminated, plan assets were insufficient to meet accrued liabilities, and participants lost all or some of their benefits.[155] Responding to this problem, ERISA requires that past service costs must be amortized, unfunded past liabilities must be gradually eliminated, and fully funded status must be attained in a prescribed number of years, under threat of excise tax penalties.[156]

Finally, pension benefits before the enactment of ERISA were sometimes lost through "the mismanagement, imprudent investment or outright theft of plan assets."[157] ERISA includes elaborate rules detailing the identity of fiduciaries, their standards of care, the scope of permissible transactions with regard to plan funds, and criminal and civil liabilities for violation of the standards.[158] Other protections of plan participants found in ERISA are: the allowance of the establishment of individual retirement accounts (IRAs),[159] the provision for plan termination insurance under the auspices of the Pension Benefit Guaranty Corporation,[160] and limited portability of pension benefits from a pension plan to an IRA.[161]

In order to establish a uniform body of pension plan regulation, ERISA specifically preempts "any and all State laws insofar as they may now or hereafter relate to any employee benefit plan."[162] To what extent ERISA preempted state domestic relations law was the subject of much litigation. Originally, ERISA contained provisions which prohibited any assignment or alienation of benefits[163] and required pension plan administrators and trustees

---

[155] Note, *supra* note 145, at 548. This note describes what occurred when Studebaker closed its South Bend, Indiana, plant in 1964. Because the plan was underfunded, full benefits were paid only to those employees who were over age 60 and had had 10 years of continuous service. Little or no payments were made to most of the plant's 8,500 workers, many of whom had vested rights.

[156] 29 USC §§1082 & 1083; 29 USC §1013(b).

[157] Note, *supra* note 145, at 549.

[158] *Id* 553 (citing 29 USC §§1101-14).

[159] IRC §219(b).

[160] 29 USC §1301-23.

[161] IRC §§402(a)(5), 403(a)(4).

[162] 29 USC §1144. However, Congress's preemption of all state laws does not extend to criminal, insurance, banking, or securities law.

[163] 29 USC §1056(d)(1) & IRC §401(a)(13).

to operate a plan solely for the benefit of participants and beneficiaries.[164] Some plan administrators contended in divorce litigation that these ERISA sections prevented them from honoring support or garnishment orders based on state domestic relations law. Their argument was that payment of retirement benefits directly to the nonemployee spouse would subject the administrators to liability for breach of their fiduciary duty to plan participants and would risk loss of the plan's tax-qualified status. However, courts generally held that court-ordered family support payments were impliedly excepted from ERISA's anti-alienation provisions.[165] This issue, now largely mooted by 1984 amendments, was an integral part of the debate as to whether pensions are marital property and is discussed in a following section.[166]

## §10.12 —Individual Retirement Accounts and Keogh Plans

The sweeping pension law changes in the Employee Retirement Income Security Act of 1974 (ERISA)[167] created the forerunner of individual retirement accounts (IRAs) for persons to establish their own funds for retirement.[168]

An IRA is a trust account established by or for an individual, solely for the benefit of that person or his or her beneficiaries.[169] Since the purpose of an IRA is to provide assets upon retirement, funds may not be withdrawn from the account until the owner or beneficiary reaches age 59-1/2.[170] A wage-earner may contribute up to $2,000 per year to an IRA and deduct the amount deposited from taxable income.[171] However, no deduction is allowed for

---

[164] 29 USC §1104(a).

[165] *See, e.g.*, Carpenter's Pension Fund v Campa, 89 Cal App 3d 113, 152 Cal Rptr 362 (1979), *appeal dismissed,* 444 US 1028 (1980); American Tel & Tel Co v Merry, 592 F2d 118 (2d Cir 1979); Cody v Reicker, 594 F2d 314 (2d Cir 1979); Senco, Inc v Clark, 573 F Supp 902 (MDFla 1978). *But see also* Francis v United Technologies Corp, 458 F Supp 84 (ND Cal 1978), which construed ERISA's preemption and antialienation clauses literally and rejected the former spouse's claim to benefits.

[166] *See* **§10.13.**

[167] Pub L No 93-406, 88 Stat 829 (codified as amended at 29 USC §§1001-1461 (1982) & IRC §§401-415 (1982)). *See* **§10.11.**

[168] *See,* §2002(a)(1), IRC §219. Originally, workers covered by government or tax-qualified private pension plans were barred from opening an IRA. In 1981, the Internal Revenue Code was amended to make an IRA available to any worker with earned income.

[169] IRC §408(a). IRAs are protected to some extent from the claims of creditors. *See* IRC §408(a)(4). *See* **app 10-2** for text of IRC §408(a), (d) & (f).

[170] IRC §408(f). Amounts improperly withdrawn are includible in gross income and a 10 percent penalty is imposed. These provisions do not apply if the withdrawal is because the taxpayer has become disabled.

[171] IRC §219(b)(1). Amounts contributed in excess of allowable limits are not deductible and are subject to a penalty tax of 6% of the excess. *See* **app 10-2** for text of IRC §219(a)-(d).

contributions made after the account-holder reaches age 70-1/2. Furthermore, distributions of the account balance *must* begin no later than the year in which the account-holder reaches that age (though they *may* begin any time after age 59-1/2).[172]

Each spouse with earned income may open an IRA, contributing a maximum of $2000 annually to each account, for a total potential annual deduction of $4000.[173] If one spouse has earned income and the other spouse has none, the wage-earner spouse may open a spousal sub-account in addition to his or her own IRA. The contributions to each account are not regulated, except that the annual total of the two accounts may not exceed $2,250, and the total in either account may not exceed $2,000.[174]

Keogh plans, or HR 10 plans,[175] are available only to self-employed persons and to partnerships, including such groups as professionals, freelancers, and owners of unincorporated businesses.[176] A person who earns some income from personal services in addition to salary from a regular job may be eligible to open a Keogh.

Like an IRA, a Keogh plan provides tax benefits for depositors. An individual may deduct contributions to a Keogh from taxable income: the limit is $15,000 or 15 per cent of self-employment income, whichever is less.[177] Furthermore, a person may take the $2,000 deduction for an IRA, *and* the $15,000 for a Keogh, for a potential deduction of $17,000. Each spouse may participate in a Keogh plan if eligible to do so, making the potential maximum deduction to a married couple $34,000 if both are self-employed and contribute the maximum allowable amounts to both types of plans.

Keogh plans are also subject to contributions and distribution rules similar to those imposed on IRA plans. A 10 per cent penalty is assessed on distributions prior to age 59-1/2.[178] Contributions to the plan must end and distributions must begin no later than the year in which the beneficiary turns

---

[172] IRC §219(d)(1). Between age 59-1/2 and age 70-1/2, a taxpayer may withdraw as much or as little as he or she wants. Beginning at age 70-1/2, the taxpayer must withdraw certain minimum amounts (based on Internal Revenue Service annuity tables) or else incur a 50% tax on amounts not withdrawn. *See* Treas Reg §1.408-2(b)(6), IRC §§408(a)(6) & 4974(a).

[173] This applies whether they file jointly or individually. Note that under IRC §219(b), neither spouse may contribute more to his or her IRA than he or she personally earned in that year.

[174] IRC §219(c).

[175] Keogh plans were named for Congressman Eugene Keogh, who authored the legislation originally establishing such plans in 1962. They are also referred to as HR 10 plans, after the bill itself.

[176] A business owner who opens a Keogh plan for his or her own benefit must also open a plan for any employees with three years or more of service, and must contribute an equal percentage of income to both accounts.

[177] IRC §404(e). *See* **app 10-2** for text of IRC §404(e).

[178] IRC §72(m)(5). This penalty does not apply if the distribution is made because of the taxpayer's death or disability. *See* **app 10-2** for text of IRC §72(m)(5).

70-1/2.[179] Contributions in excess of the $15,000 or 15 per cent of self-employment income limits are not deductible, and, if willful, may bar any further contributions on the taxpayer's behalf for the next five taxable years.[180]

## Division of IRAs and Keogh Funds at Divorce

The rules for division of IRA and Keogh plans upon divorce are found in the Internal Revenue Code and accompanying treasury regulations and revenue rulings. A couple with one IRA may transfer all or part of the account from one spouse to another pursuant to a divorce decree or a written property settlement without incurring the 10 per cent penalty for premature distributions.[181] After the division, the transferee spouse is treated as the owner of the account for all purposes and has control over the distributions, but may not withdraw funds before the age of 59-1/2 without incurring a penalty.[182] It should be noted that an owner-spouse under age 59-1/2 could not cash in the IRA and use the funds to satisfy alimony, support, or settlement obligations without incurring the substantial tax penalty.

When the divorcing couple has an IRA and a spousal sub-account, each receives the designated account as separate property. The nonearning spouse may continue to maintain the spousal account after a divorce if the following requirements are met: the spousal IRA must have been established at least five years before the divorce decree, and contributions to it must have been made in at least three of the five years next preceding the divorce.[183]

If the nonearning former spouse becomes employed, he or she may make annual contributions to the IRA of up to $2,000 from earned income. If that person is unemployed or has very little earned income, contributions may be made from qualifying alimony received during the taxable year.[184] Contributions made from alimony or from a combination of alimony and earned income are limited to $1,125 per year.[185]

It is more difficult to divide a spouse's interest in a Keogh plan. There is no such thing as a "spousal Keogh," nor are there specific rules regarding interspousal transfers, as there are with IRA plans. Furthermore, the position

---

[179] IRC §401(a)(9)(A).

[180] IRC §401(d)(5). This section only applies to excess contributions which are deliberate. Because a Keogh plan is based on self-employment income, contributions are necessarily based on estimated income. Excess contributions which are the result of a good faith estimate will not subject the taxpayer to liability under §401(d)(5), although the excess is still not deductible and must be withdrawn.

[181] IRC §219(b)(4)(A); Treas Reg §1.408-4(g)(1).

[182] Treas Reg §1.408-4(g)(2).

[183] IRC §219(b)(4). The same rules apply to a decree of separate maintenance as to a decree of divorce.

[184] IRC §219(b)(4)(B). Qualifying alimony is that which is includible in the recipient's gross income.

[185] IRC §219(b)(4)(A).

of the Internal Revenue Service on whether penalties may be assessed upon such division is not clear.[186]

Even where the plan termination or cash-out is the result of a court order incident to a divorce, receipt of the account balance constitutes a premature distribution if the owner or participant in the Keogh plan is under 59-1/2.[187] However, the penalty tax on such a distribution may be avoided if the entire amount is rolled over into an IRA within 60 days.[188] The penalty tax may also be avoided by a sequestration order protecting the nonearner spouse's interest in the Keogh plan until the earner spouse reaches age 59-1/2. In addition to tax savings, this method has the advantage of preventing termination of an ongoing plan which may cover the participant's partners or employees.[189]

## §10.13 Pension Benefits upon Divorce: Old Inequities

In the traditional nuclear family, the wife pursued a career as a homemaker and earned no credit for retirement income. She relied on her husband's retirement benefits earned by him during his employment, military service, or other governmental service to see them both through their "golden years." Even if the wife did work, she rarely accumulated pension rights.

Historically, the law has been protective of employee retirement benefits, often statutorily providing that those benefits were exempt from garnishment, levy, seizure, or any other process of law.[190] This protection was often extended by courts, which in some states interpreted those laws as preventing former wives from securing rights to those benefits to satisfy child support and alimony claims.[191] Thus, it is not surprising that the law was slow to recognize spousal rights in pension and retirement benefits upon divorce. Reasons for the perpetuation of the inequity center largely on the definitions of *property* and the characterization of the benefits.

In some title theory states, pension and retirement benefits, being titled in the name of the employee spouse, were often characterized as the separate property of that spouse. In other states, courts had difficulty construing the statute as including benefits in the definition of property. Pensions were interpreted as lacking certain attributes of property such as "cash surrender

---

[186] *See* Siegel & Buckman, *Tax Consequences of Dividing a Keogh Plan,* 3 Fairshare 4 (Feb 1983).

[187] Rev Rule 78-406, 1978-2 CB 156, IRC §401(d)(4)(B).

[188] Rev Rule 78-406, 1978-2 CB 157, IRC §402(a)(5)(A).

[189] Siegel & Buckman, *supra* note 186, at 5.

[190] Annot, 93 ALR3d 711, 716 (1974).

[191] *See, e.g.,* Watson v Watson, 424 F Supp 866 (EDNC 1976); Crane v Crane, 417 F Supp 388 (ED Okla 1976); Miller v Superior Court, 69 Cal 2d 14, 442 P2d 663, 69 Cal Rptr 583 (1968); Utley v Utley, 355 Mass 469, 245 NE2d 435 (1969); Michigan Pub School Employees' Retirement Bd v Peterson, 39 Mich App 568, 197 NW2d 854 (1972); Fowler v Fowler, 116 NH 441, 362 A2d 204 (1976); Elmwood v Elmwood, 295 NC 168, 244 SE2d 668 (1978); Prewitt v Smith, 528 SW2d 893 (Tex Civ App 1975).

value; loan value; redemption value; lump sum value; and value, realizable after death."[192] As a result, they were not divisible upon divorce.

In states where the definition of divisible property included a *present* right to enjoyment, courts held that even a fully vested but nonmatured pension was not property subject to equitable distribution.[193] The statutory requirement for such property was that it had to be "legally and beneficially acquired" by one or both parties during the marriage. Pension benefits *earned* during marriage, but not *received* until after divorce, were not acquired for the purpose of the statute.[194]

Prior to enactment of the Uniformed Services Former Spouses Protection Act,[195] some military retirement benefits were not characterized as property but as present income for reduced services. As such, they were held not subject to property division upon divorce.[196]

In addition, a few courts held that pension and retirement benefits were gifts or donations by the employer to the employee, which removed them from consideration as marital property.[197] Other courts decided that a noncontributory pension, because it consisted solely of employer payments, could not be divided upon divorce because the employee spouse did not have a present right to the funds.[198] At least one court held that unless the terms of the pension itself provided for the creation of such a right in a nonparticipant, the pension was not divisible.[199]

These interpretations of pension and retirement benefits became obsolete with development of the ideas that marriage is an economic partnership and the nonworking spouse,[200] typically the wife, makes essential contributions to

---

[192] Ellis v Ellis, 191 Colo 317, 319, 552 P2d 506, 507 (1976).

[193] Libunao v Libunao, 5 Fam L Rep (BNA) 2557 (Ind 1979); Mueller v Mueller, 166 NJ Super 557, 400 A2d 136 (1979).

[194] Mueller v Mueller, 166 NJ Super 557, 400 A2d 136 (1979). It should be noted that this is no longer the law of New Jersey. Kickert v Kickert, 177 NJ Super 471, 427 A2d 76, *affd,* 88 NJ 4, 438 A2d 317 (1981), provides that virtually all pensions are divisible under their equitable distribution statutes.

[195] 10 USC §1408 (1983). *See* **app 10-3.**

[196] McCarty v McCarty, 458 US 210 (1981); French v French, 17 Cal 2d 775, 112 P2d 235 (1941); Taggart v Taggart, 540 SW2d 823 (Tex Civ App 1976).

[197] *See, e.g.,* Daigre v Daigre, 228 La 682, 83 So 2d 900 (1955); Johnson v Johnson, 23 SW 1022 (Tex Civ App 1893). It should be noted that this viewpoint is obsolete.

[198] Phillipson v Board of Admin Pub Employee's Retirement Sys, 3 Cal 3d 32, 473 P2d 765, 89 Cal Rptr 61 (1970); Foster v Foster, 589 SW2d 223 (Ky Ct App 1979); Bolt v Bolt, 113 Mich 298, 317 NW2d 601 (1982); Tucker v Tucker, 121 NJ Super 539, 298 A2d 91 (1972).

[199] Howard v Howard, 196 Neb 351, 242 NW2d 884 (1976).

[200] The expression *nonworking spouse* is used to indicate a spouse who is not employed outside of the home. It should not be interpreted to mean that a homemaker does not work.

that partnership as a homemaker.[201] With the distinction between separate and joint blurring in common law states,[202] the category of marital property available for distribution upon divorce has been enlarged.

Despite the opening created by societal change and new legal theories, further difficulties thwarted judicial division of pension and retirement benefits upon divorce. Many courts refused to divide these benefits because the employee spouse's rights to them were contingent upon certain circumstances, and, therefore, were mere *expectancies.*

For example, in *French v French,*[203] the wife claimed a community property interest in her husband's Navy retirement benefits. He was eligible for benefits only after he completed 14 years in the Fleet Reserve in compliance with all service requirements. Since the husband had not worked the requisite time upon divorce, the California court held that the retirement pay was only an expectancy which was not subject to division. A New Jersey court held in *White v White*[204] that a husband's pension interest was not subject to equitable distribution where, at the time of divorce, the husband's right to receive retirement income in the future was contingent upon his becoming totally or permanently disabled, retiring voluntarily when he reached age 40 after 10 years of service, or retiring between the ages of 55 and 65.

Other courts have not divided an employee spouse's nonvested pension because the value of the benefit was too speculative.[205] Some early cases which did divide benefits between spouses did so specifically because the pension *was* vested, giving the spouse an existing present conditional right to immediate payments.[206]

Another barrier to nonworking spouses receiving a right to their spouses' pension and retirement benefits has been federal preemption of state domestic relations law by military and other government plans, and the Employee

---

[201] *See* Burch, *Property Rights of De Facto Spouses Including Thoughts on the Value of Homemakers Services,* 10 Fam LQ 101 (1976); Weitzman, *Legal Regulation of Marriage: Tradition and Change,* 62 Cal L Rev 1169 (1974); Comment, *Marriage Contracts for Support and Services: Constitutionality Begins at Home,* 49 NYU L Rev 1161 (1974). See also M.H. Minton & J.L. Block, What is a Wife Worth? (1983) for an analysis of the dollar value of a homemaker's contribution to the family, and M.H. Minton, *Valuing the Contribution of the Homemaker at Trial,* 1 Fair Share 10:7 (Oct 1981).

[202] See **§§10.04, 10.06,** which discuss community property theory and the development of equitable distribution.

[203] 17 Cal 2d 775, 112 P2d 235 (1941).

[204] 136 NJ Super 552, 347 A2d 360 (1975).

[205] *See* Williamson v Williamson, 203 Cal App 2d 8, 21 Cal Rptr 164 (1962); Robbins v Robbins, 463 SW2d 876 (Mo 1971); Taggart v Taggart, 540 SW2d 823 (Tex 1976).

[206] Pickell v Pickell, 76 Ill App 855, 395 NE2d 673 (1979); Savage v Savage, 176 Ind App 89, 374 NE2d 536 (1978); Ratcliff v Ratcliff, 586 SW2d 223 (Ky Ct App 1979); Marriage of Faulkner, 582 SW2d 292 (Mo 1979).

Retirement Income Security Act of 1974's[207] antialienation provisions. This issue is discussed thoroughly in the following sections.[208]

## §10.14 Private Pensions as Marital Property

The beginning of the trend recognizing pension and retirement benefits as marital property divisible upon divorce is generally marked by the California case *In re Marriage of Brown*.[209] Justice Tobriner's decision overturned *French v French*,[210] which had characterized nonvested pension rights as *expectancies* which could not be divided as community property. *Brown* held that pension benefits are a form of deferred compensation for services rendered and that an employee's rights to them are contractual rights derived from the employment contract. As contractual rights, these rights to benefits are not expectancies, but choses in action, a form of property.[211] Noting that California courts previously treated other conditional rights to income as community assets, the court rejected the theory that pensions contingent upon continuous employment could not be allocated as community property.

In his decision, Justice Tobriner discussed the inequity involved in excluding pension benefits from the community:

> Over the past decades, pension benefits have become an increasingly significant part of the consideration earned by the employee for his services. As the date of vesting and retirement approaches, the value of the pension grows until it often represents the most important asset of the marital community . . . [citation omitted]. A division of community property which awards one spouse the entire value of this asset, without any offsetting award to the other spouse, does not represent that equal division of community property contemplated by [the statute].[212]

The *Brown* decision also held that an alimony award as an offset of a nonemployee spouse's pension right was insufficient, that the difficulties of predicting future possibilities and valuing the pension could be resolved by awarding a spouse an appropriate portion of a pension as it is paid out, and that the requirement of continued supervision of division of future payments was no more onerous than supervision of alimony payments.[213]

Shortly after the *Brown* decision, the same result was reached in Texas, another community property state.[214] As of 1986, all of the community

---

207 29 USC §1001 *et seq. See* **§10.11.**

208 *See* **§§10.14-10.23.**

209 15 Cal 3d 838, 544 P2d 561, 126 Cal Rptr 633 (1976).

210 17 Cal 2d 775, 112 P2d 235 (1941). *See* **§10.13.**

211 *In re* Marriage of Brown, 15 Cal 3d 838, 845, 544 P2d 561, 565, 126 Cal Rptr 633, 637 (1976).

212 *Id* at 847, 544 P2d at 566, 126 Cal Rptr at 638.

213 *Id* at 848-49, 544 P2d at 567-68, 126 Cal Rptr at 639-40.

214 *See* Cearley v Cearley, 544 SW2d 661 (Tex 1976).

property states divide pensions earned over the course of the marriage at divorce.[215]

By 1986, pension and retirement benefits were almost universally recognized as marital property to the extent that they were earned during the marriage.[216] In fact, many state legislatures enacted pension provisions in their property division statutes.[217] Nevertheless, courts in some states continue to distinguish between vested and nonvested pensions in dividing them as marital property.[218] A new trend in this area is that equitable distribution states are beginning to broaden the distribution of pensions as marital property and recognize the divisibility of nonvested pensions.[219]

As these distinctions between vested and nonvested, contributory and noncontributory, continue to be blurred in the divorce courts, the looming problem is the valuation of pensions, particularly those based upon several contingencies. This important topic is discussed after the governmental and military pension plans and retirement benefits are reviewed.[220]

---

[215] *See* Morris & Reimer, *States Which Will Award Spouses A Share Of Retirement Benefits At Time of Divorce,* 1 Cong Research Serv (1982); Neal v Neal, 116 Ariz 590, 570 P2d 758 (1977); Day v Day, 281 Ark 261, 663 SW2d 719 (1984);*In re* Marriage of Brown, 15 Cal 3d 838, 544 P2d 561, 126 Cal Rptr 633 (1976); Shill v Shill, 100 Idaho 433, 599 P2d 1004 (1979); Sims v Sims, 358 So 2d 919 (La 1978); Duke v Duke, 98 Nev 148, 643 P2d 1205 (1982); Copeland v Copeland, 91 NM 409, 575 P2d 99 (1978); Diskrow v Thibodeaux, 596 SW2d 174 (Tex Civ App 1980); Wilder v Wilder, 85 Wash 2d 364, 534 P2d 1353 (1975).

[216] *See.,e.g.,* Malone v Malone, 587 P2d 1167 (Alaska 1978); *In re* Marriage of Mitchell, 195 Colo 399, 579 P2d 613 (1978) (en banc); Robert CS v Barbara JS, 434 A2d 383 (Del 1981); Barbour v Barbour, 464 A2d 915 (DC 1983); Arnow v Arnow, 3 Fam L Rep (BNA) 2364 (Fla Dist Ct App 1976); Tavares v Tavares, 58 Hawaii 541, 574 P2d 125 1978); *In re* Marriage of Hunt, 78 Ill App 3d 653, 397 NE2d 511 (1979); Libunao v Libunao, 388 NE2d 574 (Ind Ct App 1979); *In re* Marriage of Schissel, 292 NE2d 421 (Iowa 1980); Foster v Foster, 589 SW2d 223 (Ky Ct App 1979); Deering v Deering, 292 Md 115, 437 A2d 883 (1981); Sheskey v Sheskey, 16 Mass App Ct, 159, 450 NE2d 187 (1983); Hatcher v Hatcher, 129 Mich App 753, 343 NE2d 498 (1983); Janssen v Janssen, 331 NW2d 752 (Minn 1983); *In re* Marriage of Powers, 527 SW2d 949 (Mo Ct App 1975); Vert v Vert, 188 Mont 358, 613 P2d 1020 (1980); Kullbom v Kullbom, 209 Neb 145, 306 NW2d 844 (1981); Kruger v Kruger, 73 NJ 464, 375 A2d 659 (1977); Majauskas v Majauskas, 110 Misc 2d 323, 441 NYS2d 900 (Sup Ct 1981); Glass v Glass, 344 NW2d 677 (ND 1984); Rogers v Rogers, 45 Or App 885, 609 P2d 877 (1980); Hansen v Hansen, 273 NW2d 749 (SD 1979); Englert v Englert, 576 P2d 1274 (Utah 1978); Bloomer v Bloomer, 84 Wis 2d 124, 267 NW2d 235 (1978).

[217] *See, e.g.,* Md Fam Law Code Ann §8 203 (1984); NC Gen Stat §50-20(b)(1) (1984).

[218] *See, e.g.,* Pickell v Pickell, 76 Ill App 3d 855, 395 NE2d 673 (1979); Wilson v Wilson, 409 NE2d 1169 (Ind Ct App 1980); Ratcliff v Ratcliff, 586 SW2d 292 (Ky Ct App 1979); Powers v Powers, 527 SW2d 949 (Mo 1975); White v White, 137 NJ Super 212, 353 A2d, 144 (1976).

[219] Freed & Walker, *Family Law in the Fifty States: An Overview,* 18 Fam LQ 369, 425-26 (1985) (citing Hatcher v Hatcher, 129 Mich App 753, 343 NE2d 498 (1983); Glass v Glass, 344 NW2d 677 (ND1984); Salac v Salac, (Pa CP Mar 3, 1984).

[220] *See* **§10.25.**

## §10.15 Railroad Retirement Benefits

The Railroad Retirement Act of 1937[221] established federal retirement benefits for former railroad employees. Congress's purpose in creating this pension plan was to encourage and provide for the retirement of older workers, and to insure the retention and advancement of younger railroad employees.[222] To be eligible for benefits, an employee must work in the industry for 10 years. Absent disability, no benefit is paid until the employee either reaches age 62 or is at least 60 years old and has completed 30 years of service.[223]

In 1951, the Railroad Retirement Act was amended to provide annuities for the spouses of retired workers. Under the Act, in order to qualify for that benefit, a spouse was required to live in the employee's household, receive regular contributions for support, or be entitled to support under a court order.[224] However, a spouse's entitlement to a portion of the employee's pension, or to a survivor benefit, ended when the employee and the spouse were divorced.[225]

Like most government pension plans, the Railroad Retirement Act contains strong anti-assignment language manifesting Congress's intent to insure that railroad retirees actually receive their benefits.[226] This strong protection contrasts with the fact that railroad workers' rights to benefits are not contractual, but instead exist and may be altered by the prerogative of Congress.[227] Nevertheless, in 1975, Congress made an exception to the anti-alienation provision in the Railroad Retirement Act and all other federal benefit plans. The concern over benefits recipients who were evading family support obligations prompted an amendment of the Social Security Act to provide that federal benefits could be reached to satisfy support obligations despite existing law to the contrary.[228]

It was only a matter of time before the question would arise whether a railroad retirement pension was marital property which could be divided under state law, or whether the anti-alienation clause would federally preempt

---

[221] Pub L No 75-162, 50 Stat 307. Current version at 45 USC §§231-231u.

[222] Note, *Community Property,* Benefits Awarded Under the Railroad Retirement Act are Not Community Property Subject to Division Upon Divorce, 11 St Mary's LJ 535, 538 (1979).

[223] 45 USC §231a(a)(1).

[224] 45 USC §231a(c)(3)(i).

[225] *Id* §231d(c)(3)(B).

[226] *Id* §231m, which states as follows:

> Notwithstanding any other law of the United States, or of any State, territory, or the District of Columbia, no annuity or supplemental annuity shall be assignable or be subject to any tax or to garnishment, attachment, or other legal process under any circumstances whatsoever . . .

[227] Hisquierdo v Hisquierdo, 439 US 572, (1979).

[228] 42 USC §459.

application of state divorce law. In *Hisquierdo v Hisquierdo,*[229] the Supreme Court of the United States held that a state court award of a community property interest in a railroad pension to a divorced wife would impermissibly conflict with the anti-alienation clause of the Act and violate the Supremacy Clause of the Constitution.[230]

The Court, stating that a mere conflict in words between federal and state law was insufficient for a violation of the Supremacy Clause, decided that the inclusion of future railroad retirement benefits in community property would cause "major damage" to "clear and substantial" federal interests for several reasons. Besides contravening the direct language of the anti-alienation clause, §231m, inclusion of benefits in community property would have disrupted the uniform national scheme of protecting benefits.[231] The Court also noted that the language of §231d(d)(3) of the Railroad Retirement Act specifically denied benefits to a retiree's divorced spouse. Any award of benefits to a divorced spouse would thwart Congress's objective of encouraging retirement by forcing employees to remain on the job longer to avoid the reduced retirement income.

Finally, the Court rejected the wife's plea for an offsetting award of other community assets for her husband's expected annuity. The Court reasoned that an offsetting award would defeat the purpose of §231m, which prohibited any anticipation of benefits. Such an award would allow a nonbeneficiary, the wife, to receive an interest in benefits prior to the actual accrual date, thereby also impairing the beneficiary's economic security.[232]

After the *Hisquierdo* decision, courts in some community property jurisdictions denied community property status to expected benefits under the Railroad Retirement Act.[233] Courts in common law jurisdictions also followed the rationale of *Hisquierdo* and rejected arguments that such benefits should be included in the division of marital property upon divorce.[234]

In 1981, the Railroad Retirement Act was amended to correct the statutory inequity illuminated by the *Hisquierdo* decision. The 1981 amendments extended spousal benefits to the divorced wives or husbands of railroad employees, if certain requirements were met:

1. The divorced spouse must have been married to the employee for at least 10 years
2. He or she must be age 62 or older

---

[229] 439 US 572 (1979).

[230] *Id* 590.

[231] *Id* 583-84.

[232] *Id* 588-89.

[233] Eichelberger v Eichelberger, 582 SW2d 395 (Tex 1979); Larango v Larango, 93 Wash 2d 460, 610 P2d 907 (1980).

[234] Knopf v Knopf, 264 Ark 946, 576 SW2d 193 (1979); Pickell v Pickell, 76 Ill App 3d 855, 32 Ill Dec 443, 395 NE2d 673 (1979); Frost v Frost, 581 SW2d 582 (Ky Ct App 1979); Kendall v Kendall, 106 Mich App 240, 307 NW2d 457 (1981).

3. He or she must not have remarried prior to age 65
4. The employee must be age 62 or older.[235]

The amount of the railroad pension available to a divorced spouse is equal to the amount a divorced spouse would receive if the retiree were receiving social security benefits instead of railroad benefits.[236] Furthermore, the benefits paid to a divorced spouse are reduced by the amount of any other railroad or social security benefits he or she receives.[237]

Since the 1981 amendments, survivor benefits have also been available to divorced spouses. In order to qualify for a survivor's annuity, a divorced spouse must be over 60, and must have been married to the railroad employee for at least 10 years, unless he or she has children in his or her care, in which event the age and time of marriage standards are both waived.[238]

## §10.16 Social Security Benefits

The social security system, through the extensive legislative scheme of the Social Security Act,[239] provides old age, survivor's and disability benefits (hereinafter OASDI benefits) to American workers and their families. The Act has been amended over the years to fulfill the needs of the changing American family.

As originally enacted in 1935, the Social Security Act provided insurance benefits only for retired or disabled workers. Four years later, however, Congress supplied benefits for spouses and children as well. Spousal benefits ended upon divorce.[240] In 1965, the Act was amended to give OASDI benefits to former wives who had been married to an insured individual for at least 20 years.[241] In 1977, the 20-year requirement was reduced to 10 years.[242]

As of 1985, the Social Security Act provided that the divorced spouse of an insured person may receive benefits if he or she:

1. Was validly married to the insured under state law for more than 10 years
2. Is divorced and has not remarried
3. Is at least 62 years old
4. Is not entitled to other social security benefits either on his or her own

---

[235] 45 USC §231a(c)(4).
[236] *Id* §231(c).
[237] *Id* §231c(i).
[238] *Id* §231c(e).
[239] Current version at 42 USC §§301-1396.
[240] 42 USC §402(b) & (c).
[241] 42 USC §402(b).
[242] 42 USC §402(b). This reduction was not retroactive.

> account or an account of any other insured person, such as another previous spouse.[243]

Survivor benefits are also available to former spouses under the Social Security Act. A surviving divorced spouse who was married to an insured individual for 10 years may receive an annuity at age 60, or at age 50 if he or she is disabled.[244] The former spouse may receive death benefits at any age if he or she is caring for a child of the insured individual who is under 16 or disabled.[245]

State courts have consistently held that marital or community property laws purporting to divide future OASDI benefits are preempted by Congress's creation of such an extensive statutory scheme for the protection of workers' families. One rationale followed by other courts was provided by a California Court of Appeal in *In re Marriage of Nizenkoff*,[246] where the court stated:

> The sweep of the Social Security Act is not to be interpreted by the variations and idiosyncracies of local law. . . . As Congress expressly provided for the interests of a divorced wife in the social security system, it did not intend that they rely on state family law concepts of support, alimony and community property.[247]

Other courts relied upon *Hisquierdo v Hisquierdo*,[248] where the Supreme Court of the United States held that an award to a divorced spouse of a community property interest in a railroad retirement pension would impermissibly conflict with the anti-alienation provision of the Railroad Retirement Act[249] and violate the Supremacy Clause of the Constitution. State courts have found the *Hisquierdo* rationale useful in deciding social security benefits cases because of the similarities between the two pension systems. For example, a California Court of Appeal noted:

> Only one of the provisions relied upon by the *Hisquierdo* court appears in the Social Security Act (*i.e.*, 42 USC §662). For that reason, that decision is not controlling in the instant case, but does provide guidance for our holding. The enactment of a total OASDI family benefit scheme (42 USC

---

[243] 20 CFR §404.331.

[244] 20 CFR §404.336(2).

[245] 20 CFR §404.340.

[246] 65 Cal App 3d 138, 135 Cal Rptr 189 (1976). *See also In re* Marriage of Kelley, 64 Cal App 3d 97, 134 Cal Rptr 259 (1976); *In re* Marriage of Cohen, 105 Cal App 3d 842, 164 Cal Rptr 672 (1980).

[247] Id at 140, 135 Cal Rptr at 191 (citations omitted).

[248] 439 US 572 (1979). *See* **§10.14.**

[249] 45 USC §231m.

> §402) does, in fact, suggest to us the presence of a similar congressional intent to replace state family law as it applies to social security.[250]

The *Hisquierdo* reasoning has also been adopted in jurisdictions where the case itself has not been cited.[251]

While the majority view is that *future* OASDI benefits are not divisible property at divorce,[252] some courts have held that OASDI benefits paid and received prior to the dissolution of a marriage may be considered community or marital property subject to division.[253] Nevertheless, a few jurisdictions have classified OASDI payments received prior to divorce as separate property of the recipient spouse, not subject to division.[254]

The Social Security Act provides for benefits to a divorced spouse without any reduction in the benefits available to the insured spouse. Thus, the timing of the filing of divorce is important for the insured's spouse. As a marriage approaches the 10 years required for entitlement, a non-employee spouse should strategically delay filing for divorce in order to secure OASDI benefits.

## §10.17 Military Retirement Benefits

In the late 1960s and early 1970s, courts in some community property jurisdictions were holding that military retired pay, as an integral compensation for past service in the military, was community property which was divisible at divorce to the extent that the military spouse was married while on active

---

[250] *In re* Marriage of Hillerman, 109 Cal App 3d 567, 568, 167 Cal Rptr 240, 245 (1980).

[251] See, e.g., *In re* Marriage of Evans, 85 Ill App 3d 260, 406 NE2d 916 (1980) where the Illinois Court of Appeals concluded that since the right to receive OASDI benefits derived from statute and not from common law, the statute and not Illinois marital property law must control division of those benefits. The court stated in its holding:

> Since the statute itself provides for an equitable distribution of its benefits to dependents, spouses, divorced spouses and other family members in the event certain contingencies (such as divorce) occur, we will not disturb the statutory scheme by suggesting any award of any part of the actual social security benefits to which respondent may be entitled upon his reaching retirement age.

*Id* 919.

In *Evans* the divorced wife was entitled to benefits in any event, as the marriage had endured 28 years.

[252] Lana v Lana, 125 Ariz 120, 608 P2d 57 (1979); *In re* Marriage of Nizenkoff, 65 Cal App 3d 138, 135 Cal Rptr 189 (1976); *In re* Marriage of Evans, 85 Ill App 3d 260, 406 NE2d 916 (1980); Washington v Washington, 418 So 2d 748 (La Ct App 1982); Umber v Umber, 591 P2d 299 (Okla 1979).

[253] Guerrero v Guerrero, 18 Ariz App 400, 502 P2d 1077 (1972); Evans v Evans, 98 Mich App 328, 296 NW2d 248 (1980).

[254] Hughes v Hughes, 91 NM 339, 573 P2d 1194 (1978), where the Supreme Court of New Mexico held that the benefits that both the husband and wife received prior to divorce for the hardships they endured during the Vietnam War were the separate property of each. *See also* Umber v Umber, 591 P2d 299 (Okla 1979).

duty.[255] In the late 1970s, courts in community law jurisdictions followed the decisions of the community property states, classifying military pensions as marital property which could be divided upon divorce.[256]

Some courts in common law jurisdictions declined to follow the rationale enunciated by courts in the community property states.[257] These courts generally followed the reasoning that military retired pay was not compensation for *past* services, but continuing compensation for reduced *present* services, because retired service personnel always remained subject to recall by the armed forces. Based on this rationale, retired pay was postdivorce income if the divorce occurred before retirement, and was separate property not divisible at divorce.

The issue reached the Supreme Court of the United States in 1981. In *McCarty v McCarty,*[258] the Court reversed a decision of the California Supreme Court which had awarded a portion of the husband's military retired pay to the wife at their divorce. Characterizing military retired pay as a "personal entitlement" intended by Congress to actually reach the beneficiary without state interference,[259] the Court noted as significant the lack of statutory language conferring any personal right to retirement benefits upon the service member's spouse.[260] To award the service member's spouse a community property interest in the pension, the Court stated, would diminish the retiree portion of the benefits, disrupt military personnel management, and interfere with the goal of promoting and encouraging a youthful military.[261] Therefore, the Supreme Court held that the statutory scheme relating to military retired pay constituted a federal preemption of state community property laws. The Court left the problem of correcting any inequity to former spouses of retired service members to Congress.[262]

---

[255] Van Loan v Van Loan, 116 Ariz 272, 569 P2d 214 (1977); *In re* Marriage of Fithian, 10 Cal 3d 592, 517 P2d 449, 111 Cal Rptr 369, *cert denied,* 419 US 825, *rehg denied,* 419 US 1060 (1974); Ramsey v Ramsey, 96 Idaho 672, 535 P2d 53 (1975); Le Clert v Le Clert, 80 NM 235, 453 P2d 755 (1969); Cearley v Cearley 544 SW2d 661 (Tex 1976).

[256] *In re* Marriage of Musser, 70 Ill App 2d 706, 388 NE2d 1289 (1979); *In re* Marriage of Schissel, 292 NW2d 421 (Iowa 1980); Chisnell v Chisnell, 82 Mich App 699, 267 NW2d 155 (1978); Daffin v Daffin, 567 SW2d 672 (Mo Ct App 1978);*In re* Marriage of Miller, 187 Mont 276, 609 P2d 1185 (1980); Kruger v Kruger, 73 NJ 464, 375 A2d 659 (1977).

[257] Cose v Cose, 592 P2d 1230 (Alaska 1979); Fenny v Fenny, 259 Ark 858, 537 SW2d 367 (1980); *In re* Marriage of Ellis, 36 Colo App 234, 533 P2d 1347 (1975), *affd,* 91 Colo 317, 552 P2d 506 (1976); Hill v Hill, 47 Md App 460, 424 A2d 779 (1981); Howard v Howard, 196 Neb 351, 242 NW2d 884 (1976); Baker v Baker, 546 P2d 1325 (Okla 1976).

[258] 453 US 210 (1981).

[259] *Id* 210-11.

[260] *Id* 226-28.

[261] *Id* 233-35.

[262] *Id* 235-36, where the Court stated, "Congress may well decide . . . that more protection should be afforded a former spouse of a retired service member. This decision, however, is for Congress alone."

The *McCarty* decision raised the issue of pension rights upon divorce to public consciousness. In response to *McCarty,* and the public outcry which followed, Congress, on September 8, 1982, enacted the Uniformed Services Former Spouses Protection Act (USFSPA)[263] which accorded the state courts the power to divide military pensions under the law of the state for the purposes of alimony awards, child support payments, or property division upon the dissolution of marriage.[264]

The USFSPA, effective February 1, 1983, provides that state courts have jurisdiction to divide military retirement benefits without regard to the length of the marriage. The total amount of the disposable retired pay available to the divorced spouse may not exceed 50 per cent of the retiree's pension.[265] The divorced spouse does not lose the entitlement to a portion of the benefits upon remarriage.[266]

Enactment of the USFSPA, which was intended to negate the effect of *McCarty* in jurisdictions in which military pensions are marital property, promoted some rules as to relitigation of claims to pensions. Final court orders which had been changed to follow the *McCarty* decision were not to be recognized. Decisions made prior to *McCarty* which did not divide military retired pay were not to be reopened.[267] Indeed, some courts have ruled that those decisions are res judicata, and cannot be changed.[268] Congress did not, however, prohibit the reopening of cases *decided* after *McCarty.*

## §10.18 —Uniformed Services Former Spouses Protection Act

The Uniformed Services Former Spouses Protection Act (USFSPA)[269] has created some issues of which the practitioner should be aware. For example, under the Act, state courts may exercise jurisdiction over a service member's retired pay based on the service member's consent or based upon domicile or residence in a state not due to military assignment.[270] There is no jurisdiction

---

[263] 10 USC §1408. *See* **app 10-3,** §1316; **§10.18.**

[264] 10 USC §1408 (a)(1)(3).

[265] *Id* §1408(e)(1).

[266] *Id* §1408(d)(4).

[267] HR Rep No 112, 97th Cong, 2d Sess 5999-6000, *reprinted in* 1982 US Code Cong & Ad News 1571-72.

[268] Erspan v Bagett, 659 F2d 26 (5th Cir 1981); *In re* Marriage of Smith, 549 F Supp 761 (WD Tex 1982).

[269] 10 USC §1408. *See* **app 10-3.**

[270] 10 USC §1408(c)(4) states:

> A court may not treat the disposable retired or retainer pay of a member in the manner described in paragraph (1) unless the court has jurisdiction over the member by reason of (A) his residence, other than because of military assignment, in the territorial jurisdiction of the court, (B) his domicile in the territorial jurisdiction of the court, or (C) his consent to the jurisdiction of the court.

over the military person if he or she is residing in that state solely because of military assignment.

This rule raises serious problems of service of process. Service may not be easily effected in the domicile state if the service member is not physically present there, which may necessitate resort to the state's long-arm statute. It is conceivable that the state of the service member's domicile under the USFSPA may decline jurisdiction on the ground that there is no *residence* under its divorce statute.

The service member would be well advised, in the absence of a settlement agreement, not to facilitate jurisdiction with respect to retirement benefits by precipitously filing suit in a state which is not his or her statutory domicile. Doing so would probably constitute consent to jurisdiction.

A different issue surfaces where foreign spouses of service members file suit in their home country, where they or their local counsel feel more secure litigating custody and divorce. Divisible divorce and custody doctrines from the United States being unfamiliar to them, dependents of the military personnel risk losing what may be their most valuable right against a military spouse: an equitable share of pension rights accumulated during the marriage. A foreign court clearly does not have jurisdiction to divide the military pension under the USFSPA except where the service member consents. Although there were no regulations or reported cases on this point as of 1985, it is clear that *McCarty v McCarty*[271] still applies where the court does not have subject matter jurisdiction over the military pension.

A leading specialist in military pensions, Kathryn S. Marshall, a lawyer practicing in Waukegan, Illinois, recommends that the service member not file the initial pleading, but seek to negotiate a settlement.[272] Suggesting that "newspaper mentality"[273] notions of the pension's value should be avoided, she advises, as a negotiating technique, that the dependent spouse be asked to state a position on the worth of the pension and to negotiate down from there. Where a service member has other substantial assets, substituting them for the pension should be considered.

The formula frequently used for determining a spouse's share in a military pension, as reported by Marshall, is one-half the number of years married while on active duty divided by the total years served (if service is complete) or to be served in order to collect pension (if service is not complete).[274] Under this formula, the portion for the dependent spouse will be diminished by deliberate extension of service by the member.

In drafting agreements, it is well to keep in mind that the Department of Defense can issue separate checks to the member and the spouse if there were

---

271 McCarty v McCarty, 453 US 210 (1981).

272 Marshall, *Military Pensions in Dissolution Proceedings in Equitable Distribution States* 97, in Making Divorce into a Federal Case (Presented by the Family Law Section of the ABA 1985).

273 *Id* 98.

274 *Id* 99.

10 years of marriage during 10 years of service.[275] Although under the statute there is a limit of 50 per cent on the amount that can be paid to any one spouse, 65 per cent may be paid to more than one spouse.[276] While there is no statutory limit on a larger judgment, there is a collection problem in amounts exceeding these percentages.

Retired pay is subject to garnishment for support arrears. However, Marshall warns that the amount of disposable retired or retainer pay may be manipulated by the service member by increasing his or her withholdings for federal, state, and local taxes.[277]

Other negotiating leverage includes a service member's agreement to designate a former spouse as beneficiary under the survivor benefit plan, irrespective of court jurisdiction over the pension. Other benefits available to military spouses include medical benefits, identification cards, and exchange, commissary, and theater privileges.

Medical benefits may be available to an exmilitary spouse if the marriage has lasted at least 20 years during 20 years of service, the spouse does not remarry, and the spouse has no medical insurance pursuant to a group plan through employment. The same 20 years service during 20 years of marriage without remarriage applies for eligibility for the identification card, commissary and exchange privileges, and theater privileges. A current identification card is needed to exercise these privileges.

Sample paragraphs drafted by Kathryn Marshall for the American Bar Association Family Law Section which may be used in agreements involving military spouses are set forth in Appendix 10-4.

## §10.19 Federal Civil Service Benefits

The United States government provides pension benefits for most of its civilian employees through the Civil Service Retirement System (CSRS). CSRS annuities are administered by the Office of Personnel Management (OPM). Over the years Congress has amended the law regulating the CSRS to follow the trend increasing pension rights for former spouses of federal employees.[278]

Prior to 1978, federal law did not authorize the payment of retirement benefits to anyone other than the former or retired employee. At best, a divorcing spouse could only obtain a court order compelling the CSRS employee to pay a portion of the benefits *if* the state recognized pension benefits as marital property divisible upon divorce.[279] If payments were not

---

[275] 10 USC §1408(d)(2).

[276] *Id* §1408(e)(1) & (4)(a).

[277] Marshall, *supra* note 272, at 99.

[278] *See* **§§10.15-10.17; §§10.20-10.22.**

[279] *See* **§10.13.** Cases which have held that a CSRS pension is divisible as marital or community property include: Monsma, 618 P2d 559 (Alaska 1980); Flowers v Flowers,

made, a non-employee former spouse had few remedies since CSRS pensions were exempt from garnishment or attachment in satisfaction of a support or property division claim for many years.

In 1978 Congress amended the provisions relating to the CSRS, directing the OPM to comply with court orders dividing a CSRS pension or awarding a portion of the pension payments. The amended statute provides:

> Payments . . . which would otherwise be made to an employee . . . shall be paid (in whole or in part) by the Office to another person if and to the extent expressly provided for in the terms of any court decree of divorce, annulment, or legal separation, or the terms of any court order or court approved property settlement agreement incident to any court decree of divorce, annulment, or legal separation.[280]

This provision was designed to facilitate the enforcement of alimony or property awards in divorce cases, but does not require state courts to treat CSRS pensions as marital or community property.[281] A court order must strictly comply with the terms of the statute and corresponding regulations in order to be honored by the OPM.[282] While OPM will pay a former spouse directly if the court order "specifically provides that the former spouse is entitled to payments from the retirement benefit,"[283] if that employee objects, it will not honor an order which merely implies that payments are to be made by the federal employee.[284]

In addition, the court order must specify an amount to be paid to the former spouse which is readily ascertainable.[285] This may be accomplished by recital of a particular amount or a percentage of the total annuity. The percentage that may be awarded is virtually unlimited because of the ambiguous language of the statute, which provides that payments from a CSRS pension "shall be paid (in whole or in part)" to a former spouse according to the terms of a qualifying court order.[286] This could be interpreted as authorizing an award of any

---

118 Ariz 577, 578 P2d 1006 (1978); McCree v McCree, 464 A2d 922 (DC 1983); Gilbert v Gilbert, 422 So 2d 133 (La Ct App 1983); Woodward v Woodward, 656 P2d 431 (Utah 1982); Mack v Mack, 108 Wis 2d 604, 323 NW2d 153 (Ct App 1984). *Cf* Carter v Carter, 277 SC 277, 286 SE2d 139 (1982).

280 5 USC §8345(j)(i).

281 *See, e.g.,* Barbour v Barbour, 464 A2d 915 (DC 1983); Green v Green, 623 P2d 890 (Hawaii Ct App 1981).

282 *See* **app 10-5.**

283 5 CFR §831.1703(a).

284 *Id* §831.1703(b)(2). *See also* McDaniel v United States Office of Personnel Management, 716 F2d 1063 (Cir 1983).

285 5 CFR §831.1703(c).

286 5 USC §8345(j)(1).

portion of the annuity to the former spouse, up to the full amount payable to the retired employee.[287]

If an employee opts for lump sum withdrawal of retirement contributions, the OPM must notify the employee's former spouse. If the OPM determines, that a spouse (or exspouse) has entitlement to any portion of the retirement benefits, the lump sum withdrawal will not be permitted without consent of the spouse or exspouse.

## §10.20 —Civil Service Retirement Spouse Equity Act of 1984

In enacting the Civil Service Retirement Spouse Equity Act of 1984 (CSRSEA),[288] Congress greatly expanded the rights of former spouses to their federal employee spouses' retirement benefits.

Many changes centered on survivor benefits, which before the CSRSEA, were unavailable to former spouses.[289] The 1984 amendment shortened the length of the marriage requirement for eligibility to receive survivor benefits from one year to only nine months. The length of marriage requirement to recover survivor benefits where there is a death in service remained eighteen months. In cases where there is a marriage after retirement, the period in which a retiree must notify the Office of Personnel Management (OPM) of the desire to provide a survivor's annuity has been extended from one to two years.

While a retiring employee may designate one or more former spouses to receive survivor benefits, such a designation of a former spouse will not be valid if there is a present spouse unless that spouse consents in writing. The 1984 amendments require a surviving spouse (or exspouse) to relinquish a survivor benefit upon remarriage prior to age 60, an increase of five years. Retirees who previously waived survivor benefits for a spouse at the time of their retirement are no longer barred under the CSRSEA from making a post retirement election to provide those same benefits to a subsequent spouse, provided, of course, the retiree redeposits with interest the cumulative sum that would have been withheld had the retiree made such a designation at retirement.

The 1984 amendments made a reduction for a survivor's annuity automatic at retirement. In addition, a retiring employee is not allowed to waive the survivor benefit for a current spouse without the written consent of that spouse. Since the CSRSEA requires the OPM to recognize court orders granting survivor benefits to former spouses of federal employees, state courts may now

---

[287] 5 CFR §831.1705 specifies that the amount payable to a former spouse shall not exceed the net annuity after certain deductions required by law are made.

[288] Pub L No 98-615, 98 Stat 3195 (1984). See **app 10-5** for regulations governing apportionment of civil service benefits.

[289] In fact, until 1985, survivor benefits were not even guaranteed to widows and widowers because a CSRS retiree could unilaterally elect to receive a higher pension during his or her life and provide no death benefits. *See* HR Rep No 1054, 98th Cong, 2d Sess 10-11, *reprinted in* 1984 US Code Cong & Ad News 5540-41.

order a federal employee or retiree to provide a survivor's annuity for a divorced spouse.[290]

The 1984 law permits former spouses for the first time to enroll in the Federal Employees' Health Benefits program (FEHB).[291] Formerly, an ex-spouse could obtain only an individual policy at individual policy rates, without a physical examination, from the carrier of the employee's insurance that covered the spouse as a dependent. Now those eligible to enroll include any former spouse entitled to a portion of the retiree's or employee's annuity as part of a divorce decree or property settlement or a former spouse who became eligible for future or retroactive entitlement to a survivor's annuity *after enactment* of the 1984 amendments.

Instead of individual policy rates, the former spouse will be required to pay the premium paid by the employee plus any cost to the government. These rates should be substantially lower than individual rates and the coverage significantly broader than an individual policy. However, two additional conditions limit eligibility: the former spouse must have been covered under the employee's FEHB plan for at least 18 months immediately prior to dissolution of the marriage. This eligibility for FEHB coverage also applies to former spouses of foreign service and Central Intelligence Agency personnel.[292]

Finally, the 1984 amendments were a disappointment to spouses of civil service employees who retired or who divorced prior to May 7, 1985, the effective date of the 1984 amendments. Except for a small class of such retirees funded by a special appropriations bill, these spouses were excluded from the benefits provided to former spouses under the CSRSEA.[293]

All other persons seeking direct payments of civil service retirement benefits should submit the following information to the OPM:

1. A recently certified copy of the court order or court-approved property settlement agreement along with the order

---

[290] Civil Service Retirement Spouse Equity Act of 1984, Pub L No 98-615, §2, 98 Stat 3195.

[291] *Id* at §3, 98 Stat at 3202.

[292] *See* **§§10.21-10.22.**

[293] In order to qualify for the excepted class, the former spouse:

1. Must have had an absolute or final divorce prior to September 15, 1978
2. Must not have remarried prior to age 55
3. Must have been married to the employee during 10 years of creditable service (i.e., creditable toward the employee's pension)
4. Must be 50 years old or older
5. Must not be receiving any earned pension benefits other than social security

An application for those persons must be submitted to OPM before May 9, 1987, on the form set forth in **app 10-6.** Please note that in March, 1986, President Reagan signed into law HR 4061, which eliminated the requirement that a former spouse must not be receiving any earned pension benefits other than Social Security. As of publication, no OPM regulations had been issued on the charge.

2. A statement signed by the spouse seeking direct payment or by the spouse's attorney verifying that the order has not been amended, superseded, or set aside
3. Identifying information concerning the employee or retiree including full name, date of birth, civil service claim number, and social security number, if known
4. The complete current name and mailing address of the applicant.[294]

In preparing qualifying court orders, the attorney will take precautions to be sure that the order expressly provides that the former spouse is entitled to payments from the fund (not from the retiree), and that the United States, Office of Personnel Management, shall make the payments in the specified amounts or percentage. If the language of the order is in percentage terms, it should read that a specified "percent of the annuity unreduced for survivor's benefits shall be paid" to the former spouse "by the US Office of Personnel Management." The terms *life annuity, life rate, annuity,* and *life rate annuity* refer to the annuity computed before the reduction for survivor benefits. The term *gross annuity* refers to the annuity computed after reduction for survivor's benefits and will result in the former spouse receiving cost of living increases which the employed spouse receives. If the amount is stated in dollars instead of a percentage, no cost of living increase inures to the former spouse.

## §10.21 Foreign Service Retirement Benefits

Since 1946, career foreign service officers have received pension benefits through the Foreign Service Retirement and Disability System (FSRDS), rather than through the Civil Service Retirement System (CSRS)[295] which covers virtually all other United States government employees. Like most other government pension plans, the FSRDS, through the Foreign Service Act of 1946,[296] originally provided benefits only for foreign service employees and their widows. Pensions paid by the FSRDS were not "subject to execution, levy, attachment, garnishment, or other legal process,"[297] and were thus not available to former spouses seeking to enforce alimony, child support, or property division claims.

Survivor's annuities were also available only to widows and widowers, not to former spouses. In *Warner v United States,*[298] the United States Court of Claims interpreted a provision of the United States Code relating to the payment of survivor benefits. The court held that termination of a marriage by divorce

---

[294] Pursuant to 5 CFR pt 831, subpt Q, the address of OPM is: Allotment Section P.O. Box 17 Washington, D.C. 20044-0017.

[295] *See* **§§10.19-10.20.**

[296] Act of Aug 13, 1946, ch 957, tit VIII, §864, Pub L No 79-724, 60 Stat 999 (1946).

[297] Pub L No 79-724, 60 Stat 1024, *repealed by* the Foreign Service Act of 1980, tit II, §2205(1), Pub L No 96-465, 94 Stat 2071, 2159.

[298] 301 F2d 327, (Ct Cl 1962).

could be equated for the purpose of paying survivor benefits to termination of a marriage by death; in either event, there could no longer be any spouse eligible to receive the survivor's annuity.[299] Although *Warner v United States* involved survivor benefits, rather than pension benefits, and was not a divorce case, it was relied upon by the District of Columbia Court of Appeals in *Finch v Finch*[300] to support denial of a portion of a foreign service pension to a former wife.

In 1979, the Foreign Service Act was amended to authorize payments to be made from an FSRDS pension in satisfaction of a court order for alimony, child support, or property division.[301] This amendment permitted the FSRDS for the first time to make direct payments to a former spouse in compliance with a court order. However, it did not require state courts to divide an FSRDS pension.[302]

It soon became clear that this amendment was insufficient in light of both the trend recognizing pensions as community or marital property and the unique circumstances of foreign service wives. These women were required to serve faithfully with their foreign service husbands. Serving faithfully meant more than fidelity to the marriage. Foreign service wives frequently lived in other countries where they were expected to be models of conduct as representatives of the United States. They were required to engage in charitable activities, participate in the entertaining, and be available to assist the ambassador's wife or the charge d'affairs at any time for any reason. The foreign service wives were subject to reprimand if they did not promote their husbands' careers. They were graded on their performance, and their husbands' promotions in the service depended in part upon their spouses' rating.

Thus, these wives were performing full-time foreign service duties, and did not have time, nor were they allowed, to pursue another career, generate their own income, acquire income-producing skills, or earn credit for social security. Upon divorce, after this demanding service with their husbands, foreign service wives were without access to pension rights, marketable job skills, or survivor benefits.

Because of this grossly inequitable situation, after intensive lobbying by

---

299 *Id* 329.

300 378 A2d 1092 (DC 1977).

301 Exec Order No 12,145, §1-112, 44 Fed Reg 42653 (July 18, 1979). This executive order was made pursuant to a then-extant section of the United States Code which provided that when Congress amended a provision of general applicability in the CSRS which was "substantially identical" to a provision of the FSRDS, the amendment was deemed to extend to the FSRDS as well, and the President was authorized to prescribe by executive order regulations to maintain conformity between the two systems. 22 USC §1065(a) (repealed 1980). This order was designed to extend a similar provision relating to civil service pensions (5 USC §8345(j) to all federal employees.

302 Pub L No 96-465, 94 Stat 2071 (1980) (codified at 22 USC §4041 *et seq).*

foreign service wives, Congress enacted the Foreign Service Act of 1980,[303] which created a former spouse's entitlement to a pro rata share of an FSRDS pension, subject to modification by spousal agreement or a state court order incident to divorce or separation.[304] The pro rata share of the pension is determined by dividing the number of years of employment with the foreign service by the number of years of marriage. A former spouse is entitled to one-half of the resulting percentage of benefits. The former spouse is defined as a person who has been married to a foreign service employee for not less than 10 years during the employee's creditable service.[305]

A court order or agreement which is silent as to a former spouse's share of the pension may not necessarily be a waiver of the pro rata share of benefits. The former spouse may need only follow the State Department regulations to apply for benefits.[306] However, an agreement or court order expressly waiving all rights other than those specifically included in an agreement or order not providing for such benefits presumably would eliminate pension rights and survivor benefits.[307] Remarriage of the divorced spouse before age 60 results in loss of all rights as a former spouse.[308]

The 1980 legislation also made survivor benefits available to former spouses. A foreign service retiree must take a reduced annuity upon retirement in order to provide a survivor's annuity for a spouse or former spouse, unless both parties elect in writing to waive the survivor benefit.[309] As in the case of pension benefits, if the former spouse remarries prior to age 60, he or she loses the survivor benefit.[310]

The Department of State has issued regulations which govern payment of benefits to former spouses.[311] In general, the Department will honor a court order incident to divorce which directs it to pay a portion of regular retirement benefits to a former spouse, and will also pay survivor benefits to a divorced spouse if so directed.[312]

However, similar to civil service retirement benefits, foreign service retirement and survivor benefits will not be distributed to a former spouse unless the court order is *qualified* according to the State Department regulations.[313]

---

[303] 22 USC §4054(a).

[304] *Id* §4044(a)(10).

[305] *Id* §4054(a)(1). *See also* 22 CFR §19-6-5(b).

[306] *Cf* Williams v Williams, 472 A2d 896 (DC 1984). In this case a waiver provision in broad language executed prior to adoption of the 1980 legislation was held not effective to waive the statutory right which came into effect between the date of signing the agreement and the date of the divorce, since the right did not yet exist when the waiver was agreed upon.

[307] 22 USC §4054(b).

[308] *Id* §4046(b).

[309] *Id* §4054(b).

[310] 22 CFR §19.11-2.

[311] 22 CFR §§19.6-1, 19.6-2.

[312] 22 CFR §19.6-1.

An order is *qualified* if it directs that payment be made to the former spouse by the Department (and *not* by the retiree) and if it states the amount to be paid as a dollar figure or a percentage so that it may be readily calculated by the Department. An order will not be considered qualified if it conflicts with any previously issued court order, such as one which directs payment to a prior spouse, or if it directs payments in excess of the retiree's annuity.[314] In addition, the court order must be issued within one year after the divorce or annulment.

If a foreign service officer is disabled, the annuity to the former spouse commences when the participant would have qualified based upon his or her creditable service for an annuity or the date the disability begins, whichever is later. A foreign service employee who becomes separated from the foreign service without becoming eligible for an annuity, may elect to be paid a lump sum in lieu of receiving an annuity at retirement age. Without court order or spousal agreement, the lump sum will be paid to the former spouse, who will be entitled to 50 per cent if married to the foreign service officer throughout creditable service or a pro rata 50 per cent share based on years of marriage during service.

To receive payments pursuant to a court award, a former spouse must submit an application to the Department of State which includes the names, ages, and addresses of both spouses, the current marital status of the non-employee spouse as well as the dates of marriage and divorce and a certified copy of the divorce decree or incorporated agreement directing payment.[315]

## §10.22 Central Intelligence Agency Retirement Benefits

Central Intelligence Agency (CIA) personnel are included in the Civil Service Retirement System (CSRS)[316] unless and until they serve *overseas* for more than five years, when they become eligible to join the CIA Retirement and Disability System (CIARDS). The CIARDS is regulated by the Central Intelligence Agency Retirement Act of 1964, which was amended by Congress in 1982 to provide rights for spouses and former spouses of CIA employees.[317] Like the Foreign Service Act,[318] the CIA Act contemplates securing specific detailed benefits for spouses as a recognition of the lifestyle of compromise and sacrifice experienced by families of CIA employees with overseas service.

The amendments require that CIA spouses be notified of their rights. The

---

313 22 CFR §19.6-2(1). *See also* **§10.20.**

314 *Id* §19.6-2(a) & (b). *See also* 22 CFR §19.6-5.

315 *Id* §19.6-3.

316 *See* **§§10.19-10.20.**

317 The Central Intelligence Agency Retirement Act of 1964 For Certain Employees, *as amended,* 50 USC app §403 *et seq.*

318 Pub L No 96-465, 94 Stat 2071 (1980) (codified at 22 USC §4041 *et seq* (1982)). *See* **§10.21.**

Agency must issue a notice called *Retirement Benefits for Former Spouses.* The CIA employee or spouse must sign an acknowledgment that the spouse has been shown the notice.

A person qualifies as a CIA spouse if the following conditions are satisfied:

1. He or she was married to an agency employee during 10 years of creditable service by the employee
2. Both the employee and spouse spent at least 5 of those same 10 years outside the United States
3. They were divorced subsequent to November 15, 1982.[319]

Agency personnel who have served overseas for more than five years cannot withdraw their lump sum retirement contribution if married unless the current spouse agrees in writing. If the spouse does not consent, the agency employee will become eligible for a deferred annuity at age 62. An agency employee may withdraw his or her contribution to the CIARDS fund without the consent of the former spouse. However, a qualified former spouse has a right to a proportional share of the lump sum up to a maximum of one-half if the marriage lasted during the full period of agency service.

There is no provision for a current spouse to receive a share of the employee's retirement annuity after retirement (but before death of the employee), but a former spouse will be entitled to receive a proportionate share unless he or she has waived the right to do so. The exact amount of the former spouse's share will be the proportionate share based on the years of marriage to the employee during creditable service, up to 50 per cent.

The parties may fix or alter the proportionate share of lump sum or annuity by a valid agreement. In the absence of an agreement, a court of competent jurisdiction may determine the share of a qualified former spouse.

Under the 1982 amendments, any current or qualified former spouse is entitled to a survivor's annuity.[320] It is mandatory for agency personnel to receive a reduced annuity in order to provide a survivor benefit for a current or former spouse. The survivor's annuity will be for a maximum of 55 per cent of the CIA employee's basic annuity, if the marriage lasted the entire period of creditable service, unless the spouse agrees in writing to accept a lesser sum.

Where agency personnel have multiple exspouses, a survivor's annuity will be divided among them based on the length of time each spouse was married to the employee. Where there is a current spouse and one or more former spouses, the survivor's benefit will be paid proportionally to the former spouses based upon years of marriage during creditable service, with the remainder going to the current spouse.

The reduction in the employee's retirement annuity to provide for the

---

[319] 50 USC §403 (Supp 1985) Title II-The Central Intelligence Agency Retirement and Disability System, §204(b)(4).

[320] *Id* §221.

survivor's annuity is not greater as a result of having more than one spouse or exspouse. The former spouse loses the right to receive the survivor's annuity upon remarrying before age 60. However, the survivor's annuity may be restored if the former spouse's subsequent marriage terminates. Remarriage after age 60 does not affect the former spouse's right to the survivor benefit.

The CIA is required to provide information to former and current spouses, but discretion in communicating with the agency is essential so as not to compromise the identity of the employee or former employee when his or her relationship to the agency is not public information.

## §10.23 Retirement Equity Act of 1984

Previous sections have documented the trend towards spousal rights in retirement benefits as evinced by congressional amendment of several government pension plans.[321] This trend culminated in 1984 when Congress amended the Employee Retirement Income Security Act of 1974 (ERISA)[322] to insure that former spouses of participants in *private* pensions plans also retained retirement and survivor benefits rights.

ERISA, which expressly provides that it supersedes state law in the area of employee benefit plans, long contained an anti-alienation provision prohibiting the assignment of retirement benefits from a participant to a nonparticipant.[323] Although courts generally held that this prohibition was inapplicable to orders assigning benefits to former spouses and children under an implied exception for divorce-related transfers,[324] there was always the danger that a plan could be disqualified for certain beneficial tax treatment if the anti-alienation rule were violated.[325]

With the enactment of the Retirement Equity Act of 1984 (REA),[326] effective January 1, 1985, Congress provided that ERISA's anti-alienation rule does not apply to a limited number of domestic relations orders which divide retirement

---

[321] *See* **§§10.15-10.22.**

[322] 29 USC §1001 *et seq. See* **§10.11.**

[323] 29 USC §1144(a), which states:

> Except as provided in subsection (b) of this section, the provisions of this subchapter and subchapter III of this chapter shall supersede any and all State laws insofar as they may now or hereafter relate to any employee benefit plan described in section 1003(a) of this title. . . .

*See also* 29 USC §1056(d)(1); **§10.11.**

[324] *See, e.g.*, Carpenter's Pension Fund v Campau, 890 Cal App 3d 113, 152 Cal Rptr 362 (1979), *appeal dismissed,* 444 US 1028 (1980); American Tel & Tel Co v Merry, 592 F2d 118 (2d Cir 1979); Cody v Reicker, 594 F2d 314 (2d Cir 1979); Senco, Inc v Clark, 573 F Supp 902 (MD Fla 1978); Owens v Owens, 672 SW2d 67 (Ky Ct App 1984); General Dynamics Corp v Harris, 581 SW2d 300 (Tex 1979).

[325] Murphy, *The Retirement Equity Act of 1984 and Qualified Domestic Relations Orders,* 9 Ill Fam L Rep 94 (1985).

[326] The REA amended both the IRC and ERISA. *See* 26 USC §§72, 401, 402, 410, 411, 414, 6057, 6652; 29 USC §§1001, 1025, 1052-1056, 1144.

benefits. Domestic relations orders are defined as any judgment, decree, or order, including the approval of a property settlement agreement which relates to the provision of child support, alimony payments, or marital property rights to a spouse, former spouse, dependent, or child of a participant made pursuant to a state domestic relations law.[327]

While the anti-alienation provision is applicable to a domestic relations order under the REA, it is not applicable to what has been labeled a *qualified domestic relations order* (QDRO). A QDRO is a domestic relations order meeting the specific standards of the REA which "creates or recognizes the existence of an alternate payee's right to, or assigns to an alternate payee the right to, receive all or a portion of the benefits payable with respect to a participant under a plan."[328]

To accomplish its purpose to protect pension plans from having to pay benefits inconsistently with the plan's terms, thus balancing the plan's administrative concerns with the objective to honor all reasonable state court orders,[329] the REA lists qualifying standards for a QDRO. The order must clearly specify:

1. The name and last known mailing address (if any) of the participant and each alternate payee of the order
2. The amount or percentage of benefits to be paid by the plan to each alternate payee, or the manner in which such amount or percentage is to be determined
3. The number of payments or period to which such order applies
4. Each plan to which the order applies[330]

In addition, the order *cannot* require:

1. Any type or form of benefit, or option not otherwise provided by the plan
2. That the plan provide increased benefits (determined on the basis of actuarial value)
3. Payment of benefits to an alternate payee which are required to be paid to a different payee under another previous QDRO[331]

A QDRO may specify that benefits for the alternate payee begin on or after the date on which the participant reaches earliest retirement age, whether or not the participant actually retires on that date. This is allowed despite the rule that a QDRO may not require a plan to make a payout which would violate its

---

[327] 29 USC §1056(3)(B)(ii)(I) & (II).

[328] *Id* §1056(3)(B)(i)(I) & (II).

[329] Kittrell, *The Retirement Equity Act of 1984, Some Problems and Their Solutions* 2 (1985 ABA Annual Meeting July 9, 1985).

[330] 29 USC §1056(3)(c)(i)-(iv).

[331] *Id,* §1056(3)(D)(i)-(iii).

own rules.[332] This thwarts a participant's postponement of payout to a former spouse by not taking early retirement.

A QDRO must expressly state a former spouse's intent to seek survivor's status to retain those annuities, provided the spouses were married for one year.[333]

It has been suggested that lawyers submitting QDROs or judgments incorporating QDROS to plan administrators should also include copies of the relevant statutory sections "as a matter of prudence."[334] The plan administrator must notify the participant and any other payee of the receipt of the QDRO and the procedures for determining its validity.[335] The administrator must, within a reasonable time of receipt, determine whether the order is a QDRO and notify the participant and alternate payees of the outcome. During this decision-making process, the administrator must segregate the escrow and the alternate payee's share of the plan. The REA provides that the plan directly disburse benefits to the non-employee spouse. An alternate payee is deemed to be a beneficiary for the purposes of ERISA, is entitled to notice of plan amendments and yearly reports, and is eligible to sue in federal court to protect plan rights and collect attorneys' fees if successful.[336]

Under the Internal Revenue Code provisions amended by the REA, an alternate payee, for the most part, is to be taxed in the same manner as the employee participant.[337] Taxability is determined by the form of the payout, whether annuity or lump sum. Variations depend upon whether an employer contributed to the fund or whether the payee is the participant or the alternate payee.[338]

The REA increases pressure on attorneys to focus meticulous attention upon drafting domestic relations orders in order to insure their *qualified* status.[339]

---

[332] Kalcheim & Shapiro, *Does the Order Pass the Test?*, 8 Fam Advoc 20 (Fall 1985).

[333] 29 USC §1056(3)(F).

[334] Kalcheim & Shapiro, *supra* note 332, at 21.

[335] 29 USC §1056(3)(G)(i)(I)-(III). The REA requires that procedures to determine the status of QDROs and administer distributors:

1. Be in writing
2. Notify all persons specified in the QDRO as eligible for payment of benefits under the plan promptly of the procedure
3. Permit an alternate payee to designate a representative for receipt of copies of notices

[336] Kittrell, *supra* note 329, at 5.

[337] 26 USC §402.

[338] *See* O'Connell & Kittrell, *The Tax Effects are Easier to Predict*, 8 Fam Advoc 11 (Fall 1985).

[339] For some samples of QDROs, *see* Kittrell, *supra* note 329, at 7-11; Koretzensky, *Clause and Effect: Setting Up a QDRO*, 8 Fam Advoc 27-29 (Fall 1985).

## §10.24 —Qualified Domestic Relations Orders: Traps to Avoid

An attorney must be careful in drafting a qualified domestic relations order (QDRO), since a small slip might result in a client losing benefits and suing for malpractice. It is important to remember the following:

1. A QDRO must specify each plan to which the order applies
2. A QDRO will be disqualified if it demands a form of payout not provided by the plan to the employee
3. A QDRO must be adjusted for the rights of any other payee, such as another former spouse
4. There is the possibility that opposing counsel might commit the "naughty ploy"[340] of accepting a defective QDRO without objection, knowing it will be ineffective and that it may be too late to be corrected when the defect is discovered upon the pension administrator's refusal to honor the order
5. A fund may not be receptive to QDROs. For example, a large national fund providing retirement annuities to many colleges and private educational institutions throughout the United States, known as the Teachers Insurance Annuity Association College Retirement Equity Fund, refuses to recognize QDROs issued by Maryland courts. The TIAACREF position is based upon the peculiarity of Maryland statutory law which does not authorize its courts to change title. Although Maryland has a broad definition of marital property which has been held to include pension rights,[341] the Maryland courts can only order the spouse who *owns* the rights to pay either a lump sum or a portion of the pension if, as, and when received. Therefore, it is argued that Maryland courts have no power to issue a QDRO binding on the pension fund itself, although Maryland courts regularly purport to do so. Practitioners will need to examine their state statutes to determine whether there is authority to issue QDROs binding on third parties, as the 1984 statute leaves this question to state law

## §10.25 Valuation of Pension Plans

The acceptance of pensions as community and marital property has created another problem for judges, lawyers, and divorcing clients: valuation. Pension plans are difficult to value for several reasons discussed below. Nevertheless, courts in all jurisdictions are requiring that pension plans be valued prior to

---

[340] Troyan, *Evaluating Pensions in Light of The Retirement Equity Act of 1984*, 11 Fam L Rep (BNA) 3005, 3013 (Monograph no 2 1985).

[341] Md Fam Law Code Ann §8-203(b) (1984).

disposition at divorce.[342] Successful negotiation depends on proper valuation and allocation of pension plans and the marital portion of such plans. While it is commonly recommended that actuaries, accountants, or other experts be hired to value pension plans, it is imperative that the family law practitioner develop a basic understanding of valuation and allocation.

The lawyer must be familiar with case law in his or her jurisdiction which establishes the method of valuation of pension plans upon divorce. Generally, courts have hesitated to formulate one method for valuing pensions because of the variety of plans, the impact of a participant's personal circumstances on the plan's worth, and the inherent risk of setting a future right.[343] The most common valuation alternatives are calculation of the participant spouse's contributions to the plan, calculation of the present value of the participant's benefits when they vest, and determination of a fixed percentage of the benefits allocable to the nonparticipant spouse when they become available.

Calculation of a participant spouse's contributions to a pension fund is most useful as a method of valuation for pension plans funded by employee contributions, whether linked to income, productivity, years of service, or some other factor. It is also a useful method when the vested participant spouse has terminated employment and expects a return of contributions. It is not a good method of valuation, at least for the nonparticipant spouse, where the employee only contributes a portion of the pension.

The present cash value of vested and matured retirement benefits method of valuation has been the most commonly used alternative in the courts. It certainly is the most speculative. To reach a figure, the benefits payable in the future are discounted for interest in the future, for mortality (the probability that the participant will die before qualifying for benefits), and for vesting, if the participant has not worked the number of years necessary for full qualification for benefits.[344] The benefits are then calculated for each year, usually based on the Group Annuity Mortality (GAM) Table for the participant's life expectancy as a retiree. One consulting actuary in private practice has simplified the equation for each year of retirement as follows:

> Amount of payment in each year × interest rate per year compounded × probability that each payment will be made (taken from GAM Table) = present value for that year.[345]

There are several sources available which give examples and go into greater detail on valuation.[346] It is also important to note that it is not possible to

---

[342] B. Goldberg, Valuation of Divorce Assets 248 (1984).

[343] Berger & Eichner, *Consulting Court Decisions,* 5 Fam Advoc 26, 27 (Spring 1980).

[344] Bloomer v Bloomer, 84 Wis 2d 124, 267 NW2d 235, 240-41 (1978).

[345] Projector, *Putting A Value on A Pension Plan,* 5 Fam Advoc 37 (Spring 1983).

[346] *See e.g.,* Berger & Eichner, *supra* note 343, at 28, which summarizes the approach used by one court which will produce the present value of a contingent annuity of a defined benefit plan:

accurately provide present value figures for a deferred distribution settlement.

The deferred distribution settlement, or reserved jurisdiction method of valuation, which is also called the *as, if and when paid* alternative, is becoming more popular with the courts because the actual award is not dependent upon calculation of uncertain variables. There are two ways the reserved jurisdiction method can be applied. The pure approach requires additional litigation in that the court awards a percentage of the benefits at the time they are paid.[347] With the present percentage allocation method, at time of divorce the court awards to each party a percentage of the retirement if and when it becomes due. One court has developed the following formula for such valuation:

> The marital interest in each payment will be a fraction of that payment, the numerator of the fraction being the number of years (or months) of marriage during which benefits were being accumulated, the denominator being the total number of years (or months) during which benefits were accumulated prior to when paid. The trial court, when using this

---

> 1. Calculate the amount of monthly pension payments. Assume that the employee was at normal retirement age (usually 65 and retired with a fully vested pension on the date of separation. Later raises in wages due to merit or inflation would not be marital property. Sec. 401(e)(4).)
>
> 2. Find the employee's life expectancy at the time of separation. Subtract the normal retirement age in order to determine the probable number of months of pension benefits.
>
> 3. Select a discount rate. The legal rate (6 percent in Pennsylvania, 41 P.S. sec. 201) is clearly inappropriate, *Bouchard v. Bouchard,* 321 N.W.2d 330 (Wis. 1982), and would create too high a present value. Probably the best indicator of the true value of this tax-sheltered money is the effective interest on local high-grade municipal bonds.
>
> 4. Find the then-present value of the annuity at the normal retirement age.
>
> 5. Discount the then-present value to present value, accounting for mortality, disability, and termination, as appropriate for the specifics of the plan involved.
>
> 6. Reduce the present value of the pension to account for lack of vesting, if necessary. Some plans will be either zero or 100 percent vested. Others will be partly vested and partly not, in which case only the nonvested portion should be reduced.
>
> 7. If a portion of the pension was earned before marriage, it is not marital property, and must be excluded. Accordingly, multiply the present value by a fraction, the numerator of which is the total time of the marriage until separation, and the denominator of which is the total time of employment (assuming the employee spouse is working at the time of separation).

*Jerry L.C. v Lucille H.C.*, 448 A2d 223 (Del. 1982). *See also* Lipman, *Methodology, Valuing Deferred Contribution Plans,* 5 Fam Advoc 19 (Spring 1983); Projector, *Valuation of Retirement Benefits in Marriage Dissolution,* 50 LAB Bull 229 (1975); Tepfer, *Methodology: Valuing Defined Contribution Plans,* 5 Fam Advoc 18 (Spring 1983); Troyan, *Pension Evaluation and Equitable Distribution,* 10 Fam L Rep (BNA) 3001 (Monograph no 1, 1983).

[347] Berger & Eichner, *supra* note 343, at 40.

method of allocation, will retain jurisdiction and award the nonemployee spouse some percentage of the marital interest in each payment.[348]

Because no uniformity exists regarding pension plans, and many elements affect valuation, it is imperative that the attorney obtain a copy of the plan from the administrator and read it closely. Important information to be discovered includes:

1. The terms of vesting
2. The availability of benefits should the participant resign, be terminated or obtain disability benefits prior to retirement
3. The participant's options to elect alternative retirement plans, lump sum payment in lieu of an annuity, and provisions for survivor benefits
4. The difference between electing early retirement, the normal retirement date or late retirement
5. The benefits at retirement
6. Death benefits
7. Provisions regarding loans
8. Investment policies and procedures of the plan
9. Every other relevant factor which may influence the rights of the parties[349]

After review of the plan, it is necessary to identify the needs and desires of the client to determine which method of valuation and allocation will be most beneficial. Generally, once the marital portion of the pension plan is designated, it may be disposed of in three basic ways: a buy-out of the spouse's interest by the participant spouse, who retains exclusive right to the plan; a division of the current pension payments; or establishment of a percentage payment to the other spouse payable upon retirement.

Considerations in negotiating the terms of settlement include whether the nonemployee spouse wants to keep the marital home, the equity in which could be traded for comparable value of the spousal interest in the retirement benefits, whether the nonemployee spouse can afford the risk of the participant spouse never collecting benefits because of job termination, early death or disability, or election of a retirement option that is not beneficial to the nonemployed spouse; or whether the employed spouse will receive promotions or pay increases which will result in higher benefits, which would be beneficial

---

[348] *In re* Marriage of Hunt, 78 Ill App 3d 653, 397 NE2d 511, 519 (1979). *See also* Jerry LC v Lucille HC, 448 A2d 223, 225 (Del Super Ct 1982).

[349] B. Goldberg, *supra* note 342, at 249; Schwecter, *Defining Benefits as Property,* 5 Fam Advoc 9 (1983).

to a nonemployee spouse in a reserved jurisdiction percentage allocation.[350]

Another consideration may be tax consequences. While in community property states there is no tax upon equal division of property assets if no separate property is used to effect the equal division, a payout from separate sums for a pension buyout may be taxable.[351] If a court orders immediate distribution of a pension plan, individual retirement account, or Keogh, important tax advantages are lost.

It is important to remember that a successful valuation of a pension involves an actuary or accountant who is trained in this world of multiple variables. It has been noted that:

> The best expert is someone who has a broad understanding of plan design techniques, the legal effect of such plan provisions, the flexibility permitted to the participant, as well as the underlying law relating to trust administration and the governing federal law.[352]

## §10.26 Other Career Assets

The trend characterizing career assets as marital and community property has been stimulated by evidence reflecting that no-fault divorce and equitable distribution have produced inequities and unfair results. Long periods of education have become a necessary prerequisite to establishing a professional career. The traditional wife has often been the one who promoted her husband's chances of success through her work in and out of the home. She has also frequently had the responsibility for rearing the children.

Many young couples made career-investment goals, which, although reasonable when made, have produced serious and unforeseen consequences upon divorce. In the case of the classic student-spouse/working-spouse couple, family income is frequently consumed for survival and education, leaving little for division at divorce. The wife was left at divorce with limited job skills, no alimony or mere rehabilitative alimony, little if any property, and often several children to care for. The husband reaped the windfall of his career assets developed during the marriage.

As is often true in family law, the social forces eventually provoked legal changes. The concept of marriage as an economic partnership has developed, producing recognition of the nonemployee spouse's contributions to the partnership as valuable and compensable upon divorce. Because spousal self-sufficiency has also been strongly emphasized upon divorce, compensation for these services has been limited to division of property accumulated during the marriage, rather than through a continuing obligation of alimony.

Accordingly, the fairness-motivated search for community and marital property has led to consideration of the mainstay of the economic partnership:

---

[350] B. Goldberg, *supra* note 342, at 254-55.

[351] *Id* 262.

[352] Schwecter, *supra* note 349, at 11.

the career. This search has created a spousal right in pensions, as discussed in previous sections,[353] and continues to suggest consideration of spousal rights in other career assets. The family law practitioner should, in each divorce case, be aware of these career assets, and during discovery gather as much information about them as possible, ready to attribute appropriate weight to them in property settlement negotiations and litigation. The classification of such assets as property is new and controversial, but arguably will make the difference between an inadequate division of property rights and a fair one.

Some other career assets are forms of deferred compensation similar to pensions. For example, profit sharing, thrift plans, and savings plans are provided to employees in many corporations and businesses, and guarantee the employee an accumulation of income in addition to the paycheck. Employee stock ownership plans (ESOPs and TRASOPs) also exist in many corporations as a method for employees to accumulate stock as additional assets.[354]

Stock options are another potential career asset. However, the timing of the purchase of the stocks usually determines whether stock options can be included as community or marital property. For example, some courts have held that future stock options in which the employee has no present interest at the time of his or her divorce are not divisible because they are future earnings.[355] Other possibilities of marital property include stock appreciation rights, commissions, fringe benefits, and insurance.

Additional assets discussed in the following sections include workers' compensation benefits, personal injury awards, and professional degrees and licenses.[356]

## §10.27 —Workers' Compensation Awards

All states have workers' compensation laws which provide for fixed awards to employees who are permanently or temporarily prevented from working by some job-related injury or disease. Payments are made to compensate the employee for both loss of wages and impairment of future earning capacity. The timing of the receipt of the award and the use of the money are important factors in determining the character of the award upon divorce.

Courts in common law jurisdictions have generally ruled that workers' compensation awards received by an injured spouse are marital property, divisible at divorce. Some have reasoned that because workers' compensation is not included in any statutory definition of separate property, such awards must be marital property under the presumption that all assets not separate

---

[353] *See* **§§10.14-10.23.**

[354] *See* Fullenweider, *Unlocking the Possibilities, Deferred Compensation,* 5 Fam Advoc 2, 5 (Spring 1983).

[355] Ettinger v Ettinger, 637 P2d 63 (Okla 1981); *cf* Darwish v Darwish, 100 Mich App 758, 300 NW2d 399 (1981); McDenco, Inc v Myklebust, 615 SW2d 187 (Tex 1981).

[356] *See* **§§10.27-10.30.**

are marital.[357] Courts in common law states without the presumption that all property is marital unless separate, or which do not classify property in their statutes, have also divided workers' compensation awards upon divorce, reasoning that such benefits are designed to assist not only the injured employee, but his or her dependents as well.[358]

The date of accrual of the claim, not the date the award is received, governs its classification as marital property in most common law states. Thus, an award which accrues during marriage, but which is not paid until after divorce, is still divisible marital property. In a few cases, courts have expressed concern that to hold otherwise would invite abuse of the judicial process because an injured employee could delay settlement of a workers' compensation claim until after divorce, and thereby avoid division of a substantial marital asset.[359]

Important factors in these decisions are method of payment and subsequent use of the funds. For example, in *Mosley v Mosley*,[360] the workers' compensation scheme provided the injured worker a stream of payments which began during the marriage and would continue after divorce. The Court of Appeals of Kentucky decided that the payments received during the marriage were marital property, while payments made after the divorce, like earnings after divorce, were the separate property of the injured spouse. In *Lukas v Lukas*,[361] an Appellate Court of Illinois found it significant that the husband, upon receipt of his workers' compensation award, deposited the money into a joint savings account, where it was commingled with other funds and used on a joint basis.

In community property states, courts have held that workers' compensation benefits should be classified as community property to the extent that the award compensates for loss of earning capacity during the marriage, and not to the extent that the rights vested during the marriage.[362] Termination of marriage reduces the community's interest in the workers' compensation award which is paid after divorce to compensate for lost earning power during the marriage. The remainder, as compensation for the disability after divorce and for impairment of future earnings, is the separate property of the injured spouse.

It should be noted that even when a court determines that a workers'

---

[357] *See, e.g.*, Lukas v Lukas, 83 Ill App 3d 606, 404 NE2d 545 (1980); Johnson v Johnson, 638 SW2d 703 (Ky 1982); Quiggins v Quiggins, 637 SW2d 666 (Ky Ct App 1982).

[358] *See, e.g.*, Smith v Smith, 113 Mich App 148, 317 NW2d 324 (1982); Evans v Evans, 98 Mich App 328, 296 NW2d 248 (1980); Hughes v Hughes, 132 NJ Super 559, 334 A2d 379 (1975). *See also* Golden, Equitable Distribution of Property (1983).

[359] *See, e.g., In re* Marriage of Dettore, 86 Ill App 3d 540, 408 NE2d 429 (1980); *In re* Marriage of Thomas, 89 Ill App 3d 81, 411 NE2d 552 (1980); Smith v Smith, 113 Mich App 148, 317 NW2d 324 (1982).

[360] 682 SW2d 462 (Ky Ct App 1985).

[361] 83 Ill App 3d 606, 404 NE2d 545 (1980).

[362] *See, e.g.*, Bugh v Bugh, 125 Ariz 190, 608 P2d 329 (1980); *In re* Marriage of McDonald, 52 Cal App 3d 509, 125 Cal Rptr 160 (1975); Cook v Cook, 102 Idaho 651, 637 P2d 799 (1981); Hicks v Hicks, 546 SW2d 71 (Tex Civ App 1976).

compensation award is divisible marital or community property, it will not necessarily divide the benefits. Courts in both common law and community property jurisdictions have discretion to consider many factors when dividing property, including the health and future earnings capacity of both parties, and may award the entirety of the workers' compensation benefit to the spouse who sustained the injury.

## §10.28 —Personal Injury Awards

The important relationship of personal injury awards to the ability of a spouse to earn a living as a substitute for employment makes them a career-related asset. Courts in several states have considered whether damages awarded to one spouse for a personal injury claim are community or marital property.

In some common law states, the decision whether personal injury awards are separate or marital property depends upon the property division statutes. A few states statutorily define these awards as separate property, not divisible at divorce.[363] Other states do not include personal injury awards in their definitions of separate property, which means that they will be presumed marital property if earned during the marriage.[364] At least one court has decided that the personal injury award, to the extent that it represents compensation for "pain, suffering, disfigurement, disability or other debilitation of the mind or body,"[365] represents the personal property of the injured spouse not subject to equitable distribution. To the extent that the award constitutes compensation for economic loss, the award is marital property. However, a lump sum personal injury award, despite the fact it comprises compensation for past, present, and future wages and medical expenses, is rarely divided into these individual components in most jurisdictions. There may be difficulty upon divorce allocating the personal injury award to economic loss and pain and suffering.

In most community property states, a personal injury award is considered to be the separate property of the injured spouse. Texas, Louisiana, and California have statutorily exempted personal injury awards from division in

---

[363] *See* Cal Civil Code §§4800(c), 5126 (Deering 1984); NY Dom Rel Law §236B(1)(d)(2) (McKinney Supp 1982-83); Tex Fam Code Ann §5.01(3) (Vernon 1975). Illinois excludes from marital property "any judgment or property obtained by judgment awarded to a spouse from the other spouse." Ill Ann Stat ch 40, §503 (Smith-Hurd 1980).

[364] *See, e.g., In re* Marriage of Fjeldheim, 676 P2d 1234 (Colo Ct App 1983); Gan v Gan, 83 Ill App 3d 265, 404 NE2d 306 (1980); Nixon v Nixon, 525 SW2d 835 (Mo Ct App 1975); Platek v Platek, 309 Pa Super 16, 454 A2d 1059 (1982); Mack v Mack, 108 Wis 2d 604, 323 NW2d 153 (1982).

[365] Amato v Amato, 180 NJ Super 210, 434 A2d 639, 643-44 (1981).

most cases.[366] In Washington, Nevada, and Idaho, case law has established the same rule. In other community property states, a distinction is made between reimbursement for economic loss to the community, and damages for pain and suffering. For example, in New Mexico and Arizona, a personal injury award has been held to be community property only to the extent that it is compensation for medical expenses actually paid by the community or for lost community wages. Any award for pain and suffering is the separate property of the spouse who incurred the injury.[367]

A 1984 case in the Supreme Court of Washington, *Brown v Brown*,[368] characterized a personal injury award as partly separate property and partly community property. Although Washington is a community property state, the rationale used by the court in *Brown* may prove persuasive to courts in common law jurisdictions, inasmuch as Washington's statutory definition of community property is very similar to many states' statutory definitions of marital property.[369]

*Brown* overruled a 1892 case[370] which had held that a personal injury claim was community property, not separate property, being "acquired by either spouse otherwise than by gift, bequest, devise or descent."[371] In *Brown* the court adopted a less literal reading of the community property statute and held:

> that the word "acquired" should be construed to encompass wages and other property acquired through the toil, talent or other productive

---

[366] *See* Cal Civ Code §§4800(c), 5126 (Deering 1984); La Civ Code Ann art 2344 (West Supp 1982); Tex Fam Code Ann §5.01(a)(3) (Vernon 1975). Cal Civ Code §4800(c) provides:

> (c) Notwithstanding the provisions of subdivision (a), community property personal injury damages shall be assigned to the party who suffered the injuries unless the court, after taking into account the economic condition and needs of each party, the time that has elapsed since the recovery of the damages or the accrual of the cause of action, and all other facts of the case, determines that the interests of justice require another disposition. In such case, the community property personal injury damages shall be assigned to the respective parties in such proportions as the court determines to be just, except that at least one-half of such damages shall be assigned to the party who suffered the injuries. As used in this subdivision, "community property personal injury damages" means all money or other property received or to be received by a person in satisfaction of a judgment for damages for his or her personal injuries or pursuant to an agreement for the settlement or compromise of a claim for such damages, if the cause of action for such damages arose during the marriage but is not separate property as defined in Section 5126, unless such money or other property has been commingled with other community property.

[367] Jurek v Jurek, 124 Ariz 596, 606 P2d 812 (1980); Soto v Vandeventer, 56 NM 483, 245 P2d 826 (1952). *See also* Mead v Mead, 442 So 2d 870 (La Ct App 1983).

[368] 100 Wash 2d 729, 675 P2d 1207 (1984).

[369] Wash Rev Code Ann §§26.16.010, 26.16.020 (1961 & Supp 1986).

[370] Hawkins v Front St Cable Ry, 3 Wash 592, 28 P 1021 (1892).

[371] *Id* at 595, 28 P at 1022.

faculty of either spouse, but not compensation for personal injury. Such a construction is consistent with the basic principle that, except for gifts to the community, community property consists only of that which is acquired by onerous title, or in exchange for other community property.[372]

## §10.29 —Professional Degrees and Licenses

Whether professional degrees and licenses earned by one spouse during the marriage are divisible assets upon divorce has been highly publicized. This issue encompasses all the controversial elements of the trend defining career assets as community and mental property: injustice requiring a remedy, conflict with the standard definitions of property, valuation difficulties, unpredictability of the future, and differing judicial determinations across the country. This topic is particularly interesting to lawyers, since disputes over lawyers' degrees and licenses are second only to those involving the medical profession.[373]

The typical scenario giving rise to the issue is where one spouse, typically the wife, supports the husband, forgoing her own educational and career goals and the accumulation of assets while he pursues a graduate or professional degree. The high cost of such an education often requires that the wife earn the living for both spouses at a relatively low level in reliance on the benefit that the degree or license will bring in later years.

An acute problem arises when the parties separate and file divorce proceedings before they benefit financially from the degree or license. At that point, they usually have accumulated no substantial assets, but may have significant debts. The working wife can expect to receive little compensation for her efforts from a division of property, no matter how equitable. Neither can she expect to share in the benefits of the education and concomitantly enhanced earning power she helped finance. Alimony will probably not be available because she has already demonstrated an ability to support herself, albeit at the lower standard of living enjoyed by graduate students rather than that of practicing professionals.[374]

The trend is presumably gender-neutral, in that in the future this scenario will involve husbands who have worked to put their wives through professional school.[375] The questions presented to the courts have been: is a degree or license acquired during marriage a divisible marital property interest, and, if so, how should the supporting spouse be compensated?

---

[372] Brown v Brown, 100 Wash 2d 729, 675 P2d 1207, 1212 (1984) (citations omitted).

[373] Lauter, *Whose Law Degree Is It?,* Natl LJ, Nov 28, 1983, at 1, col 1.

[374] *See In re* Marriage of McVey, 641 P2d 300 (Colo Ct App 1981); Wright v Wright, 469 A2d 803 (Del Fam Ct 1983); Pacht v Judd, 13 Ohio App 3d 363, 469 NE2d 918 (1984).

[375] Virtually all of the cases to this 1986 date have involved a wife who is now seeking to share in the benefits of her husband's degree. But see Saint Pierre v Saint Pierre, 357 NW2d 250 (SD 1984) where division of the wife's medical degree was sought.

Few courts have actually held that a degree or license is marital or community property divisible upon divorce.[376] In fact, some early cases which so held were reversed upon appeal, rehearing, or reexamination.[377] However, some courts have held that the increased future earning capacity of a professional spouse made possible by the working spouse's contributions was an asset capable of division or allocation in alimony awards.[378]

The majority rule is that professional degrees and licenses are not property. Generally, courts have been reluctant to expand the traditional definition of property to include assets which do not have the typical property characteristics such as transferability, assignability, inheritability, or the ability to be readily valued.[379] Courts have also balked at valuing a professional degree or the potential increased earning capacity because, as stated by the New Jersey Supreme Court, an attempt to value a degree "in the hands of any particular individual at the start of his or her career would involve a gamut of calculations

---

[376] *See, e.g.,* Reen v Reen, 8 Fam L Rep (BNA) 2193 (Mass P Ct & Fam Ct 1981); Woodworth v Woodworth, 126 Mich App 258, 337 NW2d 332 (1983); O'Brien v O'Brien, 12 Fam L Rep (BNA) 2001 (NY Ct App 1985); Daniels v Daniels, 20 Ohio App 2d 458, 185 NE2d 773 (1961); *In re* Neuhaus, 9 Fam L Rep (BNA) 2168 (Wash Super Ct 1982).

[377] *See, e.g.,* Sullivan, 134 Cal App 3d 634, 184 Cal Rptr 796 (1982), *vacated,* 37 Cal 3d 762, 691 P2d 1020, 209 Cal Rptr 354 (1984); Inman v Inman, 578 SW2d 266 (Ky Ct App 1979), *revd,* 648 SW2d 847 (Ky 1982); Mahoney v Mahoney, 91 NJ 488, 453 A2d 527 (1982) (reversing decisions that professional degrees were property rights in Lynn v Lynn, 153 NJ Super 377, 379 A2d 1046 (1977); Mahoney v Mahoney, 175 NJ Super 443, 419 A2d 1149 (Super Ct Ch Div 1980); Hill v Hill, 182 NJ Super 616, 442 A2d 1072 (1982).

[378] *See, e.g., In re* Marriage of Horstmann, 263 NW2d 885 (Iowa 1978); *In re* Jannsen, 348 NW2d 251 (Iowa 1984); Vaclav v Vaclav, 96 Mich App 584, 243 NW2d 613 (1980); Stern v Stern, 66 NJ 340, 331 A2d 257 (1975); Diment v Diment, 531 P2d 1071 (Okla Ct App 1974). *Contra* Hughes v Hughes, 438 So 2d 146 (Fla Dist Ct App 1983) (value of degree measured by future earning capacity is too speculative); *In re* Marriage of Goldstein, 97 Ill App 3d 1023, 423 NE2d 1201 (1981) (court refused to engage in speculation about future income); *In re* Marriage of MacNamara, 399 NE2d 371 (Ind 1980); Wilcox v Wilcox, 173 Ind App 661, 365 NE2d 792 (1977) (Indiana courts held that future earning capacity resulting from a professional degree is purely speculative); Moss v Moss, 639 SW2d 370 (Ky Ct App 1982) (pharmacy practice's earnings were merely prospective).

[379] *See, e.g., In re* Marriage of Graham, 194 Colo 429, 574 P2d 75, 77 (1978), where the Supreme Court of Colorado held that an advanced degree was not property at all:

> An educational degree . . . is simply not encompassed even by the broad views of the concept of "property." It does not have an exchange of value or any objective transferable value on an open market. It is personal to the holder. It terminates on death of the holder and is not inheritable. It cannot be assigned, sold, transferred, conveyed or pledged. An advanced degree is a cumulative product of many years of previous education combined with diligence and hard work. It may not be acquired by the mere expenditure of money. It is simply an intellectual achievement that may potentially assist in the future acquisition of property. In our view, it has none of the attributes of property in the usual sense of that term.

that reduces to little more than guesswork."[380] In addition, the valuation and award of future income acquired after a divorce are contrary to current policies of property division law.[381]

Nevertheless, the obvious unfairness of a working spouse left with no property and alimony while the other walks away with the windfall of a professional degree has not been lost on the courts.[382] Courts in many jurisdictions have focused on how best to compensate the working spouse who has sacrificed for the improvement of the other spouse's career.

The majority of courts award working spouses some compensation for their proven contributions to the acquisition of the degree or license. The contributions may be reimbursed through the division of property, if there are sufficient assets,[383] but historically the contribution has been viewed as one of many factors in making an alimony award.[384] In other jurisdictions, courts have made compensation through a monetary award, sometimes called *reimbursement alimony,* often rationalized on the theory of unjust enrichment.[385]

Courts have taken different approaches to fixing the amount of compensation for the supporting spouse. In *Woodsworth v Woodsworth,*[386] where the Court of Appeals of Michigan held that a professional degree was marital property, the court listed the following factors for consideration in valuation:

---

[380] Mahoney v Mahoney, 91 NJ 488, 453 A2d 527, 532 (1982). *See also* Wisner v Wisner, 129 Ariz 333, 631 P2d 115 (1981); DeWitt v DeWitt, 98 Wis 2d 44, 296 NW2d 761 (1980). Critics of this argument point out that "the economic value of the education is real, and no less susceptible to calculations than in personal injury and wrongful death cases." *See Professional Licenses and Educational Degrees,* Equitable Distribution J 1, 3 (Jan 1985).

[381] *See, e.g.,* Hughes v Hughes, 438 So 2d 146 (Fla Dist Ct App 1983); **§§10.06-10.07.**

[382] However, some courts have not remedied such inequitable results of divorce. *See, e.g.,* Wright v Wright, 469 A2d 803 (Del Fam Ct 1983); *In re* Marriage of Goldstein, 97 Ill App 3d 1023, 423 NE2d 1201 (1981); *In re* Marriage of MacNamara, 399 NE2d 371 (Ind 1980); Wilcox v Wilcox, 173 Ind App 661, 365 NE2d 792 (1977); Powell v Powell, 231 Kan App 2d 456, 648 P2d 218 (1982); Ruben v Ruben, 123 NH 358, 461 A2d 733 (1983); Frausto v Frausto, 611 SW2d 656 (Tex Civ App 1980).

[383] *See, e.g., In re* Marriage of Graham, 194 Colo 429, 574 P2d 75 (1978); *In re* Marriage of Estlund, 344 NW2d 276 (Iowa Ct App 1983); Roberto v Brown, 107 Wis 2d 17, 318 NW2d 918 (1982); DeWitt v DeWitt, 99 Wis 2d 44, 296 NW2d 761 (Wis Ct App 1980); Grosskopf v Grosskopf, 677 P2d 814 (Wyo 1984).

[384] *See, e.g., In re* Marriage of McVey, 641 P2d 300 (Colo Ct App 1981); Zahler v Zahler, 8 Fam L Rep (BNA) 2694 (Conn Super Ct 1982); *In re* Jannsen, 348 NW2d 251 (Iowa 1984); Diment v Diment, 531 P2d 1071 (Okla Ct App 1974); Lira v Lira, 88 Ohio App 2d 164, 428 NE2d 445 (1980).

[385] *See, e.g.,* Pyeatte v Pyeatte, 135 Ariz 346, 661 P2d 196 (1982); Severs v Severs, 426 So 2d 992 (Fla Dist Ct App 1983); Hernandez v Hernandez, 444 So 2d 35 (Fla Dist Ct App 1983); Moss v Moss, 80 Mich App 693, 294 NW2d 87 (1978); De La Rosa v De La Rosa, 309 NW2d 755 (Minn 1981); *In re* Marriage of Cropp, 5 Fam L Rep (BNA) 2957 (D Minn 1979); Mahoney v Mahoney, 91 NJ 488, 453 A2d 527 (1982); Hubbard v Hubbard, 603 P2d 747 (Okla 1979); Adair v Adair, 670 P2d 1002 (Okla Ct App 1983); Gillette v Gillette, 101 Wash 2d 168, 677 P2d 152 (Wash 1984).

[386] 126 Mich App 693, 337 NW2d 332 (1983).

> The length of marriage after the degree was obtained, the sources and extent of financial support given plaintiff during his years at law school, and the overall division of the parties' marital property. In determining the degree's present value, the trial court should estimate what the person holding the degree is likely to make in that particular job market and subtract it from what he or she would probably have earned without the degree.[387]

The New York Court of Appeals, in *O'Brien v O'Brien*,[388] a case which has received great publicity, approached the valuation of the license to practice medicine as follows:

> Turning to the question of valuation, it has been suggested that even if a professional license is considered marital property, the working spouse is entitled only to reimbursement of his or her direct financial contributions. . . . By parity of reasoning, a spouse's down payment on real estate or contribution to the purchase of securities would be limited to the money contributed, without any remuneration for any incremental value in the asset because of price appreciation. Such a result is completely at odds with the statute's requirement that the court give full consideration to both direct and indirect contributions "made to the acquisition of such marital property by the party not having title, including joint *efforts* or expenditures and *contribution and services as a spouse, parent,* wage earner *and homemaker*" (Domestic Relations Law §236(B)(d)(6)) and the sponsoring memorandum's observation that these indirect contributions as spouse, parent or homemaker "should ordinarily be regarded as equal" (Assembly Memorandum in Support, 11 C Zett-Kaufman-Kraut, NY Civ Prac, App B, at p B-8). If the license is marital property, then the working spouse is entitled to an equitable portion of it, not a return of funds advanced. Its value is the enhanced earning capacity it affords the holder and although fixing the present value of that enhanced earning capacity may present problems, the problems are not insurmountable. Certainly they are no more difficult than computing tort damages for wrongful death or diminished earning capacity resulting from injury and they differ only in degree from the problems presented when valuing a professional practice for purposes of a distributive award, something the courts have not hesitated to do. . . . The trial court retains the flexibility and discretion to structure the distributive award equitably, taking into consideration factors such as the working spouse's need for immediate payment, the licensed spouse's current ability to pay and the income tax consequences of prolonging the period of payment . . . and, once it has received evidence of the present value of the license and the working spouse's contributions toward its

---

[387] *Id* 337.

[388] O'Brien v O'Brien, 12 Fam L Rep (BNA) 2001 (NY App Div 1985).

> acquisition and considered the remaining factors mandated by the statute . . ., it may then make an appropriate distribution of the marital property including a distributive award for the professional license if such an award is warranted. When other marital assets are of sufficient value to provide for the supporting spouse's equitable portion of the marital property, including his or her contributions to the acquisition of the professional license, however, the court retains the discretion to distribute these other marital assets or to make a distributive award in lieu of an actual distribution of the value of the professional spouse's license.[389]

The Supreme Court of Wisconsin identified four ways to determine the amount of an award to a supporting spouse.[390] An award to a supporting spouse based on *lost opportunity costs* would equal the amount of income lost because the student spouse was at school instead of working. Following the *labor theory of value,* a court values the working spouse's contribution to the marriage at one-half of income for as long as he or she supported the student spouse. Another approach gives the supporting spouse a *return on investment* by awarding the present value of the student spouse's enhanced earning capacity as determined by an expert. A final method would be the *cost value approach,* by which a court calculates the value of the working spouse's contributions, in monetary terms, for education, living expenses, and services rendered during the marriage, adjusted by a fair rate of return or for inflation.

It is clear that the issue of whether degrees and licenses are marital property is derivative of the increasingly widely held concept that marriage is an economic partnership. Some state statutes do, in fact, provide that a contribution by one spouse to the education or career potential of the other is a factor to be considered by the court in its property and or maintenance determinations.[391]

---

[389] *Id* 2004 (citations omitted, emphasis added).

[390] *In re* Marriage of Hurgren, 117 Wis 2d 200, 343 NW2d 796 (1984).

[391] Freed & Walker, *Family Law in the Fifty States: An Overview,* 18 Fam LQ 369, 422 (1985) (citing California, Florida, Georgia, Indiana, Iowa, Nebraska, New York, Pennsylvania, Vermont, and Wisconsin).

# Appendix 10-1
# ERISA: Selected Sections

(Employment Retirement Income Security Act of 1974 (ERISA), as amended by the Retirement Equity Act of 1984 (REA))

SUBTITLE A–GENERAL PROVISIONS

## §1001. Congressional findings and declaration of policy

### (a) Benefit plans as affecting interstate commerce and the Federal taxing power

The Congress finds that the growth in size, scope, and numbers of employee benefit plans in recent years has been rapid and substantial; that the operational scope and economic impact of such plans is increasingly interstate; that the continued well-being and security of millions of employees and their dependents are directly affected by these plans; that they are affected with a national public interest; that they have become an important factor affecting the stability of employment and the successful development of industrial relations; that they have become an important factor in commerce because of the interstate character of their activities, and of activities of their participants, and the employers, employee organizations, and other entities by which they are established or maintained; that a large volume of the activities of such plans is carried on by means of the mails and instrumentalities of interstate commerce; that owing to the lack of employee information and adequate safeguards concerning their operation, it is desirable in the interests of employees, and their beneficiaries, and to provide for the general welfare and the free flow of commerce, that disclosure be made and safeguards be provided with respect to the establishment, operation, and administration of such plans; that they substantially affect the revenues of the United States because they are afforded preferential Federal tax treatment; that despite the enormous growth in such plans many employees with long years of employment are losing anticipated retirement benefits owning to the lack of vesting provisions in such plans; that owing to the inadequacy of current minimum standards, the soundness and stability of plans with respect to adequate funds to pay promised benefits may be endangered; that owing to the termination of plans before requisite funds have been accumulated, employees and their beneficiaries have been deprived of anticipated benefits; and that it is therefore desirable in the interests of employees and their beneficiaries, for the protection of the revenue of the United States, and to provide for the free flow of commerce, that minimum standards be provided assuring the equitable character of such plans and their financial soundness.

### (b) Protection of interstate commerce and beneficiaries by requiring disclosure and reporting, setting standards of conduct, etc., for fiduciaries

It is hereby declared to be the policy of this chapter to protect interstate commerce and the interests of participants in employee benefit plans and their beneficiaries, by requiring the disclosure and reporting to participants and beneficiaries of financial and other information with respect thereto, by establishing standards of conduct, responsibility, and obligation for fiduciaries of employee benefit plans, and by providing for appropriate remedies, sanctions, and ready access to the Federal courts.

**(c) Protection of interstate commerce, the Federal taxing power, and beneficiaries by vesting of accrued benefits, setting minimum standards of funding, requiring termination insurance**

It is hereby further declared to be the policy of this chapter to protect interstate commerce, the Federal taxing power, and the interests of participants in private pension plans and their beneficiaries by improving the equitable character and the soundness of such plans by requiring them to vest the accrued benefits of employees with significant periods of service, to meet minimum standards of funding, and by requiring plan termination insurance.

### §1025. Reporting of participant's benefit rights

**(a) Statement furnished by administrator to participants and beneficiaries**

Each administrator of an employee pension benefit plan shall furnish to any plan participant or beneficiary who so requests in writing, a statement indicating, on the basis of the latest available information–

(1) the total benefits accrued, and

(2) the nonforfeitable pension benefits, if any, which have accrued, or the earliest date on which benefits will become nonforfeitable.

**(b) One-per-year limit on reports**

In no case shall a participant or beneficiary be entitled under this section to receive more than one report described in subsection (a) of this section during any one 12 month period.

**(c) Individual statement furnished by administrator to participants setting forth information in administrator's Internal Revenue registration statement**

Each administrator required to register under section 6057 of Title 26 shall, before the expiration of the time prescribed for such registration, furnish to each participant described in subsection (a)(2)(C) of such section, an individual statement setting forth the information with respect to such participant required to be contained in the registration statement required by section 6057(a)(2) of Title 26. Such statement shall also include a notice to the participant of any benefits which are forfeitable if the participant dies before a certain date.

**(d) Plans to which more than one unaffiliated employer is required to contribute; regulations**

Subsection (a) of this section shall apply to a plan to which more than one unaffiliated employer is required to contribute only to the extent provided in regulations prescribed by the Secretary in coordination with the Secretary of the Treasury.

### §1052. Minimum participation standards

(a)(1)(A) No pension plan may require, as a condition of participation in the plan, that an employee complete a period of service with the employer or employers maintaining the plan extending beyond the later of the following dates–

(i) the date on which the employer attains the age of 21; or

(ii) the date on which he completes 1 year of service.

(B)(i) In the case of any plan which provides that after not more than 3 years of service each participant has a right to 100 percent of his accrued benefit under the plan which is nonforfeitable at the time such benefit accrues, clause (ii) of subparagraph (A) shall be applied by substituting "3 years of service" for "1 year of service".

(ii) In the case of any plan maintained exclusively for employees of any educational institution (as defined in section 170(b)(1)(A)(ii) of Title 26) by an employer which is exempt from tax under section 501(a) of Title 26, which provides that each participant having at least 1 year of service has a right to 100 percent of his accrued benefit under the plan which is nonforfeitable at the time such benefit accrues, clause (i) of subparagraph (A) shall be applied by substituting "26" for "21". This clause shall not apply to any plan to which clause (i) applies.

(2) No pension plan may exclude from participation (on the basis of age) employees who have attained a specified age, unless-

(A) the plan is a–

(i) defined benefit plan, or

(ii) target benefit plan (as defined under regulations prescribed by the Secretary of the Treasury), and

(B) such employees begin employment with the employer after they have attained a specified age which is not more than 5 years before the normal retirement age under the plan.

(3)(A) For purposes of this section, the term "year of service" means a 12-month period during which the employee has not less than 1,000 hours of service. For purposes of this paragraph, computation of any 12-month period shall be made with reference to the date on which the employee's employment commenced, except that, in accordance with regulations prescribed by the Secretary, such computation may be made by reference to the first day of a plan year in the case of an employer who does not complete 1,000 hours of service during the 12-month period beginning on the date his employment has commenced.

(B) In the case of any seasonal industry where the customary period of employment is less than 1,000 hours during a calendar year, the term "year of service" shall be such period as may be determined under regulations prescribed by the Secretary.

(C) For purposes of this section, the term "hour of service" means a time of service determined under regulations prescribed by the Secretary.

(D) For purposes of this section, in the case of any maritime industry, 125 days of service shall be treated as 1,000 hours of service. The Secretary may prescribe regulations to carry out the purposes of this subparagraph.

(4) A plan shall be treated as not meeting the requirements of paragraph (1) unless it provides that any employee who has satisfied the minimum age and service requirements specified in such paragraph, and who is otherwise entitled to participate in the plan, commences participation in the plan no later than the earlier of–

(A) the first day of the first plan year beginning after the date on which such employee satisfied such requirements, or

(B) the date 6 months after the date on which he satisfied such requirements,

unless such employee was separated from the service before the date referred to in subparagraph (A) or (B) whichever is applicable.

(b)(1) Except as otherwise provided in paragraphs (2), (3), and (4) all years of service with the employer or employers maintaining the plan shall be taken into account in computing the period of service for purposes of subsection (a)(1) of this section.

(2) In the case of any employee who has any 1-year break in service (as defined in section 1053(b)(3)(A) of this title) under the plan to which the service requirements of clause (i) of subsection (a)(1)(B) of this section apply, if such employee has not satisfied such requirements, service before such break shall not be required to be taken into account.

(3) In computing an employee's period of service for purposes of subsection (a)(1) of this section in the case of any participant who has any 1-year break in service (as defined in section 1053(b)(3)(A) of this title), service before such break shall not be required to be taken into account under the plan until he has completed a year of service (as defined in subsection (a)(3) of this section) after his return.

(4)(A) For purposes of paragraph (1), in the case of a nonvested participant, years of service with the employer or employers maintaining the plan before any period of consecutive 1-year breaks in service shall not be required to be taken into account in computing the period of service if the number of consecutive 1-year breaks in service within such period equals or exceeds the greater of–

(i) 5, or

(ii) the aggregate number of years of service before such period.

(B) If any years of service are not required to be taken into account by reason of a period of breaks in service to which subparagraph (A) applies, such years of service shall not be taken into account in applying subparagraph (A) to a subsequent period of breaks in service.

(C) For purposes of subparagraph (A), the term "nonvested participant" means a participant who does not have any nonforfeitable right under the plan to an accrued benefit derived from employer contributions.

(5)(A) In the case of each individual who is absent from work for any period–

(i) by reason of the pregnancy of the individual,

(ii) by reason of the birth of a child of the individual

(iii) by reason of the placement of a child with the individual in connection with the adoption of such child by such individual, or

(iv) for purposes of caring for such child for a period beginning immediately following such birth or placement,

the plan shall treat as hours of service, solely for purposes of determining under this subsection whether a 1-year break in service (as defined in section 1053(b)(3)(A) of this title) has occurred, the hours described in subparagraph (B).

(B) The hours described in this subparagraph are–

(i) the hours of service which otherwise would normally have been credited to such individual but for such absence, or

(ii) in any case in which the plan is unable to determine the hours described in clause (i), 8 hours of service per day of such absence,

except that the total number of hours treated as hours of service under this subparagraph by reason of any such pregnancy or placement shall not exceed 501 hours.

(C) The hours described in subparagraph (B) shall be treated as hours of service as provided in this paragraph–

(i) only in the year in which the absence from work begins, if a participant would be prevented from incurring a 1-year break in service in such year solely because the period of absence is treated as hours of service as provided in subparagraph (A); or

(ii) in any other case, in the immediately following year.

(D) For purposes of this paragraph, the term "year" means the period used in computations pursuant to subsection (a)(3)(A) of this section.

(E) A plan may provide that no credit will be given pursuant to this paragraph unless the individual furnishes to the plan administrator such timely information as the plan may reasonably require to establish–

(i) that the absence from work is for reasons referred to in subparagraph (A), and

(ii) the number of days for which there was such an absence.

### §1053. Minimum vesting standards

#### (a) Nonforfeitability requirements

Each plan shall provide that an employee's right to his normal retirement benefit is nonforfeitable upon the attainment of normal retirement age and in addition shall satisfy the requirements of paragraphs (1) and (2) of this subsection.

(1) A plan satisfies the requirements of this paragraph if an employee's rights in his accrued benefit derived from his own contributions are nonforfeitable.

(2) A plan satisfies the requirements of this paragraph if it satisfies the requirements of subparagraph (A), (B), or (C).

(A) A plan satisfies the requirements of this subparagraph if an employee who has at least 10 years of service has a nonforfeitable right to 100 percent of his accrued benefit derived from employer contributions.

(B) A plan satisfies the requirements of this subparagraph if an employee who has completed at least 5 years of service has a nonforfeitable right to a percentage of his accrued benefit derived from either employer contributions which percentage is not less than the percentage determined under the following table:

| Years of service: | Nonforfeitable percentage |
|---|---|
| 5 | 25 |
| 6 | 30 |
| 7 | 35 |
| 8 | 40 |
| 9 | 45 |
| 10 | 50 |
| 11 | 60 |
| 12 | 70 |
| 13 | 80 |
| 14 | 90 |
| 15 or more | 100 |

(C)(i) A plan satisfies the requirements of this subparagraph if a participant who is not separated from the service, who has completed at least 5 years of service, and with respect to whom the sum of his age and years of service equals or exceeds 45, has a nonforfeitable right to a percentage of his accrued benefit derived from contributions determined under the following table:

| If years of service equal or exceed– | and sum of age and service equals or exceeds– | then the nonforfeitable percentage is– |
|---|---|---|
| 5 | 45 | 50 |
| 6 | 47 | 60 |
| 7 | 49 | 70 |
| 8 | 51 | 80 |
| 9 | 53 | 90 |
| 10 | 55 | 100 |

(ii) Notwithstanding clause (i), a plan shall not be treated as satisfying the requirements of this subparagraph unless any participant who has completed at least 10 years of service has a nonforfeitable right to not less than 50 percent of his accrued benefit derived from employer contributions and to not less than an additional 10 percent for each additional year of service thereafter.

(3)(A) A right to an accrued benefit derived from employer contributions shall not be treated as forfeitable solely because the plan provides that it is not payable if the participant dies (except in the case of a survivor annuity which is payable as provided in section 1055 of this title).

(B) A right to an accrued benefit derived from employer contributions shall not be treated as forfeitable solely because the plan provides that the payment of benefits is suspended for such period as the employee is employed, subsequent to the commencement of payment of such benefits–

(i) in the case of a plan other than a multiemployer plan, by an employer who maintains the plan under which such benefits were being paid; and

(ii) in the case of a multiemployer plan, in the same industry, in the same trade or craft, and same geographic area covered by the plan, as when such benefits commenced.

The Secretary shall prescribe such regulations as may be necessary to carry out the purposes of this subparagraph, including regulations with respect to the meaning of the term "employed".

(C) A right to an accrued benefit derived from employer contributions shall not be treated as forfeitable solely because plan amendments may be given retroactive application as provided in section 1082(c)(8) of this title.

(D)(i) A right to an accrued benefit derived from employer contributions shall not be treated as forfeitable solely because the plan provides that, in the case of a participant who does not have a nonforfeitable right to at least 50 percent of his accrued benefit derived from employer contributions, such accrued benefit may be forfeited on account of the withdrawal by the participant of any amount attributable to the benefit derived from mandatory contributions (as defined in the last sentence of section 1054(c)(2)(C) of this title) made by such participant.

(ii) Clause (i) shall not apply to a plan unless the plan provides that any accrued benefit forfeited under a plan provision described in such clause shall be restored upon repayment by the participant of the full amount of the withdrawal described in such clause plus, in the case of a defined benefit plan, interest. Such interest shall be computed on such amount at the rate determined for pusposes of section 1054(c)(2)(C) of this title (if such subsection applies) on the date of such repayment (computed annually from the date of such withdrawal). In the case of a defined contribution plan the plan provision required under the clause may provide that such repayment must be made before the participant has any 1-year break in service commencing after the withdrawal.

(iii) In the case of accrued benefits derived from employer contributions which accrued before September 2, 1974, a right to such accrued benefit derived from employer contributions shall not be treated as for feitable solely because the plan provides that an amount of such accrued benefit may be forfeited on account of the withdrawal by the participant of an amount attributable to the benefit derived from mandatory contributions, made by such participant before September 2, 1974, if such amount forfeited is proportional to such amount withdrawn. This clause shall not apply to any plan to which any mandatory contribution is made after September 2, 1974. The Secretary of the Treasury shall prescribe such regulations as may be necessary to carry out the purposes of this clause.

(iv) For purposes of this subparagraph, in the case of any class-year plan, a withdrawal of employee contributions shall be treated as a withdrawal of such contributions on a plan year by plan year basis in succeeding order of time.

(v) Cross Reference . . .

(E)(i) A right to an accrued benefit derived from employer contributions under a multiemployer plan shall not be treated as forfeitable solely because the plan provides that benefits accrued as a result of service with the participant's employer before the employer had an obligation to contribute under the plan may not be payable if the employer ceases contributions to the multiemployer plan.

(I) the plan is amended to reduce benefits under section 1425 or 1441 of this title, or

(II) benefit payments under the plan may be suspended under section 1426 or 1441 of this title.

**(b) Computation of period of service**

(1) In computing the period of service under the plan for purposes of determining the nonforfeitable percentage under subsection (a)(2) of this section, all of an employee's years of service with the employer or employers maintaining the plan shall be taken into account, except that the following may be disregarded.

(A) years of service before age 18, except that in the case of a plan which does not satisfy subparagraph (A) or (B) of subsection (a)(2) of this section, the plan may not disregard any such year of service during which the employer was a participant.

(B) years of service during a period for which the employee declined to contribute to a plan requiring employee contributions,

(C) years of service with an employer during any period for which the employer did not maintain the plan or a predecessor plan, defined by the Secretary of the Treasury;

(D) service not required to be taken into account under paragraph (3);

(E) years of service before January 1, 1971, unless the employee has had at least 3 years of service after December 31, 1970;

(F) years of service before this part first applies to the plan if such service would have been disregarded under the rules of the plan with regard to breaks in service, as in effect on the applicable date; and

(G) in the case of a multiemployer plan, years of service–

(i) with an employer after–

(I) a complete withdrawal of such employer from the plan (within the meaning of section 1383 of this title), or

(II) to the extent permitted by regulations prescribed by the Secretary of the Treasury, a partial withdrawal described in section 1385(b)(2)(A)-(i) of this title in connection with the decertification of the collective bargaining representative; and

(ii) with any employer under the plan after the termination date of the plan under section 1348 of this title.

(2)(A) For purposes of this section, except as provided in subparagraph (C), the term "year of service" means a calendar year, plan year, or other 12-consecutive month period designated by the plan (and not prohibited under regulations prescribed by the Secretary) during which the participant has completed 1,000 hours of service.

(B) For purposes of this section, the term "hour of service" has the meaning provided by section 1052(a)(3)(C) of this title.

(C) In the case of any seasonal industry where the customary period of employment is less than 1,000 hours during a calendar year, the term "year of service" shall be such period as determined under regulations of the Secretary.

(D) For purposes of this section, in the case of any maritime industry, 125 days of service shall be treated as 1,000 hours of service. The Secretary may prescribe regulations to carry out the purposes of this subparagraph.

(3)(A) For purposes of this paragraph, the term "1-year break in service" means a calendar year, plan year, or other 12-consecutive month period designated by the plan (and not prohibited under regulations prescribed by the Secretary during which the participant has not completed more than 500 hours of service.

(B) For purposes of paragraph (1), in the case of any employee who has any 1-year break in service, years of service before such break shall not be required to be taken into account until he has completed a year of service after his return.

(C) For purposes of paragraph (1), in the case of any participant in an individual account plan or an insured defined benefit plan which satisfies the requirements of subsection 1054(b)(1)(F) of this title who has 5 consecutive 1-year breaks in service, years of service after such 5-year period shall not be required to be taken into account for purposes of determining the nonforfeitable percentage of his accrued benefit derived from employer contributions which accrued before such 5-year period.

(D)(i) For purposes of paragraph (1), in the case of a nonvested participant, years of service with the employer or employers maintaining the plan before any period of consecutive 1-year breaks in service shall not be required to be taken into account if the number of consecutive 1-year breaks in service within such period equals or exceeds the greater of–

(I) 5, or

(II) the aggregate number of years of service before such period.

(ii) If any years of service are not required to be taken into account by reason of a period of breaks in service to which the clause (i) applies, such years of service shall not be taken into account in applying clause (i) to a subsequent period of breaks in service.

(iii) For purposes of clause (i,) the term "nonvested participant" means a participant who does not have any nonforfeitable right under the plan to an accrued benefit derived from employer contributions.

(E)(i) In the case of each individual who is absent from work for any period–

(I) by reason of pregnancy of the individual,

(II) by reason of the birth of a child of the individual,

(III) by reason of the placement of a child with the individual in connection with the adoption of such child by such individual, or

(IV) for purposes of caring for such child for a period beginning immediately following such birth or placement.

the plan shall treat as hours of service, solely for purposes of determining under this paragraph whether a 1-year break in service has occurred, the hours described in clause (ii).

(ii) The hours described in this clause are–

(I) the hours of service which otherwise would normally have been credited to such individual but for such absence, or

(II) in any case in which the plan is unable to determine the hours described in subclause (I), 8 hours of service per day of absence,

except that the total number of hours treated as hours of service under this clause by reason of such pregnancy or placement shall not exceed 501 hours.

(iii) The hours described in clause (ii) shall be treated as hours of service as provided in this subparagraph–

(I) only in the year in which the absence from work begins, if a participant would be prevented from incurring a 1-year break in service in such year solely because the period of absence is treated as hours of service as provided in clause (i); or

(II) in any other case, in the immediately following year.

(iv) For purposes of this subparagraph, the term "year" means the period used in computation pursuant to paragraph (2).

(v) A plan may provide that no credit will be given pursuant to this subparagraph unless the individual furnishes to the plan administrator such timely information as the plan may reasonably require to establish–

(I) that the absence from work is for reasons referred to in clause (i), and

(II) the number of days for which there was such an absence.

**(4) Cross references**

(A) For definitions of "accrued benefit" and "normal retirement age", see sections 1002(23) and (24) of this title.

(B) For effect of certain cash out distributions, see sections 1054(d)(I) of this title.

**(c) Plan amendments altering vesting schedule**

(1)(A) A plan amendment changing any vesting schedule under the plan shall be treated as not satisfying the requirements of subsection (a)(2) of this section if the nonforfeitable percentage of the accrued benefit derived from employer contributions (determined as of the later of the date such amendment is adopted, or the date such amendment becomes effective) of any employee who is a participant in the plan is less than such nonforfeitable percentage computed under the plan without regard to such amendment.

(B) A plan amendment changing any vesting schedule under the plan shall be treated as not satisfying the requirements of subsection (a)(2) of this section unless each participant having not less than 5 years of service is permitted to elect, within a reasonable period after adoption of such amendment, to have his nonforfeitable percentage computed under the plan without regard to such amendment.

(2) Subsection (a) of this section shall not apply to benefits which may not be provided for designated employees in the event of early termination of the plan under provisions of the plan adopted pursuant to regulations prescribed by the Secretary of the Treasury to preclude the discrimination prohibited by section 401(a)(4) of Title 26.

(3) The requirements of subsection (a)(2) of this section shall be deemed to be satisfied in the case of a class year plan if such plan provides that 100 percent of each employer's right to or derived from the contributions of the employer on his behalf with respect to any plan year are nonforfeitable not later than the end of the 5th plan year following the plan year for which such contributions were made. For purposes of this part, the term "class year plan" means a profit sharing, stock bonus, or money purchase plan which provides for the separate nonforfeitability of employees' rights to or derived from the contributions for each plan year.

**(d) Nonforfeitable benefits after lesser period and in greater amounts than required**

A pension plan may allow for nonforfeitable benefits after a lesser period and in greater amounts than are required by this part.

**(e) Nontreatment of accrued benefit as nonforfeitable, calculation of present value**

(1) If the present value of any accrued benefit exceeds $3,500, such benefit shall not be treated as nonforfeitable if the plan provides that the present value of such benefit could be immediately distributed without the consent of the participant.

(2) For purposes of paragraph (1), the present value shall be calculated by using an interest rate not greater than the interest rate which would be used (as of the date of distribution) by the Pension Benefit Guaranty Corporation for purposes of determining the present value of a lump sum distribution on plan termination.

## §1055. Requirement of joint and survivor annuity and preretirement survivor annuity

**(a) Required contents for applicable plans**

Each pension plan to which this section applies shall provide that–

(1) in the case of a vested participant who retires under the plan, the accrued benefit payable to such participant shall be provided in the form of a qualified joint and survivor annuity, and

(2) in the case of a vested participant who dies before the annuity starting date and who has a surviving spouse, a qualified preretirement survivor annuity shall be provided to the surviving spouse of such participant.

**(b) Applicable plans**

(1) This section shall apply to–

(A) any defined benefit plan,

(B) any individual account plan which is subject to the funding standards of section 1082 of this title, and

(C) any participant under any other individual account plan unless–

(i) such plan provides that the participant's nonforfeitable accrued benefit is payable in full, on the death of the participant, to the participant's surviving spouse (or, if there is no surviving spouse or the surviving spouse consents in the manner required under subsection (c)(2)(A) of this section, to a designated beneficiary),

(ii) such participant does not elect the payment of benefits in the form of a life annuity, and

(iii) with respect to such participant, such plan is not a transferee of a plan which is described in subparagraph (A) or (B) or to which this clause applied with respect to the participant.

(2)(A) In the case of–

(i) a tax credit employee stock ownership plan (as defined in section 409(a) of Title 26), or

(ii) an employee stock ownership plan (as defined in section 4975(e)(7) of Title 26),

subsection (a) of this section shall not apply to that portion of the employee's accrued benefit to which the requirements of section 409(h) of Title 26 apply.

(B) Subparagraph (A) shall not apply with respect to any participant unless the requirements of clause (i), (ii), and (iii) of paragraph (1)(C) are met with respect to such participant.

**(c) Plans meeting requirements of section**

(1) A plan meets the requirements of this section only if–

(A) under the plan, each participant–

(i) may elect at any time during the applicable election period to waive the qualified joint and survivor annuity form of benefit or the qualified preretirement survivor annuity form of benefit (or both), and

(ii) may revoke any such election at any time during the applicable election period, and

(B) the plan meets the requirements of paragraphs (2) and (3)

(2) Each plan shall provide that an election under paragraph (1)(A)(i) shall not take effect unless–

(A) the spouse of the participant consents in writing to such election, and the spouse's consent acknowledges the effect of such election and is witnessed by a plan representative or a notary public, or

(B) it is established to the satisfaction of a plan representative that the consent required under subparagraph (A) may not be obtained because there is no spouse, because the spouse cannot be located, or because of such other circumstances as the Secretary of the Treasury may by regulations prescribe.

Any consent by a spouse (or establishment that the consent of a spouse may not be obtained) under the preceding sentence shall be effective only with respect to such spouse.

(3)(A) Each plan shall provide to each participant, within a reasonable period of time before the annuity starting date (and consistent with such regulations as the Secretary of the Treasury may prescribe) a written explanation of–

(i) the terms and conditions of the qualified joint and survivor annuity,

(ii) the participant's right to make, and the effect of, an election under paragraph (1) to waive the joint and survivor annuity form of benefit,

(iii) the rights of the participant's spouse under paragraph (2), and

(iv) the right to make, and the effect of, a revocation of an election under paragraph (1).

(B) Each plan shall provide to each participant, within the period beginning with the first day of the plan year in which the participant attains age 32 and ending with the close of the plan year preceding the plan year in which the participant attains age 35 (and consistent with such regulations as the Secretary of the Treasury may prescribe), a written explanation with respect to the qualified preretirement survivor annuity comparable to that required under subparagraph (A).

(4)(A) The requirements of this subsection shall not apply with respect to the qualified joint and survivor annuity form of benefit or the qualified preretirement survivor annuity form of benefit, as the case may be, if the plan fully subsidizes the costs of such benefit.

(B) For purposes of subparagraph (A), a plan fully subsidizes the costs of a benefit if under the plan the failure to waive such benefit by a participant would not result in a decrease in any plan benefits with respect to such participant and would not result in increased contributions from such participant.

(5) If a plan fiduciary acts in accordance with part 4 of this subtitle in–

(A) relying on a consent or revocation referred to in paragraph (1)(a), or

(B) making a determination under paragraph (2), then such consent, revocation, or determination shall be treated as valid for purposes of discharging the plan from liability to the extent of payments made pursuant to such act.

(6) For purposes of this subsection, the term "applicable election period" means–

(A) in the case of an election to waive the qualified joint and survivor annuity form of benefit, the 90-day period ending on the annuity starting date, or

(B) in the case of an election to waive the qualified preretirement survivor annuity, the period which begins on the first day of the plan year in which the participant attains age 35 and ends on the date of the participant's death.

In the case of a participant who is separated from service, the applicable election period under subparagraph (B) with respect to benefits accrued before the date of such separation from service shall not begin later than such date.

### (d) "Qualified and joint survivor annuity" defined

For purposes of this section, the term "qualified and joint survivor annuity" means an annuity–

(1) for the life of the participant with a survivor annuity for the life of the spouse which is not less than 50 percent of (and is not greater than 100 percent of) the amount of the annuity which is payable during the joint lives of the participant and the spouse, and

(2) which is the actuarial equivalent of a single annuity for the life of the participant.

Such term also includes any annuity in a form having the effect of an annuity described in the preceding sentence.

### (e) "Qualified preretirement survivor annuity" defined

For purposes of this section–

(A) the payments to the surviving spouse under such annuity are not less than the amounts which would be payable as a survivor annuity under the qualified joint and survivor annuity under the plan (or the actuarial equivalent thereof) if–

(i) in the case of a participant who dies after the date on which the participant attained the earliest retirement age, such participant had retired with an immediate qualified joint and survivor annuity on the day before the participant's date of death, or

(ii) in the case of a participant who dies on or before the date on which the participant would have attained the earliest retirement age, such participant had–

(I) separated from service on the date of death,

(II) survived to the earliest retirement age.

(III) retired with an immediate qualified joint and survivor annuity at the earliest retirement age, and

(IV) died on the day after the day on which such participant would have attained the earliest retirement age, and

(B) under the plan, the earliest period for which the surviving spouse may receive a payment under such annuity is not later than the month in which the participant would have attained the earliest retirement age under the plan.

(2) In the case of any individual account plan or participant described in subparagraph (B) or (C) of subsection (b)(1) of this section, the term "qualified preretirement survivor annuity" means an annuity for the life of the surviving spouse the actuarial equivalent of which is not less than 50 percent of the account balance of the participant as of the date of death.

### (f) Marriage requirements for plan

(1) Except as provided in paragraph (2), a plan may provide that a qualified joint and survivor annuity (or a qualified preretirement survivor annuity) will not be provided unless the participant and spouse had been married throughout the 1-year period ending on the earlier of–

(A) the participant's annuity starting date, or

(B) the date of the participant's death.

(2) For purposes of paragraph (1), if–

(A) a participant marries within 1 year before the annuity starting date, and

(B) the participant and the participant's spouse in such marriage have been married for at least a 1-year period ending on or before the date of the participant's death.

such participant and such spouse shall be treated as having been married throughout the 1-year period ending on the participant's annuity starting date.

**(g) Distribution of present value of annuity; written consent; determination**

(1) A plan may provide that the present value of a qualified joint and survivor annuity or a qualified preretirement survivor annuity will be immediately distributed if such value does not exceed $3,500. No distribution may be made under the preceding sentence after the annuity starting date unless the participant and the spouse of the participant (or where the participant has died, the surviving spouse) consent in writing to such distribution.

(2) If–

(A) the present value of the qualified joint and survivor annuity or the qualified preretirement survivor annuity exceeds $3,500, and

(B) the participant and the spouse of the participant (or where the participant has died, the surviving spouse) consent in writing to the distribution,

the plan may immediately distribute the present value of such annuity.

(3) For purposes of paragraphs (1) and (2), the present value of a qualified joint and survivor annuity or a qualified preretirement survivor annuity shall be determined as of the date of the distribution and by using an interest rate not greater than the interest rate which would be used (as of the date of the distribution) by the Pension Benefit Guaranty Corporation for purposes of determining the present value of a lump sum distribution on plan termination.

**(h) Definitions**

For purposes of this section–

(1) the term "vested participant" means any participant who has a nonforfeitable right (within the meaning of section 1002(19) of this title) to any portion of the accrued benefit derived from employer contributions.

(2) the term "annuity starting date" means the first day of the first period for which an amount is received as an annuity (whether by reason of retirement or disability), and

(3) the term "earliest retirement age" means the earliest date on which, under the plan, the participant could elect to receive retirement benefits.

**(i) Increased costs from providing annuity**

A plan may take into account in any equitable manner (as determined by the Secretary of the Treasury) any increased costs resulting from providing a qualified joint or survivor annuity or a qualified preretirement survivor annuity.

**(j) Regulations; consultation of Secretary of the Treasury with Secretary of Labor**

In prescribing regulations under this section, the Secretary of the Treasury shall consult with the Secretary of Labor.
(Pub.L. 93-406, Title I. §205, Sept. 2, 1974, 88 Stat. 862; Pub.L. 98-397, Title I, §103(a), Aug. 23, 1984, 98 Stat. 1429).

**Historical Note**

**1984 Amendment.** Subsec. (a). Pub.L. 98-397 substituted provisions dealing with provisions to be included in applicable plans for former provisions which related to form of payment of annuity benefits.

Subsec. (b). Pub.L. 98-397 substituted provisions relating to applicable plans under this section for former provisions which related to plans providing for payment of benefits before normal retirement age.

Subsec. (c). Pub.L. 98-397 substituted provisions relating to conditions under which plans meet the requirements of this section for former provisions which related to election of qualified joint and survivor annuity form.

**§1056. Form and payment of benefits**

**(a) Commencement date for payment of benefits**

Each pension plan shall provide that unless the participant otherwise elects, the payment of benefits under the plan to the participant shall begin not later than the 60th day after the latest of the close of the plan year in which–

(1) the date on which the participant attains the earlier of age 65 or the normal retirement age specified under the plan.

(2) occurs the 10th anniversary of the year in which the participant commenced participation in the plan, or

(3) the participant terminates his service with the employer.

In the case of a plan which provides for the payment of an early retirement benefit, such plan shall provide that a participant who satisfied the service requirements for such early retirement benefit, but separated from the service (with any nonforfeitable rights to an accrued benefit) before satisfying the age requirement for such early retirement benefit, is entitled upon satisfaction of such age requirement to receive a benefit not less than the benefit to which he would be entitled at the normal retirement age, actuarially reduced under regulations prescribed by the Secretary of the Treasury.

**(b) Decrease in plan benefits by reason of increases in benefit levels under Social Security Act or Railroad Retirement Act of 1937**

If–

(1) a participant or beneficiary is receiving benefits under a pension plan, or

(2) a participant is separated from the service and has nonforfeitable rights to benefits,

a plan may not decrease benefits of such a participant by reason of any increase in the benefit levels payable under Title II of the Social Security Act (42 U.S.C.A. §401 et seq.) or the Railroad Retirement Act of 1937 (45 U.S.C.A. §231 et seq.), or any increase in the wage base under such title II, if such increase takes place after September 2, 1974, or (if later) the earlier of the date of first entitlement of such benefits or the date of such separation.

**(c) Forfeiture of accrued benefits derived from employer contributions**

No pension plan may provide that any part of a participant's accrued benefit derived from employer contributions (whether or not otherwise nonforfeitable) is forfeitable solely because of withdrawal by such participant of any amount attributable to the benefit derived from contributions made by such participant. The preceding sentence shall not apply (1) to the accrued benefit of any participant unless, at the time of such withdrawal, such participant has a nonforfeitable right to at least 50 percent of such accrued benefit, or (2) to the extent that an accrued benefit is permitted to be forfeited in accordance with section 1053(a)(3)(D)(iii) of this title.

**(d) Assignment or alienation of plan benefits**

(1) Each pension plan shall provide that benefits provided under the plan may not be assigned or alienated.

(2) For the purposes of paragraph (1) of this subsection, there shall not be taken into account any voluntary and revocable assignment of not to exceed 10 percent of any benefit payment, or of any irrevocable assignment or alienation of benefits executed before September 2, 1974. The preceding sentence shall not apply to any assignment or alienation made for the purposes of defraying plan administration costs. For purposes of this paragraph a loan made to a participant or beneficiary shall not be treated as an assignment or alienation if such loan is secured by the participant's accrued nonforfeitable benefit and is exempt from the tax imposed by section 4975 of Title 26 (relating to tax on prohibited transactions) by reason of section 4957(d)(1) of Title 26.

(3)(A) Paragraph (1) shall apply to the creation, assignment, or recognition of a right to any benefit payable with respect to a participant pursuant to a domestic relations order, except that paragraph (1) shall not apply if the order is determined to be a qualified domestic relations order. Each pension plan shall provide for the payment of benefits in accordance with the applicable requirements of any qualified domestic relations order.

(B) For purposes of this paragraph–

(i) the term "qualified domestic relations order" means a domestic relations order–

(I) which creates or recognizes the existence of an alternate payee's right to, or assigns to an alternate payee the right to, receive all or a portion of the benefits payable with respect to a participant under a plan, and

(II) with respect to which the requirements of subparagraphs (C) and (D) are met, and

(ii) the term "domestic relations order" means any judgment, decree, or order (including approval of a property settlement agreement) which–

(I) relates to the provision of child support, alimony payments, or marital property rights to a spouse, former spouse, child, or other dependent of a participant, and

(II) is made pursuant to a State domestic relations law (including a community property law).

(C) A domestic relations order meets the requirements of this subparagraph only if such order clearly specifies—

(i) the name and the last known mailing address (if any) of the participant and the name and mailing address of each alternate payee covered by the order,

(ii) the amount or percentage of the participant's benefits to be paid by the plan to each such alternate payee, or the manner in which such amount or percentage is to be determined,

(iii) the number of payments or period to which such order applies, and

(iv) each plan to which order applies.

(D) A domestic relations order meets the requirements subparagraph only if such order–

(i) does not require a plan to provide any type or form of benefit, or any option, not otherwise provided under the plan,

(ii) does not require the plan to provide increased benefits (determined on the basis of actuarial value), and

(iii) does not require the payment of benefits to an alternate payee which are required to be paid to another alternate payee under another order previously determined to be a qualified domestic relations order.

(E)(i) In the case of any payment before a participant has separated from service, a domestic relations order shall not be treated as failing to meet the requirements of clause (i) of subparagraph (D) solely because such order requires that payment of benefits be made to an alternate payee–

(I) on or after the date on which the participant attains (or would have attained) the earliest retirement age,

(II) as if the participant had retired on the date on which such payment is to begin under such order (but taking into account only the present value of benefits actually accrued and not taking into account the present value of any employer subsidy for early retirement), and

(III) in any form in which such benefits may be paid under the plan to the participant (other than in the form of a joint and survivor annuity with respect to the alternate payee and his or her subsequent spouse).

For the purposes of subclause (II), the interest rate assumption used in determining the present value shall be the interest rate specified in the plan or, if no rate is specified, 5 percent.

(ii) For purposes of this subparagraph, the term "earliest retirement age" has the meaning given such term by section 1055(h)(3) of this title, except that in the case of any individual account plan, the earliest retirement age shall be the date which is 10 years before the normal retirement age.

(F) To the extent provided in any qualified domestic relations order–

(i) the former spouse of a participant shall be treated as a surviving spouse of such participant for purposes of section 1055 of this title, and

(ii) if married for at least 1 year, the former spouse shall be treated as meeting the requirements of section 1055(f) of this title.

(G)(i) In the case of any domestic relations order received by a plan–

(I) the plan administrator shall promptly notify the participant and any other alternate payee of the receipt of such order and the plan's procedures for determining the qualified status of domestic relations orders, and

(II) within a reasonable period after receipt of such order, the plan administrator shall determine whether such order is a qualified domestic relations order and notify the participant and each alternate payee of such determination.

(ii) Each plan shall establish reasonable procedures to determine the qualified status of domestic relations orders and to administer distributions under such qualified orders. Such procedures–

(I) shall be in writing,

(II) shall provide for the notification of each person specified in a domestic relations order as entitled to payment of benefits under the plan (at the address included in the domestic relations order) of such procedures promptly upon receipt by the plan of the domestic relations order, and

(III) shall permit an alternate payee to designate a representative for receipt of copies of notices that are sent to the alternate payee with respect to a domestic relations order.

(H)(i) During any period in which the issue of whether a domestic relations order is a qualified domestic relations order is being determined (by the plan administrator, by a court of competent jurisdiction, or otherwise), the plan administrator shall segregate in a separate account in the plan or in an escrow account the amounts which would have been payable to the alternate payee during such period if the order had been determined to be a qualified domestic relations order.

(ii) if within 18 months the order (or modification thereof) is determined to be a qualified domestic relations order, the plan administrator shall pay the segregated amounts (plus any interest thereon) to the person or persons entitled thereto.

(iii) If within 18 months–

(I) it is determined that the order is not a qualified domestic relations order, or

(II) the issue as to whether such order is a qualified domestic relations order is not resolved,

then the plan administrator shall pay the segregated amounts (plus any interest thereon) to the person or persons who would have been entitled to such amounts if there had been no order.

(iv) Any determination that an order is a qualified domestic relations order which is made after the close of the 18-month period shall be applied prospectively only.

(I) If a plan fiduciary acts in accordance with part 4 of this subtitle in–

(i) treating a domestic relations order as being (or not being) a qualified domestic relations order, or

(ii) taking action under subparagraph (H),

then the plan's obligation to the participant and each alternate payee shall be discharged to the extent of any payment made pursuant to such act.

(J) A person who is an alternate payee under a qualified domestic relations order shall be considered for purposes of any provision of this chapter a beneficiary under the plan. Nothing in the preceding sentence shall permit a requirement under section 1301 of this title of the payment of more than 1 premium with respect to a participant for any period.

(K) The term "alternate payee" means any spouse, former spouse, child, or other dependent of a participant who is recognized by a domestic relations order as having a right to receive all, or a portion of, the benefits payable under a plan with respect to such participant.

(L) In prescribing regulations under this paragraph, the Secretary shall consult with the Secretary of the Treasury.

## Appendix 10-2
## IRC Sections Relating to IRAs and Keogh Plans

The following selected sections are from the Internal Revenue Code (26 USC).

§219. Retirement savings

(a) Allowance of deduction

In the case of an individual, there shall be allowed as a deduction an amount equal to the qualified retirement contributions of the individual for the taxable year.

(b) Maximum amount of deduction

(1) In general

The amount allowable as a deduction under subsection (a) to any individual for any taxable year shall not exceed the lesser of–

(A) $2,000, or

(B) an amount equal to the compensation includible in the individual's gross income for such taxable year.

(2) Special rules for employer contributions under simplified employee pensions

(A) Limitation

If there is an employer contribution on behalf of the employee to a simplified employee pension, an employee shall be allowed as a deduction under subsection (a) (in addition to the amount allowable under paragraph (1)) an amount equal to the lesser of–

(i) 15 percent of the compensation from such employer includible in the employee's gross income for the taxable year (determined without regard to the employer contribution to the simplified employee pension), or

(ii) the amount contributed by such employer to the simplified employee pension and included in gross income (but not in excess of $15,000).

(B) Certain limitations do not apply to employer contributions

Paragraph (1) of this subsection and paragraph (1) of subsection (d) shall not apply with respect to the employer contribution to a simplified employee pension.

(C) Special rule for applying subparagraph (A)(ii)

In the case of an employee who is an officer, shareholder, or owner-employee described in section 408(k)(3), the $15,000 amount specified in subparagraph (A)(ii) shall be reduced by the amount of tax taken into account with respect to such individual under subparagraph (D) of section 408(k)(3).

(3) Special rule for individual retirement plans

If the individual has paid any qualified voluntary employee contributions for the taxable year, the amount of the qualified retirement contributions (other than employer contributions to a simplified employee pension) which are paid for the taxable year to an individual retirement plan and which are allowable as a deduction under subsection (a) for such taxable year shall not exceed–

(A) the amount determined under paragraph (1) for such taxable year, reduced by

(B) the amount of the qualified voluntary employee contributions for the taxable year,

(4) Certain divorced individuals

(A) In general

In the case of an individual to whom this paragraph applies, the limitation of paragraph (1) shall not be less than the lesser of–

(i) $1,125, or

(ii) the sum of the amount referred to in paragraph (1)(B) and any qualifying alimony received by the individual during the taxable year.

(B) Qualifying alimony

For purposes of this paragraph, the term "qualifying alimony" means amounts includible in the individual's gross income under paragraph (1) of section 71(a) (relating to decree of divorce or separate maintenance).

(C) Individuals to whom paragraph applies

This paragraph shall apply to an individual if–

(i) an individual retirement plan was established for the benefit of the individual at least 5 years before the beginning of the calendar year in which the decree of divorce or separate maintenance was issued, and

(ii) for at least 3 of the former spouse's most recent 5 taxable years ending before the taxable year in which the decree was issued, such former spouse was allowed a deduction under subsection (c) (or the corresponding provisions of prior law) for contributions to such individual retirement plan.

(c) Special rules for certain married individuals

(1) In general

In the case of any individual with respect to whom a deduction is otherwise allowable under subsection (a)–

(A) who files a joint return under section 6013 for a taxable year, and

(B) whose spouse has no compensation (determined without regard to section 911) for such taxable year, there shall be allowed as a deduction any amount paid in cash for the taxable year by or on behalf of the individual to an individual retirement plan established for the benefit of his spouse.

(2) Limitation

The amount allowable as a deduction under paragraph (1) shall not exceed the excess of–

(A) the lesser of–

(i) $2,250, or

(ii) an amount equal to the compensation includible in the individual's gross income for the taxable year, over

(B) the amount allowable as a deduction under subsection (a) for the taxable year (determined without regard to so much of the employer contributions to a simplified employee pension as is allowable by reason of paragraph (2) of subsection (b)).

In no event shall the amount allowable as a deduction under paragraph (1) exceed $2,000.

(d) Other limitations and restrictions

(1) Beneficiary must be under age 70-1/2

No deduction shall be allowed under this section with respect to any qualified retirement contribution for the benefit of an individual if such individual has attained age 70-1/2 before the close of such individual's taxable year for which the contribution was made.

(2) Recontributed amounts

No deduction shall be allowed under this section with respect to a rollover contribution described in section 402(a)(5), 402(a)(7), 403(a)(4), 403(b)(8), 405(d)(3), 408(d)(3), or 409(b)(3)(C).

(3) Amounts contributed under endowment contract

In the case of an endowment contract described in section 408(b), no deduction shall be allowed under this section for that portion of the amounts paid under the contract for the taxable year which is properly allocable, under regulations prescribed by the Secretary, to the cost of life insurance.

● ● ●

§401. Qualified pension, profit-sharing, and stock bonus plans

(a) Requirements for qualification

A trust created or organized in the United States and forming part of a stock bonus, pension, or profit-sharing plan of an employer for the exclusive benefit of his employees or their beneficiaries shall constitute a qualified trust under this section–

● ● ●

(9) In the case of a plan which provides contributions or benefits for employees some or all of whom are employees within the meaning of subsection (c)(1), a trust forming part of such plan shall not constitute a qualified trust under this section unless, under the plan, the entire interest of each employee–

(A) either will be distributed to him not later than his taxable year in which he attains the age of 70-1/2 years, or, in the case of an employee other than an owner-employee (as defined in subsection (c)(3)), in which he retires, whichever is the later, or

(B) will be distributed, commencing not later than such taxable year, (i) in accordance with regulations prescribed by the Secretary, over the life of such employee or over the lives of such employee and his spouse, or (ii) in accordance with such regulations, over a period not extending beyond the life expectancy of such employee or the life expectancy of such employee and his spouse.

A trust shall not be disqualified under this paragraph by reason of distributions under a designation, prior to the date of the enactment of this paragraph, by any employee under the plan of which such trust is a part, of a method of distribution which does not meet the terms of the preceding sentence. . . .

(d) Additional requirements for qualification of trusts and plans benefiting owner-employees

A trust forming part of a pension or profit-sharing plan which provides contributions or benefits for employees some or all of whom are owner-employees shall constitute a qualified trust under this section only if, in addition to meeting the requirements of subsection (a), the following requirements of this subsection are met by the trust and by the plan of which such trust is a part: . . .

(4) Under the plan–

(A) contributions or benefits are not provided for any owner-employee unless such owner-employee has consented to being included under the plan; and

(B) no benefits in excess of contributions made by an owner-employee as an employee may be paid to any owner-employee, except in the case of his becoming disabled (within the meaning of section 72(m)(7)), prior to his attaining the age of 59-1/2 years.

Subparagraph (B) shall not apply to any distribution to which section 72(m)(9) applies:

(5) The plan does not permit–

(A) contributions to be made by the employer on behalf of any owner-employee in excess of the amounts which may be deducted under section 404 for the taxable year;

(B) in the case of a plan which provides contributions or benefits only for owner-employees, contributions to be made on behalf of any owner-employee in excess of the amounts which may be deducted under section 404 for the taxable year; and

(C) if a distribution under the plan is made to any employee and if any portion of such distribution is an amount described in section 72(m)(5)(A)(i), contributions to be made on behalf of such employee for the 5 taxable years succeeding the taxable year in which such distribution is made.

Subparagraphs (A) and (B) shall not apply to contributions described in subsection (e), and shall not apply to any deductible employee contribution (as defined in section 72(o)(5)). Subparagraph (C) shall not apply to a distribution on account of the termination of the plan. . . .

§4.02. Taxability of beneficiary of employees' trust

(a) Taxability of beneficiary of exempt trust . . .

(5) Rollover amounts

(A) General rule

If–

(i) the balance to the credit of an employee in a qualified trust is paid to him in a qualifying rollover distribution,

(ii) the employee transfers any portion of the property he receives in such distribution to an eligible retirement plan, and

(iii) in the case of a distribution of property other than money, the amount so transferred consists of the property distributed, then such distribution (to the extent so transferred) shall not be includible in gross income for the taxable year in which paid.

(B) Maximum amount which may be rolled over

In the case of any qualifying rollover distribution, the maximum amount transferred to which subparagraph (A) applies shall not exceed the fair market value of all the property the employee recieves in the distribution, reduced by the employee contributions (other than accumulated deductible employee contributions within the meaning of section 72(o)(5)).

(C) Transfer must be made within 60 days of receipt

Subparagraph (A) shall not apply to any transfer of a distribution made after the 60th day following the day on which the employee received the property distributed. . . .

§404. Deduction for contributions of an employer to an employees' trust or annuity plan and compensation under a deferred-payment plan . . .

(e) Special limitations for self-employed individuals

(1) In general

In the case of a plan included in subsection (a)(1), (2), or (3), which provides contributions or benefits for employees some or all of whom are employees within the meaning of section 401(c)(1), the amounts deductible under subsection (a) in any taxable year with respect to contributions on behalf of any employee within the meaning of section 401(c)(1) shall, subject to paragraphs (2) and (4), not exceed $15,000, or 15 percent of the earned income derived by such employee from the trade or business with respect to which the plan is established, whichever is the lesser.

(2) Contributions made under more than one plan

(A) Overall limitation

In any taxable year in which amounts are deductible with respect to contributions under two or more plans on behalf of an individual who is an employee within the meaning of section 401(c)(1) with respect to such plans, the aggregate amount deductible for such taxable year under all such plans with respect to contributions on behalf of such employee shall (subject to paragraph (4)) not exceed $15,000, or 15 percent of the earned income derived by such employee from the trades or businesses with respect to which the plans are established, whichever is the lesser.

(B) Allocation of amounts deductible

In any case in which the amounts deductible under subsection (a) (with the application of the limitations of this subsection) with respect to contributions made on behalf of an employee within the meaning of section 401(c)(1) under two or more plans are, by reason of subparagraph (A), less than the amounts deductible under such subsection determined without regard to such subparagraph, the amount deductible under subsection (a) with respect to such contributions under each such plan shall be determined in accordance with regulations prescribed by the Secretary.

(3) Contributions allocable to insurance protection

For purposes of this subsection, contributions which are allocable (determined under regulations prescribed by the Secretary) to the purchase of life, accident, health, or other insurance shall not be taken into account.

(4) Limitations cannot be lower than $750 or 100 percent of earned income

The limitations under paragraphs (1) and (2)(A) for any employee shall not be less than the lesser of–

(A) $750, or

(B) 100 percent of the earned income derived by such employee from the trades or businesses taken into account for purposes of paragraph (1) or (2)(A) as the case may be.

This paragraph does not apply for any taxable year to any employee whose adjusted gross income for such taxable year (determined separately for each individual, without regard to any community property laws, and without regard to the deduction allowable under subsection (a)) exceeds $15,000. . . .

§408. Individual retirement accounts

(a) Individual retirement account

For purposes of this section, the term "individual retirement account" means a trust created or organized in the United States for the exclusive benefit of an individual or his beneficiaries, but only if the written governing instrument creating the trust meets the following requirements:

(1) Except in the case of a rollover contribution described in subsection (d)(3) in section 402(a)(5), 402(a)(7), 403(a)(4), 403(b)(8), 405(d)(3), or 409(b)(3)(C), no contribution will be accepted unless it is in cash, and contributions will not be accepted for the taxable year in excess of $2,000 on behalf of any individual.

(2) The trustee is a bank (as defined in section 401(d)(1)) or such other person who demonstrates to the satisfaction of the Secretary that the manner in which such other person will administer the trust will be consistent with the requirements of this section.

(3) No part of the trust funds will be invested in life insurance contracts.

(4) The interest of an individual in the balance in his account is nonforfeitable.

(5) The assets of the trust will not be commingled with other property except in a common trust fund or common investment fund.

(6) The entire interest of an individual for whose benefit the trust is maintained will be distributed to him not later than the close of his taxable year in which he attains age 70-1/2, or will be distributed, commencing before the close of such taxable year, in accordance with regulations prescribed by the Secretary, over–

(A) the life of such individual or the lives of such individual and his spouse, or

(B) a period not extending beyond the life expectancy of such individual or the life expectancy of such individual and his spouse.

(7) If an individual for whose benefit the trust is maintained dies before his entire interest has been distributed to him, or if distribution has been commenced as provided in paragraph (6) to his surviving spouse and such surviving spouse dies before the entire interest has been distributed to such

spouse, the entire interest (or the remaining part of such interest if distribution thereof has commenced) will, within 5 years after his death (or the death of the surviving spouse), be distributed, or applied to the purchase of an immediate annuity for his beneficiary or beneficiaries (or the beneficiary or beneficiaries of his surviving spouse) which will be payable for the life of such beneficiary or beneficiaries (or for a term certain not extending beyond the life expectancy of such beneficiary or beneficiaries) and which annuity will be immediately distributed to such beneficiary or beneficiaries. The preceding sentence does not apply if distributions over a term certain commenced before the death of the individual for whose benefit the trust was maintained and the term certain is for a period permitted under paragraph (6). . . .

(d) Tax treatment of distributions . . .

(6) Transfer of account incident to divorce

The transfer of an individual's interest in an individual retirement account, individual retirement annuity, or retirement bond to his former spouse under a divorce decree or under a written instrument incident to such divorce is not to be considered a taxable transfer made by such individual notwithstanding any other provision of this subtitle, and such interest at the time of the transfer is to be treated as an individual retirement account of such spouse, and not of such individual. Thereafter such account, annuity, or bond for purposes of this subtitle is to be treated as maintained for the benefit of such spouse. . . .

(f) Additional tax on certain amounts included in gross income before age 59-1/2

(1) Early distribution from an individual retirement account, etc.

If a distribution from an individual retirement account or under an individual retirement annuity to the individual for whose benefit such account or annuity was established is made before such individual attains age 59-1/2, his tax under this chapter for the taxable year in which such distribution is received shall be increased by an amount equal to 10 percent of the amount of the distribution which is includible in his gross income for such taxable year.

(2) Disqualification cases

If an amount is includible in gross income for a taxable year under subsection (e) and the taxpayer has not attained age 59-1/2 before the beginning of such taxable year, his tax under this chapter for such taxable year shall be increased by an amount equal to 10 percent of such amount so required to be included in his gross income.

(3) Disability cases

Paragraphs (1) and (2) do not apply if the amount paid or distributed, or the disqualification of the account or annuity under subsection (e), is attributable to the taxpayer becoming disabled within the meaning of section 72(m)(7). . . .

## Appendix 10-3
## Uniformed Services Former Spouses Protection Act
## (10 USC §1408)

§1408. Payment of retired or retainer pay in compliance with court orders

(a) In this section:

(1) "Court" means–

(A) any court of competent jurisdiction of any State, the District of Columbia, the Commonwealth of Puerto Rico, Guam, American Samoa, the Virgin Islands, the Northern Mariana Islands, and the Trust Territory of the Pacific Islands;

(B) any court of the United States (as defined in section 451 of title 28) having competent jurisdiction; and

(C) any court of competent jurisdiction of a foreign country with which the United States has an agreement requiring the United States to honor any court order of such country.

(2) "Court order" means a final decree of divorce, dissolution, annulment, or legal separation issued by a court, or a court ordered, ratified, or approved property settlement incident to such a decree (including a final decree modifying the terms of a previously issued decree of divorce, dissolution, annulment, or legal separation, or a court ordered, ratified, or approved property settlement incident to such previously issued decree), which–

(A) is issued in accordance with the laws of the jurisdiction of that court;

(B) provides for–

(i) payment of child support (as defined in section 462(b) of the Social Security Act (42 U.S.C. 662(b)));

(ii) payment of alimony (as defined in section 462(c) of the Social Security Act (42 U.S.C. 662(c))); or

(iii) division of property (including a division of community property); and

(C) specifically provides for the payment of an amount, expressed in dollars or as a percentage of disposable retired or retainer pay, from the disposable retired or retainer pay of a member to the spouse or former spouse of that member.

(3) "Final decree" means a decree from which no appeal may be taken or from which no appeal has been taken within the time allowed for taking such appeals under the laws applicable to such appeals, or a decree from which timely appeal has been taken within the time allowed for taking such appeals under the laws applicable to such appeals.

(4) "Disposable retired or retainer pay" means the total monthly retired or retainer pay to which a member is entitled (other than the retired pay of a member retired for disability under chapter 61 of this title) less amounts which–

(A) are owed by that member to the United States;

(B) are required by law to be and are deducted from the retired or retainer pay of such member, including fines and forfeitures ordered by courts-martial, Federal employment taxes, and amounts waived in order to receive compensation under title 5 or title 38;

(C) are properly withheld for Federal, State, or local income tax purposes, if the withholding of such amounts is authorized or required by law and to the extent such amounts withheld are not greater than would be authorized if such member claimed all dependents to which he was entitled;

(D) are withheld under section 3402(i) of the Internal Revenue Code of 1954 (26 U.S.C. 3402(i)) if such member presents evidence of a tax obligation which supports such withholding;

(E) are deducted as Government life insurance premiums (not including amounts deducted for supplemental coverage); or

(F) are deducted because of an election under chapter 73 of this title to provide an annuity to a spouse or former spouse to whom payment of a portion of such member's retired or retainer pay is being made pursuant to a court order under this section.

(5) "Member" includes a former member.

(6) "Spouse or former spouse" means the husband or wife, or former husband or wife, respectively, of a member who, on or before the date of a court order, was married to that member.

(b) For the purposes of this section–

(1) service of a court order is effective if–

(A) an appropriate agent of the Secretary concerned designated for receipt of service of court orders under regulations prescribed pursuant to subsection (h) or, if no agent has been so designated, the Secretary concerned, is personally served or is served by certified or registered mail, return receipt requested;

(B) the court order is regular on its face;

(C) the court order or other documents served with the court order identify the member concerned and include the social security number of such member; and

(D) the court order or other documents served with the court order certify that the rights of the member under the Soldiers' and Sailors' Civil Relief Act of 1940 (50 U.S.C. App 501 et seq.) were observed; and

(2) a court order is regular on its face if the order–

(A) is issued by a court of competent jurisdiction;

(B) is legal in form; and

(C) includes nothing on its face that provides reasonable notice that it is issued without authority of law.

(c)(1) Subject to the limitations of this section a court may treat disposable retired or retainer pay payable to a member for pay periods beginning after June 25, 1981, either as property solely of the member or as property of the member and his spouse in accordance with the law of the jurisdiction of such court.

(2) Notwithstanding any other provision of law, this section does not create any right, title, or interest which can be sold, assigned, transferred, or otherwise disposed of (including by inheritance) by a spouse or former spouse.

(3) This section does not authorize any court to order a member to apply for retirement or retire at a particular time in order to effectuate any payment under this section.

(4) A court may not treat the disposable retired or retainer pay of a member in the manner described in paragraph (1) unless the court has jurisdiction over the member by reason of (A) his residence, other than because of military assignment, in the territorial jurisdiction of the court, (B) his domicile in the territorial jurisdiction of the court, or (C) his consent to the jurisdiction of the court.

(d)(1) After effective service on the Secretary concerned of a court order with respect to the payment of a portion of the retired or retainer pay of a member to the spouse or a former spouse of the member, the Secretary shall, subject to the limitations of this section, make payments to the spouse or former spouse in the amount of the disposable retired or retainer pay of the member specifically provided for in the court order. In the case of a member entitled to receive retired or retainer pay on the date of the effective service of the court order, such payments shall begin not later than 90 days after the date of effective service. In the case of a member not entitled to receive retired or retainer pay on the date of the effective service of the court order, such payments shall begin not later than 90 days after the date of effective service. In the case of a member not entitled to receive retired or retainer pay on the date of the effective service of the court order, such payments shall begin not later than 90 days after the date on which the member first becomes entitled to receive retired or retainer pay.

(2) If the spouse or former spouse to whom payments are to be made under this section was not married to the member for a period of 10 years or more during which the member performed at least 10 years of service creditable in determining the member's eligibility for retired or retainer pay, payments may not be made under this section to the extent that they include an amount resulting from the treatment by the court under subsection (c) of disposable retired or retainer pay of the member as property of the member or property of the member and his spouse.

(3) Payments under this section shall not be made more frequently than once each month, and the Secretary concerned shall not be required to vary normal pay and disbursement cycles for retired or retainer pay in order to comply with a court order.

(4) Payments from the disposable retired or retainer pay of a member pursuant to this section shall terminate in accordance with the terms of the applicable court order, but not later than the date of the death of the member or the date of the death of the spouse or former spouse to whom payments are being made, whichever occurs first.

(5) If a court order described in paragraph (1) provides for a division of property (including a division of community property) in addition to an amount of disposable retired or retainer pay, the Secretary concerned shall, subject to the limitations of this section, pay to the spouse or former spouse of the member, from the disposable retired or retainer pay of the member, any part

of the amount payable to the spouse or former spouse under the division of property upon effective service of a final court order of garnishment of such amount from such retired or retainer pay.

(e)(1) The total amount of the disposable retired or retainer pay of a member payable under subsection (d) may not exceed 50 percent of such disposable retired or retainer pay.

(2) In the event of effective service of more than one court order which provide for payment to a spouse and one or more former spouses or to more than one former spouse from the disposable retired or retainer pay of a member, such pay shall be used to satisfy (subject to the limitations of paragraph (1)) such court orders on a first-come, first-served basis. Such court orders shall be satisfied (subject to the limitations of paragraph (1)) out of that amount of disposable retired or retainer pay which remains after the satisfaction of all court orders which have been previously served.

(3) (A) In the event of effective service of conflicting court orders under this section which assert to direct that different amounts be paid during a month to the same spouse or former spouse from the disposable retired or retainer pay of the same member, the Secretary concerned shall–

(i) pay to that spouse the least amount of disposable retired or retainer pay directed to be paid during that month by any such conflicting court order, but not more than the amount of disposable retired or retainer pay which remains available for payment of such court orders based on when such court orders were effectively served and the limitations of paragraph (1) and subparagraph (B) of paragraph (4);

(ii) retain an amount of disposable retired or retainer pay that is equal to the lesser of–

(I) the difference between the largest amount of retired or retainer pay required by any conflicting court order to be paid to the spouse or former spouse and the amount payable to the spouse or former spouse under clause (i); and

(II) the amount of disposable retired or retainer pay which remains available for payment of any conflicting court order based on when such court order was effectively served and the limitations of paragraph (1) and subparagraph (B) of paragraph (4); and

(iii) pay to that member the amount which is equal to the amount of that member's disposable retired or retainer pay (less any amount paid during such month pursuant to legal process served under section 459 of the Social Security Act (42 U.S.C. 659) and any amount paid during such month pursuant to court orders effectively served under this section, other than such conflicting court orders) minus–

(I) the amount of disposable retired or retainer pay paid under clause (i); and

(II) the amount of disposable retired or retainer pay retained under clause (ii).

(B) The Secretary concerned shall hold the amount retained under clause (ii) of subparagraph (A) until such time as that Secretary is provided with a court order which has been certified by the member and the spouse or former spouse to be valid and applicable to the retained amount. Upon being provided with such an order, the Secretary shall pay the retained amount in accordance with the order.

(4) (A) In the event of effective service of a court order under this section and the service of legal process pursuant to section 459 of the Social Security Act (42 U.S.C. 659), both of which provide for payments during a month from the retired or retainer pay of the same member, such court orders, and legal process shall be satisfied on a first-come, first-served basis. Such court orders and legal process shall be satisfied out of moneys which are subject to such orders and legal process and which remain available in accordance with the limitations of paragraph (1) and subparagraph (B) of this paragraph during such month after the satisfaction of all court orders or legal process which have been previously served.

(B) Notwithstanding any other provision of law, the total amount of the disposable retired or retainer pay of a member payable by the Secretary concerned under all court orders pursuant to this section and all legal processes pursuant to section 459 of the Social Security Act (42 U.S.C. 659) with respect to a member may not exceed 65 percent of the disposable retired or retainer pay payable to such member.

(5) A court order which itself or because of previously served court orders provides for the payment of an amount of disposable retired or retainer pay which exceeds the amount of such pay available for payment because of the limit set forth in paragraph (1), or which, because of previously served court orders or legal process previously served under section 459 of the Social Security Act (42 U.S.C. 659), provides for payment of an amount of disposable retired or retainer pay that exceeds the maximum amount permitted under paragraph (1) or subparagraph (B) of paragraph (4), shall not be considered to be irregular on its face solely for that reason. However, such order shall be considered to be fully satisfied for purposes of this section by the payment to the spouse or former spouse of the maximum amount of disposable retired or retainer pay permitted under paragraph (1) and subparagraph (B) of paragraph (4).

(6) Nothing in this section shall be construed to relieve a member of liability for the payment of alimony, child support, or other payments required by a court order on the grounds that payments made out of disposable retired or retainer pay under this section have been made in the maximum amount permitted under paragraph (1) or subparagraph (B) of paragraph (4). Any such unsatisfied obligation of a member may be enforced by any means available under law other than the means provided under this section in any case in which the maximum amount permitted under paragraph (1) has been paid and under section 459 of the Social Security Act (42 U.S.C. 659) in any case in which the maximum amount permitted under subparagraph (B) of paragraph (4) has been paid.

(f) (1) The United States and any officer or employee of the United States shall not be liable with respect to any payment made from retired or retainer pay to any member, spouse, or former spouse pursuant to a court order that is regular on its face if such payment is made in accordance with this section and the regulations prescribed pursuant to subsection (h).

(2) An officer or employee of the United States sho, under regulations prescribed pursuant to subsection (h), has the duty to respond to interrogatories shall not be subject under any law to any disciplinary action or civil or criminal liability or penalty for, or because of, any disclosure of information made by him in carrying out any of his duties which directly or indirectly pertain to answering such interrogatories.

(g) A person receiving effective service of a court order under this section shall, as soon as possible, but not later than 30 days after the date on which effective service is made, send a written notice of such court order (together with a copy of such order) to the member affected by the court order at his last known address.

(h) The Secretaries concerned shall prescribe uniform regulations for the administration of this section.

# Appendix 10-4
# Sample Paragraphs for Use in Agreements Involving Division of Military Pensions

These paragraphs, drafted by Kathryn Marshall, are used with the permission of the American Bar Association Family Law Section

**KEY**

Use t.) paragraphs in all judgments where a military pension is divided.
Use v.) paragraphs in judgments where pension property is divided.
Use w.) paragraphs in judgments where support is ordered.
Use x.) paragraphs in judgments where support is ordered.

t.) That (service member's name) was a member of the United States (branch of military) for a period in excess of _______ years and is identified by Social Security Number _____________________.

t.) That (spouse's name) agrees to notify the designated agent of the (branch of service), (insert title), promptly if the court order upon which these payments are based is vacated, modified, or set aside.

t.) That the rights of member (service member's name), (service member's Social Security number), pursuant to the Soldiers' and Sailors' Civil Relief Act of 1940 (50 U.S.C. App. 501 et seq.) were observed by this Court.

t.) That the first payment pursuant to Paragraph _______ and subparts shall be made in the first month after entry of Judgment for Dissolution of Marriage during which (service member's name) receives a pension payment.

v.) That (service member's name) shall pay to (spouse's name) the sum of $_______ per month until (spouse's name) (named event or time).

v.) That (service member's name) shall pay to (spouse's name) the sum of _______% of (service member's name) total disposable retired or retainer pay income per month as long as he receives his military pension regardless of whether (spouse's name) (name event or time).

v.) That these payments have been agreed between the parties and shall not be taxable to recipient, (spouse's name), or deductible by (service member's name).

v.) That these payments have been agreed between the parties to resolve (spouse's name) property interest in (service member's name) military pension and the payments are to be made as a division of property pursuant to the Illinois Marriage and Dissolution of Marriage Act.

v.) That (spouse's name) and (service member's name) both contemplate that these payments will not be taxable to (spouse's name), but will be received as a division of marital property of the parties.

w.) That these payments have been agreed between the parties and shall be taxable to (spouse's name) and deductible by (service member's name) pursuant to the Internal Revenue Code of 1954 as amended.

w.) That (service member's name) shall pay to (spouse's name) the sum of $_______ per month until (spouse's name) dies or (named event or time). That (service member's name) shall have no obligation for making any payments (or substitute therefor) that become due after the date of (spouse's name) death.

w.) That (service member's name) shall pay to (spouse's name) the sum of _______% of (service member's name) total disposable or retainer pay income per month for as long as he receives his military pension regardless of whether (spouse's name) remarries. That these payments shall terminate irrevocably upon the death of (spouse's name). That (service member's name) shall have no obligation for making any of these payments (or substitute therefor) to (spouse's name) estate after her death, with the exception of those payments due and owing to (spouse's name) on the date of her death.

x.) That all payments pursuant to Paragraph _______ herein and all of its subparts shall be made by the Secretary of the (military branch) directly to (spouse's name).

x.) That (spouse's name) shall have the right to garnishee the retirement pay of (service member's name) for all amounts due and owing pursuant to this Judgment and not paid within sixty (60) days of the date due according to Judgement.

x.) That (service member's name) has consented to designate (spouse's name) as beneficiary under his Survivor Benefit Plan and shall maintain that designation until his death, the death of (spouse's name) or until further Court Order.

x.) That (service member's name) shall be permanently restrained from making any written or oral request of the military to calculate deductions for monies owed by (service member's name) to the United States Government or monies other than monies received for this military pension.

x.) That disposable retired or retainer pay of (service member's name) shall be calculated by deducting appropriate deductions (withholdings for Federal, State and local income taxes) for monies owed by (service member's name) to the United States Government on gross amount of his governmental pension, only.

x.) That (spouse's name) agrees to notify the designated agent of the (branch of service), (insert title), promptly if she re-marries.

x.) That (spouse's name) agrees to notify the designated agent of the (branch of service), (insert title), promptly if an emancipation event occurs for any child whose support payments are made directly to (spouse's name).

x.) That (service member's name) shall pay (spouse's name) each monthly payment until he is notified that (spouse's name) has received the first monthly government allotment payment from the Secretary of the (military branch). In the event of duplication of monthly payments (spouse's name) shall re-pay overages pursuant to Paragraph

_______ herein and all of its subparts due and owing to (service member's name) within three days of receipt of duplicate payment.

x.) That on receipt of the first monthly government allotment payment by (spouse's name), she shall notify (service member's name) and he shall pay arrearages pursuant to Paragraph _______ herein and all of its subparts due and owing to (spouse's name), within three (3) days of notification by (spouse's name).

x.) That (service member's name) shall provide (spouse's name) with a current and effective military identification card which will entitle her to commissary, theatre, medical and post exchange privileges to the same extent and on the same basis as the surviving spouse of a retired member of the Uniformed Services as long as she shall remain unmarried.

x.) That (service member's name) shall execute all documents necessary to provide immediate enrollment of (spouse's name) into the DEERS Program.

# Appendix 10-5
# Apportionment from Civil Service Retirement Benefits

## Subpart Q - Apportionment from Civil Service Retirement Benefits

§831.1701 Purpose.

This subpart implements portions of Pub. L. 95-366 that require the Office of Personnel Management to comply with a provision for the apportionment of retirement benefits in a State court order, decree, or court-approved property settlement in connection with the divorce, annulment of marriage, or legal separation of a Federal employee or retiree. This subpart prescribes the procedures to be followed by:

(a) A former spouse when applying for apportionment of an individual's retirement benefits pursuant to section 8345(j) of title 5, United States Code.

(b) The Associate Director for Compensation in honoring the apportionment request and making payment to the former spouse.

**§831.1702 Definitions**

In this subpart:

"Court order" means any judgment or property settlement issued by or approved by any court of a State or the District of Columbia in connection with, or incident to, the divorce, annulment of marriage, or legal separation of a Federal employee or retiree.

"Expressly provided for" means a direction by court order to divide an individual's retirement benefits and awarding all or a portion of such benefits to a former spouse.

"Former spouse" means a person who has been divorced or legally separated, or whose marriage has been annulled.

"Individual" means a separated Federal employee who has filed an application for a refund of retirement contributions or a civil service annuitant.

"Retirement benefits" means employee annuities and refunds of retirement contributions but does not include survivor annuities or lump sum payments made pursuant to section 8342(c),(d)-(f) of title 5, United States Code.

§831.1703 Qualifying court order.

(a) The former spouse will be entitled to a portion of the retirement benefits only to the extent that the division of retirement benefits is expressly provided for by the court order. The order must specifically provide that the former spouse is entitled to payments from the retirement benefit.

(b) The Office of Personnel Management will review court orders as a whole to determine whether the language of the decree shows an intent by the court that the former spouse receive a portion of the individual's retirement benefits directly from the United States. Determinations as to whether an order is qualifying will be based, in part, on the following guidelines:

(1) Indications of the court's intent generally control.

(2) Absent clear indications to the contrary, an order expressly directing

the individual to make payment to the former spouse is not a qualifying court order if the individual objects to direct payment to the former spouse by the Office of Personnel Management.

(3) Orders which qualify under the requirements expressed in paragraphs (a) and (c) of this section, but imply that the individual is to be the source of the payment, are qualifying court orders if, and only if, the individual does not object to the apportionment within the 30-day notice period provided for by §831.1707(a)(3).

(c) No court order can be qualifying court order if the amount to be paid to each spouse is not readily ascertainable from the face of the order and normal Office of Personnel Management files.

**§831.1704 Application to apportion retirement benefits.**

(a) To establish the validity of a court order the former spouse must submit to the Associate Director for Compensation:

(1) A recently certified copy of the court order;

(2) A statement that the court order has not been amended, superseded, or set aside; and

(3) Identifying information concerning the employee or retiree such as his/her full name, claim number, date of birth, and Social Security Number, if available.

(b) When payments are subject to termination upon occurrence of a condition subsequent, no payment shall be made until the former spouse submits to the Associate Director for Compensation a statement

(1) That the condition has not occurred;

(2) That he/she will notify the Associate Director for Compensation within 15 calendar days of the occurrence of the condition subsequent; and

(3) That he/she will be personally liable for any overpayment to him/her resulting from the occurrence of the condition subsequent. The Associate Director for Compensation may subsequently require recertification of these statements.

**§831.1705 Retirement benefits - amount when payable.**

(a) No apportionment to a former spouse shall exceed the net annuity, computed by excluding from the gross annuity the amounts which are:

(1) Owed by the individual to the United States;

(2) Deducted for health benefits premiums pursuant to section 8906 of title 5, United States Code, and §§891.401 and 891.402;

(3) Deducted for life insurance premiums pursuant to sections 8707(b), 8714a(d), 8714b(d), and 8714c(d) of title 5, United States Code;

(4) Owed due to overpayment of annuity;

(5) Deducted for Medicare premiums; or

(6) Property withheld for Federal and State income tax purposes, if amounts withheld are not greater than they would be if the individual claimed all dependents to which he or she was entitled.

(b) Monies held by an executive agency or the Office of Personnel Management which may be payable at some future date shall not be considered payable to the individual and subject to apportionment unless all of the conditions necessary for payment of the monies to the individual have been met, including, but not limited to:

(1) Retirement;

(2) Separation from a covered position in the Federal service;

(3) Application for payment of the monies by the individual.

(c) Waivers of annuity payments under the terms of section 8345(d) of title 5, United States Code, shall exclude the waived portion of the annuity from apportionment under section 8345(j) of title 5, United States Code, if such waivers are postmarked before the expiration of the 30-day notice period stipulated by §831.1707.

**§831.1706 Preliminary Review.**

(a) Upon receipt of a court order and necessary documentation to apportion retirement benefits, the Associate Director for Compensation will make a determination whether the court order is a qualifying court order pursuant to §831.1703.

(b) Upon determination that the court order is a qualifying court order notifications required by

**§831.1707 shall be given.**

(c) Upon determination that the court order is not a qualifying court order, the former spouse shall be notified of that determination and the basis therefor.

**§831.1707 Notification.**

(a) The Associate Director for Compensation will notify the individual that a court order has been received which requires the apportionment of his/her retirement benefit and provide the individual with a copy of the court order. The notice will inform the individual:

(1) That the Office of Personnel Management intends to honor the court order;

(2) What effect it will have on the individual's retirement benefit; and

(3) That no payments will be made to the former spouse for a period of 30 days from the notice date to enable the individual to contest the court order.

(b) The former spouse will be notified:

(1) That the Office of Personnel Management intends to honor the court order;

(2) What amount he/she is entitled to receive, and in cases which require apportionment on a percentage basis, how such amount was computed; and

(3) That payment is being delayed for a period of 30 days to give the individual an opportunity to contest the court order.

**§831.1707 Decision.**

(a)(1) When the individual does not respond within the 30-day notice period provided for by §831.1707(a)(3), the apportionment will be made in accordance with the notification.

(2) When the individual responds to the notification, the Associate Director for compensation will consider the response. The former spouse's claim will be denied whenever it is shown that:

(i) The court order is not a qualifying court order; or

(ii) The court order is inconsistent with a contemporaneous or subsequent court order.

(b) If the individual objects to payment based on the validity of the court order and the record contains some support for the objection, he/she will be granted 30 days to initiate legal action to determine the validity of the objection. If evidence is submitted that legal action has been started before the 30 days have expired, money will continue to be withheld, but no payment will be made to the former spouse pending judicial determination of the validity of the court order.

**§831.1709 Effective Date.**

(a) The provisions of this subpart apply to any refund payable on or after September 15, 1978, and apply to any employee annuity which commenced before, on, or after September 15, 1978. The Associate Director for Compensation will not increase the amount apportioned from current retirement benefits in order to satisfy an arrearage due the former spouse unless the court otherwise directs. However, the Associate Director for Compensation will honor the terms of a new or revised court order which either increases or decreases an apportionment. Those changes will be prospective only.

(b) The provisions of this subpart apply to any court order issued before, on, or after September 15, 1978; however, the former spouse will not be entitled to any payments until:

(1) The individual files a claim for his/her benefit; and

(2) All submissions required by §831.1704 have been received by the Associate Director for Compensation.

**§831.1710 Limitations.**

(a) Retirement benefits are subject to apportionment by court order only while the individual is living. Payment of apportioned amounts will be made only to the former spouse and/or the children of the individual. Payment will not be made to any of the following:

(1) The heirs or legatees of the former spouse;

(2) The creditors of either the individual or the former spouse; or

(3) Other assignees of either the individual or the former spouse.

(b) The amount of any apportionment may not be less than one dollar, and, in the absence of compelling circumstances, shall be in whole dollars.

(c) In honoring and complying with the court order, the Associate Director for Compensation shall not be required to disrupt the scheduled method of accruing retirement benefits or the normal timing for making such payment, despite the existence of a special schedule of accrual or payment of amounts due the former spouse.

(d) Payment of apportionment shall be discontinued when the individual's annuity payments are suspended or terminated. If annuity payments are restored, payment of the apportionment will resume.

(e) In cases where the court order apportions a percentage of the retirement benefit, the Associate Director for Compensation will initially determine the amount of proper payment pursuant to 831.1705. That amount will only be increased by future cost-of-living increases unless the court directs otherwise.

**§831.1711 Liability.**

(a) The Office of Personnel Management shall not be liable for any payment made from retirement benefits pursuant to a court order if such payment is made in accordance with the provisions of this subpart.

(b) In the event that the Associate Director for Compensation is served with more than one court order with respect to the same retirement benefits, the benefits shall be available to satisfy the court orders on a first-come, first-served basis.

(c) Because the former spouse is entitled to payments only while the individual is living, the former spouse shall be personally liable for any payments which he/she receives after the death of the individual.

(d) The former spouse may request that an amount be withheld from the retirement benefits which is less than the amount stipulated in the court order. This lower amount will be deemed a complete fulfillment of the obligation of the Office of Personnel Management for the period in which the request is in effect.

## Appendix 10-6
## Application for Civil Service Retirement System Survivor Benefits

The attached form is an application for Civil Service Retirement System survivor benefits based on the provisions of Public Law 98-615, a new law which provides survivor annuity benefits for former husbands or wives of Federal civil service employees who retired before May 7, 1985. These benefits are effective as of the day after the date the retired employee dies, or, if the retired employee is already deceased, the first day of the second month after we receive your application. You may qualify for survivor benefits on your own and without the consent of the retired employee if you meet *all* six of the criteria listed below.

1. Your marriage to the retired employee must have dissolved after September 14, 1978
2. You must have been married to the retired employee during at least 10 years of creditable Government service, civilian and military
3. You must not be receiving any other employer-provided retirement benefits (Social Security is not an employer-provided benefit for these purposes)
4. You must not have remarried before reaching age 65
5. You must apply to the Office of Personnel Management for a survivor annuity before May 9, 1987 (you MUST apply by this date even if the retired employee is still living)
6. You must be at least 50 years old when filing this application

If you think you meet *all* six of the criteria, use the following instructions to complete the application form. Send it to the address shown below without delay.

U.S. Office of Personnel Management
Employee Service and Records Center
Attention: Spouse Equity Coordinator
Boyers, PA 16017

Signature

Employee Service & Records Center

See Reverse Side

**Section A.**

1. Enter your full legal name (e.g. Mary Jane Smith, *not* Mrs. Bill Smith.)
2. Enter your date of birth and attach a copy of your birth certificate

3. Enter your Social Security Number

**Section B.**

1. Enter the name of the retired employee
2. Enter the date of birth of the retired employee
3. Enter the Social Security Number of the retired employee, if you know it
4. Enter the Civil Service Retirement claim number (a number beginning with CSA or CSF) applicable to the retired employee, if you know it
5. Enter the former employee's date of death if he or she is now deceased

**Section C.**

1. Enter the date you were married to the former employee, the date the marriage legally ended, the place you were married, and who performed the marriage. Give this information for each marriage to the retired employee. [Attach copies of your marriage certificate(s) and divorce decree(s).]
2. Provide information on all retirement or pension benefits you are now receiving. This means all recurring retirement, pension, or survivor payments (other than Social Security) you are now receiving that are made by, on behalf of, or under the terms of a contract with an employer and are based on past service of the retired former employee or yourself. If you are receiving more than three separate benefits, list them on a separate sheet of paper and attach it to the application.
   a. Identify the type of benefit you are now receiving (for example, if it is for retirement, or disability, or as a survivor). SOCIAL SECURITY PAYMENTS ARE NOT TO BE LISTED FOR THE PURPOSES OF THIS APPLICATION.
   b. Provide the names of the systems or companies from which you are now receiving retirement pensions.
   c. For each benefit you have identified, indicate if it is totally or partially financed by a former employer. If you answer "YES," enter the amount you receive per week, month, or year
3. Indicate if you have remarried since you divorced the retired person identified in Section B above. Enter the date you remarried

**Section D.**

All information you provide must be true and you must certify that it is true. It is your responsibility to keep the Office of Personnel Management informed of any change in your status that will disqualify you for survivor annuity benefits. You are disqualified for benefits if you: (a) remarry before you are 55, or (b) begin to receive an employer financed pension or similar benefit.

1. You must *sign* the application with your current legal name
2. Enter the date you actually sign the application form. The envelope you use to mail this application must be *postmarked* before May 9, 1987, in order to receive consideration. Applications postmarked on or after May 9, 1987, will be dismissed
3. Provide the address where you want payments delivered or where we can contact you. It is your responsibility to keep us informed of your whereabouts even though we may not be paying you a benefit now. When you correspond with us, you must include the name and date of birth of the retired Federal employee on whose service this benefit is based as well as your own name and date of birth.

Retain this notice for your payment records.

# Cases

## A

A v A, 15 Or App 353, 514 P2d 358, *rehg denied,* 515 P2d 730 (Or 1973) **§8.13**

Abbott v Abbott, 40 Ill App 3d 348, 352 NE2d 404 (1976) **§8.10**

Abdul-Rahman Omar Adra v Clift, 195 F Supp 857 (D Md 1961) **§4.22**

Abney v Abney, 222 Tenn 160, 433 SW2d 847 (1968) **§2.14**

Adair v Adair, 670 P2d 1002 (Okla Ct App 1983) **§10.29**

Adams v Adams, 402 So 2d 300 (La Ct App 1981) **§2.08**

Adams v Adams, 101 Md 506, 61 A 628 (1905) **§4.01**

Adams v Adams, 86 Nev 62, 464 P2d 458 (1970) **§7.05**

Adams v Rhoades, 56 Misc 2d 249, 288 NYS2d 710 (1969) **§5.04**

Adelman v Adelman, 58 Misc 2d 803, 296 NYS2d 999 (Sup Ct 1969) **§2.14**

Agudo v Agudo, 411 So 2d 259 (Fla Dist Ct App 1982) **§8.05**

Agur v Agur, 32 AD2d 16, 298 NYS2d 772 (1969), *appeal dismissed,* 27 NY2d 643, 261 NE2d 903, 313 NYS2d 866 (1970) **§5.04**

Albanese v Richter, 161 F2d 688 (3d Cir), *cert denied,* 332 US 782 (1947) **§4.22**

Albright v Albright, 437 So 2d 1003 (Miss 1983) **§8.10**

Aldous v Aldous, 99 AD2d 197, 473 NYS2d 61 (1984) **§8.07**

Alewine v Alewine, 3 Alaska LJ 159 (No 11 Nov 1965) **§2.13**

Allen v Allen, 78 Wis 2d 263, 254 NW2d 244 (1977) **§8.14**

Allison v Ovens, 4 Ariz App 496, 421 P2d 929 (1966) **§8.07**

Alton v Alton, 207 F2d 667 (3d Cir 1953) **§4.03**

Amato v Amato, 180 NJ Super 210, 434 A2d 639 (1981) **§10.28**

American Tel & Tel Co v Merry, 592 F2d 118 (2d Cir 1979) **§§10.11, 10.23**

Anderson v Anderson, 121 Ariz 405, 590 P2d 637 (1973) **§§7.10, 8.03**

## B

## C

## D

## E

## F

# G

## H

## I



## J

## K

## L

## M

## N



## O



## P

## T

## U



## V



## W

## Y



## Z

# Statutes

## United States Code

## Internal Revenue Code

## Acts



## Uniform Laws

## State Statutes

# Regulations

## Code of Federal Regulations



## Treasury Regulations

# Authorities

H. Clarke, Social Legislation (2d ed 1968) **§§1.12, 1.20**

Cochran, Jr, & Vitz, *Child Protective Divorce Laws: A Response to the Effects of Parental Separation on Children,* 17 Fam LQ 372 (1983) **§§2.09, 2.17**

Comment, Bezio v Patenaude, *The "Coming Out" Custody Controversy of Lesbian Mothers in Court,* 16 New Eng L Rev 331 (1981) **§8.13**

Comment, *Burdens on Gay Litigants and Bias in the Court System: Homosexual Panic, Child Custody, and Anonymous Parties,* 19 Harv CR-CL L Rev 497 (1984) **§8.13**

Comment, *Child Custody: Best Interests of Children vs Constitutional Rights of Parents,* 81 Dick L Rev 733 (1977) **§8.11**

Comment, *Child Custody—Interracial Marriage May Be Considered in Framing Custody Modification Orders—Niles v Niles, 299 So 2d 162 (Fla 2d Dist Ct App 1974),* 3 Fla St UL Rev 195 (1975) **§8.08**

Comment, *Custody: Lesbian Mothers in the Courts,* 16 Ganz L Rev 147 (1980) **§8.13**

Comment, *Divorce-Insane Spouse Allowed to Sue for Divorce,* 28 Iowa L Rev 367 (1943) **§1.16**

Comment, *Doe v Doe: Destroying the Presumption That Homosexual Parents are Unfit - The New Burden of Proof,* 16 U Rick L Rev 851 (1982) **§8.13**

Comment, *Domestic Relations: Incompatibility Divorce in Kansas - A Movement Toward No-Fault Divorce,* 14 Washvurn LJ 349 (1975) **§2.13**

Comment, *Enforcing State Domestic Relations Decrees in Federal Courts,* 50 U Chi L Rev 1357 (1983) **§§4.20, 4.22, 4.23**

Comment, *Long-Arm Jurisdiction in Alimony and Custody Cases,* 73 Colum L Rev 289 (1973) **§§4.05, 4.06, 4.08**

Comment, *Marriage Contract for Support and Services: Constitutionality Begins at Home,* 49 NYU L Rev 1161 (1974) **§10.13**

Comment, *Mexican Divorces: Are They Recognized in California?,* 4 Cal WL Rev 341 (1968) **§4.10**

Comment, *Mexican Divorce — A Survey,* 33 Fordham L Rev 449 (1965) **§4.10**

Comment, *No-Fault Divorce: Modernization Long Overdue for New Jersey,* 2 Seton L Rev 63 (1970) **§2.06**

Comment, *The Custody of Children,* 2 Ind LJ 325 (1926) **§7.04**

Comment, *The Divisible Divorce Doctrine Reexamined in Light of Shaffer v Heitner,* 51 Miss L Rev 801 (1981) **§§4.02, 4.11**

Comment, *The Enforceability of Arbitration Clauses in North Carolina Separation Agreements,* 15 Wake Forest L Rev 487 (1979) **§5.03**

Comment, *The Law and the Problem Parent: Custody and Parental Rights of Homosexual, Mentally Retarded, Mentally Ill and Incarcerated Parents,* 16 J Fam L 797 (1977-78) **§8.13**

O. Coogler, Structured Mediation in Divorce Settlement (1978) **§§5.05, 5.06**

W. Cook, The Logical and Legal Bases of Conflict of Laws 460 (1942) **§4.01**

Coombs, *Noncourt-Connected Mediation and Counseling in Child-Custody*

Foster & Freed, *Child Custody,* 39 NYU L Rev 423 (1964) **§§6.03, 8.14**

Foster, *Conciliation and Counseling in the Courts in Family Law Cases,* 4 NYUL Rev 353 (1966) **§2.05**

Foster, *Current Trends in Divorce Law,* 1 Fam LQ 21 (1967) **§2.02**

Foster, *Recognition of Migratory Divorces: Rosenthiel v Section 250,* 43 NYU L Rev 419 (1968) **§4.10**

Foster & Freed, *Spousal Rights in Retirement and Pension Benefits,* 16 J Fam L 187 (1977-78) **§10.08**

Fox, *Condonation: An Obstruction to Reconciliation,* 2 Fam LQ 259 (1968) **§1.22**

Frank, Berman, & Mazur-Hart, *No-Fault Divorce Rate: the Nebraska Experiance — An Interrupted Time Series Analysis and Commentary,* 58 Neb L Rev 1 (1978) **§2.12**

S. Frasberg, Every Child's Birthright: In Defense of Mothering (1977) **§7.06**

Freed & Foster, *Divorce in the Fifty States: An Overview as of August 1, 1981,* 7 Fam L Rep (BNA) 4049 (1981) **§9.04**

Freed, *Equitable Distribution as of December 1982,* 9 Fam L Rep (BNA) 4001 (Monograph No 1, 1983) **§10.07**

Freed & Walker, *Family Law in the Fifty Winter States: An Overview,* 18 Fam LQ 369 (Winter 1985) **§§2.01, 2.06, 2.12, 2.15, 2.16, 4.03, 4.07, 9.04, 10.01, 10.03, 10.07, 10.08, 10.14, 10.29**

Freed & Foster, *Family Law in the Fifty States: An Overview,* 16 Fam LQ 289 (1983) **§§1.19, 1.24, 1.25, 2.07, 2.09, 5.05, 5.09**

Freed & Foster, *Family Law in the Fifty States: An Overview,* 16 Fam LQ 292 (1982) **§9.12**

Freed & Walker, *Family Law in the Fifty States: An Overview,* 11 Fam L Rep (BNA) 1274 (1985) **§§2.01, 2.06, 2.12**

Freed & Walker, *Family Law in the Fifty States: An Overview,* Table IX (presented to the American Bar Association Aug 5, 1984) **§§7.03, 8.02**

Freed, *Joint Custody Laws: An Analysis And Comparative Study,* 9 Fam L Rep (BNA) 4025 (1983) **§9.04**

Freed & Foster, *Life With Father,* 11 Fam LQ 321 (1978) **§§7.09, 7.10**

Fullenweider, *Unlocking the Possibilities, Deferred Compensation,* 5 Fam Advoc 2 (Spring 1983) **§10.26**

Gallagher, *No-Fault Divorce in Delaware,* 59 ABAJ 873 (1973) **§2.06**

Gardner, *Joint Custody Is Not For Everyone,* 5 Fam Advoc 7 (Fall 1982) **§9.16**

Garfield, *The Transitory Divorce Action: Jurisdiction in the No-Fault Era,* 58 Tex L Rev 501 (1980) **§§4.02, 4.03, 4.04, 4.09, 4.10, 4.12, 4.16**

Gaughan, *Taking a Fresh Look at Divorce Mediation,* 17 Trial 39 (1981) **§5.05**

2 Gibson, Codex Juris Ecclesiatici Anglecani 356 (1761) **§1.23**

Gold, *Mediation in the Dissolution of Marriage,* 36 Arb J 9 (Sept 1981) **§§5.05, 5.06, 5.07**

B. Goldberg, Valuation of Divorce Assets 248 (1984) **§10.25**

Golden, Equitable Distribution of Property (1983) **§10.27**

J. Goldstein, A. Freud, & A. Solnit, Beyond the Best Interests of the Child (1973) **§§7.01, 7.02, 7.03, 7.07, 7.08, 8.05, 9.03**

W. Goodsell, A History of Marriage and the Family (1934) **§§1.01, 1.03, 1.04, 1.06, 1.08, 6.02**

R. Gottesman, The Child and The Law (1981) **§§6.03, 7.03, 7.04, 7.07**

S. Green & J. Long, Marriage and Family Law Agreements (1984) **§§1.09, 1.24, 1.26, 2.03, 2.08, 2.16, 3.01, 4.09, 4.23, 5.02, 5.03, 6.02, 7.01, 7.02, 8.08, 8.14, 9.10, 10.02**

Green & Long, *The Real and Illusory Changes of the 1977 Marriage and Divorce Act,* 27 Cath UL Rev 469 (1978) **§§2.09, 2.10, 2.14, 2.17**

W. Greenough & F. King, Pension Plans and Public Policy 176-77 (1976) **§10.10**

J. Grief, Fathers, Children and Joint Custody 6-8 (1978) **§9.01**

Griffin, *In 44 States, It's Legal To Rape Your Wife,* 9 Student Law 20 (1980) **§1.12**

P. Grimal, The Civilization of Rome 124-25 (1963) **§1.04**

Grossman, *A Child of a Different Color: Race as a Factor in Adoption and Custody Proceedings,* 17 Buffalo L Rev 303 (1968) **§8.08**

Grote & Weinstein, *Joint Custody: A Viable and Ideal Alternative,* 1 J Divorce 43 (1977) **§9.02**

Guerin, Transmutation and Commingling of Community Property, 3, 3-4, in Transmutation of Community Property During Marriage, His, Hers or Ours (Presented by the Section of Family Law of the ABA 1985) **§10.06**

A. Haralambie, Handling Child Custody Cases (Shepard's/McGraw-Hill 1983) **§§6.03, 7.02, 8.01, 8.06, 9.10, 9.16**

Harbinson, *Family Law — Attorney Mediation of Marital Disputes and Conflict of Interest Considerations,* 60 NCL Rev 171 (1981) **§§5.05, 5.08**

A. Harrison, The Law of Athens, Family and Property 44 (1968) **§6.02**

Hawkins, *The Effect of Shaffer v Heitner on the Jurisdictional Standard in Ex Parte Divorce,* 18 Fam LQ 311 (1984) **§§4.01, 4.02, 4.11**

J. Hayes, Divorce Mediation, A Practical Guide for Therapists and Counselors (1981) **§5.05**

Hester, *Expression of Preference By Children In Child Custody Disputes in Oklahoma,* 51 Okla BJ 3097 (1980) **§8.10**

Hetherington, Cox, & Cox, *Divorced Fathers,* 25 Fam Coordinator 417 (1976) **§9.01**

E. Hetherington, M. Cox, & R. Cox, Family Interaction and the Social, Emotional and Cognitive Development of Children Following Divorce 22 (May 17-20, 1978) (paper presented at Symposium on The Family: Setting Priorities, Washington, D.C.) **§9.01**

Hitchens & Price, *Trial Strategy in Lesbian Mother Custody Cases: The Use of Expert Testimony,* 9 Golden Gate UL Rev 451 **§8.13**

1 W. Holdsworth, History of English Law 623 (7th ed 1956) **§1.08**

1 G. Howard, A History of Matrimonial Institutions 224-49 (reprinted 1964) **§1.01**

2 G. Howard, A History of Matrimonial Institutions (reprinted 1964) **§§1.05, 1.06, 1.07, 1.08, 1.09**

D. Hunt, Parents and Children in History 33-34 (1970) **§7.01**

Hunter & Polikoff, *Custody Rights of Lesbian Mothers: Legal Theory and Litigation Strategy,* 25 Buffalo L Rev 691 (1976) **§8.13**

H. Irving, Divorce Mediation: A Rational Alternative to the Adversary System (1981) **§5.05**

Irwine, *Mutual Desertion,* 30 Mod L Rev 46 (1967) **§1.14**

Jacobson, American Marriage and Divorce 90 (1959) **§3.01**

Jellinek & Slovik, *Current Concepts in Psychiatry: Divorce: Impact on Children,* 305 New Eng J Med 557 (Sept 3, 1981) **§9.01**

Johnson, *The Family Law Act: A Guide to the Practitioner,* 1 Pac LJ 147 (1970) **§2.01**

Jones, *The Tender Years Doctrine: Survey and Analysis,* 16 J Fam L 695 (1977-78) **§§7.06, 7.07**

Jordan, *When in Doubt, Keep Child Out,* 6 Fam Advoc 16 (Spring 1984) **§8.01**

Kalcheim & Shapiro, *Does the Order Pass the Test?,* 8 Fam Advoc 20 (Fall 1985) **§10.23**

Katz, *The Maternal Preference and the Psychological Parent: Suggestions for Allocating the Burden of Proof in Custody Litigation,* 53 Conn BJ 343 (1979) **§§7.06, 7.08**

S. Katz, Child Snatching, The Legal Response to the Abduction of Children (1981) **§1.26**

S. Katz, When Parents Fail: The Law's Response To Family Breakdown 4 (1971) **§§6.02, 7.01**

G. Keeton, English Law, The Judicial Constitution (1974) **§§1.06, 1.07**

Kelly, *Marriage, Divorce, and Annulment,* 4 Jurist 246 (1944) **§1.07**

2 J. Kent, Commentaries on American Law 128 (1889) **§3.02**

2 J. Kent, Commentaries on American Law 204 (1873) **§6.02**

Kittrell, The Retirement Equity Act of 1984, Some Problems and Their Solutions 2 (1985 ABA Annual Meeting July 9, 1985) **§10.23**

Klaff, *The Tender Years Doctrine: A Defense,* 70 Colo L Rev 335 (1982) **§§7.05, 7.06, 7.07, 7.11**

M. Klaus & J. Kennell, Maternal Infant Bonding (1976) **§7.06**

Knowles, *Expanding Jurisdiction Over Domestic Relations Causes,* 11 J Fam L 49 (1971) **§§4.06, 4.07**

Koretzensky, *Clause, and Effect: Setting Up a ODRO,* 8 Fam Advoc 27-29 (Fall 1985) **§10.23**

Krom, *California's Divorce Law Reform - An Historical Analysis,* 1 Pac LJ 156 (1970) **§2.01**

Lauerman, *Nonmartial Sexual Conduct and Child Custody,* 46 U Cin L Rev 647 (1977) **§8.14**

Lauter, *Whose Law Degree Is It?,* Natl LJ, Nov 28, 1983, at 1, col 1 **§10.29**

Leach, *Divorce by Plane-Ticket in the Affluent Society - With a Side Order of Jurisprudence,* 14 Kan L Rev 549 (1966) **§4.10**

R. Leflar, American Conflicts Law 5 (rev ed 1968) **§4.01**

Leonard, *Older Women and Pensions: Catch 22,* 10 Golden Gate UL Rev 1191 (1980) **§10.09**

Leonard & Provence, *The Development of Parent-Child Relationships and the Psychological Parent,* 53 Conn BJ 320 (1979) **§§7.06, 7.08**

Letter from Doris Jonas Freed, Chair, Research Committee, Family Law Section, ABA, to John V. Long, Esquire (Jan 10, 1985) **§9.04**

Levine, *Marital Cruelty: New Wine in Old Bottles,* 2 Fam LQ 296 (1968) **§§1.12, 1.13**

J. Levine, Who Will Raise the Children: New Options for Fathers (and Mothers) (1976) **§7.06**

Levy, *Comment on the Pearson-Thoennes Study and Mediation,* 17 Fam LQ 525 (1984) **§5.05**

R. Levy, Uniform Marriage and Divorce Legislation: A Preliminary Analysis (1970) **§§2.01, 2.02, 2.05**

Lewis, 16 Soc Serv Rev 7 (1964) **§1.14**

Lichtenberger, Divorce Legislation, in Selected Essays on Family Law (1950) **§§1.01, 1.10, 2.02, 2.05**

A. Lindey, Separation Agreements and Ante-Nuptial Contracts 8-6 (1983) **§1.20**

A. Lindey, Separation Agreements and Ante-Nuptial Contracts §29 (rev ed 1983) **§5.03**

1 A. Lindey, Separation Agreements and Ante-Nuptial Contracts 29-18-20 (rev 3d ed 1983) **§5.04**

Lipman, *Methodology, Valuing Deferred Contribution Plans,* 5 Fam Advoc 19 (Spring 1983) **§10.25**

Loeb, *Introduction to the Standards of Practice for Family Mediators,* 17 Fam LQ 451 (1984) **§§5.05, 5.13**

*Luke* 16:18 **§1.05**

Lupstein, *Recognition of Foreign Divorces: Retrospects and Prospects,* 2 Ottawa L Rev 49 (1967) **§4.10**

D. Lynn, The Father: His Role in Child Development 279 (1974) **§9.01**

MacDougall, *Proposals to Reform the Law of Condonation,* 39 Australian LJ 295 (1966) **§1.22**

J. Madden, Handbook of the Law of Persons and Domestic Relations (1931) **§§1.07, 1.11, 1.14, 1.15, 1.21, 1.22, 2.01, 4.02, 7.04, 8.14, 10.02**

*Malachi* 2:14-16 **§1.03**

Marshall, Military Pensions in Dissolution Proceedings in Equitable Distribution States 97 in Making Divorce into a Federal Case (Presented by the Family Law Section of the ABA 1985) **§10.18**

Marshall & Gatz, *The Custody Decision Process: Toward New Roles for Parents and the States,* 7 NC Cent LJ 50 (Fall 1975) **§7.06**

O. Maru, Supplement to Digest of Bar Association Ethics Opinions No 8000 (1975) **§5.02**

*Matthew* 19:3-9 **§1.05**

J. McCahey, M. Kaufman, C. Kraut, D. Gaffner, M. Silverman, & J. Zett, Child Custody and

Visitation Law and Practice 10-4 (1968) **§§8.03, 8.06**

1 J. McCahey, M. Kaufman, C. Kraut, & J. Zett, Child Custody and Visitation Law and Practice (1983) **§§6.03, 7.01, 7.04**

2 J. McCahey, M. Kaufman, C. Kraut, D. Gaffner, M. Silverman, J. Zett, Child Custody and Visitation Law and Practice (1983) **§§8.09, 8.14**

D. McClanahan, Pension Plans and Pension Funding (The Actuarial Basis), Simplified for Non-Actuaries 195-96 (1980) **§10.10**

McCurdy, *Divorce-A Suggested Approach with Particular Reference to Dissolution for Living Separate and Apart,* 9 Vand L Rev 685 (1956) **§2.01**

McCurdy, *Insanity as a Ground for Annulment or Divorce in English and American Law,* 29 Vand L Rev 771 (1943) **§1.16**

McDonough, *Mr. Justice Jackson and Full Faith and Credit to Divorce Decrees: A Critique,* 56 Colum L Rev 860 (1956) **§§4.12, 4.14**

D. McGill, Fundamentals of Private Pensions (3d ed 1975) **§§10.08, 10.10**

Meroney, *Mediation and Arbitration of Separation and Divorce Agreements,* 15 Wake Forest L Rev 467 (1979) **§§5.03, 5.04, 5.05**

Meyer, *Family Law,* 14 Rutgers LJ 1011 (1983) **§1.26**

Meyers, *Washington's New Domestic Relations Tribunal,* 6 Cath UL Rev 139 (1957) **§4.20**

Miller, *Bifurcation of Dissolution of Marriage Actions, Part One,* 55 Fla BJ 755 (1981) **§§4.17, 4.18**

Miller, *Bifurcation of Dissolution of Marriage Actions, Part Two,* 55 Fla BJ 831 (1981) **§4.18**

Miller, *Joint Custody,* 13 Fam LQ 345 (1979) **§§9.01, 9.02, 9.16**

M.H. Minton, *Valuing the Contribution of the Homemaker at Trial,* 1 Fair Share 10:7 (Oct 1981) **§10.13**

M.H. Minton & J.L. Block, What is a Wife Worth? (1983) **§10.13**

Mnookin, *Child-Custody Adjudication: Judicial Functions in the Face of Indeterminacy,* 39 Law & Contemp Probs 226 (1975) **§§7.04, 7.05, 7.07, 7.08**

Moore, *An Analysis of Collusion and Connivance Bars to Divorce,* 36 UMKC L Rev 193 (1968) **§1.21**

Moore, *An Examination of the Condonation Doctrine,* 2 Akron L Rev 74 (1969) **§1.22**

Moore, *An Examination of the Recrimination Doctrine,* 20 SCL Rev 685 (1968) **§1.19**

Moore, *An Examination of the Recrimination Doctrine,* 20 SCL Rev 712 (1968) **§1.24**

Moore, *Forgotten Defences to Divorce Suits,* 9 J Fam L 149 (1969-70) **§1.25**

Morris, *A Developmental Approach to Child Custody,* 53 Conn BJ 330 (1979) **§§7.06, 7.08**

Morris & Reimer, States Which Will Award Spouses A Share Of Retirement At Time of Divorce, 1 Cong Research Serv (1982) **§10.14**

Mueller, *Inquiry Into the State of a Divorceless Society,* 18 U Pitt L Rev 545 (1957) **§§1.11, 1.14**

Murphy, *The Retirement Equity Act of 1984 and Qualified Domestic*

*Relations Orders,* 9 Ill Fam L Rep 94 (1985) **§10.23**

Myerberg, *Constructive Desertion in Maryland,* 10 Md L Rev 193 (1949) **§1.14**

Nagera, *Children's Reactions to the Death of Important Objects,* 25 Psychoanalysis Study of the Child 360 (1970) **§7.06**

Neal, *An Analysis of Newly Established Vesting Requirements Under Pension Reform,* 41 J Taxation 258 (1974) **§10.08**

1 Nelson, Divorce and Annulment 358 (2d ed 1945) **§1.24**

*1983 Survey of American Family Law,* 10 Fam L Rep (BNA) 3017 (Jan 17, 1984) **§§2.07, 2.15**

J. Noble & W. Noble, The Custody Trap 138-39 (1975) **§8.13**

Note, *Are Fault Requirements in Divorce Actions Unconstitutional?,* 16 J Fam L 265 (1977-78) **§2.03**

Note, *A Survey of the Law of Condonations, Connivance and Collusion in New England,* 35 BUL Rev 99 (1955) **§1.21**

Note, *A Survey of the Law of Condonation, Collusion and Connivance in New England,* 35 BUL Rev 99 (1955) **§1.22**

Note, *Civil Death Statutes: Medieval Factor in a Modern World,* 50 Harv L Rev 960 (1937) **§1.15**

Note, *Collusive and Consensual Divorce and the New York Anomaly,* 36 Columbia L Rev 1121 (1936) **§1.20**

Note, *Community Property-Benefits Awarded Under the Railroad Retirement Act are Not Community Property Subject to Division Upon Divorce,* 11 St Mary's LJ 535 (1979) **§10.15**

Note, *Constructive Desertion — A Broader Basis for Breaking the Bond,* 51 Iowa L Rev 108 (1965) **§1.14**

Note, *Custody and the Cohabiting Parent,* 20 J Fam L 697 (1981-82) **§8.14**

Note, *Custody Disputes Following the Dissolution of Interracial Marriage: Best Interests of the Child or Judicial Racism,* 19 J Fam L 97 (1980-81) **§8.08**

Note, *Divided Custody of Children After Their Parents Divorce,* 8 J Fam L 58 (1968) **§8.17**

Note, *Divorce-Insane Persons-Incompetent Allowed to Sue for Divorce,* 56 Harv L Rev 310 (1942) **§1.16**

Note, *Domestic Relations: Divorce: Desertion: Refusal of Sexual Relations,* 10 Cornell LQ 374 (1925) **§1.14**

Note, *Domestic Relations: Judgments: Void Decree on Its Own Motion: Hartigan v. Hartigan, 128 So 2d 725 (Ala 1961),* 47 Cornell LQ 459 (1962) **§1.20**

Note, *Domestic Relations — Jurisdiction — Extension of Comity to Foreign National Divorce,* 46 Tenn L Rev 38 (1978) **§4.10**

Note, *Domestic Relations-Separation-Suit by Mentally Incompetent Wife [Sengstack v. Sengstack],* 12 Vand L Rev 493 (1959) **§1.16**

Note, *Federal Jurisdiction of "Domestic Relations" Cases,* 7 J Fam L 309 (1967) **§§4.20, 4.21**

Note, *Florida's No-Fault Divorce: Is it Really No-Fault?,* 4 Fla St UL Rev 504 (1976) **§2.02**

Note, *Imprisonment as a Ground for Divorce-"Statutory Desertion," Judicial Improvisation and a Call for*

*Reform*, 23 Rutgers L Rev 389 (1969) **§1.15**

Note, *In the "Best Interests of the Child: and the Lesbian Mother: A Proposal for Legislative Change in New York*, 48 Alb L Rev 1021 (1984) **§8.13**

Note, *Jurisdiction in the Ex Parte Divorce: Do Absent Spouses Have a Protected Due Process Interest in Their Marital Status?* 13 Mem St UL Rev 205 (1983) **§§4.01, 4.02, 4.11**

Note, *Lawyering for the Child; Principles of Representation in Custody and Visitation Disputes Arising from Divorce*, 87 Yale LJ 1126 (1978) **§8.10**

Note, *Louisiana's New Joint Custody Law*, 43 La L Rev 759 (1983) **§8.14**

Note, *Measuring the Child's Best Interests—A Study of Incomplete Considerations*, 44 Den LJ 132 (1967) **§§7.06, 7.08**

Note, *Non-Judicial Resolution of Custody and Visitation Disputes*, 12 UCD L Rev 582 (1979) **§5.01**

Note, *Pensions as Marital Property: Valuation, Allocation, and Related Mysteries*, 16 Creighton L Rev 743 (1983) **§10.08**

Note, *The Domestic Relations Exception to Diversity Jurisdiction*, 83 Colum L Rev 1824 (1983) **§§4.20, 4.21, 4.24**

Note, *The Employee Retirement Income Security Act of 1974: Policies and Problems*, 26 Syracuse L Rev 539 (1975) **§§10.09, 10.11**

Note, *The Role of the Lawyer in Divorce: Some Ethical Problems*, 21 U Pitt L Rev 720 (1960) **§4.19**

Note, *The Tender Years Presumption in Missouri: A Judicial Anachronism*, 23 St Louis ULJ 697 (1979) **§6.03**

Note, *Virginia's Domestic Relations Long-Arm Legislation: Does Its Reach Exceed Its Due Process Grasp?*, 24 Wm & Mary L Rev 229 (1983) **§4.08**

Note, *United States Recognition of Foreign Nonjudicial Divorces*, 53 Minn L Rev 612 (1969) **§4.10**

Note, 11 St Mary's LJ 535 (1979) **§10.15**

O'Connell & Kittrell, *The Tax Effects are Easier to Predict*, 8 Fam Advoc 11 (Fall 1985) **§10.23**

Ohlson, *Adultery: A Review*, 17 BUL Rev 328 (1937) **§1.11**

Okpaku, *Psychology: Impediment of Aid in Child Custody Cases?* ,29 Rutgers L Rev 1117 (1976) **§§7.06, 7.08**

Orfield, *Divorce for Tempermental Incompatibility*, 52 Mich L Rev 659 (1954) **§2.13**

Patterson, *The Added Cost of Sharing Lives*, 5 Fam Advoc 10 (Fall 1982) **§9.03**

Pearson & Thoennes, *Mediating and Litigating Custody Disputes: A Longitudinal Evaluation*, 17 Fam LQ 497 (1984) **§§5.01, 5.05**

Pearson & Thoennes, *Mediation & Divorce, The Benefits Outweigh the Costs*, 4 Fam Advoc 26 (Winter 1982) **§§5.02, 5.05**

E. Peck, The Law of Persons and of Domestic Relations §69 (1930) **§10.03**

Peters, *Iowa Reform of Marriage Termination*, 20 Drake L Rev 211 (1970) **§2.06**

Peterson, *Foreign Country Judgments and the Second Restatement of Conflict*

**§§1.01, 1.12, 1.16, 1.24, 2.04, 4.01, 4.11, 4.12**

Rheinstein, *The Constitutional Bases of Jurisdiction,* 22 U Chi L Rev 775 (1955) **§4.03**

Rheinstein, *The Law of Divorce and the Problem of Marriage Stability,* 9 Vand L Rev 633 (1956) **§§1.01, 2.02, 2.03, 2.05**

Rifkin & Barber, American Workers Own $550 Billion, in Retirement Income: A Report from the Pension Rights Center (1979) **§10.09**

*Romans* 7:2-3 **§1.05**

Rosenberg, *How Void is a Void Decree, or the Estoppel Effect of Invalid Divorce Decrees,* 8 Fam LQ 207 (1974) **§4.10**

H. Ross & I. Sawhill, Time of Transition: The Growth of Families Headed By Women 25 (1975) **§1.26**

Roth, *The Tender Years Presumption in Child Custody Disputes,* 15 J Fam L 423 (1976-77) **§§7.05, 7.08, 7.09, 7.11, 8.17**

J. Sandys, A Companion to Latin Studies 303 (3d ed 1929) **§1.04**

Santrock, *Effects of Father Absence on Sex-Typed Behavior in Male Children: Reason for the Absence and Age of Onset of the Absence,* 130 J Gentic Psychology 3 (1977) **§9.01**

Santrock, *Relation of Type and Onset of Father Absence to Cognitive Development,* 43 Child Dev 445 (1972) **§9.01**

J. Schouler, Divorce Manual §193 (1944) **§10.03**

1 J. Schouler, Divorce, Separation and Domestic Relations §247 (6th ed 1921) **§10.02**

Schulman, *Who's Looking After the Children?,* 5 Fam Advoc 31 (Fall 1982) **§§9.09, 9.10**

Schwartz, *Toward a Presumption of Joint Custody,* 18 Fam LQ 225 (1984) **§9.01**

Schwecter, *Defining Benefits as Property,* 5 Fam Advoc 9 (1983) **§10.25**

Sears, *Doll-Play Aggression in Normal Young Children: Influence of Sex, Age, Sibling Status, Father's Absence,* 6 Psych Monographs 65 (1951) **§9.01**

C. Sherman, How to Do Your Own Divorce in California With the Forms You Will Need to Do It 12 (6th ed 1975) **§2.16**

E. Shorten, The Making of the Modern Family 255-68 (1976) **§7.01**

Siegel & Buckman, *Tax Consequences of Dividing a Keogh Plan,* 3 FairShare 4 (Feb 1983) **§10.12**

Siegel & Hurley, *The Role of the Child's Preference in Custody Proceedings,* 11 Fam LQ 1 (1977) **§8.10**

Silberman, *Professional Responsibility Problems of Divorce Mediation,* 16 Fam LQ 107 (1982) **§§5.05, 5.06, 5.08, 5.09, 5.11, 5.12**

Smith & Troha, *A Survey of the Membership of the ABA Section of Family Law,* 17 Fam LQ 225 (1983) **§4.19**

Smith, *New Rules, New Burdens,* 8 Fam Advoc 4 (Fall 1985) **§10.09**

Spencer & Zammit, *Mediation-Arbitration: A Proposal for Private Resolution of Disputes Between Divorced or Separated Parents,* 1976 Duke LJ 911 **§§5.03, 5.04**

R. Spitz, The First Year of Life (1965) **§7.06**

Stack, *Who Owns the Child? Divorce and Child Custody Decisions in Middle Class Families,* 23 Soc Prob 505 (1976) **§9.03**

*Standards of Practice for Family Mediators,* 17 Fam LQ 461 (1984) **§5.08**

E. Stimson, Conflict of Laws 71 (1963) **§4.10**

L. Stone, The Family, Sex and Marriage in England, 1500-1800, at 147-81 (1977) **§7.01**

J. Story, Conflict of Laws 40 (8th ed 1883) **§§4.01, 4.02**

Swisher, *Foreign Migratory Divorce: A Reappraisal,* 21 J Fam L 9 (1982083) **§4.10**

Tenney, Jr, *Divorce Without Fault: The Next Step,* 46 Neb L Rev 24 (1967) **§2.02**

Tepfer, *Methodology: Valuing Defined Contribution Plans,* 5 Fam Advoc 18 (Spring 1983) **§10.25**

W. Tiffany, Handbook on the Law of Persons and Domestic Relations (1896) **§§7.04, 7.05**

Trombetta, *Joint Custody: Recent Research and Overloaded Courtrooms Inspire New Solutions to Custody Disputes,* 19 J Fam L 23 (1980-81) **§9.01**

Troyan, *Evaluating Pensions in Light of The Retirement Equity Act of 1984,* 11 Fam L Rep (BNA) 3005 (Monograph no 2 1985) **§10.24**

Troyan, *Pension Evaluation and Equitable Distribution,* 10 Fam L Rep (BNA) 3001 (Monograph no 1, 1983) **§10.25**

J. Udry, The Social Context of Marriage 511 (1966) **§1.01**

Uviller, *Father's Rights and Feminism: The Maternal Presumption Revisited,* 1 Harv Women's LJ 107 (1978) **§§7.04, 7.06**

Vaughn, *The Policy of Community Property and Inter-Spousal Transactions,* 19 Baylor L Rev 20 (1967) **§10.06**

2 C. Vernier, American Family Laws (1931) **§§1.10, 1.11, 2.01, 2.04, 2.13, 3.02, 4.01, 4.09, 7.04**

3 C. Vernier, American Family Laws (1935) **§§10.02, 10.03**

Vestal & Foster, *Implied Limitations on the Diversity Jurisdiction of Federal Courts,* 41 Minn L Rev 1 (1956) **§§4.20, 4.24**

Wadlington, *Divorce Without Fault Without Perjury,* 52 Va L Rev 32 (1966) **§§2.01, 2.02, 2.03, 2.04**

Walker, *Beyond Fault: An Examination of Patterns of Behavior in Response to Present Divorce Laws,* 10 J Fam L 267 (1971) **§1.10**

Walker, *Disarming the Litigious Man — A Glance at Fault and California's New Divorce Legislation,* 1 Pac LJ 182 (1970) **§§2.01, 2.02**

Wallerstein, *Children Who Cope in Spite of Divorce,* 1 Fam Adoc 2 (1978) **§9.01**

J. Wallerstein & J. Kelly, Surviving the Breakup: How Children and Parents Cope With Divorce (1980) **§§7.02, 9.01**

Wallerstein & Kelly, *The Effects of Parental Divorce: Experiences of the Child in Later Latency,* 46 Am J Orthopsychology 256 (1976) **§9.01**

Wallerstein & Kelly, *The Effects of Parental Divorce: Experiences of the Preschool Child,* 14 J Acad Child Psych 600 (1975) **§9.01**

Wallerstein & Kelly, *The Effects of Parental Divorce: The Adolescent Experience,* in 3 The Child in His Family (E. Anthony & C. Koupernik eds 1974) **§9.01**

Watson, *The Children of Armageddon: Problems of Custody Following Divorce,* 21 Syracuse L Rev 55 (1969) **§7.06**

Watson, *The Deserted Wife and the Law,* 43 Australian LJ 450 (1969) **§1.14**

Weintraub, *Texas Long-Arm Jurisdiction in Family Law Cases,* 32 Sw LJ 965 (1978) **§4.08**

Weitzman & Dixon, *Child Custody Awards: Legal Standards and Empirical Patterns for Child Custody, Support and Visitation After Divorce,* 12 UCD L Rev 473 (1979) **§§7.05, 7.08, 8.11, 8.17**

Weitzman, *Legal Regulation of Marriage: Tradition and Change,* 62 Cal L Rev 1169 (1974) **§10.13**

Weitzman & Dixon, *The Alimony Myth: Does No-Fault Divorce Make A Difference?,* 14 Fam LQ 141 (1980) **§7.08**

L. Weitzman, The Divorce Revolution: The Unexpected Social and Economic Consequences for Women and Children in America (1985) **§§10.01, 10.04, 10.07**

Weitzman, *The Economics of Divorce: Social and Economic Consequences of Property, Alimony, and Child Support Awards,* 28 UCLA L Rev 1181 (1981) **§§1.01, 2.17, 8.12**

L. Weitzman, The Marriage Contract (1981) **§4.09**

3 E. Westermarck, The History of Human Marriage (5th ed rewritten 1925) **§§1.01, 1.03, 1.04**

W. Weyrauch & S. Katz, American Family Law in Transition (1983) **§§6.03, 7.01, 7.02, 7.03, 8.03**

H. Whitney, Marriage and Divorce: The Effect of Each on Personal Status and Property Rights 317 (1873) **§10.03**

Wiley & Rosepink, *When What You Own Depends on Where You Live,* 2 Fam Advoc 20 (Winter 1980) **§10.06**

Winks, Divorce Meditation: *A Nonadversary Procedure for the No-Fault Divorce,* 19 J Fam L 615 (1980-81) **§§5.01, 5.02, 5.05, 5.13**

Winter, *UMPA Fights for Recognition,* 70 ABA J 76 (June 1984) **§10.05**

Wood, *The Child as Witness,* 6 Fam Advoc 14 (Spring 1984) **§8.01**

T.D. Woolsey, Divorce and Divorce Legislation 117 (1882) **§10.03**

1 World Book Encyclopedia 440-41 (1983) **§1.06**

Wortis, *The Acceptance of the Concept of the Maternal Role by Behavioral Scientists: Its Effects on Women,* 41 Am J Orthopsychology 733 (1971) **§7.06**

13 C. Wright, A. Miller, & E. Cooper, Federal Practice and Procedure §3609 (1975) **§§4.20, 4.23**

C. Wright, Handbook of the Law of Federal Courts 97 (2d ed 1976) **§4.21**

C. Wright, Handbook of the Law of Federal Courts 218 (2d ed 1976) **§4.22**

Yenkel, *Families: Fighting For Father's Rights,* Washington Post, Jan 13, 1982, at B5, col 1 **§9.01**

Young, Anglo-Saxon Family Law, in Essays in Anglo-Saxon Law 180 (A. Adams ed 1876) **§6.02**

Zainaldin, *The Emergence of a Modern American Family Law: Child Custody, Adoption, and the Courts, 1796-1851,* 73 Nw UL Rev 1038 (1979) **§7.01**

Zumeta, *Mediation as an Alternative to Litigation and Divorce,* 62 Mich BJ 434 (1983) **§§5.05, 5.07, 5.08**

# Index

## A

## D

# E

## F



## G



## H

## N



## O



## P

## Q



## R